Last activity 6/4/18

To Help Students Apply Theories In Their Classrooms

MODEL ACTIVITIES Guide Words

Divide the group into two or more teams. Write the word pair *Brace—Bubble* on the board or a chart. Ask the students to pretend that these words are the guide words for a page of the dictionary. Explain that you would expect the word *brick* to be on this page because *bri* comes after *bra* and *r* comes before *u*. Then write words, one at a time, from the following list on the board below the word pair:

1. beaker
2. boil
3. break
4. braid
5. brave
6. border
7. bypass
8. bud

Let each team in turn tell you if the word would be found on the page with the designated guide words. Ask them to tell why they answered as they did. The team gets a point if the members can answer the questions correctly. The next team gets a chance to answer if they cannot. The reason for the answer is the most important part of the response.

Variation: Write four guide words and the two dictionary pages on which they appear on the board or a chart. For example, you could write:

Page 300 *Rainbow—Rapid*

Page 301 *Rapport—Raven*

Write the words from the following list below the two sets of guide words, one at a time:

1. rare
2. ramble
3. ranch
4. rabbit
5. rave
6. ratio
7. range
8. raw

Ask each team in turn to indicate on which page the displayed word would be found, or if the word would be found on neither page. Have them tell why they answered as they did. (Of course, you would model the decision-making process for them, as described earlier, before the activity starts.) If the team answers the questions about a word correctly, it is awarded a point. If the team answers incorrectly, the next team gets a chance to answer.

Model Activities provides students with detailed directions for excellent activities to be used in the classroom.

CLASSROOM SCENARIO Reading Aloud to Students

Ms. Smith sits in a circle with her students and asks them if they know what an urban legend is. The students respond and are eager to share examples of what they recognize as urban legends. Ms. Smith then reads the title, *Southern Fried Rat and Other Gruesome Tales*, and asks the students to respond. After sharing the name of the author, Daniel Cohen, the discussion continues, with students predicting what they believe the book will be about and Ms. Smith recording their predictions based on the title clue. A number of predictions are recorded. Ms. Smith then reads aloud one of the stories in the book. Following the reading of the story, several students laugh and comment that even though they realized that it was an urban legend, they were familiar with the story plot because they had been told the story before as if it were true. Ms. Smith prompts the students to reflect on the commonalities of several examples of urban legends familiar to the students. The students conclude that although the urban legends originate in various geographical locations, the plots of many of the stories reflect common fears and concerns of people. The students discuss how they might observe similarities of people by reading and researching more urban legends.

Analysis of Scenario

The use of this genre of literature provided a vehicle that engaged the interest of the middle-school students and led to an understanding about human nature. Sharing the urban legend as a read-aloud encouraged social interaction and discussion among the students.

Classroom Scenario illustrate how teachers and students are likely to use key strategies.

FOCUS ON STRATEGIES Learning the Meanings of Compound Words

Mr. Clay based his lesson on the book *The Seal Mother* by Mordicai Gerstein. He introduced the story by saying that it was an old Scottish folktale. Then he wrote the word *folktale* on the board and asked, "What can you tell me about this word?"

Bobby answered, "It is made up of two words: *folk* and *tale*. That makes it a compound word."

"Good, Bobby," Mr. Clay responded. "What does that make you believe this word means?"

"A tale is a story," LaTonya replied.

"That's right," said Mr. Clay. "Can anyone add anything else to what we know about the word's meaning? What does *folk* mean?"

Carl answered tentatively, "A kind of music?"

"There is folk music, just as there are folktales, but we still need a meaning for the word *folk*," Mr. Clay responded.

After he got only shrugs, he explained, "A folktale is a tale, or story, told by the folk, or common people, of a country. Folktales were passed down orally from older *skin, without, oilcloth, inside, rayfish, everywhere, grandfather*, and *whenever*. The students who mentioned the words were allowed to go to the board and circle them, identify the two words that made up each compound, and try to define each compound word, using the meanings of the two component words. Other students helped in determining the definitions, and sometimes the dictionary was consulted.

Finally, the students were asked to copy the compound words from the board into their vocabulary study notebooks. "I'm putting three copies of *The Seal Mother* in the reading center for the rest of this week," Mr. Clay said. "When you have time, get a copy of the book from the center and read it. Each time you find one of our compound words, put a checkmark by the word in your vocabulary notebook. When you find a compound word that we didn't use in our retelling, copy it into your notebook, and write a definition for it, using the meanings of the two words and the context of the sentence in which you found it. We'll discuss the other words that you found on Friday."

Focus on Strategies provides a detailed model of how teachers can use essential techniques.

Teaching Reading in Today's Middle Schools

Betty D. Roe
Tennessee Technological University

Sandy H. Smith
Tennessee Technological University

Houghton Mifflin Company Boston New York

Dedicated to Michael H. Roe and Dr. Gene Talbert

Publisher, Editor-in-Chief: Patricia Coryell
Senior Sponsoring Editor: Sue Pulvermacher-Alt
Senior Development Editor: Lisa Mafrici
Project Editor: Lindsay Frost
Editorial Assistant: Michelle O'Berg
Manufacturing Coordinator: Renée Ostrowski
Marketing Manager: Jane Potter

Printed in the U.S.A.

Library of Congress Control Number: 2003109901

ISBN: 0-618-34585-X

123456789-CRS-08 07 06 05 04

Brief Contents

Contents

Preface

Today's middle-school teachers are faced with a great many challenges when making decisions regarding instruction. We would like to empower middle-school teachers to become informed decision makers rather than merely followers of plans provided by others. Therefore, in *Teaching Reading in Today's Middle Schools* we offer information about middle-school students, numerous methods and materials for reading instruction, and principles to help teachers choose among these methods and materials for their specific students and situations.

Most schools today are incorporating authentic literature, holistic instruction, active learning techniques, and alternative assessment into their reading instruction periods. They are also integrating instruction in language arts and integrating the language arts across the curriculum. In the middle school, students must handle reading assignments in the content areas as well as in reading periods. Our book addresses all of these needs and will help teachers implement reading instruction across the curriculum.

Teachers are employing many technological applications and incorporating computers into instructional sessions, including both use of appropriate instructional software and use of Internet resources. These teachers are also working to meet more effectively the needs of diverse populations. This text addresses all of these areas of concern. We have included up-to-date concepts, materials, techniques, and positions and have tried to integrate them with effective traditional ideas in a balanced, evenhanded way.

Audience and Purpose

Teaching Reading in Today's Middle Schools is intended for use in introductory reading education courses for both preservice and inservice middle-school teachers. It will also be beneficial in introductory courses for teachers preparing to become reading specialists, and it contains much information that will help administrators direct their schools' reading programs.

The main purpose of the book is to prepare teachers to develop their students' abilities to read fluently and to foster their students' enjoyment of reading. This book is designed to familiarize middle-school teachers with all the important aspects of reading instruction. It presents much practical information about the process of teaching reading. The theoretical background and research base behind the teaching suggestions have also been included to give the teacher or prospective teacher a balanced perspective.

Coverage

This text is composed of nine chapters. Chapter 1 discusses characteristics of middle-school students, components of the reading act, theories related to reading, and principles of teaching reading. Chapter 2 is devoted to techniques of teaching word recognition and meaning vocabulary. Comprehension strategies and skills are covered in Chapters 3 and 4. Major approaches and materials for reading instruction are described in Chapter 5. Chapter 6 deals with language and literature; Chapter 7 discusses methods of teaching reading/study techniques; and Chapter 8 tells how to present the reading skills necessary for reading in individual content areas. Assessment of student progress and text difficulty are discussed in Chapter 9. Information on use of technology in reading instruction and the teaching of reading to students with special needs is integrated throughout the book. An appendix contains answers to the Test Yourself quizzes that appear at the end of each chapter.

Features of the Text

This text provides an abundance of practical activities and strategies for improving students' reading performance. ***Illustrative lesson plans, classroom scenarios, Focus on Strategies vignettes, model activities, instructional games,*** and ***textual ties*** are all presented.

To make this text easy to use and study, we have included the following pedagogical features:

Setting Objectives, part of the opening material in each chapter, provides objectives to be met as the chapter is read.

Key Vocabulary, a list of important terms which readers should know, is included to help students focus on key chapter concepts.

Introductions to each chapter help readers develop a mental set for reading the chapter and give them a framework into which they can fit the ideas they will read about.

Marginal icons indicate the **five textual ties** that provide cross-references to topics that are integral to the entire text. The textual ties are

Examples, Model Activities, Classroom Scenarios, and Focus on Strategies sections offer practical applications to clarify the material in the text and put it into a real-life perspective.

Time for Reflection is a feature located at strategic points throughout each chapter to encourage readers to think about the subject matter that has been presented and decide where they stand on debated issues.

Test Yourself, a section at the end of each chapter, includes questions that check readers' retention of the chapter's material as a whole; these questions may also serve as a basis for discussion.

For your journal ... presents topics the readers can write about in order to further their understanding of the ideas and methods presented in the chapter.

... And your portfolio presents ideas to include in a portfolio for assessment purposes.

A **Glossary** contains meanings of specialized terms used in this book.

The **Appendix** contains answers to Test Yourself questions.

Accompanying Teaching and Learning Resources

This text is supported by a **website** that offers resources for both instructors and students:

- For Instructors, we offer a model syllabus, PowerPoint slides, and resources for each chapter that you can use when planning instruction and exams.
- For Students, we offer ACE self-quizzes for each chapter, study aids including interactive glossary flashcards, weblinks, and more.

Acknowledgments

We are indebted to many people for their assistance in the preparation of this text. Although we would like to acknowledge the many teachers and students whose inspiration was instrumental in the development of this book, we cannot name all of them. In addition, we express appreciation to those who have granted permission to use sample materials or citations from their respective works. Credit for these contributions has been given in the source lines.

We would also like to thank the reviewers of the manuscript who contributed their time and expertise to making this a more useful book: Ruth Ference, Berry College; Carol J. Fuhler, Iowa State University; Gail Loucks, Dominican University of California; Timothy J. Quezada, Utica College; and Susan J. Wegmann, Sam Houston State University.

The invaluable assistance provided by Michael Roe in proofreading is greatly appreciated. Grateful acknowledgment is also given to our editors—Sheralee Connors, Lisa Mafrici, Sue Pulvermacher-Alt, and Lindsay Frost—for their assistance throughout the development and production of the book.

Betty D. Roe
Sandy H. Smith

1 The Reading Act

KEY VOCABULARY

Pay close attention to these terms when they appear in the chapter.

affective
auditory acuity
auditory discrimination
automaticity
bottom-up models
grapheme
hearing impairment
interactive theories
kinesthetic
metacognitive strategies
modality
motivation
perception
phoneme
reinforcement
scaffolding
schemata
self-concept
semantic clues
subskill theories
syntactic clues
tactile
top-down models
transactive theories
vicarious experiences
visual acuity
visual discrimination
visual impairment

SETTING OBJECTIVES

When you finish reading this chapter, you should be able to

- Discuss characteristics of middle-school students.
- Discuss the importance of reading instruction in the middle school.
- Discuss the reading product.
- Describe the reading process.
- Explain three types of theories of the reading process: subskill, interactive, and transactive.
- Describe a balanced approach to reading instruction.
- Name some principles on which effective reading instruction is based.
- Discuss standards for the English language arts that were developed by professional organizations.

Few adults would question the importance of reading to effective functioning in our complex technological world. Educators have long made reading instruction a priority in the school curriculum, especially in the primary grades. Unfortunately, as students enter the middle grades, a systematic approach to reading instruction often greatly decreases. Today, policymakers, family, community members, and teachers are called upon to place greater priority on reading instruction in the middle grades.

In this chapter, we introduce the needs of middle-school students and the nature of the task of helping them read effectively. Middle-school students come with diverse needs, and teachers must be prepared to provide the appropriate instruction based on those needs. Middle-school teachers are challenged to help students see the importance of reading ability for performing everyday activities and the value of reading as a source of information, enjoyment, and recreation. To accomplish this task effectively, middle-school teachers need to understand the reading process and the needs of middle-school students. They must also know how to integrate reading throughout

Chapter 1 Organization

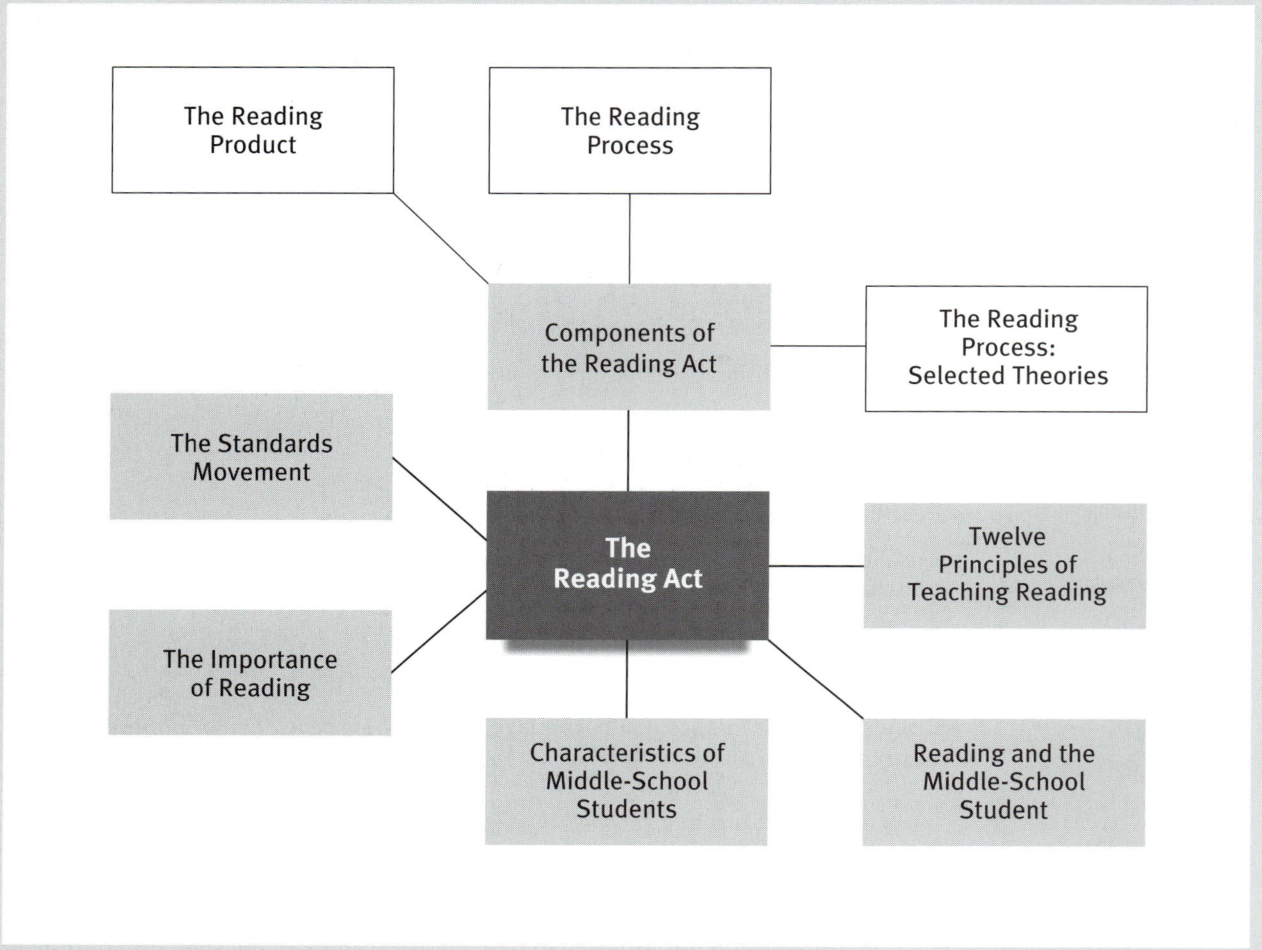

the curriculum and how to promote reading competence and the desire to read. They should be aware of the importance of a balanced approach to reading instruction. They also need to understand the standards movement that has arisen from concerns about students' academic performances.

Reading is a highly complex act, comprised of two major components: a process and a product. All teachers, including middle-level educators, need to be aware of these components and their different aspects in order to respond appropriately to their students' reading needs.

Characteristics of Middle-School Students

Middle-school students range in chronological age from eleven to fifteen years and may be assigned to various grade-span configurations. Examples of middle-school grade spans are grades five to six, seven to eight, five to eight, and sometimes six to nine. Although middle schools have these different configurations, the philosophy of middle-school education is more than just a set of grade levels or chronological age spans. Middle-school education is not just something added to particular grade levels but is a composite of ideas that focuses on how best to meet the various needs of adolescent learners through a well-developed, challenging, and complex curriculum (Doda and Thompson, 2002).

Middle-school students are most often described developmentally as adolescents. Adolescence is recognized as a developmental period of transition between childhood and adulthood (Papalia, Olds, and Feldman, 2002). Therefore, middle-school students vary widely in many areas of development. Cognitively, some are able to reason abstractly, make connections, and see relationships among ideas and concepts. Many develop metacognitive strategies, starting to think about their thinking processes. Socially, they strive for interaction with peers and seek positive social experiences that develop a sense of security and support. The numerous and rapid physical changes that they experience often leave them feeling frightened and unsure of themselves. For many, the middle-school years are dominated by the struggle to understand self and achieve autonomy (Van Hoose, Strahan, and L'Esperance, 2001).

Because middle-school students experience so many changes, the curriculum in these critical years should be organized to meet their unique needs and promote positive growth. Varying class activities that encourage positive social interactions, sharing literature that depicts characters with similar concerns or struggles, providing time for choice and exploration of interests, and structuring lessons that encourage students to take responsibility for their own learning are vital for middle-school students (Maxwell and Metser, 2001).

Reading and Middle-School Students

Cooney (1999) reports that many middle-school teachers are not adequately prepared to teach reading. Unfortunately, research reveals that 30 percent of students entering the middle grades have not mastered basic reading skills, and even with data to support the number of adolescents currently struggling to learn to read, the middle-school curriculum often does not focus on reading instruction (Jackson and Davis, 2000).

Another concern in the middle grades is that many students' reading habits change. Some studies show that students who have developed the reading skills necessary to be successful read less than they did during the primary and intermediate grades and may even respond negatively to tasks involving reading (Baker, 2002).

A position paper released jointly by the International Reading Association and the National Middle School Association (2001) provides additional information regarding the immediate need for emphasis on reading instruction in the middle schools and offers specific recommendations for the improvement of reading in the middle grades. The position paper issues this Call to Action to Schools, Policy Makers, Teacher Educators, Families, and Community Members:

Classroom teachers should:

- Engage in whole-school planning to implement components of a successful school- or district-wide literacy learning plan that is integrative and interdisciplinary.
- Collaborate with administrators, librarians, guidance counselors, intervention specialists, and other school-based educators to improve reading instruction and achievement.
- Interpret assessment data and make information available to other teachers and school-based educators.
- Provide opportunities for students to read material they choose and for students to be read to each school day.

Administrators should:

- Become knowledgeable about literacy learning.
- Provide professional development opportunities so all teachers are able to facilitate literacy learning in all curricular areas.
- Provide modeling and coaching to introduce new instructional strategies for integrating reading instruction across all subjects.
- Provide opportunities for teachers to read to students during the school day.
- Guide students in selecting books to read and provide for authentic multiple opportunities to respond in writing to texts.
- Know what to look for in good literacy learning classrooms.
- Coordinate efforts for improved literacy learning in schools and districts.
- Integrate literacy throughout the curriculum, recognizing the interdisciplinary nature of reading instruction.

Families and community members should:

- Be positive role models for reading and writing.
- Provide an abundance of reading materials and exhibit a positive attitude about reading and writing.

TIME for REFLECTION

What reasons might you offer for the decline in recreational reading reported by students in the middle grades as compared to recreational reading reported during intermediate grades?

- Encourage young adolescents to read.
- Be engaged as partners with the school in the academic lives of adolescents.

The Importance of Reading

The ability to read is vital to functioning effectively in a literate society such as ours. However, students who do not attach importance to learning to read will not be motivated to learn. Learning to read takes effort, and students who fail to see the value of reading in their personal activities will be less likely to work hard than those who do see the benefits.

Middle-school teachers should have little trouble demonstrating to students that reading is important. Every aspect of life involves reading. Road signs direct travelers to particular destinations, inform drivers of hazards, and remind people about traffic regulations. There are menus in restaurants, labels on cans, printed advertisements, newspapers, magazines, insurance forms, income tax forms, and campaign and travel brochures. These reading situations are inescapable. However, not all students automatically realize the "profusion of literacy activities in the nonschool world" (Kotrla, 1997, p. 702).

Reading tasks become increasingly complex as students advance through the grades, and attention must be given to these tasks continually. Anderson (1988) suggests sparking the interest of middle-grade students through career education activities, helping them in this way to see that reading is a life skill that is relevant to their future success. Students can identify occupations that interest them and list the

Students may read for relaxation, vicarious adventure, or aesthetic pleasure, as well as to gain information. *(© Elizabeth Crews)*

reading skills each occupation requires. They can take field trips to businesses to see workers using reading to accomplish their jobs, and they can hear resource people speak to their classes about how they personally need reading in their jobs. These resource people may bring to class examples of the reading materials they must use to perform their daily tasks. The students may also interview parents and others to learn about reading demands in a wide variety of careers. In many cases, reading activities involve such applications as use of computer databases and e-mail.

FAMILY

TECHNOLOGY

As important as functional reading is to everyday living, another important goal of reading is enjoyment. Teachers must show students that reading can be interesting to them for reasons other than strictly utilitarian ones. Students may read for relaxation, vicarious adventure, or aesthetic pleasure as they immerse themselves in tales of other times and places or those of the here and now. They may also read to obtain information about areas of interest or hobbies to fill their leisure time. To help students see reading as a pleasurable activity, middle-level teachers should read to them each day on a variety of themes and topics, from a variety of genres, and from the works of many authors. They should also make many books available for students to look at and read for themselves, and they should dedicate time for students to read from self-selected materials. Middle-school students should be given opportunities to share information from and reactions to their reading in both oral and written forms. They should be encouraged to think about the things they are reading and to relate them to their own experiences.

TIME for REFLECTION

What can you add to the list of ways to demonstrate to middle-school students the importance of reading? Can you think of more suggestions to show middle-school students the enjoyment of reading?

STANDARDS AND ASSESSMENT

The Standards Movement

Many people, aware of the importance of reading in today's society, are concerned that students are not achieving at high enough levels in reading. Policymakers and concerned community members have developed, or turned to educators to develop, standards that "define what students should learn" (Agnew, 2000, p. 1). Many states have developed literacy standards for students at each grade level.

Schmoker and Marzano (1999, p. 21) point out the importance of establishing "standards and expectations for reaching them that are clear, not confusing; essential, not exhaustive." Some states, however, have standards that cover so much that it is not realistic to expect to meet them in the available time.

Professional organizations have also sought to develop standards in their curricular areas. The National Council of Teachers of English (NCTE) and the International Reading Association (IRA) cooperatively developed a set of standards for the English language arts from kindergarten through twelfth grade (see Example 1.1). These standards specify a range of areas in the English language arts in which students must be proficient rather than specifying levels of achievement (Smagorinsky, 1999).

Components of the Reading Act

The reading act is composed of two parts: the reading process and the reading product. Nine aspects of the reading process—sensory, perceptual, sequential, experiential, thinking, learning, associational, affective, and constructive—combine to produce the

EXAMPLE 1.1 Standards for the English Language Arts Sponsored by NCTE and IRA

The vision guiding these standards is that all students must have the opportunities and resources to develop the language skills they need to pursue life's goals and to participate fully as informed, productive members of society. These standards assume that literacy growth begins before children enter school as they experience and experiment with literacy activities—reading and writing, and associating spoken words with their graphic representations. Recognizing this fact, these standards encourage the development of curriculum and instruction that make productive use of the emerging literacy abilities that children bring to school. Furthermore, the standards provide ample room for the innovation and creativity essential to teaching and learning. They are not prescriptions for particular curriculum or instruction. Although we present these standards as a list, we want to emphasize that they are not distinct and separable; they are, in fact, interrelated and should be considered as a whole.

1. Students read a wide range of print and nonprint texts to build an understanding of texts, of themselves, and of the cultures of the United States and the rest of the world; to acquire new information; to respond to the needs and demands of society and the workplace; and for personal fulfillment. Among these texts are fiction and nonfiction, classic and contemporary works.
2. Students read a wide range of literature from many periods in many genres to build an understanding of the many dimensions (e.g., philosophical, ethical, aesthetic) of human experience.
3. Students apply a wide range of strategies to comprehend, interpret, evaluate, and appreciate texts. They draw on their prior experience, their interactions with other readers and writers, their knowledge of word meaning and of other texts, their word identification strategies, and their understanding of textual features (e.g., sound-letter correspondence, sentence structure, context, graphics).
4. Students adjust their use of spoken, written, and visual language (e.g., conventions, style, vocabulary) to communicate effectively with a variety of audiences and for different purposes.
5. Students employ a wide range of strategies as they write and use different writing process elements appropriately to communicate with different audiences for a variety of purposes.
6. Students apply knowledge of language structure, language conventions (e.g., spelling and punctuation), media techniques, figurative language, and genre to create, critique, and discuss print and nonprint texts.
7. Students conduct research on issues and interests by generating ideas and questions, and by posing problems. They gather, evaluate, and synthesize data from a variety of sources (e.g., print and nonprint texts, artifacts, people) to communicate their discoveries in ways that suit their purpose and audience.
8. Students use a variety of technological and information resources (e.g., libraries, databases, computer networks, video) to gather and synthesize information and to create and communicate knowledge.
9. Students develop an understanding of and respect for diversity in language use, patterns, and dialects across cultures, ethnic groups, geographic regions, and social roles.
10. Students whose first language is not English make use of their first language to develop competency in the English language arts and to develop understanding of content across the curriculum.
11. Students participate as knowledgeable, reflective, creative, and critical members of a variety of literacy communities.
12. Students use spoken, written, and visual language to accomplish their own purposes (e.g., for learning, enjoyment, persuasion, and the exchange of information).

Source: Standards for the English Language Arts, by the International Reading Association and the National Council of Teachers of English.

reading product. When these aspects blend and interact harmoniously, good communication between the writer and reader is the product. But the sequences involved in the reading process are not always exactly the same, and they are not always performed in the same way by different readers. Because the goal of communication is central to reading instruction, we will discuss the reading product first.

The Reading Product

The product of the reading act is the communication of thoughts and emotions by the writer to the reader, resulting in the reader's own understanding of ideas that the writer has put into print. Communication results from the reader's construction of meaning through integrating his or her prior knowledge with the information presented in the text.

Today's readers have a wealth of knowledge available to them because they are able to read material that others wrote in years past. People can read of events and accomplishments that occur in other parts of the world. Knowledge of great discoveries need not be laboriously passed from person to person by word of mouth. Such knowledge is available to all who can read.

In addition to being a means of communicating generally, reading is a means of communicating specifically with friends and acquaintances. A note may inform a babysitter about where to call in case of an emergency. A memo from a person's employer can identify the work to be done. Reading can be a way to share another person's insights, joys, sorrows, or creative endeavors. Reading can also enable a person to find places he or she has never visited before (through maps and directional signs), take advantage of bargains (through advertisements), or avert disaster (through warning signs). It is difficult to imagine what life would be like without this vital means of communication.

Communication depends on comprehension, which is affected by all aspects of the reading process. Word recognition strategies, a part of the associational aspect of the reading process, are essential, but comprehension involves much more than decoding symbols into sounds; the reader must construct meaning while interacting with the printed page. Some people mistakenly view reading as a single skill, that of pronouncing words, rather than as a combination of many skills that lead to the derivation of meaning. Thinking of reading in this way may have fostered the misguided practice of using a reading period for extended drill on word calling, in which the teacher asks each student to "read" aloud while classmates follow in their books. Some students may be good pronouncers in such a situation, but are they readers? They may pronounce words perfectly, but fail to understand anything they have read. Although pronunciation is important, reading involves much more.

TIME for REFLECTION

Some people believe that just teaching students to pronounce words enables them to achieve communication with the authors of written materials. **What do *you* think, and why?**

Teachers who realize that all aspects of the reading process affect comprehension of written material will be better able to identify students' reading difficulties and offer effective instructional programs based on students' needs as a result. Faulty performance related to any aspect of the reading process may result in an inferior product or in no product at all.

The Reading Process

Reading is an extremely complex process, involving many aspects. When they read, students must be able to:

- Perceive the symbols set before them (sensory aspect).
- Interpret what they see (perceptual aspect).
- Follow the linear, logical, and grammatical patterns of the written words (sequential aspect).
- Relate words to direct experiences to give the words meaning (experiential aspect).
- Make inferences from and evaluate the material (thinking aspect).
- Remember what they learned in the past and incorporate new ideas and facts (learning aspect).
- Recognize the connections between symbols and sounds, between words and what they represent (associational aspect).
- Deal with personal interests and attitudes that affect the task of reading (affective aspect).
- Put everything together to make sense of the material (constructive aspect).

Reading seems to fit into the category of behavior called a skill, which Frederick McDonald has defined as an act that "demands complex sets of responses—some of them cognitive, some attitudinal, and some manipulative" (Downing, 1982, p. 535). Understanding, rather than simple motor behavior, is essential. The key element in skill development is integration of the processes involved, which "is learned through practice. Practice in integration is supplied only by performing the whole skill or as much as is a part of the learner's 'preliminary fix.' . . . one learns to read by reading" (Downing, 1982, p. 537). Whereas reading can be broken down into subskills, it takes place only when these subskills are put together into an integrated whole. Performing subskills individually is not reading (R. C. Anderson et al., 1985).

TECHNOLOGY

Technology has affected the teaching of reading and other literacy skills by serving as a vehicle for such instruction. However, it has also added to the literacy strategies needed for functioning in society. El-Hindi (1998, p. 694) says, "Literacy now involves being able to make sense of information including images, sounds, animation, and ongoing discussion groups." It involves navigating hypertext and hypermedia environments that deviate radically from the sequential text found in print sources.

Not only is the reading process complex, but each aspect of the process is complex as well. As Example 1.2 shows, the whole process can be likened to a series of books, with each aspect represented by a hefty volume. A student would have to understand the information in every volume to have a complete grasp of the subject. Therefore, the student would have to integrate information from all of the volumes in order to perform effectively in the area of study. The series would be more important than any individual volume.

EXAMPLE 1.2 Aspects of the Reading Process

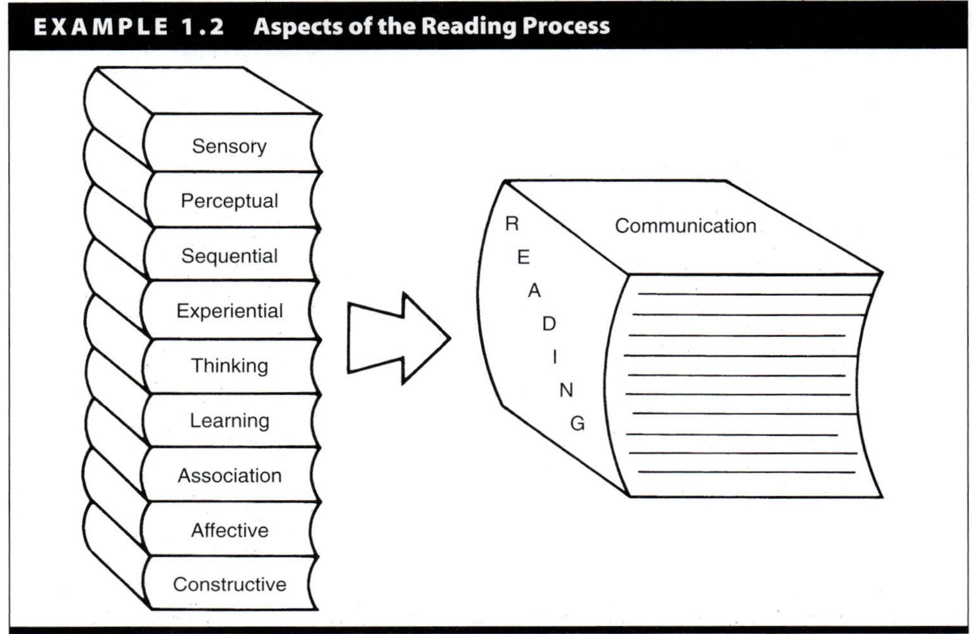

Sensory Aspects of Reading

DIVERSITY 

The reading process begins with a sensory impression, either visual (sight) or ***tactile*** (touch). A normal reader perceives the printed symbol visually; a blind reader uses the tactile sense. (Discussion of the blind reader is beyond the scope of this text.) The auditory sense is also very important, because a beginning stage in reading is the association of printed symbols with spoken language. A person with poor auditory discrimination may find some reading skills, especially those involved with phonics, difficult to master.

Vision. The reading act imposes many visual demands on students. They must be able to focus their eyes on a page of print that is generally fourteen to twenty inches away, as well as on various signs and visual displays that may be twenty or more feet away. Besides possessing ***visual acuity*** (sharpness of vision), students must learn to discriminate visually among the graphic symbols (letters or words) that are used to represent spoken language. Reading is impossible for a person who cannot differentiate between two unlike graphic symbols. Because of these demands, teachers should be aware of the way in which a student's sight develops and of the physical problems that can influence reading performance.

DIVERSITY

Uncorrected nearsightedness or farsightedness, astigmatism, problems with dual-eye coordination, and problems with tracking lines are all ***visual impairments.*** A student who is visually impaired has difficulty, but is able to learn to read print, in contrast to a student who is blind and must learn to read Braille. Teachers can make provisions for students with visual impairments by adjusting lighting and seating, providing tape-recorded stories and books with large print, and reading orally to the whole class frequently. Students who have trouble tracking print with their eyes can be

CLASSROOM SCENARIO Visual Problems

Betty Roe had a sixth-grade student in her class who had previously been identified as a behavior problem and had been suspended from school briefly. She observed that he had trouble with such tasks as hitting a ball on the playground, and she suggested that his parents take him to a vision specialist. The specialist discovered a perceptual problem and prescribed glasses and eye exercises. The boy was amazed at the difference. He told her that previously, letters had "moved around" on the page. Both his behavior and his grades improved after his vision problems were addressed.

Analysis of Scenario

Observation of the student in a variety of situations provided the clue that helped the teacher address his problem.

encouraged to follow along the line of print through the use of a pointer. The teacher can use a pointer when reading material from the board. Student-held pointers and highlight tape can also be used to assist students in following print during reading. Teachers should refer students to vision specialists if they observe such symptoms as squinting, closing or covering one eye, rubbing eyes frequently, or making frequent errors when copying board work. As described in the Classroom Scenario above, correcting vision impairments can help students in many ways.

Hearing. A student who cannot discriminate among the different sounds (***phonemes***) represented by graphic symbols will be unable to make the sound-symbol associations necessary for decoding unfamiliar words. Of course, before a student can discriminate among sounds, he or she must be able to hear them; that is, the student's ***auditory acuity*** must be adequate. Therefore, students who are deaf or hearing impaired are deprived of some methods of word identification. Students whose hearing is temporarily impaired by problems related to colds or allergies may also experience difficulties.

DIVERSITY

The term ***hearing impairment*** refers to a condition whereby an individual's sense of hearing is defective but adequate for ordinary purposes, with or without a hearing aid. When providing reading instruction for students with hearing impairments, teachers should speak slowly, clearly, and with adequate volume; seat the students as far as possible from distracting sounds; and supplement reading lessons with visual aids. Teachers should refer students to hearing specialists if they observe such symptoms as inattentiveness in class, requests for repetition of verbal information, frowning when trying to listen, or turning the head so that one or the other ear always faces the teacher. The Classroom Scenario on the next page shows how one teacher's referrals helped students with hearing impairments.

Perceptual Aspects of Reading

Perception involves interpretation of the sensory impressions that reach the brain. Individuals process and reorganize sensory data in accordance with other background experiences. When an individual reads, the brain receives a visual sensation of words and phrases from the printed page. It recognizes and gives meaning to these words and

CLASSROOM SCENARIO Hearing Problems

Two sixth-grade boys were struggling with assignments in Betty Roe's classroom. One consistently turned his head when spoken to, so that one ear was toward the speaker. The other one often failed to respond to questions and to follow directions. Betty suggested to the parents of both boys that their hearing should be checked. The first boy had impacted ear wax that caused some hearing loss in both ears, including a serious 60 percent loss in the ear he turned away from the speaker. The other boy had fused bones in his ears caused by ear infections. Both boys had been having academic problems prior to sixth grade, but their problems had been undiagnosed. Both had surgical procedures and emerged from surgery hearing well. Their grades rose dramatically.

Analysis of Scenario

The teacher recognized potential problems and alerted the parents. As a result, the students' problems were addressed.

phrases as it associates them with the reader's previous experience with the objects, ideas, or emotions represented.

Because readers' experiences vary, different readers may interpret a single text differently (R. C. Anderson et al., 1985). For example, seeing the printed words *apple pie* can result not only in a visual image of a pie but also in a recollection of its smell and taste. Of course, the person must have prior experience with the thing named by the word(s) in order to make these associations. Since different people have had different experiences with apple pies, and apple pies can vary in smell, taste, and appearance, people will attach different meanings to *apple pie*. Therefore, individuals will have slightly different perceptions when they encounter these or any other words.

The clusters of information that people develop about things (such as apple pies), places (such as restaurants or airports), and ideas (such as justice or democracy) are sometimes referred to as ***schemata.*** Every person has many schemata. Reading comprehension has been described as the act of relating textual information to existing schemata (Pearson et al., 1979).

Visual Perception. Visual perception involves identification and interpretation of the size, shape, and relative position of letters and words. ***Visual discrimination,*** the ability to see likenesses and differences in visual forms (e.g., between the printed words *brag* and *drag*), is an important part of visual perception because many letters and words are similar in form but different in pronunciation and meaning. Accurate identification and interpretation of words results from detecting the small variations in form. A student may have good visual acuity (see images clearly) but be unable to discriminate well visually. Teachers can help students develop this skill through carefully planned activities. The final step in visual perception is attaching meaning to the words by using past experiences.

Auditory Perception. Auditory perception involves ***auditory discrimination,*** detecting likenesses and differences in speech sounds (e.g., recognizing the difference in the spoken words *brag* and *drag*) and interpreting the result. Students must be able consciously to separate a phoneme (sound) from one spoken word and compare it with another phoneme separated from another word. As is true of visual discrimination, a student can have good auditory acuity (hear sounds clearly), but be unable to discriminate well auditorily. The skill can be taught, however. The final step in auditory perception is using past experiences to attach meaning to the words that are heard.

Sequential Aspects of Reading

DIVERSITY

English-language printed material generally appears on a page in a left-to-right, top-to-bottom sequence. A person's eyes must follow this sequence in order to read. Learning to follow this sequential pattern can be a new challenge for students who have not been exposed to many printed materials or who have experience with different sequences used in other languages.

Even readers who are familiar with patterns of print occasionally regress, or look back to earlier words and phrases, as they read. Although these regressions momentarily interrupt the reading process as the reader checks the accuracy of initial impressions, the skillful reader eventually returns to the left-to-right, top-to-bottom sequence.

TECHNOLOGY

The sequence of reading text from page to page in a book, front to back, has predominated in years past. Today, computer materials allow random access to information in an electronic document and offer new challenges to students, who must learn to navigate multiple sequences of text and still retain the organizational sense necessary for understanding the topic. Formats of textbooks and literature selections used in middle schools today have also begun to vary somewhat, using sidebars and presenting several levels and types of texts on the same page.

Another reason that reading is a sequential process is that oral language is strung together in a sequential pattern of grammar and logic. Since written language is a way of representing speech, it is expressed in the same manner. Readers must be able to follow the grammatical and logical patterns of spoken language in order to understand written language.

Experiential Background and Reading

As indicated in the section on perceptual aspects, meaning derived from reading is based on the reader's experiential background. If reading materials contain vocabulary, concepts, and sentence structures that are unfamiliar to students, teachers must help them develop the background they need to understand the materials. Because students' experiential backgrounds differ, some need more preparation for a particular selection than others do.

Students with rich background experiences have had more chances to develop understanding of the vocabulary and concepts they encounter in reading than have students with limited experiences. For example, a student who has actually been to an auction is more likely to be able to attach appropriate meaning to the word *auction* when he or she encounters it in a reading selection than a student who has not been to an auction. Direct experiences with places, things, and processes described in reading materials make understanding much more likely. Middle-school students from different cultures comprehend materials and remember best information from texts that are most culturally familiar and ones that have characters who are like them (Drucker, 2003).

DIVERSITY

Vicarious experiences (indirect experiences) also enhance conceptual development, although they are probably less effective than concrete experiences. Hearing other people tell of or read about a subject; seeing photos or a movie of a place, event, or activity; and reading about a topic are examples of vicarious experiences that can build concept development. Because vicarious experiences involve fewer senses than do direct, concrete experiences, the concepts gained from them may be developed less fully.

FAMILY

TECHNOLOGY

Parents who converse freely with their children, read to them, tell them stories, show them pictures, and take them to movies and on trips provide rich experiences to them. Other parents do not offer these experiences to their children. Teachers can help broaden students' concrete experiences through field trips, displays of objects, and class demonstrations. They can also help by providing rich vicarious experiences, such as photographs, videos and DVDs, CDs and tape recordings, computer software, classroom discussions, and storytelling and story-reading sessions.

Middle-school students who are English language learners (ELLs) and those who speak nonstandard dialects of English may need assistance in learning the Standard English found in many books. Teachers can help students learn Standard English by telling and reading stories, leading or encouraging class discussions, using language experience stories (accounts developed cooperatively by the teacher and class members about actual events), and using creative drama (acting out stories without set scripts, props, or costumes). The new words that students encounter during field trips and demonstrations are also valuable.

Proficient readers can skillfully integrate information in the text with their prior knowledge about the topic, but struggling readers may either overemphasize the symbols in the text or rely too heavily on prior knowledge. Poor readers who focus primarily on the text may produce nonsense words that are graphically similar to the ones in the text. This occurs because such readers are not attempting to connect what they read to their experiences and are not demanding sense from reading. Struggling readers who depend too much on prior knowledge may fail to make enough use of clues in the text to come close to the intended message (R. C. Anderson et al., 1985).

The Relationship Between Reading and Thinking

Reading is a thinking process. The act of recognizing words requires interpretation of graphic symbols. To comprehend a reading selection thoroughly, middle-school students must be able to use the information to make inferences and read critically and creatively—to understand the figurative language, determine the author's purpose, evaluate the ideas presented, and apply those ideas to actual situations. All of these skills involve thinking processes.

STANDARDS AND ASSESSMENT

Teachers can guide students' thinking by asking appropriate questions. Students will be more likely to evaluate the material they are reading if they have been directed to do so. *How* and *why* questions are particularly good. Appropriate questions can help involve a reader in the material and help the reader make personal connections with it. Questions can also limit thinking, however; if students are asked only to locate isolated facts, they will probably not be very concerned about main ideas in a passage or about the author's purpose. Test questions also affect the way students read assignments: if the usual test questions ask for evaluation or application of ideas, students will be likely to read the material more thoughtfully than they will if they are asked to recall isolated facts.

The Relationship of Reading to Learning

Reading is a complex act that must be learned. It is also a means by which further learning takes place. In other words, a person learns to read and reads to learn.

Learning to read depends on motivation, practice, and reinforcement. Teachers must show middle-school students that being able to read is rewarding in many ways: it increases success in school, helps in coping with everyday situations outside of school, bestows status, and provides recreation. Students are motivated by the expectations that they will receive these rewards, which then provide reinforcement that encourages them to continue to make associations between printed words and the things to which they refer and to practice the skills they need for reading.

After students have developed some facility in reading, it becomes a means through which they learn other things. They read to learn about science, mathematics, social studies, literature, and all other subjects, a topic treated in depth in Chapter 8.

Reading as an Associational Process

Learning to read depends on a number of types of associations. First, students learn to associate objects and ideas with spoken words. Next, they are asked to build up associations between spoken words and written words. In some cases—for instance, when a student encounters an unfamiliar written word paired with a picture of a familiar object—the student makes a direct association between the object or event and the written word without an intermediate connection with the spoken word. In teaching phonics, teachers set up associations between graphic symbols (***graphemes***) and sounds (phonemes).

When students practice the associations through classroom activities, immediate positive ***reinforcement,*** or support, of correct answers and correction of wrong ones can help to establish the associations. Positive reinforcement can include simple feedback about the correctness of an answer or a reward such as praise, a smile, or even tangible items. Practice in and of itself, however, is not always enough to set up lasting associations. The more meaningful an association is to a student, the more rapidly he or she will learn it. Students can learn words after only a single exposure if the words have vital meaning for them (Ashton-Warner, 1963).

Affective Aspects of the Reading Process

Interests, attitudes, and self-concepts are three ***affective*** aspects of the reading process that influence how hard students will work at the reading task. For example, students who are interested in the materials presented to them will put forth much more effort in the reading process than will students who have no interest in the available reading materials.

FAMILY

In the same manner, students with positive attitudes toward reading will expend more effort on the reading process than will students with negative attitudes. Positive attitudes are nurtured in home environments where the parents read for themselves and to their children and where reading materials are provided for children's use. In the classroom, teachers who enjoy reading, seize every opportunity to provide pleasurable reading experiences for their students, and allow time for recreational reading during school hours are encouraging positive attitudes. Reading aloud to the students regularly can also help accomplish this objective, and this activity should continue throughout the middle grades (Daisey, 1993; Duchein and Mealey, 1993; Schumm and Saumell, 1994). Also, if a middle-school student's peers view reading as a positive activity, that student is likely to view reading in the same way.

FAMILY

Negative attitudes toward reading may develop in a home environment where parents, for a variety of reasons, do not read. Middle-school students from some homes may be given the impression that reading is a female activity. They may bring this idea to the classroom and spread it among students who have not previously been exposed to it. This attitude affects everyone in the classroom negatively, regardless of gender. (See the Focus on Strategies below.)

Maudeville (1994) believes that when readers who have just finished a selection make decisions about what interested them or what information was important to them in their selection, they understand and retain that information better. Reflecting on changes in attitude about the topic may also help. Discussion of these personal responses is also important. Giving students opportunities for self-expression is a key

FOCUS ON STRATEGIES

Attitude Toward Reading

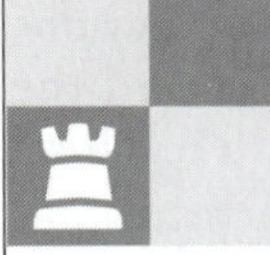

James, a sixth grader, always grumbled when he was asked to participate in reading activities. One day he told Mr. Hyde, his teacher, "I don't need to be able to read. My dad is a construction worker who drives heavy equipment, and that's what I'm going to be. I won't need to read to do that."

Mr. Hyde responded, "What will you do if you are given written instructions to get to the construction site? Won't you need to read then?"

"I'll ask somebody," James replied.

"What if nobody else is there?" Mr. Hyde persisted.

"I don't think that will happen," James countered.

"Well, what if you can't read the road signs to find the place that you are going? You might even need to read a map to find the place. Or what will you do if you get letters from people? You may not want to ask someone else to read them to you. They could be private. Can't you see some advantages to being able to read, even if you don't have to read a lot at work?"

"I guess so," James mumbled reluctantly.

Mr. Hyde had some arguments that were difficult to refute, but probably did not change James's attitude with this one conversation. James needed to be shown repeatedly the benefits that could accrue from reading ability. He also needed to be helped to see that reading can be fun. Mr. Hyde found an informational book containing lots of pictures of heavy equipment and gave James the book to look through whenever he had some time. He did not choose to look at it immediately, but a couple of days later, when the students were having a supervised study time, he took out the book in preference to doing mathematics homework. At first he just thumbed through the pages, but eventually he began to pay closer attention to specific parts of the book. After a day or two, he returned the book and remarked that it was "okay." Mr. Hyde saw a possible avenue to helping James become a reader and pursued it for the rest of the year.

to intrinsic, or internal, ***motivation*** (Oldfather, 1995). Open-ended tasks promote intrinsic motivation because they allow personal choices, challenges, and control. Social interaction during literacy tasks, book-rich environments, and teachers who model reading also enhance internal motivation (Gambrell, 1996; Turner and Paris, 1995).

Ruddell (1992) believes that internal motivation and identification with a piece of literature can take several forms: seeing oneself as a successful problem solver, viewing oneself as a person of significance, evoking an aesthetic sense, finding escape from daily life, piquing intellectual curiosity, and understanding oneself. These types of internal motivation all invite the reader to "step into the story" and be a part of it. External motivations for reading may include peer pressure, teacher expectations, and meeting one's responsibilities.

Students with poor opinions of themselves may be afraid to attempt a reading task because they are sure they will fail. They find it easier to avoid the task altogether and to develop "don't care" attitudes than to risk looking "dumb." Students with positive ***self-concepts,*** on the other hand, are generally not afraid to attack a reading task, since they believe they are going to succeed.

There are several ways to help middle-school students build positive self-concepts:

- In every possible way, the teacher should help the students feel accepted. A definite relationship exists between a teacher's attitude toward a student, as the student perceives it, and the student's self-concept. One of the best ways to make students feel accepted is for the teacher to value their interests, utilizing those interests in planning for reading instruction.
- The teacher can help students feel successful by providing activities that guarantee satisfactory completion. ***Scaffolding*** learning experiences can enhance success for students.
- The teacher should avoid comparing any student with others. Instead, reading progress should be compared with the student's own previous work.
- Teachers who use reading groups should implement flexible, not fixed, groups. Comparisons and competition among groups should be avoided, and the bases on which groups are formed should be varied.

Constructive Aspect of the Reading Process

The reader puts together input from sensory and perceptual channels with experiential background and affective responses and constructs a personal meaning for the text. This meaning is based on the printed word, but does not reside completely in it; it is transformed by the information the reader brings to the text, the reader's feelings about the material, the purposes for the reading, and the context in which the reading takes place. Readers with different backgrounds of experience and different affective reactions will derive different meanings from the same text, as may those with divergent purposes and those reading under varying conditions. A person from the Middle East, for example, will understand an article about dissension among Middle Eastern countries differently than will one from the United States. A person reading to find a single fact or a few isolated facts will derive a different meaning from an article from

DIVERSITY

someone reading to get an overall picture of the topic. A person reading a horror story alone in the house at night may well construct a different understanding of the text from one reading the same story in broad daylight in a room full of family members.

The Reading Process: Selected Theories

A theory is a set of assumptions or principles designed to explain phenomena. Theories that are based on good research and practical observations can be helpful when teachers are planning reading instruction, but teachers should not lose sight of the fact that current theories do not account for all aspects of this complex process. In addition, theories grow out of hypotheses—educated guesses. New information may be discovered that proves part or all of a theory invalid.

It would not be practical to present all the theories related to reading in the introductory chapter of a survey textbook. We have chosen to discuss three theoretical approaches—***subskill, interactive,*** and ***transactive theories***—to give you a sense of the complexities inherent in choosing a theoretical stance. The choices that teachers make about types of instruction and emphases in instructional programs are affected by their theoretical positions concerning the reading process.

Subskill Theories

Some educators see reading as a set of subskills that students must master and integrate. They believe that although good readers have learned and integrated these subskills so well that they use them automatically, beginning readers and struggling readers, including a number of middle-school students who have not learned them all, may not integrate well those that they have learned. Therefore, some middle-school students may exhibit slow, choppy reading and perhaps have reduced comprehension, because the separate skills of word recognition take so much concentration. Teaching these skills until they become automatic and smoothly integrated is thus the approach these educators take to reading instruction (Weaver and Shonhoff, 1984). ***Automaticity*** is "the ability to perform a task with little attention" (Samuels, 1994, p. 819). It is evident when a high level of accuracy is combined with speed. Readers who read orally with good expression are exhibiting automaticity in word recognition.

Smith and his colleagues (1978) assert that teachers need to teach specific skills in order to focus instruction. Otherwise, instruction in reading would be reduced to assisted practice—a long, laborious trial-and-error approach. Weaver and Shonhoff (1984) state that "although some research suggests that skilled reading is a single, holistic process, there is no research to suggest that children can learn to read and develop reading skill if they are taught using a method that treats reading as if it were a single process. Therefore, for instructional purposes, it is probably best to think of reading as a set of interrelated subskills" (p. 36).

There is research to support this approach. Samuels and Schachter (1984) report a study of one decoding subskill, recognizing words in isolation (sight words), which showed that "roughly 50 percent of the variability in oral reading of connected words is associated with how well one can read these words in isolation" (p. 40). Similarly, LaBerge and Samuels (1985) point out that a child who is slow in learning to read "often must be given extensive training on each of a variety of tasks, such as letter discrimination, letter-sound training, blending, etc. In this manner a teacher becomes aware of the fact that letter recognition can be considered a skill itself" (p. 713). LaBerge and Samuels's hierarchical model of perceptual learning suggests that students master smaller units before larger ones and integrate them into larger units after mastery.

Since fluent readers have mastered each of the subskills to the point that they use and integrate the subskills automatically, they do not clearly see the dividing lines among these skills during their daily reading. "One of the hallmarks of the reader who learned the subskills rapidly is that he was least aware of them at the time, and therefore now has little memory of them as separate subskills" (LaBerge and Samuels, 1985, p. 714). Guthrie (1973) found that reading subskills correlated highly with one another for good readers. The correlations among reading subskills for poor readers were low. These students seemed to be operating at a level of separate rather than integrated skills. Guthrie's findings led to the conclusion that "lack of subskill mastery and lack of integration of these skills into higher order units" were sources of disability among poor readers (Samuels and Schachter, 1984, p. 39).

Whereas beginning readers or struggling middle-school readers may first focus on decoding and then switch their attention to comprehension, fluent readers decode automatically, and thus can focus attention on comprehension. Samuels (1994) points out that although the meanings of familiar words may be automatic for skilled readers, "the ability to get the meaning of each word in a sentence, however, is not the same as the ability to comprehend a sentence. In comprehending a sentence one must be able to interrelate and combine the separate meanings of each of its words. From this point of view, comprehension is a constructive process of synthesis and putting word meanings together in special ways, much as individual bricks are combined in the construction of a house" (p. 820).

Those who teach a set of subskills as a means of instructing middle-school students in reading generally recognize the importance of practicing the subskills in the context of actual reading in order to ensure integration. But some teachers omit this vital phase and erroneously focus only on the subskills, overlooking the fact that they are the means to an end and not an end in themselves. Samuels (1994) points out that students can build automaticity only by spending much time reading. Although he acknowledges the need for practice with important subskills, he cautions that practice time must also be "spent on reading easy, interesting, meaningful material" (p. 834).

Adams (1994) feels much the same way. She says, "Deep and ready working knowledge of letters, spelling patterns, and words, and of the phonological translations of all three, are of inescapable importance to both skillful reading and its acquisition—not because they are the be all or the end all of the reading process, but because they enable it" (p. 859). She points out that frequent broad reading is important in developing reading proficiency.

Interactive Theories

An interactive theoretical model of the reading process depicts reading as a combination of two types of processing—***top-down*** (reader-based) and ***bottom-up*** (text-based)—in continuous interaction. In top-down processing, the act of reading begins with the reader's generating hypotheses or predictions about the material, using visual cues in the material to test these hypotheses as necessary (Walberg, Hare, and Pulliam, 1981). For instance, the reader of a folktale that begins with the words "Once upon a time there was a man who had three sons . . ." forms hypotheses about what will happen next, predicting that there will be a task to perform or a beautiful princess to win over and that the oldest two sons will fail but the youngest will attain his goal. Because of these expectations, the reader may read the material fairly quickly, giving attention primarily to words that confirm the expectations. Close reading occurs only if the hypothesis formed is not confirmed and an atypical plot unfolds. Otherwise, the reader can skip many words while skimming for key words that move the story along. Processing of print obviously cannot be a totally top-down experience, because a reader must begin by focusing on the print (Gove, 1983).

In bottom-up processing, reading is initiated by examining the printed symbols (Walberg, Hare, and Pulliam, 1981). Gove (1983) says, "Bottom-up models assume that the translation process begins with print, i.e., letter or word identification, and proceeds to progressively larger linguistic units, phrases, sentences, etc., ending in meaning" (p. 262). A reader using bottom-up processing might first sound out a word letter by letter and then pronounce it, consider its meaning in relation to the phrase in which it is found, and so on.

An interactive model assumes that students are simultaneously processing information from the print they are reading and information from their background knowledge. Recognition and comprehension of printed words and ideas are the result of using both types of information. Rumelhart's early model indicated that "at least for skilled readers, top-down and bottom-up processing occur simultaneously. Because comprehension depends on both graphic information and the information in the reader's mind, it may be obstructed when a critical skill or a piece of information is missing" (Harris and Sipay, 1985, p. 10). For example, a reader who is unable to use clues from the sentences or pictures that surround an unfamiliar word may fail to grasp the meaning of a word that is central to understanding the passage. Similarly, a reader who has no background knowledge about the topic may be unable to reconstruct the ideas the author is trying to convey.

Transactive Theories

Rosenblatt (1994) believes that "every reading act is an event, or a transaction involving a particular reader and . . . a text, and occurring at a particular time in a particular context. . . . The meaning does not reside ready-made 'in' the text or 'in' the reader but happens or comes into being during the transaction between reader and text" (p. 1061). McGee (1992) points out that readers employ knowledge gained through past experiences to help them select interpretations, visualize the message, make connections between the new information and what they know, and relate affectively to the material. The transaction between reader and text is dynamic. Thus, a single reader may construct an entirely different meaning from the same passage if he or she reads it at one time and then rereads it later, after gaining relevant personal experience that changes the initial interpretation. The context of the reading event has changed

Transactive theories of reading suggest that these two readers will each have different experiences, even though they are reading the same book. Interactive theories also suggest that they may understand the book in different ways, because the middle-school reader on the right has more background experience to help her with top-down processing. *(© Laimute E. Druskis Stock Boston)*

between these two transactions. Beach and Hynds (1991) also believe that reading must be viewed as constructing an evolving experience, instead of a static meaning. Readers' stances, beliefs, and attitudes affect their responses, as does the context.

The reader is highly important when reading is viewed as a transaction, and the stance the reader chooses must be considered. The reader may focus on obtaining information from the text (an *efferent* stance) but may also focus on the experience lived through during the reading, the feelings and images evoked, and the memories aroused by the text (an *aesthetic* stance). Both stances are appropriate at times, and it is up to the reader to choose the approach to the reading. Even when reading a single work, readers may shift their stances from more efferent to more aesthetic, or vice versa, but fiction and poetry should involve a more aesthetic stance (McGee, 1992; Probst, 1988; Rosenblatt, 1978, 1991).

Rosenblatt's idea of an efferent–aesthetic continuum helps teachers see that there are both cognitive and affective aspects of all reading activities for both fiction and nonfiction and that the relative importance of each aspect will vary with the text and the reading situation. Frager (1993) suggests encouraging a wider range of aesthetic responses to content area reading by asking readers what feelings the text aroused in them. Students should both think about the concepts and experience the feelings evoked by the words.

Goodman (1973, p. 31) sees reading as a psycholinguistic guessing game in which readers "select the fewest, most productive cues necessary to produce guesses which are right the first time." Goodman believes that although the ability to combine letters to form words is related to learning to read, it has little to do with the process of fluent reading. A person who is reading for meaning does not always need to identify individual words; a reader can comprehend a passage without having identified all the words in it. The more experience a reader has had with language and the concepts presented, the fewer clues from visual configurations (graphophonic clues) he or she will need to determine the meaning of the material. Fluent readers make frequent use of ***semantic*** (meaning) and ***syntactic*** (word-order) clues (or cues) within the material as well (Cooper and Petrosky, 1976). Goodman points out the importance of the reader's ability to anticipate material that he or she has not yet seen. He also stresses that readers bring to their reading all their accumulated experience, language development, and thought in order to anticipate meanings in the printed material (p. 34).

TIME for REFLECTION

Some people believe that meaning resides in the text. Others believe that the reader brings meaning to the text. Still others believe that for the reader to comprehend the meaning fully, reading must involve using both the information in the text and the information that the reader brings to the text in the context in which the reading takes place. **What do *you* think, and why?**

Goodman acknowledges that Rosenblatt (1938/1983) has influenced his thinking (Aaron et al., 1990), and he has moved from a strictly psycholinguistic focus to embrace a transactive focus. "The reader . . . constructs a text during reading through transactions with the published text and the reader's schemata are also transformed in the process. In the receptive processes (listening and reading), meaning is constructed through transactions with the text and indirectly through the text with the writer" (K. S. Goodman, 1985, p. 814). He now asserts that the text a writer constructs has a meaning *potential*, although the text itself does not have meaning. Readers will use this meaning potential to construct their own meaning (Goodman, 1994).

Resolving the Teacher's Dilemma: Taking a Balanced Approach

The current educational situation in many areas can pose a dilemma for teachers. Teachers and students are held accountable for meeting standards of performance set by their state or school districts. In many cases, performance is monitored by standardized tests. In general, the standardized tests of reading consist of performance of isolated skill activities rather than reading whole pieces of text and responding to the text in a variety of ways. To prepare their students to score well on standardized tests, middle-level teachers may choose to follow a subskill approach to reading even if they would otherwise be more likely to follow a more holistic interactive or a transactive theory. Such teachers might have set up classrooms filled with activities related to reading and writing whole pieces of literature rather than activities that focus on isolated skills if they had been able to make their own decisions about what would be best for their students. Mosenthal (1989) suggests that the two approaches (subskills and holistic) can work together.

Middle-school teachers should adopt a balanced approach to reading instruction in which they combine elements of direct skills instruction and elements of holistic instruction in their teaching. They should offer authentic literacy activities in the classroom, but teach skills directly to help students succeed in those activities. Spiegel (1992) sees direct instruction as teaching students strategies that they can use flexibly to meet their reading needs and suggests blending the best holistic approaches and systematic direct instruction in reading strategies to assist all students in reaching their full literacy potential. Strategies may be taught and then practiced using authentic materials rather than worksheets or other forms of isolated drill.

Educators from many philosophical backgrounds recognize the need for a balanced approach. For example, constructivist theory emphasizes student autonomy, student construction of meaning, and student interest. It depicts learners as active, involved, and creative, with the teacher coordinating and critiquing student construction. Airasian and Walsh (1997) point out that students can engage in construction of meaning as part of any teaching approach, and that even memorization and rote learning may be useful parts of learning activities under some circumstances. "One's task is to find the right balance between the activities of constructing and receiving knowledge, given that not all aspects of a subject can or should be taught in the same way or be acquired solely through 'hands-on' or student-centered means" (Airasian and Walsh, 1997, p. 447). Airasian and Walsh (1997) also advocate a balance between teacher involvement and noninvolvement in constructions.

TIME for REFLECTION

Some people think that skills instruction is unnecessary if students are surrounded by print and immersed in a literacy-rich environment. Others think that systematic, direct skills instruction is necessary for a successful reading program. **What do *you* think, and why?**

Instruction should also maintain a balance between focusing on word recognition and focusing on comprehension, with word recognition viewed as a means to enable comprehension, not as a final goal. Comprehension instruction should be emphasized from the very beginning. The principles of instruction in the next section reflect a balanced approach to reading instruction.

Twelve Principles of Teaching Reading

Principles of teaching reading are generalizations about reading instruction based on research in the field of reading and observation of reading practices. The principles listed here are not all-inclusive; many other useful generalizations about teaching reading have been made in the past and will continue to be made in the future. They are, however, the ones we believe are most useful in guiding teachers who are planning reading instruction for students in the middle grades.

Principle 1 ***Reading is a complex act with many factors that must be considered.***

The discussion earlier in this chapter of the nine aspects of the reading process makes this principle clear. Middle-school teachers must understand all parts of the reading process in order to plan reading instruction wisely.

Principle 2 ***Reading involves construction of the meaning represented by printed symbols.***

A student who fails to derive meaning from a passage has not been reading, even if he or she has pronounced every word correctly. Chapters 3 and 4 focus on constructing meaning from reading materials. "In addition to obtaining information from the letters and words in a text, reading involves selecting and using knowledge about people, places, and things, and knowledge about texts and their organization. A text is not so much a vessel containing meaning as it is a source of partial information that enables the reader to use already-possessed knowledge to determine the intended meaning" (R. C. Anderson et al., 1985, p. 8).

DIVERSITY

Readers construct the meanings of passages by using both the information conveyed by the text and their prior knowledge, which is based on their past experiences. Obviously, different readers construct meaning in somewhat different ways because of their varied experiential backgrounds. Some readers do not have enough background knowledge to understand a text; others fail to make good use of the knowledge they have (R. C. Anderson et al., 1985). For example, suppose a text mentions how mountains can isolate a group of people living in them. Students familiar with mountainous areas will picture steep grades and rough terrain, which make road building difficult, and will understand the source of the isolation, although the text never mentions it. Because students from different cultures may come to school with widely varying backgrounds of experiences, teachers must learn about the cultures from which their students come in order to understand the students' perspectives. In addition, language and culture are so tightly connected that "nothing comes from separating them because they have no meaning apart from each other" (Gunderson, 2000, p. 695). Affective factors, such as the reader's attitudes toward the subject matter, also influence the construction of meaning, as does the context in which the reading takes place.

TECHNOLOGY

Student communication is important in constructing meaning. Through use of the Internet, student talk can be extended around the world, and the social aspect of constructing meaning can be taken to extended dimensions. The Internet is also helpful in encouraging construction of meaning because it supports the natural curiosity of the students by putting a large source of information within their reach, enhancing their opportunities to discover ideas for themselves (El-Hindi, 1998).

FAMILY

DIVERSITY

STANDARDS AND ASSESSMENT

One problem with asking middle-school students to construct meaning actively, rather than "feeding" the "correct" meaning to them, occurs when this approach to instruction and learning runs counter to parents' beliefs about education and the purpose of schooling. Constructivist approaches focus on the process of meaning construction rather than on products that demonstrate acquisition of information. Families from other cultures particularly may see this emphasis on process, rather than product, as the teacher's failure to do the "teaching." They may want their children to focus on the accumulation of knowledge that will lead to high test scores and the chance for higher education (Gunderson, 2000), rather than focusing on higher-order thinking and on constructing meaning from printed sources and experience.

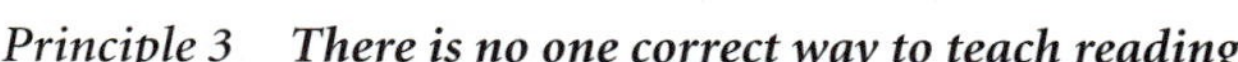

Principle 3 ***There is no one correct way to teach reading.***

Some methods of teaching reading work better for some students than for others. Each student is an individual who learns in his or her own way. Some students are visual learners; some are auditory learners; some are ***kinesthetic/tactile*** learners, who learn better through their combined senses of movement and touch. Some need to be instructed through a combination of ***modalities,*** or avenues of perception, in order to learn. The teacher should differentiate instruction to fit the diverse needs of the students. Of course, some methods also work better for some teachers than they do for others. Teachers need to be acquainted with a variety of methods, including ones that involve technology, so that they can help all of their students.

TECHNOLOGY

Principle 4 ***Learning to read is a continuing process.***

Students learn to read over a long period of time, acquiring more advanced reading skills after they master prerequisite skills. Even after they have been introduced to all reading skills, the process of refinement continues. No matter how old they are or how long they have been out of school, readers continue to refine their reading skills. Reading skills require practice. If readers do not practice, the skills deteriorate; if they do practice, their skills continue to develop.

Principle 5 ***Middle-school students should be taught word recognition strategies that will allow them to unlock the pronunciations and meanings of unfamiliar words independently.***

Students cannot memorize all the words they will meet in print. Therefore, they need to learn techniques for figuring out unfamiliar words so that they can read when the assistance of a teacher, parent, or peer is not available. Chapter 2 focuses on word recognition strategies that students need.

Principle 6 ***The teacher should assess each student's reading ability and use the assessment as a basis for planning instruction.***

Teaching all students the same reading lessons and hoping to deal with all the difficulties students encounter at a single time is a shotgun approach and should be avoided. Such an approach wastes the time of students who have attained the skills currently being emphasized and may never meet some of the desperate needs of other students. Teachers can avoid this approach by using assessment instruments and techniques to pinpoint the strengths and weaknesses of each student in the class. Then they can either group the students for pertinent instruction or give each student individual instruction. Chapter 9 describes many useful tests and other assessment procedures.

STANDARDS AND ASSESSMENT

Principle 7 ***Reading and the other language arts are closely interrelated.***

Reading—the interaction between a reader and written language through which the reader tries to reconstruct the writer's message—is closely related to the other language arts: listening, speaking, writing, viewing, and visually presenting. The strategies and skills needed for the language arts are interrelated. For example, the need to develop and expand concepts and vocabulary, which is essential to reading, is evident in the entire language arts curriculum. Spoken, written, and visual messages are organized around main ideas and supporting details, and people listen, read, and view to identify the main ideas and supporting details conveyed in the material. Chapter 4 contains many examples of reading skills that have parallel listening skills and related writing and speaking skills.

FAMILY People learn to speak before they learn to read and write. Learning to read should be treated as an extension of the process of learning spoken language, a process that generally takes place in the home with little difficulty if students are given normal language input and feedback on their efforts to use language. Students' reading vocabularies generally consist largely of words in their oral language (listening and speaking) vocabularies. These are words for which they have previously developed concepts and therefore can comprehend.

A special relationship exists among listening, reading, and viewing, which are receptive phases of language, as opposed to the expressive phases of speaking, writing, and visually presenting. Students' listening and viewing comprehension are generally superior to their reading comprehension in the elementary school years and into middle school. Mastering listening skills is important in learning to read, for direct association of sound, meaning, and word form must be established from the start. The ability to identify sounds heard at the beginning, middle, or end of a word and the ability to discriminate among sounds are essential to successful phonetic analysis of words. Listening skills also contribute to the interpretation of reading material.

Although receptive skills are not identical and each has its own advantages, they are alike in many ways. For example, all three are constructive processes. In reading, the reader constructs the message from a printed source with the help of background knowledge; in listening, the listener constructs the message from a spoken source with the help of that same background knowledge; and in viewing, the viewer constructs the message from a visual source using background knowledge.

Most people have no difficulty recognizing that the expressive phases of language—speaking, writing, and visually presenting—are also constructive processes. The speaker puts together words in an attempt to convey ideas to one or more listeners; the writer combines words in print to convey ideas to readers; and the individual giving a visual presentation arranges images, and sometimes words and sounds, to convey meaning to a viewer.

The connection between reading and writing is particularly strong. Starting with purposes for writing that affect the choice of ideas and the way these ideas are expressed, writers work to create written messages for others to read. They draw on their past experiences and their knowledge of writing conventions to complete the writing task. As they work, they tend to read and review their material in order to evaluate its effectiveness and to revise it, if necessary. Readers must evaluate the accuracy of their message construction as they monitor their reading processes; they may revise the constructed meaning if the need is apparent in order to establish communication with the writer.

DIVERSITY One means of relating writing experiences to reading experiences is the language experience approach, described in detail in Chapter 5. This approach is often used successfully with English language learners (Herrell, 2000). Writing is also sometimes used as a follow-up or enrichment activity in basal reading lessons. Chapter 6 describes instructional strategies to encourage students to construct written responses to their reading of literature.

Principle 8 Using complete literature selections in the middle-school reading program is important.

LITERATURE

Middle-school students need to experience the reading of whole stories and books to develop their reading skills. Reading isolated words, sentences, and paragraphs does not give them the opportunity to use their knowledge of language and story structure to the fullest, and reading overly simplified language both reduces the opportunities to use their language expertise and dampens interest in reading the material. Whole pieces of literature can include students' own writing and the writing of other students, as well as the works of commercial authors.

Principle 9 Reading is an integral part of all content area instruction within the educational program.

Teachers must consider the relationship of reading to other subjects within the curriculum of the middle school. Frequently, other curricular areas provide applications for the skills taught in the reading period. Textbooks in the various content areas are often the main means of conveying information to students. Students also frequently are required to read library materials, magazines, and newspapers. If they are unable to read these materials with comprehension, they may fail to master important ideas in science, mathematics, social studies, and other areas of the curriculum. Students who have poor reading skills may therefore face failure in other areas of study

TECHNOLOGY

because of the large amount of reading these areas often require. In addition, the need to write reports in social studies, science, health, or other areas can involve many reading and study skills: locating information; organizing information; and using the library and multimedia reference sources, including the Internet.

Teachers who give reading and writing instruction only within isolated periods and treat reading and writing as separate from the rest of the curriculum will probably experience frustration rather than achieve student change and growth. Although a definite period scheduled specifically for language instruction (listening, speaking, reading, writing, viewing, and visually presenting) may be recommended, this does not mean that teachers should ignore these areas when teaching content subjects. The ideal situation at any level is not "reading" and "writing" for separate time periods, followed by "study" of social science or science for the next period. Instead, although the emphasis shifts, language learning and studying should be integrated during all periods at all levels. Chapters 7 and 8 elaborate on these points.

Principle 10 Middle-school students need to see that reading can be an enjoyable pursuit.

It is possible for schools to produce capable readers who do not read; in fact, today this is common. Teachers can help students realize that reading can be entertaining as well as informative by reading stories and poems to them daily and setting aside a regular time for pleasure reading, during which many self-selected books of appropriate levels and from many interest areas are readily available. The Classroom Scenario on Sustained Silent Reading describes one formal schoolwide program of daily reading time.

Teachers can show middle-school students that reading is a recreational pursuit by describing the pleasure they personally derive from reading in their spare time and

CLASSROOM SCENARIO

Sustained Silent Reading

A group of educators visited a middle school in West Tennessee shortly after eight o'clock one morning. When they entered the school, it was extremely quiet. They went directly to the office, where they found the secretary reading a book. One member of the group explained that they had entered the building during the sustained silent reading period and would not be able to talk to anyone until it was over: interruptions to the reading of students, teachers, and staff members were not allowed. The visitors walked quietly through the school, observing the reading that was going on in every classroom. In some classrooms, students were sitting in chairs in a variety of postures or were sprawled on the carpet on their backs or stomachs. All seemed to be completely absorbed in reading books, magazines, or newspapers. At the end of the period, a bell rang, and the students, many reluctantly, put aside their reading materials and readied themselves for classwork. Some whispered excitedly to their neighbors, perhaps about the materials they had been reading. The overall impression the visitors received was that children and adults alike were pleased with the opportunity to read self-chosen material without interruption.

Analysis of Scenario

The use of sustained silent reading in this school gave students the opportunity to read entire stories independently. The students were also allowed to select their own reading material, making it more likely that the material would be more meaningful to them. Motivation to read was high under these conditions.

LITERATURE

by reading for pleasure in the students' presence. When the students read recreationally, the teacher should do this also, thereby modeling desired behavior. Pressures of tests and reports should not be a part of recreational reading times. Students in literature-based reading instructional programs that include self-selection of reading materials and group discussion of chosen reading materials are likely to discover the enjoyable aspects of reading for themselves.

Principle 11 ***Reading should be taught in a way that allows each middle-school student to experience success.***

The stage of the student's literacy development should be considered for all instructional activities throughout the middle grades. Teachers should consider each student's readiness for the instructional activity. If the student's literacy development is not adequate for the task, the teacher should adjust the instruction so that it is congruent with the student's literacy level. This may involve instruction to prepare a student to incorporate the new learning into his or her store of concepts.

Asking students to try to learn to read from materials that are too difficult for them ensures that a large number will fail. Teachers should provide students instruction at their own levels of achievement, regardless of grade placement. Success generates success. If students are given a reading task at which they can succeed, they gain the confidence to undertake the other reading tasks they must perform in a positive way. This greatly increases the likelihood of their success at these later tasks. In addition, some studies have shown that if a teacher *expects* students to be successful readers, they will in fact *be* successful. As Cambourne (2001, p. 785) has pointed out,

"We usually achieve what we expect to achieve (or are expected to achieve by others); we fail when we expect to fail (or are expected by others to fail); we are more likely to engage with the demonstrations by those whom we regard as significant and who hold high expectations for us." Therefore, teachers should always provide instruction with the expectation that the students will be successful.

Teachers should provide struggling readers with materials they can read without undue focus on word recognition. This approach allows them to focus on comprehending the text. (Chapter 9 explains how to determine text difficulty, so that teachers can match students and reading materials.) Poor readers must be convinced that they will gain greater understanding during reading if they apply strategies they have learned (Bristow, 1985).

Teachers tend to place struggling readers in materials that are too hard for them more frequently than they place proficient readers in such materials. Students who are given difficult material to read use active comprehension-seeking behaviors less often than do students who are reading material they can understand with a teacher's assistance. Placing struggling readers on levels that are too high tends to reinforce the inefficient reading strategies that emerge when material is too difficult, making it less likely that these readers will develop more efficient strategies. Although they do not have high expectations of success under any circumstances, their expectations of success decrease more after failure than do those of good readers (Bristow, 1985).

DIVERSITY

Asking students to read from materials that do not relate to their backgrounds of experiences can also result in less successful experiences. In view of the wide cultural diversity in schools today, middle-school teachers must be particularly sensitive to this problem and must provide relevant materials for students that offer them a chance for success.

Principle 12 ***Encouragement of self-direction and self-monitoring of reading is important.***

Effective middle-school readers direct their own reading, making decisions about how to approach particular passages, what reading speed is appropriate, and why they are reading the passages. They are able to decide when they are having difficulties with understanding and can take steps to remedy their misunderstandings (R. C. Anderson et al., 1985). When they do this, they are using ***metacognitive strategies.*** Chapters 3 and 7 present more information about the way good readers read flexibly and monitor their reading.

TIME for REFLECTION

Some people think reading should be taught only during reading class. Others think reading instruction should take place as needed, throughout the entire day. **What do *you* think, and why?**

No matter what teaching approaches are used in a school or what patterns of organization predominate, these twelve principles of teaching reading should apply. Each middle-school teacher should consider carefully his or her adherence or lack of adherence to such principles.

SUMMARY

Middle-school students are developmentally described as adolescents and typically range chronologically from ages eleven through fifteen. Many developmental changes occur for middle-school students, and changes in school performance can result. Middle-school literacy has become a concern due to the number of struggling readers often encountered in the middle grades, the decrease in recreational reading by many middle-school students, and the negative attitude toward reading that some middle-school students report.

The reading act is composed of two major parts: the reading process and the reading product. The reading process has nine aspects—sensory, perceptual, sequential, experiential, thinking, learning, associational, affective, and constructive—that combine to produce the reading product, communication.

Three of the many types of theories about the reading process are subskill theories, interactive theories, and transactive theories. Subskill theories depict reading as a series of subskills that students must master so that they become automatic and smoothly integrated. Interactive theories depict reading as the interaction of two types of processing: top-down and bottom-up. According to the bottom-up view, reading is initiated by the printed symbols (letters and words) and proceeds to larger linguistic units until the reader discovers meaning. According to the top-down view, reading begins with the reader's generation of hypotheses or predictions about the material and proceeds as the reader uses the visual cues in the material to test these hypotheses as necessary. Readers use both types of processing to recognize and comprehend words. Therefore, according to interactive theories, both the print and the reader's background are important in the reading process. Transactive theories depict every reading act as a transaction involving a reader and a text at a particular time in a specific context. Readers generate and test hypotheses about the reading material and get feedback from the material.

Middle-level educators should embrace the idea that standards help to produce good teaching and learning (Wormeli, 2001). Standards for literacy and other language arts have been developed by many states. The National Council of Teachers of English and the International Reading Association have cooperatively developed a set of standards for the English language arts.

Some principles related to reading instruction that may be helpful to teachers include the following:

1. Reading is a complex act with many factors that must be considered.
2. Reading involves construction of the meaning represented by printed symbols.
3. There is no one correct way to teach reading.
4. Learning to read is a continuing process.
5. Middle-school students should be taught word recognition skills that will allow them to unlock the pronunciations and meanings of unfamiliar words independently.
6. The teacher should assess each student's reading ability and use the assessment as a basis for planning instruction.

❼ Reading and the other language arts are closely interrelated.

❽ Using complete literature selections in the middle-school reading program is important.

❾ Reading is an integral part of all content area instruction within the educational program.

❿ Middle-school students need to see that reading can be an enjoyable pursuit.

⓫ Reading should be taught in a way that allows each student to experience success.

⓬ Encouragement of self-direction and self-monitoring of reading is important.

TEST YOURSELF

True or False

______ 1. Over a period of time, a single, clear-cut definition of reading has emerged.

______ 2. Reading is a complex of many skills.

______ 3. Perception involves interpretation of sensation.

______ 4. Prereading questions can affect the way students think while reading.

______ 5. The more meaningful that learning is to a student, the more rapidly associative learning takes place.

______ 6. Word calling and reading are synonymous.

______ 7. Teachers go to school so that they can learn the one way to teach reading.

______ 8. People can continue to refine their reading skills long after their formal schooling is over.

______ 9. Assessing the reading problems of every student in a class is a waste of a teacher's valuable time.

______ 10. Assessment can help a teacher plan appropriate instruction for all students in a class.

______ 11. Reading and the other language arts are closely interrelated.

______ 12. Content area instruction should not have to be interrupted for teaching of reading strategies; reading instruction should remain strictly within a special reading period.

______ 13. Understanding the importance of reading is not important to a middle-school student's reading progress.

______ 14. Middle-school teachers should stress reading for enjoyment as well as for information.

_______ 15. Reading seems to fit in the "skill" category of behavior.

_______ 16. Current theories about reading account for all aspects of the reading process. No research supports the view that reading is a set of subskills that must be mastered and integrated.

_______ 17. A bottom-up model of the reading process assumes that reading is initiated by the printed symbols, with little input required from the reader.

_______ 18. According to an interactive model of reading, parallel processing of information from print and from background knowledge takes place.

_______ 19. Reading involves constructing the meaning of a written passage.

_______ 20. Reading, writing, and viewing are constructive processes.

_______ 21. Teachers give proficient readers materials that are too hard for them more often than they give poor readers such materials.

_______ 22. Metacognitive processes are self-monitoring processes.

_______ 23. Thirty percent of adolescents entering middle grades are reported not to have the basic reading skills they need to be successful.

_______ 24. Transactive theories of the reading process take into account the reader, the text, and the context in which the reading takes place.

_______ 25. A transactive theory would support the position that the meaning resides solely in the text.

_______ 26. Professional organizations have played a part in developing standards for the English language arts.

_______ 27. The amount of instructional emphasis placed on reading instruction increases in the middle school.

_______ 28. Middle-grade students present teachers with special instructional challenges due to their varied and diverse needs.

For your journal . . .

1. Study the following definitions of reading that well-known authorities have suggested. Indicate in your journal which aspect or combination of aspects of the reading process each definition emphasizes most:
   a. "Reading is a process in which information from the text and the knowledge possessed by the reader act together to produce meaning." (R. C. Anderson et al., 1985, p. 8)
   b. Reading is "a complex process by which a reader reconstructs, to some degree, a message encoded by a writer in graphic language." (Southern Prairie Area Education Agency 15, http://www.aea15.k12.ia.us/reading.htm)
   c. Frank Smith describes reading in the following way: "In the reading process the reader's past experiences, expectations about meaning, and word recogni-

tion strategies operate simultaneously to enable the reader to obtain meaning from the printed page." (Southern Prairie Area Education Agency 15, http://www.aea15.k12.ia.us/reading.htm)

d. William S. Gray defines reading as "a process of four components (word perception, comprehension, reaction and integration) that is used to identify printed symbols and associate meaning with these symbols in order to understand ideas conveyed by the writer." (Southern Prairie Area Education Agency 15, http://www.aea15.k12.ia.us/reading.htm)

e. "Reading is thinking . . . reconstructing the ideas of others." (Karlin, 1980, p. 7)

f. "Reading involves the identification and recognition of printed or written symbols which serve as stimuli for the recall of meaning built up through past experience, and further the construction of new meanings through the reader's manipulation of relevant concepts already in his possession. The resulting meanings are organized into thought processes according to the purposes that are operating in the reader." (Tinker and McCullough, 1975, p. 9)

g. "Reading involves nothing more than the correlation of a sound image with its corresponding visual image, that is, the spelling." (Bloomfield and Barnhart, 1961, dustjacket)

h. "Reading typically is the bringing of meaning to rather than the gaining of meaning from the printed page." (Smith and Dechant, 1961, p. 22)

2. Note the points of agreement in the various definitions given in item 1.
3. Find more recent definitions of reading in this text or in journal articles, and compare them with the definitions in item 1.
4. After studying the principles of reading instruction presented in this chapter, see if you can formulate other principles based on your reading in other sources.

. . . and your portfolio

Write a description of the theoretical stance on reading instruction for the middle school that makes the most sense to you. Give reasons for your position.

2

Vocabulary Instruction

KEY VOCABULARY

Pay close attention to these terms when they appear in the chapter.

allusion
analogies
antonyms
context clues
etymology
euphemism
figurative language
homographs
homonyms
homophones
hyperbole
inflectional endings
metaphor
morphemes
personification
semantic clues
semantic feature analysis
semantic maps
sight words
simile
structural analysis
syllable
synonyms
syntactic clues
word sorts
word webs

SETTING OBJECTIVES

When you finish reading this chapter, you should be able to

- Describe ways to help a student develop a sight vocabulary.
- Discuss factors involved in the development of meaning vocabulary.
- Describe activities for teaching use of context clues.
- Discuss ways to teach the various facets of structural analysis.
- Identify the skills students need in order to use a dictionary for both word recognition and word meaning.
- Name and describe several techniques of vocabulary instruction.
- Identify special types of words, and explain how they can cause problems for students.

Vocabulary development has two facets—the ability to recognize words in print and the ability to determine word meanings. Both are essential to the success of middle-school readers. In this chapter, we address the development of both to some degree, although more attention is given to meaning vocabulary, due to the fact that word recognition is the main focus in the primary grades, and many middle-school students can recognize words without understanding their meanings.

Good readers differ from struggling readers in both the number of words they recognize instantly and the ability to decode words. Good readers tend to have larger sight vocabularies than struggling readers, thereby decreasing their need to stop and analyze words. When they do need to analyze words, good readers often have a more flexible approach than struggling readers do because generally teachers have introduced them to several strategies, and they have been encouraged to try a new approach if one strategy fails. Struggling readers frequently know only a single strategy for decoding words. No one strategy is appropriate for all words, however, and thus struggling readers are at a disadvantage when they encounter words for which their strategy is not useful. Even if they have been taught several strategies, poor readers may have failed to learn a procedure that will allow them to decode unfamiliar words as efficiently as possible.

Chapter 2 Organization

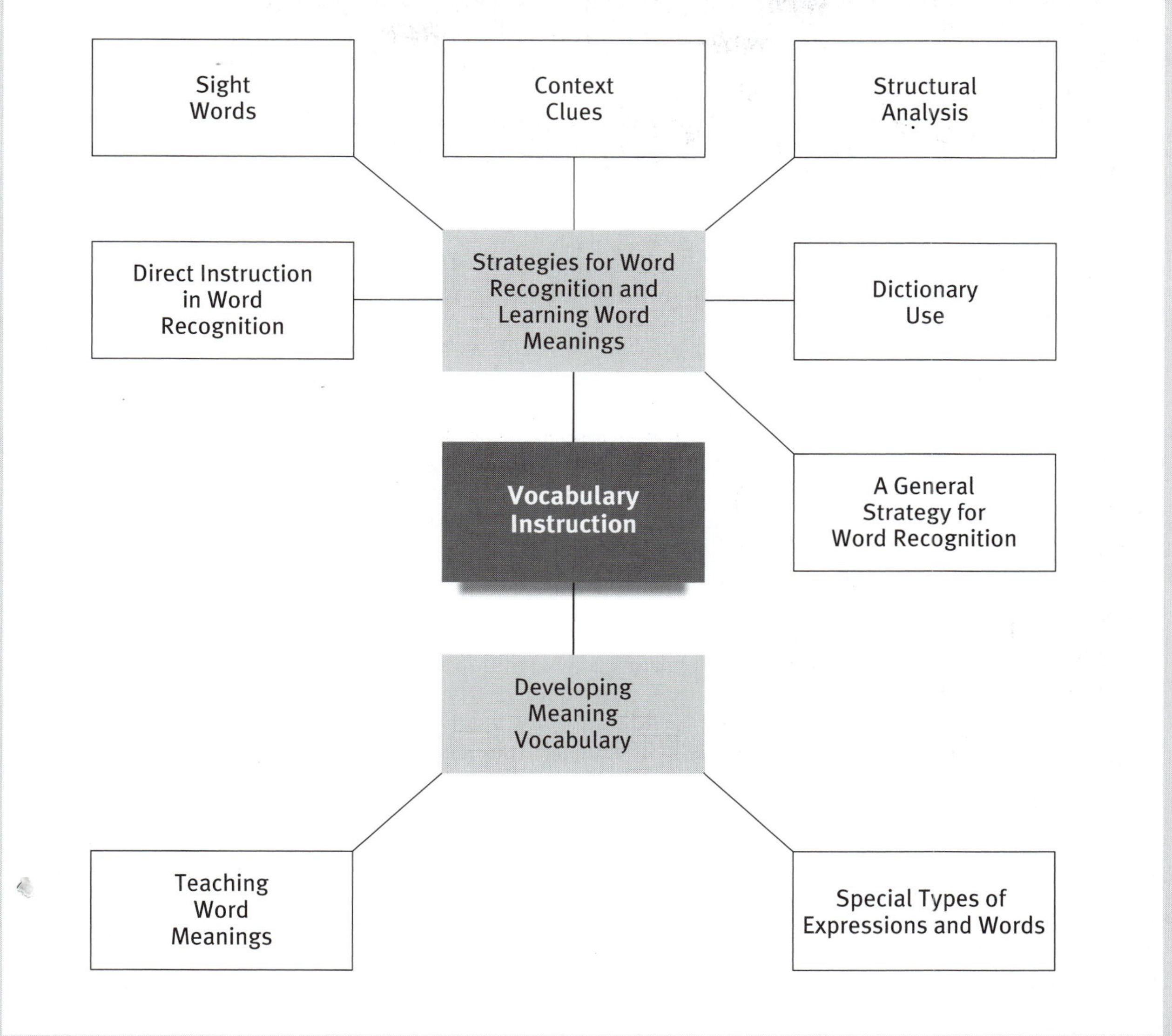

Samuels (1988) sees word recognition skills as "a necessary prerequisite for comprehension and skilled reading" and points out that "we need a balanced reading program, one which combines decoding skills and the skills of reading in context" (pp. 757, 758). He has long supported the idea that accurate and automatic word recognition is necessary for reading fluency. This automaticity (application without conscious thought) in word recognition is achieved through extended practice (*Struggling Readers, Day 1,* 2000). Repeated readings of the same passages can help move students from accuracy to automaticity in word recognition.

Adams (1991) also endorses the need for word recognition skills along with strategies for acquiring meaning. She encourages "thorough overlearning of letters, spelling patterns, and spelling-sound correspondences—and also of vocabulary, syntactic patterns, rhetorical devices, text structures, conceptual underpinnings, and modes of thought on which the full meaning of text depends." However, she denounces "'ponderous drills' on 'isolated skills'" (Adams, 1991, p. 394). She also emphasizes the need for automaticity in decoding to free students' attention for comprehension ("A Talk with Marilyn Adams," 1991). Allen (1998) also believes that decoding needs to be automatic but cautions that children must develop motivation to read, motivation that results from participation in purposeful literacy tasks. This development requires time for reading, book choice, and a chance to discuss the reading material with others.

This chapter presents a variety of methods of word recognition and stresses a flexible approach to unfamiliar words, encouraging application of those word recognition strategies that are most helpful at the moment. It also explains ways to show students how to use a number of word recognition strategies in combination to help in decoding words and discusses techniques for developing knowledge of word meanings.

Decoding words and developing a sight vocabulary are important, but these abilities have little value if students do not understand the words. Students' sight vocabularies should be built from words they already comprehend, words that are a part of their meaning vocabularies.

Meaning vocabulary (words for which meanings are understood) is essentially the set of labels for the clusters of concepts that people have learned through experience. These clusters of concepts, or knowledge structures, are called *schemata*. (Schemata are also discussed in Chapter 3.) Because students must call on their existing schemata in order to comprehend, meaning vocabulary development is an important component of comprehension (Dixon-Krauss, 2001/2002). Therefore, direct instruction in word meanings is a valuable part of reading instruction.

Strategies for Word Recognition and Learning Word Meanings

Word recognition strategies and skills help readers recognize written words. They include development of a store of words that can be recognized immediately on sight and the ability to use context clues, phonics, structural analysis, and dictionaries for word identification where each strategy is appropriate.

We will discuss all of these strategies in this chapter, except phonics. Phonics instruction is largely focused in the primary grades and will not be addressed in this text. For detailed information on phonics instruction, if you need such information as a supplement to this text, refer to *Word Recognition and Meaning Vocabulary* (Burns, Roe, and Ross, 1999). We will discuss the use of context clues, structural analysis, and dictionaries as strategies both for recognizing words and for learning their meaning.

Students need to be able to perform all of the word recognition strategies because some are more helpful than others in certain situations. Teaching a single approach to word identification is not wise, because children may be left without the proper tools for specific situations. In addition, depending on their individual abilities, children find some word recognition strategies easier to learn than others.

Direct Instruction in Word Recognition

Students must be provided with direct instruction, as needed, for skills that they lack. Many researchers have found that direct, systematic instruction in skills and strategies benefits students who have difficulty grasping important reading-writing concepts on their own (Adams, 1990; French, Ellsworth, and Amoruso, 1995; Gaskins, 1988; Sears, Carpenter, and Burstein, 1994; Wong-Kam and Au, 1988). These children seem to learn best when direct instruction in basic skills is part of their instructional program. *Direct instruction* is defined as instruction with clearly stated goals that students understand, carefully sequenced and structured materials, detailed explanations and extensive modeling of reading processes, and monitoring of student work with immediate feedback. It is generally continued until skill mastery is achieved.

Direct instruction focuses on academics and is teacher-directed. Such instruction is not a matter of asking children to complete skill sheets; instead, it is a planned instructional sequence of explaining and modeling. By modeling, the teacher is helping readers understand the "invisible mental processes which are at the core of reading" (Duffy et al., 1988, p. 762). Direct instruction enables students to become independent readers by providing them with additional strategies for attacking unknown words and applying higher-level comprehension skills.

Direct instruction is particularly helpful for students who have difficulty acquiring decoding skills that are essential for learning to read. A potential danger with direct instruction of reading skills in isolation, however, is that students may learn to recognize and pronounce words but be unable to comprehend what they read. Sears and her colleagues (1994) recommend teaching strategies explicitly or directly, but within the context of authentic reading activities. A literacy program that integrates direct instruction and holistic approaches emphasizes reading and writing with many regular opportunities for students to be actively engaged.

DIVERSITY

All students also must be provided with appropriate materials. Students who are having difficulties with word recognition need high-interest materials that they are capable of using successfully. They should not be given material with which they have previously been unsuccessful. When working with all students, but especially with students with special needs, teachers should consider learning styles when planning instruction. English language learners require instruction in use of the English language while they receive instruction in reading. They must build vocabulary and knowledge about English language features before progressing to learning sound-symbol correspondences (*Struggling Readers, Day 1,* 2000).

Use of Literature Can Help

Two uses of literature are particularly effective with middle-school students who have reading difficulties. Sustained Silent Reading (SSR) (see Chapter 8) enables them to choose familiar, predictable, or high-interest books that are easy to read. The opportunity for students to select their material makes SSR motivational for students. The basic plan for SSR can be modified for these students so that they may read their books orally to partners and discuss them in pairs (Ford and Ohlhausen, 1988; Rhodes and Dudley-Marling, 1988). Another useful strategy is repeated shared readings of predictable and repetitive stories and poetry, a procedure that enables students to sense language patterns (Ford and Ohlhausen, 1988; Wicklund, 1989). After repeated exposure, students may then compose their own pieces based on the now familiar patterns. Repeated readings encourage students to use overall contextual meaning and sentence structure to help increase their word recognition accuracy (Walker, 2000).

Sight Words

Students need to have a store of ***sight words***—words that they recognize immediately without having to resort to analysis. The larger the store of sight words a reader has, the more rapidly and fluently he or she can read a selection. Comprehension and reading speed suffer if a reader has to pause too often to analyze unfamiliar words. The more mature and experienced a reader becomes, the larger his or her store of sight words becomes. (Most, if not all, of the words used in this textbook, for example, are part of the sight vocabularies of college students.) Thus, one goal of reading instruction is to turn all the words students need to recognize in print into sight words.

Using a student's stock of sight words as a base, the teacher can present other methods of word recognition. This allows students to reason inductively about sound-symbol associations and other word elements, such as prefixes and suffixes, coming to understand generalizations and rules through experience with specific examples.

Teaching Sight Words

A potential sight word must initially be identified for learners. A teacher should show the students the printed word as he or she pronounces it or pair the word with an identifying picture or object. Reading aloud to students as they follow along in the book is one way to identify vocabulary for them within a meaningful context. Regardless of the method of presentation, one factor is of paramount importance: the students must *look* at the printed word when it is identified in order to associate the letter configuration with the spoken word or picture. If students fail to look at the word when it is pronounced, they have no chance of remembering it when they next encounter it.

Teachers can present words in conjunction with diagrams, pictures, or the actual objects the words name for words from their content area textbooks, such as *lever, divisor, stamen,* and *ballot.* Constructing picture dictionaries, in which students illustrate words and file the labeled pictures alphabetically in a notebook, is a good activity for helping to develop sight vocabulary, especially in content areas that they are studying.

DIVERSITY

This procedure has also been effective in helping students whose primary language is not English learn to read and understand English words.

The language experience approach (described in detail in Chapter 5), in which students' own words are written down and used as the basis for their reading material, is also good for developing sight vocabulary in content areas. This approach provides a meaningful context for learning sight words, and it can be used productively with individuals or groups.

Teachers can call attention to word makeup through comparison and contrast, comparing a new word to a similar known word: *tough* may be compared with *rough* if the students already have *rough* in their sight vocabularies. Either the teacher can point out that the initial letters of the words are different and the other letters are the same, or the students can discover this on their own. The latter method is preferable, because students are likely to remember their own discoveries longer than they will remember something the teacher has told them.

Few words are learned after a single presentation, although Ashton-Warner (1963) claims that students will instantly learn words that are extremely important to them. Generally, a number of repetitions are necessary before a word becomes a sight word.

Practice with Sight Words

The teacher should carefully plan practice with potential sight words. This practice should be varied and interesting, because students will more readily learn those things that interest them. Games, such as those we discuss later in this chapter, are useful if they emphasize the words being learned rather than the rules of the game.

Ceprano (1981) reviewed research on methods of teaching sight words and found that no one method alone was best for every student. She found evidence that teaching the distinctive features of words helped students learn them. Ceprano also reported that some research indicates that teaching words in isolation or with pictures does not ensure the ability to read words in context. In fact, indications are that "most learners need directed experience with written context while learning words in order to perceive that reading is a language process and a meaning-getting process" (p. 321). Readers cannot pronounce many words out of context with certainty—for example, *read.* The following sentences indicate the importance of context:

I *read* that book yesterday.   I can't *read* without glasses.

Much teaching of sight word recognition takes place as a part of basal reader lessons. For example, the teacher frequently introduces the new words, possibly in one of the ways described previously in this chapter, before reading, discussing meanings at the same time. Then students have a guided silent reading period during which they read material containing the new words in order to answer questions that the teacher asks. Purposeful oral rereading activities offer another chance to use the new words. Afterward, teachers generally provide practice activities suggested in the teacher's manual of the basal reading series. Follow-up activities may include skill sheets, games, manipulative devices, and special audiovisual materials. Writing new words is helpful for some learners, especially for kinesthetic learners (those who learn through muscle movement).

TIME for REFLECTION

Some people believe sight words should be taught in context. Others believe they should be taught in isolation. What procedures would you use?

Nicholson (1998) suggests using flashcards to foster automaticity in word recognition. He further points out that recent research indicates that "teaching children to read words faster can improve reading comprehension dramatically" (p. 188).

Context Clues

Context clues—the words, phrases, and sentences surrounding the words to be decoded—help readers determine what the unfamiliar words are. Context clues can also help students learn the meanings of unfamiliar words. We will discuss both uses of context clues in this section.

As we noted in the section on sight words, it is important that word recognition skills be introduced and practiced in context. Research shows that context clues help challenged readers recognize words more than they help better readers (Daneman, 1991; Gough, 1984).

Context clues help to verify words that have been decoded through phonics. As Heilman (2002, p. 1) points out in emphasizing the benefits of using phonics in conjunction with context clues, "English spelling patterns being what they are, children will sometimes arrive at only a close approximation of the needed sounds. . . . Fortunately, if they are reading for meaning, they will instantly correct these errors."

Context can also help readers choose the correct word from among familiar words. Some words, for example, are difficult to pronounce unless they appear in context. Many ***homographs***—words that look alike but have different meanings and sometimes different pronunciations, such as *row, wind, bow, read, content, rebel, minute, lead, record,* and *live*—are prime examples. Here are some sentences that demonstrate how context can clarify the pronunciations of such words:

1. The *wind* is blowing through the trees. Did you *wind* the clock last night?
2. She put a *bow* on the gift. You should *bow* to the audience when you finish your act.
3. Would you *rebel* against that law? I have always thought you were a *rebel.*
4. Did your father *record* his gas mileage? Suzanne broke Jill's *record* for the highest score in one game.

Locating Context Clues

Research has found that syntactic and semantic context influence readers' identification of words (Jones, 1982). ***Semantic clues*** are clues derived from the meanings of the words, phrases, and sentences surrounding the unknown word. ***Syntactic clues*** are provided by the grammar or syntax of our language. Certain types of words appear in certain positions in spoken English sentences. Thus, word order can give readers clues to the identity of an unfamiliar word. Semantic and syntactic clues should be used *together* to unlock unknown words.

Several specific kinds of context clues are found in written materials:

- *Definition clues.* A word may be directly defined in the context. Example: The *dictionary* is a book in which the meanings of words can be found.

- *Appositive clues.* An appositive may offer a synonym or a description of the word that will cue its meaning. Students need to be taught that an *appositive* is a word or phrase that restates or identifies the word or expression it follows and that it is usually set off by commas, dashes, or parentheses. Examples: They are going to *harvest,* or gather in, the season's crops. That model is *obsolete* (outdated). The *rodents*—rats and mice—in the experiment learned to run a maze.

- *Comparison clues.* A comparison of the unfamiliar word with a word the student knows may offer a clue. In the following examples, the familiar words *sleepy* and *clothes* provide the clues for *drowsy* and *habit.* Examples: Like her sleepy brother, Mary felt *drowsy.* Like all the other clothes she wore, her riding *habit* was very fashionable.

- *Contrast clues.* A contrast of the unknown word with a familiar one may offer a clue. In the following examples, the unfamiliar word *temporary* is contrasted with the familiar word *forever,* and the unfamiliar word *occasionally* is contrasted with the familiar word *regularly.* Examples: It will not last forever; it is only *temporary.* She doesn't visit regularly; she just comes by *occasionally.*

- *Example clues.* Sometimes examples are given for words that may be unfamiliar in print, and these examples can provide the clues needed for identification. Examples: Mark was going to talk about *reptiles*—for example, snakes and lizards. Andrea wants to play a *percussion* instrument, such as the snare drum or bells.

Although the examples in the list have clues in the sentences in which the new words are found, context can also offer clues in sentences other than the one in which the new words appear, so students should be encouraged to read surrounding sentences for clues to meaning. Sometimes an entire paragraph embodies the explanation of a term, as in the following example:

> I've told you before that the flu is contagious! When Johnny had the flu, Beatrice played with him one afternoon, and soon Beatrice came down with it. Joey caught it from her, and now you tell me you have been to Joey's house. I hope you don't come down with the flu and have to miss the party on Saturday.

LITERATURE

Context clues are available in both text and illustrations in many trade books. *A Gaggle of Geese,* by Philippa-Alys Browne (Atheneum Books for Young Readers, 1996); *A Gaggle of Geese,* by Eve Merriam (Knopf, 1960); and *A Cache of Jewels and Other Collective Nouns,* by Ruth Heller (Grosset & Dunlap, 1987) put collective terminology for groups into interesting contexts. Teaching the use of context clues in these meaningful settings encourages students to use such clues in their independent reading. Illustrations often provide strong context clues for English language learners.

DIVERSITY

TECHNOLOGY **DIVERSITY**

Some researchers have found that using closed-caption television programs to provide readers with both auditory and visual context was effective with below-average readers and bilingual students (Koskinen et al., 1993; Neuman and Koskinen, 1992). Such programs provided readers with print to read in a motivational format. Videotaping the programs allows repetition of the reading for different purposes and use of small segments (only a few minutes each) of video in a lesson. (Teachers must study copyright laws, however, to ensure that use is in compliance with these laws.) Teachers and students could discuss words from the programs while the students were viewing video images. Later, students could read the words again, from handouts prepared with sentences drawn from the captioned video, and finally from magazines and books on the same topic. They could also use the words in written retellings of the viewed episode. The captions presented some challenges for readers: the match between the audio and the captions seen was not exact; the captions were presented at a rapid rate for poor readers (about 120 words per minute); and the captions were in all capital letters. Nevertheless, the results teachers obtained were impressive.

Teaching Students to Use Context Clues

It is estimated that average ten- to fourteen-year-old students can acquire from 750 to 8,250 new words each year through incidental, rather than directed, contextual learning (Herman et al., 1987; Nagy, Herman, and Anderson, 1985; Schwartz, 1988). Helping students learn to use context more efficiently should therefore greatly enhance their vocabulary learning.

Teachers need to help students learn *why* and *when* to use context clues (Blachowicz and Zabroske, 1990). For word identification, context clues are best used with phonics (sound-symbol associations) and structural analysis (word part) skills. (Structural analysis is discussed in more detail later in this chapter.) Context clues help students identify words more quickly than phonics or structural analysis clues alone would by helping them make educated guesses about the identities of unfamiliar words. But without the confirmation of phonics and structural analysis, context clues provide only guesses.

For determining the meanings of words, context clues are useful when the context is explicit about word meaning, but they are less useful when the meaning is left unclear. If the clues are too vague, they may actually be misleading. Furthermore, if the word is not important to understanding the passage, the explicitness of the context is not important. Teachers should model through think-alouds (described later in this chapter) their decision-making processes about the importance of determining the meaning of the word, the usefulness of the context, and the kinds of clues available there. Students need to realize that the meanings they attribute to the words must make sense in the context.

Early exercises with context clues involve oral context, filling in missing words in oral sentences presented by the teacher. Next, written context can be presented. It is good practice for a teacher to introduce a new word in context and let students try to identify it, rather than simply telling them what the word is. Then students can use any phonics and structural analysis knowledge they have, along with context clues, to help them identify the word. The teacher should use a context in which the only unfamiliar word is the new word; for example, use the sentence "I use my *thesaurus* to find synonyms for words that I repeat too much in my writing" to present the word *thesaurus.* The students will thus have successful examples of the value of context clues in identifying unfamiliar words.

Teachers can create their own sentences to introduce new words in context by using sentences that students can relate to their own experiences and that have only one unfamiliar word each. It is best not to use the new word at the very beginning of the sentence, since the students will not have had any of the facilitating context before they encounter it (Duffelmeyer, 1982).

Context can also come from reading selections. Edwards and Dermott (1989) select difficult words from material about to be assigned, take a quotation using each word in good context from the material, and provide written comments to the students to help them use appropriate context clues or other strategies (primarily structural analysis or dictionary use). The students try to use the clues available to decide on the meanings of the words before reading. Class discussion helps the students to think through the strategy use.

Instruction that gradually moves the responsibility for determining new word meanings from the teacher to the student helps students become independent learners. Teachers can guide students to use context clues to define words independently by using a four-part procedure. First, students are given categorization tasks (described later in this chapter). Second, they practice determining meanings from complete contexts. Third, they practice determining meanings in incomplete contexts. Finally, they practice defining new vocabulary by means of context clues (Carr and Wixson, 1986).

When a student encounters an unfamiliar word while reading orally to the teacher, instead of supplying the word, the teacher can encourage the student to skip it for the time being and read on to the end of the sentence (or even to the next sentence) to see what word would make sense. Students should be encouraged to look for clues in surrounding sentences or the entire paragraph, as well as in the sentence in which the word occurs. Sometimes an entire paragraph will be useful in defining a term.

The teacher can encourage use of the sound of the initial letter or cluster of letters, sounds of other letters in the word, or known structural components, along with context. In a sentence where *hurled* appears as an unknown word in the phrase *hurled the ball,* a child might guess *held* from the context. The teacher can encourage this student to notice the letters *ur* and try a word that contains those sounds and makes sense in the context. (Of course, this approach will be effective only if the student knows the meaning of *hurled.*) Encouraging the student to read subsequent sentences could also be helpful, since these sentences might disclose a situation in which *held* would be inappropriate but *hurled* would fit.

Think-Alouds. Teachers can use a think-aloud strategy to help students see how to use context clues. (Think-aloud strategies are valuable in teaching several aspects of reading.) The Model Activities Lesson on Context Clues makes use of this strategy.

MODEL ACTIVITIES

Middle-School Lesson on Context Clues

Write on the board or display on a transparency the following sentence: "Rather than encountering hostile natives, as they had expected, many settlers found the natives to be amicable." Read the sentence aloud and say, "I wonder what *amicable* means? Let's see; the sentence says '*Rather than* encountering hostile natives.' That means the natives weren't hostile. *Hostile* means *unfriendly,* so maybe *amicable* means *friendly.*"

After several example think-aloud activities in which the teacher models the use of context clues, the teacher can ask student volunteers to think aloud the context clues for specific words. Students may work in pairs on a context clues activity and verbalize their context usage strategies to each other. Finally, the students should work alone to determine meanings from context clues.

The Cloze Procedure. A cloze passage, in which words have been systematically deleted and replaced with blanks of uniform length, can be a good way to work on context clue use. For this purpose, the teacher may delete certain types of words (e.g., nouns, verbs, or adjectives) rather than using random deletion. The students should discuss their reasons for choosing the words to be inserted in the blanks, and the teacher should accept synonyms and sometimes nonsynonyms for which the students have a good rationale. The point of the exercise is to have the students think logically about what makes sense in the context. (Other uses for the *cloze procedure* and more details about it are found in Chapters 3 and 9.)

A modified cloze procedure can be used with a story summary to develop students' skills in decoding in a meaningful context. The first letter of the deleted word is provided, helping students use their knowledge of sound-symbol relationships as well as choosing words that make sense in the context (Johnson and Louis, 1987). A student who encountered the following sentence, for example, might fill in the blank with the either *polls* or *stores:*

> After the _____ close, election officials count the ballots.

If the sentence indicated the initial sound of the missing word by presenting the initial letter *p,* the student would know that *polls,* rather than *stores,* was the appropriate word:

> After the p_____ close, election officials count the ballots.

Structural analysis clues can be used in the same way. In the following sentence, a student might insert such words as *stop* or *keep* in the blank:

> I wouldn't want to _____ you from going on the trip.

The student who had the help of the familiar prefix *pre-* to guide his or her choice would choose neither. The word *prevent* would obviously be one correct choice.

> I wouldn't want to pre_____ you from going on the trip.

Suffixes and ending sounds are also very useful in conjunction with context to help in word identification. Sample sentences for practice activities can be drawn from stories that the students are about to read in class.

An easier task is to use a maze passage, in which the deleted words are replaced by three choices. This task may work better with students who are having difficulty with reading tasks. (The maze procedure is discussed in Chapters 3 and 9.)

The cloze procedure can be combined with other teaching strategies. DeSerres (1990) introduces basal reader stories' mastery vocabulary by presenting each word on

TIME for REFLECTION

Some people believe students should learn basic skills before they begin reading selections. Others believe they should learn skills as they encounter the need for them within selections. **What do *you* think, and why?**

the board in sentence context, having students write the word in another sentence or phrase context on 3″ × 5″ word cards for their word banks, and letting them share their sentences. Later she uses modified cloze stories (in which selected words, rather than regularly spaced words, are deleted) with the mastery words as the words chosen for omission. Students fill in the blanks by choosing from their word cards as the class reads the story together. Then they fill in the blanks on individual copies of the stories and read them to partners. Partners point out parts that do not make sense. Later, students produce their own stories. This procedure gives practice with using context.

Structural Analysis

Structural analysis can help in word recognition as well as in learning word meanings. It has several significant facets:

1. Inflectional endings
2. Prefixes and suffixes
3. Contractions
4. Compound words
5. Syllabication and accents

The first four relate to meaningful word parts and are also referred to as morphemic analysis. Structural analysis strategies and skills enable students to decode unfamiliar words by using units larger than single graphemes (written symbols for sounds); this procedure generally expedites the decoding process.

Inflectional Endings

Students begin to learn about word structure very early. First, they deal with words in their simplest, most basic forms—as ***morphemes,*** the smallest units of meaning in a language. (The word *cat* is one morpheme.) Then they gradually learn to combine morphemes. If an *s* is added to form the plural, *cats,* the final *s* is also a morpheme, because it changes the word's meaning. There are two classes of morphemes, distinguished by function: *free* morphemes, which have independent meanings and can be used by themselves (*cat, man, son*), and *bound* morphemes, which must be combined with another morpheme to have meaning. ***Inflectional endings*** are one type of bound morpheme. They are added to nouns to change number, case, or gender; added to verbs to change tense or person; and added to adjectives to change degree. They may also change a word's part of speech. Since inflectional endings are letters or groups of letters added to the endings of root words, some people call them *inflectional suffixes.* Here are some examples of words with inflectional endings:

Root Word	New Word	Change
boy	boys	Singular noun changed to plural noun
host	hostess	Gender of noun changed from masculine to feminine
Karen	Karen's	Proper noun altered to show possession (change of case)
look	looked	Verb changed from present tense to past tense
make	makes	Verb changed from first- or second-person singular to third-person singular
mean	meaner	Simple form of adjective changed to the comparative form
happy	happily	Adjective changed to adverb

The Model Activity below can be used to help lower-performing middle-school students and students for whom English is a second language practice recognition of inflectional endings.

Prefixes and Suffixes

Prefixes and suffixes are *affixes*, a type of bound morpheme consisting of letters or sequences of letters that are added to root words to change their meanings and/or parts of speech. A *prefix* is placed before a root word, and a *suffix* is placed after a root word.

Students can learn the pronunciations and meanings of some common prefixes and suffixes. Good readers learn to recognize common prefixes and suffixes instantly; this helps them recognize words more rapidly than they could if they had to resort to sounding each word letter by letter.

MODEL ACTIVITIES Recognizing Inflectional Endings

Write on the board sentences containing inflectional endings that have already been discussed, taken from a book that the class has previously read. Ask the students to read the sentences silently, looking for the inflectional endings they have studied. After the silent reading, let volunteers go to the board, circle the inflectional endings in the sentences, and tell how each ending affects word meaning or word use.

You will not want to use all possible examples from the book in this activity. Instead, you can encourage students to go back to the book itself, either individually or in pairs, locate the inflectional endings under consideration, and make a list of the words they find. These words can be discussed later in a group discussion, with the students finding the words in the story and reading the sentences in which they appear.

As an example, just page 52 of Katherine Paterson's *Lyddie* could be used for sentences containing the words *clanging, girls, softened, dressing, squabbling, forced, barely, fully, coachman's, kindly, hurriedly, Charlie's, mud-caked, carried, plopped, directly, boiling, rumors, wonders, keeper's, scrubbed, straining, remaining, eyes, and stared.* From this single page, you could effectively review the inflectional endings *-ed, -s, -'s, -ly,* and *-ing*. You may decide to handle each inflectional ending in a separate lesson.

Learning common prefixes and suffixes can help students recognize unfamiliar words. *(© Elizabeth Crews)*

The suffixes *-ment, -ous, -tion,* and *-sion* have especially consistent pronunciations and thus are particularly useful to know. The suffixes *-ment* and *-ous* generally have the pronunciations heard in the words *treatment* and *joyous.* The suffixes *-tion* and *-sion* have the sound of *shun,* as heard in the words *education* and *mission.*

Whereas prefixes simply modify the meanings of the root words, suffixes may change the parts of speech as well as modify the meanings. Knowing meanings of common affixes and combining them with meanings of familiar root words can help students determine the meanings, as well as the pronunciations, of many new words. For example, if a student knows the meaning of *joy* and knows that the suffix *-ous* means *full of,* he or she can conclude that the word *joyous* means *full of joy.* Some of the resulting modifications are listed here:

Root Word	Affix	New Word	New Meaning or Change
happy	un-	unhappy	not happy
amuse	-ment	amusement	verb is changed to noun
worth	-less	worthless	meaning is opposite of original meaning

LITERATURE 

Use the Model Activity below for lessons on recognizing prefixes and suffixes.

White, Sowell, and Yanagihara (1989) have identified nine prefixes (*un-; re-; in-, im-, ir-* [meaning *not*]; *dis-; en-, em-; non-; in-, im-* [meaning *in* or *into*]; *over-* [meaning *too much*]; and *mis-*) that cover 76 percent of the prefixed words in the *Word Frequency Book* (Carroll, Davies, and Richman, 1971). They recommend that these prefixes be taught systematically, beginning with *un-*, which alone accounts for 26 percent of the prefixed words. An analysis of their word counts would lead us to add *sub-, pre-, inter-*, and *fore-* to the recommended list, since they occur as frequently as *over-* and *mis-*, thereby covering 88 percent of the prefixed words.

White et al. (1989) have identified ten suffixes and inflectional endings that are part of 85 percent of the suffixed words in the *Word Frequency Book* (Carroll, Davies, and Richman, 1971): *-s,-es; -ed; -ing; -ly; -er, -or* (agentive); *-ion, -tion, -ation, -ition; -ible, -able; -al, -ial; -y;* and *-ness.* The three inflectional endings *-s/-es, -ed,* and *-ing* alone account for 65 percent of the incidences of suffixed words in the sample.

White et al. (1989) caution teachers that prefixes may have more than one meaning. *Un-, re-, in-,* and *dis-,* the four most frequently used prefixes, have at least two meanings each. *Un-* and *dis-* may each mean either *not* or *do the opposite. In-* may mean either *not,* or *in,* or *into. Re-* may mean either *again* or *back.* Both the word parts and the context of the word should be considered in determining meanings of prefixed words.

The Classroom Scenario on page 49 shows another application of structural analysis in the classroom.

MODEL ACTIVITIES Recognition of Prefixes and Suffixes

After instruction in prefixes and suffixes, give the students duplicated sheets containing paragraphs from a story that has just been shared in class. Ask them to work independently and circle the prefixes and suffixes they see in the paragraphs. Then divide them into small groups and have them compare and discuss their responses. Each group should come to an agreement about the correct answers. Finally, check the group responses in a whole-class discussion, calling on small-group representatives to give each group's responses to various items.

For example, in *Nadia the Willful* by Sue Alexander, the following words appear: *stubbornness, willful, kindness, graciousness, return, emptiness, punishment, remind, uneasily, hardness, coldness, unhappiness, bitterness, inside, recall, recalled, unbidden, happiness, sharpness,* and *forward.* Some of the words occur several times. The paragraphs in which these words appear can be duplicated for this exercise.

Not all of the words need to be used in a single lesson. You may wish to use one prefix or suffix at a time.

CLASSROOM SCENARIO

Use of Structural Analysis Skills

A middle-school science textbook presented two theories of the solar system: a geocentric theory and a heliocentric theory. Two diagrams were provided to help the students visualize the two theories, but the diagrams were not labeled. Mrs. Brown, the teacher, asked the students, "Which diagram is related to each theory?"

Matt's hand quickly went up, and he accurately identified the two diagrams.

"How did you decide which was which?" asked Mrs. Brown.

"You told us that *geo-* means *earth. Centric* looks like it comes from *center.* This diagram has the earth in the center. So I decided it was geocentric. That would mean the other one was heliocentric. Since the sun is in the center in it, I guess *helio-* means *sun.*"

Analysis of Scenario

Mrs. Brown had taught an important science word part the first time it occurred in her class. She had encouraged her students to use their knowledge of word parts to figure out unfamiliar words. Matt followed her suggestions and managed to make decisions about key vocabulary based on his knowledge of word parts.

Contractions

The apostrophe used in *contractions* indicates that one or more letters have been left out when two words were combined into one word. Students need to learn the meanings of contractions and they need to be able to recognize the original words from which the contractions were formed. The following are common contractions, with their meanings, that teachers should present to students:

can't/cannot	I'd/I had or I would	I'll/I will	shouldn't/should not
couldn't/could not	they'd/they had or they would	I'm/I am	we've/we have
didn't/did not	they'll/they will	I've/I have	won't/will not
don't/do not	they're/they are	isn't/is not	wouldn't/would not
hadn't/had not	they've/they have	let's/let us	you'll/you will
hasn't/has not	wasn't/was not	she'd/she would or she had	you're/you are
he'll/he will	we're/we are	she'll/she will	you've/you have
he's/he is or he has	weren't/were not	she's/she is or she has	

The teacher may wish to teach contractions in related groups—for example, those in which *not* is the reduced part, those in which *have* is the reduced part, and so on. The contractions should be presented in connected text, not in list format. Students should locate these contractions and their uncontracted referents in context and use them in writing to enhance their learning.

Compound Words

Compound words consist of two (or occasionally three) words that have been joined together to form a new word. The original pronunciations of the component words are usually maintained. Students can be asked to underline or circle component parts of compound words or to put together familiar compound words as practice activities in word recognition. An exercise for compound words is in the Model Activity below.

LITERATURE

Students can often determine meanings of compound words by relating the meanings of the component parts to each other (*watchdog* means a *dog* that *watches*). After some practice, they can be led to see that the component parts of a compound word do not always have the same relationships to each other (*bookcase* means a *case* for *books*). The Focus on Strategies on compound words on page 51 provides an activity that can offer practice in determining meanings of compound words.

Syllabication/Accent

Since many phonics generalizations apply not only to one-syllable words but also to syllables within longer words, many people believe that breaking words into syllables can help determine pronunciation. Some research indicates, however, that syllabication is usually done after the reader has recognized the word and that readers use the sounds to determine syllabication rather than syllabication to determine the sounds (Glass, 1967). If students normally attack words using sounds first, then syllabication would seem to be of little use in a word analysis program. On the other hand, many authorities firmly believe that syllabication is helpful in decoding words. For this reason, a textbook on reading methods would be incomplete without discussions of syllabication and a related topic, stress or accent.

A ***syllable*** is a letter or group of letters that forms a pronunciation unit. Every syllable contains a vowel sound. In fact, a vowel sound may form a syllable by itself (*a/mong*). Only in a syllable that contains a diphthong is there more than one vowel sound. Diphthongs are treated as single units, although they are actually vowel blends. Whereas each syllable has only one vowel sound or diphthong, a syllable may have

MODEL ACTIVITIES Recognizing Compound Words

Display a page from a book (or a transparency made from a book page) that contains several compound words. Let students come to the book (or the projected image) and point out the words that are made up of two or more words—for example, on one page of *A Year Down Yonder* by Richard Peck (2000), the words *billboard, housekeeping, Grandma, hick-town, outdoors,* and *everything.* Write the words on the board. Let volunteers come to the board and circle the separate words that make up each compound word. Have a class discussion about the way to decide how to pronounce compound words and what they mean.

FOCUS ON STRATEGIES Learning the Meanings of Compound Words

Mr. Clay based his lesson on the book *The Seal Mother* by Mordicai Gerstein. He introduced the story by saying that it was an old Scottish folktale. Then he wrote the word *folktale* on the board and asked, "What can you tell me about this word?"

Bobby answered, "It is made up of two words: *folk* and *tale*. That makes it a compound word."

"Good, Bobby," Mr. Clay responded. "What does that make you believe this word means?"

"A tale is a story," LaTonya replied.

"That's right," said Mr. Clay. "Can anyone add anything else to what we know about the word's meaning? What does *folk* mean?"

Carl answered tentatively, "A kind of music?"

"There is folk music, just as there are folktales, but we still need a meaning for the word *folk*," Mr. Clay responded.

After he got only shrugs, he explained, "A folktale is a tale, or story, told by the folk, or common people, of a country. Folktales were passed down orally from older people to younger ones over the years. See how both parts of the compound word give something to the meaning?"

"Listen as I read this story to you. When I finish, we will try to retell the story by listing the main events."

The students listened intently. When he finished the story, Mr. Clay asked them to list the events in the story in order. As they suggested events, he wrote each one on the board. When he had listed all of the events they could remember, they discussed how to put some of the events in the proper order. Mr. Clay erased and moved the sentences around until the students were satisfied.

Then Mr. Clay asked the children, "Did you use any compound words to retell the story?"

Hands shot up all over the room. Mr. Clay called on them one by one, and they pointed out *fisherman, sealskin, without, oilcloth, inside, rayfish, everywhere, grandfather,* and *whenever.* The students who mentioned the words were allowed to go to the board and circle them, identify the two words that made up each compound, and try to define each compound word, using the meanings of the two component words. Other students helped in determining the definitions, and sometimes the dictionary was consulted.

Finally, the students were asked to copy the compound words from the board into their vocabulary study notebooks. "I'm putting three copies of *The Seal Mother* in the reading center for the rest of this week," Mr. Clay said. "When you have time, get a copy of the book from the center and read it. Each time you find one of our compound words, put a checkmark by the word in your vocabulary notebook. When you find a compound word that we didn't use in our retelling, copy it into your notebook, and write a definition for it, using the meanings of the two words and the context of the sentence in which you found it. We'll discuss the other words that you found on Friday."

On Friday, the students had found a number of words in the book that they hadn't used in their retelling, including *moonlit, moonlight, everything, wide-eyed, tiptoed, another,* and *into.* A discussion of the words and their meanings followed. Mr. Clay asked how use of some of these words added to the students' understanding of the story.

"*Moonlit* and *moonlight* give you a picture in your mind of the scene," Jared offered.

"*Wide-eyed* lets us know how his parents' talk made the boy feel," Marissa added.

"*Tiptoed* showed us how he walked quietly," Tyrone said.

"Watch for compound words in other books that you read, and use the meanings of the two words in each compound to help you with meanings that you don't already know," Mr. Clay told them as he ended the lesson.

more than one vowel letter. Letters and sounds should not be confused. The word *peeve,* for example, has three vowel letters, but the only vowel sound is the long *e* sound. Therefore, *peeve* contains only one syllable.

There are two types of syllables: open and closed. *Open* syllables end in vowel sounds; *closed* syllables end in consonant sounds. Syllables may in turn be classified as accented (given greater stress) or unaccented (given little stress). Accent has much to do with the vowel sound we hear in a syllable. Multisyllabic words may have primary (strongest), secondary (second strongest), and even tertiary (third strongest) accents. The vowel sound of an open accented syllable is usually long (*mi´ nus, ba´ sin*); the second syllable of each of these example words is unaccented, and the vowel sound represented is the schwa, often found in unaccented syllables. A single vowel in a closed accented syllable generally has its short sound, unless it is influenced by another sound in that syllable (*cap´ sule, cär´ go*).

Following are several useful generalizations concerning syllabication and accent:

- Words contain as many syllables as they have vowel sounds (counting diphthongs as a unit). Examples: *se/vere* (final *e* has no sound); *break* (*e* is not sounded); *so/lo* (both vowels are sounded); *oil* (diphthong is treated as a unit).
- In a word with more than one sounded vowel, when the first vowel is followed by two consonants, the division is generally between the two consonants. Examples: *mar/ry, tim/ber.* If the two consonants are identical, the second one is not sounded.
- Consonant blends (adjacent consonants whose sounds are blended, but retain their identities) and consonant digraphs (two adjacent consonants that produce a single sound) are treated as units and are not divided. Examples: *ma/chine, a/bridge.*
- In a word with more than one sounded vowel, when the first vowel is followed by only one consonant or consonant digraph, the division is generally after the vowel. Examples: *ma/jor, ri/val* (long initial vowel sounds). There are, however, many exceptions to this rule, which make it less useful. Examples: *rob/in, hab/it* (short initial vowel sounds).
- When a word ends in *-le* preceded by a consonant, the preceding consonant plus *-le* constitute the final syllable of the word. This syllable is never accented, and the vowel sound heard in it is the schwa. Examples: *can/dle, ta/ble.*
- Prefixes and suffixes generally form separate syllables. Examples: *dis/taste/ful, pre/dic/tion.*
- A compound word is divided between the two words that form the compound, as well as between syllables within the component words. Examples: *snow/man, thun/der/storm.*
- Prefixes and suffixes are usually not accented. Example: *dis/grace´ ful.*
- Words that can be used as both verbs and nouns are accented on the second syllable when used as verbs and on the first syllable when used as nouns. Examples: *pre/sent´*—verb; *pres´ ent*—noun.

- In two-syllable root words, the first syllable is usually accented, unless the second syllable has two vowel letters. Examples: *rock´ et, pa/rade´.*
- Words containing three or more syllables are likely to have secondary (and perhaps tertiary) accents, in addition to primary accents. Example: *reg´ i/men/ta´ tion.*

TIME for REFLECTION

Think back to when you were a middle-school student. Did you divide words into syllables to figure out the likely vowel sounds, or did you try sounds and see if they combined to form words that made sense?

Generalizations about syllabication can be taught by presenting many examples of a particular generalization and leading the students to state the generalization.

In dictionaries, it is the syllable divisions in the phonetic respellings, rather than the ones indicated in the boldface entry words, that are useful to students in pronouncing unfamiliar words. The divisions of the boldface entry words are a guide for hyphenation in writing, not for word pronunciation.

Accentuation generally is not taught until students have a good background in word attack skills and is often presented in conjunction with dictionary study as a tool for word attack. More will be said on this topic in the next section of this chapter.

Dictionary Use

Dictionaries are valuable tools that can help in completing many kinds of reading tasks. They can help students determine pronunciations, derivations, and parts of speech for words they encounter in reading activities. They can also help with word spellings, if students have some idea of how the words are spelled and need only to confirm the order of letters within the words. The dictionary can be an excellent source for discovering meanings of unfamiliar words, particularly for determining the appropriate meanings of words that have multiple definitions or specific, technical definitions. Either print or computerized dictionaries can be used. Hand-held computerized dictionaries are as portable as print dictionaries.

TECHNOLOGY

In some instances, students may be familiar with several common meanings of a word, but not with a word's specialized meaning found in a content area textbook. For example, a student may understand a reference to a *base* in a baseball game but not a discussion of a military *base* (social studies material), a *base* that turns litmus paper blue (science material), or *base* motives of a character (literature). Words that have the greatest number of different meanings, such as *run* or *bank,* are frequently very common. Middle-school students can develop personalized dictionaries of special terms, such as "My Science Dictionary" or "My Computer Dictionary."

Although the dictionary is undeniably useful in determining the pronunciation of unfamiliar words, students should turn to it only as a last resort for this purpose. They should consult it only after they have applied phonics and structural analysis clues along with knowledge of context clues. There are two major reasons for following this procedure. First, applying the appropriate word recognition skills immediately, without having to take the time to look up the word in the dictionary, is less of a disruption of the reader's train of thought and therefore less of a hindrance to comprehension. Second, a dictionary is not always readily available; thoroughly mastered word recognition skills, however, will always be there when they are needed.

When using other word attack skills has produced no useful or clear result, students should turn to the dictionary for help. Obviously, before students can use the dictionary for pronunciation, they must be able to locate words in it. This skill is discussed in Chapter 7.

After students have located particular words, they need two more skills to pronounce the words correctly: the ability to interpret phonetic respellings and to interpret accent marks. The pronunciation key, along with knowledge of sounds ordinarily associated with single consonants, helps in interpreting phonetic respellings in dictionaries. A pronunciation key is present somewhere on every page spread of a good dictionary. Students should not be asked to memorize the diacritical (pronunciation) markings used in a given dictionary, because different dictionaries use different markings; learning the markings for one dictionary could cause confusion when students use another. The sounds ordinarily associated with relatively unvarying consonants may or may not be included in the pronunciation key. Because they are not always included, it is important that students have a knowledge of phonics.

Here are three activities related to interpretation of phonetic spellings:

1. Have the students locate a given word in their dictionaries (example: *cheat* [*chēt*]). Call attention to the phonetic respelling beside the entry word. Point out the location of the pronunciation key and explain its function. Have the students locate each successive sound-symbol in the key—*ch, ē, t.* (If necessary, explain why the *t* is not included in the key.) Have the students check the key word for each symbol to confirm its sound value. Then have them blend the three sounds together to form a word. Repeat with other words. (Start with short words, and gradually work up to longer ones.)
2. Code an entire paragraph or a joke using phonetic respellings. Provide a pronunciation key. Let groups of students compete to see which one can be first to write the selection in the traditional way. Let each group of students who believe they have done so come to your desk. Check their work. If it is correct, keep it and give it a number indicating the order in which it was finished. If it is incorrect, send the students back to work on it some more. Set a time limit for the activity. The activity may be carried out on a competitive or a noncompetitive basis.
3. Give the students a pronunciation key, and let them encode messages to friends. Check the accuracy of each message before it is passed on to the friends to be decoded.

Some words have only one accent mark, whereas others have marks showing different degrees of accent within a single word. Students need to be able to translate the accent marks into proper stress when they speak the words. Here are two ideas for use in teaching accent marks:

1. Write several familiar multisyllabic words on the board. (*Bottle* and *apartment* are two good choices.) Explain that when words of more than one syllable are spoken, certain syllables are stressed or emphasized by the speaker's breath. Pronounce each of the example words, pointing out which part or parts of each word receive stress. Next, tell the class that the

MODEL ACTIVITIES

Accent Marks

Write the following words on the board:

1. truth ful	6. peo ple
2. lo co mo tion	7. gig gle
3. fric tion	8. emp ty
4. at ten tion	9. en e my
5. ad ven ture	10. ge og ra phy

Call on volunteers to pronounce these words and decide where the accent is placed in each one. Have them come to the board and indicate placements of the accents by putting accent marks (′) after the syllables where they think the accents belong. Then have all the students look up the words in the dictionary and check the placements of the accents. Anyone who finds an incorrectly marked word can come to the board, make the correction, and pronounce the word with the accent correctly placed.

dictionary uses accent marks to indicate which parts of words receive stress. Look up each word in the dictionary, and write the dictionary divisions and accent marks for the word on the board. Pronounce each word again, showing how the accent marks indicate the parts of the words that you stress when you pronounce them. Then have the students complete the Model Activity on Accent Marks.

2. Introduce the concept of accent in the same way described in the first activity. Then distribute sheets of paper with a list of words such as the following:
   a. des′ ti na′ tion
   b. con′ sti tu′ tion
   c. mys′ ti fy′
   d. pen′ nant
   e. thun′ der storm′

   Ask volunteers to read the words, applying the accents properly. When they have done so, give them a list of unfamiliar words with both accent marks and diacritical (pronunciation) marks inserted. (Lists will vary according to the students' ability. Use of words from their classroom reading material is preferable to use of random words.) Once again, ask the students to read the words, applying their dictionary skills.

There are some potential problems related to using dictionaries to determine word meanings. As Rhoder and Huerster (2002, p. 730) point out, "Definitions are short, abstract generalizations often written in dense embedded text. No concrete examples are offered, and ideas are never repeated in different words." Other words that are in the definition may have to be looked up in order to decipher the meaning expressed in the definition. Teaching word meanings through dictionary use has been widely criticized for these and other reasons. Nevertheless, research shows that it is a useful technique for vocabulary development if it is applied properly (Graves and Prenn, 1986).

To apply dictionary use properly, teachers should not simply assume that being able to recite a dictionary definition means that the students actually understand the word's meaning. They should point out the potential problems with dictionary definitions and model strategies for determining word meaning. Teachers should instruct students to consider the context surrounding a word, read the different dictionary definitions, and choose the definition that makes the most sense in the context. Without such instruction, students have a strong tendency to read only the first dictionary definition and try to force it into the context. The teacher should model the choice of the correct definition for the students so that they can see what the task is. Students will then need to practice the task under teacher supervision. As Nagy (1988) pointed out, combining a definitional approach to vocabulary instruction with a contextual approach is more effective than using a definitional approach in isolation. Sentences that illustrate meanings and uses of the defined words can help immensely.

The following Model Activities on Appropriate Dictionary Definitions and Multiple Meanings of Words are good to use for practice immediately following instruction in dictionary use and for later independent practice.

MODEL ACTIVITIES Appropriate Dictionary Definitions

Write the following sentences on the board:

1. Katherine's knife was very sharp.
2. There is a sharp curve in the road up ahead.
3. I hope that when I am seventy years old, my mind is as sharp as my grandmother's is.
4. We are leaving at two o'clock sharp.

Ask the students to find the dictionary definition of *sharp* that fits each sentence. You may ask them to jot down each definition and have a whole-class or small-group discussion about each one after all meanings have been located, or you may wish to discuss each meaning as it is located. The students may read other definitions for *sharp* in the dictionary and generate sentences for these as well.

MODEL ACTIVITIES Multiple Meanings of Words

Give the students a list of sentences, drawn from their textbooks, that contain words with specialized meanings for that subject. Have them use the dictionary or the textbook's glossary to discover the specialized meanings that fit the context of the sentences. After the students have completed the task independently, go over the sentences with them, and discuss reasons for right and wrong responses.

The material you give to the students may look something like this:

> *Directions:* Some words mean different things in your textbooks from what they mean in everyday conversation. In each of the following sentences, find the special meaning for the word that is underlined, and write the meaning on the line provided:

1. Frederick Smith has decided to <u>run</u> for mayor.

   ____

2. The park was near the <u>mouth</u> of the Little Bear River.

   ____

3. The management of the company was unable to avert a <u>strike</u>.

   ____

4. That song is hard to sing because of the high <u>pitch</u> of several notes.

   ____

5. That number is written in <u>base</u> two.

   ____

A General Strategy for Word Recognition

Students often know how to perform some skills that they need in word recognition, but they may not know an overall strategy for trying the skills that they do know. The Focus on Strategies on page 58 models a general strategy for decoding words that combines all of the techniques we have discussed in this section. Some of these techniques—context clues, structural analysis, and dictionaries—are also useful in determining word meaning and can be used in that order when the meaning of the word is in question.

Developing Meaning Vocabulary

Sometimes students acquire the meanings of words at the same time they decode their pronunciations, and, as you have seen, many strategies for word recognition also help students determine word meaning. It would be a mistake, however, to believe that students know the meanings of words simply because they can recognize and pronounce them.

Vocabulary building is a complex process involving many kinds of words: words with *multiple meanings* (Roberto's money is in the *bank*. Mike and Raj sat on the *bank* to fish.); words with *abstract definitions* (*Justice* must be served.); *homonyms* (She will take the *plane* to Lexington. He has on *plain* trousers.); *homographs* (Where should I hold my violin *bow* while I *bow* to the crowd?); *synonyms* (Noah was *sad* about leaving. Noah was *unhappy* about leaving.); and *antonyms* (Jamal is a *slow* runner. Lily is a *fast* runner.). In content area instruction, students must deal with *technical vocabulary* (words whose only meanings are specific to the content areas, for example, *photosynthesis*) and *specialized vocabulary* (words with general meanings as well as specialized meanings that are specific to the content area, for example, *pitch* in the area of music). Content area materials also abound with special *symbols* and *abbreviations* that students must master in order to read the materials successfully.

Wide reading is a prime method of vocabulary building. Many studies have shown that students' vocabularies increase when they read materials with many new words (Pressley, 2002). Students have many vicarious experiences through read-alouds by parents and teachers and reading for themselves. These experiences offer them a multitude of words and concepts that are not often found in their daily language interactions or experiences (Brabham and Villaume, 2002). "If we can substantially increase the reading students do, we can substantially increase the words they learn," according to Watts-Taffe (2002, p. 142). Developing enthusiasm for pleasure reading is therefore a worthy goal for teachers. Teachers can also encourage their students' parents and guardians to model and provide opportunities for pleasurable reading at home and to discuss the reading with their children.

FAMILY

Young people learn much vocabulary by listening to the conversations of those around them. Therefore, a language-rich environment promotes vocabulary acquisition (Anderson and Nagy, 1991; Brabham and Villaume, 2002). Teachers can provide such environments in their classrooms and encourage parents to do so at home. They can greatly influence students' vocabulary development simply by being good models of vocabulary use. For example, when teachers read aloud or give explanations to the class, they should discuss any new words used and encourage the students to use them.

FAMILY

FOCUS ON STRATEGIES

Word Recognition Procedure

Miss Daniel always taught students a strategy for decoding unfamiliar words independently. For students with special needs, the instruction often had to be more direct and explicit. Here are the steps that she used. (A student may discover the word at any point in the following procedure; he or she should then stop the procedure and continue reading. Sometimes it is necessary to try all of the steps.)

Step 1. Apply context clues. This may involve reading to the end of the sentence or paragraph in which the word is found to take in enough context to draw a reasonable conclusion about the word.

Step 2. Try the sound of the initial consonant, vowel, or blend along with context clues.

Step 3. Check for structure clues (prefixes, suffixes, inflectional endings, compound words, or familiar syllables).

Step 4. Begin sounding out the word using known phonics generalizations. (Go only as far as necessary to determine the word.)

Step 5. Consult the dictionary.

Miss Daniel explained this five-step strategy in the following way:

1. Try to decide what word might reasonably fit in the context in which you found the unfamiliar word. Ask yourself: "Will this word be a naming word? A word that describes? A word that shows action? A word that connects two ideas?" Also ask yourself: "What word will make sense in this place?" Do you have the answer? Are you sure of it? If so, continue to read. If not, go to Step 2.
2. Try the initial sound(s) along with the context clues. Does this help you decide? If you are sure you have the word now, continue reading. If not, go to Step 3.
3. Check to see if there are familiar word parts that will help you. Does the word have a prefix or suffix that you know? If this helps you decide on the word, continue reading. If not, go to Step 4.
4. Begin sounding out the word, using all of your phonics skills. If you discover the word, stop sounding and go back to your reading. If you have sounded out the whole word and it does not sound like a word you know, go to Step 5.
5. Look up the word in the dictionary. Use the pronunciation key to help you pronounce the word. If the word is one you have not heard before, check the meaning. Be sure to choose the meaning that fits the context.

A reader who is confronted with the unfamiliar word *chamois* might apply the strategy in the following way:

Step 1. "'He used a chamois to dry off the car.' I've never seen the word *c-h-a-m-o-i-s* before. Let's see . . . Is it a naming word? . . . Yes, it is, because *a* comes before it . . . What thing would make sense here? . . . It is something that can be used to dry a car. Could it be *towel?* . . . No, that doesn't have any of the right sounds. Maybe it is *cloth?* . . . No, *cloth* starts with *cl.*"

Step 2. "*Ch* usually sounds like the beginning of *choice* . . . I can't think of anything that starts that way that would fit here . . . Sometimes it sounds like *k* . . . I can't think of a word that fits that either . . . *Ch* even sounds like *sh* sometimes . . . The only word I can think of that starts with the *sh* sound and fits in the sentence is *sheet,* and I can tell that none of the other sounds are right."

Step 3. "I don't see a prefix, suffix, or root word that I recognize."

Step 4. "Maybe I can sound it out. *Chămois.* No, that's not a word. *Kămois.* That's not a word either. *Shămois.* I don't think so. . . . Maybe the *a* is long. *Chămois.* No. *Ka̲ mois.* No. *Sha̲ mois.* No."

Step 5. "I guess I'll have to use the dictionary. What? *Shăm´ ē?* Oh, I know what that is. I've seen Dad use one! Why is it spelled so funny? Oh, I see! It came from French."

Reminder: Students should not consider use of word recognition skills important only during reading classes. They should apply these skills whenever they encounter an unfamiliar word, whether it happens during reading class, science class, a free reading period, or outside of school. Teachers should emphasize to their students that the strategy explained here is applicable to *any* situation in which they find an unfamiliar word. Teachers should also encourage students to self-correct their reading errors when the words they read do not combine to make sense.

Teachers should not "talk down" to students, but should use appropriate terminology in describing things to them and participating in discussions with them. Graves and Watts-Taffe (2002, p. 144) also cite the importance of word consciousness—"awareness of and interest in words and their meanings"—in a vocabulary program. Modeling of precise word usage and calling attention to particularly appropriate word choices in literature encourage word consciousness. A teacher may want to have the students read the book *Miss Alaineus: A Vocabulary Disaster* by Debra Frasier for an entertaining introduction to learning word meanings and possibilities for misunderstanding word meanings. In addition to supporting wide reading and modeling correct use of words, however, teachers must also plan and provide direct vocabulary instruction.

Teaching Word Meanings

Research on vocabulary instruction indicates that "extensive reading can increase vocabulary knowledge, but direct instruction that engages students in construction of word meaning, using context and prior knowledge, is effective for learning specific vocabulary and for improving comprehension of related materials" (Nelson-Herber, 1986, p. 627). McKeown, Beck, Omanson, and Pople (1985) also offer support for this assessment.

Teachers can approach vocabulary instruction in a variety of ways, but some vocabulary instructional techniques appear to be more effective than others. The most desirable instructional techniques are those that (Beck and McKeown, 1991; Blachowicz and Lee, 1991; Carr and Wixson, 1986; Nagy, 1988):

1. Assist students in integrating the new words with their background knowledge.
2. Assist students in developing elaborated (expanded) word knowledge.
3. Actively involve students in learning new words.
4. Help students acquire strategies for independent vocabulary development.
5. Provide repetition of the words to build ready accessibility of their meanings.
6. Have students engage in meaningful use of the words.

Although procedures for vocabulary development vary widely, many of them have produced good results, and teachers should be familiar with a variety of approaches. A number of the programs described here combine several approaches, and good teachers will also use combinations of approaches in their classrooms. Graves and Prenn (1986) point out that "there is no one best method of teaching words . . . various methods have both their costs and their benefits and will be very appropriate and effective in some circumstances and less appropriate and effective in others" (p. 597).

Some research findings indicate that "vocabulary instruction improves comprehension only when both definitions and context are given, and has the largest effect when a number of different activities or examples using the word in context are used" (Stahl, 1986, p. 663). Techniques requiring students to think deeply about a term and its relationships to other terms are most effective. Class discussion seems to make students think more deeply about words as they make connections between their prior knowledge and new information. Multiple presentations of information about a word's meaning and multiple exposures to the word in varying contexts both benefit comprehension. In addition, the more time that is spent on vocabulary instruction, the better are the results. Vocabulary programs that extend over a long period of time give students a chance to encounter the words in a number of contexts and to make use of them in their own conversation and writing (Stahl, 1986). Gipe (1980) expanded a context method (in which students read new words in meaningful contexts) to include having students apply the words based on their own experiences. She then studied the effectiveness of this method, comparing it with three other methods: an association method (in which an unknown word is paired with a familiar synonym), a category method (in which students place words in categories), and a dictionary method (in which students look up the word, write a definition, and use the word in a sentence). The expanded context method was found to be the most effective of the four. The application of the new words may have been the most important aspect of the context method that Gipe used. After the students derived the meaning of the word from a variety of contexts, including a definition context, they applied the word to their personal experiences in a written response. Thus, the instruction follows the first desirable instructional technique for vocabulary listed previously in this chapter: assisting students in integrating the new words with their background knowledge.

Combining contextual and definitional approaches to vocabulary instruction has been shown to be more effective than using a contextual approach alone. In fact, "it would be hard to justify a contextual approach in which the teacher did not finally provide an adequate definition of the word or help the class arrive at one" (Nagy, 1988, p. 8). In addition, teachers can have students apply context clues in conjunction with structure clues, which we discuss next, to help them decide if a meaning suggested by the context is reasonable.

Most teachers recognize the importance of vocabulary instruction as a part of reading and language arts classes. The importance of teaching word meanings and encouraging variety in word choice and exactness in expressing thoughts is generally accepted. Teachers therefore usually give attention to many aspects of vocabulary instruction—such as structural analysis; use of context clues; and use of reference books, such as dictionaries and thesauruses—during language classes. During these lessons, teachers also need to help the students understand the real-world purpose for building vocabulary: a rich vocabulary helps us to communicate effectively. The more words we know and use appropriately, the better we are able to communicate our knowledge and our feelings to others and understand what others try to communicate to us.

Vocabulary instruction should take place throughout the day, however, not just during the language arts or reading period. Vocabulary knowledge is important in all subject areas covered in the curriculum. Students need to develop their vocabularies in every subject area so that the specialized or technical words they encounter are not barriers to their learning.

Research indicates that preteaching—teaching students new vocabulary terms before they read a selection—can result in significant gains in students' comprehension of that selection (Carney et al., 1984; Roser and Juel, 1982) and that long-term vocabulary instruction, in which words are taught and reinforced over a period of time, enhances comprehension of materials containing those words (Beck, Perfetti, and McKeown, 1982; McKeown et al., 1983; Robinson et al., 1990).

Rupley, Logan, and Nichols (1998/1999, p. 339) point out that "teaching and reviewing of key concept words prior to reading help students activate their background knowledge, relate this knowledge to new concepts, and understand how new words and concepts are related." Nelson-Herber (1986) suggests intensive direct teaching of vocabulary in specific content areas to help students read the content materials successfully. She endorses building from the known to the new, helping students understand the interrelationships among words in concept clusters (groups of related concepts), and encouraging students to use new words in reading, writing, and speaking. Leading students to construct word meaning from context, experience, and reasoning is basic to her approach. At times, the students work in cooperative groups on vocabulary exercises, and they are involved with vocabulary learning before, during, and after reading of assigned material. The techniques described in this chapter and the ideas presented in Chapter 8 will help teachers plan effectively for vocabulary instruction in various content areas.

TIME for REFLECTION

Whereas some teachers stress the need for vocabulary instruction throughout the day, others argue that such instruction logically belongs in a reading or language arts class. **What do *you* think, and why?**

Choosing words to teach can be a problem for teachers. Blachowicz and Lee (1991); Rupley, Logan, and Nichols (1998/1999); and Dixon-Krauss (2001/2002) suggest choosing terms from classroom reading materials. The terms should be central to the selections in which they appear. The teacher should activate prior knowledge related to the words before the reading begins and have students use the new vocabulary in postreading discussion. Words that students still do not understand will need further attention and elaboration. The students might use the words in retellings, dramatizations, or writings based on the story or selection for further experiences.

When commercial materials are used, teachers should use discussion to relate word meanings to the students' own experiences. Then students should use the words in some way to demonstrate their understanding of the meanings. Because multiple experiences with each word are necessary for complete learning, the number of words presented should not be overwhelming. Spaced reviews of the words over a long period of time will enhance students' retention of the word meanings.

DIVERSITY

Davis and McDaniel (1998) urge teachers to include what they refer to as "essential" vocabulary words—words important to survival in our complex society—in their instruction. This instruction is particularly important to struggling readers and English language learners. Davis and McDaniel stress teaching recognition of these words, but many are words that appear to require instruction in meanings as well—for example, *hazardous, prohibited, expiration, evacuate, infectious,* and *ventilation.*

We have already discussed the use of structural analysis, context clues, and the dictionary as ways of discovering word meanings. We now look at several additional techniques for vocabulary development.

Building Readers' Schemata

Vocabulary terms are labels for *schemata,* or the clusters of concepts each person develops through experience. Learning new vocabulary may just involve acquisition of a new label for a concept that is already known. In this case, the teacher's task is simple. The teacher provides the new term (such as *expedition*) and tells the students it has a meaning similar to a familiar term (such as *trip*) (Armbruster and Nagy, 1992).

Other times, however, students cannot understand the terms they encounter in books because they do not know the concepts to which the terms refer. In this case, concept or schemata development involving the use of direct and vicarious experiences is necessary. Thelen (1986) found that meaningful learning is enhanced by teaching general concepts before specific concepts. Using this approach, the teacher presents the concept of *machine* before the concept of *lever,* for example. In this way, the students have the schemata they need to incorporate new facts they encounter. For example, they have a prior pool of information about machines to which they can relate the new information about *lever.* Isabel Beck has stated that *ownership* of a word, or the ability to relate the word to an existing schema, is necessary for meaningful learning. In other words, students need to relate the word to information they already know. Several instructional approaches encourage teachers to be aware of and use students' experience base when they teach new word meanings, to prevent students' acquiring a store of words for which they have only superficial understanding. Duffelmeyer (1985) suggests four techniques to link word meaning and experience: use of synonyms and examples, use of positive and negative instances of the concepts, use of examples and definitions, and use of definitions together with sentence completion. His techniques are all teacher-directed and involve verbal interaction between the teacher and the students.

Several techniques discussed later in this chapter are good methods for accomplishing this goal, including semantic mapping, semantic feature analysis, and brainstorming about words and webbing the responses. Students learn new connections as their classmates contribute new related words.

Providing Direct Experiences. A good technique for concept development is to offer as concrete an experience for the concept as possible. The class should then discuss the attributes of the concept. The teacher should give examples and nonexamples of the concept, pointing out the attributes that distinguish examples from nonexamples. Next, the students should try to identify other examples and nonexamples that the teacher supplies and give their reasons. Finally, the students should suggest additional examples and nonexamples.

For example, to develop the concept of *banjo,* the teacher could bring a banjo to class. The teacher would show it to the students, play it for them (or get someone to do so), and let them touch it and pluck or strum the strings. A discussion of its attributes would follow. The students might decide that a banjo has a circular body and a long neck, that it has a tightly stretched cover over the body, that it has strings, and that one can play music on it. The teacher might show the students pictures or real examples of a variety of banjos, some with five and some with four strings, and some with enclosed backs and some with open backs. Then the teacher might show the students a guitar, pointing out the differences in construction (e.g., different shape, different material forming the front of the instrument, different number of strings). The teacher might also show several other instruments, at first following the same procedure and then letting the students identify how they are different from and similar to banjos. The students can provide their own examples of banjos by bringing in pictures or actual instruments. They will note that although there may be some variation in size and appearance, the essential attributes are present. They can also name and bring pictures or actual examples of instruments that are not banjos, such as harps, mandolins, or violins, and explain why these instruments do not fit the concept.

As students progress in school, they are introduced to a growing number of abstract concepts. Concrete experiences for abstract concepts are difficult to provide, but the teacher can use approximations. For example, to develop the concept of *freedom,* the teacher can say, "You may play with any of the board games in the room for the next twenty minutes, or you may choose not to play at all." After twenty minutes have passed, the teacher can tell the class that they were given the freedom to choose their activity; that is, they were not kept from doing what they chose to do. The teacher may then offer several examples of freedom. One might be the freedom to choose friends. No one else tells the students who their friends have to be; they choose based on their own desires. The teacher should also offer several nonexamples of freedom, perhaps pointing out that during a game, players are restrained by a set of rules and do not have the freedom to do anything they want to do. Then the teacher should ask the students to give examples of freedom and explain why these examples are appropriate. A student may suggest that the freedom we have in the United States to say what we think about our leaders is a good example, because we are not punished for voicing our views. After several examples, the teacher can ask the students for nonexamples. Students may suggest that people in jail do not have freedom, because they cannot go where they wish or do what they wish. After students have offered a number of nonexamples, the teacher may ask them to be alert for examples and nonexamples of freedom in their everyday activities and to report their findings to the class. Some may discover that being "grounded" by their parents is a good nonexample of freedom.

Firsthand experiences, such as field trips and demonstrations, can help students associate words with real situations. These experiences can be preceded and followed up by discussion of the new concepts, and written accounts of the experiences can help students gain control of the new vocabulary. Before a field trip, for example, a teacher may discuss the work that is done at the target location. During the field trip, the teacher or the field trip host can explain each activity to students as they watch it. This explanation should include the proper terms for the processes and personnel involved. After the trip, the students can discuss the experience. They can make graphic displays of the new terms (see the sections later in this chapter on semantic maps and word webs), classify the new terms (see the section on categorization), make comparison charts for the words (see the section on semantic feature analysis), analyze the structure of the words (see the section on structural analysis), or manipulate the new terms in some other way. They may write individual summaries of the experience or participate in writing a class summary. They may wish to use reference books or the Internet to expand their knowledge about some of the new things they have seen. All of these activities build both the students' concepts and their vocabularies, thereby enhancing their comprehension of material containing this vocabulary.

TECHNOLOGY

Providing Vicarious Experiences. Vicarious experiences can also help to build concepts and vocabulary. Audiovisual aids, such as pictures, films, videotapes, and computer displays, can be used to illustrate words that students have encountered in reading and provide other words for discussion. Books such as thesauruses, dictionaries, and trade books about words are also useful sources of information about words.

Using Active Approaches to Learning Vocabulary

Beck and McKeown (1983) described a program of vocabulary instruction that emphasized relating vocabulary to students' preexisting word knowledge and experiences. Students generated their own context for the terms being taught by answering questions about the words (e.g., the teacher might say, "Tell about something you might want to *eavesdrop* on" [p. 624]). The program also helped students to further their word knowledge by introducing new words in global semantic, or meaning, categories, such as *people* or *places,* and by requiring the students to work

Field trips and demonstrations provide firsthand experiences that help students increase their schemata and expand their vocabularies. *(© 2004 Suzie Fitzhugh)*

with the relationships among words. The students were asked to differentiate among critical features of words and to generalize from one word to similar ones. They were also asked to complete analogies involving the words and to pantomime words. These activities were in keeping with suggestions 2 and 3 about vocabulary instruction presented in the list on page 59; the students were active participants in the activities described rather than passive observers. Students were given a number of exposures to each word in a variety of contexts. The final aspect of the program was development of rapid responses to words by using timed activities, some of which were gamelike. These activities kept the students actively involved and probably increased their interest as well.

The students in Beck and McKeown's program learned the words taught, developed speed and accuracy in making semantic decisions, and showed comprehension of stories containing the target words superior to that of a control group. They also learned more than the specific words taught, as indicated by the size of their gains on a standardized measure of reading comprehension and vocabulary.

A closely related procedure, developed by Blachowicz (1986), also helps teachers focus on vocabulary instruction. First, teachers activate what the students know about the target words in the reading selection, using either exclusion brainstorming (in which students exclude unrelated words from a list of possible associated words) or knowledge rating (in which students indicate their degree of familiarity with the words). Then the teachers can elicit predictions about "connections between words or between words and the topic and structure of the selection" (p. 644), emphasizing the words' roles in semantic networks. (Word webs or semantic feature analysis, discussed later in this chapter, may be used.) Next, the students are asked to construct tentative definitions of the words. They read the text to test these definitions, refining them as they discover additional information. Finally, the students use the words in other reading and writing tasks to make them their own.

Blachowicz (1985, p. 877) points out that "the harder one works to process stimuli . . . the better one's retention." Blachowicz's approach causes the students to work harder by predicting and constructing definitions rather than merely memorizing the material presented.

Dramatizing Words. Another active way to clarify word meanings by associating situations with them is dramatization of words. This technique is more effective than mere verbal explanations of terms. Under some circumstances, dramatization of words has proved to be more effective than use of context clues, structural analysis, or dictionaries (Duffelmeyer, 1980; Duffelmeyer and Duffelmeyer, 1979).

Expanding Sentences. Cudd and Roberts (1993/1994) use sentence expansion activities to work on vocabulary. They create sentence stems composed of syntactic structures and vocabulary the students have encountered in classroom reading materials. Then they display the stems on the board and lead a discussion of them. Students supply endings for the sentences and then read the completed sentences. Students write their own sentences based on the stems, working with peer-editing partners. Then they illustrate one or two of their sentences. In this way, students become actively involved in using the target vocabulary.

Using Manipulatives. Manipulatives are helpful in explaining or demonstrating meanings of content area vocabulary. Teachers can use tape measures to show the meanings of certain lengths (e.g., *foot, yard*), use cotton balls and water to demonstrate *absorption,* or use a rubber band to demonstrate the concept of *elasticity* (Petrick, 1992). They can use geoboards in teaching geometric concepts, such as *congruent.*

Concept Cards. Students can also become highly involved in learning vocabulary through creating their own learning aids. Davis (1990) has pairs of students construct concept cards for new vocabulary terms. On the cards, they list definitions, synonyms, and examples for the terms. She has the students supplement their own knowledge by consulting dictionaries and thesauruses. Then she has them discuss the various connotations of the synonyms provided. Following the discussion, the class is divided into teams that compete to supply the most definitions, synonyms, or examples for words from the cards.

Making Possible Sentences. A technique called "possible sentences" is effective in teaching content area vocabulary. In this activity, the teacher chooses six to eight difficult words and four to six familiar words that are important to a reading selection. The teacher writes these words on the board and may offer a definition of each one. Students are asked to supply possible sentences for these terms that include at least two of the words. This causes them to think about the relationships among the terms. When all words are represented in the possible sentences, the students read the selection. After reading, each possible sentence is discussed and either accepted as true or changed to make it true. This technique requires much active processing of the vocabulary (Stahl and Kapinus, 1991).

LITERATURE

Connecting to Literature. Iwicki (1992) and her colleagues found that they could enhance vocabulary learning through an activity called "vocabulary connections." They put the vocabulary terms and definitions on wall charts and then asked students to relate each term to situations in the literature selection they were reading and situations in previously read books. For example, the word *pandemonium* is used in *Welcome Home, Jelly Bean* by M. F. Shyer. It can later be related to events in *The Black Stallion* by Walter Farley. This activity can be motivational and can encourage use of higher-level thinking skills.

DIVERSITY

Illustrating Words. Students whose primary language is not English can be asked to illustrate new vocabulary words to show their understanding. Then the students' illustrations can be shown to a small group of other class members, who try to identify the word being illustrated in each picture and record it on their papers. Finally, each artist tells which word each of his or her pictures represented. This procedure gets the students very actively involved with words (Baroni, 1987).

Categorization

Categorization is grouping together things or ideas that have common features. Classifying words into categories can be a good way to learn more about word meanings.

An activity such as this is referred to as a ***word sort.*** Students can begin placing the words they see in print into teacher-provided categories according to their meanings. They may discover that they want to put a word in more than one category. This desire will provide an opportunity for discussion about how a word may fit in two or more places for different reasons. The students should give reasons for all of their placements.

Classifying words into categories supplied by the teacher is a *closed-ended sort.* After the students become adept at closed-ended sorts, they are ready for the more difficult task of generating the categories needed for classifying the words presented—an *open-ended sort.* The teacher may give them a word list such as the one that follows and ask them to place the words in groups of things that are alike and to name the trait the items have in common.

List for Word Sort

horse	cow	goose	stallion	foal
gosling	mare	filly	chick	calf
colt	gander	bull	hen	rooster

Students may offer several categories for these words: various families of animals; four-legged and two-legged animals; feathered and furred animals; winged and wingless animals; or male animals, female animals, or animals that might be either sex. They may also come up with a classification that the teacher has not considered. As long as the classification system makes sense and the animals are correctly classified according to the stated system, it should be considered correct. Teachers should encourage students to discover various possibilities for classifications.

There are several benefits to a classification task such as this. Discussion of the different classification systems may help to extend the students' concepts about some of the animals on the list, and it may help some students develop concepts related to some of the animals for the first time, especially for inner-city students who have not had contact with farm animals. The classification system allows them to relate the new knowledge about some of the animals to the knowledge they already have about these animals or others. If some of the animal terms are new to students, putting these new words into categories can help students remember their meanings. The usefulness of categorization activities is supported by research indicating that presenting words in semantically related clusters can lead to improvement in students' vocabulary knowledge and reading comprehension (Marzano, 1984).

A classification game such as the one in the Model Activity on page 68 provides an interesting way to work on categorization skills.

The ability to classify is a basic skill that applies to many areas of learning. Many of the other activities described in this chapter, including those for analogies, semantic maps, and semantic feature analysis, depend on categorization.

Analogies and Word Lines

Analogies compare two relationships and thereby provide a basis for building word knowledge. Educators may teach analogies by displaying examples of categories,

MODEL ACTIVITIES

Classification Game

Divide the class into groups of three or four, and make category sheets like the one shown here for each group. When you give a signal, the students start writing as many words as they can think of that fit in each category; when you signal that time is up, a student from each group reads the group's words to the class. Have the students compare their lists and discuss why they placed particular words in particular categories.

Appropriate categories other than the ones used below are mammals, reptiles, and insects; or liquids, solids, and gases.

Meats	Fruits	Vegetables

relationships, and analogies; asking guiding questions about the examples; allowing students to discuss the questions; and applying the ideas that emerge.

Students may need help in grouping items into categories and understanding relationships among items. For example, the teacher might write *nickel, dime,* and *quarter* on the board and ask, "How are these things related? What name could you give the entire group of items?" (Answer: *money, coins,* or *change.*) Then he or she can ask students to apply the skill by naming other things that would fit in the category (*penny, half-dollar,* and *dollar,* for the category *money; penny* and *half-dollar* for the categories *coins* or *change*). Or the teacher could write *painter* and *brush* and ask, "What is the relationship between the two items?" (Answer: A *painter* works with a *brush.*) Teachers should remember to have students give other examples of the relationship (*dentist* and *drill*). After working through many examples such as these, the students should be ready for examples of simple analogies, such as, "Light is to dark as day is to night," "Glove is to hand as sock is to foot," and "Round is to ball as square is to block." Students can discuss how analogies work: "How are the first two things related? How are the second two things related? How are these relationships alike?" They can then complete incomplete analogies, such as "Teacher is to classroom as pilot is to ________." Middle-school students can understand the standard shorthand form of *come:go::live:die* if they are taught to read the colon (:) as *is to* and the double colon (::) as *as* (Bellows, 1980).

Teachers may use word lines to show the relationships among words, just as they use number lines for numbers. They can arrange related words on a graduated line that emphasizes their relationships. The students can then be asked to arrange a specified list of words on a word line themselves. Word lines can concretely show antonym, synonym, and degree analogies, as in this example:

The teacher can eventually have the students make their own word lines and analogies. Analogies that they could develop based on the word line example above include "enormous is to large as small is to tiny" (synonym), "enormous is to tiny as large is to small" (antonym), and "large is to medium as medium is to small" (degree).

Dwyer (1988) suggests mapping analogies, as shown in Example 2.1. The map in Example 2.1 provides the relationship involved, a complete example, two incomplete examples for the students to complete, and one space for an example that comes entirely from the student.

Semantic Maps and Word Webs

Semantic maps are diagrams that show how words are connected in meaning to one another (Heimlich and Pittelman, 1986; Johnson and Pearson, 1984; Johnson, Pittelman, and Heimlich, 1986;). They can be used to teach related concepts or to expand

EXAMPLE 2.1 Analogy Map

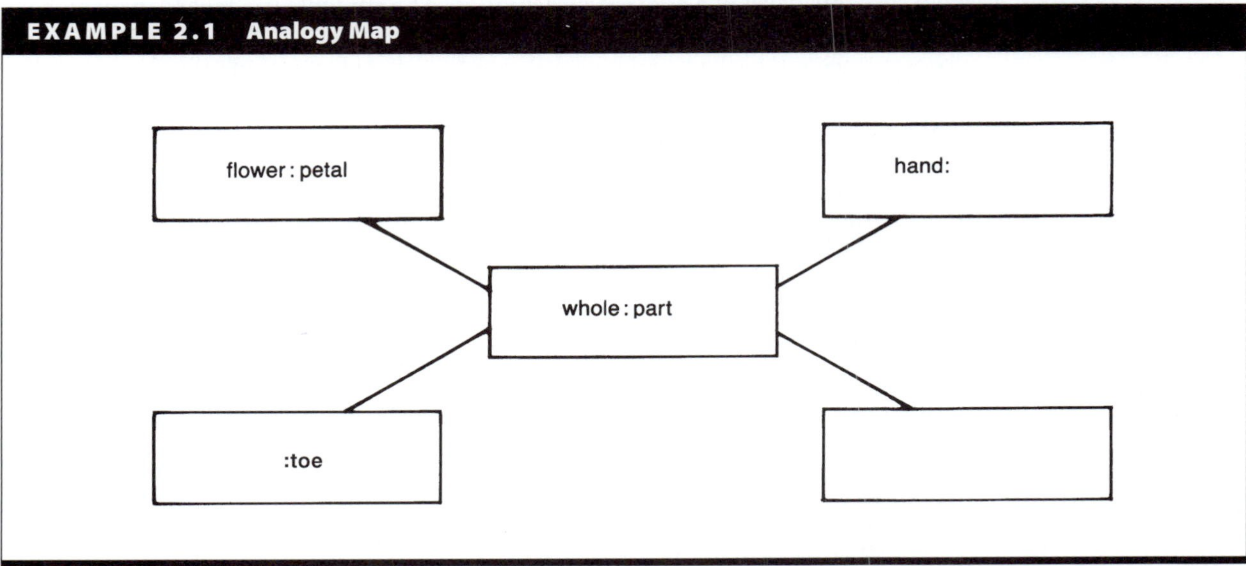

or activate students' knowledge about a single concept. To construct a semantic map with a class, the teacher writes on the board or a chart a word that represents a concept that is central to the topic under consideration. The teacher asks the students to name other words related to this concept. The teacher groups the students' words into broad categories while listing them on the board or chart. Then students name the categories. They may also suggest additional categories. A discussion of the central concept, the listed words, the categories, and the interrelationships among the words follows.

The discussion step appears to be the key to the effectiveness of this method, because it allows the students to be actively involved in the learning. After the class has discussed the semantic map, the teacher can give an incomplete semantic map to the students and ask them to fill in the words from the map on the board or chart and add any categories or words that they wish. The students can work on their maps as they read an assigned selection related to the central concept. Further discussion can follow the reading, and more categories and words can be added to the maps. The final discussion and mapping allow the students to recall and graphically organize the information they gained from the reading (Johnson et al., 1986; Stahl and Vancil, 1986). Example 2.2 shows a semantic map constructed by one class.

Because a semantic map shows both familiar and new words under labeled categories, the process of constructing one helps students make connections between known and new concepts (Johnson et al., 1986). The graphic display makes relationships among terms easier to see. Discussion of the map allows the teacher to assess the students' background knowledge, clarify concepts, and correct misunderstandings.

Schwartz and Raphael (1985) used a modified approach to semantic mapping to help students develop a concept of *definition.* The students used word maps to help them learn what types of information are needed for a definition and learn how to use context clues and background knowledge to help them better understand word meanings. Word maps are graphic representations of definitions. The word maps Schwartz and Raphael used were like the one in Example 2.3, which defines the concept *snake.* Each map contained information about the general class to which the target concept belonged, answering the question "What is it?"; the properties of the concept, answering the question "What is it like?"; and examples of the concept. With the basic information contained in such a map, students have enough information to construct definitions.

The approach that Schwartz and Raphael used started with strong teacher involvement, but control was gradually transferred to the students. Students were led to search the context of a sentence in which the word occurred for the elements of definition needed to map a word. Eventually the teachers provided only partial context for the word, leading the students to go to outside sources, such as dictionaries, for information to complete the maps. Finally, teachers asked the students to write definitions, including all the features previously mapped, without actually mapping the word on paper. This procedure for understanding the concept of *definition* is effective from the fourth-grade level through college.

EXAMPLE 2.2 Semantic Map of the Concept *Tennis*

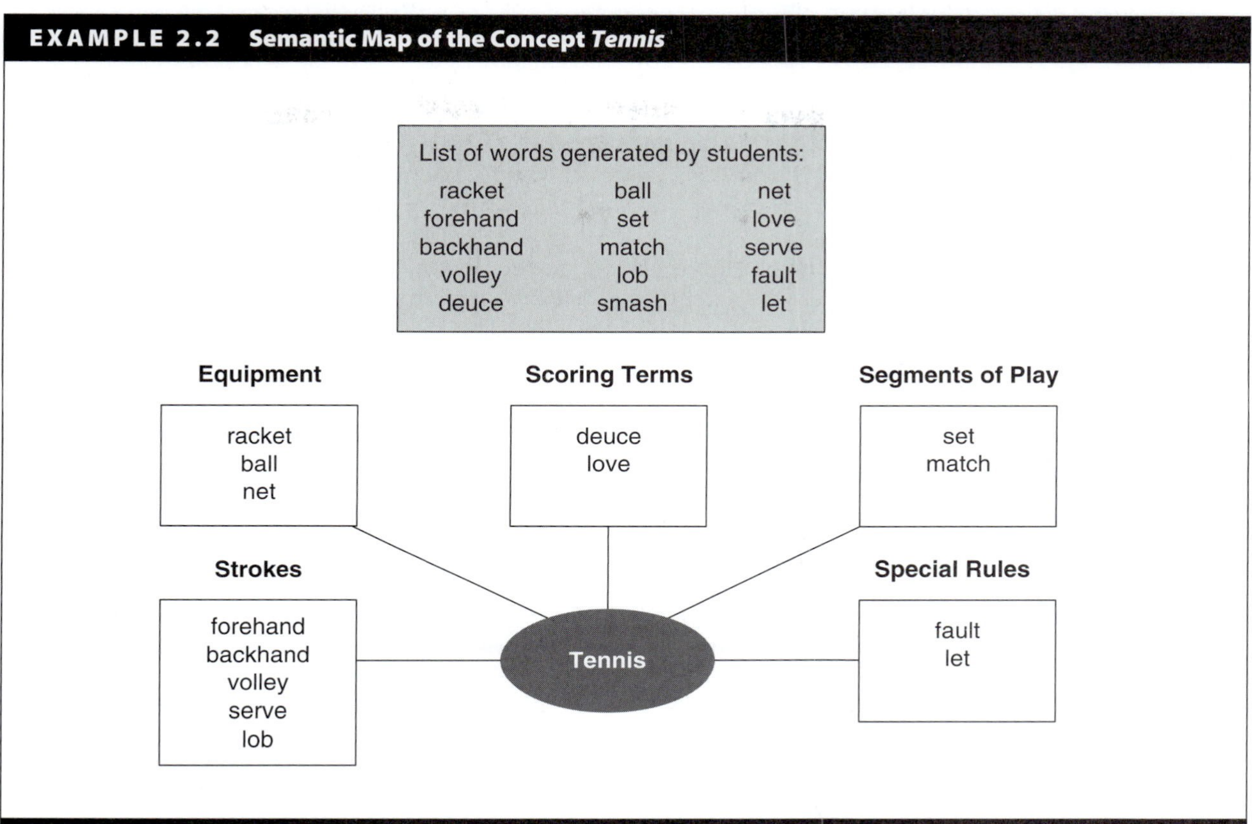

Word webs are another way to represent the relationships among words graphically. Students construct these diagrams by connecting related words with lines. The words used for the web may be taken from material students have read in class.

Semantic Feature Analysis

Semantic feature analysis is a technique that can help students understand the uniqueness of a word as well as its relationships to other words (Johnson and Pearson, 1984). To perform such an analysis, the teacher lists in a column on the board or a chart some known words with common properties. Then the students generate a list of features that the various items in the list possess. A feature needs to apply to only one item to be listed. The teacher writes these features in a row across the top of the board or chart, and the students fill in the cells of the resulting matrix with pluses or minuses to indicate the presence or absence of each feature.

Example 2.4 shows a partial matrix developed by students for various buildings. "Walls" and "doors" were other features the students suggested for the matrix; they

EXAMPLE 2.3 Word Map for Definition

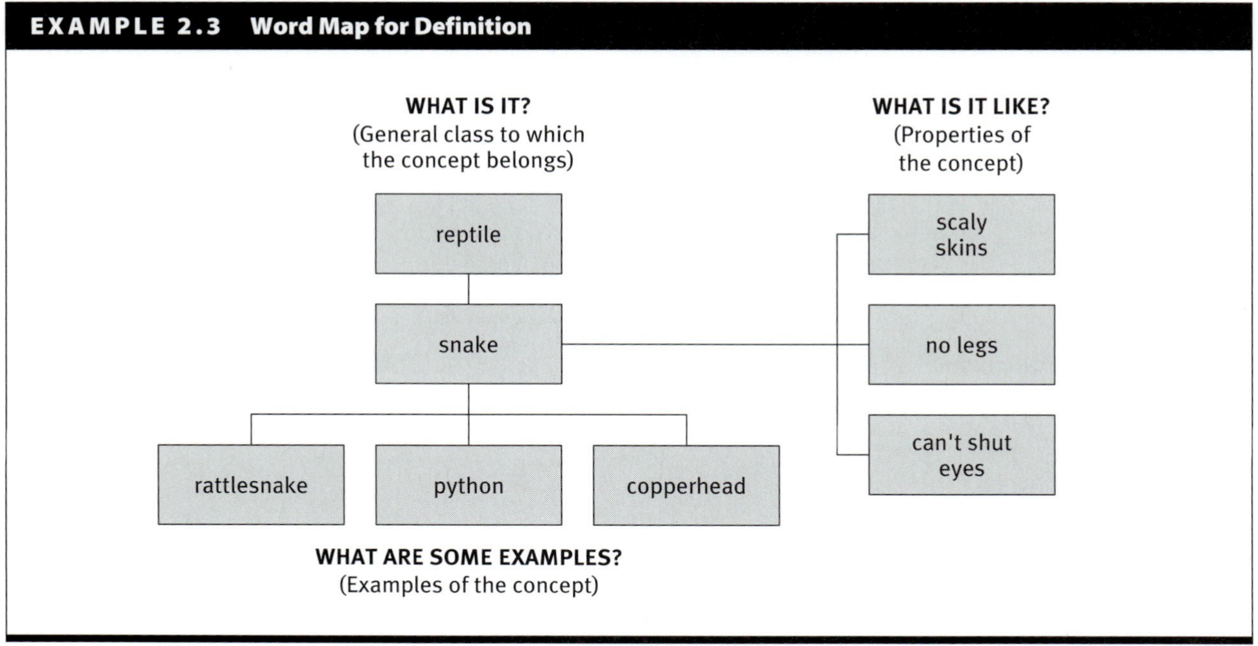

EXAMPLE 2.4 Semantic Feature Analysis Chart

	barred windows	exhibits	steeple	cross	cars	lift-up doors	guards	oil stains
jail	+	–	–	–	–	–	+	–
garage	?	–	–	–	+	+	–	+
museum	?	+	–	–	?	–	+	–
church	–	–	+	+	–	–	–	–

were omitted from the example only for space considerations. Both of these features received a plus for each building, emphasizing the similarities of the terms *jail, garage, museum,* and *church.*

The students discussed the terms as they filled in the matrix. In the places where the question marks occur, the students said, "Sometimes it may have that, but not always. It doesn't have to have it." The group discussion brought out much information about each building listed and served to expand the students' existing schemata.

Students can continue to expand such a matrix after initially filling it out by adding words that share some of the listed features. For example, the students added *grocery store* to the list of buildings in Example 2.4 because it shared the walls and doors, and they added other features showing the differentiation, such as *food, clerks,* and *checkout counters.* Johnson and Pearson (1984) suggest that after experience with these matrices, students may begin to realize that some words have different degrees of the same feature. At this time, the teacher may want to try using a numerical system of coding, using 0 for *none,* 1 for *some,* 2 for *much,* and 3 for *all.* Under the feature "fear," for example, *scared* might be coded with a 1, whereas *terrified* might be coded with a 3.

Semantic feature analysis can be used with vocabulary needed for content area reading assignments. It activates the students' prior knowledge through discussion and relates prior knowledge to new knowledge, making the material seem more relevant to the students and increasing the likelihood of retaining the information. This technique can be used before, during, and after the reading. A chart can be started in the background-building portion of the lesson, added to or modified by the students as they read the material, and refined further during the follow-up discussion of the material.

Word Origins and Histories

Students in middle school can enjoy learning about the histories and origins of words (***etymology***) and the kinds of changes that have taken place in the English language. They can learn more about etymology by studying words and definitions that appear in very old dictionaries and by studying differences between American English and British English. Charles Earle Funk's *Curious Word Origins, Sayings and Expressions* (1993) is a good reference.

Teachers need to help students understand the different ways English words have been created. *Portmanteau* words are formed by merging the sounds and meanings of two different words (for example, *smog,* from *smoke* and *fog*). *Acronyms* are words formed from the initial letters of a name or by combining initial letters or parts from a series of words (for example, *radar,* from *ra*dio *d*etecting *a*nd *r*anging). Some words are just shortened forms of other words (for example, *phone,* from *telephone; flu,* from *influenza;* and *piano,* from *pianoforte*). Both shortened forms and acronyms are ways our language has become more compact (Richler, 1996). Some words are borrowed from other languages (for example, *lasso,* from the Spanish *lazo*). The teacher can discuss the origins of such terms when they occur in students' reading materials. In addition, students should try to think of other words that have been formed in a similar manner. The students can combine structural analysis and etymology by studying words derived from Latin or Greek word parts, such as *prescription* and *scripture.* They can be encouraged to think of other examples and asked to use the derived words in sentences. The teacher may also wish to contribute other examples from familiar sources.

Word Play

Word play is an enjoyable way to learn more about words. It can provide multiple exposures to words in different contexts that are important to complete word learning. In order to understand puns, for example, a student must know the multiple meanings of a word.

FAMILY

The following activities present some other ways that teachers can engage students in word play. Students can also share many of these activities with family members:

1. Ask students silly questions containing new words. Example: "Would you have a terrarium for dinner? Why or why not?"
2. Discuss what puns are, and give some examples. Then ask students to make up or find puns to bring to class. Let them explain the play on words to classmates who do not understand it. Example: "What is black and white and read all over?" Answer: A newspaper (word play on the homonyms *red* and *read*).
3. Use Hink Pinks, Hinky Pinkies, and Hinkety Pinketies—rhyming definitions for terms with one, two, and three syllables, respectively. Give a definition, tell whether it is a Hink Pink, Hinky Pinky, or Hinkety Pinkety, and let the students guess the expression. Then let the students make up their own terms. Several examples follow.

   Hink Pink: Unhappy father—Sad dad

   Hinky Pinky: Late group of celebrators—Tardy party

   Hinkety Pinkety: Yearly handbook—Annual manual
4. Locate words from a current reading selection that have synonyms, antonyms, and homonyms. Give the students a list of synonyms, antonyms, and homonyms for these target words, and tell them to find the target words from the selection and write these words beside the appropriate clue words on the list. For example, the list might have the words *hotel* (synonym), *fare* (homonym), *sense* (homonym), and *calm* (antonym) for a selection from *Lyddie* that contained the words *inn, fair, cents,* and *panic.*
5. Students might enjoy crossword puzzles that highlight new words in their textbooks or other instructional materials.
6. Mountain (2002) has students start with four syllables on two poker chips—two prefixes on one and two roots on the other, or two suffixes on one and two roots on the other. The students flip the two chips until they form four different words. They discuss the meanings of the words and then place them in appropriate blanks in cloze passages (described earlier in this chapter). Later the students can make their own "flip-chip" pairs and cloze passages.

Riddles are a very effective form of word play. To use riddles, students must interact verbally with others; to create riddles, they have to organize information and decide on significant details. Riddles can help students move from the literal to the interpretive level of understanding. They provide both context clues and high-interest material, two factors that promote vocabulary learning.

TIME for REFLECTION

What forms of word play are particularly effective in enhancing vocabulary development? Why do you believe this is so?

Riddles can be classified into several categories: those based on homonyms, on rhyming words, on double meanings, and on figurative and literal meanings, for example. (See the section "Special Types of Expressions and Words" later in this chapter.) An example of a homonym riddle is: "What does a grizzly *bear* take on a trip? Only the *bare* essentials" (Tyson and Mountain, 1982, p. 170).

TECHNOLOGY

Computer Techniques

Computers are present in many middle-school classrooms in this age of high technology, and the software available includes many programs for vocabulary development. Although some of them are simply drill-and-practice programs, which are meant to provide practice with word meanings the teacher has already taught, some tutorial programs provide initial instruction in word meanings. (These programs may also include a drill-and-practice component.) Programs focusing on synonyms, antonyms, homonyms, and words with multiple meanings are available, as are programs providing work with classification and analogies. Semantic mapping programs allow students to work with word relationships.

Word-processing programs can be profitably used in vocabulary instruction. A student may be given a disk that has files containing paragraphs with certain words used repeatedly. The student may use the find-and-replace function to replace all instances of a chosen word with a synonym and then read the paragraph to see if the synonym makes sense in each place it appears. If it does not, the student can delete the synonym in the inappropriate places and choose more appropriate replacements for the original word or put the original word back into the paragraph. Then the student can read the file again to see if the words chosen convey the correct meanings and if the variation in word choices makes the paragraph more interesting to read.

A paragraph such as the following one could be a starting place:

> Shonda had to run to the store for her mother because her mother got a run in her pantyhose just before the party. Shonda had to listen to her mother run on and on about her run of bad luck that day before she was able to leave the house. When she arrived at the store, she saw her uncle, who told her he had decided to run for office, delaying her progress further. She finally bought the last pair of pantyhose in the store. There must have been a run on them earlier in the day.

Student-Centered Vocabulary Learning Techniques

Some vocabulary learning techniques focus on students and their individual needs and interests. Explanations of several of these techniques follow.

The *Vocabulary Self-Collection Strategy (VSS)* fits the belief that some educators have that "vocabulary instruction should feature student-selected words" (Brabham and Villaume, 2002, p. 266). Haggard (1986) suggests the following approach for general vocabulary development:

1. Ask each student to bring to class a word that the entire class should learn. (The teacher brings one too.) Each student should determine the meaning of his or her word from its context rather than looking it up in the dictionary.

2. Write the words on the board. Let each participant identify his or her word and tell where it was found, the context-derived meaning, and why the class

should learn the word. The class should then discuss the meaning of the word, in order to clarify and extend it and to construct a definition on which the class agrees. The result may be checked against a dictionary definition.

3. Narrow the list down to a manageable number, and have the students record the final list of words and definitions in their vocabulary journals. Some students may want to put eliminated words on their personal lists.
4. Make study assignments for the words.
5. Test the students on the words at the end of the week.

Ruddell and Shearer (2002, p. 354) believe that "students learn new words not by hearing them explained with other new words, but rather from ongoing and extended transaction with the words, their peers, and their teacher within the context of life and classroom experience." Such transactions increase word awareness and word learning strategies. Ruddell and Shearer used the VSS as a vehicle to accomplish these goals with at-risk middle-school students. The word study during the week involved such techniques as discussion, semantic mapping, and semantic feature analysis. Students chose many words from their content area classes, but also chose words from nonschool sources. Ruddell and Shearer found that the students chose important and challenging words, learned these words, and retained the words over time.

Rosenbaum (2001) used eight techniques for clarifying word meanings of self-selected words for students that Harmon (1998) had identified. Rosenbaum developed a word map for her students to use daily with words they located during independent reading. They included "synonyms, brief descriptions, examples and nonexamples, rephrasing, repetition, associations, and unique expression" (Rosenbaum, 2001, p. 45). Example 2.5 illustrates a word map.

Vocabulary notebooks are useful for recording new words found in general reading or words heard in conversations or on radio or television. New words may be alphabetized in the notebooks and defined and illustrated.

TIME for REFLECTION

Some teachers think that having students learn the dictionary definitions of weekly teacher-chosen vocabulary words is a good approach to vocabulary instruction. Others believe in more use of student-centered methods to help students acquire meaning vocabulary. **What do *you* think, and why?**

Special Types of Expressions and Words

Figurative language and certain special types of words can present extra problems in vocabulary learning for students. Teachers may wish to plan special instruction, in addition to the techniques described earlier in the chapter, to help students understand these types of vocabulary.

Figurative Language

Figurative language, or nonliteral language, can be a barrier to understanding written selections. Students tend to interpret literally many expressions that have meanings different from the sums of the meanings of the individual words. For example, the expression "the teeth of the wind" does not mean that the wind actually has teeth, nor does "a blanket of fog" mean a conventional blanket. Context clues indicate the meanings of such phrases in the same ways that they cue the meanings

EXAMPLE 2.5 Word Map Completed by Student

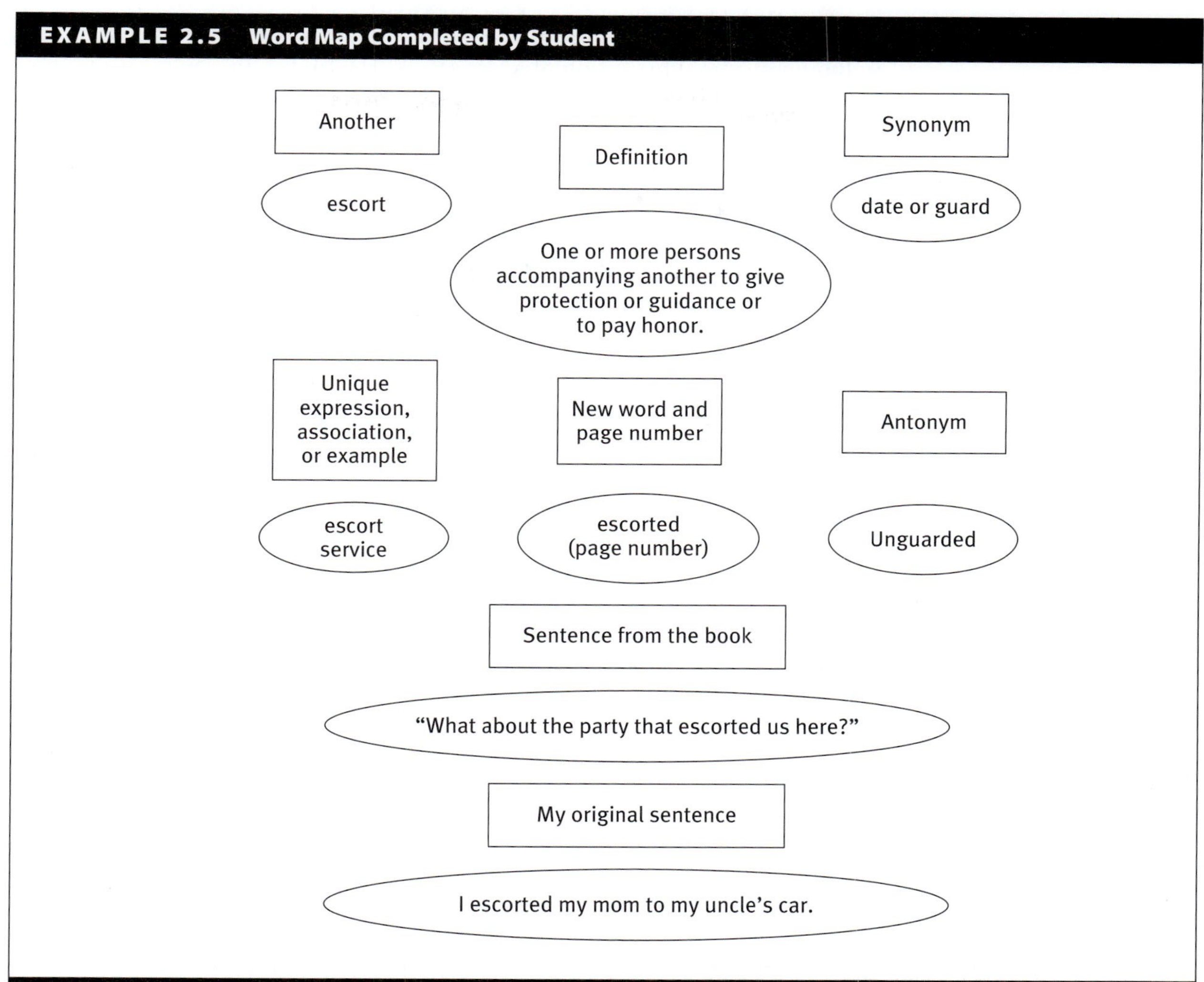

Source: Catherine Rosenbaum, "A Word Map for Middle School: A Tool for Effective Vocabulary Instruction," *Journal of Adolescent & Adult Literacy* 45(1) (September 2001), pp. 44–49. Reprinted with permission of the International Reading Association and the author.

DIVERSITY

of individual words. English language learners have special difficulties interpreting figurative language because of their lack of background exposure to such usage.

Adults often assume students have had exposure to expressions that in fact are unfamiliar to them. Students need substantial help in order to comprehend figurative language. Even basal readers present many of these expressions. Some common figures of speech cause trouble—for example:

- ***Simile***—a comparison using *like* or *as*
- ***Metaphor***—a direct comparison without the words *like* or *as*
- ***Personification***—giving the attributes of a person to an inanimate object or abstract idea

- ***Hyperbole***—an extreme exaggeration
- ***Euphemism***—substitution of a less offensive term for an unpleasant term or expression
- ***Allusion***—an indirect reference to a person, place, thing, or event considered to be known to the reader

Teaching students to recognize and understand similes is usually not too difficult, because the cue words *like* and *as* help to show the presence of a comparison. Metaphors, however, may cause more serious problems. A metaphor is a comparison between two unlike things that share an attribute. Sometimes students do not realize that the language in metaphors is figurative; sometimes they do not have sufficient background knowledge about one or both of the things being compared; and sometimes they simply have not learned a process for interpreting metaphors.

The two things compared in a metaphor may seem to be incompatible, but readers must think of past experiences with each, searching for a match in attributes that could be the basis of comparison. For example, a man might be compared to a mouse based on the characteristic of timidity.

Readence, Baldwin, and Head (1986, 1987) suggest the following instructional sequence for teaching metaphorical interpretation:

1. The teacher displays a metaphor, such as, "Her eyes were stars," together with the more explicit simile, "Her eyes were as bright as stars," and explains that metaphors have missing words that link the things being compared (such as *bright* does). Other sentence pairs can also be shown and explained.
2. Then the students are asked to find the missing word in a new metaphor, such as, "He is a mouse around his boss." They offer guesses, explaining their reasons aloud.
3. The teacher explains that people have lists of words related to different topics stored in their minds. The teacher models examples, and then the students produce examples. At this point, the students try to select the attribute related to the new metaphor. If there are two incorrect guesses, the attribute *timid* can be supplied and the reason for this choice given. This process can then be repeated with another metaphor.
4. As more metaphors are presented, the teacher does less modeling, turning over more and more control of the process to the students.

After explaining each type of figurative language, modeling its interpretation, and having students interpret it under supervision, the teacher may provide independent practice activities such as the Figures of Speech Model Activity. Ideally, the teacher should take examples of figurative expressions from literature the students are currently reading and use these expressions in constructing practice activities. For example, *Maniac Magee* by Jerry Spinelli contains an abundance of good examples, such as the following: "The book came flapping like a wounded duck," "He's paralyzed, a mouse in front of the yawning maw of a python," "The phantom Samaritan stuck the book between his teeth, . . . and hauled him out of there like a sack of flour." All of these appear

MODEL ACTIVITIES

Figures of Speech

Display the following cartoon on a transparency:

DENNIS THE MENACE® used by permission of Hank Ketcham Enterprises and © by North America Syndicate.

Lead a discussion about the cartoon using the following questions as a guide:

1. What does "been through the mill" really mean, as Dennis's mother used it?
2. What does Dennis think it means?
3. How is the woman likely to react to Dennis's question?
4. How does Dennis's mother probably feel about the question?
5. Can misunderstanding figurative language cause trouble at times? Why do you say so?

Have the students suggest other figurative expressions that could produce misunderstandings. As a follow-up activity, let them draw funny scenes in which the misunderstandings occur.

Also have the students look for other examples in newspaper comics. Ask them to cut out the examples and bring them to school for discussion.

in the first nineteen pages of the book, and there are many more throughout the book. Teachers could also give each student a copy of a poem that is filled with figures of speech, and have the class compete to see who can identify all of them first. You may require students to label all figures of speech properly as to type and to explain them.

Homonyms, or Homophones

Many ***homonyms,*** or ***homophones,*** can cause trouble for students because they are spelled differently but pronounced the same way. Some common homonyms are found in the following sentences:

I want to *be* a doctor.

That *bee* almost stung me.

She has *two* brothers.

Will you go *to* the show with me?

I have *too* much work to do.

I can *hear* the bird singing.

Maurice, you sit over *here.*

Mark has a *red* scarf.
Have you *read* that book?

I *ate* all of my supper.
We have *eight* dollars to spend.

LITERATURE

Fred Gwynne's *The King Who Rained* and *A Chocolate Moose for Dinner* both have homonyms in their titles, as well as throughout their texts. Although these are picture books, middle-school students enjoy their humor. Pettersen (1988) suggests letting the students look for homonyms in all of their reading materials. Students can construct lists of homonym pairs that mean something to them because they discovered at least one of the qualifying words in each pair themselves. If you would like to try this for yourself, the paragraph you are currently reading is a good one to use as a starter for such an exercise. (Hint: *all-awl* is a good start.) Expanding Pettersen's activity to require the use of each homonym in a meaningful sentence is a way to keep the focus on meaning.

Have students web homonyms in the following way:

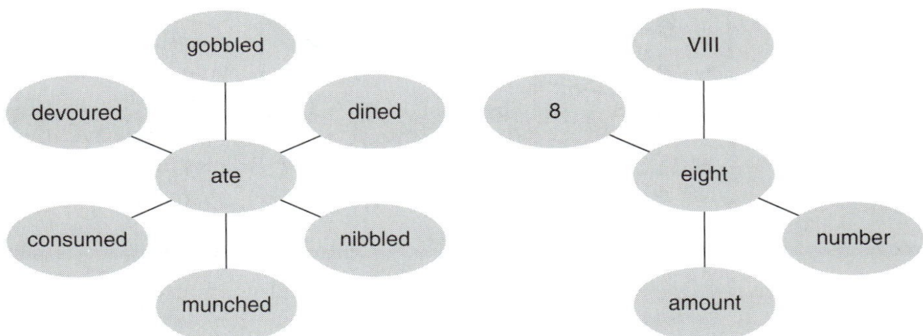

Homographs

Homographs are words that have identical spellings but not the same meanings. Their pronunciations may or may not be the same. Readers must use context clues to identify the correct pronunciations, parts of speech, and meanings of homographs. Examples include:

I will *read* my newspaper. (pronounced as if it were *reed*)
I have *read* my newspaper. (pronounced like the color *red*)

I have a *contract* signed by the president. (noun: pronounced *con′ trakt;* means a document)

I didn't know it would *contract* as it cooled. (verb: pronounced *cən/trakt′;* means to reduce in size)

The books by Fred Gwynne mentioned in the section on homonyms are also rich sources of homographs.

Synonyms

Synonyms are words that have the same or very similar meanings. Work with synonyms can help expand students' vocabularies.

Study of the sports page of the newspaper for ways that writers express the ideas of *win* and *lose* can be a good way to introduce synonyms. The teacher should take this opportunity to show the students the different shadings of meaning that synonyms may have. For example, the headlines "Cats Maul Dogs" and "Cats Squeak by Dogs" both mean that the Cats beat the Dogs, but one indicates a win by a large margin, whereas the other indicates a close game. In addition, some synonyms are on varying levels of formality (for example, *dog* and *pooch*) (Breen, 1989).

A teacher can also provide a stimulus word and have the students find as many synonyms as they can. The class can discuss the small differences in meaning of some words suggested as synonyms. For example, the teacher can ask, "Would you rather be called *thrifty* or *stingy*? Why?"

Antonyms

Antonyms are two words that have opposite meanings. Their meanings are not merely different; they are balanced against each other on a particular feature. In the continuum *cold, cool, tepid, warm,* and *hot,* for example, *cold* is the opposite of *hot,* being as close to the extreme in a negative direction as *hot* is in a positive direction. Thus, *cold* and *hot* are antonyms. *Tepid* and *hot* are different but not opposites. *Cool* and *warm* are also antonyms. Similarly, *buy* and *sell* are antonyms because one is the reverse of the other. But *buy* and *give* are not antonyms, because no exchange of money is involved in the giving. The words are different, but not opposite. Powell (1986) points out that the use of opposition (citing antonyms) in defining terms can help to set the extremities of a word's meaning and provide its shadings and nuances. Research has shown that synonym production is helped by antonym production, but the reverse has not been shown to be true. Therefore, work with antonyms may enhance success in synonym exercises.

New Words

New words are constantly being coined to meet the changing needs of society and are possible sources of difficulty. Have students search for such words in their reading and television viewing and then compile a dictionary of words so new that they are not yet in standard dictionaries. The class may have to discuss these words to derive an accurate definition for each one, considering all the contexts in which the students have heard or seen it. These new words may have been formed from Latin and Greek word elements, from current slang, or by shortening or combining older words (Richek, 1988).

SUMMARY

Vocabulary development includes both the ability to recognize words in print and to determine word meanings. Word recognition techniques (particularly phonic analysis) generally receive extensive attention in the primary grades. Methods of determining word meanings are introduced in the primary grades and receive extensive attention in the middle school. Some techniques, such as use of context clues, structural analysis, and dictionary skills, are useful in both word recognition and determination of word meanings, and these should continue to be emphasized in middle-school classes. Additionally, since the greater the store of sight words a person has, the more fluent his or her reading is likely to be, middle-school teachers should continue to help students add to their stores of sight words.

Acquiring a meaning vocabulary involves developing labels for the schemata, or organized knowledge structures, that a person possesses. Because vocabulary is an important component of reading comprehension, direct instruction in vocabulary can enhance reading achievement.

There are many ways to approach vocabulary instruction. The best techniques link new terms to the students' background knowledge, help them expand their word knowledge, actively involve them in learning, help them become independent in acquiring vocabulary, provide repetition of the words, and have them use the words meaningfully. Techniques that cause students to work harder to learn words tend to aid retention. Teachers may need to spend time on schema development before working with specific vocabulary terms.

Vocabulary development should be emphasized throughout the day, not just in reading and language classes; students can learn much vocabulary from the teacher's modeling of vocabulary use. Categorization, analogies and word lines, semantic maps and word webs, semantic feature analysis, study of word origins and histories, study of a number of student-centered learning techniques, word play, and computer techniques can be helpful in vocabulary instruction.

Figurative language and some special types of words, including homonyms, homographs, synonyms, antonyms, and newly coined words, can cause comprehension problems for students. They need to receive special attention.

TEST YOURSELF

True or False

______ 1. It is wise to teach only a single approach to word recognition.

______ 2. All word recognition strategies are learned with equal ease by all students.

______ 3. Sight words are words that readers recognize immediately without needing to resort to analysis.

______ 4. Most practice with sight words should involve the words in context.

______ 5. Structural analysis skills include the ability to recognize prefixes and suffixes.

______ 6. The addition of a prefix to a root word can change the word's meaning.

______ 7. Inflectional endings can change verb tenses.

______ 8. The apostrophe in a contraction indicates possession or ownership.

_____ 9. Every syllable contains a vowel sound.

_____ 10. There is only one vowel letter in each syllable.

_____ 11. Open syllables end in consonant sounds.

_____ 12. Prefixes and suffixes generally form separate syllables.

_____ 13. Prefixes and suffixes are usually accented.

_____ 14. Context clues used by themselves provide only educated guesses about the identities of unfamiliar words.

_____ 15. Students should be expected to memorize the diacritical markings used in their dictionaries.

_____ 16. Accent marks indicate which syllables are stressed.

_____ 17. Some words have more than one accented syllable.

_____ 18. Writing new words is helpful to some learners in building sight vocabulary.

_____ 19. The language experience approach is good for developing sight vocabulary.

_____ 20. One method of teaching sight words is best for all students.

_____ 21. For students with special needs, instruction often needs to be more direct and explicit.

_____ 22. Context clues are of little help in determining the meanings of unfamiliar words, although they are useful for recognizing familiar ones.

_____ 23. Structural analysis can help in determining meanings of new words containing familiar prefixes, suffixes, and root words.

_____ 24. When looking up a word in the dictionary to determine its meaning, a student needs to read only the first definition listed.

_____ 25. Homonyms are words that have identical, or almost identical, meanings.

_____ 26. Antonyms are words that have opposite meanings.

_____ 27. Word play is one good approach to building vocabulary.

_____ 28. The development of vocabulary is essentially a student's development of labels for his or her schemata.

_____ 29. Work with analogies bolsters word knowledge.

_____ 30. Semantic maps show how words are connected in meaning to one another.

_____ 31. Instruction in vocabulary that helps students relate new terms to their background knowledge is helpful.

_______ 32. Active involvement in vocabulary activities has little effect on vocabulary learning.

_______ 33. Pantomiming word meanings is one technique to produce active involvement in word learning.

_______ 34. Students should have multiple exposures to words they are expected to learn.

_______ 35. Working hard to learn words results in better retention.

_______ 36. There are many ways to teach the meanings of words.

_______ 37. Both concrete and vicarious experiences can help to build concepts.

_______ 38. Vocabulary instruction should receive attention during content area classes.

_______ 39. "Think-aloud" strategies can help students see how to use context clues.

_______ 40. Although use of categorization activities is motivational, it is not an effective approach, according to current research findings.

_______ 41. Semantic mapping can help students develop a concept of *definition.*

_______ 42. Semantic feature analysis is the same as structural analysis.

_______ 43. Semantic feature analysis can help students see the uniqueness of each word studied.

_______ 44. The study of word origins is called *etymology.*

_______ 45. A word-processing program can facilitate certain types of vocabulary instruction.

_______ 46. Students instinctively understand figures of speech; therefore, figurative language presents them with no special problems.

_______ 47. Wide reading is a prime method of vocabulary building.

_______ 48. Being able to recite a dictionary definition means that the students understand the word's meaning.

For your journal . . .

1. Reflect on the value of context clues for vocabulary development.
2. React to commercial computer software for vocabulary development that you have used. Include strengths and weaknesses of the programs. Which one would you recommend to parents who ask about buying software for home use? Why?

. . . and your portfolio

1. Plan a lesson on dictionary use that requires students to locate the meaning of a word that fits the context surrounding that word.
2. Plan a lesson designed to teach the concept of *justice* to a group of sixth-grade students.
3. After collecting examples of figurative language from a variety of sources, use them as the basis for a lesson on interpreting figurative language.
4. Plan a lesson to teach one or more word recognition strategies, using a library book that contains appropriate examples of structural analysis elements.

3

Comprehension: Part 1

KEY VOCABULARY

Pay close attention to these terms when they appear in the chapter.

- anticipation guide
- cloze procedure
- Investigative Questioning (InQuest)
- knowledge-based processes
- K-W-L teaching model
- metacognition
- multiple intelligences
- reciprocal teaching
- relative clause
- schema (and schemata)
- semantic webbing
- story grammar
- story mapping
- text-based processes
- think-alouds

SETTING OBJECTIVES

When you finish reading this chapter, you should be able to

- Explain how schema theory relates to reading comprehension.
- Explain how a reader's purpose and other aspects of the situation in which reading takes place affect comprehension.
- Describe some characteristics of text that affect comprehension.
- Discuss some prereading, during-reading, and postreading activities that can enhance comprehension for middle-school students.

The objective of all readers is, or should be, comprehension of what they read. Comprehension is understanding. Wiggins and McTighe (1998) point out that understanding involves the abilities to explain, interpret, apply, have perspective, empathize, and have self-knowledge. Shanklin and Rhodes (1989) see comprehension as an evolving process, often beginning before a book is opened, changing as the material is read, and continuing to change even after the book is completed. This developmental nature of comprehension is enhanced when the student interacts with others about aspects of the material after it has been read. Therefore, classroom interaction related to reading materials is important to comprehension development and should be planned carefully.

As Pearson and Johnson (1978) point out, "reading comprehension is at once a unitary process and a set of discrete processes" (p. 227). We discuss the individual processes separately; yet teachers must not lose sight of the fact that there are many overlaps and interrelationships among the processes. Close relationships even exist between comprehension and decoding. Research has shown that good comprehenders are able to decode quickly and accurately ("A Talk with Marilyn Adams," 1991; Eads, 1981). Thus, developing decoding strategies to the automatic stage is important. Teachers should always keep in mind, however, that use of decoding strategies is merely a means of accessing the meaning of the written material.

When good decoders have problems with comprehension, they need help in developing language proficiency and listening comprehension. Teachers can help them

Chapter 3 Organization

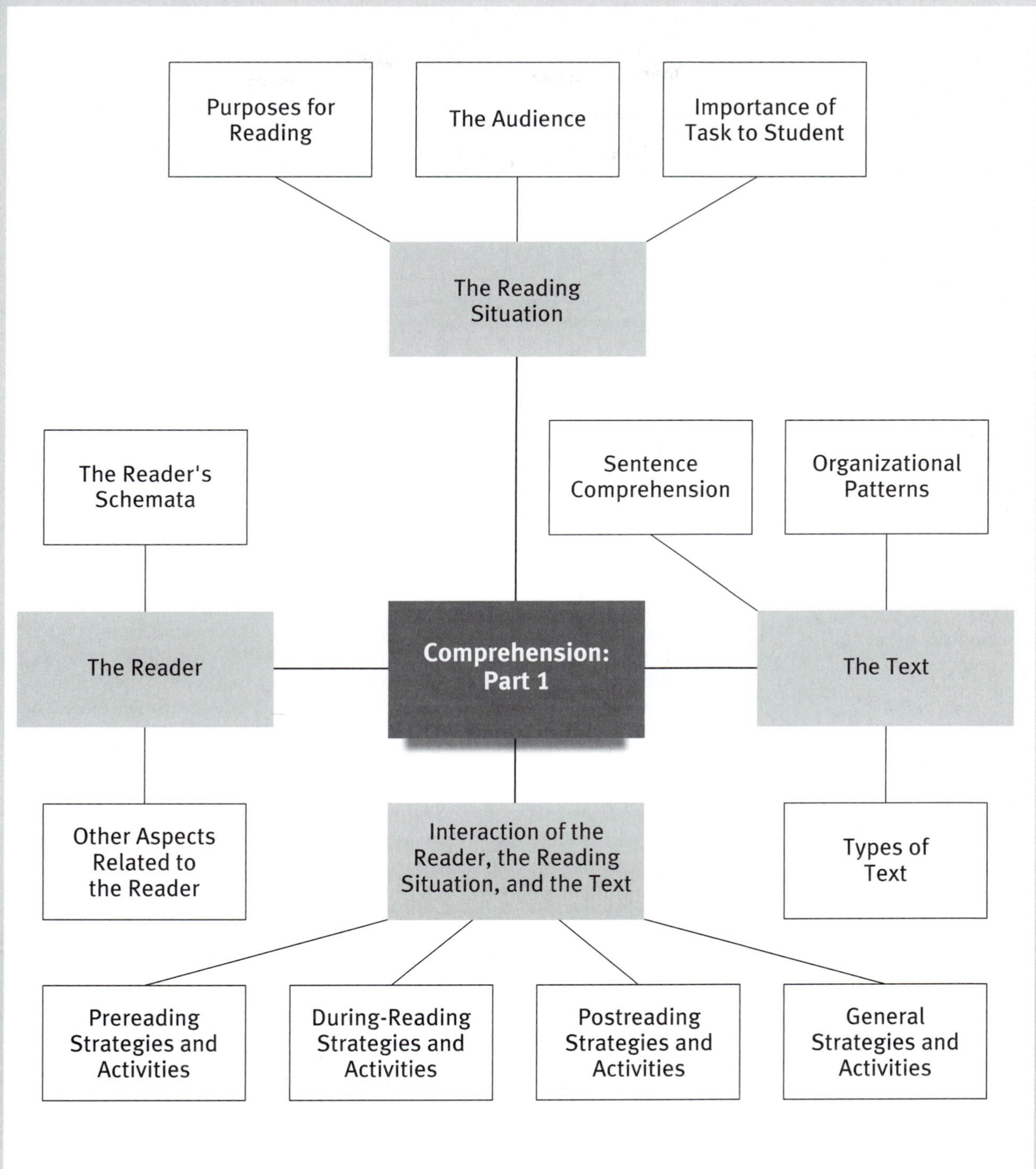

develop these skills by combining instruction in vocabulary and comprehension strategies with encouragement to increase their reading of material written at levels that yield good comprehension (Dymock, 1993).

Allington (2002) and his colleagues studied effective teachers of reading and writing. The students in their classes spent much of the school day reading and writing. This extensive practice gives the students a chance to internalize the skills and strategies that they have been taught. Much of this reading should be done in materials that the students can read with accuracy, fluency, and understanding. The lowest achievers benefited the most from this exemplary teaching.

Villaume and Brabham (2002, p. 673) point out that "[t]hrough strategic reading, students gain access to the rights, responsibilities, and benefits accorded to skillful readers." Just as we do, Villaume and Brabham see the need for explicit instruction that is not heavily scripted, but is *clear,* involving modeling of strategies, supervised practice of these strategies, and follow-up assistance that clarifies areas where students may encounter problems. Such effective comprehension instruction is presented in a logical and purposeful manner; the interrelated strategies are addressed over time, and learning is monitored, with instruction based on exhibited student needs. Strategy instruction should center on tasks that are of appropriate difficulty for the particular students. Practice with the strategies in the context of real-world tasks should take place. Strategy use should be practiced until it becomes automatic (Pressley, 1995; Rhoder, 2002). Allington (2002, p. 743) says that the exemplary teachers in his study "routinely gave direct explicit demonstrations of the cognitive strategies that good readers use when they read."

Villaume and Brabham (2002) make a good point when they say "that strategies do not exist in neat boxes and that the boundaries between them are blurred" (p. 647). We isolate strategies for purposes of discussion in this textbook, but it is very important to remember that readers use them in combination when reading. Like Pressley (1995) and Rhoder (2002), however, we feel that the strategies are more durable when they are initially learned individually. Comprehension strategy instruction should make use of the students' own textbooks (Roe, 1992) or trade books they are reading (Baumann, Hooten, and White, 1999). The teacher should tell the students what strategy they are going to learn and how it will help them in their reading. Then the teacher should describe the strategy, model it, guide practice with it, and provide cooperative and independent practice opportunities (Roe, 1992). About one-fifth of each reading period should be spent on explicit strategy instruction, with the rest spent on reading, responding to, analyzing, and discussing the reading material (Baumann, Hooten, and White, 1999).

Middle-school readers approach a text with much background knowledge concerning their world, and they use this knowledge along with the text to construct the meanings represented by the printed material that meet their purposes for reading. To access the information supplied by the text, they must use word recognition strategies (covered in Chapter 2) and comprehension strategies (covered in Chapter 2, this chapter, and Chapter 4). They combine their existing knowledge with new information supplied by the text in order to achieve understanding of the material.

This chapter discusses the importance to comprehension of the interaction among the reader, the reading situation, and the text. It explores the importance of the reader's prior knowledge, the reader's purposes for reading, the audience for reading, and the characteristics of the text to be read. It also presents strategies to be used before, during, and after reading.

This chapter is a logical continuation of Chapter 2, "Vocabulary Instruction," because vocabulary knowledge is a vital component of comprehension. Therefore, these chapters cannot truly be considered separately and are divided here only for convenience of presentation. Similarly, the coverage of the types of comprehension in Chapter 4 is a continuation of the topic that is separated for ease of treatment.

The Reader

This section discusses factors related to the reader that affect his or her comprehension, including the reader's background knowledge, sensory and perceptual abilities, thinking abilities, word recognition strategies, and affective aspects, such as attitudes, self-concepts, and interests.

The Reader's Schemata

Educators have long believed that if a reader has not been exposed to a writer's language patterns or to the objects and concepts to which the writer refers, the reader's comprehension will at best be incomplete. This belief is supported by theories holding that reading comprehension involves relating textual information to preexisting knowledge structures, or schemata (Pearson et al., 1979). ***Schemata*** are a person's organized clusters of concepts related to objects, places, actions, or events. Each schema represents a person's knowledge about a particular concept and the interrelationships among the known pieces of information. For example, a schema for *car* may include a person's knowledge about the car's construction, its appearance, and its operation, as well as many other facts about it. Two people may have quite different schemata for the same basic concept; for example, a race-car driver's schema for *car* (or, to be more exact, the driver's cluster of schemata about cars) will differ from that of a seventh grader.

Types of Schemata

People may have schemata for objects, events, abstract ideas, story structure, processes, emotions, roles, conventions of writing, and so forth. In fact, "schemata can represent knowledge at all levels—from ideologies and cultural truths . . . to knowledge about what patterns of excitations are associated with what letters of the alphabet" (Rumelhart, 1981, p. 13). Each schema a person has is incomplete, as though it contains empty slots that could be filled with information collected from new experiences. Reading of informational material is aided by the existing schemata and also fills in some of the empty slots in them (Durkin, 1981).

Students need schemata of a variety of types to be successful readers. They must have concepts about the arrangement of print on a page, the purpose of printed material (to convey ideas), and the relationship of spoken language to written language. They need to be familiar with vocabulary and sentence patterns not generally found in oral language and with the different writing styles associated with various literary genres.

A *story schema* is a set of expectations about the internal structure of stories (Mandler and Johnson, 1977). Readers find well-structured stories easier to recall and summarize than unstructured passages. Possession of a story schema appears to have a positive effect on recall, and good readers seem to have a better grasp of text structure than poor readers do. Having students retell stories is a good way to discover their grasp of a story schema (Rand, 1984). (A rubric for analyzing retelling is found in Chapter 9.)

STANDARDS AND ASSESSMENT

LITERATURE

Having many experiences with well-formed stories helps students develop a story schema. Storytelling and story reading are excellent ways to develop students' schemata related to stories or other materials they will be expected to read. Hearing teachers read different genres of stories helps students develop a variety of story schemata that allows them to anticipate or predict what will happen next in different types of literature. This ability enables students to become more involved in stories they read and more effectively to make and confirm or reject predictions, a process that fosters comprehension. The sentence structures in the stories told and read to students expose them to patterns they will encounter when they read literature on their own and will help make these patterns more understandable (Roe, 1985, 1986). Middle-school students will benefit from hearing stories that have multiple story lines and ones that contain advanced literary elements such as flashbacks. Another way to help develop students' story schemata is direct teaching of story structure and story grammars, covered later in this chapter in the section "Story Grammar Activities." Perhaps the most important concept students need to have in their "reading schema" is the understanding that reading can be fun and can help them do things.

Hearing teachers read different genres of stories helps students develop a variety of story schemata.
(© Elizabeth Crews)

Research Findings About Schemata

Many research studies have supported schema theory. Anderson and colleagues, for example, discovered that recall and comprehension of passages with two possible interpretations (in one case, wrestling versus a prison break; in another, card playing versus a music rehearsal) were closely related to the readers' background knowledge or the testing environment (cited in Pearson et al., 1979). Bransford and Johnson discovered that recall of obscure passages increased if a statement of the passage's topic or a picture related to the passage was provided.

Studies have shown that the provision of background information on a topic before reading is likely to enhance reading comprehension, especially inferential comprehension, the ability to determine information implied in the text (Pearson et al., 1979; Stevens, 1982). These findings indicate that teachers should plan experiences that will give students background information to help them understand written material they are expected to read and help them choose appropriate schemata to apply to the reading.

When students have trouble using their experiential backgrounds to assist in reading comprehension, teachers need to find out if the students lack the necessary schemata or if they possess the needed schemata but are unable to use them effectively when reading. If the students lack the schemata, the teacher should plan direct and vicarious experiences to build them, such as having the students examine and discuss pictures that reveal information about the subject, introducing new terminology related to the subject, taking field trips, giving demonstrations, or having students read about particular topics in other books. Struggling readers frequently need more help with concept development and more discussion time before reading than teachers provide. If students already know about the subject, letting them share their knowledge, preview the material to be read, and predict what might happen can encourage them to draw on their existing schemata.

Readers vary in the relative degree to which they use two processes of comprehension (Spiro, 1979). ***Text-based processes*** are those in which the reader is primarily trying to extract information from the text. ***Knowledge-based processes*** are those in which the reader primarily brings prior knowledge and experiences to bear on the interpretation of the material. For example, consider this text: "The children were gathered around a table on which sat a beautiful cake with *Happy Birthday* written on it. Mrs. Jones said, 'Now, Maria, make a wish and blow out the candles.'" Readers must use a text-based process to answer the question, "What was written on the cake?" because the information is directly stated in the material. They must use a knowledge-based process to answer the question, "Whose birthday was it?" Prior experience will provide them with the answer, "Maria," because they have consistently seen candles blown out by the child who is celebrating the birthday at parties they have attended. Of course, before they use the knowledge-based process, they must use a text-based process to discover that Maria was told to blow out the candles.

Skilled readers may employ one type of process more than the other when the situation allows them to do this without affecting their comprehension. Less able readers may tend to rely too heavily on one type of processing in all situations, resulting in poorer comprehension (Walker, 2000). Unfortunately, some students have the idea that knowledge-based processing is not an appropriate reading activity, so they fail to use knowledge they have.

Rystrom (cited in Strange, 1980) presents a good argument that reading cannot be exclusively knowledge-based, or "top-down": if it were, two people reading the same material would rarely arrive at the same conclusions, and the probability that a person could learn anything from written material would be slight. Rystrom has an equally convincing argument that reading is not exclusively text-based, or "bottom-up": if it were, all people who read a written selection would agree about its meaning. It is far more likely that reading is interactive, involving both information supplied by the text and information brought to the text by the reader, which combine to produce the reader's understanding of the material. (See Chapter 1 for a detailed discussion of this idea.) Example 3.1 illustrates this process.

If reading performance results from interaction between information in the text and information the reader possesses, anything that increases a reader's background knowledge may also enhance reading performance. Increased exposure to social studies, science, art, music, mathematics, and other content areas should therefore enhance reading achievement. In general, this seems to be the case: students at schools with broad curricular scopes have been found to score higher on inferential reading comprehension than students at schools with narrow curricular scopes (Singer, McNeil, and Furse, 1984). Teachers can also encourage family members to involve students in a wide variety of activities outside of school.

FAMILY

Helping Students Use Their Schemata

Teachers need to help students activate whatever background knowledge they already possess about a selection to be read, as well as help them develop important concepts,

EXAMPLE 3.1 Flow of Information During Reading

A reader uses information stored in the brain in the form of schemata to help in understanding the message conveyed by the print. The new information gained from the page is then stored in the brain, connected in an organized manner to the schema that it enriched.

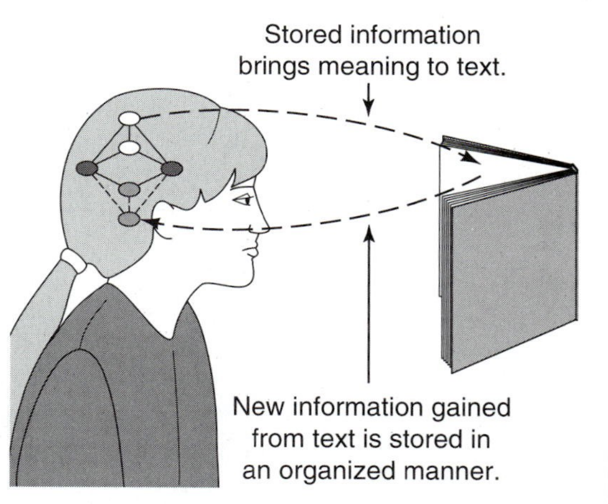

related to the reading material, that they do not currently possess. The students need to understand that they can use what they already know to help comprehend reading materials.

Teachers can use ***think-alouds*** with the students to illustrate or demonstrate the process that they use in activating schemata for a passage being read, modeling the mental process so that the students can emulate it. (An example of a think-aloud session appears on pages 110–111.) Some other techniques that may be used for schema activation include the prediction strategies in a Directed Reading-Thinking Activity (described in Chapters 5 and 8), the preview step of the SQ3R study method (described in Chapter 7), and the purpose questions of the Directed Reading Activity (described in Chapter 5).

Teachers should make sure the material students are asked to read is not too difficult for them. Difficult materials tend to work against students' use of meaning-seeking activities because they cause students to focus too much on decoding and not enough on comprehension.

Other Aspects Related to the Reader

Experiential background is the basis for readers' schemata. The discussion in Chapter 1 of the many aspects of the reading process includes this vital aspect, as well as a number of other aspects related to the reader that affect comprehension. These additional aspects are readers' sensory and perceptual abilities, their thinking abilities, and affective aspects, such as self-concepts, attitudes, and interests. Readers' attitudes and interests affect motivation to read, and readers who are not motivated to read are not likely to give the reading task the degree of attention needed to result in high levels of comprehension. Facility with word recognition strategies also enhances comprehension because it releases the students' attention from the word recognition task and allows the students to apply it to the task of comprehension. Some educators have been concerned that nonstandard dialects could be a major barrier to comprehension. Goodman and Buck (1997, p. 459) assert, however, that "dialect-involved miscues do not interfere with the reading process or the construction of meaning, since they move to the readers' own language."

DIVERSITY

Teachers may find Howard Gardner's theory of ***multiple intelligences*** of interest. Gardner (1995, p. 202) defines an intelligence as follows: "an *intelligence* is a biological and psychological potential; that potential is capable of being realized to a greater or lesser extent as a consequence of the experiential, cultural, and motivational factors that affect a person." It is not the same as a learning style; it is applied to a more narrow range of activities.

Gardner recognizes several distinct areas of potential that readers possess to different degrees (Armstrong, 1994; Gardner, 1995; Lazear, 1992). These areas of potential are *linguistic intelligence,* the ability to use written and spoken words effectively; *logical-mathematical intelligence,* the ability to reason, think deductively, and use numbers effectively; *spatial intelligence,* the capacity to perceive visual-spatial aspects of the world accurately and to create mental images; *bodily-kinesthetic intelligence,* knowledge of one's body and its physical movements; *musical intelligence,* recognition of tonal patterns and sensitivity to rhythm; *interpersonal intelligence,* the capacity to understand

and relate to other people; *intrapersonal intelligence,* knowledge of self, including metacognition, spirituality, and self-reflection; and *naturalist intelligence,* the ability to problem-solve, observe, classify, and categorize. Lessons that incorporate use of more than one type of intelligence, or potential, are likely to be appropriate for more students than lessons that involve only one. Several of the techniques described later in this chapter encourage students to use multiple intelligences.

Gardner believes that there is no single right way to use the multiple intelligences theory in education. Furthermore, he says that not every topic can be taught through all intelligences. Trying to teach every topic that way is a waste of time, and some efforts to force attention on particular intelligences are pointless. Playing music in the background while students work in areas other than music does not use musical intelligence, for example. Gardner (1995) does believe that concepts should be taught in a variety of appropriate ways, so that more students will be reached.

TIME for REFLECTION

Gardner does not believe that every topic can be taught through all intelligences, yet some teachers disagree. Gardner, for example, doesn't believe that the mathematical skill of a person who is strong in musical intelligence is enhanced by music being played in the background while the person is doing math problems. **What do *you* think, and why?**

The Reading Situation

The *reading situation* includes purposes for the reading, both self-constructed and teacher-directed; the audience for the reading; and the importance the reading task has for the individual.

Purposes for Reading

All of the reading that middle-school students do should be purposeful, because students who read with a purpose tend to comprehend what they read better than those who have no purpose. This result may occur because the students are attending to the material rather than just calling words. Purpose-setting activities can help students activate their existing schemata about the topic of the material. For this reason, teachers should set purposes for students by providing them with pertinent objectives for the reading or help them set their own purposes by deciding on their own objectives. There are many possible objectives for reading (Blanton, Wood, and Moorman, 1990; Dowhower, 1999; Irwin, 1991):

- For enjoyment
- To perfect oral reading performance or use of a particular strategy
- To update knowledge about a topic by linking new information to that already known
- To obtain information for an oral or written report
- To confirm or reject predictions
- To perform an experiment or apply information gained from the text in some other way

- To learn about the structure of a text
- To answer specific questions

Teacher-constructed purpose questions can help students focus on important information in the selection and should replace such assignments as "Read Chapter 7 for tomorrow." Providing specific purposes avoids presenting students with the insurmountable task of remembering everything they read and allows them to know whether they are reading to determine main ideas, locate details, understand vocabulary terms, or meet some other well-defined goal. As a result, they can apply themselves to a specific, manageable task. However, if teachers always use the same types of purpose questions and do not guide students to set their own purposes, the students may not develop the ability to read for a variety of purposes.

Cunningham and Wall (1994, p. 481) suggest always setting a purpose for student reading that is either "(a) a clear and precise statement of what the students are to focus on while they read or (b) a clear preview of the task they will be asked to perform after reading." This allows students to use the purpose to help them choose reading strategies. Cunningham and Wall also suggest making purposes more specific for more difficult texts to guide the students to the important and challenging content.

For maximum effectiveness, Blanton and colleagues (1990) recommend setting a single purpose for reading rather than multiple purposes. A single purpose may be especially effective for struggling readers because it can help to avoid cognitive confusion from the overload of multiple purposes. The purpose should be one that is sustained throughout the entire selection, not met after reading only a small portion of the material; in other words, the purpose should be fairly broad in scope. Purposes should be formed carefully, because poor ones can misdirect the students' attention by focusing on information that is not essential to the passage and slighting important information. Purposes should help readers differentiate between relevant and irrelevant information.

Even when teachers set purposes for students initially, responsibility for setting purposes should gradually shift from the teacher to the students. Middle-school students are capable of setting their own purposes, and they will be more committed to purposes they have set than to ones set by the teacher. When teachers set purposes for reading, they may then "think aloud" how the purpose was developed, thus modeling the purpose-setting procedure for later independent use by students. (An example of a think-aloud session appears on pages 110–111.)

Having students predict what will happen in a story or what information will be presented in an informational selection is a step in helping students set for themselves the purpose of reading to find out if their predictions are accurate. Such purposes engage the students in the reading more than teacher-generated ones do. The Directed Reading-Thinking Activity, described further in Chapters 5 and 8, encourages such personal purpose setting through predictions on the part of the students. Fielding, Anderson, and Pearson (1990) found that prediction questions were more effective than traditional basal reader questions if the predictions were compared with the actual text after reading (Pearson and Fielding, 1991). Therefore, teachers should be sure to follow up on predictions if this type of purpose is used. Actually, all purposes should be discussed immediately after the reading is completed. Neglecting this procedure may cause students to ignore the purposes and merely try to pronounce all the words in the selection.

Commercial reading materials tend to offer a variety of types of purpose questions. However, teachers sometimes do not make use of these ready-made questions, or they may paraphrase them. If teachers are going to use self-constructed questions, they should give careful thought to the desired outcomes of the reading and the types of purpose questions most likely to lead to these outcomes.

Prereading questions should focus on predicting and on relating text to prior knowledge. Students should be asked about the details that relate to problems, goals, attempts to solve problems, characters' reactions, resolutions, and themes (Pearson, 1985). (More about this type of questioning appears in the section "Story Grammar as a Basis for Questioning" in Chapter 4.)

STANDARDS AND ASSESSMENT

TIME for REFLECTION

Some teachers believe that middle-school students should always set their own purposes for reading. Others believe that teachers should set the purposes. Still others believe that sometimes it is appropriate for teachers to set purposes, but that much of the time, the students should do the purpose setting. **What do *you* think, and why?**

Even when teachers do not provide purpose questions, students are often guided in the way they approach their reading assignments by the types of questions that teachers have used in the past on tests, using this knowledge to set their own purposes for reading. If a teacher tends to ask for factual recall of small details in test questions, students will concentrate on such details and perhaps overlook the main ideas entirely. In class discussion, the teacher may be bewildered by the fact that the students know many things that happened in a story without knowing what the basic theme was. Teachers need to be aware that their testing procedures affect the purposes for which students read content material in their classrooms.

The Audience

The audience for the reading may consist of only the reader, reading alone for personal or teacher-directed purposes. In this case, the reader is free to use his or her available reading strategies as needed to meet the purposes. The degree to which the reader has accepted the purposes as valid will affect his or her comprehension of the material.

Sometimes the audience for the reading is the teacher. Teachers have been found to focus more on word recognition concerns with lower-achieving groups of students and more on meaning with higher-achieving groups (Irwin, 1991), a tendency that could be detrimental to the students in lower groups. Anderson, Mason, and Shirey (1983) found that a meaning focus was more effective than a word recognition focus with both struggling readers and good readers.

Sometimes the audience is other students. In school, a common audience is the reading group. Some students may comprehend less well when reading to perform in a reading group than when reading independently. They may even react differently to different groups of students, for example, younger students as opposed to students of their own age. Teachers should be aware of this possibility and assess reading comprehension in a variety of settings.

STANDARDS AND ASSESSMENT

Importance of Task to Student

The degree to which students embrace the purposes for reading the material will affect the attention they give to the task and the perseverance with which they attempt it. The level of risk involved will have an additional effect on the results of the reading. Mosenthal and Na (1980a) found that students performed differently on reading tasks in high-risk situations, such as tests, than in low-risk situations, such as normal classroom lessons. In high-risk situations, low-ability and average-ability students tended to reproduce the text, whereas high-ability students tended to reproduce and embellish it. In low-risk situations, the students tended to respond according to their typical verbal interaction patterns with the teacher (Mosenthal and Na, 1980b).

STANDARDS AND ASSESSMENT

The Text

Reading a text involves dealing with its specific characteristics and deriving information from it using word recognition and comprehension strategies. Texts are made up of words, sentences, paragraphs, and whole selections. Since vocabulary is one of the most important factors affecting comprehension, Chapter 2 was devoted to vocabulary instruction. Sentence difficulty and organizational patterns are other text characteristics. Although some suggestions in this section focus on comprehension of sentences or paragraphs, comprehension is a unitary act, and eventually all the procedures discussed here must work together for the reader to achieve comprehension of the whole selection.

People who choose texts and supplementary material for students must be aware of the difficulty of the material they choose, especially when students will use it independently. The directions provided for students and the instructional language used in such materials should be of high quality. The language of the directions should be at least as clear as the language of the exercises.

Sentence Comprehension

Students may find complicated sentences difficult to understand, so they need to know ways to derive sentence meanings. Research has shown that systematic instruction in sentence comprehension increases reading comprehension. For example, Weaver (as cited in Durkin, 1978/1979) had students arrange cut-up sentences in the correct order by finding the action word first and then asking *who, what, where,* and *why* questions. This activity may work especially well when the sentences are drawn from literature selections the teacher has already shared with the students. Another approach is to have students discover the essential parts of sentences by writing them in telegram form, as illustrated in the Model Activity on Telegram Sentences.

Teachers should help students learn that sentences can be stated in different ways without changing their meanings. For example, some sentence parts can be moved around without affecting the meaning of the sentence, as in these two sentences:

> On a pole in front of the school, the flag was flying.
>
> The flag was flying on a pole in front of the school.

MODEL ACTIVITIES

Telegram Sentences

Write a sentence like this one on the board: "The angry dog chased me down the street." Tell the students that you want to state what happened in the fewest words possible because, when you send a telegram, each word used costs money. Then think aloud about the sentence: "Who did something in this sentence? Oh, the dog did. My sentence needs to include the dog . . . What action did he perform? He chased. I'll need that action word too. 'Dog chased . . .' That doesn't make a complete thought, though. I'll have to tell whom he chased. He chased me. Now I have a complete message that leaves out the extra details. My telegram is: 'Dog chased me.'"

Then let the students write a telegram based on a story they have read or heard. For example, have them write the telegram that Parvana in Ellis's *The Breadwinner* might have sent to her mother after her father was released from prison.

Nevertheless, teachers should acknowledge that moving sentence parts *can* affect the meaning. For example, the following two sentences have distinctly different meanings:

Carla helped Teresa.

Teresa helped Carla.

Sentence Difficulty Factors

A number of types of sentences are difficult for students to comprehend, including

- those with relative clauses,
- other complex sentences,
- those with missing words,
- those in the passive voice, and
- those expressing negation.

Students understand material better when the syntax is like their oral language patterns, but the text in some reading material is syntactically more complex than the students' oral language.

Relative clauses are among the syntactic patterns that do not appear regularly in some students' speech. Relative clauses either restrict the information in the main clause by adding information or simply add extra information. Both types may be troublesome. In the example, "The man *who called my name* was my father," the relative clause indicates the specific man to designate as "my father" (Kachuck, 1981).

STANDARDS AND ASSESSMENT

Teachers should ask questions that assess students' understanding of particular syntactic patterns in the reading material, and when misunderstanding is evident, they should point out the clues that can help students discover the correct meanings (Kachuck, 1981). Teachers may find it necessary to read aloud sentences from assigned passages to students and explain the functions of the relative clauses found in the sentences. Then they may give other examples of sentences with relative clauses and ask the students to explain the meanings of these clauses. Feedback on correctness or incorrectness and further explanation should be given at this point. Finally, teachers should provide students with independent practice activities to help them set the new skill in memory.

Students who need more work with relative clauses can be asked to turn two-clause sentences into two sentences (Kachuck, 1981). Teachers can model this activity also, as in the earlier example: "The man called my name. The man was my father." Supervised student practice with feedback and independent practice can follow, using progressively more difficult sentences. Students can move from this activity into sentence combining, which we examine next. Finally, they should apply their understanding in reading whole passages (Kachuck, 1981). Until they have used the skill in interpreting connected discourse, it is impossible to be sure they have mastered it.

Sentence combining involves giving students two or more short sentences and asking them to combine the information into a single sentence. For example, they might be asked to combine these two sentences: "Joe has a motorcycle. It is red." Responses might include "Joe has a red motorcycle." "Joe has a motorcycle, and it is red." "Joe has a motorcycle that is red." "Joe's motorcycle is red." Wilkinson and Patty (1993) have found that students can learn to attend to elements of text related to connectives through sentence-combining practice, but not just through reading texts written by other students during sentence-combining practice activities.

Discussion of a number of sentence combinations may reveal much about the students' syntactic knowledge. Sentence-combining activities also bring out the important fact that there are always multiple ways of expressing an idea in English (Pearson and Camperell, 1981).

Punctuation

Punctuation can greatly affect the meaning a sentence conveys; it represents pauses and pitch changes that would occur if the passage were read aloud. While punctuation marks represent the inflections in speech imperfectly, they greatly aid in turning written language into oral language.

Commas and dashes indicate pauses within sentences. Periods, question marks, and exclamation points all signal pauses between sentences and also alter the meaning:

He's a crook. (Making a statement)

He's a crook? (Asking a question)

He's a crook! (Showing surprise or dismay at the discovery)

To help students see how punctuation can affect the meaning of the material, use sentences such as the following:

Mother said, "Joe could do it."

Mother said, "Joe could do it?"

"Mother," said Joe, "could do it."

We had ice cream and cake.

We had ice cream and cake?

We had ice, cream, and cake.

Discuss the differences in meaning among the sentences in each set, highlighting the function of each punctuation mark.

Underlining and italics, which are frequently used to indicate that a word or group of words is to be stressed, are also clues to underlying meaning. Here are several stress patterns for a single sentence:

Pat ate one snail.

Pat *ate* one snail.

Pat ate *one* snail.

Pat ate one *snail.*

In the first pattern, the stress immediately indicates that Pat, and no one else, ate the snail. In the second variation, stressing the word *ate* shows that the act of eating the snail was of great importance. In the third variation, the writer emphasizes that only one snail was eaten. The last variation implies that eating a snail was unusual and that *snail* is more important than the other words in the sentence.

Teachers need to be sure that students are aware of the aids to comprehension that punctuation provides and that they practice interpreting punctuation marks. To make students more aware of punctuation such as quotation marks, periods, and commas, teachers can have students read chorally, do readers' theater, or read plays.

TIME for REFLECTION

Some teachers think there should be much work with sentence-level comprehension before moving on to whole selections. Others think they should address sentence-level comprehension only within the context of whole selections. **What do *you* think, and why?**

Organizational Patterns

The internal organization of paragraphs in informational material can have a variety of patterns (for example, listing, chronological order, comparison and contrast, and cause and effect). In addition, paragraphs of each of these types also generally have an underlying organization that consists of the main idea plus supporting details. Whole selections contain these same organizational patterns and others, notably a topical pattern such as the one used in this textbook. Students' comprehension of informational material can be increased if they learn these organizational patterns. The Model Activities in this section show two examples of procedures for teaching paragraph patterns.

Similar exercises may be constructed with longer selections as well, preferably ones drawn from books available for the students to read. Kane (1998) suggests using quality literature to teach organizational patterns. Many stories are told in straight chronological order, for example, *A Year Down Yonder* by Richard Peck. Time-travel books, such as Jane Yolan's *The Devil's Arithmetic,* show movement back and forth in time. Mysteries often exhibit cause-and-effect patterns; for example, *Who Really Killed Cock Robin?* by Jean Craighead George is good for cause and effect. The McKissacks' *Christmas in the Big House, Christmas in the Quarters* is an advanced-level picture book that works well for comparison and contrast. Examples of several patterns may be located in a single book, as well. Teachers may introduce complex structures through read-alouds.

MODEL ACTIVITIES Chronological Order Paragraphs

Write the following paragraph on the board:

Jonah wanted to make a peanut butter sandwich. First, he gathered the necessary materials—peanut butter, bread, and knife. Then he took two slices of bread out of the package and opened the peanut butter jar. Next, he dipped the knife into the peanut butter, scooping up some. Then he spread the peanut butter on one of the slices of bread. Finally, he placed the other slice of bread on the peanut butter he had spread, and he had a sandwich.

Discuss the features of this paragraph, pointing out the functions of the sequence words, such as *first, then, next*, and *finally*. Make a list on the board, showing the sequence of events, numbering the events appropriately, or simply number them directly above their positions in the paragraph. Next, using another passage of the same type, preferably from a literature or content area selection that the students have already read, have them discover the sequence under your direction. Sequence words should also receive attention during this discussion. Then have the students detect sequence in other paragraphs from literature or content area selections that you have duplicated for independent practice. Discuss these independent practice paragraphs in class after the students have completed the exercises. Finally, alert students to watch for sequence as they do their daily reading.

MODEL ACTIVITIES Cause-and-Effect Paragraphs

Write the following paragraph on the board:

Jean lifted the box and started for the door. Because she could not see where her feet were landing, she tripped on her brother's fire truck.

Discuss the cause-and-effect relationship presented in this paragraph by saying: "The effect is the thing that happened, and the cause is the reason for the effect. The thing that happened in this paragraph was that Jean tripped on the fire truck. The cause was that she could not see where her feet were landing. The word *because* helps me to see that cause."

Then lead class discussions related to the cause-and-effect paragraph pattern by using other cause-and-effect paragraphs with different key words (such as *since* or *as a result of*) or with no key words at all. These examples should preferably be chosen from the students' classroom reading materials.

Types of Text

Narrative (storylike) selections generally consist of a series of narrative paragraphs that present the unfolding of a plot. They have a number of elements (setting, characters, theme, and so on) that have been described in story grammars (discussed later in this chapter). Although they are usually arranged in chronological order, paragraphs may be flashbacks, or narrations of events from an earlier time, to provide readers with the background information they need to understand the current situation.

Expository (explanatory) selections are composed of a variety of types of paragraphs, usually beginning with one or more introductory paragraphs and composed primarily of a series of topical paragraphs, with transition paragraphs to indicate shifts from one line of thought to another and illustrative paragraphs to provide examples to clarify the ideas. These selections generally conclude with summary paragraphs. Most content area textbooks are made up of primarily expository text.

Teaching students to make use of paragraphs that have specific functions can be beneficial. For example, students can be alerted to the fact that *introductory paragraphs* inform the reader about the topics a selection will cover. These paragraphs usually occur at the beginnings of whole selections or at major subdivisions of lengthy readings.

If students are searching for a discussion of a particular topic, they can check the introductory paragraphs of selections to determine if they need to read the entire selections. (The introductory sections that open each chapter in this book are suitable for use in this manner.) Introductory paragraphs can also help readers establish a proper mental set for the material to follow and may offer a framework for categorizing the facts readers will encounter in the selection.

Summary paragraphs occur at the ends of whole selections or major subdivisions and summarize what has gone before, stating the main points of the selection in a concise manner and omitting explanatory material and supporting details. They offer a tool for rapid review of the material. Students should be encouraged to use these paragraphs to check their memories for the important points in the selection.

To carry the reader through the author's presentation of an idea or a process, the topical paragraphs within an expository selection are logically arranged in one of the organizational patterns discussed earlier in this chapter. The writer's purpose will dictate the order in which he or she arranges the material—for example, chronologically or in a cause-and-effect arrangement. A history textbook may present the causes of the Civil War and lead the reader to see that the war was the effect of these causes. At times, a writer may use more than one form of organization in a single selection, such as combining chronological order and cause-and-effect organization in history materials.

One way to work on recognition of text patterns is to write examples of text patterns on index cards and give them to small groups of students who work cooperatively to sort them into the patterns represented. Discussion of the reasons for the classifications can take place in a whole-class setting. Students can move from this activity to locating the patterns in their content textbooks (Kuta, 1992).

Regardless of the approach, attention needs to be given to text structure. Pearson and Fielding (1991, p. 832) state, "It appears that any sort of systematic attention to clues that reveal how authors attempt to relate ideas to one another or any sort of systematic attempt to impose structure upon a text . . . facilitates comprehension as well as both short-term and long-term memory for the text." Chapter 8 discusses text patterns in more detail.

Interaction of the Reader, the Reading Situation, and the Text

Factors related to the reader, the reading situation, and the text all interact as the middle-school student reads in instructional settings. To encourage comprehension of whole selections, teachers usually incorporate prereading, during-reading, and postreading activities into lessons. Some techniques are more general and include activities for more than one of these lesson parts. Example 3.2 shows some techniques applicable to various parts of a lesson.

EXAMPLE 3.2 Interaction of Reader, Reading Situation, and Text

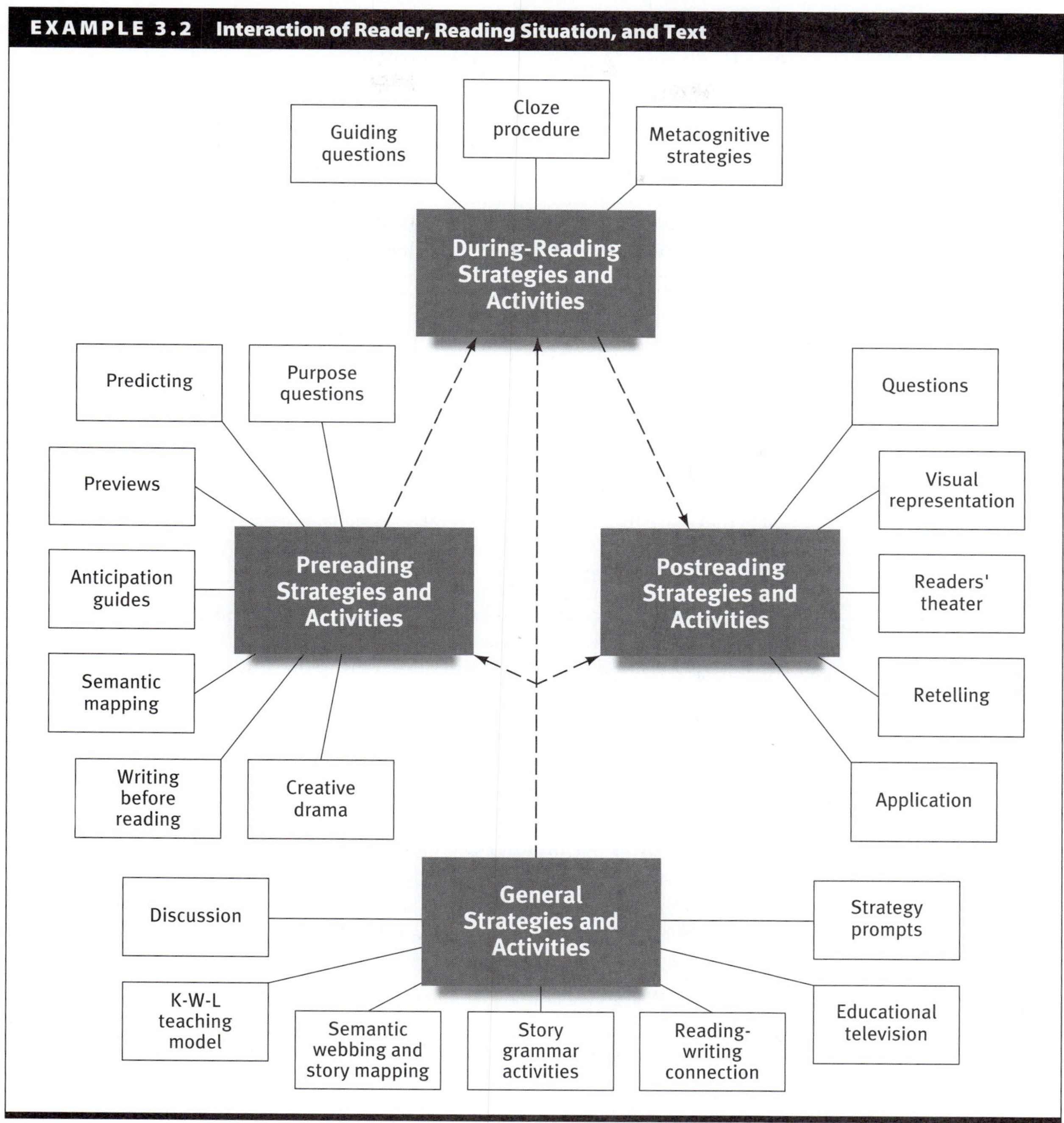

Prereading Strategies and Activities

Prereading activities are often intended to activate students' prior knowledge related to the reading, as well as their problem-solving behavior and their motivation to examine the material. The making of predictions in the Directed Reading-Thinking Activity described in Chapter 5 is a good example of this type of activity. The use of purpose questions, as described earlier in this chapter, is another example. The following activities can also enhance comprehension of the material by activating schemata related to the subject or type of text to be read, or they can be used to help students expand their schemata by building background for topics covered by the reading material.

Previews

Story previews, which contain information related to story content, can benefit comprehension. Research has shown that having students read story previews designed partially to build background knowledge about the stories increases students' learning from the selections impressively and that story previews can help students make inferences when they read. The previews help students to activate their prior knowledge and focus their attention before reading (Tierney and Cunningham, 1984). Story previews of trade books are often found on the back cover of the book. For other selections, teachers may have to write short previews.

Anticipation Guides

Anticipation guides can be useful prereading devices. Designed to stimulate thinking, they consist of declarative statements related to the material about to be read. Some of the statements are true, and some are not. Before the students read the story, they respond to the statements according to their own experiences and discuss them (Wiesendanger, 1985). The value of anticipation guides can be extended into the postreading part of the lesson by repeating the process after reading, considering the input from the reading, resulting in a combination anticipation-reaction guide.

DIVERSITY

Merkley (1996/1997) suggests adding an "I'm Not Sure" column to anticipation guides. She thinks it causes students who choose this option to attend more carefully to the text to discover the answer. (See the next Classroom Scenario for an example of an anticipation-reaction guide for a multicultural reading selection.)

Semantic Mapping

Semantic mapping (discussed in Chapter 2) is a good prereading strategy because it introduces important vocabulary that students will encounter in the passage and activates their schemata related to the topic of the reading assignment. This makes it possible for them to connect new information in the assignment to their prior knowledge. The procedure may also motivate them to read the selection (Johnson, Pittelman, and Heimlich, 1986).

Writing Before Reading

Hamann, Schultz, Smith, and White (1991) found that having students write about relevant personal experiences before they read a selection resulted in more on-task

CLASSROOM SCENARIO Use of Anticipation-Reaction Guide

Ms. Bucholtz's sixth-grade class had been studying the many cultures that make up U.S. culture. To introduce the Chinese culture to a group of students who had no Chinese American classmates, she decided to have them read *Child of the Owl* by Laurence Yep, a book for which she had a classroom set. She had prepared an anticipation-reaction guide that was designed to help them banish stereotypes and see the commonalities among all people.

Ms. Bucholtz began the lesson by holding up the book. She said, "Look at the cover of the book I have just given to you. From what you see on the cover, what do you think the book will be about?"

Blake said, "Maybe it will be about a baby owl."

Krystal looked at him disdainfully and said, "Oh, don't be silly. The picture is of a Chinese girl and an owl necklace. She's in front of a Chinese store. I think it's about her getting that necklace."

Ms. Bucholtz looked at Krystal and said, "Your prediction is reasonable, but you shouldn't say someone else's is silly. We don't have enough information yet to know if live owls will be in the story."

"I'm sorry, Blake," Krystal said. "Sometimes the cover does fool you, and it almost looks like an owl is flying behind her."

"That looks like a ghost owl. It looks spooky," said DeRon. "Maybe this is a ghost story."

"*Yep* sounds Chinese," Marie said.

"It is," Pete replied. "This guy wrote *Dragonwings* too, and it was great. It was about Chinese who came to America. I guess this one will be too, but the main character will be a girl in this one."

"You'll have to read the book to see if your predictions are right," said Ms. Bucholtz, "but first I want you to turn over that paper I put on your desk."

The students turned over the following anticipation-reaction guide:

Anticipation-Reaction Guide

Directions: As you read *Child of the Owl* by Laurence Yep, you will find out some things about Chinese and Chinese American people and some things about people in general. Before you read the book, write *Yes, No,* or *Sometimes* on the line under the word *Before* to show what you believe to be true at this time. After you read the book, write *Yes, No,* or *Sometimes* on the line under the word *After* to show what you believe then.

Before	*After*	
_____	_____	1. Chinese Americans can speak Chinese.
_____	_____	2. Chinese Americans can write Chinese.
_____	_____	3. Chinese Americans live in Chinatowns.
_____	_____	4. Chinese Americans are very close to family members and take care of them when they need help.
_____	_____	5. Chinese Americans live just like other Americans.
_____	_____	6. Chinese Americans are wealthy.
_____	_____	7. All it takes to fit in in Chinatown is to look Chinese.
_____	_____	8. Chinese owls are supposed to be evil.
_____	_____	9. Chinese Americans eat with chopsticks instead of forks and knives.
_____	_____	10. People can hurt people whom they care about.
_____	_____	11. The way people look and act on the outside is the way they are inside.

Continued

Anticipation-Reaction Guide (cont.)

Before	*After*	
_____	_____	12. Chinese Americans have feelings that are like other Americans' feelings.
_____	_____	13. People make sacrifices for people whom they love.
_____	_____	14. Chinese Americans have been treated fairly since they came to the United States.

"Bryan, read the directions for us," Ms. Bucholtz requested.

Bryan read the directions.

Then Ms. Bucholtz said, "Please follow the directions and fill in the *Before* column now. Then break into your cooperative groups, and discuss the reasons for your answers with your classmates. When all of you have discussed your answers, you may begin reading. A few minutes before the period ends today, I'll stop you, and let you discuss your predictions with your group and set new ones if your old ones no longer seem likely. You'll be reading this book all week. We'll discuss and revise predictions every day and jot down our new predictions. When you finish reading, fill in the *After* column on your guide. You may want to look back in the book for evidence for your responses to share later. When your entire group is finished, discuss those responses with your classmates. Then we'll talk about the guide as a whole class. Happy reading!"

The students quickly read and completed the guide, but their small-group discussions were filled with uncertainty about the items that specified Chinese Americans, since none of the students knew any. Statements such as the following were heard: "Of course, a person who looked Chinese would fit in in Chinatown. I'd stick out like a sore thumb though." "The Chinese in that book I read weren't wealthy, but that was a long time ago." "Sure, they do; they always have chopsticks in Chinese restaurants." "They can speak Chinese, because we can speak American." They were quick to support the answers they had given for more general categories with statements such as the following: "Mr. Woolly looks mean, but he gives us candy when we are in his store." "But Mr. Lynn looks nice, and he is super." "Guess that means 'Sometimes,' right?" "Yeah, 'Sometimes.'" "My mom bought me a boom box with her new dress money because she felt sorry for me." "My brother spent *all* of his paycheck to buy flowers for this girl he is crazy about, even though he couldn't go to the ballgame with his friends after he did it."

Predictions were quickly revised after the day's reading, and they continued to be revised every day.

On Friday, the students independently filled out the *After* column on the guide, some of them mumbling about how wrong they had been originally. Their discussions of the responses in their small groups were lively, with reading from the text to support many points. Some of the comments were as follows: "Casey couldn't even speak Chinese." "Her Uncle Phil and his family were wealthy, but her grandmother wasn't. So 'Sometimes.'" "Look at how different Gilbert was than he seemed to be." (This was followed by the reading of several example passages.) The whole-class discussion was rich, featuring comments such as the following: "People are a lot alike in how they feel, even if they look different on the outside." "I felt like she did when her grandmother was in the hospital when my dad got hurt on the job." "Gilbert is like my cousin. He wants to act cool too."

Ms. Bucholtz ended the focus on the book by inviting the students to read individually other books about the Chinese or Chinese American culture for comparisons and contrasts with this book the next week.

Analysis of Scenario

Ms. Bucholtz began the lessons by eliciting from the students predictions, based on the book cover, that activated the schemata they had for the story. Then she gave them an anticipation-reaction guide that elicited further predictions and led them to commit their predictions to paper. The small-group discussions of the predictions and adjustment of predictions throughout the week kept the students involved in the reading. Returning to the anticipation-reaction guide at the end caused them to revise predictions based on their reading. They were encouraged to be ready to defend their answers with evidence.

behavior, more sophisticated responses to characters, and more positive reactions to the selections. As a result, the students became more involved with their reading.

Creative Drama

Although creative drama is most often used as a postreading activity, it also may be used *before* a story is read to enhance comprehension. The teacher may describe the situation developed in the story and let the students act out their own solutions. Then they can read the story to see how their solutions compared with the actual story. The teacher can take the parts of various characters to help move the drama along and to pose questions related to setting, characters, emotions, and critical analysis (Flynn and Carr, 1994). Drama may be particularly effective with students who have strong interpersonal skills and are kinesthetic learners.

During-Reading Strategies and Activities

Some strategies and activities can be used during reading to promote comprehension.

Metacognitive Strategies

Metacognition refers to a person's knowledge of the intellectual functioning of his or her own mind and that person's conscious efforts to monitor or control this functioning. It involves analyzing the way thinking takes place. In reading tasks, the reader who displays metacognition selects skills and reading techniques that fit the particular reading task (Babbs and Moe, 1983; Barton and Sawyer, 2003/2004).

Much attention has been given to students' use of metacognitive strategies during reading. Certainly, effective use of metacognitive techniques has a positive effect on comprehension. Since learning metacognitive strategies enhances study skills, this topic will be covered in detail in Chapter 7. Some information related to the use of metacognitive skills during reading as an aid to comprehension is included here to show the interrelationships of these two aspects of reading.

Part of the metacognitive process is deciding what type of task the reader needs to complete in order to achieve understanding. Readers need to ask themselves:

- Is the answer I need stated directly? (If so, the reader looks for the author's exact words for an answer.)
- Does the text imply the answer by giving strong clues that help determine it? (If so, the reader searches for clues related to the question and reasons about the information provided to determine an answer.)
- Does the answer have to come from my own knowledge and ideas as they relate to the story? (If so, the reader relates what he or she knows and thinks about the topic to the information given and includes both sources of information in the reasoning process in order to come to a decision about an answer.)

Direct instruction in which teachers model reasoning processes to help students understand how reading works may be particularly effective for helping struggling readers become more strategic. It is not possible, however, to reduce the mental processes associated with strategic reading to a fixed set of steps, because, for example, "what an expert reader does when encountering an unknown affixed word in one text situation may differ from what is done when an unknown affixed word is met in another textual situation" (Duffy, Roehler, and Herrmann, 1988, p. 765). Struggling readers often do not grasp the need for variation from situation to situation. After demonstrating their own metacognitive strategies, teachers may ask the students to explain how they made sense of material they have read and then provide additional help if the students' responses indicate the need (Herrmann, 1988).

Teaching students to combine the two metacognitive strategies of self-questioning and prediction can result in better comprehension scores for middle-school students who are reading below grade level than using only a self-questioning strategy or traditional vocabulary instruction. This may be because the combination strategy causes them to monitor the information more actively as they read to confirm predictions (Nolan, 1991).

Good readers monitor their comprehension constantly and take steps to correct situations when they fail to comprehend. They may reread passages or adjust their reading techniques or rates. Struggling readers, in contrast, often fail to monitor their understanding of the text. They make fewer spontaneous corrections in oral reading than good readers do and also correct miscues that affect meaning less frequently than do good readers. They seem to regard reading as a decoding process, whereas good readers see it as a comprehension-seeking process (Bristow, 1985).

DIVERSITY

Studies have shown that gifted students tend to be more efficient in the use of strategies, learn new strategies more easily, are more likely to transfer them to new situations, and are better at discussing their understanding of their cognitive processes than average students. There are, however, indications that gifted students, like other students, can benefit from instruction in metacognition (Borkowski and Kurtz, 1987; Cheng, 1993).

Englot-Mash (1991) helps students learn to tie strategies together in a usable manner by presenting them with the flowchart in Example 3.3.This chart helps the students to think about their fix-up strategies (corrective strategies) in a concrete way.

Think-Alouds. Baumann, Jones, and Seifert-Kessell (1993) advocate using think-alouds to enhance students' comprehension monitoring: "Think alouds involve the overt, verbal expression of the normally covert mental processes readers engage in when constructing meaning from texts" (p. 185). They studied the teaching of think-alouds using an instructional format in which teachers tell the students *what* the strategy is, *why* it is important and helpful for them to know, *how* it functions, and *when* it should be used (Baumann and Schmitt, 1986). In their study, Baumann and colleagues used think-alouds to model for the students the asking of questions about the material, accessing prior knowledge about the topic, asking if the selection is making sense, making predictions and verifying them, making inferences, retelling what they have already read, and rereading or reading further to clear up confusion. They had the students use think-alouds as they applied the strategies to their own reading. At times, the students were divided into small groups or pairs to apply the think-alouds, and this collaborative activity appeared to be especially helpful. The researchers helped build student interest by comparing the students as readers to newspaper or television reporters: they interview writers as they read, just as reporters interview people.

EXAMPLE 3.3 Strategy Use

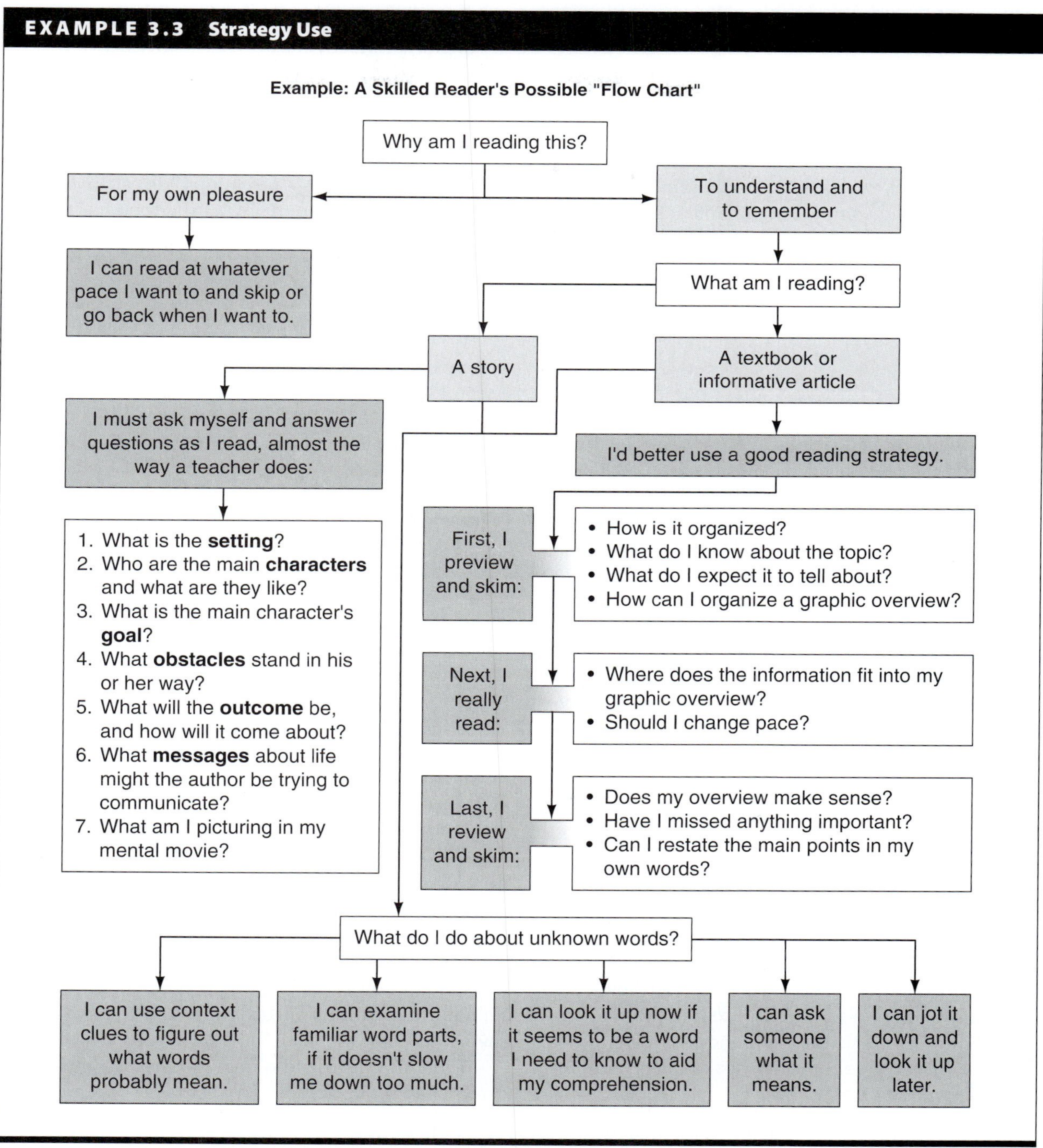

Source: Christine Englot-Mash. "Tying Together Reading Strategies," *Journal of Reading*, 35 (October 1991), 151. Reprinted with permission of the International Reading Association.

FOCUS ON STRATEGIES

Think-Aloud Session

Mr. Barr's class was beginning a unit on elderly people. Mr. Barr had assembled a number of books featuring elderly characters for the unit study. The books covered a wide range of reading levels, and some presented complex or unfamiliar concepts. Mr. Barr wanted to encourage students to use their metacognitive skills as they read from this collection of books. He decided to use one book, *The Hundred Penny Box* by Sharon Bell Mathis, for which he had a class set, to model his own metacognitive processes when reading texts.

First, he read the title, author's name, and illustrators' names from the book cover. "I'll bet this will be a good book," he said. "I've read other books by this author, and they were good. These illustrators are always good too. I loved their illustrations in *Why Mosquitoes Buzz in People's Ears*. Let's see what this book is likely to be about. The picture shows a little boy looking into a box and either getting a penny out or putting one in, while an elderly woman sits in a chair in the background. That box must be the one mentioned in the title. I guess it has a hundred pennies in it. I wonder if they belong to the boy or to the woman, and I wonder if the woman is his grandmother. Maybe she has saved the pennies for him. I'll have to read to find out."

Opening the book to the first page of text, Mr. Barr remarked about the facing page, "I liked the picture on the front better than this one. This one looks a little depressing. I wonder if the book is going to be sad."

Then Mr. Barr read the first paragraph of the text aloud and said, "If Michael is sitting on the bed 'that used to be his' in the room with his great-great-aunt, he probably had to let her have his room. She must have moved in with his family. I wonder how he felt about giving up his bed? . . . Great-great-aunt . . . A great-aunt is the sister of a grandparent, so a great-great-aunt must be the sister of a great-grandparent. Aunt Dew must be pretty old."

Mr. Barr read the next paragraph and said, "I guess the hundred penny box is Aunt Dew's, and she lets Michael play with it sometimes. . . . Sometimes she would forget who Michael was. I had an elderly uncle who forgot who we were sometimes. He called me by my dad's name. . . . I wonder what the song has to do with forgetting."

After he read the third and fourth paragraphs, he said, "She called him by his dad's name too. I think it irritated Michael's mother."

Mr. Barr continued to model his thinking for the students for several more pages. Then he said, "So far, it seems that Michael's mother is frustrated with trying to take care of Aunt Dew, but Michael likes to get her to play with him with the box. I think that there is going to be trouble between Michael's mother and Aunt Dew, and I think it will have something to do with that box. I'll have to read on if I want to find out."

Then Mr. Barr asked for a volunteer to read and think aloud about the next part. After reading the second paragraph on page 14, Susan said in alarm, "Is Michael stealing the box? He didn't seem like he would steal from his aunt. I don't think that's it. I'll read on to see."

Several paragraphs later, Susan exclaimed, "Oh, no! His mother is going to burn the box!"

After the next paragraph, Susan said, "But Michael won't let her have it. Is he protecting it from her, or does he want it for himself? I think he's protecting it."

After the next paragraph, Susan said with more assurance, "He *is* protecting it. But I can't believe his mother burned someone else's things up. He's been helping Aunt Dew hide some of her other stuff. Maybe he was going to hide the box. But, if he was, why did he go in the kitchen with it? I'm confused. I'll have to read more."

Mr. Barr stopped her there and asked her to make a prediction about what would happen next. She replied, "I think he will run away with the box and save it."

Then Mr. Barr told the class to break up into preestablished groups of four and complete reading the book aloud, taking turns reading and thinking aloud about it as they read. At the end of each person's turn (about two pages each time), that person would summarize the situation and make a prediction about what would happen next.

Eager to read on, the students quickly formed their groups and began to read. The book was short enough to be completed that day.

The next day, the students were reminded of the questioning, predicting, connecting to prior knowledge, and summarizing that they had done in the think-alouds the day before. Mr. Barr encouraged them to continue to do these things silently as they read their individually chosen selections for that day.

Reciprocal Teaching. Palincsar and Brown (1986) suggest ***reciprocal teaching*** as a means to promote comprehension and comprehension monitoring. In this technique, the teacher and the students take turns being the "teacher." The "teacher" leads the discussion of material the students are reading. The participants have four common goals: "predicting, question generating, summarizing, and clarifying" (p. 772). When using reciprocal teaching, the teacher must explain to the students each component strategy and the reason for it:

- The predictions that the students make provide them with a purpose for reading: to test their predictions. Text features such as headings and subheadings help students form predictions.
- Generating questions provides a basis for self-testing and interaction with others in the group.
- Summarizing, which can be a joint effort, helps students to integrate the information presented.
- Clarifying calls attention to reasons the material may be hard to understand. Students are encouraged to reread or ask for help when their need for clarification becomes obvious.

Instruction in each strategy is important. At first, the teacher leads the discussion, modeling the strategies for the students. The students add their predictions, clarifications, and comments on the teacher's summaries and respond to the teacher's questions. Gradually the responsibility for the process is transferred from the teacher to the students. The teacher participates, but the students take on the "teacher" role too. The interactive aspect of this procedure is very important. Rosenshine and Meister (1994) reviewed research on reciprocal teaching and concluded that such instruction should be incorporated into ongoing practice. Hashey and Connors (2003) found that when they gave students time to learn the process, introducing the steps one at a time and allowing sufficient practice with feedback, students used reciprocal teaching successfully. The reciprocal teaching procedure may need to be modified for English language learners. Some of them may be unable to assume the role of "teacher" but may

serve different useful functions, such as translator for other English language learners. Some English language learners may need to answer questions by drawing pictures or pointing (Herrell, 2000).

Paragraph-by-Paragraph Reactions. Richards and Gipe (1992) describe another active during-reading strategy. They suggest asking students to consider after each paragraph an idea in that paragraph that they know about, appreciate, or understand and an idea they dislike, dispute, or don't understand. They must also give reasons for these reactions. They may share their responses with other students as they go or record them to share after the entire selection has been read. For each paragraph, students may also indicate a connection with their own experiences by telling what the paragraph reminds them of. All of these activities help middle-school students connect their knowledge to the text and expand comprehension.

Simply reminding and encouraging students to use metacognitive strategies, such as making connections among different reading selections, can also lead to their increased use. The Classroom Scenario below shows how one child used her metacognitive skills.

Guiding Questions

During reading, guiding questions are often used to enhance comprehension. Research indicates that questions posed by the teacher when students are reading seem to facilitate comprehension (Tierney and Cunningham, 1984). Some authorities have suggested that extensive use of self-questioning while reading also facilitates comprehension. Teachers can enhance students' learning of the factual information by showing them how to turn each factual statement they need to remember into a *why* question that they then attempt to answer (for example, "Why did Davy Crockett leave Tennessee to fight at the Alamo?"). Better answers to the *why* questions result in better memory for the facts (Menke and Pressley, 1994).

Shoop (1986) describes the ***Investigative Questioning Procedure (InQuest),*** a comprehension strategy that combines student questioning with creative drama and

CLASSROOM SCENARIO Metacognition

As Ina Maxwell works at her desk one January morning, a student comes by to share a discovery about her reading. The girl is currently reading *Dark Hour of Noon.*

"*Dark Hour of Noon* reminds me of *Number the Stars,* that book we read last fall," she says. "In *Number the Stars,* the Nazis came and told the Jews to move to camps. They took butter and other food. The Nazis were killing Jews. Adolf Hitler was in charge of the Germans."

Analysis of Scenario

Ms. Maxwell encourages her students to make connections with life experiences and previous reading material as they read. Her encouragement and openness to students' comments lead students to share these connections with her, even when they are unsolicited.

encourages reader interaction with text. In this technique, the teacher stops the reading at a critical point in the story. One student takes the role of a major character, and other students take the roles of investigative "on-the-scene" reporters. The reporters ask the character interpretive and evaluative questions about story events. More than one character may be interviewed to delve into different viewpoints. Then the students resume reading, although the teacher may interrupt their reading several more times for other "news conferences." When introducing the procedure, the teacher may occasionally participate as a story character or a reporter, in order to model the processes involved. The class should evaluate the process when the entire story has been covered.

InQuest lets students monitor comprehension. They actively keep up with what is known. Before this procedure can be effective, however, students must have had some training in generating questions. One means to accomplish this training is to give students opportunities to view and evaluate actual questioning sessions on television news shows. They need to learn to ask questions that produce information, evaluations, and predictions, and they need to ask a variety of types of questions and to use *why* questions judiciously to elicit in-depth responses. We also discuss student-generated questions in Chapter 4.

TECHNOLOGY

Cloze Procedure

The ***cloze procedure*** is sometimes used as a strategy for teaching comprehension, as well as for word recognition, as we described in Chapter 2. In using the cloze procedure, the teacher deletes some information from a passage and asks students to fill it in as they read, drawing on their knowledge of syntax, semantics, and graphic clues. (See Chapter 8 for an example of a cloze passage.) Use of cloze techniques can help English language learners understand that a reader does not have to be able to read every word of a passage to grasp the meaning (Herrell, 2000).

DIVERSITY

Cloze tasks can involve deletions of letters, word parts, whole words, phrases, clauses, or whole sentences. In macrocloze activities, entire story parts are deleted. The deletions are generally made for specific purposes to focus on particular skills. Although either random or regularly spaced deletions can lead students to make predictions and confirm predictions based on their language knowledge, such systems of deletion will not focus on one particular skill.

To focus on specific skills, teachers can vary the sizes of blanks. When a whole word is deleted and a standard-sized blank is left, the readers must use semantic and syntactic clues to decide on a replacement. If the blanks vary in length according to word length, word recognition skill also can be incorporated. Teachers can make the task of exact replacement easier by providing the additional clue of a short underline for each letter in the deleted words. However, the discussion of alternatives likely to be generated when standard-sized blanks are used can be extremely beneficial in developing comprehension skills. Teachers should always ask students to state their reasons for making particular choices and give positive reinforcement for good reasoning.

Teachers can offer a multiple-choice set of answers for completing each blank, a task referred to as a *maze* procedure. Maze techniques may simplify the task for readers who need scaffolding and may prepare students for participating in cloze activities. (See Chapters 8 and 9 for more on the cloze procedure and Chapter 9 for more on the maze procedure.)

Postreading Strategies and Activities

Postreading strategies help students integrate new information from the reading they just completed into their existing schemata. They also allow students to elaborate on the learning that has taken place. Middle-school students should be given an opportunity to decide what further information they would like to have about the topic and where they can find out more. They may, for example, read about the topic and share their findings with the class.

Questions

Prereading questions may focus students' learning more than postreading questions do, but research indicates that postreading questions may facilitate learning for all information in the text. There appears to be an advantage to using higher-level, application-type, and structurally important questions rather than questions that focus on facts or details. Students obtain greater gains from postreading questions if feedback on answers is provided, especially feedback on incorrect answers (Tierney and Cunningham, 1984).

Visual Representation

After reading, students may be asked to sketch or paint what they learned from the text or what it made them think about and then share their sketches with a group, explaining how the sketches relate to the text. The sharing can extend the comprehension of all participants (Shanklin and Rhodes, 1989).

Quiocho (1997) had students work in groups. One student would read a section of a text aloud while other group members made sketches based on what they were hearing. Group members discussed the accuracy of each sketch, and the sketches were revised on the basis of the discussion.

The teacher may draw a step-by-step sketch of what is happening in a reading selection or of where the selection takes place to show the students how picturing what they are reading can be helpful. The teacher can have the students create drawings based on read-alouds by the teacher or material that the students are reading for themselves. These drawings may expose misconceptions that can be cleared up by the teacher. They may also help students retain information, but only if they are accurate (Hibbing and Rankin-Erickson, 2003).

Readers' Theater

After the students read a story, they can work together, or with the teacher's guidance, to transform the story into a readers' theater script. The act of developing the script from a story involves deciding on important dialogue and narration and thereby increases comprehension (Walker, 2000). Once the script is designed, the students take specific parts and practice reading the script together. Finally, they read the script for an audience (Shanklin and Rhodes, 1989).

Retelling

Talking about reading material has been shown to have a positive effect on reading comprehension. Therefore, an appropriate comprehension enhancement technique is *retelling* of the important aspects of the material that has been read. To retell a story or selection, the reader must organize the material for the presentation (Walker, 2000). Students are generally paired with partners for this activity. After silent reading of a section from the text, one child retells what has been read, while the other listens. Tellers and listeners alternate. This technique has been used with intermediate-grade students, resulting in better comprehension than did producing illustrations or answering questions about the text.

TECHNOLOGY

Teachers should introduce the retelling technique by explaining that it will help the students become better storytellers, in the case of presentation of narrative retellings, and help them see how well they understand the reading selections. They should model good retellings for the students, provide guided practice, and then allow independent practice. When the procedure is first used, short, well-constructed reading selections should be chosen. Prereading and postreading discussions of the story frequently help students improve their retellings. The teacher may wish to tape retellings and play them back to allow students to identify their strengths and weaknesses (Koskinen, Gambrell, Kapinus, and Heathington, 1988; Morrow, 1989).

Students can retell stories for teachers, classmates, or younger children in the school, or they can retell stories into a tape recorder. They can also practice and improve retelling skills at home with family members. Story retellings can be done unaided or with the assistance of the pictures in the book. Retellings can also be done with flannel boards, with props (for example, stuffed animals), as chalk talks, or as sound stories in which sound effects are added to the telling of the story. Teachers can use retelling to assess student progress (discussed in Chapter 9).

Application

A good postreading activity for use with content area selections that explain how to do something (for example, how to work a certain type of math problem or how to perform a science experiment) is to have the students perform the task, applying the information that they read. Postreading activities that are often appropriate for social studies reading include constructing time lines of events discussed in the reading selection and creating maps of areas discussed. Many of the activities described in the "Creative Reading" section of Chapter 4 are good postreading activities that ask the students to go beyond the material they have read and create something new based on the reading.

TIME for REFLECTION

How can comprehension strategies be integrated into authentic learning situations across the curriculum?

General Strategies and Activities

Some types of strategies are useful throughout the reading process: before, during, and after reading. Several of these are discussed next.

Discussion

Goldenberg (1992/1993) advocates what he calls "instructional conversations." Basically these are highly interactive discussions among the teacher and the students. Students focus on a topic chosen by the teacher and are gently guided by the teacher's questions and probing for elaboration and text support for their positions, but the discussion is not dominated by the teacher. Students are encouraged to use their background knowledge to contribute to the discussion, and in some cases the teacher provides needed background information that the students do not have. Sometimes the teacher offers direct teaching of a needed skill or concept.

The discussions generally center on questions for which a number of correct answers may exist. The teacher encourages participation from the students, but does not determine the order of speaking. Ideas are built on previously shared ones, and the teacher is responsive to students' contributions in order to build a positive climate for students' efforts to construct meaning. It can be helpful for the teacher or students to record on the board, in a list or on a semantic map, the key points that students make during the discussion. Having students write about the topic after the discussion can show what they have learned.

STANDARDS AND ASSESSMENT

LITERATURE

Informational storybooks that present facts through fictional situations have been found to enhance discussion more than books that were all fiction or all fact (Leal, 1993). The students discussed these books more, made more predictions about them, and connected more outside information to them.

Cornett (1997) allows only students who have read the material to participate in story discussions. Before the discussion, students think of parts of the story that are exciting or puzzling or that connect to their lives to read aloud or discuss. They also list questions they have about the book, to ask the others. They look for special language in the book and decide what truths the book holds. Then they meet with three to five other students for student-led discussions.

K-W-L Teaching Model

Ogle (1986, 1989) has devised what she calls the ***K-W-L teaching model*** for expository text. The *K* stands for "What I *Know*," the *W* for "What I *Want* to Learn," and the *L* for "What I *Learned*." The *K* and *W* steps take place before reading. In the first step, the teacher and the students discuss what the group already knows about the topic of the reading material. The teacher may ask the students where they learned what they know or how they could verify the information. Students may also be asked to think of categories of information that they expect to find in the material that they are about to read.

The second step is to hold a class discussion of what the students want to learn. The teacher may point out disagreements about the things that the students think they already know and may call attention to gaps in their knowledge. Each student writes down personal questions to be answered by the reading. Students then read the material. After they have finished reading, they record what they have learned from the reading. If the reading did not answer all of their personal questions, students can be directed to other sources for the answers. (Example 3.4 shows a K-W-L study sheet that was filled out by a girl who was working with teacher Gail Hyder.) Weissman

The K-W-L teaching model involves students in planning and monitoring their comprehension before, during, and after reading.
(© Elizabeth Crews)

(1996) adapts paragraph frames (as described in Chapter 8) to help her students complete the "What I Learned" step of the K-W-L, and Sippola (1995) adds a column labeled "What I Still Need to Learn" to the original three columns.

Semantic Webbing and Story Mapping

Semantic webbing is a way of organizing terms into categories and showing their relationships through visual displays that can help students integrate concepts. Each web consists of a core question, strands, strand supports, and strand ties. The teacher chooses the core question, which becomes the center of the web, to which the entire web is related. The students' answers are web strands; facts and inferences taken from the story and students' experiences are the strand supports; and the relationships of the strands to one another are strand ties (Freedman and Reynolds, 1980).

EXAMPLE 3.4 Completed K-W-L Sheet

K-W-L Welcome to the Green House by: Jane Yolen

What I Know	What I Want to Know	What I Learned
a lot of animal live there.	What kind of animal live there.	butter flys, snakes, frogs, bats, fish, bees, wild pigs, tamarin toucan, herons, Ocelot, lizirds, humino binds, sloth.
Plant live there.	What kind of plants grow there.	flowers crimson, orchid trees, vines lianas, very hot
A Green house is very hot.	How hot it is in there.	A wet house,

Source: Stephanie Hunsucker, Crossville, Tennessee.

LITERATURE 

Example 3.5 shows a semantic web, based on *Prince Caspian* by C. S. Lewis, developed by Winter Howard, a sixth grader. Before constructing webs like this one, Winter and her classmates read a portion of the book to a point where the hero found himself in a difficult situation. Then their teacher, Natalie Knox, asked the students to predict what would happen next. The core question ("What will the Old Narnians do with or to Prince Caspian?") focuses on this prediction. Students answered the question individually, and their answers became web strands (for example, "Nikabrik will try to kill Caspian"). They drew support for strands from the story and from their own experiences. Then the strands were related through strand ties (shown with broken lines in the example). Finally, students used the webs as motivation for reading the end of the story to see what happened.

EXAMPLE 3.5 Semantic Web

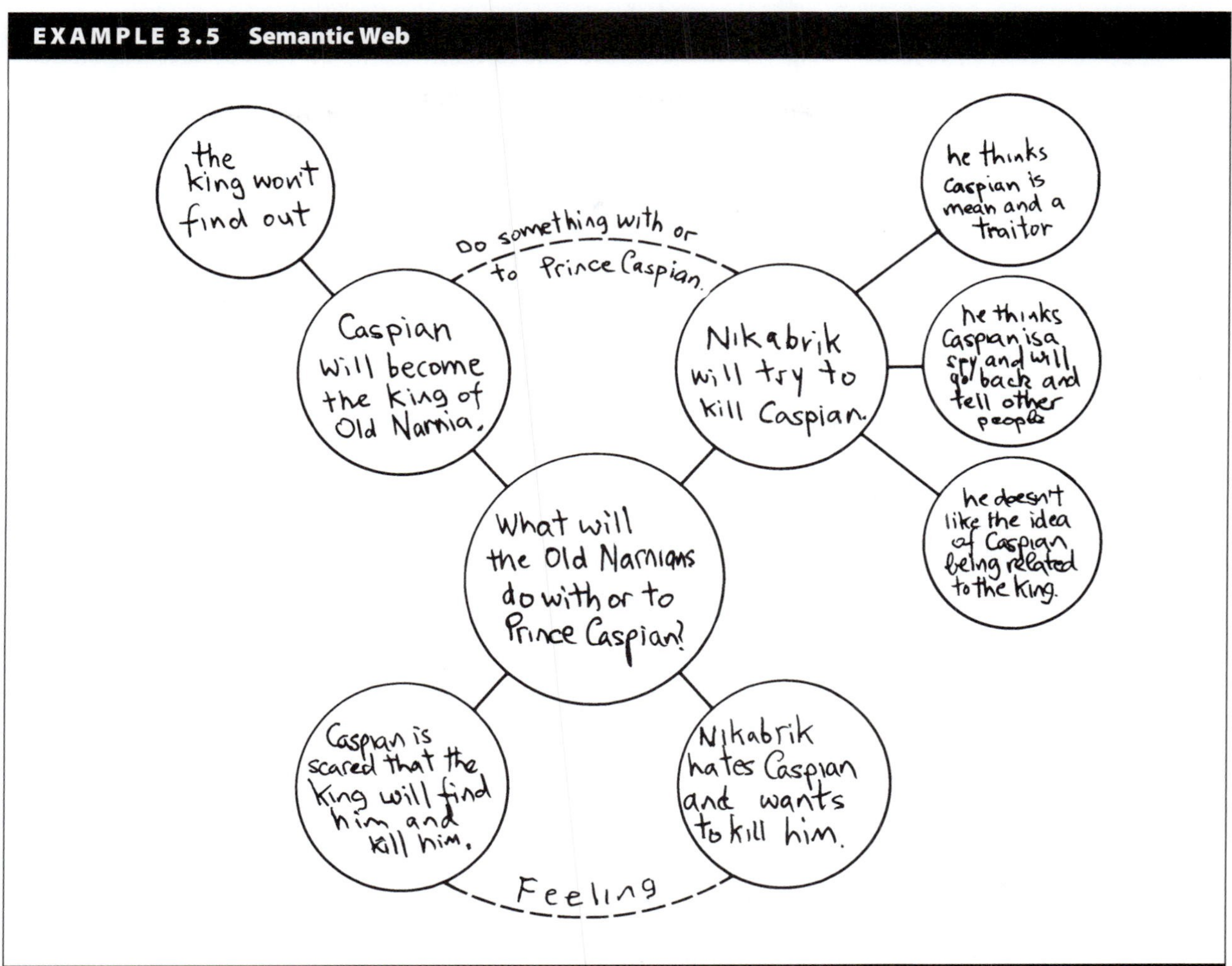

Source: Winter Howard, sixth grade, Central Intermediate School, Harriman, Tennessee.

LITERATURE

Instruction in ***story mapping*** can benefit reading comprehension, since mental representations of story structures can aid comprehension (Davis and McPherson, 1989; Fitzgerald, 1989a; Gordon and Pearson, 1983). A story map is "a graphic representation of all or part of the elements of a story and the relationships between them" (Davis and McPherson, 1989, p. 232). In addition to representing plots, settings, characterizations, and themes of stories visually, these maps (sometimes called *literature webs*) can emphasize the authors' writing patterns in predictable books.

Story maps, which resemble semantic maps or webs (described in Chapter 2 and in this chapter), help readers perceive the way their reading material is organized. They can be used to activate schemata for a story that is about to be read, to help students follow the sequence during reading, or as a means to focus postreading discussion.

When the story map is used to activate schemata, students may try to predict the contents of the story from it and then read to confirm or reject their predictions. Students may also refer to the map as reading progresses to help them keep their thoughts organized. After reading, the students can try to reconstruct the map from memory or can simply discuss it and its relationship to the story events.

Some webs are based on plot structure or story grammar (discussed in the next section), but some are more like structured overviews. One way to construct story maps is to put the theme in the center and arrange main events or settings sequentially in a second level of circles. Circles with characters, events, and actions may be connected to these second-level circles, and each may have additional circles attached to them, arranged in a clockwise order. Teaching readers to fill in story structure components on story maps while reading is beneficial to the students' comprehension (Davis and McPherson, 1989). Bluestein (2002) suggests another type of story map. She asks students to create word webs to describe characters. The map would include a character's words, feelings, and actions that show what he or she is like.

Staal (2000) has developed an adaptation of the story-mapping strategy called the Story Face and found that it is useful with fifth graders, because it is easy to construct and remember. The technique is based on the shape of a face, with two circles for the eyes that contain the setting and the main characters, respectively. Eyelashes (radiating lines) can be added to the eyes for descriptive words about the setting and other characters. The nose is a square in which the problem is written. The mouth is a semicircle of small circles that contain the main events and solution. This semicircle can curve up for a happy story and down for a sad one, and the number of circles for events can vary. This graphic can serve as a visual aid for retelling a story or a framework for narrative writing. The story face functions as a framework for narrative writing when the graphic is filled in with the student's own story plan.

Story Grammar Activities

STANDARDS AND ASSESSMENT

A *story schema* is a person's mental representation of story structures, the elements that make up a story, and the way they are related. As we noted earlier in this chapter, knowledge of such structures appears to facilitate both comprehension and recall of stories. Students' written stories can serve as a source for understanding their concepts of story, and their retellings of stories also reveal story knowledge (Golden, 1984).

A ***story grammar*** provides rules that define these story structures. Educational researchers have developed different story grammars. Jean Mandler and Nancy Johnson include six major structures in their story grammar: setting, beginning, reaction, attempt, outcome, and ending (Whaley, 1981). In a simplified version of Perry Thorndike's story grammar, the structures are setting, characters, theme, plot, and resolution (McGee and Tompkins, 1981).

Teachers may be able to use story grammars as part of many activities to help students develop a concept of story. For instance, they can read stories and talk about the structure in terms students understand (folktales and fairy tales are good choices because they have easily identifiable parts), or they can have students retell stories. Reading or listening to stories and predicting what comes next is a good activity, as is discussion of the predicted parts. Teachers may give students stories in which whole sections are left out, indicated by blank lines in place of the material (macrocloze activity), ask the students to supply the missing material, and then discuss the appropriateness of their answers. By dividing a story into different categories and scrambling the parts, teachers can give students the opportunity to rearrange the parts to form a good story. Or they can give the students all of the sentences in the story on strips of paper and ask them to put together the ones that are related (Whaley, 1981).

Students may enjoy a turn-taking activity for working on the concept of story. Each student starts by writing a setting for a story and then passing his or her paper to a classmate, who adds a beginning and passes the paper along to another classmate. As the papers are passed from student to student, each one contributes a reaction, attempt, outcome, or, finally, an ending. When the stories are complete, they are read aloud to the class (Spiegel and Fitzgerald, 1986).

Fowler (1982) suggests the use of *story frames* to provide a structure for organizing a reader's understandings about the material. Frames are sequences of blanks linked by transition words that reflect a line of thought. Frames like the ones in Example 3.6 can be used with a variety of selections. Oja (1996, p. 129) says, "Using story frames along with basic elements of story grammar directs both students' and teachers' attention to the actual structure of the story and how the content fits that structure."

EXAMPLE 3.6 Sample Story Frames

Frame 1: Setting

The setting for the story is ______________________ (where) ______________________ (when)

I could tell where the story took place because the story said "____."

I could tell when it took place because the story said "____."

Frame 2: Characters

The main character in this story is ______________________ (name).

I could tell that ______________________ (name) was ______________________ (trait)

because the story said "____."

I could tell that ______________________ (name) was ______________________ (trait)

because the story said "____."

Students can fill out story frames as they read or after reading. The frames can be the basis for the postreading class discussion of a story. Because the frames are open-ended, the discussion will include much varied input. The teacher should stress that the information used in subsequent blanks should relate logically to the material that came before it. Students may use frames independently after the process has been modeled and practiced in class, and the class may also discuss the results. This technique is especially useful with struggling readers (Fowler, 1982).

Creative dramatics can help middle-school students comprehend stories. The active reconstruction of a story through drama focuses students' minds on the characters, setting, and plot. Students can resolve conflicts among different interpretations through discussion. Stories with a lot of dialogue are good for use with drama. As students read these stories, they must use their knowledge of such print conventions as quotation marks to interpret what each speaker is saying (Bidwell, 1992; Miller and Mason, 1983).

Students benefit from drawing plot diagrams and relating these diagrams to characterizations and themes. The plot diagram of *Mufaro's Beautiful Daughter* by John Steptoe, in Example 3.7, shows how the plot relates to the characters of the two daughters and to the overall theme that kindness and generosity are good and will be rewarded, whereas greed and selfishness are bad and will be punished (Norton, 1992b).

To help students comprehend stories that start and end at the same place, with a series of events in between, the *circle story* can be effective (Jett-Simpson, 1981; Smith and Bean, 1983). The teacher draws a circle on a large sheet of paper and divides it into a number of pie-shaped sections corresponding to the number of events in the story. The teacher reads the story to the students, who then decide which events need to be pictured in each section of the circle. Circle story completion can be done in small groups, with each student responsible for illustrating a different event. If the paper is large enough, all of the students can work at the same time.

TECHNOLOGY

Teachers can improve understanding of story features such as plots, themes, characters, and setting by using movies, a medium in which students generally have high interest. For example, they can list types of plots that movies may have and let the students match movies to plots (Sawyer, 1994). This understanding can then be transferred to stories in books through parallel techniques. Teachers can also use story grammars to help students focus on particular elements of a story, including setting, character, and themes.

Focus on Settings. Settings may serve simply as backdrops for stories, or they may be integral to the narrative, influencing characters, action, and theme. The author's use of sensory imagery helps to make the setting clear. Pictures in the book also enhance the effect of the words in the text in clarifying setting (Watson, 1991).

Focus on Characters. To fully comprehend a story, the readers must understand the characters. Preadolescents often focus on what is happening in a story rather than on the reasons behind the actions. They may assume that story characters think and feel the same way they do, even if the characters come from very different backgrounds. Story maps that include character perspectives that go with each story event can help students understand stories more fully (Emery, 1996). Having students create a collage of words

EXAMPLE 3.7 Plot Diagram of *Mufaro's Beautiful Daughter*

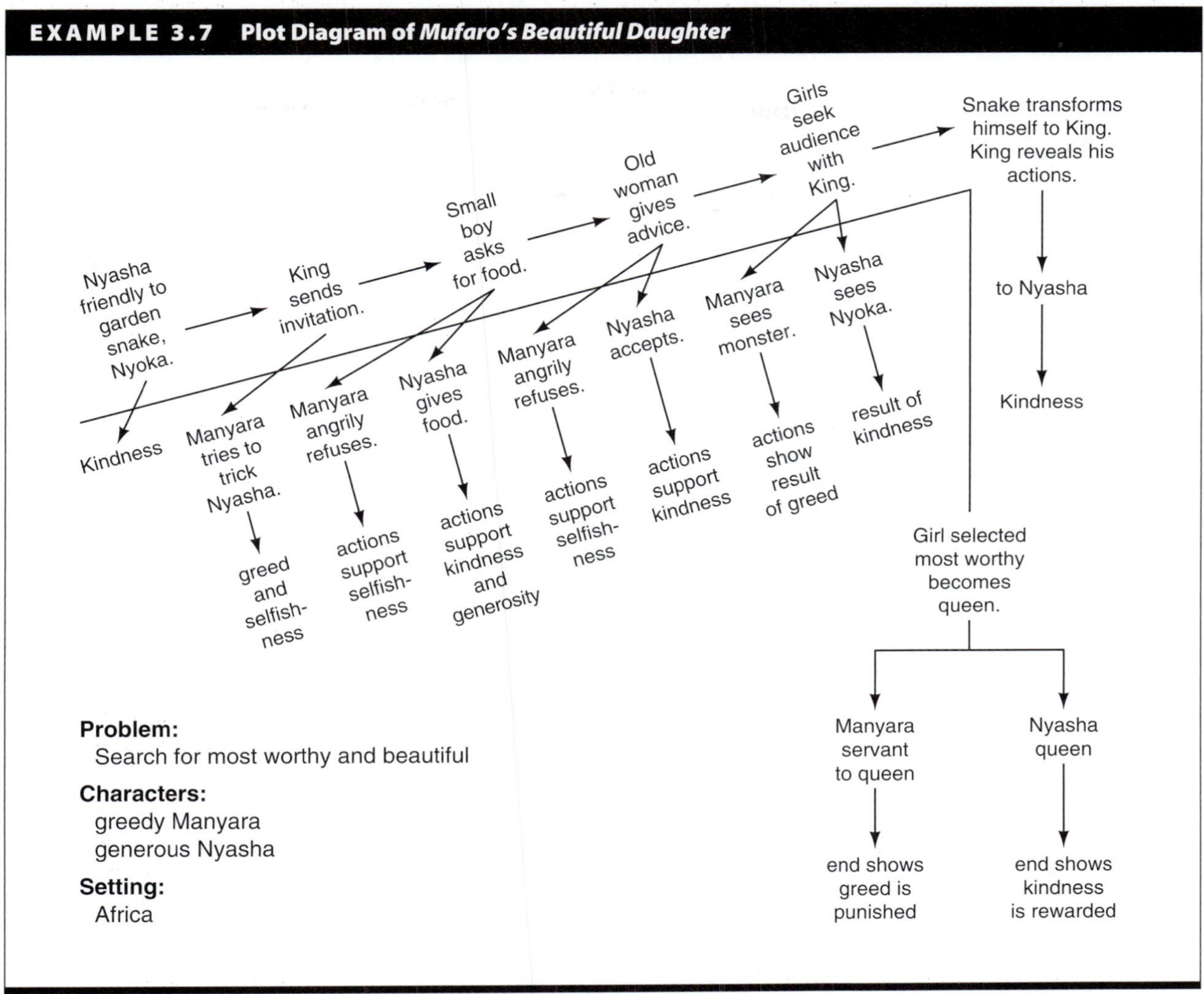

Source: Donna E. Norton, "Understanding Plot Structures," *The Reading Teacher*, 46 (November 1992), p. 256. Reprinted with permission of the International Reading Association.

describing a character's traits, drawn from both text and pictures and superimposed on a drawing of the character, can also be helpful (Golden, Meiners, and Lewis, 1992). Use of character interrogations, in which one student plays the character and other students question him or her, is another valuable way to work on understanding characterization, as is use of character journals, discussed in the next section (Van Horn, 1997).

Awareness of story characters' emotions is particularly helpful in understanding cause-and-effect relationships in the stories. Students need instruction in understanding emotional words and finding clues to characters' emotional states, and they need to realize that story characters may experience several emotions simultaneously (Barton, 1996). Word lines, such as those described in Chapter 2, and word webs can be used to show the relationships among the words. Barton (1996) uses the categories of "strong," "moderate," and "mild" to organize related emotion words in word webs. For example, *ecstatic* would be placed under "strong" in a web for the word *happiness*.

Teachers can ask students questions to help them make connections between their own emotions and those of story characters. One question Barton (1996, p. 25) suggests is: "Has anyone ever treated you like this character is being treated by the people around him/her? How did it feel?" Teachers can also alert students to clues authors supply about characters' emotions, such as explicit character statements and actions, explicit plot events, text features, and emotional words. Implicit clues that need attention may come from the setting, the characters' thoughts, the story mood, or the author's style (Barton, 1996).

Focus on Themes. Middle-school students need to be able to identify themes. Au (1992, p. 106) states that "themes are often implicit and emerge gradually as the story unfolds." The theme is "an idea that encompasses the text as a whole." (Some stories have several themes.) The teacher can offer support through questions and comments as students work at constructing the theme of a story. Gradually, the students can take more responsibility for the construction. Students learn from opportunities to discuss themes with peers.

Cautions About Story Grammars. Although there is much interest among educators in the use of story grammars, questions about this technique remain. Results of studies on the effectiveness of story grammar instruction in increasing reading comprehension have been contradictory (Dreher and Singer, 1980; Greenewald and Rossing, 1986; Sebesta, Calder, and Cleland, 1982; Spiegel and Fitzgerald, 1986). Some have shown positive effects, and others have shown no benefits. It must be remembered that story grammars describe only a limited set of relatively short, simple stories, ones derived from a fairy tale or folktale tradition, and are unable to describe stories that have characters with simultaneously competing goals (Fitzgerald, 1989b; Mandler, 1984; Schmitt and O'Brien, 1986).

Reading-Writing Connection

Composition and comprehension both involve planning, composing, and revising. Although these steps may seem clear in composition, their equivalents in reading may be less obvious. Teachers may need to think of the prereading activities related to background building, schema activation, and prediction as the planning phase in comprehension; developing tentative meanings while reading as the composing phase; and revising the meanings when new information is acquired as the revision phase.

Writing can be involved with reading comprehension instruction at each phase. In the prereading phase, students can write story predictions based on questioning or prereading word webs. During reading, they can take notes in the form of outlines or series of summary statements. Macrocloze activities related to story grammars and the use of story frames are other ways to use writing to enhance reading. Interpretive reading activities, such as rewriting sentences containing figurative expressions into literal forms and rewriting sentences containing pronouns by using their referents instead, are composition activities.

A *character journal* is composed of diary entries from the viewpoint of a character in a story. Students can be asked to write a diary entry for each chapter in a book. The entries are written in the first-person voice. Students are encouraged to write as the character might have written, without concern for mechanics and spelling. Personal comments not in the voice of the character can be allowed, but they should be put in parentheses or brackets to set them apart from regular entries. Teacher responses to the entries can help encourage the students and reassure them about their competence. When students are asked to compose diary entries for characters in the literature they are reading, they become more intensely involved in the reading. To accomplish this, the students must get inside the character's head and experience the events through his or her eyes, a perspective that produces improved comprehension (Hancock, 1993).

TECHNOLOGY

Writing comments about reading may be facilitated through use of a computer. Bernhardt (1994) suggests putting a reading passage on the computer and allowing students to interact with it by breaking it into meaningful or difficult chunks. Then they mark, number, or reorder these chunks and intersperse their own comments and questions in the text. Comments are written in all capital letters or in different colors or fonts so that they stand out from the original text. The active involvement with the text can promote better understanding.

Writing in cooperative groups works well for helping students understand elements of a story. For example, after students have read a selection, the teacher can give each group a character to describe. He or she can instruct the students to web the characters' characteristics and evidence from the story and then write character descriptions based on the web (Avery and Avery, 1994).

Many writing activities are a part of instruction in creative reading instruction, as described in Chapter 4.

TECHNOLOGY

Educational Television

FAMILY

DIVERSITY

Many excellent adolescent literature selections have been made into movies that are available through regular television programming or can be rented from video stores and played at home. Many cable channels have documentary programs that relate to curricular studies. Parents and teachers can encourage their children to watch such sound programming. It may be particularly helpful for English language learners and perhaps other members of their families. These students may even benefit from such educational programs as *Reading Rainbow* and *Between the Lions,* even though these programs are aimed at younger children who have English language skills.

Strategy Prompts

Physical objects can provide prompts to help readers who are learning new strategies or struggling to use particular strategies in their reading. The physical prompts provide scaffolding to support the students as they work on developing and integrating comprehension strategies. Fournier and Graves (2002) found that a scaffolded reading experience throughout prereading, during-reading, and postreading activities increased seventh graders' comprehension of short stories.

Strategy access rods are instructional aids for struggling readers (Worthing and Laster, 2002). Each rod has a one-sentence reading strategy printed on it. The strategies are written in first person. The reader has a personalized collection of rods that represent different strategies in front of him or her for easy reference. Comprehension strategies can be color-coded to represent before-, during-, and after-reading strategies. An example of a before-reading strategy is "I predict" (Worthing and Laster, 2002, p. 123). Struggling readers who encounter comprehension difficulties can then choose from available strategies ones that are appropriate for the reading event.

Newman (2001/2002) developed comprehension strategy gloves that could serve a similar purpose. She had a prereading glove, a narrative structure glove, and an expository structure glove with icons on the gloves to prompt recall of questions that need to be answered by the students.

SUMMARY

The central factor in reading is comprehension. Since reading is an interactive process that involves the information brought to the text by readers, the information supplied by the text, and the reading situation, good comprehension depends on many factors. Among them are readers' backgrounds of experience, sensory and perceptual abilities, thinking abilities, and word recognition strategies, as well as their purposes for reading, their audience for the reading, the importance of the reading to them, and their facility with various comprehension strategies that will help them unlock the meanings within the text. Students' schemata, built through background experiences, aid comprehension of printed material and are themselves modified by input from this material.

Having a purpose for reading enhances comprehension. Teachers should learn how to set good purposes for students' reading assignments and discover how to help them learn to set their own purposes.

The audience for reading affects the reading strategies used. The audience may be the reader himself or herself, the teacher, or other students.

The importance the reading has for the reader is also a factor. High-risk reading for a test may be done differently from low-risk reading in the classroom setting.

Features of the text itself also affect comprehension. Sentences that are complex, contain relative clauses, are in the passive voice, have missing words, or express negation may need special attention because students may have difficulty comprehending them. The meaning conveyed by punctuation in sentences should receive attention. Students also need help in understanding the functions of paragraphs and the organizational patterns of paragraphs and whole selections.

Prereading, during-reading, and postreading activities can foster middle-school students' comprehension of reading selections. Prereading activities such as previews, anticipation guides, semantic mapping, writing before reading, and creative drama can be helpful. Metacognitive strategies, questioning, and the cloze procedure are among the techniques that can be used during reading. Postreading activities usually involve questioning, making visual representations, using readers' theater, retelling, and application of concepts. Some activities—such as discussion; the K-W-L procedure; semantic webbing and story mapping; story grammar, story frame, and other story structure activities; writing activities related to reading; educational television; and strategy prompts from physical objects—may be involved in prereading, during-reading, and postreading activities at various times.

TEST YOURSELF

True or False

______ 1. Each schema that a person has represents what the person knows about a particular concept and the interrelationships among the known pieces of information.

______ 2. Anything that increases a reader's background knowledge may also increase reading comprehension.

______ 3. An intelligence is the same as a learning style.

______ 4. Previews for stories that build background related to the stories have a positive effect on comprehension.

______ 5. Character journals are journals filled with character sketches.

______ 6. Comprehension-monitoring techniques are metacognitive strategies.

______ 7. Punctuation marks do not function as clues to sentence meaning.

______ 8. Reading comprehension involves relating textual information to preexisting knowledge structures.

______ 9. Comprehension strategies should be taught in a way that emphasizes their application when students are actually reading connected discourse.

______ 10. Less able readers may rely too heavily on either text-based or knowledge-based processing.

______ 11. Richard Rystrom argues that reading is exclusively a top-down process.

______ 12. InQuest combines student questioning with creative drama.

______ 13. Story grammar activities can increase students' understanding of story structure and serve as a basis for questioning.

______ 14. Relative clauses cause few comprehension problems for students.

______ 15. Punctuation marks are clues to pauses and pitch changes.

______ 16. Semantic webbing involves systematically deleting words from a printed passage.

______ 17. Think-alouds are useless in teaching metacognitive strategies.

______ 18. The K-W-L teaching model for expository text is strictly a prereading strategy.

For your journal . . .

1. Choose a short selection about an uncommon subject. Question your classmates to find out how complete their schemata on this topic are, and give them copies of the selection to read. Later, discuss the difficulties that some of them had because of inadequate prior knowledge. In your journal, write your observations about this activity, and indicate what you could have done to develop schemata before the reading took place.
2. Read Margaret Egan's article "Capitalizing on the Reader's Strengths: An Activity Using Schema" (*Journal of Reading, 37* [May 1994], pp. 636–640), and try the check activity "Travail in Nova Scotia" with a group of middle-school students. Write your results in your journal.

. . . and your portfolio

1. Construct a time line for a chapter in a social studies textbook that has a chronological-order organizational pattern. Write a description of how you could use the time line with students to teach this organizational pattern.
2. Construct an anticipation guide for a well-known folktale.
3. Construct a story map for a story.
4. Read Egan's article, cited in item 2 of "For your journal . . . ," and compose a check story to use with students in a specific grade.

4

Comprehension: Part 2

KEY VOCABULARY

Pay close attention to these terms when they appear in the chapter:

anaphora
creative reading
critical literacy
critical reading
ellipsis
idiom
interpretive reading
literal comprehension
media literacy
propaganda techniques
schema (and schemata)
story grammar
topic sentence
visualization

In addition, when you read the section on propaganda techniques, pay close attention to the terms used there.

SETTING OBJECTIVES

When you finish reading this chapter, you should be able to

- Describe ways to promote reading for literal meanings.
- Explain the importance of being able to make inferences.
- Discuss some of the ways to help a student become a critical reader.
- Explain what creative reading means.
- Explain how to construct questions for discussions and assessments.

Whereas Chapter 3 emphasized the role of the reader, the text, and the reading situation, as well as some comprehension strategies, Chapter 4 examines two types of comprehension—literal and higher-order—and describes approaches for developing each type. Although the two chapters look at different aspects of comprehension, the material in both chapters is necessary to understanding the overall process.

To take in ideas that are directly stated is literal comprehension; this is the most basic type. Higher-order comprehension includes interpretive, critical, and creative comprehension. To read between the lines is interpretive reading; to read for evaluation is critical reading; and to read beyond the lines is creative reading. Example 4.1 shows these types of comprehension and their elements. Regardless of the type of comprehension involved, "instructional methods that generate high levels of student involvement and engagement during reading can have positive effects on reading comprehension" (Williams, 2002, pp. 253–254).

This chapter also discusses questioning techniques that can be used to guide reading, enhance comprehension and retention, and assess comprehension. Three important activities related to effective questioning are discussed: preparing questions, helping students answer questions, and helping students question.

Chapter 4 Organization

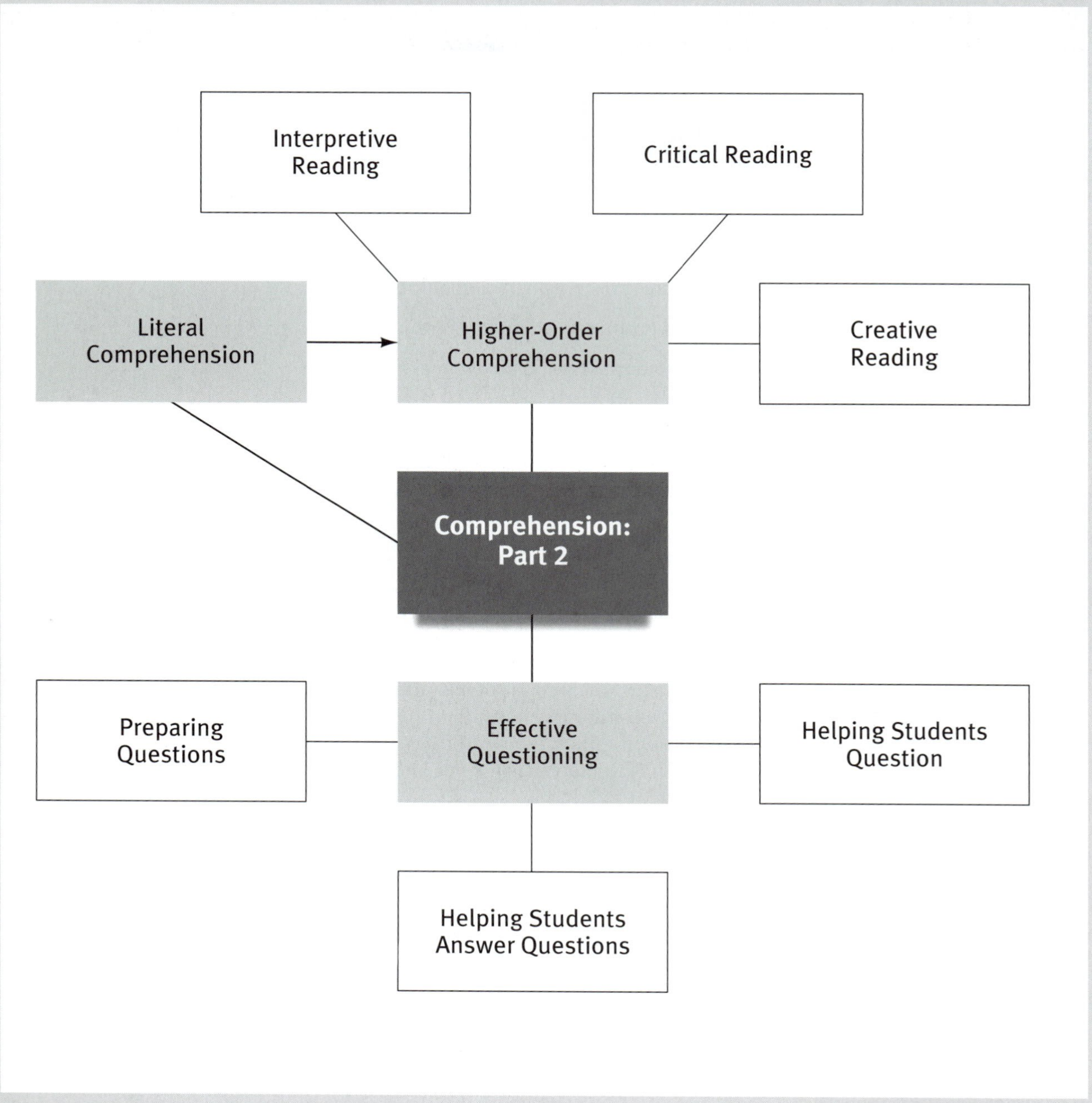

EXAMPLE 4.1 Types of Comprehension

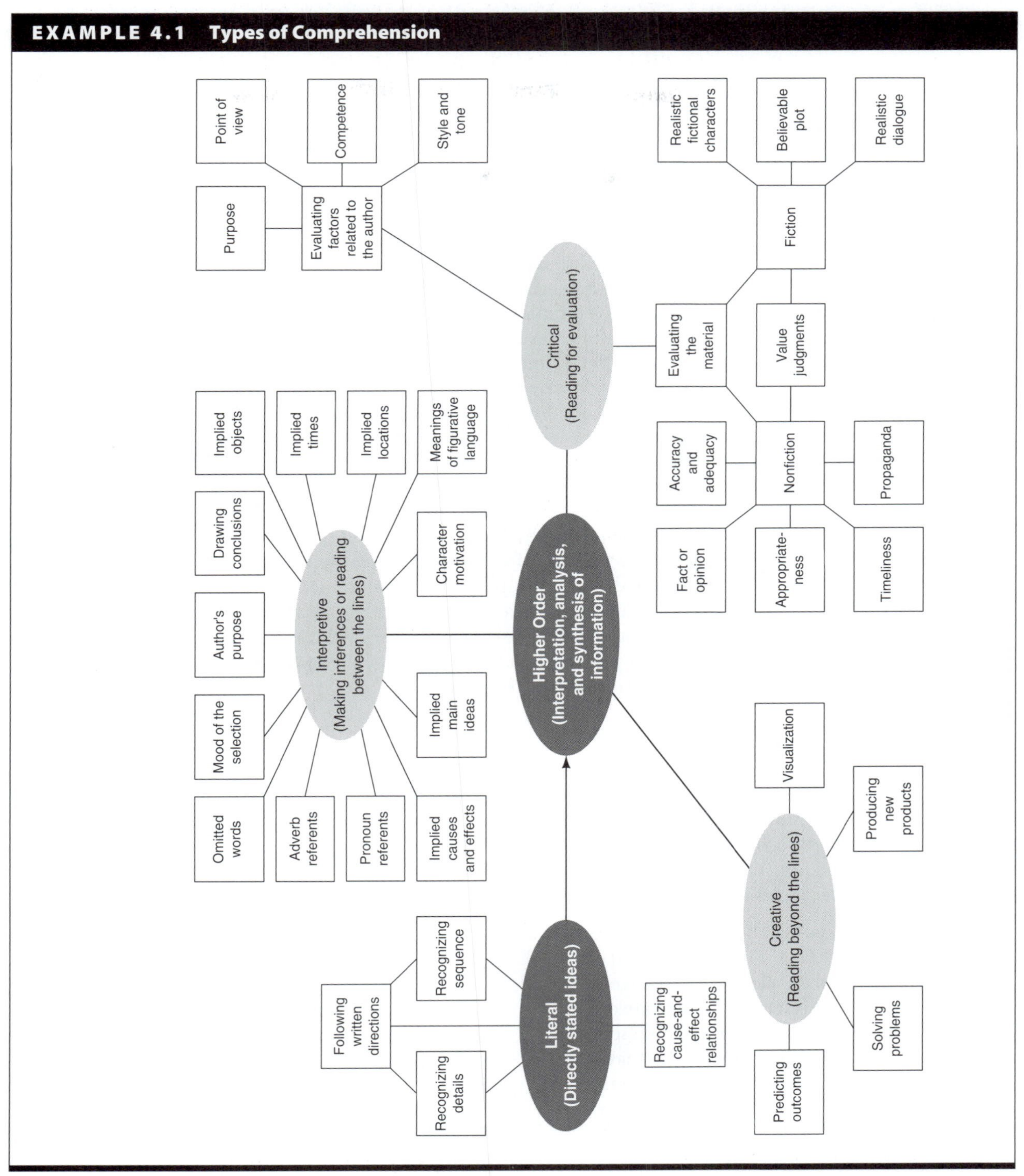

Literal Comprehension

Reading for ***literal comprehension,*** or acquiring information that is directly stated in a selection, is important in and of itself and is also a prerequisite for higher-level comprehension. Recognizing stated information is the basis of literal comprehension. The specific, explicitly stated parts of a paragraph or passage that contain the basic information are the details on which main ideas, cause-and-effect relationships, inferences, and so on, are built. For example, in the sentence "The man wore a red hat," the fact that a red hat was being worn is one detail that readers can note. Literal comprehension involves several skills, including locating details, understanding sequences, following directions, and recognizing cause-and-effect relationships. To locate details effectively, students may need some direction about the types of details that specific questions elicit. For example, a *who* question asks for the name or identification of a person; a *what* question asks for a thing or an event; a *where* question asks for a place; a *when* question asks for a time; a *how* question asks for the way something is or was accomplished; and a *why* question asks for the reason for something. After discussing these question words and their meanings, the teacher can model for the students the locations of answers to each type of question in a passage displayed on the board or projected on a screen. Then the students can participate in an activity such as the following Model Activity to practice the skill. Newspaper articles are good for practice of this sort, since lead paragraphs tend to include information about *who, what, where, when, why,* and *how.* The teacher should provide feedback on the correctness of responses as soon as possible after the students complete the activity. Students may also practice finding details in newspaper articles at home, with family members.

FAMILY

Sequence, the order in which events in a paragraph or passage occur, is signaled by time-order words such as *now, before, when, while, yet,* and *after*. Readers must learn to recognize straightforward chronological sequence, as well as flashbacks and other devices that describe events "out of order."

MODEL ACTIVITIES — Locating Details in a Newspaper Story

Have the students read the following newspaper article and answer the questions in small groups, making sure that every group member agrees to each answer chosen:

> The Live Wire Singers will be performing in concert at Lowe's Auditorium on First Street at 7:00 p.m. this Friday, to benefit the Children's College Fund. Admission is $10 per person or $15 per couple. This group presents programs of current pop songs and old standards. They have performed in thirty-six states to sell-out crowds during the past year.

1. Who is involved in this event?
2. What is about to take place?
3. Where will it take place?
4. When will it take place?
5. How or why will it take place?

Have a whole-class discussion of the article, with members from the different groups giving their groups' answers and reasons for their answers.

Teachers must model the process of finding the correct sequence of events in a passage before expecting students to locate such sequences independently. Helpful time-order words should be discussed and pointed out in selections. Then students need to engage in practice activities related to this skill, such as the one in the following Model Activity "Placing Story Events in Order."

The ability to read and follow directions is a prerequisite for virtually all successful schoolwork. It involves understanding details and sequence.

The teacher should take a set of directions for performing a task and model following these directions carefully, reading the directions aloud as each step is completed and commenting on the meaning of each instruction. Then he or she should follow the directions again, leaving out a vital step. Class discussion about the results of not following directions carefully should follow. After several modeling episodes, the teacher should consistently refer students to written directions instead of telling them orally how to do everything. Students can be asked to read the directions silently and then repeat them in their own words. There are numerous opportunities for students to practice following directions outside of school. With family members, they may read and follow directions for using public transportation, cooking, or participating in games and crafts.

FAMILY

MODEL ACTIVITIES Placing Story Events in Order

Discuss the meaning of sequence with the students. Give an example of the sequence in a very familiar story, such as "King Midas and the Golden Touch" or *The Wizard of Oz*. Then ask the students to read the following story and place the list of story events in order:

> We were all excited on Friday morning because we were going to go to Disney World. We were in a hurry to leave, but Mother wouldn't allow us to leave the table before we finished breakfast.
>
> Immediately after breakfast, we piled into the van. Everyone was talking at once and bouncing around on the seats as Dad started the van and backed out of the driveway. We were making so much noise and moving around so much that Dad didn't hear or see the truck turn the corner. The truck driver honked his horn, but it was too late. Dad backed right into the side of the truck.
>
> The angry driver jumped out of his truck, but when he saw all of us in the van, he calmed down. He and Dad talked to each other awhile, staring at the damaged side of the truck occasionally. Then they went into the house to report the accident to the police.
>
> Mother recovered from the shock and told us to get out of the van. "We'll have a long wait before we will be able to leave," she said.

Story Events

The family got into the van.

The truck driver honked his horn.

The family ate breakfast.

Dad backed out of the driveway.

Dad and the truck driver talked.

Mother told the children to get out of the van.

Dad backed into the side of the truck.

Dad and the truck driver went into the house.

The driver jumped out of his truck.

After everyone has finished the exercise independently, discuss the students' results in class. Be sure to have the students give the reasons for their decisions.

Recognizing and understanding a cause-and-effect relationship in a written passage is an important reading skill. It is considered a literal skill when the relationship is explicitly stated ("Bill stayed home because he was ill") and an interpretive skill if the relationship is implied.

Following are some activities for working with literal comprehension:

1. After students have read a paragraph, preferably from a book they have chosen themselves, ask them questions whose answers are directly stated in the paragraph. These are often *who, what, where,* and *when* questions. Have them show where they found the answers in the paragraph.

2. Give the students a set of directions for a task that they need to complete, and have them number the important details (or steps), as has been done in the following example. Go through one or more examples before you ask them to work alone or cooperatively with partners or small groups.

   To make a good bowl of chili, first (1) sauté the onions for about ten minutes. Then (2) add the ground beef and brown it. (3) Stir the mixture frequently so that it will not burn. Finally, (4) add the tomatoes, tomato sauce, Mexican-style beans, salt, pepper, and chili powder. (5) Cook over low heat for 45 minutes to 1 hour.

3. Make some copies of a menu. After modeling for the students how to locate items and prices, ask them to read the menu and answer specific questions such as these:

   a. What is the price of a soft drink?

   b. Can you order a baked potato separately? If so, under what heading is it found?

   c. What else do you get when you order a rib steak?

   d. How many desserts are available?

4. Using a description like the following one and reading each step aloud, draw an object on the board. Then give the students a written description of another object and ask them to draw it:

   The flower has five oval petals. The petals are red. The center, at which the petals meet, is brown. The flower has a long green stem. At the bottom of the stem are overlapping blade-shaped leaves, which are half as tall as the stem.

5. Display (by writing on the board or by projecting the material on a screen) a paragraph from a book the students have read that contains a cause-and-effect relationship. Model the process of locating the cause and the effect. Point out clue words, such as *because*, if they are present, but make sure the students know they cannot always expect such clues to be present. Then show the students another paragraph from the same book or a different one. State the cause of the action, and have them identify the effect. Discuss the students' responses. A paragraph similar to the following one could be used for instruction:

Rashad, Jill, Leon, and Maya were playing baseball in Rashad's yard. Maya was at bat and hit the ball squarely in the direction of Rashad's bedroom window. As the group watched in horror, the ball crashed through the window, shattering the glass.

Question: What happened when the baseball hit the window? [or What caused the window to break?]

6. Have the students read a selection such as "The Legend of Sleepy Hollow." Then list the events in the story out of sequence, and show students how to reorder them, explaining why the events came in that order. Using another selection, such as that in the Model Activity Placing Story Events in Order, ask the students to list the events in sequence.
7. Discuss with the students the functions of such key words as *first, next, last,* and *finally*. Then give them a paragraph containing these words, and ask them to underline the words that help to show the order of events.
8. Use an activity similar to the Model Activity Following Directions on page 135.
9. Write directions for an activity, and have the students perform it. Construction projects, science experiments, and magic tricks can be used. Discussion can center on the results that occur if the correct sequence is not followed. Directions can be cut apart, scrambled, and reconstructed to show comprehension of the necessary sequence.

Perhaps because literal comprehension is the easiest to deal with in the classroom, teachers have given it a disproportionate amount of attention; but students

MODEL ACTIVITIES

Following Directions

Give the students handouts with the following information printed on them:

Directions: Read all the items before you begin to carry out each instruction. Work as quickly as you can; you have five minutes to finish this activity.

1. Write your name at the top of the paper.
2. Turn the paper over, and add 15 and 25. Write the answer you get on this line: ________.
3. Stand up and clap your hands three times.
4. Count the number of times the word *the* is written on this page. Put the answer on this line: ________.
5. Go to the board and write your name.
6. Count the people in this room. Put the answer under your name at the top of the page.
7. Now that you have read all of the directions, take your paper to the teacher. It should have no marks on it.

After the students have finished the exercise, hold a discussion about why some of them made marks on the paper that they should not have made. Emphasize the importance of reading and following directions carefully to avoid errors.

need to achieve higher-order reading comprehension to become thoughtful and effective citizens.

Higher-Order Comprehension

Higher-order reading comprehension goes beyond literal understanding of a text. It is based on the higher-order thinking processes of interpretation, analysis, and synthesis of information. In this chapter, we discuss the higher-order comprehension processes of interpretive reading, critical reading, and creative reading.

Good readers employ a variety of higher-order strategies. They interpret and evaluate the material that they read. They adjust the way they read to the type of text they are reading. They paraphrase ideas accurately, relate the ideas to their background knowledge, draw conclusions about the ideas, consider the author's purpose, and consider the accuracy of the material. They monitor their understanding as they read, and adjust reading strategies accordingly. In other words, they are active readers (Duke and Pearson, 2002; Pressley, 2002).

Knowledge is necessary to higher-order thinking, but students do not always use the knowledge they possess to think inferentially, critically, and creatively (Beck, 1989). They may have the background knowledge needed for comprehending a text but fail to use it, or they may have misconceptions about certain topics that are more detrimental to comprehension than no background knowledge at all. Students in all groups, regardless of socioeconomic level or ethnic origin, vary in background knowledge, but it is true that "membership in specific cultural groups goes far in determining what a reader knows that can be related to text—and thus goes far in determining a reader's interpretation of text" (Pressley, 2001, p. 8). Semantic mapping (described in Chapter 3) accompanied by group discussion can help students who have little individual knowledge about a topic to pool their information and expand their knowledge (Maria, 1989).

Making predictions about reading material is an important higher-order reading strategy. Predicting what will happen in a story or other reading selection engages students' interest and leads them to organize their thinking. A hypothesis-testing process is initiated in which students make predictions and then read to confirm or reject them. If the predictions must be rejected, the students revise them. In all cases, they must be ready to explain why they made the predictions and why they believe the predictions can be accepted or must be rejected.

Students need to realize that any evidence that refutes a prediction is enough to show the prediction is not valid, but even a great deal of supporting evidence in favor of a prediction may not conclusively prove that it is true. They also need to realize that just because a prediction has not been refuted at one point in the reading does not mean that evidence to refute it will not appear later. Readers tend to overlook refuting evidence while noticing confirming evidence, and students must be taught to avoid doing this. By refuting unsupportable predictions, students reduce uncertainty about the story's outcome. Teachers should ask students if their predictions have been proven wrong yet, and other similar questions, to encourage them to search for refuting evidence (Garrison and Hoskisson, 1989).

Asking for predictions when the text offers clues about what will happen helps make students aware of the usefulness of text information in making inferences. Asking for predictions when there are no text clues about what will happen encourages creative thinking on the part of the students. Both types of prediction activities are good to include in lessons over time (Beck, 1989). Before students are asked to make and verify predictions, the teacher should model the strategy with a variety of materials. Reading response activities can also help students develop higher-order comprehension skills. Ollmann (1996) tried seven types of open-ended reading response formats with her middle-school students: literary letters to the teacher; reading response questions; two-column responses, in which quotations from a book are written on one side and personal responses to the quotations on the other; letters to an author with questions about the development of a book; hexagonal essays, in which students respond to a book from the perspective of each of the six levels of Bloom's Taxonomy; buddy journals, in which partners who have read the same book write about it in a journal and respond to each other's entries; and character journals, in which each student writes a first-person diary entry as a main character in the book. The hexagonal essay worked best at promoting higher-order thinking: with it, students "summarize the plot, make a personal association with text, analyze the theme, analyze literary techniques, compare and contrast with other literature, and evaluate the work as a whole" (Ollmann, 1996, p. 579). The two-column response format also did well. Character journals led to development of empathy with the characters.

LITERATURE

Interpretive Reading

Interpretive reading is reading between the lines or making inferences. It is the process of deriving ideas that are implied rather than directly stated. Interpretive reading includes making inferences about main ideas of passages, cause-and-effect relationships that are not directly stated, referents of pronouns, referents of adverbs, and omitted words. It also includes detecting the mood of a passage, detecting the author's purpose in writing a selection, drawing conclusions, and interpreting figurative language.

No text is ever fully explicit. Some relationships among events, motivations of characters, and other factors are left out, with the expectation that readers will figure them out on their own. Readers therefore must play an active role in constructing the meanings represented by the text. They must infer the implied information by combining the information in the text with their background knowledge of the world. Stories that require more inferences are more difficult to read (Pearson, 1985).

Lange (1981) has pointed out that "readers make inferences consistent with their ***schemata***" (p. 443). It is important to realize, however, that middle-school students have less prior knowledge than adults do and that even when they possess the necessary background knowledge, they do not always make inferences spontaneously, without teacher direction. As students get older, their ability to make inferences improves, possibly because of their increased knowledge of the world.

Comparing events in students' own lives with events that might occur in stories they are about to read is one way to help the students see the thinking processes they should use when they read. Even struggling readers show the ability to make inferences about the material they are reading when such a procedure is used (Hansen and Hubbard, 1984).

Students are expected to make inferences about a number of things: locations, people who act in certain ways, time, actions, devices or instruments, categories, objects, causes and effects, solutions to problems, and feelings. To make these inferences, they can relate important vocabulary in the reading material to their backgrounds of experience. First, the teacher should explain how readers can use important words in a passage to help them make a particular inference about the passage. Then the teacher should have students practice and apply this procedure. During the application phase, students are asked to make an inference based on the first sentence and then retain, modify, or reject it as each subsequent sentence is read (Johnson and Johnson, 1986).

Such instruction is needed because some students will make hypotheses about the reading material but fail to modify them when additional information shows them to be incorrect. Instead, they may distort subsequent information in an attempt to make it conform to their original hypotheses. These students may have problems with passages that present one idea and follow it with a contrasting idea or passages that present an idea and subsequently refute it. They may also have difficulty with passages that give examples of a topic, followed by a topic statement, or with passages that give no topic statement (Kimmel and MacGinitie, 1985).

To help students learn to revise their hypotheses as they read, teachers can use a passage that contains a word with multiple meanings, asking students to hypothesize about possible meanings for the word based on initial sentences. Then they can have students read to confirm or disprove these predictions. Reading stories written from unusual points of view can also help; for example, *The True Story of the 3 Little Pigs* by Jon Scieszka is written from the wolf's point of view. Although this example is a picture book, middle-school students and even adults enjoy the way the author has presented the wolf's case in a hilarious manner.

The information needed to make inferences is not always adjacent in the text. When this situation exists, the teacher can use guiding questions to lead students to such information. This type of instruction helps students become aware of the need to search actively for the meanings of written passages.

Active involvement with the printed message enhances students' abilities to make inferences related to it. Pearson (1985) succinctly describes a method related to teaching inference skills that Gordon and Pearson (1983) developed. Students should "(1) ask the inference question, (2) answer it, (3) find clues in the text to support the inference, and (4) tell how to get from the clues to the answer (i.e., give a 'line of reasoning')" (Pearson, 1985, p. 731). First, the teacher models all four steps; then the teacher performs steps 1 and 2, while requiring the students to complete steps 3 and 4; then the teacher performs steps 1 and 3, requiring the students to complete steps 2 and 4; and finally, the teacher asks the question (step 1), and the students perform all the other steps. The responsibility for the task is thus gradually transferred from teacher to students. This procedure can be used for other skills as well. Providing practice in answering inferential questions is important to helping students improve in this skill.

Interpreting Anaphora

Interpreting anaphora is another task that requires students to make inferences. ***Anaphora*** refers to the use of one word or phrase to replace another one (Irwin, 1991). Examples are using pronouns in place of nouns (*he* for a noun such as *Bill*), using adverbs for nouns or noun phrases (*here* for a phrase such as *in the kitchen*), letting adjectives stand for the nouns that would have followed them (*several* for *several people*), using a superordinate term to stand for a subordinate one (*reptile* for *rattlesnake*), using an inclusive term to stand for an extended section of text (*This* for *a disturbance in the neighborhood* presented in an earlier sentence), and letting referents in another sentence or clause represent deleted items (*I will too*, following *Mom will bake brownies for the sale. Bake brownies for the sale* is "understood").

At some point, teachers will probably need to address all forms of anaphora, but the approaches used can be similar. Modeling of the thought processes used is important. Because some students, especially English language learners (Herrell, 2000), frequently have trouble identifying the noun to which a pronoun refers, they need practice in deciding to whom or to what pronouns refer. Some other forms of anaphora are discussed in subsequent sections.

DIVERSITY

Pronoun Referents. Few, if any, pieces of writing explicitly state the connections between pronouns and their referents (anaphoric relationships), so the task of determining the referent is an inferential one. After reading, students recall structures in which the referent is a noun or a noun phrase more easily than they remember structures in which the referent is a clause or a sentence (Barnitz, 1979)—for example:

> Mark wanted an ice-cream cone but did not have enough money for it. (noun phrase referent)
>
> Mike plays the guitar for fun, but he does not do it often. (sentence referent)

Similarly, students find it easier to remember structures in which the pronoun follows its referent than ones in which the pronoun comes first (Barnitz, 1979)—for example:

> Marcia wanted the blouse because it was pretty.
>
> Because it was pretty, Marcia wanted the blouse.

Teachers should give attention to the structures just described. They should use stories or content selections the students are currently reading and explain the connections between the pronouns and referents in a number of examples before asking students to determine the relationships themselves.

TIME for REFLECTION

Some people believe that students intuitively know the referents for pronouns. Others say that they need instruction to help them recognize referents. **What do *you* think, and why?**

Adverb Referents. At times, adverbs refer to other words or groups of words without an explicitly stated relationship. Teachers can explain these relationships, using examples such as the following, and then let students practice making the connections independently:

> I'll stay at home, and you come here after you finish. (The adverb *here* refers to *home*.)
>
> I enjoy the swimming pool, even if you do not like to go there. (The adverb *there* refers to *swimming pool*.)

Omitted Words. Sometimes words are omitted and said to be "understood," a structure known as ***ellipsis.*** Ellipsis can cause problems for some students, so again teachers should provide examples, explain the structure, and then give students practice in interpreting sentences:

Are you going to the library? Yes, I am. (In the second sentence, the words *going to the library* are understood.)

Who is going with you? Colin. (The words *is going with me* are understood.)

I have my books. Where are yours? (Here the second sentence is a shortened form of *Where are your books?*)

After this structure has been thoroughly discussed, students may practice by restating the sentences, filling in the deleted words.

Main Ideas

The main idea of a paragraph is the central thought around which the whole paragraph is organized. It is often, but not always, expressed in a ***topic sentence*** in expository writing; fewer topic sentences are found in narrative writing.

To understand written selections fully and to summarize long selections, students must be able to determine the main ideas in their reading materials. Teachers should provide them with opportunities to practice recognizing main ideas and help them to realize the following facts:

- A topic sentence often states the main idea of the paragraph.
- The topic sentence is often, though not always, the first sentence in the paragraph; sometimes it appears at the end or in the middle.
- Not all paragraphs have topic sentences.
- The main idea is supported by all of the details in a well-written paragraph.
- When the main idea is not directly stated, readers can determine it by discovering the topic to which all the stated details are related.
- The main idea of a whole selection may be determined by examining the main ideas of the individual paragraphs and deciding to what topic they are all related.

Individual teachers mean different things when they request main ideas from students, and when students are asked to give the main idea of a passage, some produce topics, some topic sentences, and some brief summaries. A description of the task expected, however, may be all students need to lead them to produce the desired response.

A topic merely identifies the subject matter; a main idea also includes the type of information given about the topic. For example, a topic of a paragraph or selection might be "football," whereas the main idea might be "There are several ways to score in football."

To give students a concrete analogy for main ideas and details, a teacher can use a familiar object such as a bicycle. The whole bicycle can be identified as the main idea, and the handlebars, seat, pedals, gears, wheels, and chain can represent the supporting details that together make up the main idea.

In many selections, readers must infer the main idea from related details. Even in selections in which the main idea is directly stated, readers generally must make inferences about which sentence states the main idea. The teacher should model the thought process students need to follow in deciding on the main idea of a selection before asking them to try this task independently. For paragraphs with topic sentences, the teacher can show students that the topic sentence is the main idea and that the other sentences in the paragraph relate to it by taking a paragraph, locating the topic sentence, and showing the relationship of each of the other sentences to the topic sentence. Then the teacher can give the students paragraphs and ask them to underline the topic sentences and tell how each of the other sentences relates to each topic sentence.

The teacher can help develop students' readiness to make inferences about unstated main ideas by first asking them to locate the main ideas of pictures. Then the teacher can ask them to listen for main ideas as he or she reads to them. Finally, the teacher can have students look for main ideas of passages they read themselves.

Activities such as those illustrated in the following Focus on Strategies and the Model Activity on Inferring Unstated Main Ideas on page 142 can give students practice in locating main ideas in paragraphs.

Showing students how to infer unstated main ideas is a more difficult process than showing them how to decide which stated sentence represents the main idea. In situations such as the one shown in the Model Activity, the teacher could compare each of the possible choices to the details in the selection, rejecting those that fail to encompass the details. As students practice and become more proficient at identifying implied main ideas, the teacher should omit the choices and ask them to construct the

FOCUS ON STRATEGIES

Finding Main Ideas

Mrs. Braswell wrote the following paragraph on the board:

> Edward Fong is a good family man. He is well educated, and he keeps his knowledge of governmental processes current. He has served our city well as a mayor for the past two years, exhibiting his outstanding skills as an administrator. Edward Fong has qualities that make him an excellent choice as our party's candidate for governor.

She said to the class, "I am going to try to locate the topic sentence—the one to which all of the other sentences are related. The topic sentence provides one type of main idea for the paragraph. . . . Now, let's see, is it the first sentence? No. None of the other sentences appear to support his being a good family man. . . . Is it the second sentence? No. It isn't supported by the first sentence . . . . Is it the third sentence? No. It may be supported by the second sentence, but not by the others . . . . Is it the fourth sentence? Yes, I think it is. A candidate for governor would do well to be a good family man, be well educated and knowledgeable about government, and have experience as a city administrator. All the other sentences support the last one, which is broad enough in its meaning to include the ideas expressed in the other sentences."

After this demonstration, Mrs. Braswell let one student "think aloud" the reasoning behind his or her choice of a topic sentence for another paragraph. Finally, she had students work on this process in pairs, "thinking aloud" to each other.

main idea themselves. Teachers can also increase passage length as the students gain proficiency, beginning with paragraphs that have directly stated topic sentences, moving to paragraphs that do not have directly stated topic sentences, and finally moving gradually to entire selections.

LITERATURE

Because of their obvious morals, Aesop's fables are good for teaching implied main ideas. The teacher can give students a fable and ask them to state the moral, then compare the morals given in the fables with the ones stated by the students, discuss any variations, and examine reasoning processes. Students may have fun using Arnold Lobel's *Fables* (Harper & Row, 1980) with this activity as well.

Finding the main idea in whole selections of nonfiction generally is a categorizing process in which the topic is located and the information given about the topic is then examined. In fiction, however, there is not a "topic" but a central problem, which is rarely stated explicitly. To help students learn to locate a central problem in a fictional work, the teacher should first activate their schemata for problems and solutions, perhaps by talking about background experiences or stories they have previously read. Then the class may identify and categorize types of problems. Finally, the teacher should model the process of identifying a central story problem using a familiar, brief story. Pauses during reading to hypothesize about the central problem and to confirm or modify hypotheses can show the students how to search for the thing the central character wants, needs, or feels—the thing that provides the story's problem. The teacher should let the students see how the story's events affect the hypotheses they have made. Events of a story may be listed on the board to be analyzed for the needs or desires of the main character (Moldofsky, 1983).

MODEL ACTIVITIES Inferring Unstated Main Ideas

Model the generation of a main idea for a paragraph from one of the students' textbooks that has an unstated main idea. Be sure to show how each sentence in the paragraph supports the main idea you generated. Then display a copy of the following paragraph (or a similar one from one of their textbooks) and main idea choices on the board or a transparency:

> The mayor of this town has always conducted his political campaigns as name-calling battles. Never once has he approached the basic issues of a campaign. Nevertheless, he builds himself up as a great statesman, ignoring the irregularities that have been discovered during his terms of office. Do you want a person like this to be reelected?

The main idea of this selection is:

1. The current mayor is not a good person to reelect to office.
2. The mayor doesn't say nice things about his opponents.
3. The mayor is a crook.
4. The mayor should be reelected.

Say, "In this selection, the main idea is implied but not directly stated. Choose the correct main idea from the list of possible ones. Try to use a thinking process similar to the one I used in the example that I gave for you. Be ready to explain the reason for your choice to your classmates."

Two activities using newspaper articles can provide enjoyable practice in identifying main ideas:

1. Gather old newspapers and cardboard for mounting. Cut from the newspapers a number of articles that you think will interest the students, and separate the text of each article from its headline. Mount each article and title on cardboard. The students' task is to read each article and locate the most suitable headline for it. To make the task easier, have them begin by matching captions to pictures, use very short articles, or use articles that are completely different in subject matter. Have the students discuss the reasons for their choices. Make the activity self-checking by coding articles and headlines. To follow up, you might use these ideas: (a) have students make pictures and captions to share in the reading center, or (b) have them try to match advertisements to pictures or captions to cartoons.
2. Collect newspaper articles and cut off headlines. Then have students construct titles using the information in the lead paragraph. Show them how to do this before you ask them to work on the task alone.

Cause and Effect

Sometimes a reader needs to infer a cause or an effect that has been implied in the material. Cause-and-effect relationships can be taught using cause-and-effect chains in real life and in stories. Brainstorming out loud about causes and effects may help students develop skill in this area. The teacher can ask, "What could be the effect when a person falls into the lake?" or "What could be the cause of a crying baby?" Then the teacher should elicit the reasoning behind students' answers. The Classroom Scenario on page 144 describes a practice activity for this skill.

Detecting Mood

Certain words and ways of using words tend to set a mood for a story, poem, or other literary work. Teachers should have students discuss how certain words trigger certain moods—for example, *ghostly, deserted, haunted,* and *howling* convey a scary mood; *lilting, sparkling, shining,* and *laughing* project a happy mood; *downcast, sobbing,* and *dejected* indicate a sad mood. They should model for the class the process of locating mood words in a paragraph and using these words to determine the mood of the paragraph. Then they can give the students copies of selections in which they have underlined words that set the mood and let them decide what the mood is, based on the underlined words. Finally, teachers can give the students a passage such as the one provided in the Classroom Scenario on page 145 and tell them to underline the words that set the mood. After the students complete the practice activity, they should discuss the mood that the words established.

Detecting the Author's Purpose

Writers always have a purpose for writing: to inform, entertain, persuade, or accomplish something else. Teachers should encourage their students to ask, "Why was this

CLASSROOM SCENARIO

Inferring Cause-and-Effect Relationships

Mrs. Rodriguez stacked three books on the edge of her desk as the class watched. Then she said, "Cover your eyes or put your heads down on your desks so that you can't see the books anymore. Don't peek!"

When all eyes were covered, Mrs. Rodriguez knocked the books off the desk. Then she said, "You can open your eyes now."

The students opened their eyes and saw the books on the floor.

"What caused the books to be on the floor?" Mrs. Rodriguez asked.

Rob immediately responded, "You knocked them off."

"How do you know that I knocked them off?" Mrs. Rodriguez persisted. "You didn't see me do it."

"Nobody except you was up there," Rob replied.

"How do you know that I didn't just lay them gently on the floor?" the teacher then asked.

"Because they made such a loud noise," Rob answered. "If you had put them down gently, there wouldn't have been much noise."

"That's right," said Mrs. Rodriguez. "You used clues to figure out something that you didn't actually see. When you read, you can use that skill, too. Sometimes the author leaves clues about what he or she wants you to know, but doesn't come right out and say it. You have to use clues the author gives and read between the lines to find out what happened. We're going to try doing that right now."

Mrs. Rodriguez passed out a handout with the following paragraphs on it. She said, "Read the following paragraphs and answer the question."

> Caitlin was playing a computer game when her mother called to her that it was time for bed. Caitlin was winning the game, and she had never done as well before. She ignored her mother's warning and continued to play until midnight.
>
> The next morning Caitlin found it hard to get out of bed. Furthermore, she felt groggy in class all day. Her teacher commented that she needed to pay more attention to the lesson.
>
> "I don't know what's wrong with me today," she told her teacher. "I just don't seem to feel well."
>
> *Question:* What caused Caitlin to feel the way she did today?

When everyone had finished reading and had answered the question independently, Mrs. Rodriguez had one student answer the question aloud. The other students verified the answer, and several pointed out the clues in the material that helped them to decide on the answer.

Analysis of Scenario

Mrs. Rodriguez used a concrete experience to show the class how they made inferences about events every day. Then she had them try to apply the same kind of thinking to a reading experience, analyzing their thinking and pointing out the clues they used, so that classmates who were having trouble with the skill could see how they processed the information.

---

written?" by presenting them with a series of stories and explaining the purpose of each one, then giving them other stories and asking them to identify the purposes. The class should discuss reasons for the answers. The Model Activity on page 146 gives students practice in detecting purpose.

TECHNOLOGY

Students can also be led to detect the purposes of the authors and producers of television shows and advertisements. Many middle-school students have a good background for doing this, but they have not been led to do it consciously and to see how knowledge of the ways other authors transmit information to meet specific purposes can help them do so in their own writing. "By being asked to explain how they recognized the target audience [for a show or commercial], students can be helped to realize

CLASSROOM SCENARIO Detecting Mood

Mrs. Vaden read the following excerpt from *Homesick: My Own Story* by Jean Fritz (1982, p. 138) to her class:

> By the time we were at the bottom of the hill and had parked beside the house, my grandmother, my grandfather, and Aunt Margaret were all outside, looking exactly the way they had in the calendar picture. I ran right into my grandmother's arms as if I'd been doing this every day.
>
> "Welcome home! Oh, welcome home!" my grandmother cried.
>
> I hadn't known it but this was exactly what I'd wanted her to say. I needed to hear it said out loud. I was home.

Mrs. Vaden said, "In this passage, the mood of happiness is effectively developed by describing the girl's running into her grandmother's arms, the cries of 'welcome' from her grandmother, and the statement 'I was home.' All these things combine to help us feel the happy mood. Some authors carefully choose words to help readers feel the mood they want to share. Read the paragraph on the board, decide what mood the author wanted to set, and be ready to tell the class which words helped you to decide about the mood."

The following paragraph was on the board:

> Jay turned dejectedly away from the busy scene made by the movers as they carried his family's furniture from the house. "We're going away forever," he thought. "I'll never see my friends again." The corners of his mouth turned down, and he stared glumly at the ground.

Steve raised his hand. When the teacher called on him, he said, "The mood is sad."

"That's right," Mrs. Vaden responded. "What clues did you use to decide that?"

"*His mouth turned down* and *stared glumly at the ground*," he replied.

Sharon chimed in, "I see another one. *Dejected* is a sad word, too."

"Very good," said Mrs. Vaden. "You both found clues to the mood of this paragraph. Next, we will look for the mood as we begin to read our story for this week. Jot down the clue words and phrases as you find them to help you decide on the mood."

Analysis of Scenario

Mrs. Vaden first showed the class how she decided about the mood of a passage in a literature selection with which they were familiar. Then she gave them an opportunity to determine the mood for another selection, under her supervision. Finally, she asked them to apply the skill in further purposeful reading activities.

that in writing for a particular audience the writer has to make assumptions about the audience's values, knowledge, and interests" (Williams, 2003, p. 552). Students can also identify different media genres (for example, sitcom, documentary, soap opera) and talk about the characteristics of the different genres in preparation for understanding the genres of printed text and the genres available to them for their own writing (Williams, 2003).

Drawing Conclusions

To draw conclusions, a reader must put together information gathered from several sources or from several places within the same source. Students may develop readiness for this skill by studying pictures and drawing conclusions from them. Answering

MODEL ACTIVITIES

Detecting the Author's Purpose

Display the following list of reading selections on the board, or display the actual books. Ask the students to consider the selections and decide for each one whether the author was trying to inform, entertain, persuade, or accomplish a combination of purposes:

The New Way Things Work by David Macaulay. New York: Houghton Mifflin, 1998.

The Long Road to Gettysburg by Jim Murphy. New York: Scholastic, 1992.

Never Trust a Dead Man by Vivian Vande Velde. San Diego, CA: Harcourt, 1999.

Help! I'm Trapped in My Gym Teacher's Body by Todd Strasser. New York: Scholastic, 1996.

"Put Safety First." (a pamphlet)

After each student has had time to make a decision about each selection, ask volunteers to share their responses and the reasons for each one. Clear up any misconceptions through discussion.

questions like the following may also help. The teacher should model the process before having the students attempt it.

1. What is taking place here?
2. What happened just before this picture was taken?
3. What are the people in the picture preparing to do?

Cartoons may be used to good advantage in developing this comprehension skill. The teacher can show the students a cartoon like the one shown on page 147 and ask a question that leads them to draw a conclusion, such as, "What kind of news does Dennis have for his father?" Putting together the ideas that an event happened today and that Dennis's father needs to be relaxed to hear about it enables students to conclude that Dennis was involved in some mischief or accident that is likely to upset his father. The teacher can model the necessary thinking process by pointing out each clue and relating it to personal knowledge about how parents react. Then students can practice on other cartoons.

Riddles offer good practice in drawing conclusions. Commercial riddle books, which allow readers to answer riddles and explain the reasoning behind their answers, may be used for developing this skill.

Another way to help students draw conclusions is to ask questions about sentences that imply certain information. For example, the teacher can write on the chalkboard, "The two men in uniforms removed a stretcher from the back of their vehicle." Then the teacher can ask: "What kind of vehicle were these men driving? What are your reasons for your answers?" Although the sentence does not directly state that the vehicle is an ambulance, the details lead to this conclusion. With help, students can become adept at detecting such clues to implied meanings. The Model Activity on Drawing Conclusions offers practice with this skill. (See the Model Activity on page 147.)

To draw conclusions about characters' motives in stories, students must have some knowledge about how people react in social situations. This knowledge comes from their backgrounds of experience. Teachers' questions can encourage inferences by

requiring students to consider events from the viewpoints of different characters; to think about the characters' likely thoughts, feelings, and motives; and to anticipate consequences of the actions of various characters (Moss and Oden, 1983).

MODEL ACTIVITIES Drawing Conclusions

Divide the class into small cooperative groups. Give each group a copy of a handout containing the following two paragraphs. Tell the class: "Individually read each paragraph, and come up with an answer to the question that follows it. After each person in your group has finished reading and has an answer, discuss the answers in your group, and explain why you answered as you did. Modify your answers if you believe your thinking was wrong originally. Be ready to share your decisions with the rest of the class."

> Ray went through the line, piling his plate high with food. He then carried his plate over to a table, where a server was waiting to find out what he wanted to drink.
>
> Where was Ray?
>
> ______________________________
>
> ______________________________
>
> Cindy awoke with pleasure, remembering where she was. She hurried to dress so that she could help feed the chickens and watch her uncle milk the cows. Then she would go down to the field, catch Ginger, and take a ride through the woods.
>
> Where was Cindy?
>
> ______________________________
>
> ______________________________

Hold a whole-class discussion in which representatives from each small group share their group's answers.

Interpreting Figurative Language

Interpreting figurative language is an inferential task. Idioms abound in the English language. An ***idiom*** is a phrase that has a meaning different from its literal meaning. A person who "keeps his eyes peeled," for example, does not actually peel his eyes, but uses them intently. Idioms make language more difficult to comprehend, but they also add color and interest.

DIVERSITY

Students who are not part of the mainstream culture often lack the backgrounds of experience with the culture to help them interpret idioms. They may be confused over the idea that a word or phrase has different meanings in different contexts, and its meaning in an idiomatic context may be very different from any of its denotative meanings.

It may be helpful to teach idioms by defining and explaining them when they occur in reading materials or in oral activities. Studying the origins of the expressions may also be helpful. After an idiom's meaning has been clarified, students need to use it in class activities. They may rewrite sentences to include newly learned idioms or replace these idioms with more literal language. Deaton (1992) found that doing writing that makes use of idioms can help students better understand the meanings. Illustrating idioms is another helpful activity. Students can also listen for idioms in class discussion or try using them. Creative writing about possible origins of idioms may elicit interest in discovering their real origins (Bromley, 1984).

One of the best ways to teach figurative language, as well as all interpretive reading strategies and skills, is through think-alouds. More extensive coverage of figurative expressions appears in Chapter 2. That discussion identifies different types of figures of speech and offers teaching suggestions.

Critical Reading

Critical reading is evaluating written material—comparing the ideas presented in the material with known standards and drawing conclusions about their accuracy, appropriateness, and timeliness. The critical reader must be an active reader, questioning, searching for facts, and suspending judgment until he or she has considered all the material. Critical reading depends on both literal and interpretive comprehension; grasping implied ideas is especially important.

People must read critically to make intelligent decisions based on the material they read, such as which political candidate to support, which products to buy, which movies to attend, and which television programs to watch. Because students face many of these decisions daily, they should receive instruction in critical reading.

TECHNOLOGY

Critical literacy for today's middle-school students should probably be interpreted more broadly than critical reading. Students are exposed to television shows and movies that are not primarily involved with printed text, but require the same critical thinking skills that critical reading does. "The National Council of Teachers of English and International Reading Association Standards for the English Language Arts (1996) mentions popular film and television as visual texts worthy of study in K–12 classrooms" (Morrell, 2002, pp. 74–75). ***Media literacy*** entails questioning the selections and programs that a

Students need instruction in critical reading because they must read critically to make intelligent decisions based on the material they read.
(© Elizabeth Crews)

person sees, hears, and reads. Students today are deluged with media messages of various types, and they must become critical listeners and viewers (Scharrer, 2002/2003).

Eken (2002, p. 221) believes that "in the contemporary world, literacy is not limited to the printed page and students need to interpret a variety of audio and visual texts." He showed movies and excerpts of movies in class and led students to analyze them. They considered the story lines, the characters, the settings, the themes, symbolism, the genres, the quality of the acting, the costumes and makeup, and such cinematic aspects as camera angles and movement, sound, special visual effects, and lighting. Eken used small-group and class discussions in which he was a participant, rather than a director, and written film reviews. The study resulted in improved higher-order thinking skills among his students. Students with experiences like these become critical media users. Since computer media include audio and visual texts to analyze, they should also be included, as should radio broadcasts (often accessed over the Internet) and sound recordings. Taken together, these applications of literacy have been referred to as media literacy.

Critical listening instruction and critical reading instruction are appropriate for readers at all levels of proficiency. Instruction in critical listening has been shown to improve critical reading and general reading comprehension for low-performing readers in grades four through six (Boodt, 1984).

Critical reading is closely related to revision in writing. Both activities require critical thinking. Students must evaluate their own writing to improve it, just as they evaluate the writing of others as they read.

Group thinking conferences can help students become better critical readers and writers. In these small-group conferences, students read their own written materials aloud. After a piece has been read, the teacher motivates discussion by asking what the piece was about, what the students liked about it, and what questions or suggestions the students might have for the author. The students revise their own pieces after the group conferences. The same type of conference can be held about a published work by a professional author. This process gives student writers insight into what readers expect of writers. If students fail to respond in ways that alert their classmates to missing or inappropriate aspects of the written pieces, the teacher can ask questions aimed at helping them make these discoveries (Fitzgerald, 1989a).

As Robertson and Rane-Szostak (1996) have done with older students, middle-school teachers can use short written dialogues between two people who have different positions on the issue being discussed to help students develop critical thinking skills. The students, in collaborative learning groups, can be asked to evaluate the dialogues by identifying each person's viewpoint, biases in the presentations, evidence for positions, evidence that was excluded, misstated facts, and mistaken reasoning. The groups then can choose the most reasonable position. Each group can act out its dialogue and explain its decision. The other class members can then add to the analysis.

Critical literacy instruction is sometimes avoided because it addresses issues that are controversial and potentially disturbing. Foss (2002, p. 402) said of her work with eighth graders that "although our critical conversations make students uncomfortable and push them to think more deeply, those discussions tend to be the ones students remember the most." Teachers, as well as students, may find these discussions uncomfortable, but ultimately valuable, educational experiences.

To foster critical reading skills in the classroom, teachers can encourage pupils to read with a questioning attitude and can lead them to ask questions such as the following when they are reading nonfiction:

1. Why did the author write this material?
2. Does the author know what he or she is writing about? Is he or she likely to be biased? Why or why not?
3. Is the material up to date?
4. Is the author approaching the material logically or emotionally? What emotional words does he or she use?
5. Is the author employing any undesirable propaganda techniques? If so, which ones? How does he or she use them? (Several propaganda techniques are described later in this chapter.)

Fiction can also be read critically, but the questions that apply are a little different:

1. Could this story really have happened?
2. Are the characters believable within the setting furnished by the story? Are they consistent in their actions?
3. Is the dialogue realistic?

4. Did the plot hold your interest? What was it that kept your interest?

5. Was the ending reasonable or believable? Why or why not?

6. Was the title well chosen? Why or why not?

Groups may be used for discussion of the reading material, whether all of the students have read the same selection or some of them have read different selections on a common topic or from a common genre. The students compose questions to be discussed by the group, with the group making the decision about which questions to consider. When questions have been selected, the students prepare for the group meeting by reading and/or rereading material to answer the questions, taking notes about their findings, and marking (with strips of paper or sticky notes) passages in the book that support their answers. During group discussions, students talk without holding up their hands for a turn or being called on. They respond to the comments and questions of the other group members. In this activity, analysis of the material is meaningful to the students: they decide what is significant in the material, and they relate the material to matters of importance to them, for example, how the author's use of language affects the story.

LITERATURE

Many excellent books for middle-school students have themes of honesty and dishonesty, courage and cowardice, and consequences of thoughtless or thoughtful behavior. Discussion of these themes in the context of the stories' characters, with consideration of alternatives available to them and of the appropriateness or inappropriateness of their actions, can build skill in critical reading. The students can be asked to compare the actions of the characters to standards of behavior set by the law, the school, parents, and so forth.

Resnick (1987) points out that "[h]igher order thinking often yields multiple solutions, each with costs and benefits, rather than unique solutions" and that "[h]igher order thinking involves imposing meaning, finding structure in apparent disorder" (p. 3). Literature analysis can help students become skillful in performing these tasks.

TECHNOLOGY

Computer simulations can give students the opportunity to use critical reading skills. Computer simulation programs set up situations that simulate real-life activities, such as running a business or traveling west in a wagon train, that cannot be offered in other ways in the curriculum because of limited time, changed conditions (when the past is being simulated), or limited financial and physical resources. Students examine the current situation and their options and make decisions about how to proceed. The computer responds to the students' decisions and presents different outcomes, depending on these decisions. This practice in evaluating options and drawing conclusions often seems more like play than study to students.

Geisert and Futrell (1995, p. 93) point out that a computer model "is not a complete rendition of reality, but it can be made sufficient to enable users to examine events and study relationships, such as the behavior of objects when colliding." Simulation programs can also be time-consuming to use, but if the programs can be saved and reentered from the same place in a later session, students will be likely to stay with them until a conclusion is reached. Motivation for using these programs is often high.

Students enjoy cooperative work with simulation programs (with discussion about each needed decision and collaborative decision making). Even university students can feel the excitement as they work as a group to complete a simulation activity designed for middle-school students. Discussion becomes animated and thoughtful, and logic is applied in arguments that try to sway others toward a particular decision.

Critical thinking is often important to the interpretation of humor. Therefore, humorous literature can be an enjoyable vehicle for teaching critical reading skills. It is especially good for determining the author's purpose (often to entertain, but sometimes also to convince through humor) and for evaluating content (especially distinguishing fact from fantasy and recognizing assumptions).

LITERATURE

To analyze characterization in literature selections, students must be able to make inferences about characters. Norton (1992a) believes teachers need to model the process of making inferences about characters for the students. They can read examples from a text, pause and verbalize a question that requires an inference, and answer the question, using supporting data from the text and making their reasoning process clear to the students. They can tell how their prior knowledge and beliefs affected the answer. Then students can be asked to attempt these same steps. Norton suggests the story *Shiloh* by Phyllis Reynolds Naylor as a good one for helping students learn to make inferences about characters.

Norton (1992a, p. 65) says that students must understand that making inferences requires going beyond the information stated in the text and that "they must use clues from the text to hypothesize about a character's emotions, beliefs, actions, hopes, and fears. Students must also be aware that authors develop characters through dialogue, narration, thoughts, and actions." This activity leads directly into character analysis.

Commeyras (1989) suggests the use of literature selections and a grid developed by Ashby-Davis (1986) to help students learn about character analysis. Example 4.2 shows a completed grid based on the character of Tom Sawyer. Such a grid leads students to collect evidence about a character, interpret the evidence, and make a generalization about the evidence after all of it has been collected. Looking for commonalities and discrepancies in the data and considering the amount of evidence available for a conclusion drawn are important to good critical analysis. When readers draw evidence from reactions of other characters in the story, they must evaluate the credibility of the sources before accepting the evidence.

DIVERSITY

Careful questioning by the teacher to extend limited and stereotyped depictions of people in reading materials can help students develop expertise in critical reading. Students must be encouraged to relate their personal experiences to the materials. They can examine stereotyped language in relation to stories in which it occurs, and teachers can point out the problems caused by looking at people and ideas in a stereotyped way (Zimet, 1983). For example, some books give the impression that certain nationalities have particular personality characteristics, but it should be easy to demonstrate that not all people of that nationality are alike, just as not all Americans are alike. Multicultural literature can be a vehicle through which teachers can create awareness of cultural variations and of negative biases that exist toward some groups, allowing progress to be made toward elimination of these biases (Barta and Grindler, 1996).

DIVERSITY

Having students compare different versions of folktales with Venn diagrams and comparison charts can help improve the students' comprehension and help them to see commonalities in stories from different cultures. Example 4.3 shows a comparison of a Russian folktale with an Appalachian one.

EXAMPLE 4.2 Sample Grid on Tom Sawyer

External clues	Student's interpretation
(1) Frequent kinds of statements made by this character	
A. Fibs	A. Tom gets his way.
B. Commands	B. Tom is confident.

My summary of these interpretations of statements:
Tom is bold and daring.

External clues	Student's interpretation
(2) Frequent actions of the character	
A. Mischievous	A. Tom likes to fool around.
B. Heroic	B. Tom isn't afraid.

My summary of these interpretations of actions:
Tom's good deeds are more important than his misbehavior.

External clues	Student's interpretation
(3) Frequent ways of thinking by this character:	
A. He schemes.	A. Tom finds solutions.
B. He's optimistic.	B. Tom has confidence.

My summary of these interpretations of thought:
Tom is smart.

External clues	Student's interpretation
(4) What do others frequently say to the character:	
A. What have you done?	A. Tom is unpredictable.
B. This is fun!	B. Tom has good ideas.

Summary of my interpretations of these statements:
Tom is independent in his actions.

External clues	Student's interpretation
(5) What do others do to this character:	
A. They get mad at him.	A. Tom upsets people.
B. They follow his lead.	B. Tom gets respect.

Summary of my interpretation:
Tom gets to people one way or another.

External clues	Student's interpretation
(6) What do others say about the character:	
A. He's stubborn.	A. Tom doesn't give up.
B. He's brave.	B. Tom helps others.

Summary of my interpretation:
Tom isn't all good or all bad.

My final generalization concerning the personality of Tom Sawyer:
Tom Sawyer is a boy who gets into trouble, but ends up doing the right thing in the end.

Source: Michelle Commeyras, "Using Literature to Teach Critical Thinking," *Journal of Reading*, 32 (May 1989), 703–707. Reprinted with permission of Michelle Commeyras and the International Reading Association.

EXAMPLE 4.3 Comparison of Folktales

Comparison of Two Stories

	Hardy Hardhead	Fool of the World and the Flying Ship
QUEST	To break enchantment and marry King's daughter	To provide flying ship to Czar and marry Czar's daughter
CHARACTERS	Two older brothers (Tom & Will) favored by parents	Two older brothers favored by parents
	Younger brother (Jack) – thought to be foolish	Younger brother – Fool of the World
	Old Man: Tom and Will didn't share; Jack shared food; Gave Jack a flying ship and money (Take in everyone)	Old man: Fool shared food; Showed Fool how to get flying ship (Take in everyone)
	[1]Hardy Hardhead	
	[2]Eatwell	[4]Man with bread
	[3]Drinkwell	[5]Man walking around lake
	[4]Runwell	[3]Man on one leg (other tied to head)
	[5]Harkwell	[1]Man listening to all that is being done in the world
	[6]Seewell	
	[7]Shootwell	[2]Man with gun
		[6]Man with wood on shoulders
		[7]Man with sack of straw
ACTION	Each person Jack picked up helped Jack win a bet with the witch.	Each person the Fool picked up helped him perform a seemingly impossible task for the Czar.
RESOLUTION	Jack paid back old man and kept ship. Enchantment on King's girl was broken.	Fool married princess. They fell in love with each other.

Note: The numbers beside the character names indicate the order in which the characters appear in the respective stories.

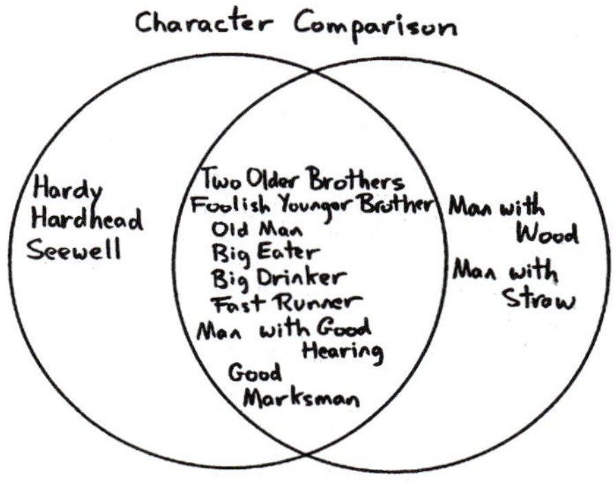

TECHNOLOGY

Teachers can also encourage students to think critically by having them compare film versions of stories with the text versions. Some movies are based on children's books and can serve as an introduction or follow-up to the reading of those books. Some books that have related movies are Patricia MacLachlan's *Sarah, Plain and Tall;* Louis Sachar's *Holes;* Wilson Rawls's *Where the Red Fern Grows;* Frances Hodgson Burnett's *The Secret Garden;* Katherine Paterson's *Bridge to Terabithia;* Natalie Babbitt's *Tuck Everlasting;* and Louise Fitzhugh's *Harriet, the Spy*. Students can use Venn diagrams to show how characters were alike and different in film and text versions of stories. They can also write film reviews, including notes about how true the film was to the book. These activities can help the students hone critical reading skills as they compare and contrast the books and films.

DIVERSITY

If the students have adequate schemata for understanding the text, it is better to have them read the text before seeing the film. Sometimes the story may be presented on film, but only a portion of the text version may be used in instruction. Then some students may be motivated to finish the text on their own. Most film versions are necessarily abbreviated versions. However, seeing an abbreviated presentation of a story that provides a knowledge of its basic structure may provide needed support for disabled readers, giving them confidence to attempt to read the text (Duncan, 1993).

Evaluating Factors Related to the Author

Krieger (1990) found that middle-school students paid no attention to the identities of the authors of the material they read and were not aware of the devices the authors used (flashbacks, foreshadowing, and so forth) for special purposes. She read to these

FOCUS ON STRATEGIES

Comparing Books and Videos

Two classes of middle-school students and their partners in a university methods class read the book *Bridge to Terabithia* at the same time. The middle-school students and the university students e-mailed each other about each section of the book as they read it. Both groups also viewed a videotape of a movie based on the book. They compared and contrasted the book and the video in e-mail messages. The middle-school students came out firmly in favor of the book. They felt that the movie at times differed from the book "for no reason at all," although they saw that some changes had been made because of time constraints. They commented, too, that many important details had been left out of the movie, making the character portrayals weaker.

A similar e-mail exchange took place with the same partners later for the book *Tuck Everlasting.* The participants also viewed a videotape of the movie based on this book. Once again, they compared and contrasted the movie and the book, with similar results. The middle-school students found many changes to be unnecessary and inexplicable and even decided that the impact of the plot, as it unfolded, was lessened because the movie contained some foreshadowing that was not in the book. The middle-school students' e-mail communications reflected thinking on all levels of Bloom's Taxonomy, and the university students were sometimes surprised at the higher-order thinking that their younger partners displayed (Roe and Smith, 1997).

students, modeling as she read her thinking processes concerning why the author included certain details. She asked them to make predictions about what might happen next from clues left by the author. Outside assignments based on the material allowed for further thinking about the story or the author by the students; students might be asked to keep listening journals with reactions to the stories, for example. Through this listening experience, Krieger opens the students' minds to the ways authors express ideas, making it more likely that they will be able to read stories with understanding later.

A critical literacy curriculum emphasizes discussion, both aloud and mental. "Students involved in a critical literacy curriculum read the world and the word, by using dialogue to engage texts and discourses inside and outside the classroom" (Cadiero-Kaplan, 2002, p. 377). Students who take this approach to reading history, for example, see it "as a record told from one perspective that can be examined from other perspectives" (p. 378). Acknowledging the bias that may be present in a particular point of view allows students to draw more valid conclusions from reading than they would if they accepted everything that is in print as true.

McKeown, Beck, and Worthy (1993) have developed a technique called Questioning the Author to help students access ideas in a text. They point out that someone wrote the ideas in the text and that some people do not write as clearly as others. Students are invited to figure out the ideas behind the author's words, determine the author's reasons for presenting the particular information, and decide whether the author has presented the ideas clearly. Then students are asked to state confusing material in a clearer way. Teachers should model this process for students before asking them to do it independently.

The mature critical reader must consider and evaluate factors related to the person who wrote the material, taking into account the following four categories.

Author's Purpose. The critical reader will try to determine whether the author wrote the material to inform, to entertain, to persuade, or for some other purpose. This is an interpretive reading skill.

Author's Point of View. The critical reader will want to know if the writer belonged to a political group, lived in a particular geographical area, or held a strong view that would tend to bias any opinions about a subject in one way or another. Two accounts of the Revolutionary War might be very different if one author was from Canada and the other from the United States.

Students can learn more about point of view by writing letters or essays about issues from different points of view. For example, they might take the point of view of a middle-school student, a concerned parent, or a principal when a school dress code is being considered.

Author's Style and Tone. The author's style is the manner in which he or she uses vocabulary (vividness, precision, inclusion of emotional words, use of figurative language) and sentence structure (the order within the language). Special attention should be given to use of figurative language, that is, language that is not meant to be taken literally, and use of emotional words, which do much to sway the reader toward or away from a point of view or attitude. (More information on figurative language is found in Chapter 2.) Note the effects of these two sentences:

Author 1: Next we heard the heart-rending cry of the wounded tiger.

Author 2: The tiger let out a vicious roar when it was shot.

Teachers should be aware of undesirable aspects of the style or tone of some writers of material for adolescents. Readers will quickly sense and resent a condescending tone.

Author's Competence. The reliability of written material is affected by the author's competence to write about the subject in question. If background information shows that a star football player has written an article on the nation's foreign policy, middle-school students will have little trouble determining that the reliability of the statements in this article is likely to be lower than the reliability of a similar article written by an experienced diplomat.

To determine an author's competence, students should consider his or her education and experience, referring to books such as *Current Biography Yearbook: 2002* (H. W. Wilson, 2002) and *Eighth Book of Junior Authors and Illustrators* (H. W. Wilson, 2000) or to book jacket flaps to find such information. Teachers can give students a topic and ask them to name people who might write about it. Students can discuss which people might be most qualified, or they can compare two authors of books on the same subject and decide which one is better qualified.

TECHNOLOGY

In these days of heavy use of Internet sites, determining the competence of authors is made more difficult. Students should be taught to be wary of material posted on the Internet by unknown authors or on sites that do not screen the material and provide information about the authors.

Evaluating the Material

Besides comprehending the material literally, the critical reader needs to be able to determine and evaluate several factors.

Timeliness. The critical reader will wish to check the date the material was published, because the timeliness of an article or a book can make a crucial difference in a rapidly changing world. An outdated social studies book, for example, may show incorrect boundaries for countries or fail to show some countries that now exist; similarly, an outdated science book may refer to a disease as incurable when a cure has recently been found.

Accuracy and Adequacy. Nonfiction material should be approached with this question in mind: "Are the statements presented here true?" The importance of a good background of experience becomes evident in this situation. A reader who has had previous experience with the material will have a basis of comparison not available to one lacking such experience. A person with even a little knowledge of a particular field can often spot such indications of inadequacy as exaggerated statements, one-sided presentations, and opinion offered as fact. Readers without experience in the subject can always check reference books to see if the statements in the material are supported elsewhere.

TECHNOLOGY

Material found on the Internet can pose a problem. As Owens, Hester, and Teale (2002, p. 623) point out, "Just because a site is listed in the first set of hits that appear on the search screen does not mean it is a legitimate or useful site." In some cases, companies or organizations pay fees to ensure that their site turns up at or near the top of specific searches. Students need to be led to see the potential biases that might be associated with such sites. Double-checking information in other reference materials is highly advisable when material from Internet sites is used. Brainstorming about the biases that are most likely to appear on specific sites is a good classroom activity.

Appropriateness. Critical readers must be able to determine whether the material is suitable for their purposes. A book or an article can be completely accurate and not be applicable to the problem or topic under consideration. For example, a student looking for information for a paper about Cherokee ceremonies needs to realize that an article on the invention of the Cherokee alphabet is irrelevant to the task at hand.

Inquiry Charts can be constructed in order to promote use of critical reading strategies (Hoffman, 1992). First, the class identifies a topic and formulates the questions that will be the basis of the inquiry. The teacher records these on a large I-Chart (see Example 4.4 for a sample I-Chart). Materials such as textbook selections, trade books, encyclopedia articles, magazine articles, and websites that pertain to the topic are also collected and listed on the I-Chart as they are used.

Next, the teacher questions the students to discover their prior knowledge about the topic and enters their responses, whether correct or incorrect, on the I-Chart under the identified questions. Information the students have that is not related to the identified questions is recorded under "Other Interesting Facts and Figures." If students have other questions that have not been identified, these are listed under "New Questions." Then the students read the source material independently or in a group, or the teacher reads it to them. Each source is discussed, and decisions are made about the appropriateness of the information in answering the identified questions. Information pertinent to the questions is recorded in the proper spaces. More "Interesting Facts" and "New Questions" may also be added.

After all sources have been read and information from them recorded, the students write summary statements to answer each question, considering the information from all of the sources. They also summarize the "Interesting Facts." Then the students compare what they had listed as prior knowledge with the newly acquired information and note the differences, clarifying any misconceptions previously held. Unanswered "New Questions" are researched further by individuals or small groups, who must decide about appropriate sources for the information, and findings are reported to the class.

Differentiating Fact from Opinion. This skill is vital for good critical reading. People often unquestioningly accept as fact anything they see in print, even though printed material is often composed of statements of opinion. Some authors intermingle facts and opinions, giving little indication that they are presenting anything but pure fact.

Some readers have trouble reading critically because they lack a clear idea of what constitutes a fact. Facts are statements that can be verified through direct observation, consultation of official records of past events, or scientific experimentation. The statement "General Lee surrendered to General Grant at Appomattox" is a fact that can be verified by checking historical records. For various reasons, opinions cannot be directly verified. For example, the statement "She is the most beautiful girl in the world" is unverifiable and is therefore an opinion. Even if every girl in the world could be

EXAMPLE 4.4 I-Chart

I - CHART

GUIDING QUESTIONS

TOPIC: Columbus	1. Why did Columbus sail?	2. What did he find?	3. What important things did he do when he got there?	4. How was Columbus regarded by others?	Other Interesting Facts & Figures	New Questions
WHAT WE KNOW	to prove the world was round	America	... not sure	He was a hero	He sailed in 1492 He was Spanish	Did he have a family?
SOURCES 1. Meet Christopher Columbus, de Kay New York: Random House, 1989	He was trying to find a new route to the Indies	He found friendly Indians... some pieces of gold... different islands. He found America	He named the islands. He claimed the land for Queen Isabella and King Ferdinand. He brought back gold for Isabella	At the beginning people regarded him as a normal person. Later, when he got back, they thought he was a great man.	C.C. had asked the King of Portugal for ships. He was turned down. When he came back he landed in Portugal and was taken to the King. The King was mad that he didn't help him.	Whatever happened to his son?
2. The World Book Encyclopedia. World Book Childcraft, Inc. 1979	to find riches... and a shorter route to the Indies. He wanted to be famous... to be known as a great sailor and explorer.	He found America. Indians... new islands.	He named the islands. He captured some Indians as slaves. He became the governor.	He was an "understanding... dreamy" person. It sounds like he had a lot of friends	In other books I've read he wasn't very popular. He had 2 sons, not 1... Six brothers and a sister. He was born in Italy.	Whatever happened to his sons?
3. Where do You Think You're Going Christopher Columbus? Jean Fritz. New York G.P. Putnam's Sons, 1980	Because he liked to travel and explore they said they would give a big reward for finding a new route to the Indies	He found Indians... Some small hunks of gold	He talked to the Indians. He asked for directions to the Palace of the Khan. He named the islands	Before he went he was wealthy because he had married a rich woman. He was famous after he sailed, but a couple of years later, everyone forgot about him.	Columbus sounded greedy in this book. He said he saw land first and claimed the prize money. He claimed that all of this was God's work.	Was he really cruel to the Indians? Whatever happened to the slaves he brought back to Spain?
SUMMARY	To find a new route to the Indies... He hoped to find riches and become famous as an explorer. He already knew the world was round.	He found America and the Indians living there. He found a little gold.	He claimed the new land for Spain. He named the islands. He met with the Indians. He took some back to Spain as slaves. He became Governor.	Before he sailed he was normal... a dreamer. After he came back he was famous and a hero. He seemed greedy. Everyone forgot about him after a while.	He claimed he was doing God's work. His family supported him. He tried to get money for his voyage from lots of people. He was born an Italian.	Find out more about his family and what happened to them. Was he cruel to the Indians? What happened to the slaves?

Source: James V. Hoffman. "Critical Reading/Thinking Across the Curriculum: Using I-Charts to Support Learning." *Language Arts*, February 1992.

assembled for comparison, people's standards of beauty differ and a scale of relative beauty would be impossible to construct.

Many readers are not alert to clues that signal opinions. Knowledge of key words that signal opinions, such as *believe, think, seems, may, appears, probably, likely,* and *possibly,* can be extremely helpful to readers. By pointing out these clues and providing practice in discrimination, teachers can promote the ability to discriminate between facts and opinions.

Students must also understand that not all opinions are of equal value, since some have been based on facts, whereas others are unsupported. Critical readers try to determine the relative merit of opinions as well as to separate the opinions from the facts.

Newspaper editorials offer one good way for students to practice distinguishing fact from opinion. They can underline each sentence in the editorial with colored pencils—one color for facts and another for opinions. They can then be encouraged to discuss which opinions are best supported by facts.

Furleigh (1991) has students read and analyze an editorial for the subject or main idea, the writer's opinion about the subject, and their own opinions about the subject. The teacher or peers then evaluate the answers each student provides. When peers do the evaluations, the evaluations become additional practice sessions for them.

Activities similar to the Model Activity below may also be used to help students make this difficult differentiation.

LITERATURE 

Recognition of Propaganda Techniques. Middle-school students, like adults, are constantly deluged with writing that attempts to influence their thinking and actions. Some of these materials may be used for good purposes and some for bad ones. For example, most people would consider propaganda designed to persuade people to protect their health as "good" and propaganda intended to persuade people to do things that are harmful to their health as "bad." Since propaganda techniques are often used to sway people toward or away from a cause or point of view, students should be made aware of these techniques so that they can avoid being unduly influenced by them.

The Institute for Propaganda Awareness has identified seven undesirable ***propaganda techniques*** that good critical readers should know about:

1. Name-calling—using derogatory labels (*reactionary, troublemaker*) to create negative reactions toward a person without providing evidence to support such impressions

MODEL ACTIVITIES

Fact and Opinion

Give the students copies of the following paragraph, which opens the book *Homesick: My Own Story* by Jean Fritz (1982, p. 9):

> In my father's study there was a large globe with all the countries of the world running around it. I could put my finger on the exact spot where I was and had been ever since I'd been born. And I was on the wrong side of the globe. I was in China in a city named Hankow, a dot on a crooked line that seemed to break the country right in two. The line was really the Yangtse River, but who would know by looking at a map what the Yangtse River really was?

Ask students to read this opening paragraph carefully, underlining any part or parts that are statements of opinion, based on the definition of opinion that was discussed in class. Ask them to decide what they can tell about the main character from both the facts and the opinions revealed in this opening paragraph. Then have them decide how the located opinion or opinions are likely to affect the story about to be read.

Let the students share their reactions to this opening passage before they begin to read the book. After they have finished reading the book, have them discuss whether or not their initial reactions were accurate.

2. Glittering generalities—using vague phrases to influence a point of view without providing necessary specifics
3. Transfer technique—associating a respected organization or symbol with a particular person, project, product, or idea, thus transferring that respect to the person or thing being promoted
4. Plain-folks talk—relating a person (for example, a politician) or a proposed program to the "common people" in order to gain their support
5. Testimonial technique—using a highly popular or respected person to endorse a product or proposal
6. Bandwagon technique—playing on the urge to do what others are doing by giving the impression that everyone else is participating in a particular activity
7. Card stacking—telling only one side of a story by ignoring information that favors the opposing point of view

Teachers should describe propaganda techniques to the class and model the process of locating these techniques in printed materials such as advertisements. Then the students should practice this skill. They can learn to detect propaganda techniques by analyzing newspaper and magazine advertisements, printed political campaign material, and requests for donations to various organizations.

LITERATURE

Making Value Judgments. Readers need to be able to determine whether the actions of both fictional and real-life characters are reasonable or unreasonable. To help students develop this ability, teachers may ask questions such as the following:

Should Maniac Magee have left the Beales' house when he did? Why or why not? Did he do it for a good reason? Why or why not?

In *On My Honor,* was it reasonable for Joel to lie about Tony's drowning? Why did he do it?

Was it a good thing for Heidi to save bread from the Sesemanns' table to take back to the grandmother? Why or why not?

Readers draw on their schemata related to right and wrong actions in order to complete this type of activity. Because of their varying schemata, not all students will answer in the same way.

Activities like the following ones can be used to provide students with practice in critical reading strategies:

- Have a propaganda hunt. Label boxes with the names of the seven propaganda techniques listed earlier. Then ask students to find examples of these techniques in a variety of sources; cut out, photocopy, or hand-copy each example; and drop their examples into the boxes. As a class activity, evaluate each example for appropriateness to the category in which it was placed.
- Have students compare editorials from two newspapers with different viewpoints or from different cities. Have them decide why differences exist and which stand, if either, is more reasonable, based on facts.

- Ask students to compare two biographies of a well-known person by answering questions such as "How do they differ in their treatment of the subject? Is either of the authors likely to be biased for or against the subject? Are there contradictory statements in the two works? If so, which one seems more likely to be correct? Could the truth be different from both accounts?"
- Use computer simulation programs for practice in making critical judgments. These programs provide simulated models of real-life experiences with which students can experiment in a risk-free manner.
- Ask students to examine newspaper articles for typographical errors and to determine whether or not each typographical error changed the message of the article.
- Have the class interpret political cartoons from various newspapers.
- Ask students to examine the headlines of news stories and decide if the headlines fit the stories.
- Ask students to write editorials about topics of interest. Their editorials should include facts, their own opinions, and their reasons for the opinions.
- Locate old science or geography books containing statements that are no longer true, and use them to show the importance of using current sources. Let students compare old and new books to find the differences (for example, new material included or "facts" that have changed), and discuss what types of material are most and least likely to be dependent on recent copyright dates for accuracy (Ross, 1981).
- Direct students to write material that will persuade their classmates to do something. Then examine the material for the techniques they used.
- Discuss the nutritional aspects of sugar and chemical food additives and the foods that contain them. Then have students examine the ingredient lists from popular snacks, asking themselves what food value various snacks have, according to their labels (Neville, 1982).

TIME for REFLECTION

Some teachers tell students that they should believe certain things "because it says so in the book." Others tell them, "Don't believe everything that you read." **What would *you* tell students, and why?**

Creative Reading

Creative reading involves going beyond the material presented by the author. Like critical reading, creative reading requires readers to think as they read, and it also requires them to use their imaginations. Such reading results in the production of new ideas.

Teachers must carefully nurture creative reading, trying not to ask only questions that have absolute answers, since such questions may discourage the diverse processes characteristic of creative reading. To go beyond the material in the text, readers must make use of their background schemata, combining this prior knowledge with ideas from the text to produce a new response based on, but not completely dictated by, the text. Creative readers must be skilled in predicting outcomes, visualizing the things they read about, solving problems, and producing their own creations.

Predicting Outcomes

Predicting outcomes, discussed earlier as a good purpose-setting technique, is a creative reading skill. In order to predict outcomes, readers must put together available information and note trends, then project the trends into the future, making decisions about what events might logically follow. A creative reader is constantly predicting what will happen next in a story, reacting to the events he or she is reading about and drawing conclusions about their results.

An enjoyable way to work on this skill is to have students read an action comic strip in the newspaper for several weeks and then predict what will happen next, based on their knowledge of what has occurred until that time. The teacher can record these predictions on paper and file them; later, students can compare the actual ending of the adventure with their predictions. The teacher should be sure students can present reasons to justify what they predict. When judging their theories, the teacher should point out that some predictions may seem as good a way to end the story as the one the comic strip artist used. Other predictions may not make sense, based on the evidence, and reasons for this should be made clear.

Another way to work on prediction is to stop students at particular points in their reading of a literature selection and let them predict what will happen next. In the book *The Great Gilly Hopkins* by Katherine Paterson, for example, the teacher would stop when Gilly finds out that she is being sent to her grandmother's house and ask what the students think will happen next. They should be asked to give reasons for their answers.

To help students acquire creative reading skill, teachers can also model the thought processes involved in answering "what if" questions. After the students practice on various texts, the teacher can ask them to explain their reasons for thinking as they did. Some questions they might answer for Johanna Spyri's *Heidi,* for example, are as follows:

- What would have happened in the book if Peter had not pushed Klara's wheelchair down the side of the mountain?
- What would have happened if Herr Sesemann had refused to send Heidi back to the Alm, even though the doctor advised it?

A possible question from Andrew Clements's *Frindle* is:

- What would have happened if the students had not defied the teacher and continued to use the word *frindle*?

Possible questions from Mildred Taylor's *The Land* are as follows:

- What would have happened differently in the book if Paul had not taken the blame for riding Ghost Wind and allowing him to be injured, even though it was Mitchell who had caused the injury?
- What would have happened in the book if Miz Crenshaw hadn't hidden Paul and Mitchell on the train?

Visualization

When readers draw on their existing schemata to see pictures in their minds, they are engaging in ***visualization.*** By vividly visualizing the events depicted by the author's words, creative readers allow themselves to become a part of the story; they see the colors, hear the sounds, feel the textures, taste the flavors, and smell the odors the writer describes. They will find that they are living the story as they read. By doing this, they will enjoy the story more and understand it more deeply.

Students can be encouraged to see pictures in their minds as they read silently. Such *guided imagery* has been shown to enhance comprehension and can help with later recall of events read. Guided imagery can be used before reading, as well as during or after reading. Guided imagery activities before reading a story can help readers draw on their past experiences to visualize events, places, and things in a story. Creating such images before reading has been shown to result in better literal comprehension than is produced by creating the images after reading (Fredericks, 1986; Harp, 1988).

Dee Mundell suggests four steps for helping students develop techniques for visualization. First, teachers should lead students to visualize concrete objects after they have seen and closely examined them in the classroom. Then teachers can ask students to visualize objects or experiences outside the classroom. They can draw the objects they visualize and compare their drawings to the actual objects later. Next, teachers can read high-imagery stories to their classes, letting individuals share their mental images with the group and having small groups illustrate the stories after the reading. Finally, teachers should encourage students to visualize as they read independently (Fredericks, 1986).

Open-ended questions can aid development of imagery. For example, if a student says she sees a house, the teacher can ask, "What does it look like?" If she replies that it is white with green trim, the teacher may ask, "What is the yard like?"

Following are activities that encourage visualization:

- Give students copies of a paragraph from a book that vividly describes a scene or a situation, and have them illustrate the scene or situation in a painting or a three-dimensional art project.
- Using a paragraph or statement that contains almost no description, ask students questions about details they would need in order to picture the scene in their minds. An example follows.

  The dog ran toward Shyra and Susan. Shyra held out her hands toward it and smiled.

  Questions: What kind of dog was it? How big was it? Why was it running toward the girls? What happened when the dog reached the girls? Where did this action take place? Was the dog on a leash, behind a fence, or running free?

- Have the students dramatize a story they have read, such as the scene in *Bridge to Terabithia* in which Leslie races the boys.

- Compare the characters, action, and scenery in a movie with mental images formed from reading a book or story (Rasinski, 1988).

Solving Problems

LITERATURE 

Creative readers relate the things they read to their own personal problems, sometimes applying the solution of a problem they encounter in a story to a different situation. For instance, after reading the chapter in *Tom Sawyer* in which Tom tricks his friends into painting a fence for him, a student may use a similar ruse to persuade a sibling to take over his or her chores or homework.

To work on developing this problem-solving skill, teachers need to use books in which different types of problems are solved, choosing an appropriate one to read or to have the class read. Then the teacher can ask the class questions such as the following:

1. What problem did the character(s) in the story face?
2. How was the problem handled?
3. Was the solution a good one?
4. What other possible solutions can you think of?
5. Would you prefer the solution in the book or one of the others?

Literature selections abound with characters trying to solve problems in efficient and inefficient ways. Students can analyze these problem-solving situations. Problems in a story can be identified as they occur. Discussion of the situation can take place at each problem occurrence. Some element of the story can be changed, and the students can then be asked how the character would have handled the new situation (Beck, 1989). The *Encyclopedia Brown* mysteries by Donald Sobol offer good problem-solving opportunities for students in intermediate grades and less proficient students in middle school; more proficient middle-school students may find *The Westing Game* by Ellen Raskin and *Wolf Rider* by Avi to be interesting problem-solving mysteries.

Bransford and Stein's IDEAL approach to problem solving is good to use in conjunction with cooperative learning techniques (Bransford and Stein, 1984; Flynn, 1989). The *I* stands for *identifying* the problem, the *D* for *defining* the problem more clearly, the *E* for *exploration* of the problem, the *A* for *acting* on ideas, and the *L* for *looking* for the effects. Cooperative learning techniques encourage the development of problem-solving skills through discussion, negotiation, clarification of ideas, and evaluation of the ideas of classmates. These activities help students meet their group and individual goals.

Producing New Creations

Art, drama, and dance can be useful in elaborating on what students read. By creating a new ending for a story, adding a new character, changing some aspect of a character, or adding an additional adventure within the framework of the existing story, students approach reading creatively. Following are some possible activities:

- Ask students to illustrate a story they have read, using a series of pictures or three-dimensional scenes. These pictures may be displayed on a webpage, on a bulletin board, or in a class or personal book.

TECHNOLOGY

- Have students write plays or poems based on works of fiction they have read and enjoyed. These productions may be published on a webpage, in a class or personal book, or in a class literary magazine.
- Have the students write prose narratives based on a poem they have read. These narratives may be shared orally or in writing.

TECHNOLOGY

- After the students have read several stories of a certain type (such as mysteries), ask each of them to write an original story of the same type. These stories may be collected in a class or personal book or displayed on a webpage.
- Have the students transfer the story of *Heidi* to the Rocky Mountains or to Appalachia. Ask them to describe what caused them to make various changes.

TECHNOLOGY

- Have the students make their own videotapes of class presentations or field trips. They can write scripts for skits or plays, do the casting, rehearse for the performances, videotape the productions, and edit the tapes until they have polished products. Creative drama and readers' theater performances can also be videotaped. Simulated newscasts can be written, dramatized, and videotaped, with editing as a final step. These activities involve many technological and higher-order thinking skills. A reference for teachers interested in creation of such tapes is *Creating Videos for School Use* (Valmont, 1995).

TECHNOLOGY

As described in the Focus on Strategies on Creating Multimedia Productions on page 167, students can also gain and use computer skills while producing new creations. Sefton-Green (2001, p. 728) points out, however, that "working in new media needs to be taught. The skill will not spontaneously erupt from young people, even from the ones who gain other kinds of literacy learning beyond school." This instruction should include work with video productions and work with computer presentations and productions. Teachers may want to guide their classes in developing their own Web home pages (Cotton, 1996). Many classes have done this, and the students have posted everything from creative writing to research reports to results of scientific experiments. Materials produced by students in the course of some of the activities listed above can be included in the class website. Class newspapers or magazines may be published on the webpages. It is possible to include text, graphics, photographs, and animations. Since webpages can be accessed from all over the world, the motivation for accuracy and clarity of information presented is great. Students may therefore be more inclined to revise and edit material.

Effective Questioning

STANDARDS AND ASSESSMENT

All teachers use both written and oral questions as a part of class activities. They may ask questions as a way of setting purposes for students' reading, in discussions, or on tests and quizzes. Regardless of when they are used, questions have been found to foster increased comprehension, apparently because readers give more time to the material related to answering them (Durkin, 1981). Students also remember best information about which they have been directly questioned. Additionally, the types of

FOCUS ON STRATEGIES

Creating Multimedia Productions

The two middle-school classes described in the previous Focus on Strategies on comparing and contrasting books and videos developed a computer multimedia presentation on each of the books that they read along with their university partners, and the university partners viewed the presentations just before the end-of-semester meetings.

The middle-school classroom teachers organized their classes into cooperative groups to work on specific portions of the multimedia presentation and developed a schedule for the group assignments. Each group produced a rough draft to show what it planned to do. Then each group used the computer to create its portion of the presentation. To do this, the students had to make decisions about important incidents to include, sequence to follow, visual and sound features to incorporate, transitions to use, and other considerations. They used *mPower,* a multimedia publishing program, to develop a series of carefully designed and sequenced slides that represented main events and characters in the books. They incorporated student-produced drawings, photography, and music to develop powerful presentations of content. The university students were impressed by the professional appearance and the thoroughness of the presentations. Such productions required a depth of understanding of the material that went far beyond the ability to describe the stories in words (Roe and Smith, 1997).

questions that teachers ask about selections affect the type of information that students recall about selections (Wixson, 1983). Research indicates, for example, that asking more inference questions during and after reading stories results in improved inferential comprehension (Hansen and Pearson, 1983; Pearson, 1985). Because questions have such a strong influence on student learning, teachers need to understand thoroughly the process of preparing questions.

Farrar (1984a) asserts that the phrasing of questions should depend on the amount of challenge individual students need. Questions can be phrased differently and still address the same content. The phrasing can make questions easier or harder to answer and can require simple or complex answers. It may take several questions requiring simple responses to elicit all the information obtainable from one question that requires a complex response.

Wiggins and McTighe (1998, p. 28) assert, "To get at matters of deep and enduring understanding, we need to use provocative and multilayered questions that reveal the richness and complexities of a subject. We refer to such questions as 'essential' because they point to the key inquiries and the core ideas of a discipline." Wiggins and McTighe recommend using essential questions as the central focus of courses, units, and lessons. They suggest that teachers use relatively few of these questions for a unit (two to five) and that they plan concrete activities and inquiries related to each one. Teachers should word essential questions so that students can understand them and should develop initial assessment tasks to show if students understand the question focus. In addition, teachers should order questions about a central concept from simple to complex. The questions asked early in the unit should always point toward the larger essential questions, and teachers should lead the students to ask broader questions

The types of questions that teachers ask about selections affect the type of information that students recall about selections, and students remember best the information about which they have been directly questioned.
(© Elizabeth Crews)

prompted by their answers to ones more narrowly cast. Wiggins and McTighe (1998, p. 35) suggest introductory questions such as "In what ways is a fairy tale 'true'? In what ways is any documentary 'false'? (Can be used to compare myths, novels, biographies, histories, and docudramas.)" Guiding a unit of study through essential questions can also help address diversity in academic ability in a classroom, since essential questions can prompt gifted and talented students to explore the central, significant ideas of a discipline through independent learning and inquiry.

DIVERSITY

Preparing Questions

Teachers often ask questions they devise on the spur of the moment. This practice no doubt results from the pressure of the many different tasks a teacher must perform during the day, but it is a poor one for at least two reasons. First, questions developed hastily, without close attention to the material, tend to be detail questions ("What color was the car? Where were they going?"), since detail questions are much easier to construct than most other types. But detail questions fail to measure more than simple recall. Second, many hastily constructed questions tend to be poorly worded, vague in intent, and misleading to students. Example 4.5 shows some options on which to base questioning.

Questions Based on Comprehension Factors

One basis for planning questioning strategies is to try to construct specific types of questions to tap different types of comprehension and different factors related to comprehension. Seven major types of questions are generally useful in guiding reading: main idea, detail, vocabulary, sequence, inference, evaluation, and creative response.

EXAMPLE 4.5 Options for Questioning

Questions Based on Comprehension Factors

Main idea—identify the central theme or idea of selection

Detail—identify the directly stated facts

Vocabulary—define words to fit the context of the selection

Sequence—identify the order of events in selection

Inference—infer information implied by the author

Evaluation—judge ideas presented, based on a standard

Creative response—go beyond the material and create new ideas based on the material read

Questions Based on Source of Answers

Textually explicit—answers directly stated in the text

Textually implicit—answers implied by the text that require inferences on the part of the reader

Scriptually implicit—answers come from the reader's background knowledge

Questions Based on Story Grammar

Setting—when and where the story took place and who was involved

Initiating event—event that started the story sequence

Reaction—the main character's reaction to the initiating event

Action—the main character's actions caused by the initiating event and subsequent events

Consequence—the result of main character's actions

Main Idea Questions. Main idea questions ask readers to identify the central theme of the selection. These questions may give readers some direction toward the nature of the answer. The question "What caused Crystal to act so excited?" could direct readers toward the main idea of a passage in which Crystal was very excited because she was going to meet her newly adopted sister. An example of a question that offers no clues to the main idea is "What is a sentence that explains what this selection is about?" Main idea questions help students to become aware of the relationships among details.

Detail Questions. Detail questions ask for bits of information covered by the material, such as "Who was coming to study with Maria? What was Betty bringing with her? What happened to Betty on the way to Maria's house? When did Betty finally arrive? Where had Betty left her bicycle?" Whereas it is important for students to assimilate the information these questions cover, very little depth of comprehension is necessary to answer them all correctly. Therefore, although these questions are easy to construct, they should not constitute the bulk of the questions the teacher asks.

STANDARDS AND ASSESSMENT

Vocabulary Questions. Vocabulary questions check readers' understanding of word meanings, generally as used in a particular selection. For discussion purposes, a teacher might ask students to produce as many meanings of a specific word as they can, but purpose-setting questions and test questions should ask for the meaning of a word as it is used in the selection being read.

Sequence Questions. Sequence questions check the readers' knowledge of the order in which events occurred in the story. The question "What did Alex and Robbie do when their parents left the house?" is not a sequence question, since students are free to list the events in any order they choose. The question "What three things did Alex and Robbie do, in order, when their parents left the house?" requires students to display their grasp of the sequence of events.

Inference Questions. Inference questions ask for information that is implied but not directly stated in the material. These questions require some reading between the lines. The following is an example:

> Margie and Jan were sitting on the couch listening to Linkin Park CDs. Their father walked in and announced, "I hear that there is a Linkin Park concert at the Municipal Auditorium next week." Both girls jumped up and ran toward their father. "Can we go? Can we go?" they begged.
>
> *Question:* Do you think Margie and Jan liked to hear the music of Linkin Park? Why or why not?

Evaluation Questions. Evaluation questions require readers to make judgments about the material. Although these judgments are inferences, they depend on more than the information implied or stated by the story; the readers must have enough experience related to the situations involved to establish standards for comparison. An

STANDARDS AND ASSESSMENT

example of an evaluation question is "Was the method Kim used to rescue Dana wise? Why or why not?" These questions are excellent for open-ended class discussion but hard to grade as test questions.

STANDARDS AND ASSESSMENT

Creative Response Questions. Creative response questions ask readers to go beyond the material and create new ideas based on the ideas they have read. Questions requiring creative response are also good for class discussions. As a means of testing comprehension of a passage, however, they are not desirable, since almost any response could be considered correct. Examples of creative response questions include "If the story stopped after Jimmy lost his money, what ending would you write for it?" and "If Meg had not gone to school that day, what do you think might have happened?"

Other Categorizations of Question Types

Pearson and Johnson (1978) suggest three question types. They label questions as *textually explicit* when they have answers that are directly stated in the text, *textually implicit* when they have implied answers (but the text contains clues for making the necessary inference), and *scriptually implicit* when the reader must answer them from his or her background knowledge.

The reader's own characteristics interact with the text and the question to determine the actual demands of the question-answering task. A reader's interest, background knowledge, and reading skill affect the difficulty and type of question for each reader. The structure of a question may lead a teacher to expect a textually explicit response, whereas the student's background may cause him or her to give a scriptually implicit response (Wixson, 1983). For example, if the text tells readers how to construct a kite, a student who has actually made a kite before reading the material may answer the question on the basis of direct experience rather than from information presented in the text.

Inability to take the perspective of another person can affect comprehension. Students who can take the perspective of another person do better on scriptually implicit questions than those who cannot (Gardner and Smith, 1987).

Story Grammar as a Basis for Questioning

Another basis for questioning deserves attention: use of story grammar. A story is a series of events that are related to one another in particular ways. As people hear and read many stories, they develop expectations, sometimes called story schemata, about the types of things they will encounter; these help them organize information. Related story schemata are described by a ***story grammar.*** (The influence of story grammars on comprehension is discussed in Chapter 3.) As Sadow (1982) suggests, questions based on a story grammar may help readers develop story schemata. The questions should be chosen to reflect the logical sequence of events.

David Rumelhart proposed a simple story grammar that "describes a story as consisting of a setting and one or more episodes" (Sadow, 1982, p. 519). The setting includes the main characters and the time and location of the events, and each episode contains an initiating event, the main character's reaction to it, an action of the main character caused by this reaction, and a consequence of the action, which may act as an initiating event for a subsequent episode. (Sometimes some of the elements of an episode are not directly stated.) Sadow suggests the following five generic questions as appropriate types to ask about a story:

1. Where and when did the events in the story take place, and who was involved in them? (setting)
2. What started the chain of events in the story? (initiating event)
3. What was the main character's reaction to this event? (reaction)
4. What did the main character do about it? (action)
5. What happened as a result of what the main character did? (consequence) (Sadow, 1982, p. 520)

Such questions can help students see the underlying order of ideas in a story, but of course teachers should reword them to fit the story and the particular students. For example, question 1 can be broken into three questions (*where, when, who*), and the teacher can provide appropriate focus by using words or phrases from the story. After students address these story grammar questions, which establish the essential facts, they should answer questions that help them relate the story to their own experiences and knowledge (Sadow, 1982).

Marshall (1983) has also suggested using story grammar as a basis for developing comprehension questions. In Marshall's questioning scheme, *theme* questions are similar to main idea questions and ask about the major point or moral of the story. As in Sadow's questioning scheme, *setting* questions are *where* and *when* questions, but *character* questions ask about the main character and other characters. *Initiating events* questions often ask about a problem that a particular character faces. *Attempts* questions ask what a character did about a situation or what he or she will do. *Resolution* questions ask how a character solved the problem or what the reader would do to solve the problem. *Reaction* questions focus on what a character felt, the reasons for a character's actions or feelings, or the feelings of the reader.

STANDARDS AND ASSESSMENT

Guidelines for Preparation

Some guidelines for preparing questions may be useful to teachers who wish to improve their questioning techniques. The following suggestions may help teachers avoid some pitfalls that other educators have detected:

1. In trying to determine overall comprehension skills, ask a variety of questions designed to reflect different types of comprehension. Avoid overloading the evaluation with a single type of question.
2. Don't ask questions about obscure or insignificant portions of the selection. Such questions may make a test harder, but they don't convey realistic indications of comprehension. "Hard" tests and "good" tests are not necessarily synonymous.
3. Avoid ambiguous or tricky questions. If a question has two or more possible interpretations, more than one answer for it has to be acceptable.

4. Avoid useless questions. Questions that a person who has not read the material can answer correctly offer no valuable information about his or her comprehension.

5. Don't ask questions in language that is more difficult than the language of the selection the question is about. Sometimes you can word questions in a way that prevents a student who knows the answer from responding appropriately.

6. Make sure the answers to sequence questions require knowledge of the order of events. Don't confuse questions that simply ask for lists with sequence questions.

7. Don't ask for unsupported opinions when you are testing for comprehension. Have students give support for their opinions, by asking them, "Why do you think that?" or "What in the story made you think that?" If you ask for an unsupported opinion, any answer will be correct.

8. Don't ask for opinions if you want facts. Ask for the type of information you want to receive.

9. Avoid questions that give away information. Instead of asking, "What makes you believe the boy was angry?" ask, "How do you think the boy felt? Why?" Questions may lead students to the answers by supplying too much information.

10. Use precise terms in phrasing questions related to reading. Ask students to compare or contrast, predict, or draw conclusions about the reading (Smith, 1989).

Helping Students Answer Questions

DIVERSITY

Some students lack familiarity with the question-answer-feedback sequence often used for instructional purposes. They may not have been exposed to this language pattern at home and find it strange and confusing that the teacher is asking for information he or she already knows. Teachers may need to teach the question-answer-feedback strategy in oral and written situations directly so that students will respond appropriately (Farrar, 1984b). Teacher modeling of the answers to questions is helpful. In the process, the teacher can explain how to interpret the question, how and where to find the information, and how to construct the answer after the information is located (Armbruster, 1992).

Raphael and Pearson (1982) taught students three types of Question-Answer Relationships (QARs). QAR instruction encourages students to consider both information in the text and their own background knowledge when answering questions (Raphael, 1986). The relationship for questions with answers directly stated in the text in one sentence was called "Right There." The students looked for the words in the question and read the sentence containing those words to locate the answer. The relationship for questions with an answer in the story that required information from multiple sentences or paragraphs was called "Think and Search," and the relationship for questions for which answers had to come from the reader's own knowledge was called "On My Own" (Raphael and Pearson, 1982). Modeling the decision about question-answer relationships and correct answers based on them was an important part of the teaching. Supervised practice following the modeling, with immediate feedback on student responses, was also important. The practice involved gradually increased passage lengths, progressing from simpler to more difficult tasks (Raphael, 1982). Learning the three types of QARs enhanced students' success in answering questions. The training appeared to help average- and low-ability students most (Raphael, 1984).

Raphael (1986) subsequently modified QAR instruction to include four categories, clustered under two headings. Example 4.6 illustrates this modification.

In the modified scheme, the "In My Head" category is divided into questions that involve both the text information and the reader's background of experiences (Author and You) and those that can be answered from the reader's experience without information from the story (On My Own) (Raphael, 1986).

Discussing the use of the QAR categorization to plan questioning strategies, Raphael (1986) states:

> Questions asked prior to reading are usually On My Own QARs. They are designed to help students think about what they already know and how it relates to the upcoming story or content text. In creating guided reading questions, it is important to balance text-based and inference questions. For these, Think and Search QARs should dominate, since they require integration of information and should build to the asking of Author and

EXAMPLE 4.6 Question-Answer Relationships (QARs)

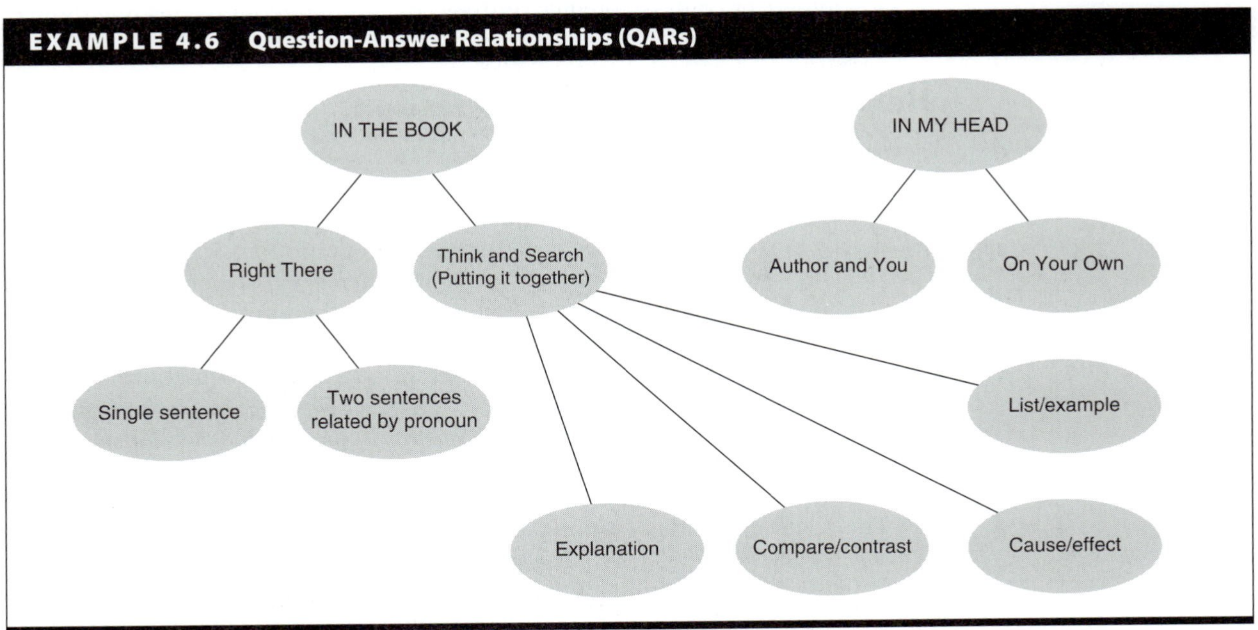

Source: Taffy E. Raphael. "Teaching Question-Answer Relationships, Revisited," *The Reading Teacher*, 39 (February 1986), 516–522. Reprinted with permission of Taffy E. Raphael and the International Reading Association.

> You QARs. Finally, for extension activities, teachers will want to create primarily On My Own or Author and You QARs, focusing again on students' background information as it pertains to the text. (p. 521)

Mesmer and Hutchins (2002) discovered that a group of fifth-grade students had problems interpreting graphic aids in order to answer questions about them. (See Chapter 7 for a discussion of the attributes of graphic aids.) The educators realized that a complex, multistep process is involved in answering questions from the information in graphic aids. "Students must first read a related question, then read and analyze the graphic, determine the answer, locate the answer within a list of options, and record the selection on an answer sheet" (p. 22). Mesmer and Hutchins had been trying to teach students to use a QAR framework to answer questions from graphic aids in expository materials. They found that the students tended to treat all questions related to a graphic aid as Right There types, when they could be any type, including those that require use of background knowledge, and that they did not pay attention to the details on the graphics, such as units of measure and titles. The students often assumed that the graphic's information was going to answer the question and failed to pay close attention to the question itself. Learning the characteristics of different kinds of graphic aids was important to helping students answer questions about the aids. After receiving instruction about graphic aids, students were given direct instruction in using the QAR strategy to answer questions about these aids. This proved to be a useful strategy that improved metacognitive and test-taking skills.

STANDARDS AND ASSESSMENT

Helping Students Question

Active readers constantly question the text. As they construct meaning, they ask themselves, "Does this make sense?" Questions about why the material being presented makes sense, also referred to as *elaborative interrogation,* can help students remember the texts better, perhaps because these questions cause students to consider their prior knowledge and relate it to the material (Pressley, 2001).

Many authorities advocate teaching the reader to generate questions throughout the reading process to enhance comprehension, and such training has proven to be effective. Students who are trained to ask literal questions about material they are reading have learned to discriminate questions from nonquestions and good literal questions from poor ones. After they practiced the production of good literal questions for paragraphs and then for stories that they read to answer the questions, their comprehension improved (Cohen, 1983). Other students who were taught (through modeling, with gradual phasing out of teacher involvement) to generate their own questions based on a story grammar also had better comprehension (Nolte and Singer, 1985). Fischer (2003) teaches students to ask and answer questions about single sentences, then multiple sentences through modeling and discussion and active involvement by the students through writing answers and discussing the answers. Bristow (1985) believes that provision of interspersed questions in the text to provide a transition from teacher questioning to self-questioning may be helpful.

Questioning and sharing responses in small groups can help students improve critical insights into texts. Student-generated questions can motivate peers to respond and cause the questioner to have more interest in the response. Both Commeyras (1994, p. 519) and Simpson (1996, p. 124) conclude that "good discussion questions are the ones students want to discuss."

Kitagawa (1982, p. 43) encouraged students to become questioners by asking questions that had to be answered by a question, such as "What question did the author mainly answer in the passage we just read?" She also encouraged them to develop questions they wished to have answered through educational activities, such as field trips, and to construct preview questions, based on titles and pictures, for reading selections. Students were asked what questions they would ask the author of a selection or a character, if they could, and they were asked to predict the questions that would be answered next in the selection.

TIME for REFLECTION

Under what conditions would you encourage students to construct their own questions, and under what conditions would you use teacher-generated questions in your classroom? What are the reasons for your choices?

Busching and Slesinger (1995) also led students to ask their own questions about their readings. The students wrote, in their reading response journals or notebooks, questions that selections raised. This preserved the questions for ongoing reflection. Busching and Slesinger (p. 344) discovered that "[w]hether a question is about facts or concepts is less important than whether a question is a part of something significant. The outward form of the question may have little to do with the level, the depth, or the importance of thinking that has occurred." When reading *Rose Blanche* by Roberto Innocenti, middle-school students first raised factual questions because of their limited backgrounds of experience. Later, more of their questions were on higher levels. Some of their questions became "what if" questions.

LITERATURE

SUMMARY

This chapter examines types of reading comprehension. Literal comprehension results from reading for directly stated ideas. Higher-order comprehension goes beyond literal comprehension to include interpretive, critical, and creative reading. Interpretive reading is reading for implied ideas; critical reading is reading for evaluation; and creative reading is reading beyond the lines. Teachers can generally teach strategies in all of these areas most effectively through explanation and modeling, guided student practice, and independent student practice.

Questioning techniques are important to instruction because teachers use questions to provide purposes for reading, elicit and focus discussion, and check students' comprehension of material they have read. Questions may be based on comprehension factors or story structure. Students may need to be taught how to approach answering questions. Self-questioning by the reader is also a valuable comprehension and comprehension-monitoring technique. Teachers can help students develop the skill of self-questioning.

TEST YOURSELF

True or False

______ 1. Literal comprehension involves acquiring information that is directly stated in a selection.

______ 2. Students must attend to details when they follow directions.

______ 3. Critical reading is reading for evaluation.

______ 4. Critical reading strategies are easier to teach than literal reading strategies.

______ 5. Higher-order comprehension may involve determining the author's purpose.

______ 6. Critical readers are not interested in copyright dates of material they read.

______ 7. An inference is an idea that is implied in the material, rather than being directly stated.

______ 8. Studying propaganda techniques is not appropriate for middle-school students, since they do not often have to deal with such techniques in daily life.

______ 9. A bandwagon approach takes advantage of the desires of people to conform to the crowd.

______ 10. Hexagonal essays promote higher-order thinking.

______ 11. Critical readers read with a questioning attitude.

______ 12. Creative reading involves going beyond the material presented by the author.

______ 13. Teachers should give little class time to creative reading because it is not practical.

______ 14. In composing comprehension questions for testing purposes, teachers should use several types of questions.

______ 15. A good test is a hard test, and vice versa.

______ 16. Listing questions and sequence questions are the same thing.

______ 17. The main idea of a paragraph is always stated in the form of a topic sentence.

______ 18. Readers make inferences that are consistent with their schemata.

______ 19. Some students have difficulty determining referents of pronouns and adverbs.

______ 20. "Essential" questions, as defined by Wiggins and McTighe, point to the core ideas of a discipline.

For your journal . . .

1. Using the seven question types based on comprehension factors that are described in this chapter, compose some questions about the content of this chapter or of another chapter in this book. Answer the questions.
2. After you have read a novel written for middle-school students, write story grammar-based questions about the story. Answer the questions.

. . . and your portfolio

1. Make a comprehension board game based on a favorite book for middle-school students.
2. Gather examples of each propaganda technique listed in the chapter in order to create a file for each type. Describe instructional uses for your file.

5

Major Approaches and Materials for Reading Instruction

KEY VOCABULARY

Pay close attention to these terms when they appear in the chapter.

- computer-assisted instruction
- desktop publishing
- directed reading activity
- directed reading-thinking activity
- eclectic approaches
- hypermedia
- hypertext
- individualized reading approach
- language experience approach
- literature-based approaches
- literature circles
- programmed instruction
- thematic literature units
- trade books
- videoconferencing
- webbing
- WebQuests
- word bank

SETTING OBJECTIVES

When you finish reading this chapter, you should be able to

- Discuss the characteristics of different types of published reading series.
- Compare and contrast a directed reading activity with a directed reading-thinking activity.
- Discuss the characteristics of literature-based approaches to reading instruction.
- Explain the rationale behind the language experience approach.
- Discuss the place of computers in reading instructional programs.
- Discuss how a middle-school teacher might use elements of several approaches in a single classroom.

Over the years, educators have developed many approaches to teaching reading. This chapter discusses some of the more widely accepted approaches appropriate for middle-school students. These approaches are not mutually exclusive; many teachers use more than one method simultaneously. They often select the best techniques and materials from a number of approaches to meet the varied needs of individual students in their classrooms. We take the position that no one approach is best for all students or all teachers. Therefore, we acquaint teachers with the characteristics of different approaches so that they will be able to choose intelligently the procedures they will use in their classrooms.

Just as there are many approaches, there are many types of materials that can be used for reading instruction, varying from teacher-made materials to published reading series, library books, and computers. All are tools to help teachers present reading instruction effectively in the middle school.

Chapter 5 Organization

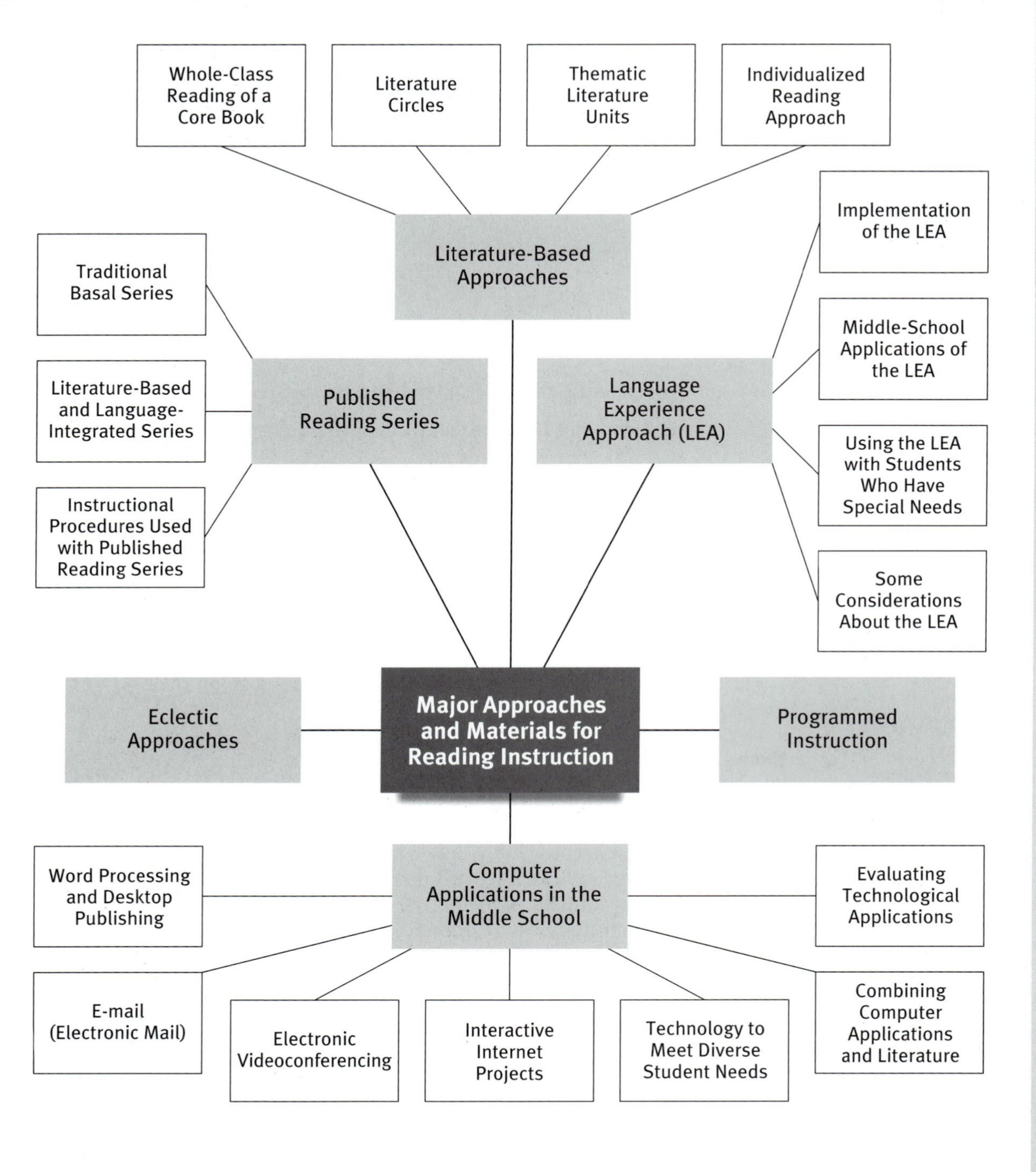

Published Reading Series

Many schools depend on published reading series for materials to support reading instruction. These series have evolved over time. For many years, the published reading series were like the traditional basal series described here. Now many publishers are producing more literature-based and language-integrated series as they respond to criticisms of the traditional series, taking into account current theory and research in reading.

Traditional Basal Series

For many years, basal reader series have been the most widely used materials for teaching reading in the United States. They provide materials for development and practice of reading strategies in each grade.

STANDARDS AND ASSESSMENT

TECHNOLOGY

In addition to the student books, basal reader series include teacher's manuals with detailed lesson plans to help teachers use the material effectively. Teachers who follow these plans use what is called a *directed reading activity* (DRA), described later in this chapter. Basal reader series also include workbooks and/or blackline duplicating masters of skill sheets that students can use to practice skills and strategies they have previously learned in class. Many publishing companies offer other supplementary materials to use in conjunction with basal series, such as student journals; read-aloud libraries for the teacher; unit tests; and computer management, reinforcement, and enrichment activities.

LITERATURE

Basal reading series are quite useful for middle-school teachers. They provide anthologies of stories, content area selections, poems, plays, and so on, that can be the basis for enriching classroom reading activities. Many of these pieces are whole selections or excerpts from high-quality literature. The new basals contain much literature because the publishers are trying to provide material that teachers want (Cullinan, 1992). Many basal reading programs present integrated, thematic approaches to reading. Moreover, as Wiggins (1994) points out, when a basal reading program is used schoolwide, teachers have an idea of what the students have been taught in past years. This can aid in curricular planning.

STANDARDS AND ASSESSMENT

The teacher's manuals offer many valuable suggestions for teaching reading lessons and thus can save much lesson preparation time. Such suggestions offer positive guidance for teachers, helping them to include all aspects of reading (word recognition, comprehension, oral reading, silent reading, reading for information, and reading for enjoyment) in their reading lessons. Manuals allow for systematic teaching and reteaching of skills and strategies and for systematic review. They provide strategy and skill scope and sequence charts that show what strategies are introduced, taught, and reinforced at different grade levels throughout the series. They also offer ways to monitor the success of the instruction (Wiggins, 1994).

The wealth of material provided in the teacher's manuals allows teachers to choose from among the offered suggestions those that fit their needs and discard the ones that do not. If, however, teachers try to do everything suggested, they may use valuable time for activities that are inappropriate for some groups of students, leaving inadequate time for appropriate ones. Teachers should not use basal readers from front to back in their entirety without considering the special needs of their students. A teacher might use one set of activities from the basal one year and a different set the next year to accommodate the different needs of the two classes.

Teachers should also be aware that the skill sheets and workbooks in basal series are not designed to teach the skills and strategies and should not be used for this purpose. They are designed to provide practice in skills that have been taught. Some educators have pointed out that basal reader workbook pages may fail to relate directly to the story in the reader and may give insufficient attention to higher-level comprehension skills. Therefore, teachers may want to have students write responses to the selections in reading logs and let students discuss the selections in literature circles, as described later in this chapter, or use a variety of other literature response activities, such as drama, art, and storytelling, rather than depending on workbook activities that are unrelated to the stories or that cover comprehension superficially.

LITERATURE

DIVERSITY

Publishers of basal readers are continually working to improve them. Some people equate basal readers with overly simplified texts that have received much negative media attention. Many publishers today, however, consider factors other than readability formulas to aid in placement. They include good literature, often without adaptation, as well as more content area material. Stories in these readers have diverse characters—both male and female main characters, people of various racial and ethnic groups, elderly people, and people with disabilities—and depict them in less stereotyped ways than in the past.

STANDARDS AND ASSESSMENT

Basal publishers have put many research findings about reading into practice in basal lessons within the context of the pressures classroom teachers face. Basal readers address considerations from diagnosis to reading appreciation and offer suggestions for both instructional techniques and guided practice. Teachers should make their instructional needs known to publishers. Publishers have been responsive to user reactions in the past and are likely to continue to be responsive.

Uses and Misuses of Basal Materials

Much of the criticism of basal readers has focused on less-than-desirable uses of the materials. Teachers have a responsibility to plan the use of all materials in their classrooms, including the basal readers, regardless of the presence or absence of guiding suggestions accompanying the materials.

If teachers perceive basals as *total* reading programs, they may fail to provide the variety of experiences students need for a balanced program. Basals can never provide all of the reading situations a middle-school student needs to encounter.

Some teachers form basal reading groups based on achievement. They place the best readers in the top group, the average readers in a middle group or groups, and the poorest readers in the lowest group. In this way, these teachers believe they can provide all of the students with basal materials that are appropriate for their reading levels. In actuality, however, the match of materials with students is not always good. Forell (1985) has pointed out that good readers are often placed in comfortable reading materials in which word recognition problems are not frequent and attention can be given to meaning, using context clues to advantage. Poor readers, however, are often placed in "challenging" material that causes frustration and is not conducive to comprehension, because they need to pay so much attention to word recognition, an arrangement that denies them a chance for fluent reading. All readers should be given material that is comfortable enough to allow reasonable application of comprehension skills. Teachers may be reluctant to place students in materials at as low a level as they need in order to allow this to happen, but doing so can be beneficial to these students in the long run.

STANDARDS AND ASSESSMENT

Blanton, Moorman, and Wood (1986) suggest that teachers use direct instruction in basal reader skill lessons by assessing the students' background knowledge related to the skill; explaining the skill in detail, including when it is needed and why it is important; having the students explain the skill in their own words; modeling the use of the skill for the students and then providing them with guided practice with the skill; having students apply the skill in regular reading materials; and leading the students in discussion of real-world encounters with the skill. Some of these steps may already be included in basal manual instructions. Teachers can add the other steps for more complete skills lessons. Of course, teachers need to provide much time for actual reading of connected text.

Teachers may ask students to illustrate scenes from the story, write questions for other class members to answer, write other adventures for story characters, read books by the author of the story or books related to the story, or engage in many other activities that encourage active participation and interaction with the selection.

Educators have expressed considerable concern about the misuse of workbooks or skill sheets that accompany basal readers; some teachers use them to keep students busy while they meet with other students or do paperwork. Wiggins (1994) decries the fact that some teachers assign all pages sequentially to all students, regardless of appropriateness to the individual student's needs. It is important to note that the fault here is with the teachers' procedures, not with the workbooks. Workbook activities should always be purposeful, and teachers should never assign workbook pages simply to keep students occupied. Teachers should also grade and return completed workbook assignments promptly, since students need to have correct responses reinforced immediately and need to be informed about incorrect responses so that they will not continue to make them.

In summary, teachers do not have to follow all suggestions in the manuals—or, indeed, *any* of the suggestions—in order to use basal materials to provide students with a variety of reading materials that would not otherwise be available in many schools. They are also not limited to using the suggestions in the manuals. The manner in which basal materials are used, not the basals themselves, has often been the main concern about basal programs.

TIME for REFLECTION

Would you ask all students in your middle-school classroom to complete all workbook pages, to ensure learning? Why, or why not? If not, what would you do?

Variations in Basal Reading Programs

Although the preceding discussion of basal reading programs contained some generalizations about them, the intention is not to imply that all basal reader series are alike. On the contrary, these series differ in basic philosophies, order of presentation of strategies and skills, degree and type of vocabulary control, types of selections, and number and types of practice activities provided. Some supplement workbook/skill sheet material with student journals that call for more varied responses. Most are eclectic in approach, but some emphasize a single method.

Literature-Based and Language-Integrated Series

One of the most widely heralded changes that educational publishers have made is the creation of *literature-based* reading series. These programs offer quality literature selections for students to read, often in their entirety and without adaptation. In addition, some series integrate instruction involving listening, speaking, and writing activities to accompany the literature selections, making the lessons true communication experiences. Having students write in journals and participate in unit studies that tie together selections with similar themes, by the same author, or of the same genre is common in the literature-based and language-integrated series.

Instructional Procedures Used with Published Reading Series

A number of instructional procedures can be used with published reading series. Some are built into the manuals included in the series, and some can be easily adapted for use with these materials.

Directed Reading Activity (DRA)

The ***directed reading activity*** (DRA) is a teaching strategy used to extend and strengthen a student's reading abilities. It can be used with a story from a published reading series or with any other reading selection, including content area materials or ***trade books*** (books not written primarily for instructional purposes). The DRA is the strategy that is generally built into basal reading series' teacher's manuals. Following are five components often included in the DRA:

1. *Motivation and development of background (activating and building schemata).* The teacher attempts to interest students in reading about the topic by helping them associate the subject matter with their own experiences or by using audiovisual aids to arouse interest in unfamiliar areas. It may not be necessary to work on motivation for all stories. At this point, the teacher can determine whether the students have the backgrounds of experience and language needed for understanding the story, and, if necessary, he or she can help them develop new concepts and vocabulary before they read the story.

2. *Directed story reading (silent and oral).* Before students read the story silently, the teacher provides them with purpose questions (or an anticipation guide or study guide, as described in Chapter 4) or helps them to set their own purposes (by questioning or predicting) to direct their reading (on a section-by-section basis, if needed). Following the silent reading, the teacher may ask students to read aloud their answers to the purpose or study-guide questions, read aloud to prove or reject their predictions, or read orally for a new purpose. Oral reading

is not always included in middle-school lessons, although it may be helpful to English language learners. This section of the lesson is designed to aid students' comprehension and retention of the material.

3. *Strategy- or skill-building activities.* At some point during the lesson, the teacher provides direct instruction in one or more word recognition or comprehension strategies or skills.
4. *Follow-up practice.* Students practice strategies and skills they have already been taught, frequently by doing workbook exercises or engaging in skill-oriented games.
5. *Enrichment activities.* These activities may connect the story with art, music, or creative writing or may lead the students to read additional material on the same topic or by the same author. Creative drama is often included as an enrichment activity, linking the reading with speaking and listening.

Although the steps may vary from series to series, most basal reading lessons have parts that correspond to this list of components. Directed reading of a story generally involves the teacher's asking questions and the students' reading to find the answers, or the teacher's asking the students to make predictions and read to confirm or reject them. Traditional basal readers tend to give the teacher responsibility for purpose setting. Literature-based and language-integrated series, in contrast, have moved toward giving students more responsibility for purpose setting and stress the making and confirming of predictions.

Adaptations of the DRA. Rearranging a basal reading lesson so that the activities labeled *enrichment activities* are completed before, rather than after, the story is read can produce better results than presentation in the traditional order. These activities can help the students build and integrate background knowledge (Pearson and Fielding, 1991).

Comprehension monitoring (metacognitive activities) can be made a natural part of a DRA by using student *predictions,* rather than teacher questions, as the purpose-setting vehicle for the lessons, using the title, pictures, and students' background information about the general topic that has been activated as a basis for the predictions. The predictions are revised as necessary as the students read the material, much as is done in a directed reading-thinking activity, discussed in the next section. *Self-questioning* before and during the reading is encouraged. In addition, readers can stop at logical story breaks to *summarize* the main points as a check for ongoing comprehension. Summarization of the entire selection can follow completion of the reading. Some basal series incorporate some of these activities into their teacher's manual suggestions, and the literature-based and language-integrated readers tend to use the predicting and confirming techniques regularly.

Guided Reading

Guided reading, as developed in New Zealand, has become a popular means of reading instruction. According to Fawson and Reutzel (2000, p. 84), "When implementing guided reading in classrooms, students are matched with books that provide a level of challenge and familiarity that appropriately support the development of each student's self-extending reading strategies. In short, students receive instruction during guided reading that focuses on their use of specific reading strategies so that they are able to choose from and apply a variety of reading strategies." The groups for guided reading are flexible, just as we have advocated in this text for all grouping practices. Although guided reading is sometimes characterized by teachers as being very different from the use of DRAs, we believe that good teachers generally use DRAs in a very similar manner.

Guided reading lessons begin with an introduction to the story that is focused on concepts important to the story. Just as in a DRA, the purpose is to build background for the material in the story. Then students read the story aloud quietly, with the teacher observing their application of reading strategies and providing support. In a DRA, silent reading generally precedes oral reading, but there is follow-up oral reading for purposes. The teacher circulates to provide support during silent reading and observes oral reading to provide support as needed. Finally, the students may take part in extension activities, such as additional instruction on strategies, dramatizations, and writing, serving the same purpose as extension activities in the DRA.

The Directed Reading-Thinking Activity (DR-TA)

One alternative to the DRA is the ***directed reading-thinking activity*** (DR-TA). The DR-TA focuses on student control instead of primarily teacher guidance of the reading. The DR-TA is a general plan for directing students' reading of stories in published reading series, trade books, or content area selections and for encouraging students to think as they read and to make predictions and check their accuracy. The steps in a DR-TA are listed in Example 5.1. Stauffer (1968) offered some background for understanding the DR-TA:

> Children are by nature curious and inquiring, and they will be so in school if they are permitted to inquire. It is possible to direct the reading-thinking process in such a way that children will be encouraged to think when reading—to speculate, to search, to evaluate, and to use. (p. 348)

Stauffer (1969) further pointed out that teachers can motivate students' effort and concentration by involving them intellectually and encouraging them to formulate questions and hypotheses, to process information, and to evaluate tentative solutions. The DR-TA is directed toward accomplishing these goals. The teacher observes the students as they read, in order to diagnose difficulties and offer help. Perhaps because the student is interacting with the material during reading, the DR-TA is extremely useful for improving students' comprehension of selections. Making predictions about what will occur in a text encourages students to think about the text's message. In making predictions, students use their background knowledge about the topic and their knowledge of text organizational patterns. This step provides purposes for reading: trying to confirm one or more predictions from other students in the group and to confirm or reject their own. It also encourages students to apply metacognitive skills as they think through their lines of reasoning. If students are unable to make predictions as requested, the teacher can model his or her thinking in making a prediction,

STANDARDS AND ASSESSMENT

EXAMPLE 5.1 Steps in a DR-TA

Step 1: Making Predictions from Title Clues

Write the title of the story or chapter to be studied on the chalkboard, and have a student read it. Ask the students, "What do you think this story will be about?" Give them time to consider the question thoroughly, and let each student have an opportunity to make predictions. All student predictions should be accepted, regardless of how reasonable or unreasonable they may seem, but the teacher should not make any predictions during this discussion period.

Step 2: Making Predictions from Picture Clues

Have the students open their books to the beginning of the selection. If there is a picture on the first page, ask them to examine it carefully. After they have examined it, ask them to reconsider the predictions they made earlier, using the additional information in the picture, and make any appropriate revisions to their predictions.

Step 3: Reading the Material

Have the students read a predetermined amount of the story to check the accuracy of their predictions.

Step 4: Assessing the Accuracy of Predictions and Adjusting Predictions

When all of the students have read the first segment, lead a discussion by asking such questions as "Who correctly predicted what the story was going to be about?" Ask the students who believe they were right to read orally to the class the parts of the selection that support their predictions. Students who were wrong can tell why they believe they were wrong. Let them revise their predictions, if necessary, and then ask them to predict what will happen next in the story.

Step 5: Repeating the Procedure Until All Parts of the Lesson Have Been Covered

Have the students read the next predetermined segment of the story to check the accuracy of their predictions. Have them read selected parts orally to justify the predictions they think were correct and tell why they believe other predictions were incorrect. Have them revise or adjust their predictions, based on their reading. Repeat the prediction and checking of predictions steps until all predetermined segments of the story have been read.

using a think-aloud, or can provide several possible predictions for the student to choose from and ask for the reason a particular one is chosen. The teacher should accept all predictions and encourage the students to reflect on their accuracy later. It may help to have the students summarize what has happened before making predictions (Johnston, 1993).

In preparing a DR-TA, the teacher should select points at which to pause so that the students can make predictions. These points should probably be ones where the story line changes, points of high suspense, or other logical spots, and there should be no more than four or five stops in a story (Haggard, 1988). During pauses, the teacher may use one or more open-ended questions to elicit student predictions about the next part of the story (Blachowicz, 1983). After the reading, skill-building activities take place. (See Chapter 8 for an example of the DR-TA applied to a content area lesson.)

TIME for REFLECTION

Some teachers think a DRA is too prescriptive to use, but consider a DR-TA acceptable because it gives middle-school students some control over their own learning. Other teachers believe that there is a place for each technique. **What do *you* think, and why?**

Literature-Based Approaches

Most educators recognize the value of using quality literature as a basis for reading instruction. A ***literature-based approach*** places emphasis on connecting stories to students' personal background knowledge, analyzing stories and selections for particular elements, and monitoring students' understanding of the reading materials. In addition, "good literature offers readers opportunities to engage in life experiences that they would otherwise miss" (Barone, Eeds, and Mason, 1995, p. 31).

The foundation of a literature-based program is trade books. Most teachers have always made use of trade books for students in their classrooms. They have read aloud to the students from these books, urged students to read the books in the classroom reading center or to check them out from the school library for recreational reading, and used them as supplements to basal instruction. In a literature-based program, the teacher uses knowledge of students' backgrounds and attempts to "hook" them on reading selections. The teacher may give book talks that are based on marketing procedures, as Shiflett (1998) suggests, finding a book that draws the students' interest and using techniques that are often used in advertising, such as hyperbole, to focus students' attention on the book.

To use literature-based approaches effectively, teachers need to understand theoretical perspectives on literature and reading. They also need to know reasons for using particular books and particular instructional approaches (McGee and Tompkins, 1995). They need clear instructional plans and clear goals and expectations for students. Books of all types should be read aloud to students and be made available for students to read independently.

Essential reading skills and strategies can be taught within the context of material the students are actively involved in reading. Baumann, Hooten, and White (1999) found that students understood material better and enjoyed reading more when they incorporated comprehension strategy instruction within the context of literature. During reading, students' strategy use is monitored by both teacher and students, who share in responsibility for learning (Ruddell, 1992). After reading, students may participate in activities such as retelling stories, writing reactions to books, and conversing about books with the teacher and other students. Students can study writers' styles and use them as models for their personal writing (Fuhler, 1990). For example, Lunsford (1997) found that minilessons based on literature enhanced her writing workshops.

DIVERSITY

Literature-based instruction has been successful with a wide range of students. Zucker (1993) found that a literature-based whole language teaching-learning philosophy applied in classes with students who had language and learning disabilities resulted in positive gains in listening, speaking, reading, and writing. Stewart and others (1996, p. 476) found that literature-based developmental reading programs resulted in improved reading performance by seventh and eighth graders. They believe that "choice leads to interest and ownership, interest and ownership to practice, and practice to speed and fluency. Speed and fluency result in increased comprehension and retention (i.e., reading proficiency)." Time for reading is, of course, necessary for this model to work.

On the other hand, Scharer and Detwiler (1992) point out some concerns regarding literature-based instruction. When it is used, teachers find it hard to be sure they

STANDARDS AND ASSESSMENT

are covering all needed strategies and skills, hard to know how to assess progress, and hard to know how to handle the struggling readers. Certainly teachers need to be well prepared as language teachers to use the approaches effectively.

Literature-based programs may be conducted in a number of ways, and combinations of these approaches are common in most literature-based classrooms. Four such approaches are whole-class reading of a core book, use of literature circles with multiple copies of several books, use of thematic literature units, and individualized reading approaches (Henke, 1988; Hiebert and Colt, 1989). Each of these approaches will be discussed in turn. A common adjunct to all of them is *Sustained Silent Reading* (SSR), in which students and teachers alike are allowed time to read materials of their own choice without interruption. (SSR is described in detail in Chapter 6.)

Whole-Class Reading of a Core Book

Generally, core books used for whole-class reading are acquired in classroom sets so that every student has a personal copy. Teachers often select these books for the quality of the material and because they fit into the overall classroom curriculum by relating to studies in other curricular areas, such as social studies and science. It is a further advantage if the teacher personally likes the book, for the teacher's attitude is communicated to the students as the reading progresses.

Whole-class reading of a core book provides an opportunity for an entire class to analyze a book in depth, sharing information and insights. *(© Elizabeth Crews)*

Prereading Activities

Before a book is presented to the class, there may be prereading activities in which the students share personal experiences related to the book's content and activate information they possess about the topics or themes covered in it. (See Chapter 4 for information about techniques for schema activation.) The teacher may also present a minilesson on some literary element that is important in the book, such as characterization or flashbacks (Atwell, 1987). Purposes for listening to or reading the material are often set by having students predict what will happen in the story, based on the title and possibly on the picture on the book's cover or the first page of the story. At other times, purposes may be set by having students generate questions about the story that they expect to answer from reading. Occasionally the teacher may suggest some purpose question that will focus the readers on a key element in the book, such as, "How is the setting of the story important to its plot?" At times some students may present the book or a portion of it in a readers' theater as an introduction for other students. Such a presentation could help the other students activate their schemata for the reading to come.

During-Reading Activities

Sometimes the teacher first presents the book to the students by reading aloud part or all of it, depending on the students' reading abilities and the difficulty of the book. A novel may be read in installments over a period of days. After the teacher's oral reading, silent reading of the book by the students follows. More often at the middle-school level, the students read the book silently with no more than limited introductory reading by the teacher to build interest in the story.

At strategic points in the initial reading or independent rereading, there are usually pauses for small-group or whole-class discussion of the material. If students initially made predictions, these discussions may focus on the predictions, which can be evaluated, retained for the time being, altered slightly, or changed completely, based on the new information. The discussion may also focus on the purpose questions that were generated or on students' personal reactions to the story. To guide these discussions, the teacher may design questions that help the students to relate the story to their own experiences and to think critically and creatively about the material.

Between reading sessions, students may write reactions to the story in literature logs. The literature logs may be written just for the individual students, to help them think through what they are reading; or they may be dialogue logs, addressed to the teacher or a buddy. If the logs are part of a written dialogue with the teacher, the teacher must respond to each entry with his or her own reaction to the story and/or to the student's reaction. Students should be free to write any honest response to the material without concern for negative teacher reaction. For example, a student who is bored by the story should feel free to say so in the log. Thus, the teacher's comments should be encouraging, thought provoking, and nonjudgmental. The teacher should not be looking for predetermined responses, but should respond with genuine interest in the students' comments (Fuhler, 1994; Wollman-Bonilla, 1989). Students should be encouraged to link the reading material with personal experiences. The teacher should model such entries for students by sharing his or her personal log entries orally. Students should also be encouraged to note phrases and expressions that appealed to them, statements that caused personal confusion, and predictions about what will happen next. Many different learning goals may be met through this student-teacher interaction. One type of literature log is presented in Example 5.2 and another type in Example 5.3, in the section on literature circles.

Postreading Activities

After the book has been read, follow-up activities should be used to extend the students' understanding and help them elaborate on the ideas they gained from the shared book. These activities often involve writing—for example, composing another episode for the characters in the story, another story of the same genre, or a character sketch of a favorite character. Swindall and Cantrell (1999) ask sixth graders to write questions for well-developed characters in the literature selections they are reading, and then to impersonate characters of their choice and answer questions that their classmates, acting as interviewers, ask them.

Retelling the story in various ways is a follow-up activity. Students may simply retell the story to partners, who may ask questions about missing events or ideas; or they may act out the story through creative dramatics or puppetry. Illustrating the story sequence or selected parts of the story is a good follow-up activity that causes the students to reflect on the story and provides the teacher with insight into the students' degrees of comprehension of the story. This is especially effective if the students add

EXAMPLE 5.2 Literature Log

EIGHT COUSINS Read to 53
10-8-86

Each time I read this book it seems to get easier to read. I guess it is because I'm getting used to the proper English used. I enjoy it a lot and Feel so carried off when I read it. So far the story is very good and I just want to always know whats going to happen next.

Anita

Anita,

I haven't read <u>Eight Cousins</u>, but I sure would like to after reading your enthusiastic responses. I must confess that Louisa May Alcott is one author I've never read. I think I'll read <u>Eight Cousins</u> and give her a try.

Can you discover what or how the author is creating such a wonderful feeling for you?

Mrs. H.

Source: Jill Dillard, "Lit Logs: A Reading and Writing Activity for the Library/Media Center and the Classroom." Reprinted with permission of the author and the Ohio Educational Library/Media Association's *Ohio Media Spectrum* journal, from the Winter 1989 issue, Vol. 41, No. 4, p. 39.

commentary to their illustrations. Middle-school students may, however, be self-conscious about their drawings if they are expected to show them to others.

The students may construct group or individual story maps after the reading. The maps can be displayed in the classroom or shared during discussions or oral presentations. Students may apply information learned in the story (for example, how to do origami), or they may read related materials because of aroused interest in the topic.

Modifications of Whole-Class Reading of a Core Book

Teachers have made many individual modifications of the procedures for close, careful reading of a book by a class. Shaw (1988) had fifth graders keep narrative journals in which they wrote after reading each chapter of their book, taking the perspective of the main character to relate that character's adventures. Through this activity, they learned much about summarizing and the first-person narrative form. Journal writing is a powerful way to reflect and discover insights about material read. It encourages active reading and gives the teacher a glimpse of the students' personal transactions with the story (Fuhler, 1994).

Dugan (1997, p. 87) uses transactional literature discussions that include "getting ready, reading and thinking aloud, wondering on paper, and looking back." Getting ready includes reviewing and making predictions during the reading, predictions that the students then try to confirm or reject. Teachers need to model the think-aloud process and encourage students to think aloud as they read. (This step eventually evolves into thinking silently as they read.) As they read, or just after they finish, students write responses to the reading on sticky notes that are placed on the pages to which they refer. These written responses can provide fodder for talk sessions in which students respond, question, listen to their classmates, and make links between the events in the story, the story and their personal experiences, or their ideas and their classmates' ideas. After their talk sessions, the students write in their journals. Finally, the students review what they have learned. Teachers offer scaffolding throughout this process, but scaffolds are not used when students no longer need them. This procedure has produced a positive effect on students' reading abilities and pleasure in reading.

Wertheim (1988) created a personal teaching guide for the novels she had her students read, by listing difficult vocabulary at the beginning of each chapter, underlining important vocabulary in the text, writing discussion questions on the pages to which they pertained (coded as literal, inferential, and critical); writing more inclusive questions at ends of chapters, and listing follow-up activities at the end of the book. This plan can be efficient, but some educators feel that it is too structured.

The Focus on Strategies on page 193 describes one way to do close reading of a core book. This example is not a prescribed procedure; many variations are possible.

LITERATURE

Literature Circles

In ***literature circles,*** the teacher generally chooses several books for which multiple copies are available, introduces each one, lets students choose which book to read, and presents the books to the students if they are unable to read them independently first. The structured book choices lead students to try books in a variety of genres and by a

FOCUS ON STRATEGIES

Whole-Class Reading of a Core Book

In this lesson, the teacher has chosen the book *The War at Home* by Connie Jordan Green because of the way it shows relationships among the characters and because of the importance of setting to the story.

The teacher opens with a minilesson on character development, leading the students to see how authors reveal characterization through the things the character says and does, the things other characters say about the character, and the ways they react to him or her.

Next, she reviews the fact that the setting of a story relates to the time and place in which the story unfolds.

Then the teacher asks the students to brainstorm their personal associations for the words and phrases *World War II, security, taunts, greenbelt, torrent,* and *atomic bomb*. Webs of these associations are written on the board or on a chart.

Now the teacher invites the students to predict what the story will be about. They write down their predictions or share them orally with partners or the whole group. The teacher tells the students that, as they read the story, they should look for clues that will either confirm or disprove their predictions and that they should also look for the characteristics of the characters, noticing what is said about and to them, what they say, and what they do.

The teacher may ask the students to read just the first chapter of the story and stop to discuss these questions with others at their tables:

- What is the relationship between Mattie and Virgil like?
- Have you ever had to deal with someone new coming to live with you? How did you handle it?
- When does this story take place?
- Where does this story take place? How was it different from other U.S. cities? How would you feel about living in a place like that?

Now students may read the rest of the story, with the amount read each time varying with the maturity of the students. Some possible stopping points and questions for discussion in the small groups include the following:

After Chapters 2–4

- What is the relationship between Mattie and Janie Mae like? Have you ever had a relationship like that with someone?
- What kind of person is Eddie? How does he make Virgil feel? What does he do that lets you know?
- What mistake has Virgil made?
- How does Virgil feel about Oak Ridge? Why does he feel this way?

After Chapters 5–9

- How are Mattie's feelings for Virgil changing?
- What do the young people in Oak Ridge do for fun? How is it like what you do today, or how is it different?
- How does Mattie try to comfort Virgil? Why doesn't she know what to say to him?
- How does Virgil feel about his father? How can you tell?
- What is Virgil's relationship with his grandmother like? How can you tell?
- What does Mattie's father think about the sheriff? How can you tell?
- Where does Mattie think Gran and Gramps will sleep in her house?

After Chapters 10–12

- Why does Gran work so much at Mattie's house? Does working ever make you feel better? Why, or why not?
- How is Fred's house different from Mattie's?
- Why does Mattie take up for Virgil? Does Virgil appreciate it? How can you tell?

Continued

After Chapters 13–14

- What is working on Fred's farm like? How does Mattie feel about it?
- What does "her arms felt as if she'd been picking up elephants" mean?
- Why does Mattie go hunting with Virgil? What does the hunting make her think about?

After Chapter 15

- How did Mattie's father feel about Virgil's having to leave?
- Why was Mattie so absent-minded?
- Why does Mattie's mother tell her to throw salt over her shoulder? Have you ever seen anyone do that?

After the story is finished

- What was Oak Ridge's secret?
- Why does Mattie's mother have mixed feelings about the atomic bomb?
- How is Mattie beginning to feel about Robert?
- What is the relationship between Mattie and Virgil at the end of the book?

Follow-up activities after the reading may include some of the following:

1. Find another book that tells about the United States during World War II. Compare and contrast the stories.
2. Write a diary entry that Mattie might have made when Virgil had to go away. Have Mattie tell her diary how she felt about her cousin.
3. Pick a character and describe him or her. List his or her characteristics and why you did or did not like him or her.
4. Compare and contrast living in Oak Ridge in the early 1940s and living where you live today.
5. Compare and contrast the way the characters in this book and the characters in another book, such as *Bridge to Terabithia* by Katherine Paterson, deal with death.

variety of authors. Based on their choices, the teacher has the students form groups to hold discussions about the books, and he or she may participate as a member in these group discussions. Students respond in response journals or literature logs. The teacher then lets the students help decide how to share the experience of the books (Heald-Taylor, 1996). In this process, teachers make a number of decisions that touch on many aspects of instruction, such as their own roles in the groups, when and how much teacher-directed instruction should be involved, how books will be chosen, how students can be helped to respond more effectively, and how groups should be structured (Spiegel, 1998).

Groups should be formed after the teacher and students have established rapport, so that they feel comfortable exchanging thoughts and ideas. Usually there are four or five groups in a class, each consisting of four to six members. Martinez-Roldan and Lopez-Robertson (1999/2000) discovered that English language learners are capable of participating productively in literature circles in classrooms, so this activity can have groups that are heterogeneous in terms of cultural composition, as well as in terms of reading ability, as long as the students have chosen the same book.

DIVERSITY

Groups generally meet two to five times a week, with each group lasting about two to three weeks. When they meet, students look through their books, decide how far to

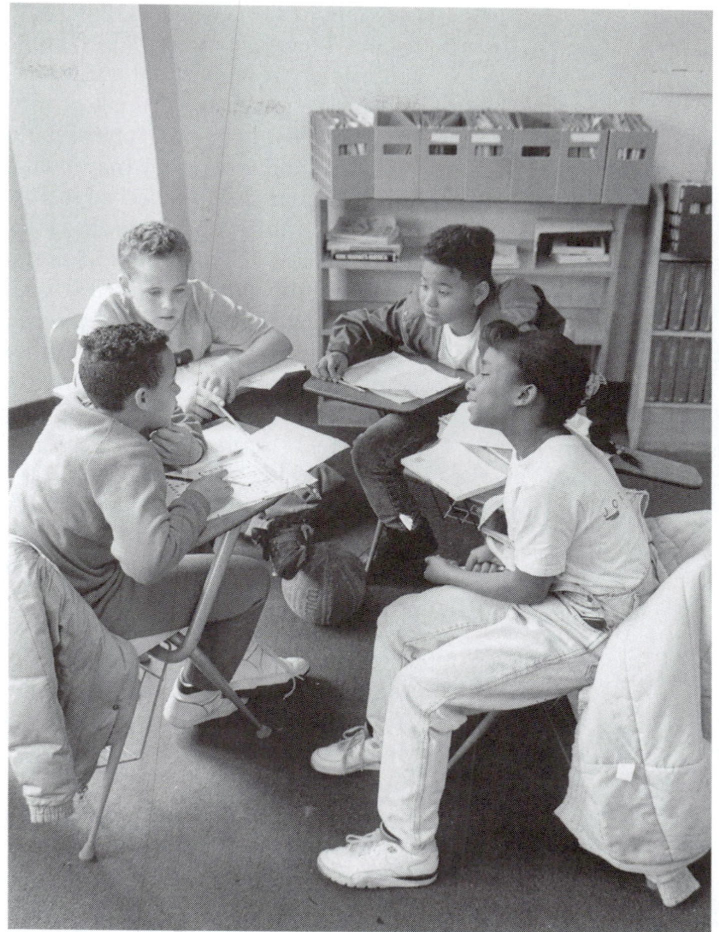

In literature circles, students can share their personal views of the books they read. *(© Elizabeth Crews)*

read each time (in order to finish the reading by the deadline and to have enough material for good discussions at each meeting), and begin reading. During group sessions, a student leader can conduct the activities, which may consist of silent reading, writing in and sharing literature logs, asking open-ended questions, discussing what was read, and doing extension activities. In their groups, students initiate and sustain discussion topics, connect literature selections to their lives, compare literature selections and authors with each other, note authors' styles, and consider authors' intents. Discussions are directed by the insights and ideas that the students bring to the group, instead of a list of teacher-supplied questions (Brabham and Villaume, 2000). Personal responses to literature replace "correct" answers to questions about the stories. Participation in an interpretive community of readers allows half-formed ideas to be explored from different perspectives. Students are required to provide substantiation for their contributions to the group. They should be receptive to the interpretations of their classmates, but they should also feel free to disagree (Spiegel, 1996). (See Chapter 9 for a teacher's checklist for literature circles.) Literature logs, or literature response journals, allow the collection of reactions to the reading throughout the reading process, not just at the end, and can be the basis for small-group discussions. When writing in their literature logs, students record personal interpretations, strategies for constructing meaning, questions that arise, and issues they may want to discuss with others (Popp, 1997). Since spelling and grammar are not checked in any way, the students feel freer to communicate. One type of literature log or response journal was shown in the section on whole-class reading of a core book. Example 5.3 is another type that can be used.

STANDARDS AND ASSESSMENT

From reading these entries, teachers not only become aware of ways that students are reacting to literature but also gain insight into each student's literacy processes (Handloff and Golden, 1995). Supportive comments by the teacher can encourage students to react honestly to the material and to persevere in the reading. Sometimes students need encouragement to be more specific in their entries (Fuhler, 1994; Hancock, 1992; Raphael et al., 1992). To provide such encouragement, Berger (1996, p. 381) had her students respond to these questions: "What do you notice? . . . What do you question? . . . What do you feel? . . . What do you relate to?" These questions led the students to do more than just summarize the reading.

Hancock (1992) believes awareness of typical response patterns in literature response journals can help teachers encourage extensions of response types. Some possible response types involve interaction with the characters, empathy with the characters, prediction and validation of predictions, personal experiences that relate to the reading, and philosophical reflections.

TECHNOLOGY

Technology can provide ways for students to respond to their reading. Margaret Moore (1991) had teachers in a graduate methods course take part in electronic dialogue journals with fifth-grade students (using computers). The partners discussed the book *Superfudge* by Judy Blume. The teachers modeled good discussions of characters and setting through their entries, and the quality of students' entries improved. Both groups enjoyed the interaction. We conducted a similar project and had a high level of success (Roe and Smith, 1997). The Focus on Strategies on page 198 describes the project.

TECHNOLOGY

LITERATURE

Art provides another option for responding. Whitin (2002) has her students try to show their ideas about the books through sketching. She says, "It's called sketch-to-stretch because as we sketch and talk about our sketches, our minds are stretched to think in new ways" (p. 445). Students use colors, shapes, lines, or complete pictures to represent their thinking and are asked to give reasons for their representations. They also write brief statements that explain their thoughts. Whitin emphasizes that story ideas can be represented in many ways—some students use colors and shapes, some more detailed drawings. The symbolism they use often exhibits deep understanding.

As groups finish their books, the teacher can encourage students to create extension projects individually, in pairs, or as a group. Examples include reading a similar book or a book by the same author, creating a drama, and writing an epilogue for the story.

Thematic Literature Units

Thematic literature units center around themes based on topics such as homes, families, survival, taking care of our earth, wild animals, pets, specific geographical regions

EXAMPLE 5.3 Literature Log

Part 1

Amaroq, the Wolf

NAME: Katie Smith
DATE: September 11

TITLE OF BOOK: Julie of the wolves
PAGE STARTED: 20
PAGE STOPPED: 45

RETELL:

Miyax is still looking for food. No matter what she will not give up. Now she is communicating with the wolves. She talks and acts like them.

Jello, one of the wolves, brings food back from the hunt and Miyax gets offered some.

COMMENTS:

- p. 20 How many wolves? Have I missed missed something?
- p. 22 Does Miyax think the wolves can understand her? Can they?
- p. 23 Eelie? Excitement = Eelie?
- p. 24 Why does she try to make the wolves get food for her when she has an ulo?
- p. 25 Sunny Night?
- p. 27 "learn about her family" Does that mean her wolf family?

REACTION:

Exciting!

FOCUS ON STRATEGIES E-mail Conversations About Literature

During each of two semesters, students from Livingston Middle School, a rural public school in Tennessee, were paired with teacher education students enrolled in Betty Roe's reading and language arts methods classes at Tennessee Technological University to discuss literature selections that both groups were reading. In the fall semester both groups read Paterson's *Bridge to Terabithia*, and in the spring semester both groups read Babbitt's *Tuck Everlasting*. The books were read on a predetermined schedule, and the partners communicated about their reading each week for seven weeks. During the fall semester, the university students also posted comments about literary features of the book to a newsgroup that was limited to the university students in the project. After both groups viewed a videotape of the book that had been read, they communicated with partners by e-mail, comparing and contrasting the book and the video. (See the Focus on Strategies on Comparing Books and Videos in Chapter 4 for more detail about this facet of the project.) The middle-school students also prepared an *mPower* presentation about each book at the conclusion of the reading. (See the Focus on Strategies on Creating Multimedia Productions in Chapter 4 for more detail on this part of the program.)

Evaluations of the program by public-school and university teachers and students were positive. The public-school teachers felt that receiving e-mail motivated their students and enhanced the students' self-esteem. They felt that interacting with college students gave their students a sense of status and of doing high-level work. Some of the middle-school students had never read a novel before, but they read these books in order to communicate with their partners. Of course, they got additional reading practice when they read the e-mail correspondence from their partners in order to respond. These students had rarely done much writing, and the teachers saw the writing skills of many increase during the project. The university students had been encouraged to model good writing for their partners in their e-mail exchanges, and most did. Some partners continued to correspond after the semesters had ended. The e-mail communications reflected thinking on all levels of Bloom's taxonomy of cognitive objectives of instruction, and the university students were sometimes surprised at the higher-order thinking that their partners displayed.

The university students gave the project high evaluations, also. One wrote, "This particular project not only introduced students to a good piece of literature; it introduced them to interactive technology, which is a skill that will be useful and probably necessary to their futures. It provided feedback that was fun and involving. I would definitely use this technique again" (Roe and Smith, 1997, p. 372).

(for example, South America), or specific groups of people (for example, Japanese); genres, such as biography, science fiction, or folktales; authors, such as Cynthia Voigt, Katherine Paterson, Gary Paulsen, Christopher Paul Curtis, or Walter Dean Myers; or single books. Barton and Smith (2000, p. 55) urge teachers to avoid the use of simple topics that "organize content and activities together simply because they contain or mention a similar subject—bears, cats, dragons, leaves."

Thematic units allow students to delve more deeply into ideas and thus develop deeper understandings and see connections between ideas. With themes, students can support or challenge a position and think more deeply about it. Themes can help teachers and learners focus on meaning making. A theme offers a *focus* for instruction and activities, making it easier for students to see the reason for classroom activities, acquire an integrated knowledge base, achieve depth and breadth of learning, and connect with real audiences. The variety of materials used allows for these accomplishments (Bergeron, 1996; Lipson et al., 1993).

There are other values as well. The reflection involved in studying themes can enhance metacognition, but perhaps the biggest advantage of thematic teaching is the promotion of positive attitudes toward reading and writing. The range of topics covered and the opportunity for self-selection promote student interest and positive attitudes. Another advantage is that time is less fragmented in a classroom in which the teacher uses thematic units. The number of subjects to be taught is reduced by embedding one subject in another one (Lipson et al., 1993).

Norton (1993) suggests a procedure for developing a unit. The first step is to identify a theme that can be enriched with literature. Then the teacher and students construct a web with subtopics that become the subjects of study for groups of students. Students locate books and other resources that will help them investigate their subjects; then they share their findings creatively with the rest of the class.

A single book or story can be used as the focus for curricular integration (Lauritzen, Jaeger, and Davenport, 1996). (Example 5.4 shows a web for a unit based on the book *Number the Stars* by Lois Lowry.) ***Webbing*** is a technique that connects a central topic or perhaps a book to related ideas. A web is a framework that can cut across curricular areas. Emphasizing that no two webs are alike, Huck, Hepler, and Hickman (1997) recommend webbing as a plan for literature study that grows out of students' interests and the strengths of the books. During the process of creating a web, teachers become aware of the many directions in which books can lead students. Although the teacher uses the web as an overall plan, students contribute their own ideas as the theme unfolds, so the study becomes learner centered.

TECHNOLOGY

STANDARDS AND ASSESSMENT

For help in planning units that are based on a single piece of literature, teachers may find SCORE CyberGuides useful. The guides, based on California's Language Arts standards, contain online activities for award-winning books. They are located at **http://www.Sdcoe.k12.ca.us/SCORE/cyberguide.html** (Leu, Castek, Henry, Coiro, and McMullan, 2004).

Teachers can also develop literature units using books that share similar characteristics. *Textsets* are books that have the same author, theme, topic, genre, or some other characteristic. They can set the stage for critical thinking by students as they look for connections. Textsets encourage discussion and varied interpretations (Heine, 1991). A textset on Katherine Paterson's books might include *Bridge to Terabithia, Lyddie, The Great Gilly Hopkins, Jacob Have I Loved,* and *The Sign of the Chrysanthemum.* Use of textsets allows small-group discussion in which students can compare and contrast a variety of related books and write in response journals about the relationships they have discovered. Roser and colleagues (1992) incorporated literature comparison charts (which they called *language charts*) into thematic units to facilitate the making of connections among the stories. The charts seemed to enhance the students' reactions to the literature.

Gallagher (1995) suggests hooking the interest of adolescent readers with one or more young adult novels, then including in the textset a classic that is related in some way to the young adult literature. The connections made between or among the books can enrich the reading. For example, Katherine Paterson's *Park's Quest* could lead to the reading of Charles Dickens's *Great Expectations.* Both books are concerned with a

EXAMPLE 5.4 Literature Web

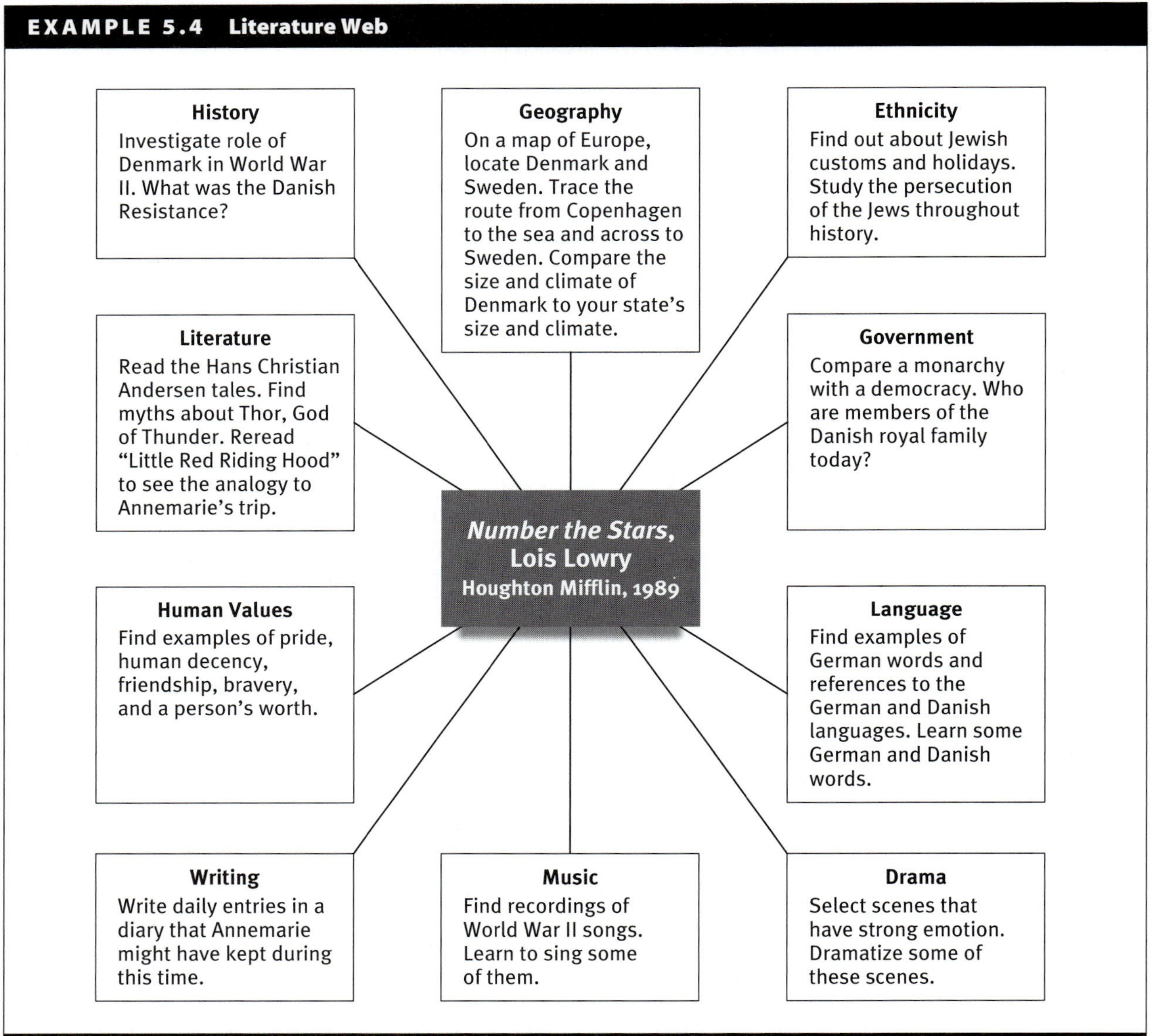

Source: Web based on *Number the Stars* by Lois Lowry. Boston: Houghton Mifflin, 1989.

young man's search for his own identity. S. E. Hinton's *The Outsiders* could also be paired with *Great Expectations,* since Ponyboy says he feels like Pip. Joan Lowery Nixon's *The Name of the Game Was Murder* could be paired with Agatha Christie's *And Then There Were None*. Books may be paired according to theme, setting, mood, or some other element. Thematic units are often opened with prereading activities for developing background, such as those mentioned earlier for the core book, in which students discuss what they already know about the focus of the unit. Students may brainstorm terms they associate with the theme, and these terms may be organized into a semantic web. (See Chapters 2, 3, and 8 for more on semantic webs and literature webs.) The teacher may read aloud one or more books that fit the focus of the unit before allowing students to form small groups to read from multiple copies of other related books. One fifth-grade teacher read aloud Freedman's *Lincoln: A Photobiography* at the beginning of a unit based on the genre of biography and let the students form small groups to read such books as Fritz's *What's the Big Idea, Ben Franklin?;* Winner's *Eleanor Roosevelt: First Lady of the World;* Aliki's *A Weed Is a Flower: The Life of George Washington Carver;* and others for which she had secured multiple copies. Single copies of other biographies were also available for independent reading, as well as short biographies in basal readers, anthologies, and periodicals (Zarillo, 1989).

Any *genre,* or type of literature, can be a focus for study. In Example 5.5 the genre is folktales. Other viable genres are poetry, historical fiction, biography, and fantasy,

EXAMPLE 5.5 Thematic Unit on Folklore

1. Let students read and compare folktale variants, beginning with the Brothers Grimm tales and moving toward contemporary versions.
2. Encourage students to tell stories, repeating familiar favorites or creating new tales.
3. Read or tell classic folktales to the students.
4. Provide opportunities for discovering word origins and literary allusions, especially in myths (e.g., echo, Pandora's box, Mercury, Atlas).
5. Let students dramatize folktales using puppets, pantomime, readers' theater, and creative dramatics.
6. Encourage students to write creatively. Have them
   a. Study the characteristics of a fable (brevity, animal characters, a moral) and create new fables.
   b. Write modern versions of fairy tales.
   c. Make up a ballad based on folklore and set it to music.
   d. Make up original *pourquoi* tales that explain the origins of natural phenomena, such as "Why the Rabbit Has Long Ears."
   e. Write new endings for folktales after changing major events in the stories.
   f. Select a newspaper story, find a moral for it (e.g., "theft doesn't pay"), and write a fable about this moral.
7. Help students find out how folktales were originally communicated and how they came to be written.
8. Invite storytellers to the class. Ask students to interview the storytellers about techniques and the origins of the tales they tell.
9. Encourage students to compare similarities in characters and motifs of folktales from around the world (e.g., the Jackal in India, the Weasel in Africa, and Br'er Rabbit in the United States).
10. Have students locate the places of origin of various versions of folktales on a map.
11. Provide tapes of music and dance based on folktales, such as selections from Stephen Sondheim's *Into the Woods.*

each of which may be divided into subtopics. For instance, types of fantasy that may be studied are (1) modern literary tales based on folktales; (2) fantastic stories, which are basically realistic but contain elements of fantasy; (3) science fiction; and (4) high fantasy with heroes and heroines who confront evil for the sake of humanity.

The teacher may read aloud to the entire class the selection or selections chosen to open the unit. Some selections may be presented through videotapes or audiotapes. Each reading should be accompanied by or followed by discussion of the material, writing in literature logs, and other activities, such as those listed for follow-up activities in the section on whole-class reading of a core book.

TECHNOLOGY

The teacher may then give book talks about the books that are available in multiple copies to help students make decisions about the groups in which they will work. Students should have choices regarding these books, although it may be necessary to let them give their top three choices and be assigned a book from these choices, because of the limited number of copies available for each book. Book talks may also be given for some of the single-copy books. In addition, as students finish reading certain books, they may give book talks to entice their classmates to read these books.

Some unit activities should be designed for whole-group participation (for example, the read-alouds), some for small-group participation (for example, activities related to the multiple-copy books), and some for independent work (for example, literature logs about books read individually). Whole-group activities are likely to include minilessons related to the reading that the students are doing. These minilessons may focus on literary elements or reading strategies.

When small groups meet about the books they are reading in common, activities such as those described in the section on literature circles can be used. As small-group and independent reading progress, students may continue to build on the webs they started during the introductory activities. At the end of the unit, culminating activities may include comparing and contrasting the books read and some elements of the books, such as characters, settings, plots, and themes; construction of time lines related to the unit theme; creative dramatics based on readings; writing related to the theme; and so on. For example, students may cooperatively write a story with the same theme that appears in the books they have read in the unit (Marzano, 1990).

Example 5.6 shows a thematic literature unit plan that is based on a theme focus from a core book.

Individualized Reading Approach

The ***individualized reading approach*** encourages students to move at their own paces through reading material they have chosen rather than requiring them to move through teacher-prescribed material at the same pace as other students placed in the same group for reading instruction. With the individualized reading approach, which is designed to encourage independent reading, each student receives assistance in improving performance when the need for such assistance becomes apparent.

EXAMPLE 5.6 Thematic Literature Unit Plan

Book: *The Breadwinner* by Deborah Ellis

Focus: Survival in a War-Torn Land

Grade: Sixth or Seventh

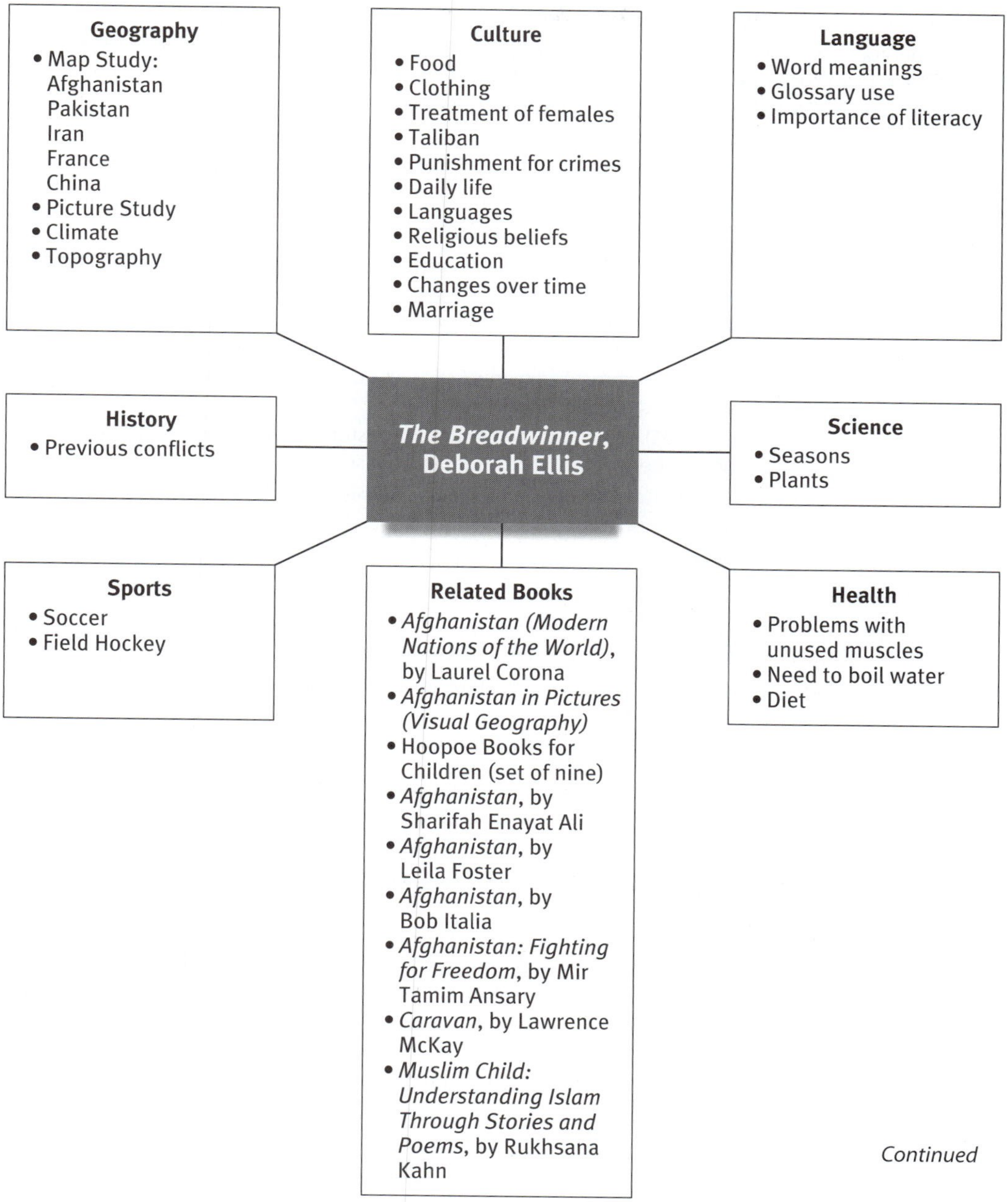

Geography
- Map Study:
  Afghanistan
  Pakistan
  Iran
  France
  China
- Picture Study
- Climate
- Topography

Culture
- Food
- Clothing
- Treatment of females
- Taliban
- Punishment for crimes
- Daily life
- Languages
- Religious beliefs
- Education
- Changes over time
- Marriage

Language
- Word meanings
- Glossary use
- Importance of literacy

History
- Previous conflicts

***The Breadwinner*, Deborah Ellis**

Science
- Seasons
- Plants

Sports
- Soccer
- Field Hockey

Related Books
- *Afghanistan (Modern Nations of the World)*, by Laurel Corona
- *Afghanistan in Pictures (Visual Geography)*
- Hoopoe Books for Children (set of nine)
- *Afghanistan*, by Sharifah Enayat Ali
- *Afghanistan*, by Leila Foster
- *Afghanistan*, by Bob Italia
- *Afghanistan: Fighting for Freedom*, by Mir Tamim Ansary
- *Caravan*, by Lawrence McKay
- *Muslim Child: Understanding Islam Through Stories and Poems*, by Rukhsana Kahn

Health
- Problems with unused muscles
- Need to boil water
- Diet

Continued

EXAMPLE 5.6 Thematic Literature Unit Plan *(cont.)*

Prereading

1. Ask: "Have you heard of Afghanistan? Where did you hear about it? What did you learn from this source?" (Most students will have heard of it from television, newspapers, radio, magazines, or their parents.)
2. Start a K-W-L chart of things the students know about Afghanistan and things they want to learn. (See Chapter 3 for a discussion of the K-W-L Procedure.)
3. Point out the glossary in this book, and discuss glossary use.
4. Preteach general vocabulary words from the book that your students may find problematic, for example, *decreed, smuggling,* and *stench,* as well as alerting them to difficult words that appear in the glossary.
5. Let students browse through books related to Afghanistan that you place in a classroom display. Examples:
   - *Afghanistan (Modern Nations of the World)*, by Laurel Corona (2002). For general background.
   - *Afghanistan in Pictures (Visual Geography),* edited by Camille Mirepoix (1997). To help them visualize the location.
   - Set of nine children's books by Idries Shah: *The Man with Bad Manners; The Old Woman and the Eagle; The Boy Without a Name; Neem the Half-Boy; The Farmer's Wife; The Clever Boy and the Terrible, Dangerous Animal; The Magic Horse; The Lion Who Saw Himself in the Water;* and *The Silly Chicken*. (This set has a manual for parents and teachers available on the Internet at **www.hoopoekids.com/.** The manual suggests questions for before-, during-, and after-reading activities.) Easy reading for struggling students.
   - *Afghanistan*, by Sharifah Enayat Ali (1995). Describes the geography, history, government, economy, and culture of this country, located on the crossroads between Europe and the Far East.
   - *Afghanistan*, by Leila Foster (1996). An introduction to the geography, history, culture, and people of Afghanistan.
   - *Afghanistan: Fighting for Freedom*, by Mir Tamim Ansary (1991). Background information.
   - *Caravan,* by Lawrence McKay (1995). Easy reading for struggling readers. A teacher's guide for this book is available at **http://www.leeandlow.com/teachers/guide6.html.**
   - *Afghanistan,* by Bob Italia (2002). Background information.
   - *Muslim Child: Understanding Islam Through Stories and Poems*, by Rukhsana Kahn (2002).
6. Discuss the cover photo on the book *The Breadwinner.* Pay attention to the manner of dress of the people in the picture.
7. Discuss the maps on pages 4 and 5 of *The Breadwinner.* Emphasize the location of Afghanistan and the surrounding countries.

During Reading

1. Have students keep literature logs about their reading. Periodically ask students to share entries from these logs with their classmates.
2. Have students add to the K-W-L chart as they read.
3. Have students, as they read, look for material on the areas of concern in the web: climate, topography, food, clothing, treatment of females, Taliban, punishments for crimes, daily life, languages, religious beliefs, education, changes over time, marriage, importance of literacy, seasons, plants, health, sports, and history. Suggest that they make notes on each of these topics in their literature logs.

Continued

EXAMPLE 5.6 Thematic Literature Unit Plan *(cont.)*

After Reading

1. Form small groups to discuss what they have learned about Afghanistan for each category on the web from reading *The Breadwinner.*
2. Have the students read *Parvana's Journey,* the sequel to *The Breadwinner.* Let them add information to their literature logs on each web category. Hold a class discussion.
3. Let each student choose a book from the book display to read or—in the cases of the longer nonfiction books—read selected sections and share with the class through individual reports.
4. Have each group take the category that they have examined and develop a presentation about it, using information from *The Breadwinner, Parvana's Journey,* books from the class display, and other books they have located.

Characteristics of an individualized reading approach include the following:

- *Self-selection.* Students choose material they are interested in reading. Each student may choose a different book. The teacher may offer suggestions or give help if it is requested, but the choice ultimately rests with the student. Thus, an individualized reading approach has built-in motivation: students want to read the material because they have chosen it themselves.
- *Self-pacing.* Each student reads the material at his or her own pace. Struggling readers are not rushed through material in order to keep up with the faster ones, and advanced readers are not held back until others have caught up with them.
- *Strategy and skill instruction.* The teacher helps students, either on an individual basis or in groups, develop their word recognition and comprehension strategies and skills as needed.

- *Recordkeeping.* The teacher keeps records of each student's progress. He or she must know the levels of a student's reading performance to know which books the student can read independently, which are too difficult or frustrating, and which can be read with the teacher's assistance. The teacher must also be aware of a student's reading strengths and weaknesses and should keep a record of the strategies and skills help the student has received. Each student should keep records of books read, new words encountered, and new strategies learned.
- *Student-teacher conferences.* Once or twice a week, the teacher schedules a conference with each student, varying from three to fifteen minutes, depending on

STANDARDS AND ASSESSMENT

the purpose. Teachers act as collaborators in the reading of text, as demonstrators of strategies, and as observers and assessors of reading behaviors during conferences (Gill, 2000).

- *Sharing activities.* The teacher plans some time each week for the students to share books they have read individually. The students may share with the entire class or with a small group. Sharing can sometimes take the form of book auctions in which the students bid with play money on the opportunity to read a book next. The "auctioneer" tries to interest the students in bidding by telling about the book (Bagford, 1985).

- *Independent work.* The students do a great deal of independent work at their seats, rather than spending most of the assigned reading period in a group with the teacher. Better readers can benefit more from time spent in individualized reading than can poorer readers, who need more teacher direction.

Exposure to different types of literature helps students build schemata for these types and should thus increase their efficiency in processing texts. In addition, the variety of material students read provides them with vicarious experiences that help build other schemata and thus contribute to future comprehension. Students encounter words in a variety of meaningful contexts, thus extending their vocabulary knowledge.

To set up an individualized reading program, a teacher must have available a large supply of books, magazines, newspapers, and other reading materials covering a variety of reading levels and many different interest areas. This collection will need to be supplemented continuously after the program begins, for many students will quickly read all the books that are appropriate for them.

STANDARDS AND ASSESSMENT

The teacher should have read a large number of the books available in the classroom, since familiarity with the books makes it much easier to check the students' comprehension. Starting a file of comprehension questions and answers for books being used in the program is a good idea; these questions will be available year after year and will help refresh the teacher's memory of the books. The teacher will also find it convenient to have a file of strategy- and skill-developing activities, covering the entire spectrum of word recognition and comprehension strategies and skills and a wide range of difficulty levels.

When starting an individualized program, the teacher should determine the students' reading levels and interests in order to choose books for the program that cover a sufficiently broad range of topics and difficulty levels. Two articles that can be helpful in choosing materials at appropriate levels are "Caldecott Medal Books and Readability Levels: Not Just Picture Books" (Chamberlain and Leal, 1999) and "A Newbery Medal-Winning Combination: High Student Interest Plus Appropriate Readability Levels" (Leal and Chamberlain-Solecki, 1998), both of which provide readability information

DIVERSITY

for excellent book choices. There are many sources that can help teachers find books appropriate for various cultural backgrounds, such as books featuring Hispanic culture or characters (Martinez-Roldan and Lopez-Robertson, 2000; Smolen and Ortiz-Castro, 2000).

Before initiating an individualized program, the teacher can plan routines to follow in the classroom, considering questions such as: (1) How are books to be checked out? (2) How will conferences be set up? (3) What should students who are working independently at their desks do when they need assistance? The room arrangement should be planned to allow for good traffic flow. If books are categorized and located in a number of places instead of bunched together in a single location, students will have less trouble finding them, and the potential noise level in the room will be lower.

STANDARDS AND ASSESSMENT

The teacher may find that having a file folder for each student helps in organizing and recordkeeping. Each folder can contain both checklists on which to record the student's strategy and skill strengths and weaknesses and a form noting conference dates and instructional help given. Students can keep their own records in file folders that are accessible to both them and the teacher. These records of books read, opinions, and difficulties encountered will have different content and more or fewer specific details, depending on the maturity of the students.

Student-teacher conferences serve a variety of purposes, including the following:

- *To help with book choices.* Teachers should spend some time showing students how to choose appropriate books. Teachers can encourage them to read one or two pages of the books they think might appeal to them and consider the number of unfamiliar words they encounter. If there are more than five unfamiliar words per page, the book might be too difficult; if there are no unfamiliar words, the student should consider the possibility that he or she could read more difficult material. A teacher can suggest potentially interesting books to students who find it hard to make a choice. Student-written book reviews may be provided for students who are having trouble deciding about books. Students can learn to write good reviews by examining models of written reviews and receiving assistance from the teacher or librarian (Jenks and Roberts, 1990).

STANDARDS AND ASSESSMENT

- *To check comprehension.* Conferences help determine how well the students are comprehending the books and other materials they are reading. Much of the time, the teacher and students may have authentic discussions about issues in the book during the conferences. Sometimes, however, the teacher may ask a student to retell all or part of the story or ask a variety of types of comprehension questions. (See Chapter 4 for information on question types.)

STANDARDS AND ASSESSMENT

- *To check word recognition strategies and oral reading skills.* The teacher can ask a student to read orally, observing his or her methods of attacking unfamiliar words and using oral reading skills, such as appropriate phrasing and good oral expression.
- *To give strategy and skill assistance.* If a student is the only one in the room who needs help with a particular strategy or skill, the teacher can help that student on a one-to-one basis during a conference.
- *To plan for sharing.* Some conferences are designed to help students prepare for sharing their reading experiences with others. If a student wishes to read a portion of a book to the class, the teacher might use a conference to listen to that student practice audience reading and give help with the presentation.

There is nothing contradictory about using group instruction in an individualized reading program. A teacher can group students with similar skill difficulties to give help. The important thing is to be sure that all students get the instruction they need when they need it and are not forced to sit through instruction they do not need.

In an individualized reading program, each student is expected to be involved in independent silent reading a great deal of the time. This time should not be interrupted by noisy surroundings or non-task-oriented activities. The teacher should make the rules for the reading time very clear and indicate acceptable activities, such as taking part in student-teacher conferences, selecting a book, reading silently, giving or receiving specific reading assistance, taking part in a reading group, completing a strategy- or skill-development practice activity, or keeping records on reading activity.

Individualizing a reading program is a huge undertaking. Such a program can be introduced gradually by using it only one day a week, while using the basal program the other four days, and increasing time spent in the individualized program one day at a time over a period of weeks until all five days of the week are devoted to it or by introducing the program to one reading group at a time while the remaining groups continue the basal program. After one group has become familiar with the approach, other groups can be introduced to it, until the entire class is participating in the individualized reading program. Teachers whom Harris (1996) worked with thought that using the basal for part of the week and literature-based instruction for the other part of the week would be a good way to start.

The main advantages of an individualized reading approach follow:

1. Students have built-in motivation to read books they have chosen themselves.
2. Students are not compared negatively with one another because every student has a different book and the books are primarily trade books, which have no visible grade designations.
3. Each student has an opportunity to learn to read at his or her own rate.
4. Student-teacher conferences create a great deal of personal contact between the teacher and students.
5. Reading books at comfortable reading levels develops fluency and can contribute to improved reading rates.
6. Students realize that reading is enjoyable.

Characteristics of this approach that some educators have considered to be disadvantages include the following:

1. The teacher must amass and continually replenish a large quantity of reading material.
2. The need to schedule many individual conferences and small-group meetings can create time difficulties.
3. An enormous amount of recordkeeping is necessary.
4. The program lacks a systematic approach to strategy and skill development.

TIME for REFLECTION

Some teachers believe that literature-based instruction using trade books should completely replace the use of published reading series that contain anthologies of literature. Others believe that use of both will result in the best instruction. **What do *you* think, and why?**

The Focus on Strategies below demonstrates the effectiveness of an Individualized Reading Approach in a middle-school classroom.

Language Experience Approach

The ***language experience approach*** (LEA) interrelates the different language arts and uses the students' experiences as the basis for reading materials. A student's background may be limited, but every student has experiences that can be converted into stories. In addition, the teacher can plan interesting firsthand experiences that can result in reading material that is meaningful for all middle-school students.

FOCUS ON STRATEGIES

Individualized Reading Approach

Mr. Neal is sitting at a table with Paul, a student who has been reading the book *Maniac Magee* by Jerry Spinelli. They are having a lively discussion about which characters in the story value reading and how they show that they do. Mr. Neal is able to tell from this discussion how well Paul has comprehended aspects of the book, but he is also engaged in a valid discussion of the content about which he has a personal opinion with a boy who has his own opinion, feels free to share it, and knows how to use events from the book to back up his ideas.

In the meantime, most of the other class members are reading from self-selected books at their desks or on the carpeted area of the reading center. When Megan has problems with a word in her book, she quietly leans over and asks for assistance from her assigned buddy, Tracy. When Tracy fails to be of help, Megan lists the word, page, and paragraph and reads on in her book.

Trey, who has a great deal of trouble sustaining independent reading over a period of time, is sitting at the computer, reading from a book on *CD-ROM* that allows him to click on words he doesn't know to obtain pronunciations and definitions. With this assistance, Trey is able to remain focused on his reading for the entire period.

Jason and Joshua are sitting close together discussing the mock interview they plan to use during the book-sharing time on Friday. Both have read *Hatchet* by Gary Paulsen, and have decided to share with the rest of the class by having Jason play a reporter and Joshua play Brian. They are intently listing interview questions and answers to use for this purpose.

As Mr. Neal finishes the conference with Paul, he asks who needs some help. Megan and Mark hold up their hands, and Mr. Neal moves to their desks to offer assistance. Then he returns to the conference table and calls Michael, who is scheduled for the next conference, to come up. Michael has been having difficulty with word recognition skills, and Mr. Neal asks him to read orally from some new material in the book he is currently reading, in order to assess the particular difficulties that he is having.

After Michael's conference, Mr. Neal will meet with a small group of students who need help in making inferences when they read. He will model the process for them and have them engage in some directed practice activities.

Each student in Mr. Neal's class has self-selected material to read when he or she is not involved in a teacher-student conference, a peer-planning session, or a needs-group session. The students know the procedures to use when they have trouble, and they know they can receive individual attention during conferences or at intervals during class time if they follow accepted procedures. The fact that they have chosen their own reading material heightens their motivation to read it and makes student engagement more likely.

This approach to reading is not new, although its implementation has changed over the years. Today the experience charts used in the approach may be either group or individual compositions; stories about field trips, school activities, or personal experiences outside school; or charts that contain directions, special words, observations, job assignments, questions to be answered, imaginative stories or poems based on experiences, or class procedures and routines.

Because the stories used in the language experience approach are developed by the students, they are motivational, and because they use the language of the students, the reading material is meaningful to the students. The language experience approach has been used effectively with students who speak English as a second language, providing material for reading instruction that they can understand (Moustafa, 1987; Moustafa and Penrose, 1985).

DIVERSITY

The language experience approach is consistent with schema theory. Because it uses the student's experiences as the basis for written language, the student necessarily has adequate schemata to comprehend the material. Students can use compound and complex sentences and a wide vocabulary in their stories, and they seem to find their own language patterns much easier to read than those in basal readers, probably because clues in a familiar context are easier to use.

STANDARDS AND ASSESSMENT

With the language experience approach, reading grows out of natural, ongoing activities. Observations made during dictation and reading of a language experience story and during the follow-up activities can provide the teacher with diagnostic insights into students' reading difficulties (Waugh, 1993).

Implementation of the LEA

Implementation of the language experience approach with a group of middle-school students for whom the process is new may take a number of forms, but the following steps are common:

1. Participating in a shared experience
2. Discussing the experience
3. Cooperative writing of the story on a chart, the board, or a computer
4. Participating in extension activities related to the story

After the students have participated in a common experience and have talked it over thoroughly, they are ready to compose a group experience story. First, the teacher may ask for suggestions for a title, allowing the students to select their favorite by voting. Then the teacher or a class member records the title on the board or a transparency. Each student offers details to add to the story, which the teacher or a student also records. After recording each idea, the teacher reads it aloud. After all contributions have been recorded, the teacher reads the entire story to the class. Then the teacher may ask the class to read the story in unison. Under cover of the group, no student will stand out if he or she does not know a word. Then the students may copy the chart on their own papers.

If the students have had experience with this type of activity, the teacher may proceed to other activities involving the story. The class can be divided into three or four groups with which the teacher can work separately. To begin each group session, the students may reread the story together, using the copies that they made the day before, or a volunteer may read it aloud to the group. Group charts can be useful in developing many skills and are commonly used for lessons in word endings, compound words, not-yet-mastered phonics skills, capitalization, punctuation, and other areas, because the students have identical material that is of interest to them.

If the teacher makes a copy of the story for each student, it is possible for the teacher to underline on each individual's copy the words that the student recognizes while reading the story. The teacher may then make word cards of these words for struggling readers, which serve as the beginnings of ***word banks*** of known words for them. After their first experience story, students will write most experience stories in small groups, sometimes working on a story together and sometimes producing and sharing individual stories. Some teachers use audiotape recorders for dictation for students who need assistance in transcribing their stories.

TECHNOLOGY

Class stories do not always have to be in the same format. They may take the form of reports, newspaper articles, descriptive essays, or letters, or they can be creative in content while using a particular writing style to which the students have been exposed.

TECHNOLOGY

Computers can be useful in a language experience lesson. The teacher can type into the computer student-dictated material and modify it as the students direct. A large monitor or projection device is needed for this approach. Teachers can print individual copies to be used in strategy or skill instruction. The students may be able to enter their stories into the computer themselves. Students can write stories on the computer individually or in small groups. A group of students can collectively decide what to say, taking turns entering sentences as they are composed, or some students can be in charge of keyboarding and others in charge of content and mechanics, spelling, and grammar.

The experience stories written by the group as a whole may be gathered into a booklet under a general title chosen by the group, and individuals may also bind their stories into booklets. Students will enjoy reading one another's booklets, and a collection of their own stories provides both a record of their activities and evidence of their growth in reading and writing.

In some schools, students write language experience stories, illustrate them, make them into books, and set them up in a classroom library with library pockets and check-out cards, as they might have in a regular library. Students assume jobs as librarians.

Middle-school students may want to write some experience stories by themselves, turning to their word banks or dictionaries for help in spelling. If other students are going to read an individual's experience story, the story must be proofread and edited for spelling, grammar, and punctuation. Rereading and editing also generally involve the students in more extensive revision, making judgments about syntax, semantics, and the topic and about whether or not others will understand the written account. These activities provide ways to emphasize comprehension when using language experience stories.

Word banks offer many opportunities for instructional activities. When students have accumulated a sufficient number of word cards in their word banks, they can use them to compose new stories. To develop comprehension skills, a teacher can use classification games, asking questions such as "How many of you have an adjective? A verb? A noun?" When each student has as many as ten word cards, the students can alphabetize them. Students can also develop dictionaries of the words on their cards, or they can search for their words in newspapers and magazines.

Middle-School Applications of the LEA

The LEA has many applications in the middle school. These applications are often in content area instruction: writing the results of scientific experiments; comparing and contrasting people, things, or events; writing directions for performing a task; and so forth.

Text structures found in content area textbooks, such as comparison-and-contrast patterns, can initially be taught through language experience activities. Then students will be more likely to understand these structures when they encounter them in content materials. First, the teacher can present students with two items and ask them how these items are alike. Then the teacher can ask how the items are different. The class can construct a chart of these likenesses and differences during the discussion. After the discussion, the students can dictate a language experience story based on the information listed on their chart. The teacher can encourage them to write first about likenesses and then about differences.

Heller (1988) has pointed out that direct teaching of story structure during language experience activities that are used with older remedial learners can be helpful. She also emphasizes the inclusion of revision and editing as natural extensions of experience story writing.

TECHNOLOGY

Many computer applications lend themselves to middle-school activities, for they allow students to enter their stories easily and provide ease of revision without the drudgery of recopying. A good computer application is the production of a newspaper based on experiences around the school. Programs are available that make the production of a nice-looking newspaper relatively easy for middle-school students. Students can be reporters, who initially write the stories and enter them into the computer; editors, who edit the work of the reporters; and layout specialists, who format the edited material (Mason, 1984).

DIVERSITY

Using the LEA with Students Who Have Special Needs

The language experience approach can be used to help students with special needs learn how to read. Teachers must weigh the general benefits and drawbacks of this approach for these students, as well as for other students in the class. It offers something for students regardless of the modes through which they learn best because it incorporates all modes. For instance, the learners use the auditory mode when stories are dictated or read aloud, the kinesthetic (motor) mode when they write stories, and the visual mode when they read stories.

The LEA promotes a good self-concept. It shows students that what they have to say is important enough to write down and that others are interested in it. It also promotes close contact between teachers and students. This approach has been highly successful as a remedial technique in the middle school and above, allowing low-achieving readers to read material that interests them rather than lower-level materials that they quickly recognize as being written for younger students.

As noted above, the LEA is a good approach to use with English language learners (Heald-Taylor, 1989). Students who know very little English, however, need to acquire additional vocabulary and knowledge of oral language before they dictate sentences (Moustafa and Penrose, 1985). To increase students' vocabularies, teachers can ask them to touch, name, label, and talk about concrete objects.

The language experience approach also offers many advantages as a method for teaching reading to students whose dialect differs considerably from standard English. A *dialect* is a variation of a language that is sufficiently different from the original to be considered a separate entity but not different enough to be classified as a separate language. Dialectal variations are usually associated with socioeconomic level, geographical region, or national origin. In truth, we all speak a dialect of some sort, and differences exist even within a regional pattern.

Each dialect is a complete and functional language system, and no dialect is superior or inferior to another for purposes of communication. However, for individuals to be accepted in some social classes and attain certain career goals, use of standard English is desirable. Teachers should accept and respect students' dialects as part of their cultures and environments, but should make them aware of standard English as an important alternative. Perhaps the most widely accepted view among linguists and educators is support of *bidialectalism,* which affirms both the value of the home dialect and its use within the community and the value of teaching students standard English (Ovando and Collier, 1985).

Critics point out that the LEA might simply reinforce students' dialects without providing contact with standard English. Gillet and Gentry (1983) propose a variation of this approach that values students' language but also provides exposure to standard English. The teacher transcribes the students' story exactly as dictated. The process continues in the traditional way, but later the teacher writes another version of the dictated chart in standard English with conventional sentence structure, using the same format and much of the same vocabulary. The teacher presents it as another story, not a better one, and students compare the two versions. The students then revise the original chart, making their sentences longer, more elaborate, and more consistent with standard English. They practice echo reading and choral reading with this version until they can read it fluently and have acquired additional sight words.

Some Considerations About the LEA

The LEA does not facilitate development of reading skills in a predetermined sequence. Therefore, all skill areas may not be covered. This problem is not likely to occur, since the LEA is generally used in conjunction with other approaches.

The LEA also does not offer systematic repetition of new words or vocabulary control in general. Still, structure words, which are important and need to be learned in context, are generally repeated quite often.

If no other approach were used along with the LEA, the limitations of the students' backgrounds of experience might drastically limit reading content, and the materials used in

TIME for REFLECTION

Some teachers think the language experience approach is too unstructured in relation to skill development to be useful. Others think it is valuable only as a supplement to other approaches. Still others think it is a valuable tool for use with struggling readers. **What do *you* think, and why?**

reading would also rarely be of good literary quality. However, this situation is highly unlikely to occur.

Programmed Instruction

Some approaches are particularly helpful for individualizing instruction—one is programmed instruction. ***Programmed instruction*** is sometimes used to offer individualized instruction. Programmed materials instruct in small, sequential steps, each of which is referred to as a *frame*. The student is required to respond in some way to each frame and is instantly informed of the correctness of his or her response (given immediate reinforcement). Because the instruction is presented to an individual student rather than to a group, each student moves through the material at his or her own pace, thereby benefiting from some individualization. Branching programs provide an even greater degree of individualization by offering review material to students who respond incorrectly to frames, thereby indicating that they have not mastered the skills being presented.

Programmed instruction in print or electronic form can also provide follow-up reinforcement for instruction presented by the teacher, freeing the teacher from many drill activities and allowing him or her more time to spend on complex teaching tasks. The programmed materials are designed to be self-instructional and do not require direct teacher supervision.

Programmed instruction does not, however, lend itself to teaching many complex comprehension skills, such as those involving analysis and interpretation, nor does it promote flexibility of reading rate. It also does not encourage student-to-student interaction. Word analysis and vocabulary-building skills are most prominently treated in programmed materials, so teachers may wish to use other materials (for example, basal texts) or techniques (for example, semantic webbing) to present and provide practice in the complex comprehension skills.

TECHNOLOGY

Materials used with programmed instruction may consist of print materials such as programmed texts, or they may exist in electronic format, presented on computers. The delivery of programmed instruction on a computer is known as ***computer-assisted instruction*** (CAI). Because of the interactive characteristics of the computer—it can provide immediate responses to input from student users—teachers find that it is a good tool for individualizing instruction. Because of its ability to repeat instructions patiently without showing irritation or judging students negatively, it is also useful for remedial instruction. Students who need extra practice on a particular skill or need to receive instruction that they missed during absences will benefit most from CAI. Computers are valuable tools for the reading teacher in ways other than CAI also.

Computer Applications in the Middle School

TECHNOLOGY

The computer generation is indeed here. Leu (2000) points out that "the Internet is entering classrooms at a faster rate than books, newspapers, magazines, movies, overhead projectors, televisions, or even telephones." Today's middle-school students expect to use computers, which now pervade every aspect of life.

Word processing, database applications, and computerized literature presentations allow teachers to plan many meaningful learning experiences for students. *World*

Wide Web browsers that give students access to information on the *Internet* can be powerful research tools. There is also a great deal of software available to help teachers with recordkeeping and other class-management tasks.

Computer applications may be made basically linear or highly interactive. Anderson-Inman (1998, p. 679) points out that "any chunk of electronic text (e.g., a character, word, phrase, or paragraph) can be linked to any other chunk, allowing non-linear movement through an electronic text document. This linking mechanism is the foundation for materials referred to as ***hypertext*** (or hypermedia)." With ***hypermedia,*** a variety of media—including text, full-motion video, sound clips, graphics, and still images—can be viewed and/or heard in an order chosen by the user (Poole, 1997; Wilhelm, 2000). *Multimedia* refers to the mixing of different media. Multimedia computer programs generally have interactive capabilities. For example, a student who is reading an entry from a multimedia encyclopedia may click on a word or symbol to view a picture, see a definition, see a video clip, or hear an audio clip related to the topic.

Hypertext allows enhancements to text that assist comprehension; with hypertext and hypermedia applications, for example, a student can use a mouse pointer and click when the cursor is over boldfaced words in the material. This may cause the program to display a glossary text that defines the word, provide a picture, or read the word aloud. In this sense, hypertext is similar to footnotes in showing relationships between texts (Klein and Olson, 2001). (Books on CD-ROM are examples of hypertext and hypermedia applications.) Hypertext applications may also provide graphic organizers or interspersed questions. They may offer options for taking notes as the reading progresses and printing out notes for review or as a basis for developing essays.

Hypertext materials present new reading challenges. Readers may continue to click on keywords that lead them further away from the original text; then they may have trouble returning to their points of origin, a situation referred to as a "navigational problem" (Reinking, 1997). There is also the danger that hypertext and hypermedia lead students to read about an extensive number of topics superficially, rather than reading in depth about any single topic (Leu, 1996). Obviously, hyperlinks and hypermedia found in electronic texts complicate the process of comprehending text material for those who are accustomed to reading traditional print, which is linear in nature (Coiro, 2003; RAND Reading Study Group, 2002).

Word Processing and Desktop Publishing

Word-processing software is an excellent tool for both creative writing and writing of a functional nature, such as the writing of research reports. This software takes much of the dreaded labor out of editing and revising written products. Since words, sentences, and longer passages can be moved around with a few clicks of a mouse, students are less reluctant to reconsider the content, organization, and mechanical aspects of their papers and to make needed changes. Freedom from recopying an entire document is a definite plus, especially for reluctant and struggling writers.

There are word-processing programs on many different levels of difficulty, so it is possible to find tools easy enough for middle-school students and powerful enough to meet their needs. In fact, many word-processing programs can fulfill the capabilities of producing special print applications, such as newsletters and advertisements, that once required special ***desktop-publishing*** software. Desktop-publishing programs and multimedia programs are often used to set up special formats for such applications as banners and greeting cards. The programs usually have clip art, ready-made images that can be used for illustrations, and students may be able to create their own illustrations or modify the available clip art. (Many word-processing programs offer the ability to use clip art and integrate drawing as well.) *The Print Shop Deluxe* (Broderbund) allows students to produce signs, posters, and banners, as well as to combine text and graphics to customize reports. With *Imagination Express* (EdMark) students can make electronic books with sound effects and animation. A variety of *Imagination Express Series* titles can be used in social studies and science classes. *Creative Writer* (Microsoft Corp.) is a creative-writing and desktop-publishing program, and *Classroom Publisher* (Staz Software) is an easy-to-use desktop-publishing program suitable for middle-school students (Cowan, 1996). Lee (2000) found that use of desktop-publishing software helped fifth graders feel like "real writers" and that book reports posted on the World Wide Web caused sixth graders to care about the grammar, accuracy, and tone of their writing.

The full facilitative effects of word processing on the quality of student writing may not be evident, however, until students become proficient in the use of the program and the equipment (Owston, Murphy, and Wideman, 1992; Schumm and Saumell, 1993). Peer assistance with computer tasks can help alleviate problems with use of programs and equipment. Such assistance often appears to occur spontaneously, but teachers can capitalize on students' expertise by assigning peer tutors. There are particular advantages when lower-achieving students get the chance to be the experts (Sandholtz, Ringstaff, and Dwyer, 1997).

Many word-processing programs include dictionaries and thesauruses, which students can use to help them make decisions about their word choices. The dictionary can be used in deciding if a word has the correct meaning for the context; the thesaurus can be used in choosing a synonym when a word has been overused in a selection or to pick a word that fits the situation exactly.

Use of spelling checkers and grammar checkers alerts students to words that *may* be misspelled or constructions that *may* need modification, but the checkers do not make the decisions about what will actually be done. Students have to look at each comment and decide on its merits. This is a critical reading activity that is a natural part of the writing process.

E-mail (Electronic Mail)

LITERATURE

E-mail has many applications for literacy instruction in the middle school. Students can e-mail other students in different classes, states, or countries. They can discuss the locales in which they live, customs of their countries, current events, topics being studied in school, and literature they are reading. (See the Focus on Strategies on E-mail Conversations About Literature earlier in this chapter.) E-mail correspondence with other students, teachers, mentors, and resource people can result in improvement in writing skills, for it is writing for an authentic audience and a real purpose. Use of such experiences has resulted in lengthier writing and improved attitudes and performance in reading and writing for middle-grade students (Moore, 1991).

DIVERSITY Stivers (1996) paired college students taking a methods course with middle-school students with special needs for e-mail conversation and skill instruction about writing. The public-school students responded well, and the college students showed enhanced self-esteem as a result of the program.

Electronic Videoconferencing

Most middle-school classrooms do not yet have the cameras and software needed for ***videoconferencing,*** but this may be an application on the horizon for literacy instruction. In videoconferencing, individuals hold conferences over the Internet with others who can be seen on their computer monitors and heard through their speakers. The advantages of this method for bringing such people as authors of children's books, scientists, and historians into contact with elementary-school students are obvious. Students could be responsible for researching the person, literature, or topic of conversation ahead of time, writing interview questions, conducting a controlled interview, taking notes on the discussion, and writing reports on the results—all valid literacy activities. This type of interaction could also take place between two groups of middle-school students from different parts of the world. Maring (2002) has used videoconferencing in his cyber mentoring projects at Washington State University in which preservice education students and K–12 students work together.

Interactive Internet Projects

DIVERSITY There are many interactive Internet projects that allow students to work with other students from around the United States and even worldwide. Kidlink (**http://www.kidlink.org**) is a site for an organization focused on enhancing global communication among children up through secondary school. The International Telementor Program "facilitates electronic mentoring relationships between professional adults and students worldwide." The mentors communicate through "a secure Web-based messaging system" (**http://www.telementor.org/program.cfm**).

DIVERSITY Leu, Castek, Henry, Coiro, and McMullan (2004) describe Book Raps (**http://rite.ed.qut.edu.au/oz-teachernet/projects/book-rap/index1.html**), which are online versions of literature circles or response groups. "In a Book Rap, classes from around the world read together and then exchange responses by e-mail through a listserv or common mailing list. Classes in Australia, Germany, Japan, and Chile might, for example, sign up to read and exchange responses to a work such as *The Giver* by Lois Lowry during a common three-week period" (p. 502).

To locate collaborative projects with schools in other countries, Leu, Karchmer, and Leu (1999) suggest checking out the Intercultural E-mail Classroom Connection (**http: //www.iecc.org/**). Global Schoolhouse Projects and Programs Main Page (**http://www. gsn.org/**) is a resource for permanent, ongoing Internet projects. These authors also list many other literacy-rich Internet projects that are worthy of attention.

In addition to communication with students at other schools, students can develop literacy and technology skills as they build their own websites or a class website. Students in one middle-school Web-design course were presented with authentic tasks and software tools to learn about Web design. The students worked in small groups to make decisions about how to complete real-world tasks, including planning, creating, and publishing an electronic tour of their school on the Web. They used digital cameras, computers with Web authoring software, and school blueprints. Students acquired technological skills as well as improving other language skills through activities such as speaking and listening in groups, reading blueprints, and writing (Basden, 2001).

DIVERSITY

Technology to Meet Diverse Student Needs

Technology can be used to help address the diverse needs of students in a classroom. Many computer applications, for example, can be used by students working at a variety of reading levels. Gifted and talented students can pursue independent inquiry through Internet research or creating their own websites, activities that often require both divergent and convergent thinking skills. Supportive technology can also help students overcome some reading problems. Computer-supported instruction can help "at-risk" students who have reading difficulties (McKenna, Reinking, Labbo, and Kieffer, 1999).

Many computers are capable of reading texts aloud, using synthetic speech. This enhances the utility of computer programs for second language learners and readers with visual disabilities. Computers can also provide larger print for visually impaired readers, and the color and typeface of print shown on the monitor can be changed.

Other computer technologies are available for students who have physical problems. There are special pads that serve as input devices for students with physical disabilities that affect their motor control. Voice recognition programs are becoming more widely available, allowing speech input for students who lack motor control. Zorfass, Corley, and Remz (1994) describe a computer keyboard with Braille overlays on the keys used in conjunction with a word-processing program with speech feedback to allow a blind girl with cerebral palsy to type and monitor her writing. An application referred to as *word prediction* allows students who have fine-motor difficulties to begin typing words. As the students type, lists of words beginning that way appear, allowing the students to choose the desired words without having to type them in their entirety. Another application, called *abbreviation expansion,* allows whole messages to be encoded and retrieved with a given keystroke combination. Headsticks, mouthsticks, and customized hand-held pointers are also available for students with physical problems. Any student who can make a consistent movement of some kind can use a computer. Braille translation programs are available to allow printouts on Braille printers (Zorfass, Corley, and Remz, 1994).

LITERATURE

Combining Computer Applications and Literature

Literature-oriented teachers often use computer programs, such as interactive fiction programs, that are more open-ended than drill-and-practice programs. Especially popular are programs that allow construction of semantic maps, story maps, and interactive branching stories, as well as programs that offer onscreen activities tied in with popular trade books.

WebQuests, learning activities developed by Bernie Dodge (1997), are good tools to use with literature selections. "A WebQuest is an inquiry-based approach to learning that helps students explore essential questions" (Teclehaimanot and Lamb, 2004,

p. 1). WebQuests promote skills in navigating the Internet, as well as critical thinking skills (Dodge, 1998). They also generally require students to perform more complex tasks than just doing a report. Possible tasks in WebQuests include "creation of a hyperstudio project, videoconferencing, and using email, databases, and spreadsheets" (Watson, 1999).

WebQuests that focus on literature selections provide activities that involve the students in exploring literary elements, such as theme, plot, characters, or setting. In fact, WebQuests can be developed that focus on a single book or on a number of books on various difficulty levels, allowing for differentiation of instruction within the coverage of a single theme unit. Each WebQuest has an introduction, a task, a process to follow, resources to search for information, guidance on organizing the information that is collected, an evaluation, and a conclusion. Dodge (1997) sees WebQuests as usually being group activities. They may provide the learners with roles to play, such as reporter or detective. There are many WebQuests on the Internet that teachers have created and posted. Using a ready-made one can be a time-saver. However, if there isn't an appropriate one already developed, a number of websites contain detailed information about how to construct WebQuests. Teclehaimanot and Lamb (2004) offer excellent ideas for developing WebQuests for literature.

Many teachers use combinations of computer applications, along with other media, in their lessons regularly. Wepner and Ray (2000) tell about Mr. Xavier, a fifth-grade teacher, who uses the computer program *Reading Galaxy* to introduce two survival novels, Paulsen's *Hatchet* and George's *Julie of the Wolves*. His students read these two novels as part of a combined language arts–social studies unit. The computer "program is designed to stimulate interest in reading, using a game-show format to present character, setting, initial conflicts, and author backgrounds" (p. 77) for these and other middle-school novels. The teacher is also using Internet and CD-ROM maps in the unit, as well as Internet sites to check on facts about Alaska, and he sets up Alaskan keypals for his students.

Evaluating Technological Applications

All applications of technology in the classroom need to be evaluated for appropriateness and effectiveness, just as other materials should be. Teachers should not decide to use material or equipment simply because it is there. There are some specific concerns in evaluating computer software, such as the ones in Example 5.7.

Websites used for educational purposes must be carefully evaluated, as well. Example 5.8 presents some questions to ask when evaluating websites.

Eclectic Approaches

Eclectic approaches combine the desirable aspects of a number of different methods rather than strictly adhering to a single one. Research has not found one method that works for everyone, but has repeatedly pointed to the teacher as the key factor in effective programs. An effective teacher integrates materials and methods as is appropriate to meet students' needs. As Duffy and Hoffman (1999) point out, laws that mandate a single method for reading instruction keep teachers from adjusting instruction for

EXAMPLE 5.7 Evaluating Computer Software

When evaluating computer software, ask the following questions:

1. Is the program compatible with the available hardware and operating system?
2. Does the program meet a curricular need better than another approach would?
3. Is the program well documented?
   a. Are the objectives of the program clearly presented?
   b. Are steps for running the program clearly stated?
   c. Are hardware requirements for the program clearly specified, and is this hardware available?
   d. Are time requirements for program use described, and are they reasonable for classroom use? (If a program can be saved at any time and reentered at the same place, some of the problems with time are alleviated.)
4. Is the program user-friendly?
5. Is there a management system that keeps up with a student's performance on the program, if that would be appropriate?
6. Are the screens well designed and readable?
7. Is the program essentially crash-proof?
8. Is feedback about performance offered to the students? Is the feedback appropriate for them?
9. Do the students have control over the
   a. speed of the program presentation?
   b. level of difficulty of the program?
   c. degree of prompting offered by the program (including seeing instructions for use)?
   d. sequence of presentation of material?
10. Is the program highly interactive, requiring more of the student than just page-turning?
11. Is sound used appropriately, if at all? Can the sound be turned off without destroying the effectiveness of the program?
12. Is color used effectively, if at all?
13. Is the program adaptable for a variety of levels of students? Are your students within this range?
14. Is the material free of stereotypes and bias?
15. Is there a way that the teacher can modify the program for a particular class, set of data, or student? Is this procedure protected against student tampering?
16. Is information presented in the program accurate, clear, and grammatically correct?

EXAMPLE 5.8 Website Evaluation Questions

Evaluating Websites

When you are evaluating websites, you must consider the reliability of the sources of the material, accuracy of the content, clarity of the material presented, and purposes of the sites. Ask yourself the following questions when judging a website:

1. Can you determine who has developed the site? (If not, you may not want to place undue confidence in its contents.) If so, is the developer a reliable source for the information you are seeking? (A noted authority on the topic or an agency of the government would be considered reliable. Someone you have not heard of before may need to be investigated.)
2. Is there enough information given on the site developer that qualifications can be checked? (If not, be cautious.)
3. Are sources provided for information displayed on the site, so the user can cross-check information? (If they are, this is a definite plus.)
4. Does any of the information conflict with reliable sources that you have consulted? (If some of the information is in question, all of it is suspect.)
5. Is the layout of the site busy and confusing, making information difficult to evaluate? (Disorganization, particularly, is a bad sign.)
6. Is site navigation easy? (Sloppy navigational methods sometimes indicate a lack of attention to detail.)
7. Is the presented material grammatically correct, and is it free from errors in spelling and mechanics? (If it is not, the clarity is badly affected.)
8. Is the site free of advertising? (If not, look for possible bias of information presented, based on the advertising present.)
9. If currency of information is important, can you tell when the page was developed and last updated? (If not, be careful in accepting the information. If currency is not a factor—for example, for a Civil War site on which the material is not likely to become dated—this will not be a major concern.)

Source: Betty D. Roe, "Using Technology for Content Area Literacy." In *Linking Literacy and Technology: A Guide for K–8 Classrooms*. Shelley B. Wepner, William J. Valmont, and Richard Thurlow, Eds. Newark, Delaware: International Reading Association, 2000, p. 155. Reprinted with permission.

students who would learn better from another approach. They downgrade the professional nature of teaching and discourage innovation in the field. Duffy and Hoffman have in fact concluded that "effective teachers are eclectic" (p. 11), echoing findings of Shanahan and Neuman (1997) and Stahl (1997). Thoughtful eclecticism is based on experience, professional studies and research, and analysis and reflection, and it requires teachers who are adaptive decision makers (Duffy and Hoffman, 1999).

Teachers often take an eclectic approach in choosing instructional materials and techniques to fit their unique situations and provide a variety of reading experiences for students. The following examples are only possibilities, and teachers should remember that the only limitations are school resources and their own imaginations:

1. Language experience stories can be based on characters, events, or ideas in either trade books or basal stories. The teacher can plan an experience related to the story, lead a discussion of the experience, and record the students' dic-

tated account. If an experience such as this is used prior to reading the book or basal story, it can help to activate the students' schemata related to the story. It will also probably involve use of some of the same vocabulary in the story, providing an introduction to this vocabulary in context. The story may also be used as a basis for skills instruction suggested in the basal reader (Jones and Nessel, 1985).

LITERATURE

2. In a class in which whole-class reading of a core book is taking place, language experience stories can be written, based on material from the particular book being read. For example, if the core book is *The Cay*, by Theodore Taylor, the experience might be to try to weave a mat while blindfolded. The students could write a story about the experience and in the process develop a better understanding of the difficulty Phillip had when Timothy asked him to weave a mat, even though he was blind.

TECHNOLOGY

3. Computers can be used with any approach. Word-processing software, for example, makes the computer a natural tool for implementing the language experience approach.

4. Teachers can use the individualized reading approach for two or three days each week and the basal program for the rest of the week, or they can alternate weeks with the individualized reading approach and the basal. They may supplement either or both with occasional language experience activities, either on or off of the computer.

LITERATURE

TECHNOLOGY

5. Teachers can use a thematic literature unit approach to reading instruction, making use of pertinent basal reader stories as they are available and using language experience activities as appropriate to the planned curriculum. They may use database software to store information about the unit on the computer in an organized way, and they may use word-processing software to produce written reports about aspects of the theme.

LITERATURE

6. Walker-Dalhouse, Dalhouse, and Mitchell (1997) conducted a literature-based reading program that employed basal themes with middle-school students. Some of the selections were from the Houghton Mifflin literature-based reading program; others were theme-related trade books. Writing, language, oral reading, and independent reading were taught in the communications area. Writing and grammar lessons were related to the literature theme, although a grammar textbook was used. Oral reading groups read a common book and discussed it. Students also chose independent books from a group designated by the teachers, and the teachers developed instructional packets for each group. Students chose books, completed the activities in the packets, and had conferences with the teachers about the reading. Students responded well to the program.

TIME for REFLECTION

Some teachers believe that they should use a single approach to reading instruction. Others believe that using the best ideas from all approaches is preferable. **What do *you* think, and why?**

SUMMARY

Published reading series are the most widely used materials for teaching reading in elementary schools in this country. Basal readers have been improved in recent years and provide teachers with anthologies of reading materials, detailed teacher's manuals, and many supplementary materials. Some published series are called literature-based and/or language-integrated series because of their greater focus on quality literature selections and integration of other types of language activities with the reading. Literature-based and language-integrated series focus on more student-generated prediction and more instructional options for the teacher than are found in traditional basal reader manuals.

The directed reading activity (DRA) is the teaching strategy presented in traditional basal manuals. This strategy can be used with other reading materials as well. Teachers can use the enrichment activities of the DRA before the story to help build and integrate background. Comprehension monitoring can also be made a natural part of a DRA. An alternative to the DRA is the directed reading-thinking activity (DR-TA). Another alternative, guided reading, involves similar steps to a DRA, but focuses on matching students with reading material in leveled books.

Literature-based reading approaches include whole-class reading of a core book, literature circles reading several books for which there are multiple copies, thematic literature units, and the individualized reading approach. All of these approaches include various types of responses to literature. Whole-class reading of a core book, thematic literature units, and the individualized reading approach include use of minilessons. Thematic literature units center around a theme, a genre, an author, or a book. The individualized reading approach allows students to move at their own paces through reading material that they have chosen. Student-teacher conferences help the teacher monitor progress and build rapport with the students. Sharing activities allow group interaction.

The language experience approach interrelates the different language arts and uses students' experiences as the basis for reading materials. This approach has many advantages: it incorporates the visual, auditory, and kinesthetic modes of learning; it promotes a positive self-concept and fosters close contact between teachers and students; and it serves as an effective remedial technique in the middle school. This approach is also effective to use with content area activities for all middle-school students.

Some approaches are particularly helpful for individualizing instruction. Among these are programmed instruction and computer use, in addition to the individualized reading approach. Programmed instruction is administered through materials that present information in small, sequential steps. The student responds at each step and receives immediate feedback about the correctness of the response. Students are allowed to learn at their own paces. Computers are ideal for delivering programmed instruction.

Computers are used in literacy instruction for word processing and desktop publishing; to access databases, electronic books and reference works, and the Internet; for electronic communications such as e-mail and videoconferencing; for computer-assisted instruction; and for multimedia applications. Some computer applications and materials make possible the participation of students with special needs. Synthetic speech and large print on computer screens and printouts, as well as special input devices and output systems, are available.

An eclectic approach combines desirable aspects of a number of different methods. The only limitation to possible combinations is the teacher's imagination.

TEST YOURSELF

True or False

_______ 1. All published reading series are alike.

_______ 2. Teacher's manuals in basal reading series generally provide detailed lesson plans for teaching each story in a basal reader.

_______ 3. Basal reader workbooks are designed to teach reading skills and do not require teacher intervention.

_______ 4. Workbook activities are useful only for keeping students busy while the teacher is engaged in other activities.

_______ 5. The language experience approach is not useful in the middle school.

_______ 6. The language experience approach uses student-created material for reading instruction.

_______ 7. A word bank is a collection of words that the teacher believes students should learn.

_______ 8. The language experience approach promotes a better self-concept in many students.

_______ 9. The individualized reading approach includes self-selection and self-pacing.

_______ 10. The individualized reading approach involves no direct skills instruction.

_______ 11. Student-teacher conferences are an integral part of the individualized reading approach.

_______ 12. When literature-based reading programs are used, students interact with texts in meaningful ways.

_______ 13. Close reading of core books, discussion, and writing related to the reading take place in many literature-based classrooms.

_______ 14. Thematic literature units involve the reading of a single book by all class members and the writing of a book report on it.

_______ 15. Programmed instruction presents instructional material in small, sequential steps.

_______ 16. An eclectic approach combines features from a number of different approaches.

_______ 17. The language experience approach is not consistent with schema theory.

_______ 18. The directed reading-thinking activity is a good alternative to the directed reading activity to provide a more student-centered experience.

_______ 19. Word processing on the computer is useful for writing language experience stories.

_______ 20. Hypertext and hypermedia allow text and media, respectively, to be accessed in a nonsequential manner.

_______ 21. Hypertext and hypermedia usage may lead to "navigational problems" for users.

_______ 22. *Multimedia* refers to the mixing of different media.

_______ 23. Computers are now capable of reading texts aloud, enhancing their utility for struggling readers and readers with visual disabilities.

_______ 24. Any student who can make a consistent movement of some kind can use a computer.

For your journal . . .

1. Visit a middle-school classroom and then write about the instructional materials used in the reading program.
2. Visit a middle school and watch an experienced teacher use a DRA. Write your reactions.
3. In a section in your journal, keep reviews of pertinent websites and computer programs that you might wish to use in your literacy program. If you can, try each one with students, and write a reaction about its effectiveness in the journal. You may want to include your reviews in your portfolio.

. . . and your portfolio

1. Plan an individualized reading approach for a specific group of middle-school students. Explain what materials will be used (include reading levels and interest areas of the materials) and where they will be obtained. Outline the recordkeeping procedures; explain how conferences will be scheduled and the uses to which they will be put; and describe the routines students will follow for selecting books, checking out books, and receiving help while reading.
2. Develop a directed reading-thinking activity (DR-TA) for a trade book.
3. Choose a basal reader for a middle-school grade level you might teach. Examine it for variety of writing types (narrative, expository, poetry). Make a chart showing the frequency of the various types. Note also the frequency of different types of content (language skills, social studies, science, art, mathematics, music, and so on).
4. Plan a thematic literature unit for a middle-school grade level of your choice. Think about ways that you can actively involve the students with the books.
5. Develop a multimedia presentation on a literacy topic of your choice for a middle-school grade level and include a copy of it on disk or videotape in your portfolio.
6. Produce a series of transparencies or a computer-driven slide presentation, using a computer program such as *PowerPoint* or *mPower,* to help explain a literacy topic,

such as "Propaganda Devices in Advertising." Use the transparencies or slide show with a group of students to teach a lesson. Evaluate the results in your journal. Put a printout of your transparencies or slide show in your portfolio, along with the lesson plan that you taught.

7. Develop a WebQuest related to a literature selection or to a thematic literature unit for a middle-school grade level. Include a copy of it in your portfolio.

6

Language and Literature

LITERATURE 

KEY VOCABULARY

Pay close attention to these terms when they appear in the chapter.

- Caldecott Medal
- content literacy
- Coretta Scott King Awards
- cumulative tales
- fables
- fantasy
- fiction
- genre
- journal
- legends
- myths
- Newbery Medal
- nonfiction
- *pourquoi* tales
- readers' theater
- reading and writing workshops
- Sustained Silent Reading
- tall tales
- traditional literature (folklore)
- webbing
- writing process

SETTING OBJECTIVES

When you finish reading this chapter, you should be able to

- Explain the importance of integrating instruction in the language arts for middle-level students.
- Identify some relationships between reading and writing.
- Understand how to implement the writing process and list the major steps in this process.
- Discuss procedures for using journals and for implementing writing and reading workshops.
- Design a middle-level classroom environment conducive to reading and writing for a diverse population of students.
- Select appropriate literature of good quality and high interest, and read or tell stories expressively.
- Discuss a variety of ways to respond to literature.
- Identify the characteristics of a variety of literary genres.

This chapter presents a brief description of today's middle-school students and reasons for integrating the language arts throughout the middle-school curriculum. Reading-writing connections are demonstrated through discussions of process writing, journal writing, and reading and writing workshops. The chapter also supports the concept of enabling all students to make choices and to assume responsibility for their learning.

The chapter focuses on the use of literature to integrate the curriculum and offers ideas to assist the teacher in creating a classroom environment where students support one another's efforts and experience a sense of ownership in their reading and writing. It provides suggestions for selecting appropriate literature for middle-school students and suggestions for helping students choose books for themselves. The chapter also presents a discussion of literary genres and of many ways to respond to

Chapter 6 Organization

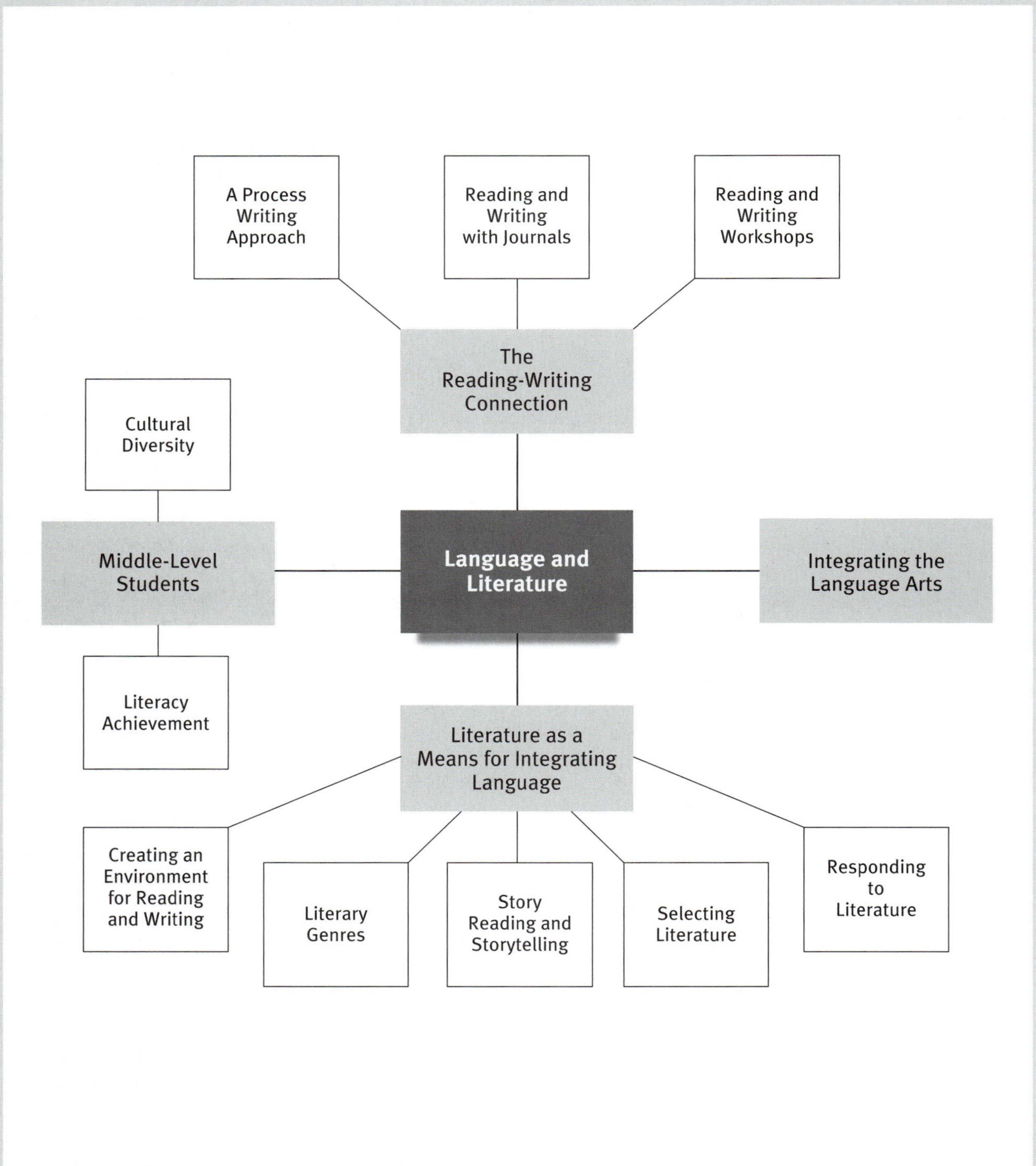

literature, including participation in literature circles, oral interpretation, drama, written expression, art, music, and the creation of multimedia presentations.

Middle-Level Students

DIVERSITY

Middle-school teachers today find that they are teaching diverse groups of students from many cultures and with a wide span of achievement levels.

Cultural Diversity

Middle-school classrooms are now composed of students whose values, orientations toward school, and speech patterns may differ greatly. Culturally diverse students come from many regional cultures, ethnic groups, and religions. In recent years, the enrollment of culturally diverse students in schools has increased dramatically (Wood, 1993), and the ethnic and racial composition of students has changed. Cultural and linguistic divergences influence how students learn and how they should be taught.

Multicultural education involves developing an understanding and appreciation of various cultural groups. However, simply having awareness and good intentions to be just and fair are not enough to achieve the level of changes necessary in classrooms. Students should be taught with consideration for their cultural heritages and their language preferences. Teachers need to concentrate on teaching the strategies and content necessary for all students to achieve success in American society.

Following are some general guidelines for creating a learning environment inclusive of students with diverse cultural backgrounds (Au, 1993; Coelho, 1994; Wood, 1993):

1. *Learn about students' cultures.* Find out about the students' language, and learn cultural variations in word meanings. Learn about students' living conditions and what things are important to them. Identify and be aware of cultural traits that affect how students learn. Show that you accept and value their cultures, even though they may differ from your own.

FAMILY

2. *Value their contributions.* Take an interest in what students bring to share, and listen to what they say. Create opportunities for their families to share their cultural heritages through learning experiences in the curriculum.

3. *Provide a supportive classroom environment.* Let the environment reflect the various cultures represented in the classroom by displaying multicultural literature and materials and including instruction related to multicultural education.

4. *Provide opportunities for cooperative learning.* Let students work collaboratively to develop social and academic skills, understand and appreciate the diversity among themselves, and learn strategies to use in their interactions outside school.

5. *Use multicultural literature.* When possible, choose stories related to students' cultural backgrounds. Exposure to such stories benefits all students. They

gain self-esteem by reading about their own heritage and broaden their concepts of the world and the people in it as they read about other cultures.

Marianne Baker (2002) shares her insights as to what can be done to improve the level of reading resistance often encountered during the middle-school years. Based on responses from interviews with two students, she has identified a definite need to create respectful classrooms where all students feel represented and accepted. She suggests using literature as a vehicle to provide students the opportunities to make personal connections. During her interviews, one student indicated that the only materials about African American males read during one particular year were "really dumb." This student response prompted her to emphasize the importance of personalizing the selections of reading materials available for middle-school students as well as providing student choice and adequate time for active reading.

The use of multicultural literature merits special attention because it affirms and legitimizes various cultures (Diamond and Moore, 1995). It helps students connect with people of different cultures and provides them with information and insights about their own heritages. Because it implicitly acknowledges individuals' rights to be who they are, multicultural literature increases understanding of and respect for differences. Ultimately, literature can contribute to the reduction of fear and prejudice.

We provide some guidelines for evaluating multicultural literature later in this chapter.

Literacy Achievement

STANDARDS AND ASSESSMENT

Middle-school students have improved their reading skills in recent years. According to *The Nation's Report Card: Reading 2002,* the average eighth-grade reading achievement score was higher in 2002 than in previous years with an increase in the percentage of students at or above the basic or proficient levels (*Reading Today,* 2003). Approximately one-third of the 115,000 eighth-grade students tested in the most recent National Assessment of Educational Progress performed at or above the "proficient" level in reading and math. Although these results indicate a positive trend in achievement growth at the eighth-grade level, middle-school educators continue to voice concerns for meeting the challenges of the middle-school student.

Jackson and Davis (2000) suggest that schools implement integrated, relevant curricula, supported by purposeful assessment and instruction based on the knowledge of students' development needs. Middle-school teachers must encourage students to become engaged in authentic, integrated situations. Integration means coordinating activities so that students can see the natural connections among the various forms of language as they work to achieve goals. Learning is centered on the student, and the student learns strategies and skills through verbal interaction with others. The following basic tenets for middle-school literacy instruction are congruent with the *Standards for the English Language Arts* (1996):

STANDARDS AND ASSESSMENT

- *Learning is integrated.* Students learn more effectively when they can see connections and relationships among ideas and subjects than when they learn bits and pieces of information in isolation.

- *Tasks are authentic.* Authentic activities relate to real-world tasks such as writing letters and reading for information. When students can see the purpose and meaning of the work they do, they understand why it is important.
- *Learning is social.* The purpose of language is to communicate with others. Students therefore learn to use language by sharing ideas, working cooperatively, and becoming part of a community of learners.
- *Classrooms are learning centered.* Students need to be actively involved in the learning process by accepting such responsibilities as making choices, taking part in negotiating decisions regarding procedures and curriculum, and self-evaluation.
- *Learning is holistic.* Students are actively engaged in tasks that promote understanding and meaning making. They learn literacy skills and strategies in meaningful context.

- *Literature is an integral part of the curriculum.* Since a widely accepted premise is that students learn to read by reading, classrooms should offer a wide variety of books and related materials. Good books and quality literature can be used across the curriculum as sources of information and pleasure, and they can provide the tools necessary to meet the specific instructional needs of all readers, including those who may be struggling.

Integrating the Language Arts

STANDARDS AND ASSESSMENT

TECHNOLOGY

Listening, speaking, reading, and writing have long been accepted as the language arts, but developers of the *Standards for the English Language Arts* expanded the concept to include viewing and visually representing. "Being literate in contemporary society means being active, critical, and creative users not only of print and spoken language but also of the visual language of film and television, commercial and political advertising, photography, and more" (*Standards,* 1996, p. 5). As teachers challenge students to integrate visual communication with other language forms, students are learning to use, interpret, and create illustrations, graphs, charts, videos, and electronic displays.

TIME for REFLECTION

Some middle-school students have difficulty seeing authentic purposes for language arts. In what ways might you help all students see the importance of literacy in their daily lives?

Middle schools vary widely in their organizational and instructional patterns. Teachers may work in self-contained classrooms, team-teach, or teach in a departmentalized setting. The most recent pattern found in middle schools is an interdisciplinary team approach, which often combines the areas of English or language arts, social studies, science, and math. Teachers working as an interdisciplinary team share a group of students and work together to create communities of learners. A shared block of instructional time provides opportunities for the team of teachers to plan together and develop interdisciplinary units of instruction (Jasmine, 1994).

In a well-planned middle-school program, integrated language experiences extend throughout the day into every area of the curriculum. For example, reading, writing, speaking, listening, and viewing are essential for learning about ideas that have changed history and science concepts that have resulted in new discoveries. In the model activity

MODEL ACTIVITIES

Integrated Language Arts Lesson

After reading Katherine Paterson's *Park's Quest* to the class, ask: "What do you think the title means? What is a quest?" Discuss the responses. If the students wish to pursue various aspects of the book, form groups to investigate topics that interest them. These topics may lead to such activities as a debate over U.S. involvement in the Vietnam War, a student-made book that connects the quest of King Arthur with that of Park, a diary in which students write from Park's perspective after each day on the farm, a report on the causes and effects of a stroke on a person's health, or an annotated bibliography of books about the Vietnam War.

LITERATURE

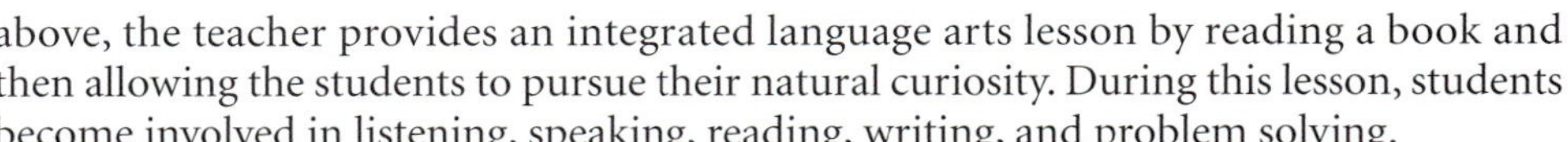

above, the teacher provides an integrated language arts lesson by reading a book and then allowing the students to pursue their natural curiosity. During this lesson, students become involved in listening, speaking, reading, writing, and problem solving.

The Focus on Strategies on page 233 shows how a single book can become the center for learning in many areas. The teacher may introduce a book that so intrigues the students that they assume an active role in developing meaningful related activities. They contribute their own ideas so that their investigation is truly learner centered rather than teacher directed.

The Reading-Writing Connection

TIME for REFLECTION

Some teachers believe they need to teach each language art separately each day in order to be sure to cover each subject. Other teachers feel that integration of the language arts is more meaningful and that eventually every subject will be covered. **What do *you* think, and why?**

Many educators have viewed both reading and writing as composing processes (Butler and Turbill, 1987; Flood and Lapp, 1987). Based on prior knowledge, attitudes, and experiences, the reader constructs meaning from text, and the writer composes meaningful text. Both reading and writing require the use of similar thinking skills, such as analyzing, selecting and organizing, making inferences, evaluating, problem solving, and making comparisons.

Reading and writing tend to reinforce each other. According to Smith (1983), students must learn to read like writers in order to write like writers. By offering a model, good literature instructs young authors through example and inspires them to try their hand at creating stories of their own (Lancia, 1997). Students quickly detect patterns in predictable and repetitive books, which they imitate as they write (Saccardi, 1996a). By carefully observing an author's use of dialogue in a story, a student begins to learn how to create dialogue when writing a story. Or in trying to write a description of the setting for a piece of writing, a student reads and rereads the setting from another selection to get ideas.

Table 6.1 on page 234 shows examples of links between reading and writing. Stotsky (1983) warns, however, that although similarities exist in the ways in which reading and writing are learned, research shows there are sufficient differences to warrant attention to each independently, as well as in combination.

FOCUS ON STRATEGIES

Developing a Literature-Based Thematic Unit That Integrates the Language Arts

LITERATURE Ms. Brison introduced Chris Van Allsburg's *The Wretched Stone* to her students by asking them to listen for clues that tell what the stone represents. This story was one of her favorites, and she hoped the students would like it too. When she finished reading it aloud, the students raised their hands to tell what they thought the stone really was. Isaac, the class scientist, thought it was malachite, and Katrina said it must be a mirror. Others thought it was an object from outer space.

The students begged Ms. Brison to reread the story, and she agreed to do so if they would listen again for clues. This time Janis solemnly said, "I believe it's a television because that's how television makes some people act." The others quickly agreed as they noted the similarities between a television set and the stone in the story.

Still fascinated, the students wanted to know more about the story, so Ms. Brison asked them what they would like to do with it. Mike suggested finding other books by Van Allsburg to read, and Beth wanted to learn more about the way sailors lived and worked long ago. Tim said he could teach a group how to make sailors' knots, and Molly said they could write logs as if they were sailors on the ship.

Ms. Brison recorded the ideas on the board, then placed each idea at the top of a piece of chart paper. She wrote *Other* at the top of one chart to allow the students to come up with other creative responses. She told the students to think about what they would like to do and then sign up to work on a topic. Those responsible for finding other books by Van Allsburg checked the school library, the neighborhood branch library, and the downtown library. They found *The Widow's Broom, The Stranger,* and *Two Bad Ants.* They also borrowed books that Ms. Brison checked out at the Teacher Center. Each day the students read a different story until they became quite familiar with Van Allsburg's style. "His books always have something mysterious in them," Jack said. "Yes," Connie continued, "and they start like it's for real, and then something happens that makes you know it has to be fantasy."

The students who signed up to research the lives of sailors years ago collected books about sailing, took notes, and compiled an illustrated informational book that told of the hardships of sea travel: the food sailors ate, the length of their journeys, weather signs, the consequences of storms at sea, and the stars they used to chart their courses. Some students, intrigued by pirates on the high seas, found stories and legends about pirates, particularly Blackbeard. Students who had read *Jumanji* decided to make their own board game with penalties and rewards. As their projects neared completion, most groups decided to put their work at a center so that they could see what others were doing. Another group showcased their work by dramatizing *The Wretched Stone* for the class next door.

This integrated language arts unit involved thoughtful listening as the students tried to identify the elements of mystery, defending their views with well-supported points about Van Allsburg's use of fantasy, reading related books and reference materials, and writing an informational book that portrayed the harsh life at sea. The logs they wrote as sailors impressed Ms. Brison most of all. The students had used such vivid descriptive words to express their feelings as they moved from being lively, active sailors to entranced viewers of the stone.

STANDARDS AND ASSESSMENT While the students were having fun investigating Van Allsburg, they were learning a great deal about language and literature. Mrs. Brison got out her curriculum guide and checked off several language skills for her grade level: making inferences, recognizing elements of fantasy, identifying an author's style, locating information, and using reference materials. Of course, there were other skills as well.

Writing and reading are closely connected language arts processes, and practice in one can help students in the other.
(© Elizabeth Crews)

TABLE 6.1 Links Between Reader and Writer

Reader	Writer
Brings, uses prior knowledge about topic	Brings, uses prior knowledge about topic
Reconstructs another's meaning	Constructs own meaning
Predicts what comes next	Predicts what should come next
Has expectations for text, based on experiences	Has expectations for how text might develop
Modifies comprehension of text as reading	Develops and changes meaning while writing continues
Engages in "draft reading"—skimming	Engages in "draft writing"—getting ideas, writing notes, making sense
Rereads to clarify	Rewrites to clarify
Uses writer's clues to help make sense of reading	Uses writing conventions to assist readers
Responds by talking, doing, and/or writing	Gets response from readers

Source: Based on Butler and Turbill (1987) and Hornsby, Sukarna, and Parry (1986).

Educators have explored many ways of using the linkage between reading and writing. A literacy program that integrates direct instruction and holistic approaches emphasizes reading and writing, with many regular opportunities for students to be actively engaged. Involving students in authentic tasks is motivating and promotes their understanding of reading and writing as meaning-making processes. The functional situations given in Example 6.1 are appropriate for any learner but particularly for struggling readers and writers

EXAMPLE 6.1 Imaginary Functional Situations

Directions: Please read the following situations. Think about your responses and write your reactions to the questions.

- Your dog is sick. What number do you call for help? Where could you take your dog?
- Choose a magazine you would like to order. Fill out the order form.
- Your mother is coming home on the bus that leaves at 5:30 pm, but you forgot what time she is supposed to arrive. Look it up in the bus schedule.
- You want to watch a movie special on television, but you can't remember the time. Find it in the media guide.
- Look through a catalogue, and choose four items you would like to have for less than $100 in all. Fill out the order blank.
- If a house catches fire, what number would you call? What are other important emergency numbers you need to know?
- You want to order a game that is advertised on the back of a cereal box. Follow the directions for placing the order.
- Look at a menu and order a meal for yourself. Find out how much it costs.
- You want to go to a football game in a nearby town. Find the stadium on the map, and be able to give directions to a friend.

TECHNOLOGY

Teachers and students have used message boards, or centrally located bulletin boards, for sending and receiving messages, and some students correspond with other students through pen-pal programs. Pen-pal programs are sometimes conducted electronically. These are generally referred to as keypal programs. Computers make it possible for young authors to share their work on electronic bulletin boards, class websites, and other maintained sites (Greenlaw, 2001). Several types of young authors' programs exist for various purposes, including encouraging students to write illustrated bound books and to share their writing with other authors outside their schools. Following are some class activities for combining writing with reading:

1. Provide opportunities for students to publish: (a) news stories that are modern adaptations of fairy tales and Mother Goose rhymes, (b) news stories written at the same time and place as the setting of the book the teacher is reading to the class, (c) a literary digest of news about books, or (d) advertisements for favorite books.

TECHNOLOGY 

2. Encourage students to write a radio or television script based on a story they have read. (First, they should read some plays to become familiar with directions for staging and appropriate writing style for dialogue.) Students could videotape the performance of their created script or record it as a digital movie and share it on their class website.
3. Arrange for students to correspond with pen pals or keypals from other regions of the country. As they interact, they are likely to become interested in those geographical areas, so provide resource materials for them to read about their pen pals' or keypals' homes.
4. Organize a young authors' conference in which students display and read from books they have published. The conference could take place among classes within a single school, or it could be district-wide.

TECHNOLOGY

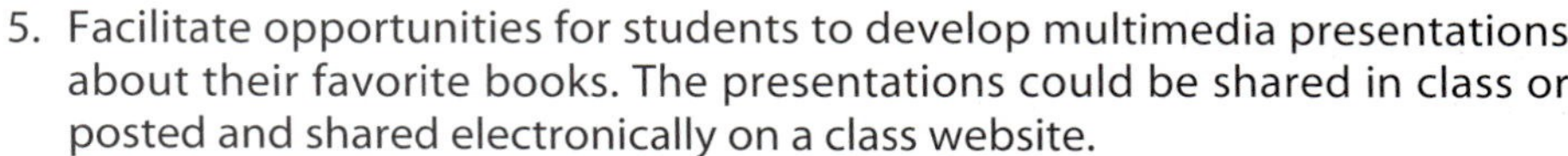

5. Facilitate opportunities for students to develop multimedia presentations about their favorite books. The presentations could be shared in class or posted and shared electronically on a class website.

Struggling readers and writers benefit from personalized reading and writing strategies (Walker, 2000). Literature circles (described in Chapter 5) offer students the opportunities to interact and discuss selections while assuming a variety of roles. SQ3R, K-W-L, and Question and Answer Relationship (QAR) strategies provide effective models for the organization and comprehension of large amounts of information. Repeated readings encourage students to use sentence structure and context clues to help increase their word recognition accuracy (Walker, 2000). Semantic mapping (as described in Chapters 2 and 3) is another particularly useful strategy for struggling readers because it helps them visualize relationships among concepts, as well as providing practice in reading and writing (Flood and Lapp, 1988; Pehrsson and Denner, 1989).

A Process Writing Approach

A *process writing approach* is a learning-centered approach to writing in which students create their own pieces of writing based on their choice of topic, their awareness of audience, and their development of ideas from initial stages through revisions to final publication. The process is ongoing and recursive, with writing in some form generally occurring every day and with pieces in various stages of development. The first and final drafts of a composition written during process writing instruction by a student who is an English language learner appears in Example 6.2.

DIVERSITY

Cross-grade process writing programs provide opportunities for middle-school students to act as literary advisers and attentive audiences for younger students and

EXAMPLE 6.2 Process Writing Drafts by an English Language Learner

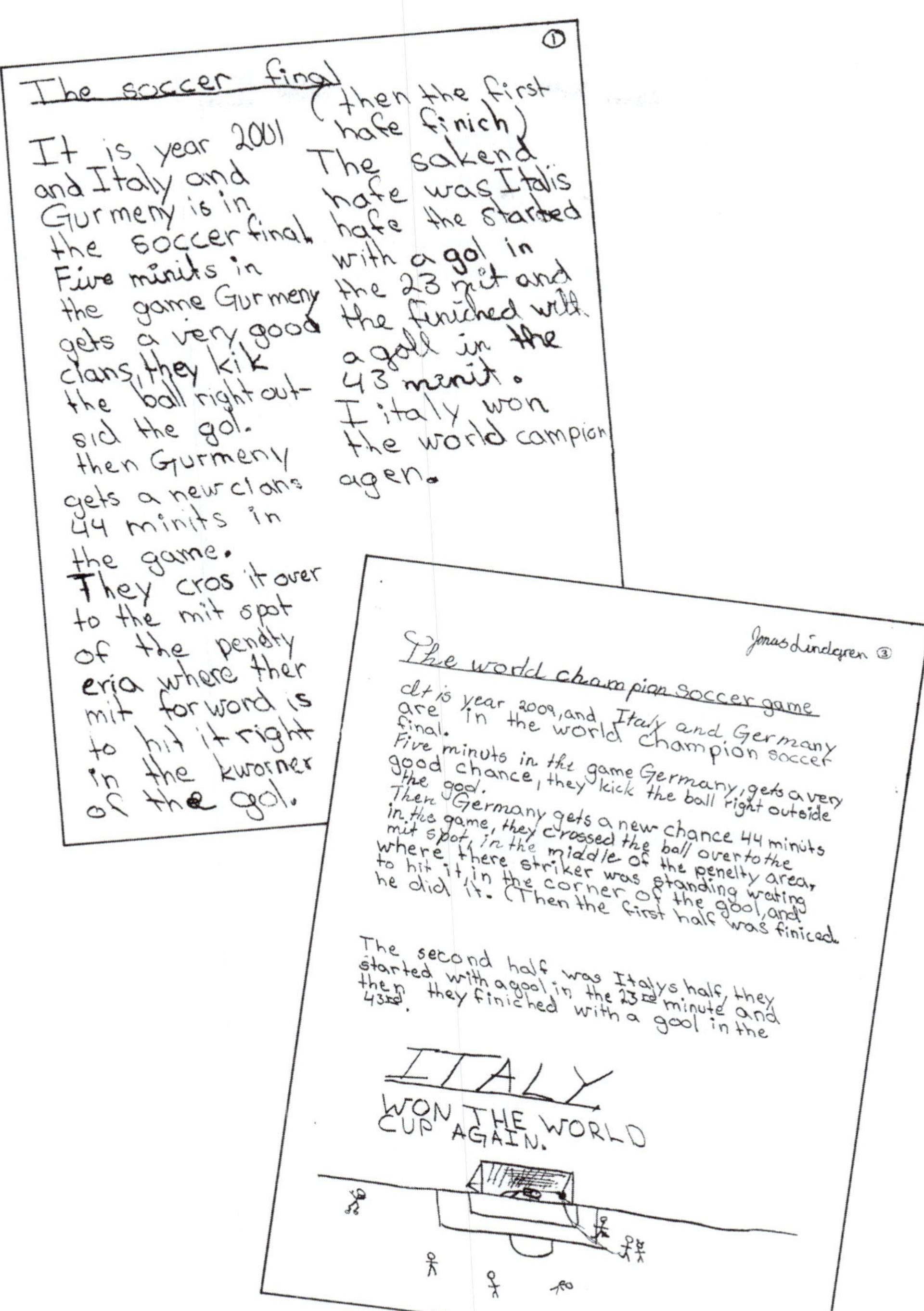

①

The soccer final

It is year 2001 and Italy and Gurmeny is in the soccer final. Five minits in the game Gurmeny gets a very good clans, they kik the ball right outsid the gol. then Gurmeny gets a new clans 44 minits in the game. They cros it over to the mit spot of the pendty eria where ther mit forword is to hit it right in the kworner of the gol. (then the first hafe finich) The sakend hafe was Italis hafe the started with a gol in the 23 mit and the finiched with a goll in the 43 minit. I italy won the world campion agen.

Jonas Lindgren ③

The world champion soccer game

It is year 2009, and Italy and Germany are in the world champion soccer final.
Five minuts in the game Germany, gets a very good chance, they kick the ball right outside the gool.
Then Germany gets a new chance 44 minuts in the game, they crossed the ball over to the mit spot, in the middle of the penelty area, where there striker was standing wating to hit it in the corner of the gool, and he did it. (Then the first half was finiced.

The second half was Italys half, they started with a gool in the 23rd minute and then they finiched with a gool in the 43rd.

ITALY WON THE WORLD CUP AGAIN.

for younger students to act as audiences for older writers. Roe (1990) conducted such a program involving partnerships between fifth graders and second graders; it is described in the Classroom Scenario on cross-grade process writing.

Stages of the Writing Process

The ***writing process*** consists of the following major stages: prewriting, drafting, revising, editing, and sharing and publishing. These stages may be used at any grade level. As students progress through the grades, they will be capable of producing more complex, more carefully edited works. The stages of the writing process may be briefly described as follows:

Prewriting. The author prepares for writing by talking, drawing, reading, and thinking about the piece and by organizing ideas and developing a plan.

Drafting. The author sets ideas on paper without regard for neatness or mechanics.

Revising. After getting suggestions from others, the author may wish to make some changes in the initial draft. These changes may include adding dialogue, deleting repetitious parts, adding depth to a character, clarifying meaning, providing needed information, or changing the ending of the story.

Editing. With careful proofreading and the help of peers and the teacher, the author corrects spelling and mechanics.

CLASSROOM SCENARIO

Cross-Grade Process Writing

During a cross-grade writing project at Crossville Elementary School, Austin Hamby's fifth graders were preparing to give their completed books to Ann Norris's second graders, who were their partners. It was the fifth graders' first attempt at process writing, and most of them were somewhat amazed at how well their stories had developed with input from classmates and teachers during conferences. One boy said, "This is a good story. I'd really like to keep it for myself." Nevertheless, he gave his book to his partner, who was delighted with it and told the story to anyone who would listen. A couple of times, fifth graders excitedly showed the program director their writing, saying, "Look what I wrote for my partner! It wasn't part of an assignment; I just wanted to do it."

Analysis of Scenario

Awareness of their audience for the stories caused students to devote much attention to the development process. The students were much more concerned about revising their stories to improve them and copying them neatly for their partners than they had been about polishing stories that were written before the project began. The fifth graders produced whole books for their young partners, complete with title pages, copyright dates, dedications, and "about the author" sections. Writing for authentic purposes made a difference in the quality of these students' writing.

Sharing and Publishing. After thoughtful revisions, the authors share finished pieces with real audiences. Pages can be fastened with brads, taped together, sewn, or professionally bound. Finished books may be kept in the classroom or taken to the school library, fitted with pockets, and checked out.

TECHNOLOGY

Word-processing programs simplify the writing process. They enable students to enter rough drafts quickly, revise frequently, and print their final copies. Students revise by inserting or deleting material and moving chunks of text, and they edit by correcting spelling and mechanics.

The process approach to writing provides a supportive format for struggling readers and writers. The revision and editing stages provide opportunities for all students to become published authors. Of special benefit during the writing process is peer conferencing, in which students assist one another by offering suggestions and asking questions that lead to better composition.

Reading and Writing with Journals

Students write in ***journals*** to record their thoughts and ideas, without concern for correctness of form or mechanics. Writers determine the audience; sometimes journals or designated pages within them are personal, and other times they are meant to be shared. Journals may be spiral notebooks or simply papers stapled together with student-decorated construction-paper covers, or they may be kept in word-processing files or folders. Students must have time for journal writing, preferably on a daily basis.

TECHNOLOGY

To introduce middle-school students to journal writing, the teacher might discuss diary writing and read books written in letter or journal form, such as Joan Blos's *A Gathering of Days: A New England Girl's Journal, 1830–32* or Beverly Cleary's *Dear Mr. Henshaw*. The teacher should write in a journal as the students write, to model the importance of recording thoughts and ideas. Teachers can encourage parents and family members who write in journals to model their writing habits at home. If students have trouble finding topics, the teacher might offer such suggestions as an important event, a perplexing problem, or a really good friend. Writers should understand that journals are a place where they can complain, ask questions, or express their true feelings.

FAMILY

Journal writing can take many forms:

- *Dialogue journals* are interactive, with the teacher or other reader responding to the student's writing. The responder should never correct the student's writing but can model proper spelling and writing conventions in the response.
- *Reading* or *literary journals* enable students to write responses to what they have read and receive the teacher's supportive feedback as a guide for further reading.
- In *buddy journals* (see Example 6.3 on page 240), student pairs "converse" in writing on a continuing basis, thus engaging in a meaningful writing and reading exchange (Bromley, 1989).
- A *double entry journal* enables the student to respond to a passage of particular interest. The student writes what the author says on one side of the page and

EXAMPLE 6.3 Buddy Journal Entries

Fri, 16, Feb, 1990

Erin,

You are a very good reader. You are going to be a better reader if you keep practicing.

do you like school? What is your favorite subject? My favorite subject is spelling.

Your partner,
Lesley Ann Richards

Wed. 21, 1990

Lesley,

I do not like school very much. My favorite subject is scisce.

do you like school?

Your Partner,
Erin Young

Source: Lesley Ann Richards and Erin Young, Crossville Elementary School, Crossville, Tennessee.

enters a personal response on the other side. Responses may be drawings, graphics, opinions, questions, reflections, or connections to personal experiences (Popp, 1997). In Example 6.4 on page 241, sixth grader Madyson Burgess responds to *The Westing Game,* by Ellen Raskin.

DIVERSITY Journal writing is an effective strategy for all middle-school students but especially beneficial for students who are acquiring English. Teachers should encourage English language learners to write for authentic purposes even before they are proficient in English. Students may use a combination of symbols, drawings, and invented

EXAMPLE 6.4 Double Entry Journal

Quote	My Opinion
"He found Madame Hoo in their rear fourth-floor apartment kneeling before her bamboo trunk, fingering mementoes from her childhood in China".	This in my opinion is saying Madame Hoo is missing her home in China or maybe she is missing her child hood.

Source: Madyson Burgess, Prescott Central Middle School, Cookeville, Tennessee. Used with permission.

TIME for REFLECTION

What are the advantages of encouraging all students to write freely in journals without regard for mechanical accuracy?

spellings to communicate their ideas. Dialogue journals enable teachers to move English language learners toward competency by providing them a nonthreatening, unstructured medium for exchanging ideas.

Reading and Writing Workshops

Reading and writing workshops provide opportunities for teachers to teach specific strategies directly during brief minilessons and for students to spend most of their time actually reading and writing.

"Writing workshops consist of four steps: a minilesson, a status-of-the-class report, the actual writing workshop, and sharing time" (Atwell, 1987). The minilesson lasts only a few minutes and deals with issues such as following procedures, writing realistic dialogue, using mechanics correctly, or starting with good leads (Clemmons and Laase, 1995). The status-of-the-class check is made as the teacher calls each student's name and records what the student will be doing during the workshop. The writing workshop, when most students write and/or confer, consumes most of the class time. Group sharing occurs during the last few minutes when students share their writing, try out ideas, and respond to one another's writing.

TIME for REFLECTION

In reading and writing workshops, teachers present skills and strategies during five- or ten-minute minilessons, then allow students to read or write during the remaining class time. Some teachers spend an entire class period (forty-five minutes or so) teaching skills and strategies, believing they need this much time to provide instruction. What do you think should be done, and why?

Although formats differ, most reading workshops operate in a similar manner, beginning with a minilesson that might be about comprehension strategies, literary appreciation, or genres. After the teacher records student-selected tasks on the status-of-the-class record sheet, students spend most of their time with self-selected reading and responses. During this time, the teacher may hold conferences with some of the students. Before the end of class, students spend five to ten minutes sharing their activities, books, or projects with one another (Atwell, 1985, 1987; Ross, 1996). Such workshops promote inquiry by letting students reflect on literature, interpret it, seek deeper meanings for it, and respond to it in various ways (Heald-Taylor, 1996).

Literature as a Means for Integrating Language

Literature can be the basis for learning to read and write and for developing positive attitudes toward further language learning. Teachers who integrate literature with language arts give purposes and opportunities for all students to engage in reading and writing throughout the day and across all areas of the curriculum. They read aloud to students daily from various genres of literature and provide a variety of good books for classroom library shelves.

Creating an Environment for Reading and Writing

The classroom environment should be supportive and free from the risks that inhibit honest expression. To help students feel a sense of ownership in their reading, teachers should allow some time for them to choose books. Middle-school students should also have input into how they are to respond to what they have read and how their own related work is to be displayed or published. They should be provided opportunities to decide the way that they share their own writing with their peers or others. In an effort to encourage adolescents to read, some schools report the organization of an "open mike" event where both students and staff share poetry selections. The selections are often original works but may also include selections from published sources.

Sustained Silent Reading (SSR), or Drop Everything and Read (DEAR), occurs in classrooms where students are given time, a wide selection of books, and encouragement to read. The teacher sets aside a period of time each day, usually from fifteen to thirty minutes, for silent reading. SSR can be used by a single classroom or by the entire school (students and staff). The teacher also reads to model the value of reading for everyone. Since there is no formal reporting or assessment at the conclusion of SSR periods, students feel no pressure as they read. This strategy is easily modified for students with special needs. During SSR, students are encouraged to choose familiar, predictable, or high-interest books that are easy to read. They may be encouraged to read their books orally to partners and to discuss them in pairs (Ford and Ohlhausen, 1988; Rhodes and Dudley-Marling, 1988). Adding Sustained Silent Writing and encouraging the use of invented spelling can also be effective for struggling readers and writers,

STANDARDS AND ASSESSMENT

because it includes the same element of student choice as SSR. Students who have been engaging in SSR and have teachers who read to them score significantly higher on standardized tests than students who are deprived of these benefits (Trelease, 1995).

Literary Genres

A teacher's knowledge of literary genres is essential for selecting literature and for establishing an environment that supports both reading and writing. Harris and Hodges define ***genre*** as "a category used to classify literary works, usually by form, technique, or content" (1995, p. 94). Following are characteristics of a number of literary genres or categories.

Fiction is written in a narrative style designed to entertain. Characters, setting, plot, author's style, and theme are elements often identified in fictional writing. Fantasy stories, folklore, realistic fiction, and mysteries are all types of fiction.

Fantasy stories are written in a narrative style, and a number of titles with enduring popularity may be categorized in this genre. Harris and Hodges (1995, p. 82) define fantasy as a "highly imaginative story about characters, places, and events that, while sometimes believable, do not exist."

Traditional literature (folklore) may include folktales, cumulative tales, *pourquoi* (why) tales, fables, myths, and legends. Traditional tales are often passed from generation to generation through oral narration and have no identifiable author (Norton, 1999). Folklore presents many possibilities for introducing different literary forms. Many students are familiar with the repetitive plot sequence in ***cumulative tales*** such as "The Gingerbread Boy." Such materials are useful for teaching reading to English language learners. Middle-school students are often entertained by ***tall tales,*** which feature individuals who accomplish astonishing feats. Students especially enjoy locating the exaggerations in tall tales such as those about Paul Bunyan or Pecos Bill.

DIVERSITY

Another form of folklore is the ***fable,*** which is usually characterized by brevity, a moral, and use of animal characters. Students can practice identifying the morals of the fables before they read the ones stated in the books.

Myths, legends,* pourquoi *tales, some Native American folklore, Rudyard Kipling's *Just So Stories,* and various "trickster" tales from all over the world involving characters such as Anansi provide explanations of universal origins. These are excellent sources for helping students to understand different cultures and become familiar with literary classics.

Teachers can introduce students to *poetry* by reading and rereading selections of all kinds and asking students to respond freely and with feeling. Students should then have opportunities to read much poetry for themselves and to participate in choral reading and speaking of poetry. Poems to which middle-school students respond positively are characterized by rhythm and rhyme, alliteration and onomatopoeia, and metaphors and imagery, to name only a few elements.

Nonfiction may include biographies, autobiographies, and informational books. The purpose of nonfiction literature is to inform and/or to instruct. Nonfiction selections are especially helpful for developing curriculum ties with various content areas and for designing inquiry-based lessons. Elements of style and degree of accuracy of the content of nonfiction selections offer middle-school students the opportunities to develop critical and analytical reading skills. When middle-school students are actively engaged with nonfiction selections, they can develop content literacy skills. ***Content literacy*** involves the reader's ability to read information and write information on a variety of topics through strategically selected organizational structures and appropriate styles. It requires the reader to gather, organize, summarize, and synthesize information (Fountas and Pinnell, 2001).

Reading *play scripts* is quite different from reading narrative prose and expository material. Bringing a play to life involves many interpretive and creative decisions about the elements of setting, action, and characters. Discussion about the way dialogue should be delivered helps students become more sensitive to language styles and usages that fit the context and the characters. Engaging students in activities involving the reading of scripts can help demonstrate the development of characterization. Middle-school students are often interested in reading about individuals like themselves. Strong, well-defined characters provide models for dealing with contemporary issues and encourage readers to reflect and problem-solve as well as introduce different perspectives and points of view.

Comparisons of narrative and script versions of the same stories can help middle-school students identify differences in the writing styles and help them learn to look for information in the appropriate places. Many plays based on children's stories are readily available. Basal readers often include play selections, as do some trade books.

Understanding different genres assists readers in the recognition of text structure and story elements. Readers who successfully identify common elements can use this knowledge to construct their own stories, strengthening the connection between reading and writing (Buss and Karnowski, 2000).

Story Reading and Storytelling

Reading aloud to students of all ages fulfills many purposes. Oral reading by the teacher serves as a model and allows students to experience literature they might not be able or inclined to read for themselves. It can encourage students to read more on their own, since an exciting chapter or section of a book often stimulates students to read the entire book themselves. Besides providing exposure to specific books, reading to students can introduce them to creative use of language in prose and poetry, present new vocabulary and concepts, and acquaint them with the variety of language patterns found in written communication. Hearing literature read aloud gives English language learners opportunities to hear the intonation and rhythm of the English language in meaningful contexts and to become familiar with the structure of the language.

DIVERSITY

Research supports the benefits of reading aloud to students. In *Becoming a Nation of Readers*, Richard Anderson and colleagues (1985) conclude, "The single most important activity for building the knowledge required for eventual success in reading is reading aloud to children" (p. 23). In addition, Michener (1988) finds research support for many benefits of reading aloud to students, including the following:

- Improves their listening skills
- Increases their ability to read independently

- Expands their vocabularies
- Improves their reading comprehension
- Helps them to become better speakers
- Improves their abilities as writers
- Improves the quantity and quality of independent reading

Teachers approach read-aloud events in different ways (Barrentine, 1996). Some limit interactions during story reading and focus on reflective after-reading discussions. Other teachers read stories interactively, encouraging students to respond verbally to their peers, the text, and the teacher as they listen. During interactive read-alouds, teachers ask questions to guide students in constructing meaning and making personal responses. Both approaches enable students to connect stories to their lives, explore layers of meaning, develop knowledge about literary elements, and personalize story meanings. Just before reading a story aloud to the class, the teacher might ask students to listen to how the author uses a lead sentence to create interest in the story or uses dialogue to develop characterization. During the story, the teacher can stop occasionally to point out a literary technique or ask students to visualize a descriptive passage. After completing the story or chapter, the teacher might ask students what they specifically liked or disliked about the way the author wrote. When the teacher points out such features to the class, students learn to evaluate material, thus making them more critical readers and improving their writing abilities as well. It is also often helpful to provide English language learners a copy of the selection being read aloud, so they can observe English print characteristics and directional patterns, as well as developing an appreciation for literature (Heald-Taylor, 1989). The Classroom Scenario on page 246 shows how one teacher reads aloud to her seventh-grade students.

DIVERSITY

When reading aloud, teachers should read in natural tones and with expression, providing time for sharing the illustrations, exploring key words and phrases, and evaluating reactions. The best stories to read aloud to middle-level students are those that motivate students to read, that the teacher personally likes and is thoroughly familiar with, and that possess the qualities characteristic of the best literature. Jim Trelease's *The New Read-Aloud Handbook* (1995) and *Read All About It! Great Read Aloud Stories, Poems, and Newspaper Pieces for Preteens and Teens* (1993) are excellent sources for how and what to read aloud to students.

The middle-school curriculum should include the reading aloud of nonfiction as well as fiction. When reading nonfiction, teachers can respond to students' special interests, relate books to thematic units, probe into student-initiated inquiries, read high-interest excerpts selectively, and expand students' knowledge of a variety of topics. As students listen to informational books and discuss ideas from them, they may find it easier and more natural to read expository text for their own pleasure. More middle-school educators have begun to recognize the importance of including nonfiction trade books for self-selection during in-class reading, and as a result students often respond more favorably to reading and demonstrate a greater interest in reading (Moss and Hendershot, 2002).

CLASSROOM SCENARIO Reading Aloud to Students

Ms. Smith sits in a circle with her students and asks them if they know what an urban legend is. The students respond and are eager to share examples of what they recognize as urban legends. Ms. Smith then reads the title, *Southern Fried Rat and Other Gruesome Tales*, and asks the students to respond. After sharing the name of the author, Daniel Cohen, the discussion continues, with students predicting what they believe the book will be about and Ms. Smith recording their predictions based on the title clue. A number of predictions are recorded. Ms. Smith then reads aloud one of the stories in the book. Following the reading of the story, several students laugh and comment that even though they realized that it was an urban legend, they were familiar with the story plot because they had been told the story before as if it were true. Ms. Smith prompts the students to reflect on the commonalities of several examples of urban legends familiar to the students. The students conclude that although the urban legends originate in various geographical locations, the plots of many of the stories reflect common fears and concerns of people. The students discuss how they might observe similarities of people by reading and researching more urban legends.

Analysis of Scenario

The use of this genre of literature provided a vehicle that engaged the interest of the middle-school students and led to an understanding about human nature. Sharing the urban legend as a read-aloud encouraged social interaction and discussion among the students.

Storytelling, like story reading, acquaints students with literature and provides good listening experiences. Listeners visualize the story through a "transfer of imagery" (Lipman, 1999). The storyteller uses oral language to prompt the listener to develop personal images of the story. Folktales are especially good for telling because they were told and told again long before they were captured in print.

Both teachers and students can successfully tell stories. Students as storytellers can develop fluency and expression in oral language. By preparing and telling stories, they also can develop poise and build self-esteem. As storytellers, students must be aware of pitch, volume, timing, and gesture, as well as the responsiveness of the audience. A logical progression is for students to move from hearing, reading, and telling stories to writing original stories, which are often based on literary patterns they already know (Peck, 1989; Roe, Alfred, and Smith, 1998).

Selecting Literature

From the thousands of books published annually for children and adolescents, teachers and media specialists must select quality literature that they think students will want to read. Making such decisions is a challenge and a responsibility. Teachers can assess students' personal reading interests by simply asking them to list three things that interest them or by administering an interest inventory. A useful source in selecting books is a listing of Newbery and Caldecott Award winners presented by the American Library Association. The ***John Newbery Medal*** is awarded annually to the author whose book is selected as the year's most distinguished contribution to American literature for children. Excellence in illustration is the criterion used in granting the annual ***Randolph Caldecott Medal.***

LITERATURE

Some educators advocate classics, quality books that exhibit enduring excellence, as the foundation for reading. Not all classics are popular with middle-school students, however, so it is important to choose appropriate works and avoid those that may discourage students from reading. Some favorite classics are: *The Borrowers* (by Mary Norton); *The Secret Garden* (by Frances Hodgson Burnett); *Where the Red Fern Grows* (by Wilson Rawls); and *Little House in the Big Woods* (by Laura Ingalls Wilder).

DIVERSITY

Another consideration in choosing books is their social significance in relation to human values, cultural pluralism, and aesthetic standards (Norton, 2003). For minority students, multicultural literature based on familiar traditions and values provides for and validates their own cultural experiences. For all students, such books can offer insights into less familiar cultures (Cox and Galda, 1990). Teachers can ask themselves the following questions to help them choose books that promote cultural pluralism and avoid portraying negative stereotypes:

- Do the illustrations and text depict the character in the story as a distinct individual, or as a stereotype of a particular ethnic group?
- Is dialect used as a natural part of the story, or contrived to reinforce a stereotype?
- Is the culture treated respectfully, or portrayed as inferior?
- Are the people and the settings described authentically?

One valuable instructional resource when searching for multicultural literature is the annual ***Coretta Scott King Awards*** presented annually by the American Library Association. The recipients are authors and illustrators of African descent whose books promote peace and world brotherhood.

Hadaway and Florez (1990) point out several ways to use multicultural literature. Teachers, with the help of librarians or media specialists, should select books that represent cultural groups realistically and integrate these books into literature and social studies programs. As they tell or read the stories to the class, teachers can promote vocabulary, comprehension, and writing skills, along with values education. Despite adult critics' recommendations, many children prefer to make their own choices. Each year, the International Reading Association–Children's Book Council Joint Committee publishes an annotated list of "Children's Choices," which appears in the October issue of *The Reading Teacher*. Each list is compiled by approximately 10,000 children who, working in teams, read new books and vote for their favorites. Since children are the ultimate critics of their literature, teachers and librarians should consider their choices seriously when purchasing and recommending books.

In helping students select books, teachers need to know both the books that are available and their students' needs and interests. Teachers can guide students' choices by helping them locate books on special topics, sampling new books to pique their interest, allowing time for students to browse in the library, and suggesting titles on occasion. Regardless of this assistance, however, most middle-school students value the freedom to choose their own books.

LITERATURE

Selecting appropriate poetry for students is especially difficult. Poorly chosen poems can prejudice students against poetry, whereas suitable poems will amuse, inspire,

Middle-school students are likely to have more lively responses to literature when they can follow their own interests in choosing reading selections. *(© Elizabeth Crews)*

emotionally move, or intellectually interest them. Middle-school students prefer poems with rhyme, rhythm, humor, and narration; works by Shel Silverstein (*Where the Sidewalk Ends, A Light in the Attic*) and Jack Prelutsky (*The New Kid on the Block, Something Big Has Been Here*) are favorites. The humor they use comes from alliteration, plays on words, or highly exaggerated situations, as in "Sarah Cynthia Sylvia Stout Who Would Not Take the Garbage Out" (from *Where the Sidewalk Ends*). Kupiter and Wilson (1993) contend, however, that teachers must sensitively cultivate an interest in poetry that goes beyond Silverstein and Prelutsky; they must build bridges from these popular poems to the rich array of diverse poetry waiting to be discovered.

Not to be overlooked are the intriguing nonfiction selections that can supplement textbooks or even substitute for them. So many appealing, well-illustrated informational books on nearly any topic are available that choosing the best books can be difficult. When selecting nonfiction, teachers should look for the following characteristics (Sudol and King, 1996):

- Content that is accurate and current
- Organization and layout that facilitate easy use
- Cohesive text in which ideas are arranged logically
- Specialized vocabulary that is clearly defined
- Attention-grabbing content and illustrations

Because informational books can be read or viewed at varying levels, most are appropriate for many ability levels. Struggling readers can examine illustrations in David Macaulay's *Cathedral, Pyramid,* and *Mosque,* for example, whereas more proficient readers can find out how these structures were built. Worthy (1996) found that nonfiction selections, particularly those dealing with sports, animals, drawing, or cars, are popular with struggling readers. Fascinating books about animals—books useful for enriching a thematic unit—include *Summer Ice: Life along the Antarctic Peninsula* (Bruce McMillan), a combination of text and photographs about animal life in Antarctica; *Raptor Rescue: An Eagle Flies Free* (Sylvia Johnson), detailing the work of Minnesota's Raptor Center in rehabilitating injured raptors; and *Dolphin Man: Exploring the World of Dolphins* (Laurence Pringle), a photobiography of Randy Wells, an authority on dolphins. Many teachers prefer paperback books, because multiple copies of one book cost the same as a single library edition, allowing teachers to order enough for small groups of students to read and use in follow-up activities and discussions. Paperback books are often available at special reduced rates through book clubs.

Magazines and newspapers, appropriate for middle-school students, are available for different reading levels and different areas of interest. These periodicals are excellent classroom resources and offer several benefits for the reading program: (1) the material is current and relevant; (2) the reading range varies in levels of difficulty and content presented; (3) several genres usually appear in a single issue; (4) language activities, such as crossword puzzles, contests, and students' writings, are often included; (5) the illustrations and photographs are excellent and can improve comprehension; (6) their low cost makes them easily accessible; and (7) they are popular with reluctant readers (Seminoff, 1986; Worthy, 1996). Classroom subscriptions to two or three favorites will enrich the reading program. Some popular choices are listed in Stoll's *Magazines for Kids and Teens* (1997).

Knickerbocker and Rycik (2002) examine Conley's description of middle-school students. He noted that middle-school students are readers who are still struggling to develop important reading strategies, while at the same time are confronted with demands of content presented through textbooks and various classroom assignments. He suggests that it is of paramount importance that teachers emphasize and model the relevance of reading while guiding the student through the reading process. The development of strategies, high level of motivation, and successful experience with reading all lead to success in the understanding and interpretation of literature.

Responding to Literature

According to reader response theory, readers are actively constructing meaning as they read. Since each reader differs in terms of background experiences and preformed attitudes, each interprets the text somewhat differently (Cox, 1997).

Rosenblatt (1978) proposed that any text can be read efferently (for information) and aesthetically (as a lived-through experience). Usually readers move back and forth along a continuum between an efferent stance and an aesthetic stance until they settle on a single predominant stance (Cox, 1997). They may be getting information as they read, but they may also be experiencing the emotions of the characters, the mood of the story as the plot unfolds, or a sense of morality toward an episode in history. For example, Lloyd Alexander's *The King's Fountain* gives a historical perspective of village life, but the courageous poor man's efforts to save his village tug at the heart. Both types of responses are important, but teachers tend to ask questions that call for efferent responses (Zarillo and Cox, 1992), even though aesthetic responses may be more meaningful and more enduring. Students need to have adequate time for reflecting on and responding to books in different ways (Cox and Many, 1992; Hickman, 1995). Students can express their responses by answering teacher questions, participating in literature circles, interpreting literature orally, dramatizing reading selections, writing, or creating art or music. For English language learners, reader response is especially beneficial because it allows each student to respond to literature uniquely in terms of his or her own cultural background and level of English proficiency (Cox and Boyd-Batstone, 1997).

DIVERSITY

TIME for REFLECTION

Some teachers' manuals—and often teachers themselves—identify a single theme or a single correct interpretation for a literary selection. Should teachers accept as correct other themes or interpretations that students discover for themselves? Can more than one answer be acceptable? **What do *you* think, and why?**

Responding to Questions

Teachers can prepare generic questions to encourage students to respond thoughtfully to literature. These questions may be used during conferences, for written responses, for group activities, or during class discussions. Questions should be open-ended, not limited to a single correct answer. Popp (1997) suggests four categories of questions, which are given here with sample prompts for each category:

Evaluation

What did you like or dislike about this book? Why?

Why do you think the main character acted in such a way?

Connection

How did a character make you think of someone you know?

Has anyone you know faced a similar challenge? What was it?

Comprehension

What is a theme of this story?

What does this story mean to you?

Strategy

How did you figure out an unfamiliar word in this story?

What special features helped you understand the story?

Literature Circles

An organized procedure for responding to literature is use of *literature circles* (Bell, 1990; Strube, 1996; Zogby, 1990). Chapter 5 provides guidelines for using literature circles. These groups give students opportunities to read and respond to literature, engage in high-level thinking about books, and engage in extensive and intensive reading. The formation of literature circles not only encourages discussion of the material but also meets the needs of middle-level students to interact socially.

Oral Interpretation of Literature

Fluent oral reading with intonation and phrasing that accurately reflect the mood and tone of the story or poem is another way to respond to literature. Oral reading is more difficult than silent reading because, in order to convey the author's message to an audience, the reader must pronounce words correctly, phrase appropriately, enunciate distinctly, use proper intonation, and pace the reading appropriately. To accomplish these goals, the oral reader should have an opportunity to read silently first to become acquainted with the author's style of writing, determine the author's message, and check the correct pronunciation of unfamiliar words. If the passage is particularly difficult, the reader may need to practice it aloud to ensure proper phrasing and intonation.

STANDARDS AND ASSESSMENT

Oral reading skills require special attention. The teacher may demonstrate fluent and poor oral reading, let the students analyze these performances, and then help students develop a rubric or draw up a list of standards or guidelines like the following:

1. Be sure you can pronounce each word correctly before you read your selection to an audience. If you are not sure of a pronunciation, check the dictionary, or ask for help.
2. Say each word clearly and distinctly. Don't run words together, and take care not to leave out word parts or add parts to words.
3. Pause in the right places. Pay attention to punctuation clues.
4. Emphasize important words. Help the audience understand the meaning of the selection by the way you read it. Read slowly enough to allow for adequate expression, and speak loudly enough to be easily heard.
5. Prepare carefully before you read to an audience.

When well-rehearsed oral reading occurs, there should be one or more people with whom the reader is attempting to communicate through reading. Audience members should not have access to the book from which the performer is reading so they cannot follow the reading with their eyes. Instead, they should listen to the reader to grasp the author's meaning and, if the reader is reading to prove a point, to agree or disagree. The reader must attempt to hold the audience's attention through oral interpretation of the author's words. A stumbling performance will lead to a restless, impatient audience and a poor listening situation.

Some examples of purposes for audience reading include:

- Confirming an answer to a question by reading the portion of the selection in which the answer is found
- Sharing a part of a published story, a poem (most poems are written to be read aloud), or an experience story that the reader has enjoyed
- Participating in choral reading or readers' theater
- Sharing riddles, jokes, and tongue twisters to entertain classmates
- Reading stories aloud to students in lower grades
- Reading the part of a character in a play or the narration for a play or other dramatic presentation

LITERATURE 

Books by Paul Fleischman contain poems for two voices that invite students or groups of students to collaborate in reading aloud. Sometimes passages are to be read singly and sometimes in unison, but students must read expressively and fluently to achieve the proper effect. *Joyful Noise* contains poems about insects that think and act as humans; *I Am Phoenix* consists of poems that celebrate a variety of birds.

Responses Through Drama

DIVERSITY

Dramatic interpretations of literature are aesthetic responses, and they help students find success because there are no right or wrong answers (Fennessey, 1995). Through drama, students can deepen their responses to literature and discover underlying meanings. Drama helps students become aware of different points of view and develops imagination and critical thinking. Through creative drama, bilingual students can interpret the stories they hear, thereby clarifying their understanding of story structure and vocabulary. Role-playing enables them to experiment with vocabulary and sentence structure as they explore their feelings.

Drama can take many forms. In *pantomime,* students speak no lines but show what is happening through their gestures and body movements. Fables are good for pantomiming. *Characterization* focuses on revealing the way characters feel, act, and relate to other characters in the story, and students attempt to speak, move, and modify their facial expressions as they become the story characters. *Creative dramatics* means acting out a story without using a script, and *choral speaking* or *choral reading* is the dramatic interpretation of poetry or other literature with two or more voices. In ***readers' theater,*** students read aloud in dramatic style from scripts; no sets, costumes, or props are necessary, and the emphasis is on interpretive oral reading (Cullinan and Galda, 1994; Savage, 1994).

Responses Through Written Expression

Traditional written book reports in which students merely summarize plots of stories have in many cases been replaced by more authentic responses to literature. Students

EXAMPLE 6.5 Book Recommendation

Hatchet by Gary Paulsen (1988)

A really great survival story! You can almost see inside Brian's mind as he tries to figure out what to do to stay alive. He has so many problems—a bear, a tornado, no food. It's amazing the way he solves his problems. Very exciting!

are encouraged to react thoughtfully to what they read by writing in literature logs or critically reviewing books on note cards that are filed for other students to read. In one class, students place minireviews of favorite books they want to recommend on a bulletin board. Example 6.5 is a sample of one student's recommendation.

Several ideas for activities that combine reading and writing were presented earlier in this chapter. Here are some additional activities that focus on written responses to literature:

LITERATURE

1. Ask students to collect as many Newbery Award books and Honor books (runners-up to Award books) as they can find, read several of them, and ask their friends to read others. After making up and filling out an evaluation checklist for each book, including such criteria as characterization, author's style, authenticity of setting, and plot development, they may add to the checklist their own comments about the merit of each book.
2. Let each student read a biography of a famous historical figure and write a story about what would happen if that person lived today—for example, how he or she would bring peace to the world, solve medical problems, or protect the environment. The popular *Lincoln: A Photobiography*, by Russell Freedman, would be a good choice.
3. Choose an environmental book, such as Chris Van Allsburg's *Just a Dream*, and have students discuss the issues it raises. Ask them each to choose one issue that especially concerns them and write letters to their legislator describing the issue and recommending solutions.
4. Read *War with Grandpa* by Robert Kimmel Smith or a similar book about elderly people to the class, and discuss both the contributions and special needs of older people. Ask each student to identify an elderly person to whom he or she can write a letter or send a story. Help the students follow through with their plans.

5. After reading several selections of multicultural literature, keep a continuing record on a world map of the settings featured in the selections. Encourage students to identify the sites of their family origins.

Responses Through Art and Music

Many students who have difficulty expressing themselves with words prefer to respond to literature in other ways (Hoyt, 1992). Art and music offer creative options for these students. Through exposure to well-illustrated picture books, students learn to appreciate the artists' work and begin to see themselves as illustrators capable of creating their own art (Galda and Short, 1993). They can interpret stories through many art media, including clay, paint, papier-mâché, scraps of felt and ribbon, colored pencils and pens, computer drawing programs, and three-dimensional objects. Using such media, they create collages and montages, dioramas and puppet figures, mobiles and stabiles, and illustrations for their own storybooks (Russell, 1994).

TECHNOLOGY

There are songs that can be related to many literature selections. Students have a natural tendency to respond to the rhythm and melody of music, so it can be effective to combine music with literature and language activities (Kolb, 1996).

Middle-level teachers are currently faced with a diverse population of students. Many middle-school classrooms are composed of students who have wide ranges of instructional needs. Cultural and linguistic divergencies influence how students learn and how they should be taught.

SUMMARY

Some basic tenets of facilitating literacy development are that learning is integrated, tasks are authentic, learning is social, classrooms are learning centered, and literature is an integral part of the curriculum. Applications of these principles are found throughout the text.

Instead of separating the language arts into discrete time periods, teachers should integrate instruction in reading, writing, listening, speaking, viewing, and visually representing. When students learn language as an integrated whole, they are likely to view reading and writing as meaningful events.

Many similarities exist between reading and writing. Both are composing processes in which meaning is constructed. Teachers can use this natural connection by guiding students into activities that call for both reading and writing. Process writing is an approach to writing that consists of five steps: prewriting, drafting, revising, editing, and sharing and publishing. Journal writing and reading provide students the opportunities to record their ideas and, in many cases, read responses from their teacher. Writing and reading workshops provide minilessons and large blocks of time for students to concentrate on actual writing and reading.

Literature is useful for integrating language. Story reading and storytelling provide multiple benefits by enticing students to read and providing them with knowledge. Teachers should be aware of the characteristics of a variety of literary genres, and they should consider both literary merit and students' interests when helping them choose books. Teachers should also establish environments with an abundance of interesting books and attractive displays that create interest in reading.

Students may respond to literature aesthetically (by making emotional responses) and efferently (by seeking information). Their responses may take place in literature circles, or through oral reading, drama, written expression, art, and music.

TEST YOURSELF

True or False

_______ 1. Ideally, language arts instruction should be integrated throughout the middle-school curriculum.

_______ 2. Reading and writing are both composing processes.

_______ 3. The *writing process* refers to the way students use punctuation, grammar, and spelling.

_______ 4. Middle-school students generally prefer poems with thoughtful, serious themes.

_______ 5. During the drafting stage of writing, students must be careful to observe correct use of spelling and mechanics.

_______ 6. Students must work alone when doing revisions.

_______ 7. In dialogue journals, usually the student writes some thoughts, and the teacher responds in writing.

_______ 8. Journal writing is a good opportunity for teachers to correct students' handwriting, spelling, and grammar.

_______ 9. In writing and reading workshops, students complete workbook exercises.

_______ 10. Middle-school students are capable of using word processors to write and edit compositions.

_______ 11. Literature can be an effective vehicle for integrating the instruction in language arts across the curriculum.

_______ 12. When readers take an aesthetic stance as they respond to literature, they read to gain information.

_______ 13. When reading aloud, teachers should speak in natural tones and with expression.

_______ 14. In a double entry journal, the student writes on one side of the page, and the teacher writes on the other.

_______ 15. The Newbery Medal is awarded for excellence in illustration.

_______ 16. Many appropriate, high-quality, magazines are being published for middle-school students.

______ 17. Silent reading is more difficult than oral reading.

______ 18. Performers in readers' theater memorize their parts.

______ 19. When writing responses to literature, a student's first priority should be the mechanics of writing.

______ 20. There is no need for teachers to read aloud to students after they learn to read for themselves.

______ 21. Award-winning trade books can be found for nearly every period in history.

______ 22. The Coretta Scott King Awards are given to selections by authors and illustrators of African descent.

For your journal . . .

1. Read a novel appropriate for middle-grades students, such as *Holes* (Louis Sachar) or *The Sign of the Beaver* (Elizabeth George Speare), and respond to it both aesthetically and efferently. If you could choose, how would you prefer to respond to literature: through writing, oral expression, art, music, drama, or in some other way? Why?

. . . and your portfolio

1. Begin an annotated list of books you would like to have in your middle-school classroom library, and add to the list as you find other selections you wish to include.
2. When you are visiting schools, jot down literature-related ideas that you see middle-school teachers using. These might include bulletin-board displays, classroom library corners, theme-related book collections, and students' responses to literature.
3. As you come across books you might like to use during thematic units, copy the bibliographic information and brainstorm ways to connect each book to different areas of the curriculum.

7

Reading/Study Techniques

KEY VOCABULARY

Pay close attention to these terms when they appear in the chapter.

- bar graphs
- circle or pie graphs
- database
- graphic organizers
- guide words
- legend of a map
- line graphs
- metacognition
- picture graphs
- reading rate
- reading/study techniques
- scale of a map
- SQRQCQ
- SQ3R

SETTING OBJECTIVES

When you finish reading this chapter, you should be able to

- Discuss the features of the SQ3R study method.
- Explain the importance of developing flexible reading habits.
- Name some skills students need in order to locate information in a variety of print and nonprint sources.
- Describe how to help students learn to organize, outline, and summarize information.
- Discuss metacognitive strategies students need.
- Explain how to teach students to use graphic aids in textbooks.

Jerry L. Johns (International Reading Association, 2003) described elements of a comprehensive literacy program, pointing out that adolescent literacy should include reading instruction that emphasizes "comprehension, interpretation, and analysis of text that is individually appropriate." He also addressed the need to provide opportunities for adolescents to "read and discuss reading with others" (p. 17).

All students must develop reading and study skills necessary to gather information, organize it, and evaluate it in a variety of contexts. ***Reading/study techniques*** are strategies that enhance comprehension and retention of information in print and nonprint sources and thus help students cope successfully with assignments in content area classes and with informational reading throughout their lives. To succeed in their schoolwork, middle-school students need a variety of skills. They need to use study methods that can help them retain material they read, take tests effectively, exercise flexibility in their reading habits, locate and organize information effectively, and use metacognitive strategies when studying. They also need to learn the skills necessary to derive information from graphic aids (maps, graphs, tables, and illustrations) in content area reading materials.

Teachers may present study techniques during a content class when the need arises or during reading classes, but they should be sure the strategies are applied to content soon, if they are taught during reading class. Middle-school students will retain study

Chapter 7 Organization

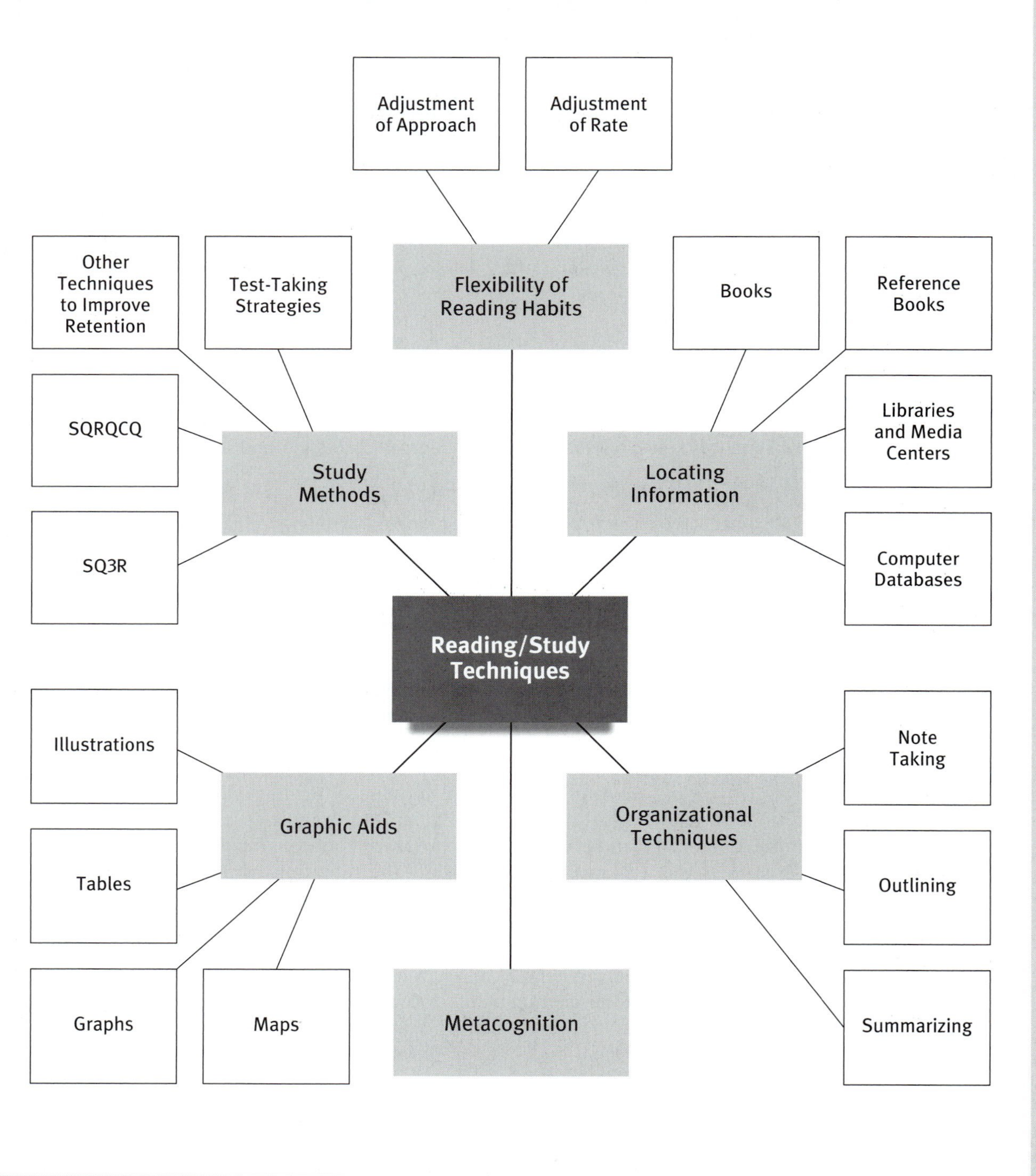

techniques longer if they apply them, and they will see these skills as useful tools rather than busywork exercises. They are more likely to apply their new knowledge if they practice the techniques in the context in which they will use them. Therefore, a teacher may find it very effective to set aside time during a content class to teach a study strategy that students will need to use immediately in that class.

Study Methods

Study methods are techniques that help students read, listen to, or view material in a way that enhances comprehension and retention. Unlike the directed reading activities (DRAs) found in teacher's manuals in basal reading series, study methods are student directed, rather than teacher directed.

SQ3R

Probably the best-known study method is Robinson's ***SQ3R*** method: Survey, Question, Read, Recite, Review (Robinson, 1961). For this method, the steps given to the students are as follows:

1. *Survey.* As you approach a reading assignment, you should notice the chapter title and main headings, read the introductory and summary paragraphs, and inspect any visual aids such as maps, graphs, or illustrations. This initial survey provides a framework for organizing the facts you later derive from the reading.
2. *Question.* Formulate a list of questions you expect to be answered in the reading. The headings may give you some clues.
3. *Read.* Read the selection in order to answer the questions you have formulated. Since this is purposeful reading, making brief notes may be helpful.
4. *Recite.* After reading the selection, try to answer each of the questions you formulated earlier without looking back at the material.
5. *Review.* Reread to verify or correct your recited answers and to make sure that you have the main points of the selection in mind and that you understand the relationships among the various points.

Students who use a study method such as SQ3R will remember content material better than they would if they simply read the material. Consequently, it is worthwhile to take time in class to show students how to go through the various steps. Teachers should have group practice sessions on SQ3R, or on any other study method, before expecting the students to perform the steps independently.

Material chosen for SQ3R instruction should be content material on which the students should normally use the method. The teacher should ask all the students to survey the selection together—reading aloud the title and main headings and the introductory and summary paragraphs, and discussing the visual aids—in the first practice session.

The step that needs most explanation by the teacher is the Question step. The teacher can show students how to take a heading, such as "Brazil's Exports," and turn it into a question: "What are Brazil's exports?" This question should be answered in the section, and trying to find the answer provides a good purpose for students as they read. A chapter heading, such as "The Westward Movement," may elicit a variety of possible questions: "What is the westward movement?" "When did it take place?" "Where did it take place?" "Why did it take place?" "Who was involved?" The teacher can encourage students to generate questions like these in a class discussion during initial practice sessions.

After they have formulated questions, students read to find the answers. The teacher might make brief notes on the board to model behavior the students can follow. Then he or she can have students practice the Recite step by asking each student to respond orally to one of the purpose questions with the book closed. During the Review step, the students reread to check all the answers they have just heard.

In subsequent practice sessions, the teacher can merely alert the students to perform each step and have them all perform the step silently at the same time. Students will probably need several practice sessions before the steps are thoroughly set in their memories.

SQRQCQ

Another effective method for middle-school students is one developed especially for use with mathematics materials: ***SQRQCQ*** (Fay, 1965). *SQRQCQ* stands for Survey, Question, Read, Question, Compute, Question. This approach may be beneficial because students frequently have great difficulty reading statement problems in mathematics textbooks. For this method, the steps given to the students are as follows:

1. *Survey*. Read through the problem quickly to gain an idea of its general nature.
2. *Question*. Ask, "What is being asked in the problem?"
3. *Read*. Read the problem carefully, paying attention to specific details and relationships.
4. *Question*. Make a decision about the mathematical operations to be carried out and, in some cases, the order in which they are to be performed.
5. *Compute*. Perform the computations you decided on in the preceding step.
6. *Question*. Decide whether or not the answer seems to be correct, asking, "Is this a reasonable answer? Have I accurately performed the computations?"

As with SQ3R, the teacher should have the whole class practice the SQRQCQ method before expecting students to use it independently. Teaching the method takes little extra time, since it is a good way to manage mathematics instruction.

Other Techniques to Improve Retention

In addition to providing students with effective study strategies, a teacher can improve their abilities to retain content material by following these suggestions:

1. Conduct discussions about all assigned reading material. Talking about ideas they have read helps to fix these ideas in students' memories.

2. Teach students to read assignments critically. Have them constantly evaluate the material they read, and avoid giving them the idea that something is true "because the book says so" by encouraging them to challenge any statement in the book if they can find evidence to the contrary. The active involvement with the material that is necessary in critical reading aids retention.
3. Encourage students to apply in authentic situations the ideas about which they have read. For example, after reading about parliamentary procedure, students can conduct a club meeting; after reading about a simple science experiment, they can conduct the experiment. Students learn those things they have applied in real life better than those about which they have only read.
4. Assist students in identifying a purpose for reading before beginning each reading assignment, since this increases their ability to retain material. You may supply them with purpose questions or encourage them to state their own purposes.
5. TECHNOLOGY — Use audiovisual aids to reinforce concepts presented in the reading material.
6. Read background material to students to give them a frame of reference to which they can relate the ideas they read.
7. Prepare study guides for content area assignments. Study guides (described in more detail in Chapter 8) help students retain their content area concepts by setting purposes for reading and providing appropriate frameworks for organizing material.
8. Teach students to look for the author's organization of material. Have them outline the material or construct a diagram of the organizational pattern. (Outlining is discussed later in this chapter.)
9. TECHNOLOGY — Encourage students to picture the ideas the author is describing. Visualizing information will help them remember it longer. Some students will find it helpful to draw, sketch, graph, or chart the ideas they visualize. Semantic webs are particularly useful. *Inspiration* is a computer program that facilitates webbing of ideas.
10. Teach note-taking procedures and encourage note taking. Writing down information often helps students retain it. (Note taking is discussed later in this chapter.)
11. After students have read the material, have them paraphrase and summarize the information in either written or oral form. (Later in this chapter, we discuss summarizing skills in more detail.)
12. Have students use spaced practice (a number of short practice sessions extended over a period of time) rather than massed practice (one long practice session) for material you wish them to retain over a long period of time.
13. Encourage overlearning (continuing to practice a skill for a while after it has been initially mastered) of material you wish students to retain for long periods of time.

14 When appropriate, teach some simple mnemonic devices (short phrases or verses used as memory aids)—for example, "There is *a rat* in the middle of sep*arat*e."

15 Offer positive reinforcement for correct responses to questions during discussion and review sessions.

16 Encourage students to look for words and ideas that are mentioned repeatedly, because they are likely to be important ones.

17 Encourage students to study more difficult and less interesting material when they are most alert (Memory and Yoder, 1988).

18 Teach students to ask and answer *why* questions about each factual statement in an informational passage (Menke and Pressley, 1994).

Test-Taking Strategies

Students need to retain what they have read in order to do well on tests, but sometimes students who know the material fail to do as well as they could because they lack good test-taking strategies. Students may study in the same way for essay tests and objective tests, for example. Helping them understand how to study for and take different types of tests can improve their performances.

Teachers can help students prepare for taking essay tests by helping them understand the meanings of certain words, such as *compare, contrast, describe,* and *explain,* that frequently appear in essay questions. This is especially important for English language learners. The teacher can state a potential question using one of these terms and then model the answer to the question, explaining what is important to include in the answer. If a contrast is requested, the differences in the two things or ideas should be explained. If a comparison is requested, likenesses should be included. The use of visual/graphic aids such as Venn diagrams can support the concept of comparison/contrast relationships.

DIVERSITY

To prepare for objective tests, teachers should encourage students to learn important terms and their definitions, study for types of questions that have been asked in the past, and learn to use mnemonic devices to help in memorizing lists.

Providing students focused instruction on taking standardized tests can help them perform better on these tests. Teachers should discuss with the students the purpose of the tests and the special rules that apply during testing well before they take the standardized tests. They should provide practice in completing test items within specified time limits. A practice test with directions, time limits, and item formats as similar as possible to those of the actual test should be given to familiarize the students with the overall testing environment.

Armitage (2000) suggests alternatives to students practicing commercially prepared testing exercises. Rather than falling prey to the pressure of using valuable instructional time for test preparation and review, she suggests that certain strategies be modeled and taught consistently throughout the year and not just prior to the administration of a standardized test. She recommends that students be taught to analyze the types of passages that appear on standardized tests and construct their own questions. She also recommends that students be given frequent opportunities to compete cloze passages to help prepare for the format of many standardized tests. (See Chapter 9 for more on cloze passages.)

Students need to learn to follow the directions for testing exactly, including those related to recording answers. They should learn to answer first those items they can answer quickly and to check answers if they have time left. Teachers can also encourage students to consider the words *always, never,* and *not* carefully when answering true-false questions, since these words have a powerful effect on the meaning. They can make sure students realize that if any part of a true-false statement is false, the answer must be false. They can also caution students to read and consider all answers to a multiple-choice question before choosing an answer, and encourage them to guess rather than leave an answer blank if there is not a severe penalty for guessing.

Flexibility of Reading Habits

Flexible readers adjust their approaches and rates to fit the materials they are reading. Effective readers continually adjust their reading approaches and rates without being aware of it.

Adjustment of Approach

Flexible readers approach material according to *their purposes for reading* and the *type of material.* For example, they may read poetry aloud to savor the beauty of the words, or they may read novels for relaxation in a leisurely fashion, giving attention to descriptive passages that evoke visual imagery and taking time to think about the characters and their traits. If they are reading novels simply to be able to converse with friends about the story lines, they may read less carefully, wishing only to discover the novels' main ideas and basic plots.

Flexible readers approach informational reading with the goal of separating the important facts from the unimportant ones and paying careful attention in order to retain what they need from the material. Rereading is often necessary if the material contains a high density of facts or very difficult concepts and interrelationships. With such material, reading every word may be highly important, whereas it is less important with material containing few facts or less difficult concepts. Flexible readers approach material for which they have little background with greater concentration than material for which their background is extensive.

Some reading purposes do not demand the reading of every word in a passage. Sometimes *skimming* (reading selectively to pick up main ideas and general impressions about the material) or *scanning* (moving the eyes rapidly over the selection to locate a specific bit of information, such as a name or a date) is sufficient. Skimming is the process used in the Survey step of SQ3R, when students are trying to orient themselves to the organization and general focus of the material. Scanning is useful when searching for names in telephone books or entries in dictionaries or indexes.

Adjustment of Rate

Students often make the mistake of trying to read everything at the same rate. Some of them read short stories as slowly and carefully as they read science experiments, and they may not enjoy recreational reading because they have to work so hard and it takes them so long to read a story. Other students read everything rapidly, often failing to grasp essential details in content area reading assignments even though they complete the reading. ***Reading rate*** should not be considered apart from comprehension. The optimum rate for reading a particular piece is the fastest rate at which the reader maintains an acceptable level of comprehension.

Middle-school students will use study time more efficiently if they are taught to vary their rates to fit their reading *purposes* and *materials.* Students should read light fiction for enjoyment much faster than a mathematics problem that they must solve. When reading to find isolated facts such as names and dates, they will do better to scan a page rapidly for key words than to read every word of the material. When reading to determine the main ideas or organization of a selection, they will find skimming more practical than reading each word of the selection.

One way to help students fit appropriate rates to materials is to give them various types of materials and purposes, allow them to try different rates, and then encourage them to discuss the effectiveness of different rates for different purposes and materials. This will be particularly helpful if regular classroom materials are used for the practice. Emphasis on increasing reading speed is best left until students have well-developed basic word recognition and comprehension skills. By the time they reach middle grades, some will be ready for assistance in increasing their reading rates. It is important to remember that speed without comprehension is useless, so the teacher must be sure students maintain comprehension levels as they keep working to increase their reading rates. Techniques teachers can use with students to help them increase their reading rates include the following:

1. To encourage students to try consciously to increase their reading rates, time their reading for three minutes. At the end of that period, have the students count the total words read, divide by three, and record the resulting number as their rate in average words per minute. To ensure that they are focusing on understanding, follow the timed reading with a comprehension check. The students can graph the results of these timed readings over a period of time, along with the comprehension results. Ideally, students will see their rates increase without a decrease in comprehension. If the students' comprehension does decrease, encourage them to slow down enough to regain an appropriate comprehension level.
2. To help students cut down on unnecessary regressions (going back to reread), have them use markers to move down the page, covering the lines just read.
3. To help decrease students' anxiety about comprehension that could impede their progress, give them material written at their independent reading levels for practice in building their reading rates.

TIME for REFLECTION

Some teachers spend time on development of reading rate, but do not address flexibility. Other teachers address flexibility, but give little attention to increasing rate. Some teachers work on both aspects. Still others dismiss rate considerations entirely, as inappropriate for middle-school instruction. **What do *you* think, and why?**

Locating Information

To engage in many study activities, middle-school students need to be able to locate the necessary material. Inquiry learning, for example, requires students to locate applicable information. A recent review of exemplary classrooms and teachers concluded that students in these classes were encouraged to view themselves as researchers and approach learning through inquiry (Allington, 2002). Teachers who create inquiry-based classrooms do more than just pose carefully designed questions; they encourage students to approach learning in an inquisitive manner. They facilitate independent learning and provide opportunities for students to discover knowledge. Tower (2000) described the need for the preparation of students involved in the inquiry process. She emphasized the need for students to have experience with nonfiction reading and writing before the inquiry process can be a successful strategy for gathering information. A teacher can help prepare students by pointing out the location aids in textbooks, reference books, and libraries and by showing them how to access databases.

Books

Most nonfiction books offer students several special features that are helpful for locating needed information, including prefaces, tables of contents, index, appendices, glossary, footnotes, and bibliography. Teachers should not assume that students make the adjustment from the basal reader or trade book format to the format of content subject textbooks without assistance. Basal readers have a great deal of narrative (story-like) material that, unlike most content material, is not packed with facts to be learned. When the trade books used in a program are primarily fiction, they will also be narrative in format. Although most basals have tables of contents and glossaries, they may not contain as many helpful special features as content textbooks; and, although some nonfiction trade books have tables of contents and/or glossaries, not all do.

DIVERSITY

Teachers should present content textbooks to students carefully. Such instruction is particularly important for struggling readers and English language learners. Manz (2002) describes a strategy useful for students' introduction to expository text. The strategy is introduced early in the school year with each step modeled explicitly by the teacher. The steps are identified by the acronym THIEVES with the following key words for each step:

T Title
H Headings
I Introduction
E Every first sentence in a paragraph
V Visuals and vocabulary
E End-of-chapter questions
S Summary

At each step questions help develop previewing skills by engaging the reader, activating background knowledge, and providing purpose.

Preface or Introduction

When presenting textbooks to students in the middle school, the teacher can ask them to read the preface or introduction to get an idea of why the book was written and of the manner in which the author or authors present the material.

Table of Contents

On the day a new textbook is distributed, the teacher can lead students in an examination of its table of contents. The teacher can help students discover information about their new textbooks by asking questions such as the following:

- What topics are covered in this book?
- What is the first topic discussed?
- On what page does the discussion about __________ begin? This question can be repeated several times with different topics inserted in the blank.

Indexes

Students in the middle school should become familiar with indexes. They should understand that an index is an alphabetical list of items and names mentioned in a book and the pages where these items or names appear, and that some books contain one general index and some contain subject and author indexes as well as other specialized ones (for example, a first-line index in a music or poetry book). Most indexes contain both main headings and subheadings, and students should be given opportunities to practice using these headings to locate information within their books. The teacher can lead students to examine the index of a book to make inferences about which topics the author considers to be important, based on the amount of space devoted to them. The Focus on Strategies on page 267 shows use of the index to locate information.

Thinking skills become important when the word being sought in an index is not listed. Readers must then think of synonyms for the word or another form of the word that might be listed. Brainstorming possibilities for alternative listings for a variety of terms could be a helpful class activity to prepare students to be flexible when such situations occur.

Appendices

Students can be shown that the appendices of books contain supplementary information that may be helpful to them, for example, maps or tabular material.

Glossaries

Textbooks often contain glossaries of technical terms that can greatly aid students in understanding the book's content. The skills necessary for proper use of a glossary are the same as those needed for using a dictionary (described later in this chapter).

FOCUS ON STRATEGIES Using the Index to Locate Information

Several students in Ms. Rand's class needed to find out how to check division problems completed the previous day, but they had trouble locating the part of the book they wanted and spent too much time on the task. Ms. Rand noticed that none of the students used the index to find the pages. When she questioned a couple of them, she found out that they had only a hazy concept that the index was in the back of the book, and they didn't know how to use it.

The next day, Ms. Rand set out to remedy this situation. "Turn to page 315 of your math books," she told her class. "Tell me what you find there."

Here is a portion of what the children found:

Sample Index

"It's called the *index*," Tommy replied, as he located the page.

"Right, Tommy," said Ms. Rand. "The index is a part of the book that can help you find information that you need to locate in the book. It lists the topics in the book in alphabetical order, and after the topic it has the pages on which the topic is discussed in the book. For example, in your index, you can see that information about graphs is found on pages 300 through 306. The dash shows that all the pages in between 300 and 306 are about graphs too. If it had been written this way—[*she writes on board*] 300, 306—that would mean the information would be on just those two pages. Who can tell me which pages have information about circles?"

"Pages 204 and 206," Tamara said.

"What about page 205?" asked Ms. Rand.

Ramón broke in: "It is about circles, too. You said the dash meant all of the pages between the ones listed."

"Oh, yeah," agreed Tamara. "Page 205 is part of it too."

"Very good," Ms. Rand replied. "Now look under the listing for Graph, and notice that there are some words indented there. These are types of graphs, and the particular types are listed with their own page numbers. When there is a list of indented terms under the main term, those terms are related to the main term, but they are there to help you find more specific topics. If I wanted to find out about bar graphs, I could look on pages 303 through 306. I wouldn't have to look at the other pages about graphs, because bar graphs wouldn't be discussed there. What if I wanted to read about picture graphs?"

"You would read pages 300 through 303," Penny replied.

"Right! And what if I wanted to find out about regrouping in addition?" Ms. Rand asked.

"Pages 80 through 104," said Morgan.

"All of them?" asked Ms. Rand.

"Well, there are dashes," Morgan replied.

"What else do you see besides the dashes?" Ms. Rand asked.

Continued

"There is a comma between the 91 and the 103," Morgan reported.

"What do you think that tells you?" Ms. Rand asked.

"I guess that 92 through 102 don't have anything about regrouping on them," Morgan answered hesitantly.

"Good thinking," Ms. Rand replied. "You are getting that punctuation figured out."

Then she told the class, "Now get in your math work groups and see if you can answer the questions on this sheet about the index in your math text." (The sheet asked the students to locate pages on which specific math topics were covered.)

After the small groups had all reached agreement on the answers, the whole class discussed the items to ensure that everyone had been successful in understanding the process.

At the end of the lesson, Ms. Rand said, "Find the meaning of division, and read it to me."

Mark did so.

"Did you look in the index to find the page number?" she asked.

"Yes, I did," Mark said.

"Do you think you found it more quickly by looking in the index than you would have by turning through the book to find it?"

"Yes," Mark replied.

"When you need to look things up in your textbooks, remember that the index can be helpful to you," Ms. Rand reminded the group as the lesson ended.

Footnotes and Bibliographies

Footnotes and bibliographies refer students to other sources of information about the subject being discussed in a book. Teachers should encourage students to turn to these sources for clarification, for additional information on a topic for a report, or simply for their own satisfaction.

Reference Books

Middle-school students often need to find information in encyclopedias, dictionaries, almanacs, atlases, and other reference books. Unfortunately, many students reach high school still unable to use such aids effectively. Important skills for effective use of reference books include the following:

General

- Knowledge of alphabetical order and understanding that encyclopedias, dictionaries, and some atlases are arranged in alphabetical order
- Ability to use ***guide words,*** knowledge of their location on a page, and understanding that they represent the first and last entry words on a dictionary or encyclopedia page
- Ability to determine key words under which related information can be found

Encyclopedias

- Ability to use cross-references
- Ability to determine which volume of a set of encyclopedias will contain the information needed

Dictionaries

- Ability to use pronunciation keys
- Ability to choose from several possible word meanings the one that most closely fits the context in which a word is found

Atlases

- Ability to interpret the legend of a map
- Ability to interpret the scale of a map
- Ability to locate directions on maps

Because encyclopedias, almanacs, and atlases are often written at much higher readability levels than other materials used in the classroom, teachers must use caution when assigning work in these reference books. Students are not likely to profit from looking up material in books that are too difficult for them to read. When asked to do so, they tend to copy the material word for word without trying to understand it.

However, teachers should keep in mind the difference between *assigning* students to use a particular reference work and letting the students *choose* to use any work that interests them. Readers can handle much more difficult levels of high-interest material than of low-interest material. Therefore, a student who is intensely interested in the subject matter of an encyclopedia article may be able to glean much information from it, even if his or her usual reading level for school materials is lower. For this reason, teachers should never forbid students to try to use material that *may be* too difficult for them. They should, however, avoid *forcing* students to struggle with material that is clearly beyond their range of understanding.

Many skills related to the use of an atlas are included in the section on map reading in this chapter. Some factors related to dictionary and encyclopedia use are discussed in the following sections.

Dictionaries

Before a student can use a dictionary for any of its major functions, he or she must be able to locate a designated word with some ease. Three important skills are necessary to do this: using alphabetical order, using guide words, and locating variants and derivatives.

Using Alphabetical Order. Since the words in a dictionary are arranged in alphabetical order, students must learn to use alphabetical order to find the words they seek. Beginning with the first letter of the word, they gradually learn alphabetization by the first two or three letters, discovering that sometimes it is necessary to work through every letter in a word in the process.

Using Guide Words. Students need to learn that the guide words at the top of a dictionary page tell them the first and last words on that page. If they are proficient in using alphabetical order, they should be able to decide whether or not a word will be

MODEL ACTIVITIES Guide Words

Divide the group into two or more teams. Write the word pair *Brace—Bubble* on the board or a chart. Ask the students to pretend that these words are the guide words for a page of the dictionary. Explain that you would expect the word *brick* to be on this page because *bri* comes after *bra* and *r* comes before *u*. Then write words, one at a time, from the following list on the board below the word pair:

1. beaker
2. boil
3. break
4. braid
5. brave
6. border
7. bypass
8. bud

Let each team in turn tell you if the word would be found on the page with the designated guide words. Ask them to tell why they answered as they did. The team gets a point if the members can answer the questions correctly. The next team gets a chance to answer if they cannot. The reason for the answer is the most important part of the response.

Variation: Write four guide words and the two dictionary pages on which they appear on the board or a chart. For example, you could write:

Page 300 *Rainbow—Rapid*

Page 301 *Rapport—Raven*

Write the words from the following list below the two sets of guide words, one at a time:

1. rare
2. ramble
3. ranch
4. rabbit
5. rave
6. ratio
7. range
8. raw

Ask each team in turn to indicate on which page the displayed word would be found, or if the word would be found on neither page. Have them tell why they answered as they did. (Of course, you would model the decision-making process for them, as described earlier, before the activity starts.) If the team answers the questions about a word correctly, it is awarded a point. If the team answers incorrectly, the next team gets a chance to answer.

found on a certain page by checking to see if the word falls alphabetically between the two guide words.

The Model Activity on Guide Words above describes a way to practice with guide words.

Locating Variants and Derivatives. Variants and derivatives are sometimes entered alphabetically in a dictionary, but more often they are either not listed or are listed in conjunction with their root words. If they are not listed, the reader must find the pronunciation of the root word and combine the sounds of the added parts with that pronunciation. This procedure requires advanced skills in word analysis and blending.

An exercise on determining the correct entry word in the dictionary is shown in the Model Activity on page 271.

Bilingual Dictionaries. English language learners would benefit from instruction in the use of bilingual dictionaries. English speakers, as well, could gain in vocabulary understanding from use of these resources.

MODEL ACTIVITIES

Determining the Correct Entry Word

As the students are reading a story that contains many words with affixes, call their attention to the affixed words as they occur in the text. Tell the students that, if they wanted to look up the words in the dictionary, they might not be able to find them listed separately. These words have prefixes, suffixes, and inflectional endings added to root words, so students might need to locate their root words to find them. Choose one word from the text, perhaps *happily*. Point to the word, and say: "I recognize the *-ly* ending here. The rest of the word is almost like *happy*. The *y* was changed to *i* when the ending was added. So the root word is *happy*." Repeat this procedure for one or two other words from the text.

Later, as a follow-up activity, write on the board the following list of words:

1. directness
2. commonly
3. opposed
4. undeniable
5. gnarled
6. customs
7. cuter
8. joyfully
9. comradeship
10. concentrating

For each word, ask the students to find the root word and tell about the other word parts that made the root word hard to find. They may also discuss the spelling changes made in the root word when endings were added.

TECHNOLOGY 

Using Electronic Dictionaries. Some dictionaries are available on CD-ROMs, DVD-ROMs, or the Internet. They may provide definitions, spellings, pronunciations, and idioms. Some feature interactive multimedia. Users may be able to hear words pronounced when they click on them with the mouse, hear sound effects related to the words, and play word games. There may be color illustrations for many words, in addition to the standard definitions, sentences using the words, syllabic breakdowns, spellings, pronunciations, and plural forms (Johnson, 1994).

Encyclopedia Use

Since encyclopedias vary in content and arrangement, students should be exposed to several different sets. Teachers should have them compare the entries from different encyclopedias on a specified list of topics. The Model Activity on page 272 can provide children with instruction and practice in the use of the encyclopedia as they work on a thematic unit on the Revolutionary War.

Encyclopedia articles are often very difficult for many middle-school readers to comprehend. This difficulty makes putting the information they find into their own words harder. To encourage appropriate encyclopedia use, the teacher can work with the students to construct a list of things the students should look for about their topics, and the students can list what they already know about each category of information. Next, the children can examine the graphic aids in the encyclopedia article to gather information. Then they can skim the written material to gather main ideas. Finally, they should read the material carefully and put it into their own words. They should be encouraged to consult other sources to check their facts and obtain additional information.

TECHNOLOGY

Electronic encyclopedias have become widely available and are located in many school settings. These encyclopedias are available on CD-ROMs, DVD-ROMs, or the

MODEL ACTIVITIES

Encyclopedia Skills

Have students find the correct volume for each of the following topics without opening the volume:

Revolutionary War

George Washington

Declaration of Independence

Muskets

British Parliament

Battle of Bunker Hill

Have them check their choices by actually looking up the terms. If they fail to find a term in the volume where they expected to find it, ask them to think of other places to look. Let them check these possibilities also. Continue the process until each term has been located. Here is a possible dialogue between teacher and student:

Teacher: In which volume of the encyclopedia would you find a discussion of George Washington?

Student: In Volume 23.

Teacher: Why did you choose Volume 23?

Student: Because *W* is in Volume 23.

Teacher: Why didn't you choose Volume 7 for the *G*s?

Student: Because people are listed under their last names.

Teacher: Look up the term, and check to see if your decision was correct.

Student: It was. I found "George Washington" on page 58.

Teacher: Very good. Now tell me where you would find a description of the Battle of Bunker Hill.

Student: In Volume 2 under "Battle."

Teacher: Check your decision by looking it up.

Student: It's not here. It must be under "Bunker."

Teacher: Good idea.

Student: Here it is. It's under "Bunker Hill, Battle of."

Internet. Some of these encyclopedias have text, pictures, sound, and animation. They can be searched through use of key words and phrases, alphabetical title searches, and topical searches. They are motivational and easy to use (Roe, 2000).

Other Reference Materials

Middle-school students often use materials other than books, such as newspapers, magazines, catalogues, transportation schedules, and pamphlets and brochures, as reference sources. For a thematic unit on pollution, for example, students might search through newspapers, magazines, and government pamphlets for stories and information about pollution and groups that are trying to do something about it, in addition to using trade books related to this problem.

To help students learn to locate information in newspapers, teachers can alert them to the function of headlines and teach them how to use the newspaper's index. Teachers also should devote some class time to explaining journalistic terms, which can help students better understand the material in the newspaper, and to explaining the functions of news stories, editorials, columns, and feature stories. Some of this instruction could be a part of a thematic unit on the newspaper. Students are often fascinated by the procedures involved in publishing a newspaper and the techniques used to design and produce a good newspaper. Activities such as the one on using a newspaper's index would be appropriate. Whenever possible, teachers should use actual newspapers as a basis for activities similar to the Model Activity "Using a Newspaper's Index."

Other instruction could take place as an integral part of other units being used in the classroom. For example, before the students search the newspaper for information on pollution for the unit mentioned earlier, the teacher could introduce activities related to developing the concept of *main idea*. This could help make their newspaper searches more efficient and meaningful.

In helping students to obtain information from magazines, teachers can call attention to the table of contents and give the students practice in using it, just as they do with textbooks. Distinguishing between informational and fictional materials is important in reading magazines, as is analyzing advertisements to detect propaganda.

To obtain information from many catalogues, students again need to be able to use indexes. Activities suggested in this chapter for using indexes in newspapers and textbooks can be profitably used here also. The ability to read charts giving information about sizes and about shipping and handling charges may also be important in reading catalogues.

A variety of transportation schedules, pamphlets, and brochures may be used as reference sources in social studies activities. Since their formats may vary greatly, teachers will need to provide practice in reading the specific materials they intend to use in their classes.

MODEL ACTIVITIES

Using a Newspaper's Index

Hand out copies of the following newspaper index, or write the example on the board or a chart:

Index

Classified Ads	B5–10
Comics	B11–12
Crossword	B11
Editorials	A2–3
Entertainment	B3–4
Finance	A4–7
Horoscope	A8
Obituaries	A11

Have a class discussion based on the following questions:

1. Where in the newspaper would you find information about the stock market? Why would you look there?
2. In what section would you look to find a movie that you would like to see or to find the television schedule? How did you know to look there?
3. On what page is the crossword puzzle found? How did you know?
4. How many pages have comics on them? How did you know?
5. Where would you look to find out who has died recently? How did you know to look there?

Libraries and Media Centers

Libraries or media centers are key locations in schools. Teachers and librarians/media specialists should work together as teams to develop the skills that students need to use libraries effectively. (The librarian/media specialist will hereafter be referred to as *librarian* for ease of reference, but the expanded role this person plays in dealing with multimedia should be kept in mind.)

Librarians can be helpful in many ways. They can show students the locations of books and journals, card catalogs, and reference materials (such as dictionaries, encyclopedias, atlases, and the *Reader's Guide to Periodical Literature*) in the library; explain the procedures for checking books in and out; and describe the rules and regulations regarding behavior in the library. Demonstrations of the use of the card catalog (either print or electronic version) and the *Reader's Guide* and explanations of the arrangement of books in libraries are also worthwhile. Prominently displayed posters can remind students to observe checkout procedures and library rules.

Students need to be taught to use libraries and media centers effectively.

LITERATURE 

Librarians are more frequently using library periods not only to help students locate and select books, but also to share literature with them. Librarians may introduce students to book reviews that can guide them in their selection of materials. The students can also be guided to write reviews that they can share with other students.

By familiarizing students with reasons for using the library and explaining to them why they may need to use such aids as manual and computerized card catalogs and the *Reader's Guide,* teachers can prepare students for a visit to the library. While they are still in the classroom, the students can learn that cards in the manual card catalog are arranged alphabetically and that the card catalog contains subject, author, and title cards. Sample cards of each type can be drawn on posters and placed on the bulletin board. In addition, fifth and sixth graders will benefit from a lesson that explains the use of cross-reference cards.

TECHNOLOGY

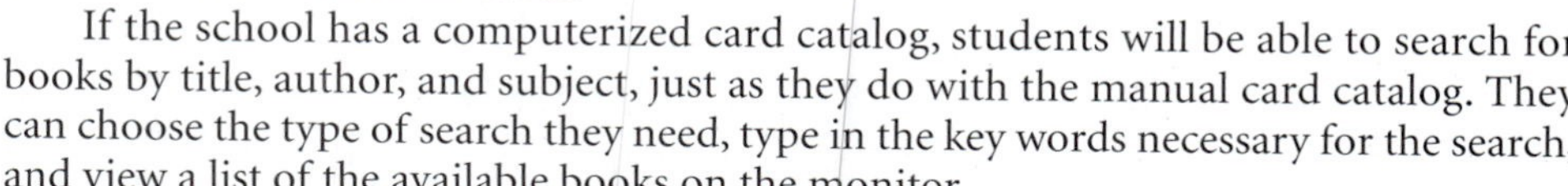

If the school has a computerized card catalog, students will be able to search for books by title, author, and subject, just as they do with the manual card catalog. They can choose the type of search they need, type in the key words necessary for the search, and view a list of the available books on the monitor.

Here are two other suggestions for practice with library skills:

1. The teacher can send the students on a scavenger hunt that requires using the library by dividing the class into teams and giving the teams statements to complete or questions to answer. (Example: The author of *The Secret Garden* is_______________.)
2. The teacher can give students questions and ask them to show on a map of the library where they would go to find the answers (Muller and Savage, 1982).

The Classroom Scenario on locating information on page 276 shows how one class put their research skills to work.

The librarian is an important partner for the teacher as thematic units are planned, for no unit will be successful if the needed reading materials are not available in a reasonable supply. Both books and other media are needed for these units, and the books need to be on a variety of levels. The librarian is also a valuable helper as students search the library for this related material as the unit progresses. Librarians provide useful help to teachers and students alike about books that are good for reading aloud, for sustained silent reading, and as reference sources. Cooperative planning between teachers and librarians can ensure that activities in the library and activities in the classroom are connected (Hughes, 1993; Lamme and Ledbetter, 1990).

TIME for REFLECTION

Some teachers think that the librarian should have the complete responsibility for teaching library skills. Others think the teaching of library skills should be a team effort. **What do *you* think, and why?**

In many schools, students are moving in and out of the library all the time. The library is used as "an extension of the classroom" (Hughes, 1993, p. 294) and frequently remains open to students all day, allowing access when they need it (Hansen, 1993). Many students use the library to find books, to read, to write, and to interact with classmates about books. Many also use it to do research on questions they need to answer, and their research is specific and of personal interest (Hughes, 1993). Valenza (1996) points out that since multimedia production is a research process, it belongs in the school library, where audiovisual and print resources are located, most schools have

TECHNOLOGY

CLASSROOM SCENARIO

Locating Information

Students in a fifth-grade classroom are about to begin a study of World War II. They have formed into groups, each of which will research a different topic related to the war. One group will research transportation methods for troops.

When the students in Keith's group meet, Keith says, "First we need to know the different types of transportation that were used. I think we can find that in the encyclopedia under 'World War II.' Who would like to check that out?"

"I will," replies Rosa. "I'll look in all of the different encyclopedias and see if they all have the same information or if they have different stuff. That will help us when we divide up jobs later."

"Good," Keith says. "Then we can make a list of the types of transportation, and each one of us can look up one or two of them and get more details. We can use the dictionary for a basic definition and the encyclopedia for more details on the type of transportation we are looking for, like 'Jeeps.' Where else will we get information?"

"We can check the card catalog," Charmaine suggests. "The subject cards on 'World War II' and things like 'jeeps' would give us some leads."

"I have a book at home on airplanes," Randy says. "Some of them were from World War II. Can I draw some for our report?"

"Great!" Keith says. "We need some visuals for our report, and you are better at drawing than the rest of us. We'll want some drawings of those planes and tanks and probably some other stuff. We'll all be on the lookout for examples that you can use for models. I'll also ask my Great Uncle Joe about it. He was in the army in World War II."

Analysis of Scenario

These students have received instruction that made them aware of places to find information for class studies, and they are putting that information to use as they work in their research group. Randy does not have ideas about where to find information in the library, but he recognizes that he has a valuable personal resource and offers it for the study. The students have been taught that there are sources of information other than school materials, and they freely plan to use personal books and even primary sources.

Internet connections, and librarians are available. When students need a research skill, librarians now often teach it or direct them to other students who can help with that skill.

TECHNOLOGY

Computer Databases

Students need to be able to locate and retrieve information from computer ***databases,*** in addition to performing more traditional activities. A computer database is a collection of related information that has been organized to facilitate retrieval through an electronic search. Each database is somewhat like a filing cabinet or several filing cabinets, with separate file folders for the different articles in the database. The information is categorized and indexed for easy retrieval. Users may create their own databases or use existing ones. Using databases, students pose questions, decide on keywords to access the data, read, follow directions, collect and categorize data, summarize material, and make comparisons and contrasts (Layton and Irwin, 1989; Roe, 2000). The electronic encyclopedias discussed earlier are examples of databases that are available in some schools. In addition, many databases can be accessed through the Internet.

Organizational Techniques

When engaging in such activities as writing reports, middle-school students need to organize the ideas they encounter in their reading. Too often teachers at the middle-school level give little attention to organizational techniques such as note taking, outlining, and summarizing, and too many students enter secondary school without knowing how to perform these tasks.

Note Taking

Teachers may present note-taking techniques in a functional setting when students are preparing written reports on materials they have read. Students should be taught to

- Include key words and phrases in their notes.
- Include enough of the context to make the notes understandable after a period of time has elapsed.
- Include a bibliographical reference (source) with each note.
- Copy direct quotations exactly.
- Indicate carefully which notes are direct quotations and which are reworded.

Key words—the words that carry the important information in a sentence—are generally nouns and verbs, but they may include important modifiers. Example 7.1 shows a sample paragraph and a possible set of notes based on this paragraph. Laase (1997) suggests using sample paragraphs and an overhead projector to model note

EXAMPLE 7.1 Sample Paragraph and Notes

A restaurant is not as easy a business to run as it may appear to be to some people, since the problem of obtaining good help is ever-present. Cooks, servers, and cleaning personnel are necessary. Cooks must be able to prepare the food offered by the restaurant. Servers need to be able to carry out their duties politely and efficiently. Cleaning personnel need to be dependable and thorough. Poorly prepared food, inadequate cleaning, and rude help can be the downfall of a restaurant, so restaurant owners and managers must hire with care.

SAMPLE NOTE CARD

Problem for restaurant owner or manager—good help: good cooks; polite, efficient servers; dependable, thorough cleaning personnel. Hire with care.

taking. Seitz (1997) also uses the overhead projector to model note taking for his middle-school students.

After reading the paragraph shown in Example 7.1, the note taker first thinks, "What kind of information is given here?" The answer, "Problem for restaurant owner or manager—good help," is the first note. Then the note taker searches for key words to describe the kind of help needed. For example, cooks who "are able to prepare the food offered by the restaurant" can be described as "good cooks"—ten words condensed into two that carry the idea. In the case of the nouns *server* and *cleaning personnel,* descriptive words related to them are added; condensation of phrases is not necessary (although the *and*s between the adjectives may be left out) because the key words needed are found directly in the selection. The last part of the paragraph can be summed up in the warning, "Hire with care." It is easy to see that key-word notes carry the message of the passage in a very condensed or abbreviated form.

A teacher can go through an example like this one with the students, telling them what key words to choose and why, and then provide another example, letting the students decide as a group which key words to write down and having them give reasons for their choices. Finally, each student can do a selection individually. After completing the individual note taking, the students can compare their notes and discuss reasons for choices.

Fisk and Hurst (2003) describe a paraphrasing strategy designed for middle-school students to aid in the comprehension of information. They suggest that paraphrasing integrates reading, writing, listening, and speaking and thus results in a deeper understanding of text. Their strategy begins with an explicit initial step that includes prereading questions, silent reading, and postreading discussion of the material. The objectives of the initial step are to familiarize the students with the material and identify both the main idea and author's voice.

Step two includes a second reading of the text. During this second reading, students are instructed to read each paragraph carefully and take detailed notes. This is followed by a third step where students turn in their original text and use only their notes as the reference for a paraphrased version. They are instructed to be sure to relate the main idea and to communicate with the original author's voice. The fourth and final step involves a sharing of their paraphrased versions either in pairs or small groups. According to Fisk and Hurst, paraphrasing is an interactive and effective comprehension aid that encourages students to process and comprehend both what they are reading and writing. Paraphrasing is also a key component of good note taking.

Students can take notes in outline, sentence, or paragraph form. Beginners may even benefit from taking notes in the form of semantic webs or maps.

Outlining

Teachers can lead students to understand that outlining is writing down information from the material they read in a way that shows the relationships among the main ideas and the supporting details. To create an outline, the students must already know how to recognize main ideas and details. Two types of outlines that are important for students to understand are the *sentence* outline, in which each point is a complete sentence, and the *topic* outline, which is composed of key words and phrases. Since choosing key words and phrases is in itself a difficult task for many students, it is wise to present sentence outlines first.

The first step in forming a traditional outline is to extract the main ideas from the material and list these ideas beside Roman numerals in the order in which they occur. Supporting details are listed beside capital letters below the main idea they support and are slightly indented to indicate their subordination. Details that are subordinate to the main details designated by capital letters are indented still further and preceded by Arabic numerals. The next level of subordination is indicated by lowercase letters, although middle-school students will rarely need to make an outline that goes beyond the level of Arabic numerals. A model outline form like the one shown in Example 7.2 may help students understand how outlines may be arranged.

The teacher can supply students with partially completed outlines of chapters in their content textbooks and ask them to fill in the missing parts, gradually leaving out more and more details until the students are doing the complete outline alone. To develop students' readiness for outlining, the teacher can use the "Readiness for Outlining" Model Activity on page 280.

This Model Activity can be used as a first step in teaching the concept of outlining to middle-school students. The next step might be to have the students make free-form outlines, or story webs, in which they use words, lines, and arrows to arrange key words and phrases from the story in a way that shows their relationships. Example 7.3 on page 280 shows a web based on *The Sign of the Beaver* by Elizabeth George Speare.

Teachers should model web construction during initial instruction. Then one or more story webs may be constructed cooperatively by the whole class. The teacher may need to provide the key words and phrases in early experiences with webbing. The students can then cooperatively develop webs in small groups with help from the teacher's probing questions about connecting lines, directions of arrows, and

EXAMPLE 7.2 Sample Outline

TITLE

I. Main idea
  A. Detail supporting I
  B. Detail supporting I
    1. Detail supporting B
    2. Detail supporting B
      a. Detail supporting 2
      b. Detail supporting 2
    3. Detail supporting B
  C. Detail supporting I

II. Main idea
  A. Detail supporting II
  B. Detail supporting II
  C. Detail supporting II

MODEL ACTIVITIES

Readiness for Outlining

1. Provide the students with a set of items to be categorized.
2. Ask them to place the items in categories. More than one arrangement may be possible; let them try several.
3. Provide the students with a blank outline form of this type:

4. Have the students fill in the outline.

EXAMPLE 7.3 Story Web

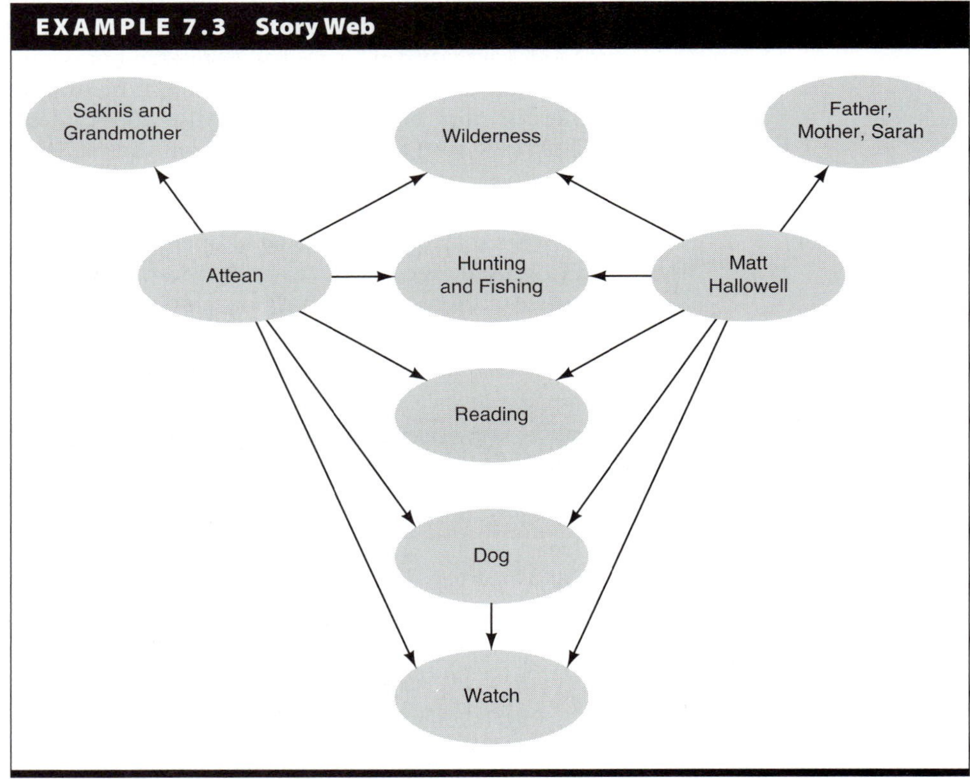

positions of phrases. The students may also ask the teacher questions about their decisions. As they develop proficiency with the task, the teacher can allow them to choose key words and phrases themselves, at first with assistance and then independently. After mastering this step, the students can move on to forming webs without assistance (Hansell, 1978).

TECHNOLOGY

Students can obtain outlining practice by outlining material the teacher has entered into a computer file. The students can move phrases and headings around with a word-processing program and create an outline relatively easily. Computer software such as *Inspiration* and *PowerPoint* also provides students with support for the creation of outlines of information.

TIME for REFLECTION

Some teachers believe in teaching only formal outlining. Others think students can benefit from organizational techniques such as webs. **What do *you* think, and why?**

Summarizing

In a summary, a student is expected to restate what the author has said in a more concise form. Main ideas of selections should be preserved, but illustrative materials and statements that merely elaborate on the main ideas should not be included.

Students should be led to see that they should delete trivial and redundant material when writing summaries. Superordinate terms can be used to replace lists of similar items or actions (for example, *people* for *men, women, and children*). Steps in an action may be replaced by a superordinate action (*baked a cake* for *took flour, butter, . . . and then placed it in an oven*). Each paragraph can be represented with its topic sentence or implied main idea sentence (Brown and Day, 1983; Brown, Day, and Jones, 1983; Recht, 1984).

The teacher should model the deletion of nonessential material when constructing summaries and then should have students practice this activity under supervision. Choosing superordinate terms and actions and choosing or constructing topic sentences should also be modeled and practiced. Teachers can use a think-aloud process to demonstrate how to delete "redundant, trivial, and subordinate information" (Allington, 2002, p. 744). Easy material should be used for beginning instruction, and paragraphs should be used before proceeding to longer passages.

One way the teacher can build students' experience with summarizing is to give them a long passage to read and three or four sample summaries of the passage. The teacher can let the students examine the summaries and decide which one is best and why each of the others was not satisfactory. The teacher can help in this exploration process by asking appropriate questions if the students appear confused about what to consider. For example, the teacher may ask, "Does this sentence tell something different, or is it just an example?" After the students have been successful in differentiating between the satisfactory and unsatisfactory summaries, the teacher can refer them to a passage in one of their textbooks, along with several possible summaries, and have them choose the best summary and tell why they did not choose each of the others. In addition, the Model Activity "Single-Sentence Summaries" on page 282 can provide practice with summarizing.

Metacognition

Metacognition involves knowing what is already known, knowing when understanding of new material has been accomplished, knowing how the understanding was reached, and knowing why something is or is not known (Guthrie, 1983). Metacognitive strategies are important in reading for meaning and in reading for retention.

MODEL ACTIVITIES

Single-Sentence Summaries

Have the students read a short passage like the following one and try to summarize its content in a single sentence:

Sometimes your hair makes a noise when you comb it. The noise is really made by static electricity. Static electricity collects in one place. Then it jumps to another place. Rub your feet on a rug. Now touch something. What happens? Static electricity collects on your body, but it can jump from your finger to other places. Sometimes you can see a spark and hear a noise.

Have students compare their answers and revise them as they discuss the merits of different answers.

Students who monitor their own comprehension and use fix-up strategies such as rereading, self-questioning, retelling, predicting and verifying, and reading further while withholding judgment are more likely to comprehend and retain the information they read. Recognizing important ideas, checking mastery of the information read, and developing effective strategies for study are metacognitive techniques involved in reading for retention (Baumann, Jones, and Seifert-Kessell, 1993; Paris, Wasik, and Turner, 1991). Schwartz (1997, p. 43) points out that "monitoring strategies involve checking one's attempts to coordinate the variety of cues found in texts." Self-correction behaviors are indications that monitoring strategies are occurring.

The RAND Reading Study Group report (Perkins-Gough, 2002) reinforces the importance of metacognitive strategies to comprehension. Students who approach their reading with a purpose and actively monitor their understanding as they read comprehend the material that they are reading better than those who do not. The report suggests that explicit instruction in the use of metacognitive strategies, such as creating and understanding graphic organizers, questioning, and summarizing, can assist students in the development of their abilities to locate, organize, and analyze information.

Research indicates that comprehension monitoring is a developmental skill that is not fully mastered until adolescence. Ann Brown and Sandra Smiley discovered that students with low abilities did not always benefit from instruction in monitoring strategies. These strategies may be beneficial only if students possess the background and understanding to use them effectively. With attention to students' levels of maturity, however, aspects of comprehension monitoring can be taught. It is important for teachers to guide students toward actually using these strategies rather than just to teach them *about* the strategies (Meir, 1984). Rhoder (2002) describes a model of strategy instruction designed to promote "mindful reading" during which students understand, select, and monitor strategies. The model involves instruction within the students' zone of proximal development (the area of skills they are capable of learning with the help of an expert), explicit modeling, practice, and opportunities to transfer metacognitive strategy use into new situations.

To help students develop metacognitive strategies, the teacher must convince them of the need to become active learners. Students need to learn to set goals for their reading tasks, plan how they will meet their goals, monitor their success in meeting their goals, and remedy the situation when they do not meet their goals.

To plan ways to meet their goals, students need to know certain techniques, such as relating new information to their background knowledge, previewing material to be read, paraphrasing ideas presented, and identifying the organizational pattern or patterns of the text. Students should learn the value of periodically questioning themselves about the ideas in the material to see if they are meeting their goals (Babbs and Moe, 1983). They need to learn to ask if the information they have read makes sense. If it does not make sense, they need to learn to ask why it does not make sense. They should decide if they have a problem with decoding a word, understanding what a word means, understanding what a sentence is saying, understanding how a sentence relates to the rest of the passage, or grasping the focus or purpose of the passage (Wilson, 1983). If they have not met their goals because they did not recognize certain words, they need to use context clues, structural analysis, phonics, and possibly the dictionary. If word meaning is the problem, they can use any of these techniques, except phonics. If sentence structure or sentence relationships are the problem, they can try identifying key words, breaking down sentences into separate meaning units, locating antecedents for pronouns, and other such techniques.

Teachers often use ***graphic organizers*** (visual depictions of text material, such as webs) before, during, or after reading to assist students in the comprehension of expository material. Combined with other metacognitive strategies, graphic organizers can help students activate their recall of background information, identify essential information in the reading, and recognize relationships among concepts. Reviewing the research on the growth and development of graphic organizers, Merkley and Jefferies (2000–2001) suggest the following guidelines for teachers who plan to use graphic organizers:

- Conduct a prereading dialogue to discuss the relationships illustrated by the graphic.
- Encourage student input throughout the discussion.
- Connect to previous learning by correcting errors in understanding and challenging thinking.
- Reference the upcoming text as a source for additional information.
- Reinforce decoding and structural analysis without distracting from the emphasis on comprehension.

Teachers should teach specific strategies for students to use when they do not comprehend material. Moderately difficult material should be used for this instruction so that they will have some actual comprehension problems to confront, although it should not be too difficult to be useful. Teachers should present background information before the students read, so that they have the information needed to apply comprehension strategies.

Teacher modeling and student practice of think-alouds can help students learn metacognitive strategies. "Think alouds require a reader to stop periodically, reflect on how a text is being processed and understood, and relate orally what reading strategies are being employed" (Baumann, Jones, and Seifert-Kessell, 1993, p. 185). Students have to be told what each strategy is and why it is important. Then the teacher can model

TIME for REFLECTION

Some teachers believe that students should enter middle school with the comprehension strategies to understand text when reading independently, and that reading instruction should not be their responsibility. **What do *you* think, and why?**

strategies for monitoring comprehension by reading a passage aloud and "thinking aloud" about his or her own monitoring behaviors and hypotheses. Noting things that are currently known and unknown and modifying these notes as more information is added can be helpful. Students should be drawn into the process in subsequent lessons by practicing the think-aloud strategy with the teacher's guidance at first and then independently. Eventually they need to apply the monitoring strategy independently (Baumann, Jones, and Seifert-Kessell, 1993; Fitzgerald, 1983; Oster, 2001).

To check students' comprehension monitoring, teachers can ask students to read difficult passages and then ask questions about them. The students write their answers and indicate their degree of confidence in the answers. Incorrect answers should have low confidence ratings, and correct answers should have high ratings in order to indicate good comprehension monitoring (Fitzgerald, 1983).

Graphic Aids

Textbooks contain numerous reading aids that students often disregard because they have had no training in how to use them. We have already discussed glossaries, footnotes, bibliographies, and appendices in this chapter, but we also need to consider graphic aids such as maps, graphs, tables, and illustrations. Teachers should explain how these aids function, model their use for the students, and provide students with supervised practice in extracting information from them. Making their own graphic aids is also a good technique to help students develop their communication abilities.

Maps

Many maps appear in social studies textbooks, and they are also sometimes found in science, mathematics, and literature books. The use of maps will increase in frequency, and the maps will increase in complexity, as students progress through school.

A first step in map reading is to examine the title (for example, "Annual Rainfall in the United States") to determine what area is being represented and what type of information is being given about the area. The teacher should emphasize the importance of determining the information conveyed by the title before moving on to a more detailed study of the map. The next step is to teach students how to determine directions by helping them to locate directional indicators on maps and to use these indicators to identify the four cardinal directions.

Interpreting the map's ***legend*** is the next reading task. The legend contains an explanation of each symbol used on the map. The reader must be able to interpret these symbols in order to understand the information the map contains.

Learning to apply a map's ***scale*** is fairly difficult. Because it would be highly impractical to draw a map to the actual size of the area represented (for instance, the United States), maps show areas greatly reduced in size. The scale shows the relationship of a given distance on the map to the same distance on the earth.

Middle-school students should understand the concepts of latitude and longitude, the Tropic of Cancer and the Tropic of Capricorn, the north and south poles, and the equator. They should also be acquainted with map terms such as *hemisphere, peninsula, continent, isthmus, gulf, bay,* and many others.

Each time students look at a map of an area, the teacher should encourage them to relate it to a map of a larger area—for example, to relate a map of Tennessee to a map of the United States. This points out the position of Tennessee within the entire United States.

Students need practice in thinking critically about the information that maps can provide. For example, the teacher may provide students with a map of the United States in the early 1800s that shows waterways, bodies of water, and population distributions and ask the students to draw conclusions about the population distributions. The effect of the bodies of water should be evident to the students.

Some suggestions for teaching map-reading skills follow. These skills are best taught when the students need to read maps for a purpose in one or more of their classes. Map skills should be immediately applied to these authentic materials after instruction takes place:

1. To teach students to apply a map's scale, help them construct a map of their classroom to a specified scale. Provide step-by-step guidance.
2. Model the use of a map's legend. Then have the students practice using the map's legend by asking them questions such as the following:

   Where is there a railroad on this map?

   Where is the state capital located?

Students can construct maps that illustrate information found in content area textbooks. *(© Jean Claude LeJeune)*

Where do you see a symbol for a college?

Are there any national monuments in this area? If so, where are they?

3. Give the students a map of their county or city, and let them locate their homes on the map.
4. Give the students maps such as the one presented in Example 7.4, and have them answer questions about them.

DIVERSITY 

5. Have English language learners label parts of maps to become familiar with map terminology.

LITERATURE 

6. Have students map the locale in a piece of literature that they are reading.

EXAMPLE 7.4 Sample Map and Questions: Trails West

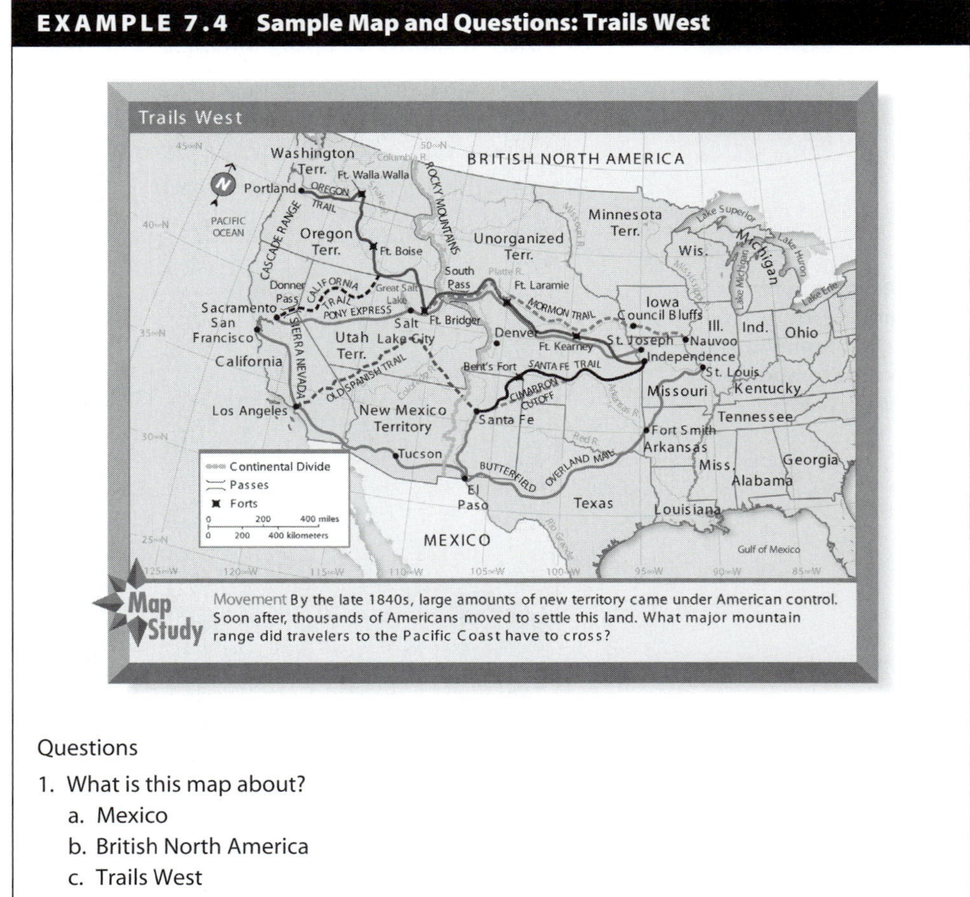

Map Study Movement By the late 1840s, large amounts of new territory came under American control. Soon after, thousands of Americans moved to settle this land. What major mountain range did travelers to the Pacific Coast have to cross?

Questions

1. What is this map about?
   a. Mexico
   b. British North America
   c. Trails West

2. What two cities indicate the eastern beginning point and the western destination for travelers on the Oregon Trail?
   a. Independence, Missouri, and Portland, Oregon
   b. Independence, Missouri, and Sacramento, California
   c. Independence, Missouri, and Los Angeles, Callifornia
3. What trail led travelers through Donner Pass in the Sierra Nevada mountain range?
   a. Cimarron Cutoff
   b. Old Spanish Trail
   c. California Trail
4. On what trail would travelers going west cross the Red River?
   a. Cimarron Cutoff
   b. Butterfield Overland Mail
   c. Mormon Trail
5. Approximately how many miles was it from Santa Fe, New Mexico, to Salt Lake City, Utah?
   a. 100 miles
   b. 200 miles
   c. 400 miles
6. Which of the following features is not identifiable from the map?
   a. Continental Divide
   b. Mountain ranges
   c. Routes for major cattle drives
7. What city served as the eastern origin for mail carriers for the Pony Express?
   a. Fort Smith, Arkansas
   b. St. Joseph, Missouri
   c. St. Louis, Missouri

Source: Davidson, *American History: The Early Years to 1877,* Woodland Hills, Ca.: Glencoe / McGraw Hill, 2001, p. 448. Reprinted with permission.

Graphs

Graphs often appear in social studies, science, and mathematics books to clarify written explanations. Four basic types of graphs are described as follows and are illustrated in Example 7.5 on page 288:

1. ***Picture graphs*** express quantities through pictures.
2. ***Circle or pie graphs*** show relationships of individual parts to the whole.
3. ***Bar graphs*** use vertical or horizontal bars to compare quantities. (Vertical bar graphs are easier to read than horizontal ones.)
4. ***Line graphs*** show changes in amounts.

EXAMPLE 7.5 Sample Picture, Pie, Bar, and Line Graphs

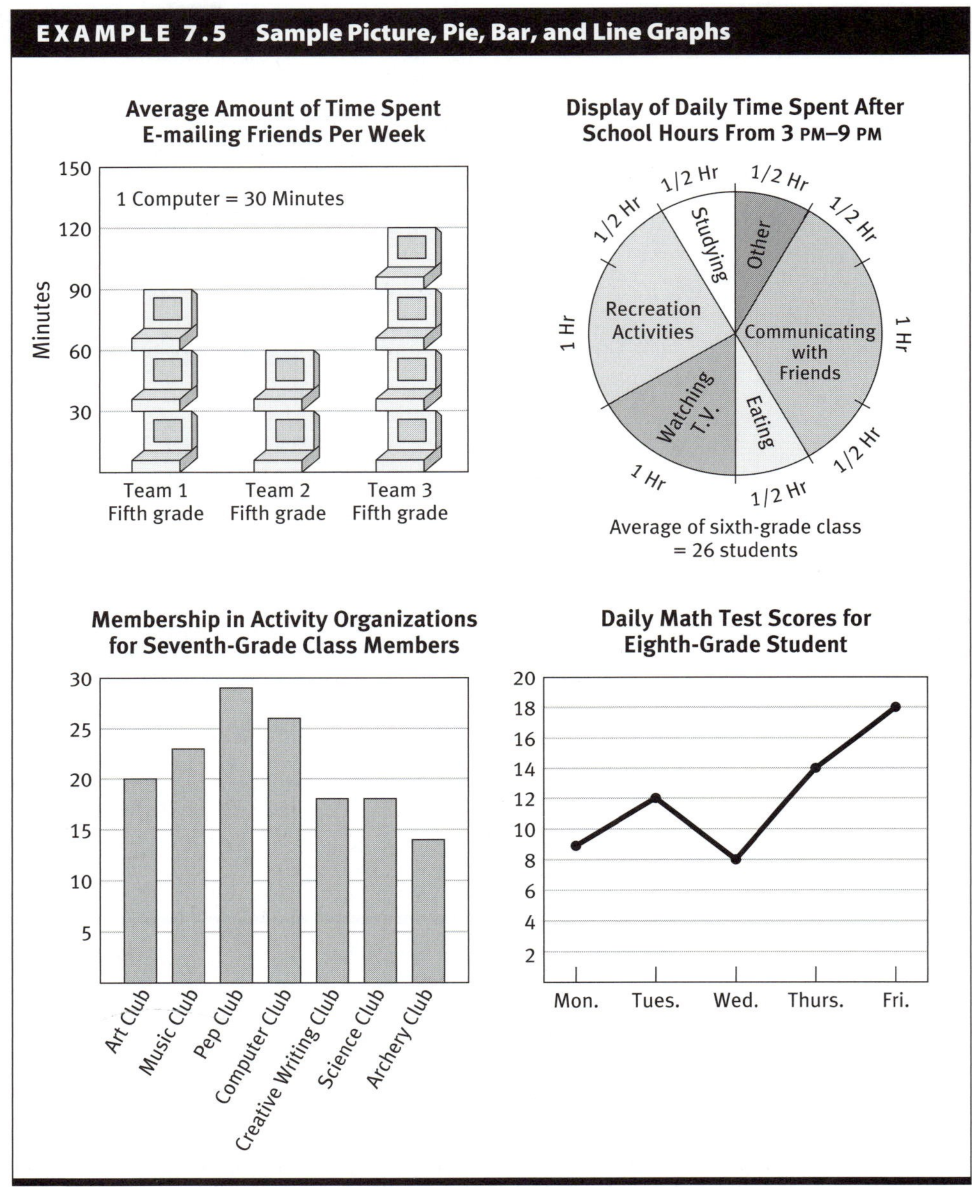

Students can learn to discover from the graph's title what comparison is being made or information is being given (for example, time spent in various activities during the day or populations of various counties in a state), to interpret the legend of a picture graph, and to derive needed information accurately from a graph.

One of the best ways to help students learn to read graphs is to have them construct meaningful graphs (Hadaway and Young, 1994). Following are some examples of graph construction activities:

1. A picture graph showing the number of dance tickets sold by each class. One picture of a ticket could equal five tickets.
2. A circle graph showing the percentage of each day that a student spends sleeping, eating, studying, and in recreation.

3. A bar graph showing the number of books class members read each week for six weeks.
4. A line graph showing the weekly test scores of one student over a six- or nine-week grading period.
5. A picture graph, bar graph, or circle graph of students' predictions about a story (McDonald, 1999).

Tables

Tables, which appear in reading materials of all subject areas, may present a problem because students have trouble extracting specific facts from a large mass of available information. The great amount of information provided in the small amount of space on tables can confuse students unless the teacher provides a procedure for reading tables.

Just as the titles of maps and graphs contain information about their content, so do the titles of tables. In addition, since tables are arranged in columns and rows, the headings can provide information. To discover specific information, students must locate the intersection of an appropriate column with an appropriate row. The teacher can model reading tables, verbalizing the mental processes involved in locating the information. Then the students can be asked to read a table, such as the multiplication table shown in Example 7.6 on page 290, and answer related questions. Some sample questions are provided.

Illustrations

DIVERSITY

Various types of illustrations, ranging from photographs to schematic diagrams, are found in textbooks. Too often students see illustrations merely as space fillers, reducing the amount of reading they will have to do on a page. As a result, they tend to pay little attention to illustrations even though illustrations are a very good source of information. A picture of a jungle, for example, may add considerably to a student's understanding of that term; a picture of an Arabian nomad may illuminate the term *Bedouin* in a history class. Diagrams of bones within the body can show a student things that cannot readily be observed firsthand. Having English language learners and students with special needs label illustrations is particularly helpful to their comprehension of content material.

EXAMPLE 7.6 Sample Table and Questions

Multiplication Table

	1	2	3	4	5	6	7	8	9
1	1	2	3	4	5	6	7	8	9
2	2	4	6	8	10	12	14	16	18
3	3	6	9	12	15	18	21	24	27
4	4	8	12	16	20	24	28	32	36
5	5	10	15	20	25	30	35	40	45
6	6	12	18	24	30	36	42	48	54
7	7	14	21	28	35	42	49	56	63
8	8	16	24	32	40	48	56	64	72
9	9	18	27	36	45	54	63	72	81

Questions

1. What is the product of 5×6?
2. What is the product of 9×3?
3. Is the product of 5×4 the same as the product of 4×5?
4. Which number is greater: the product of 3×8 or the product of 4×7?
5. When a number is multiplied by 1, what will the product always be?
6. Why is 24 where the 4 row and the 6 column meet?
7. How do the numbers in the 2 row compare with the numbers in the 4 row?

SUMMARY

Reading/study techniques enhance middle-school students' comprehension and retention of printed material. Study methods, such as SQ3R and SQRQCQ, can help students comprehend and retain material that they read. A number of other techniques can also help students with organization and retention.

Developing test-taking strategies can allow students to show more accurately what they have learned. Students need strategies for taking objective and essay tests, and they need special strategies for standardized testing situations.

Flexible reading habits can help students study more effectively. Students need to be able to adjust their approaches to the reading and adjust their reading rates.

Students need to learn strategies for locating information in both print and nonprint sources: in library books and textbooks using the important parts of the books; in reference books, such as dictionaries and encyclopedias; in the library; and in computer databases. They need to learn how to design and use graphic organizers. They also need to learn how to organize the information when they find it and to learn how to monitor their comprehension and retention of material (metacognition).

In addition, students need to know how to obtain information from the graphic aids found in textbooks. They must be able to read and understand maps, graphs, tables, and illustrations.

TEST YOURSELF

True or False

______ 1. SQ3R stands for Stimulate, Question, Read, Reason, React.

______ 2. SQ3R is a study method useful in reading social studies and science materials.

______ 3. SQRQCQ is a study method designed for use with mathematics textbooks.

______ 4. Students remember material better if they are given opportunities to discuss it.

______ 5. Study guides are of little help to retention.

______ 6. Writing information often helps students to fix it in their memories.

______ 7. Massed practice is preferable to spaced practice for encouraging long-term retention.

______ 8. Students should read all reading materials at the same speed.

______ 9. Rereading is often necessary for materials that contain a high density of facts.

______ 10. Many content area textbooks offer glossaries of technical terms as reading aids.

______ 11. Index practice is most effective when students use their own textbooks rather than a worksheet index that has no obvious function.

______ 12. Middle-school students have no need to learn how to take notes, since they are not asked to use this skill until secondary school.

______ 13. Subordination in outlines is indicated by lettering, numbering, and indentation.

______ 14. The legend of a map tells the history of the area represented.

______ 15. A good way to help students develop an understanding of graphs is to help them construct their own meaningful graphs.

______ 16. Middle-school students may use newspapers, magazines, catalogues, and brochures as reference sources.

______ 17. Teachers do not need to teach journalistic terms to middle-school students; this is a higher-level activity.

______ 18. Using catalogues often requires the ability to read charts.

_______ 19. Key words are the words that carry the important information in a sentence.

_______ 20. The ability to recognize main ideas is a prerequisite skill for outlining.

_______ 21. Guide words indicate the first two words on a dictionary page.

_______ 22. Summaries should include redundant material.

_______ 23. Some students fail to do well on essay tests because they do not understand such terms as *compare* and *contrast.*

_______ 24. Students need to practice under standardized testing conditions so that they will be familiar with the testing situation when they take a standardized test.

_______ 25. Rereading can be a useful metacognitive strategy.

_______ 26. Graphic organizers are designed to provide visual representations of key concepts or terms.

_______ 27. In an inquiry-based learning environment, locating and organizing information is primarily the responsibility of the teacher.

For your journal . . .

1. Visit a middle-school library, and listen as the librarian or media specialist explains the reference materials and library procedures to students. In your journal, evaluate the presentation, and decide how you might change it if you were responsible for it.
2. Choose a textbook from a subject area and middle-school grade level of your choice. Examine closely the material on twenty consecutive pages, and list the study skills needed to obtain information from these pages effectively.

. . . and your portfolio

1. Using materials of widely varying types, develop and document a procedure to help middle-school students learn to be flexible in their rates of reading.
2. Choose a content area textbook at the middle level, and plan procedures to familiarize students with the parts of the book and the reading aids the book offers.
3. Collect materials that middle-school students can use as supplementary reference sources (such as newspapers, magazines, catalogues, and brochures), and develop several short lessons to help the students read these materials effectively.
4. Make a variety of types of graphs into a display that you could use in a unit on reading graphs. Photograph the display.
5. Collect pictures and diagrams that present information. Ask several students to study these pictures and extract as much information from them as possible. Provide a written summary of your analysis.

8 Reading in the Content Areas

KEY VOCABULARY

Pay close attention to these terms when they appear in the chapter.

- content area textbook
- directed reading-thinking activity
- expository text
- figurative language
- frustration level
- guided reading procedure (GRP)
- independent level
- instructional level
- language arts
- language experience approach (LEA)
- narrative text
- readability level
- study guides

SETTING OBJECTIVES

When you finish reading this chapter, you should be able to

- Describe several general techniques for helping middle-school students read content area materials.
- Describe some procedures and materials that are helpful in presenting material in language arts, social studies, mathematics, and science and health books.

Reading in ***content area textbooks,*** such as those for social studies, science, mathematics, and other curricular areas, and in supplementary materials used in content classes is often difficult for students. Content textbooks and other informational materials contain ***expository*** (explanatory) ***text*** that can be more difficult for students to read than ***narrative*** (story) ***text.*** These materials also contain many new concepts. As Yopp and Yopp (2000) point out, the different text features and structures found in informational text pose problems that are different from those found in narrative text, and the ability to read narrative text is no guarantee that students can read informational text with the same competence.

Students' reading strategies are often initially acquired in reading class, using basal readers. Because content area books and supplementary materials present special reading problems, however, teachers should be aware that simply offering their students instruction in basal readers, even though today's basal readers contain more content-oriented text than did the readers in the past, is not sufficient if the students are to read well in content area texts and other nonfiction materials.

To read well in content area textbooks, students need good general reading strategies, including word recognition and comprehension, and reading/study strategies. If they cannot recognize the words they encounter, they will be unable to take in the information from the material. Without good literal, interpretive, critical, and creative reading comprehension strategies, as described in Chapter 4, they will not understand the textbook's message. And if they lack good reading/study strategies, they will be less likely to comprehend and retain the material. Special help with content area reading, at the time students are expected to do such reading, is important, for this is when students most effectively learn how to apply the strategies and techniques. Classrooms in

Chapter 8 Organization

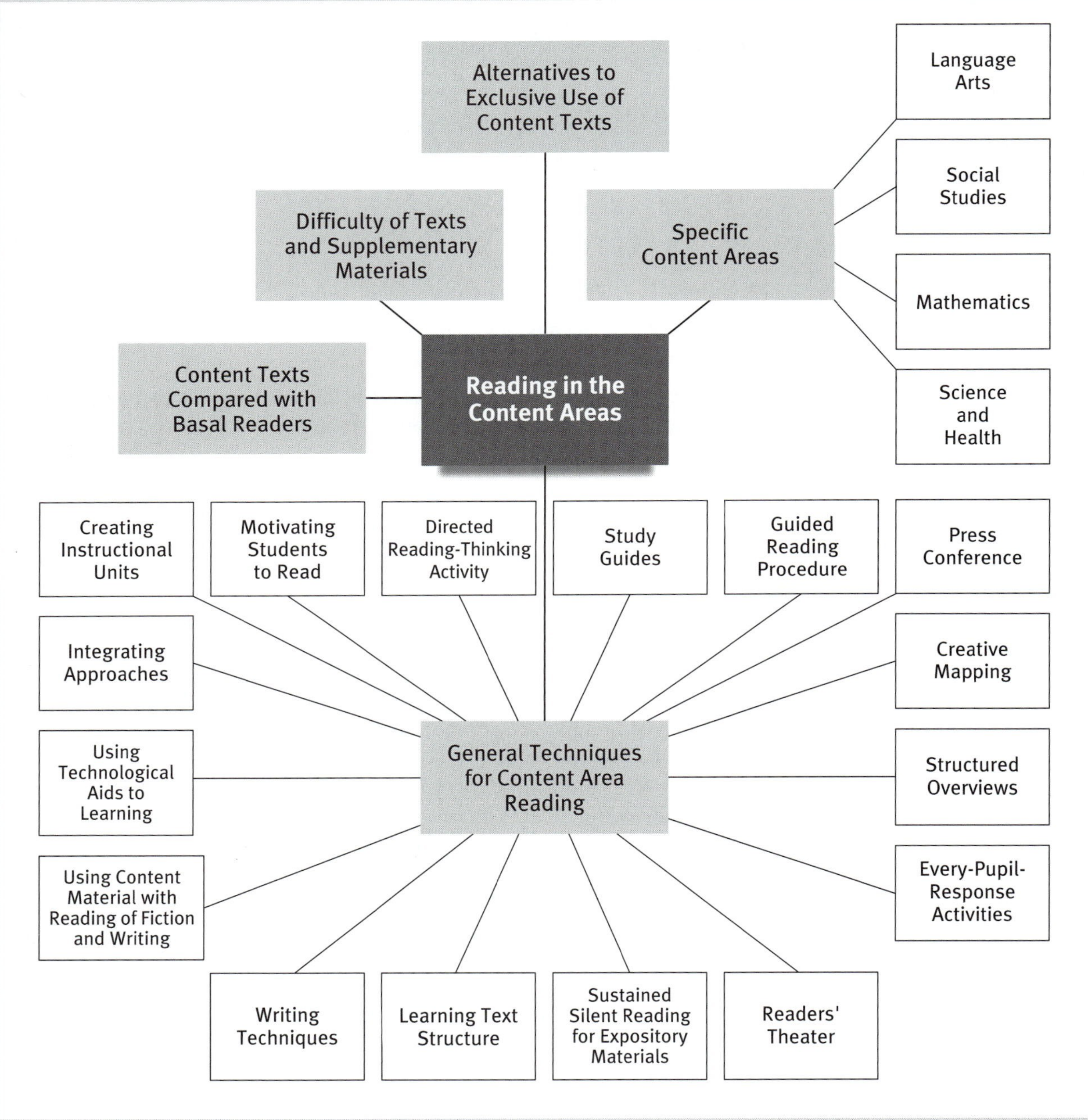

which the teachers integrate learning activities across the curriculum, rather than scheduling separate periods for language, science, social studies, and so on, offer opportunities throughout the day to help students read and comprehend the expository texts generally used in content areas.

Instead of relying solely on textbooks, we will see later in this chapter that teachers may choose nonfiction trade books (library books), newspapers, brochures, and other factual materials to supplement the curriculum in some classes and as the core of the curriculum in others. Students often need to apply the same strategies to reading many of these informational materials as they do to reading content area textbooks. Goldman (1997) described a project in which middle-school students searched for information in print texts, on CDs, and on the Internet, taking notes in field journals. They evaluated the resulting information and developed the trustworthy results into written projects that integrated the relevant data (Wade and Moje, 2000).

TECHNOLOGY

Because of the special challenges posed by reading in content area textbooks and other factual materials, teachers need to know a variety of techniques for helping students understand their reading. Teachers often use concrete manipulatives (such as maps and pictures) to develop concepts. Manipulatives are especially helpful with struggling readers. The teachers encourage students to visualize information, which can be helped by use of manipulatives, and brainstorm about the topics, and they often provide narratives on the same topic and use audiotaped, videotaped, or computer-based materials to aid comprehension. Semantic mapping of the main topic, use of the K-W-L procedure, and use of expository paragraph frames are other good techniques. Teachers may also require retellings of text material and have students summarize the material to check understanding.

DIVERSITY

TECHNOLOGY

STANDARDS AND ASSESSMENT

This chapter concludes with an examination of several content areas—language arts, social studies, mathematics, and science and health—along with their specific reading difficulties and activities to promote readiness and good comprehension. In addition, it presents general content area reading strategies to use in conjunction with the many strategies already described in Chapters 3 and 4 as comprehension aids in reading content area material.

Content Texts Compared with Basal Readers

Much material in basal readers is written in a narrative style that describes the actions of people in particular situations, while textbooks are generally written in an expository style, with heavy concentrations of facts. Students find narrative material easier to read than expository material. Narrative selections often have entertaining plots that can be read for enjoyment. Content selections rarely offer this enticement.

Many students are unfamiliar with the organizational structures of expository texts. Therefore, they are left without a predictable structure to use when they are asked to read such materials (Beck and McKeown, 1991a).

Basal readers do not present the density of ideas typical of content textbooks. Students must give attention to each sentence in a content book, for nearly every one carries important information. In addition, students must acquire the information presented early, so they can understand later passages. This is rarely true of basal readers, in which each selection is generally a discrete entity.

Whereas basal readers may have planned repetition of key words to encourage their acquisition, content area texts present many new concepts and vocabulary terms with little planned repetition. All of the content areas have specialized and technical vocabularies that students must acquire. Generally, basal readers contain little specialized or technical vocabulary. (See Chapter 2 for a discussion of specialized and technical vocabulary.)

Content textbooks contain a large number of graphic aids that students must interpret, whereas basal readers contain fewer of these aids. The illustrations in basal readers at the middle-school level are often included primarily for interest value, but those in content books are designed to help clarify concepts and need to be studied carefully.

Whereas content area textbooks have abundant headings that signal the organization of the selection, few such headings are used in basal readers, and the ones that are used may be less informative than those in the content books. In reading content books, students should be helped to see that sometimes the headings outline the material for them, indicating main ideas and supporting details.

Organizational patterns of some newer content textbooks are changing, however, and the changes may signal even more reading difficulties for students if their teachers do not properly prepare them for the reading. Walpole (1998/1999) examined a traditional and a newer science textbook and found that the newer text had a less linear, less predictable format and did not lend itself as well to traditional outlining. Subheads in the newer text did not have a hierarchical order, and the format was more varied. Compared with the newer text, the traditional text had more signal words to help students make connections between ideas. The newer text posed more unanswered questions and asked the reader to perform actions or think about something more frequently. Captions for pictures in the traditional text generally paraphrased the main text, whereas in the newer text, the captions contained new information. Teachers must adjust instruction to fit the formats and organizational patterns of the textbooks they must use.

Difficulty of Texts and Supplementary Materials

STANDARDS AND ASSESSMENT

The teacher's first step in helping students to read content material is to be aware of the level of difficulty of the textbook and other reading assignments they make. Teachers must adjust their expectations for each student according to that student's reading ability, so that no student is assigned work in material on his or her ***frustration level***—that is, the level at which the material is so difficult that it will immediately be frustrating and the student will be unable to comprehend it. Trying to read from material that is too hard for them can prevent students from learning the content. If students are required to try to read a book or other material at this difficulty level, they may develop negative attitudes toward the subject, the teacher, and even school in general. Students probably learn best from printed material that is written on their ***independent levels,*** or the levels at which they read with ease and comprehension. They can also learn from textbooks written on their ***instructional levels,*** or the levels at which they read with understanding when given sufficient help by the teacher. (See Chapter 9 for further discussion of independent, instructional, and frustration levels and techniques for determining readability.)

After determining each student's ability to benefit from the class textbook and chosen supplementary materials, the teacher has the information needed to make instructional decisions. For some students, the content area reading assignments will be on their independent level. They will be able to read the assignments and prepare for class discussion independently, and they will often be able to set their own purpose questions to direct their reading. For other students, the material will be at their instructional level. These students need to have the teacher introduce material carefully, build concepts and vocabulary gradually, and assign purpose questions. For still other students, the material will be at their frustration level. These students need to be introduced to the subject and, in order to understand the concepts and information involved, be given some simpler materials with a lower readability level than that of the text or supplementary material that their classmates are using.

All students can participate together in discussing the material, and the teacher can record significant contributions on the board in the same way as in recording a language experience story. (Detailed discussions of the language experience approach appear later in this chapter and in Chapter 5.) When the teacher asks students to read the contributions from the board at the end of the discussion period, even poor readers may be able to read fairly difficult contributions because they have heard the sentences being dictated and have seen them being written down. Before the next class, the teacher can duplicate the class summary for each student to use in reviewing for tests. During study periods, he or she can help the students who are at their frustration levels to reread the notes, emphasizing the new words and concepts.

Not only are many content area textbooks written at much higher ***readability levels*** than basal readers for the corresponding grades, but subject matter textbooks also often vary in difficulty from chapter to chapter. If teachers are aware of various levels of difficulty within a text, they can adjust teaching methods to help students gain the most from each portion of the book, perhaps by teaching easier chapters earlier in the year and more difficult chapters later on. Of course, this technique is not advisable for teaching material in which the concepts in an early, difficult chapter are necessary for understanding a later, easier chapter.

A good way to decrease the difficulty of content passages for students is to teach the content vocabulary thoroughly before the material containing that vocabulary is assigned to be read. The unfamiliar content vocabulary is a major factor in the higher difficulty levels of many content area materials.

Alternatives to Exclusive Use of Content Texts

Some students find textbooks difficult to read or are unmotivated to read them because they find them dull and dry. For such students, supplementary trade books offer one viable option for learning content area material. Many students experience their first serious difficulties with reading as they begin reading content textbooks, but the continued use of high-interest trade books along with textbooks may ease the transition.

Regardless of whether or not the students have trouble reading the textbooks, teachers can use trade books to enhance the study of textbook topics and help students learn more about the content. Trade books can be chosen to coincide with students' reading levels, easing one typical problem. These books can be visually appealing to students and therefore can spark their interest. They can also cover a topic in greater depth than the length limits of a textbook would allow, and they frequently have coherent organizational patterns. Newer books ensure access to timely information.

Some nonfiction books make use of a narrative format, with which students are often more familiar than they are with nonfiction organizational patterns, although others will have topical, comparison/contrast, problem/solution, cause/effect, or other expository patterns. Regardless of the organizational pattern, the nonfiction selections can provide more elaboration on a single topic than can a standard textbook description.

After identifying concepts in the content textbooks that need elaboration, teachers locate suitable trade books that include these concepts. They may read aloud from these books in class or obtain multiple copies of the books for independent reading by the students prior to completing textbook assignments or for an enrichment activity after reading the textbook materials.

Camp (2000) suggests use of "twin texts" of fiction and nonfiction to present content. Such trade books are available on a wide variety of topics. For some middle-school students, the fiction selection *Hiroshima* by Laurence Yep could be paired with the nonfiction *Sadako and the Thousand Paper Cranes* by Eleanor Coerr. Each book presents pertinent information that helps students build a framework for understanding content lessons. The fiction selection has factual material woven into a fictional setting and narrative format, and many fiction selections are less packed with new concepts and vocabulary than are nonfiction books. Teachers must be aware, however, as Guillaume (1998) cautions, that the fiction selected should help students understand the topics and should not perpetuate faulty concepts.

Use of the twin texts before the textbook material is read will lead to better understanding of the material because students will have activated or expanded their schemata before reading the textbook and because the twin texts provide elaboration on the topic. Teachers may wish to use Venn diagrams (see Chapter 4 for an example) to compare and contrast the fiction and nonfiction selections on the same topic. The K-W-L technique (see Chapter 3) could also be used before students read the twin texts. A DR-TA (discussed in Chapter 5 and this chapter) could be employed in guiding the reading of the trade books. Writing about the central topic and webbing key vocabulary in the books are good follow-up activities (Camp, 2000).

TECHNOLOGY

Information from Internet sites can supplement the textbook information. Teachers may wish to bookmark appropriate sites and provide guidance for the students in how to use them. Middle-school students may also use search engines to locate sites that have appropriate information.

Videotapes, CDs, and DVDs can also provide supplementary information. Teachers may want to suggest appropriate videotapes, CDs, and DVDs for the school librarian or media specialist to purchase.

Hibbing and Rankin-Erickson (2003) used movies with struggling middle-school readers before having them read about content area topics. The movies provided the students with important background information that helped them understand the novels, nonfiction trade books, and the textbook material. These movies helped students understand time contexts, details related to settings, and language in the written materials. They also provided the students with "memory pegs" for information, that is, ideas to which information in the written texts could be attached.

General Techniques for Content Area Reading

When working with students who are reading in the content areas, teachers should do many of the things suggested in earlier chapters for directing the reading of any material, such as developing vocabulary knowledge, activating background knowledge about the topic, and providing purposes for reading. They should also suggest use of a study method, such as SQ3R or another appropriate one, encourage note taking, and provide suggestions to promote retention of the material. Prior knowledge can be accessed and/or developed through such techniques as provision of firsthand experiences, discussion, brainstorming, mapping, and the K-W-L procedure. (Information about these activities appears in Chapters 3, 4, 5, and 7.) Teachers may also use a number of other techniques, such as the ones in this section, to help their students read in content areas more effectively.

The teacher should make reading materials available at a variety of difficulty levels, so that all students can participate in acquiring information from print sources. They should systematically include nonfiction selections in their daily read-aloud sessions in order to expose students to nonfiction material, organizational patterns, and authors. Dreher (1998/1999) suggests keeping a log of read-aloud selections to help in balancing types of material read.

Motivating Students to Read

Middle-school students are frequently less motivated to read than are younger students. Moss and Hendershot (2002) believe that nonfiction trade books have tremendous potential to motivate middle-school readers, especially reluctant readers. Unmotivated seventh graders reported that among activities that would motivate them to read would be reading nonfiction and reading self-selected material.

With all of the high-quality nonfiction books available for this age group, teachers should be able to provide some choice in reading material in each content area on topics that are in the year's curriculum. Many of the available books are well-written, attractive, and up-to-date—all prerequisites for good, motivational learning experiences. When allowed to choose nonfiction books to read, students sometimes select books based on visuals that cause them to reflect upon the possible content, sometimes on their desire to know what topics or titles mean, sometimes on the authors' or the books' relationships to topics that they have previously read about, sometimes on awards that the books have won, and sometimes on the recommendations of others.

Mathison (1989) found that teachers can stimulate interest in reading content area materials in a number of ways. Two strategies are using analogies to help give new ideas familiar connections and telling personal anecdotes that can help personalize reading material. For example, a study of arteries and veins in a sixth-grade class could be motivated by drawing an analogy to roads leading into the downtown area; or, in a study of a particular climate, the teacher might share a personal anecdote about a camping trip in such a climate. Teachers should examine each reading assignment for possibilities for motivational introductions. Glynn (1996) also suggests ways to use analogies in science instruction.

Stories can help students see the connections that exist among people across time and from different places because of common needs people share. Participation in storytelling sessions helps the students develop shared experiences that create bonds among classmates (Combs and Beach, 1994). Such bonds allow the students to cooperate more freely as they work toward common goals in the classroom.

Directed Reading-Thinking Activity

The ***directed reading-thinking activity*** (DR-TA) can be used to direct students' reading of either basal reader stories or content area selections. (A complete discussion of the DR-TA is found in Chapter 5.) As Harp (1989a) points out, in this activity students predict, read, and prove predictions as the teacher asks them what they think, why they think that, and how they can prove their points.

Study Guides

Study guides are prepared by the teacher to guide expository reading in content fields. They can set purposes for reading, as well as provide aids for interpreting material through suggestions about how to apply reading strategies. These guides also serve as vehicles for group discussions and cooperative learning activities. Discussion of the questions or items after reading the material is very important to the learning process. There are many kinds of study guides, and the nature of the material and the reason for reading it can help teachers determine which kind to use.

Content-process guides, as shown in Example 8.1 on page 301, focus on both the content and process aspects of reading. The study guide in Example 8.1 directs students' reading in the following ways:

1. The overview question offers an overall purpose for the reading, helping students read the material with the appropriate mental set.
2. The first item after the overview question gives students content purposes for reading the first section. Notice that the questions are phrased to elicit thought about the information in the passage.
3. Following the purposes are two questions about vocabulary meanings. The students are encouraged to use their skills in structural analysis to help them understand the vocabulary presented. This is process guidance.
4. The second item offers purposes for reading the second main section. Notice that it specifies the groups under consideration.
5. The second item is followed by a vocabulary question and a process suggestion to use context clues.

Pattern guides are study guides that stress the relationship among the organizational structure, the reading/thinking skills needed for comprehension, and the important concepts in the material. The first step in constructing such a guide is to identify the important concepts in the material. Then information about each concept must be located within the selection, and the author's organizational pattern must be

EXAMPLE 8.1 Sample Selection and Content-Process Study Guide

[*Note:* The material in this passage is part of a discussion of the Seven Years' War.]

The Proclamation of 1763 With the French defeat, many colonists eagerly prepared to move across the Appalachian Mountains. However, the British were worried. They knew that new settlements would anger the Iroquois, Delaware, Shawnee, and other Indian tribes who already lived there. To prevent fighting, the British issued the Proclamation of 1763. This act saved all land west of the Appalachians for Indians. Colonists could not settle there.

The Proclamation upset many colonists. Earlier, the French had blocked new settlements. The French had been defeated. Now, though, the British also stopped people from moving west. Many colonists wondered why they had fought the war.

The Cost of Victory Colonial anger at Britain's Proclamation of 1763 was just one hardship the war caused. The British, the Indians, and the colonists each faced new troubles.

In Britain, the war had caused the government to borrow money. Between 1754 and 1763, the money Britain owed doubled. The country needed money to pay back its many loans.

Britain also had to pay the 10,000 soldiers it sent to North America. These troops were needed to protect the large new British empire. Britain now had to spend three times as much to defend its American empire as it did before the war.

For many Indian tribes, the war brought a loss of power. They could no longer use the French to help them against the British. And even 10,000 British soldiers could not stop settlers from moving onto Indian lands.

In the colonies, the war caused great suffering. Boston, a city of about 2,200 families, lost 700 men during the war. These deaths left many widows and orphans who needed help just to buy food.

Study Guide

Overview Question: What were the effects of the war on the people of America and Great Britain?

1. Read the section titled "The Proclamation of 1763" to find out what effect this action had on the colonists. Were the colonists pleased with the effect? How can you tell?
   What is a settlement? What is a proclamation? If you don't know, locate the root words to help you figure this out.

2. Read the section titled "The Cost of Victory" to discover other hardships the war caused. Look for hardships faced by the British, the Indian tribes, and the people of the colonies.
   What is a synonym for *hardship*? Look for a context clue to this word's meaning.

Source: From *America Will Be* in *Houghton Mifflin Social Studies* by Armento et al. Copyright 1994 by Houghton Mifflin Company. Reprinted by permission of Houghton Mifflin Company.

identified. The teacher then integrates the identified concepts, the writing pattern, and the skills necessary for reading the material with understanding in a guide that offers as much direction as specific students need—whether it be the section of text in which the information is located; the page number; or the page, paragraph, and line numbers.

Conrad (1989) found that her students were able to work more effectively with cause-and-effect relationships if the effects were listed on the left side of the page and

EXAMPLE 8.2 Cause-and-Effect Pattern Guide

Causes	*Effects*		
	On British	**On Indians**	**On Colonists**
Proclamation of 1763	Drew colonists' anger	Land west of Appalachians saved for them	Denied right to settle on land west of Appalachians
Seven Years' War	Needed money to pay back loans Had to pay larger number of soldiers	Loss of power Not enough British soldiers to keep settlers off their lands	Widows and orphans who needed help to buy food

the causes on the right side. She believed this was because students tend to want to tell what happened and then add a *because* phrase.

Example 8.2 above shows a completed complex cause-and-effect pattern guide that also has an implicit comparison-contrast element, since effects on three populations are compared. This pattern guide is based on the text selection in Example 8.1 on page 301. The guide had the two causes listed for the students, and they had to fill in the multiple effects.

Anticipation guides, which are used before reading a selection, require students to react to a series of statements related to the selection to be read. The students can react to the anticipation guide again when they have finished reading to see the differences, if any, between their initial opinions and the correct responses. When the teacher asks for responses both before and after reading, the guide is generally referred to as an anticipation/reaction guide.

The statements in an anticipation guide should relate to major concepts and significant details in the reading material. They may reflect common misconceptions about the topic, challenging students' beliefs. They should link students' prior knowledge with text concepts, and they should be general (Duffelmeyer, 1994). The guide may be used in a group setting, with students discussing and justifying their responses. See Chapter 3 for an example of an anticipation/reaction guide.

Duffelmeyer and Baum (1992) suggest extending the anticipation guide by having students decide if the text supported each of their choices and having them indicate why their choices were correct or incorrect by citing evidence from the text. This seems to be a good addition to the procedure. Merkley (1996/1997) suggests adding a prereading "I'm Not Sure" option to the "True and False" or "Yes and No" choices if the questions involve factual information. In postreading, "I'm Not Sure" should no longer be an option.

Guided Reading Procedure

Anthony Manzo's ***guided reading procedure (GRP)***, designed to help readers improve organizational skills, comprehension, and recall, is appropriate for content area reading in middle schools and high schools. The steps in the procedure follow:

1. Set a purpose for reading a selection of about 500 words, and tell the students to remember all they can about it. Tell them to close their books when they finish reading.
2. Have the students tell everything they remember from the material, and record this information on the board.
3. Ask students to look at the selection again to correct or add to the information they have already offered.
4. Direct the students to organize the information in an outline (see Chapter 7), semantic web (see Chapter 3), or some other arrangement.
5. Ask synthesizing questions to help students integrate the new material with previously acquired information.

6. Give a test immediately to check on the students' short-term recall.
7. Give another form of the test later to check medium- or long-term recall (Ankney and McClurg, 1981).

Press Conference

Press Conference is a strategy in which some students take the parts of characters in material that has been read (literature, science, social studies, current events) and others take the parts of reporters interviewing the characters. The interviews must have carefully planned questions, and the interviewers must take detailed notes from which they compose news stories about the interviewees and the events in which they have been involved. These stories are taken through a process writing approach, and the final versions are published in a class newspaper (Dever, 1992).

Creative Mapping

Naughton (1993/1994) suggests *creative mapping* to enhance content area reading. Creative mapping combines semantic mapping with pictures to display material in a way that helps students see relationships and also helps them recall it.

First, a picture that represents the topic or main idea is drawn. Then supporting details are arranged on or around the image in an organized manner. Students use their background knowledge and the text to complete the map.

Structured Overviews

Structured overviews are graphic organizers that show hierarchical and/or linear relationships among key concepts. Structured overviews of the vocabulary from a content area reading assignment can help students learn the terms and concepts. Initially, the teacher can project an overview on a screen, with students answering questions about how the vocabulary is related to the concepts in the assignment as the overview is developed in front of them, or the overview can be placed on strips on the bulletin board. Later the students can work cooperatively in small groups to form overviews, or they can make individual overviews from a chapter they read (Wolfe and Lopez, 1992/1993).

Every-Pupil-Response Activities

Gaskins and her colleagues (1994) found that use of *every-pupil-response activities*, such as engaging in written responses to text, facilitated participation in discussion about the text. These responses were not graded, but were used to help students assess their own understanding of the text and sometimes of its organizational structure. Partner discussions followed the writing and in turn were followed by whole-class discussions. The students helped one another to clarify their understandings and to see alternate interpretations.

Teachers reminded the students to support their positions with evidence from the text. Teachers also presented the students with real-life problems to which they could apply information from the text, eliciting enthusiastic small-group discussions. They talked about the strategies that would best fit the solution of the particular problem, why these strategies should help, when they should be used, and how to use them. Teachers modeled strategy use for the students before asking them to participate in guided practice.

Readers' Theater

Young and Vardell (1993) suggest using *readers' theater* with nonfiction trade books to increase active involvement with the material and add to their enjoyment of it. Books with dialogue are especially easy to adapt to readers' theater scripts. Some other types of text may be rewritten as dialogue, or multiple narrators may be assigned. Prologues may be added to introduce the material in the scripts, and/or postscripts may be added to bring some scripts to a close. Students should have an active part in developing the scripts, making their production as much of a learning experience as the performances.

Suggestions of books to use for readers' theater include David M. Schwartz's *How Much Is a Million?* for math; Joanna Cole's books about the Magic School Bus for science; Russell Freedman's *Buffalo Hunt* and Jean Fritz's *And Then What Happened, Paul Revere?* for social studies.

Sustained Silent Reading (SSR) for Expository Materials

In regular Sustained Silent Reading (SSR) periods, students have free choice of materials to read, and they generally choose narrative materials. Teachers can encourage students to read both fiction and nonfiction during SSR periods; there may even be separate SSR periods for each of the two types of text. Having many nonfiction titles easily accessible to students in the classroom, school library, or media center facilitates nonfiction reading (Dreher, 1998/1999; Joranko, 1990). This approach should help students become familiar with many expository text structures without the pressure that accompanies assigned reading.

Learning Text Structure

Many students do not use text structure to help them comprehend and retain information from content area textbooks, but research has shown that text structure can be taught (McGee and Richgels, 1985). Systematic attention to clues about the organizational structure of a text and creation of visual representations of the relationships among ideas aid both comprehension and retention (Pearson and Fielding, 1991). Five of the more common expository text structures are cause/effect, comparison/contrast, problem/solution, description, and collection.

Using Graphic Organizers

Using graphic organizers (such as webs), teachers can show how passages with the same text structure can have different content. Then they can prepare a graphic organizer for each structure to be taught. Focusing on one structure at a time, they can present students with the graphic organizer for a passage and have them construct a passage based on this organizer (See the section "Webs Plus Writing" later in this chapter.), which will include appropriate clue words, such as *because* and *different from*. Teachers should emphasize how the clue words help both readers and writers. After revising and refining their passages, students can compare them with the passage on which the graphic organizer was based (McGee and Richgels, 1985).

Hadaway and Young (1994) encourage the use of visual representations to help students grasp organization and content. They suggest the use of index cards to assist in the construction of time lines, especially when multiple sources are used. Venn diagrams can help students see common elements of concepts and can help them visualize similarities and differences in order to make comparisons and contrasts. Flowcharts help students visualize a sequence of events, such as the sequence of steps in a science experiment. (See Chapter 7 for more information on graphic organizers.)

Maps of the content may be used before, during, and/or after students read it. (See Chapter 3 for a discussion of semantic mapping and some examples.) Sometimes the teacher can construct the maps, and at other times students can do so. The teacher should also ask appropriate questions before, during, and after reading. (See Chapter 4 for a discussion of questioning techniques.)

Using Paragraph Frames

Another way to work on students' knowledge of text structure is through the use of expository paragraph frames. *Expository paragraph frames* are similar to the story frames described in Chapter 5. They provide sentence starters that include signal words or phrases to fit the paragraph organization. To clarify meanings of the signal words, the teacher can show the students a frame with the signal words and then model filling in the frame with responses elicited from students.

The sequential pattern is a good place to start. The teacher can write a sequential paragraph that uses the cue words for sequence: *first, next, then, finally.* The sentences can be copied onto index cards, the sequential nature of the material can be discussed in the group, and the students can be asked to arrange the sentences in sequential order on their desks. Then they can copy the sentences on their papers in paragraph form.

Any expository structure can be used with appropriate frames. Lewis, Wray, and Rospigliosi (1994) have found sequential, enumeration, comparison, contrast, and reaction frames to work well. They also have had success with getting students to draw pictures depicting sequential text after they read, but before they write about, the material; having them transform the information in the text into a graphic form (for example, a chart or a map); and having them rewrite material in another genre, such as a job advertisement.

Cudd and Roberts (1989) suggest the use of reaction frames that are elaborations of enumeration frames. One type leads the students to tie prior knowledge to new information—for example:

Before I started reading about China, I knew____________________________
____.

In the book I read, I learned that _________________________________.

I also learned____.

The thing that surprised me most was_______________________________.

Cairney (1990) says that these frames provide probes that encourage text recall.

Writing Techniques

A number of writing techniques may be used to advantage in helping students learn to read effectively in the content areas. Probably the best known is the language experience approach. Others include feature analysis plus writing, webs plus writing, and keeping learning logs.

Language Experience Approach (LEA)

The ***language experience approach (LEA)*** is a good basic method to use in content area teaching. Expository text structure can be taught through the LEA. For example, a teacher who wishes to have students learn the comparison-and-contrast pattern of writing can have them discuss how two objects are alike and different, make a chart showing the likenesses and differences, and dictate a written selection based on the chart. The teacher can ask first for likenesses and then for differences as the dictation takes place. Then the students can use their own written selection to locate the two related parts of a contrast and do other activities related to the structure. (This chapter contains several examples of applying the LEA to specific content areas to promote learning of the content.)

Feature Analysis Plus Writing

A *feature matrix* can be helpful for gathering, comparing, and contrasting information about several items in the same category (Cunningham and Cunningham, 1987). The teacher first reads through the material and selects the members of the category and specific features that some, all, or none of them have. Then he or she forms them into a matrix like the one in Example 8.3 and displays the matrix to the class. The students fill in the matrix in the same way that the semantic feature analysis chart in Chapter 4 was completed, leaving blanks when they are unsure about a feature. Then the students read the assigned material to confirm or revise their original markings and to fill in any empty spaces. They are encouraged to erase and change marks if the information they read refutes initial ideas. During class discussion following the reading, the students and teacher complete the class matrix cooperatively. If there is disagreement, students return to the text to find support for their positions. Some points may require library research.

The information on the feature matrix can be used as a basis for writing about the reading material. For instance, in Example 8.3 below, the teacher can choose one geometric shape and model the writing of a paragraph about it. Students and teacher can then cooperatively write another paragraph about another shape. Then each student or small group of students may choose other shapes to write about. (The matrix can be expanded to include many more shapes and features.) Using the information from a feature matrix for paragraph writing promotes retention of information covered in the matrix.

EXAMPLE 8.3 Semantic Feature Matrix for Geometric Shapes

	Straight lines	Curved lines	Four sides	Three sides	All sides must be equal in length
Triangle					
Rectangle					
Circle					
Square					

Webs Plus Writing

Webs are useful organizers in the content areas. Before the reading of the content material, the teacher records the information the students think they know about the topic of the chapter in the form of a web like the one shown in Example 8.4 on page 308.

The students may make individual webs, containing only the points they think are correct. Then they read the material, checking the information on the web and adding the new information they find. In class discussion following the reading, the class web is revised, and disagreements are settled by consulting the text. The class can write paragraphs about different strands of the web—for example, about famous leaders from Tennessee.

Keeping Learning Logs

Using *learning logs* or journals to promote content area learning is a highly effective technique. Students can follow the reading or discussion of a content topic with written summaries, comments, or questions related to the reading or class discussion. The content teacher can read the comments and adjust future lessons in response to the degree of understanding or confusion reflected in the logs.

EXAMPLE 8.4 Web for Content Material

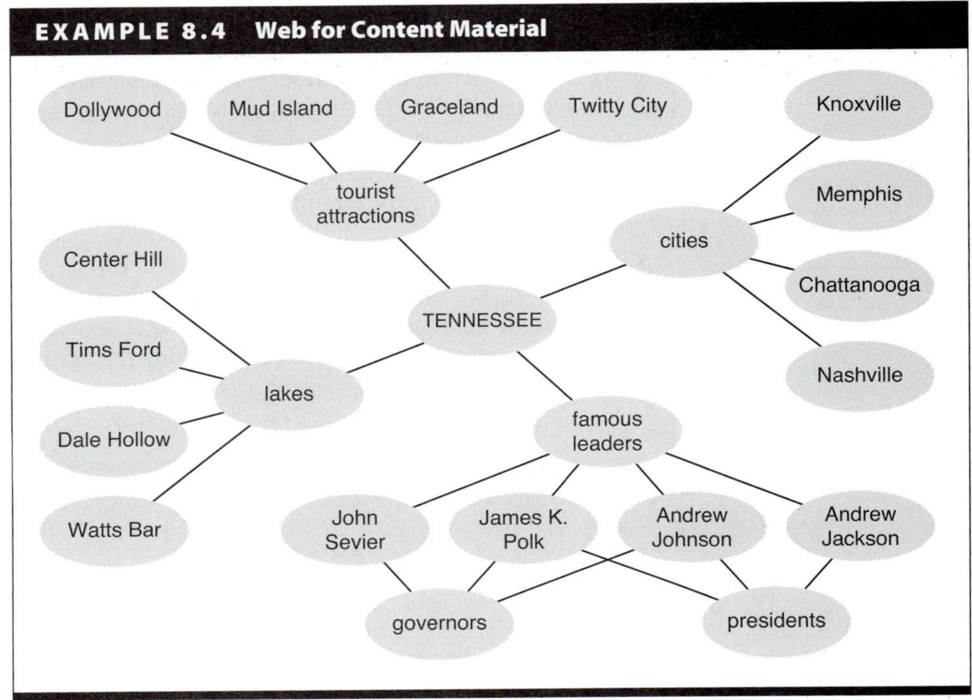

In social studies and science classes, students can be encouraged to observe things around them, record their observations (in pictures or writing), and associate what they observe with their past experiences and prior knowledge. When students keep observation notebooks, the teacher can lead them to draw conclusions about word parts in words chosen from their notebooks, thereby allowing them to work with words they can already identify. This enhances students' decoding skills while they are engaged in content learning (Sullivan, 1986).

Using Content Material with Reading of Fiction and Writing

Ollmann (1991) suggests using factual content material as part of the prereading phase to prepare students for reading literature that involves content concepts. Encyclopedia articles, travel magazines and brochures, *National Geographic,* and other material can often provide background information related to settings or to scientific concepts involved in stories. When the prereading material is being examined, the teacher can emphasize strategies needed for reading content material, such as skimming, scanning, use of alphabetical order and guide words, and others in a realistic setting.

Besides reading factual content material, students can read poems and other literature related to the content, think about the content from an aesthetic perspective, and write poetry related to the topic. For example, they can read poems such as David

McCord's "This Is My Rock" and Lisa Peters's book *The Sun, the Wind, and the Rain* when they are studying geology. Then they can write in descriptive or poetic form about the things they have discovered from the more factual books (McClure and Zitlow, 1991). Long (1993) suggests using acrostic poems, rather than formal written reports, to share information gained from researching a topic.

TECHNOLOGY

Using Technological Aids to Learning

DIVERSITY

Reference works and movies are educational applications available on videotapes, CDs, or DVDs. One reference work on CD and DVD is *The Complete National Geographic: 109 Years of National Geographic Magazine* (National Geographic Society), a natural literacy support for thematic studies in science and social studies. These materials are particularly useful in illustrating text materials for less proficient readers or students with limited experiential backgrounds. They may help to bring a literary selection to life for students or help them understand a process that is described in a content area textbook.

Wepner (1992b, 1992c) suggests using cross-curricular content units that include books, computer software, magazines, and musical recordings. Sometimes teachers overlook software when planning thematic units. Dowd and Sinatra (1990) point out, for example, that there are three kinds of computer software designed to help students learn about text structure. One type models the different text structures, then has the students write something based on the model. Another type includes interactive/prompt tutorials on particular types of discourse. Some of these allow students to write working outlines for papers; and others allow students to process a complete draft, revise it, and edit it. The last type lets students use their knowledge of text structure to do real-life activities requiring use of that knowledge, such as writing a class newspaper.

Integrating Approaches

Because no single technique will enable all students to deal with the many demands of content material, a teacher must know many approaches, teach them directly, and let the students know why they help. Students need to be able to pick out an appropriate approach for a particular assignment.

A procedure similar to the DRA may provide structure. First, the teacher may plan activities to prepare the students to read the material and build their background for reading it, including teaching vocabulary through context clues or by relating the words to ones the students already know. Students may discuss what they already know about the topic, web this information, and survey the material to be read. After the survey, they may be asked to predict what information is going to be presented. Then purposes for reading need to be set by the students, the teacher, or both cooperatively. The teacher may provide a study guide for the reading, focusing attention on important concepts and/or appropriate reading processes. Students may read to answer *who, what, when, where, how,* and *why* questions; to verify hypotheses; or to discover important material to add to information already collected about a topic. After the students have completed the reading, the teacher should plan activities that guide students to organize and synthesize information. They may write content-based language experience stories on the material or make graphic representations of the content (graphs, charts, diagrams); for example, for some material, the students may be able to apply the concepts presented.

Creating Instructional Units

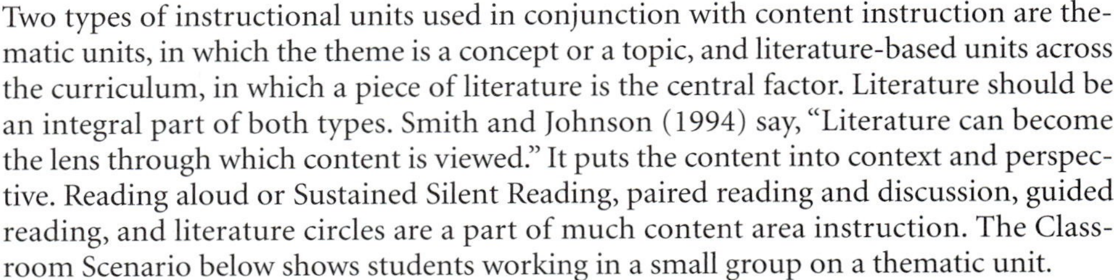

LITERATURE

Two types of instructional units used in conjunction with content instruction are thematic units, in which the theme is a concept or a topic, and literature-based units across the curriculum, in which a piece of literature is the central factor. Literature should be an integral part of both types. Smith and Johnson (1994) say, "Literature can become the lens through which content is viewed." It puts the content into context and perspective. Reading aloud or Sustained Silent Reading, paired reading and discussion, guided reading, and literature circles are a part of much content area instruction. The Classroom Scenario below shows students working in a small group on a thematic unit.

Thematic Content Units

LITERATURE

The use of thematic units was discussed as one approach to literature-based reading instruction in Chapter 5. The same concept can apply to teaching content units.

CLASSROOM SCENARIO

Thematic Unit on Survival

The students in Ms. Ling's sixth-grade class had been reading books related to the theme of survival. Several of them were seated around a table, beginning to discuss how their books related to the theme.

"In *Julie of the Wolves,* Miyax has to survive by herself on the Alaskan tundra," Tonya began.

"In *Hatchet,* Brian has to survive by himself after his plane crashes in the Canadian wilderness," David said.

"Karana was left alone on an island off the coast of California," Zack said, referring to the main character in *Island of the Blue Dolphins.*

"Well, Phillip wasn't all alone on the Caribbean island in *The Cay* at first, but he did need help because he was blind after the blow to his head," David said. "Timothy, the black man, was really the one who made sure Phillip would survive. He used a lot of survival techniques."

"Let's list the survival techniques the characters used," Bruce said. "We could web them like Ms. Ling had us do with settings last month. We could use headings like 'Food' and 'Clothing.'"

"That's a good idea!" Tonya chimed in. "How about 'Shelter' for another heading?"

"Karana ate abalones and scallops from the sea," Zack said, "and she made herself a fenced-in house and a shelter in a cave."

"That's a good start," said Tonya. "Let's get that down on paper before we go on." She went to the storage shelf and returned with a piece of drawing paper and a black marker. She handed the materials to Bruce, the group member with the best handwriting skills. "Put your ideas and Zack's down before we forget them," she said. "Then we'll add more things from other people."

As Bruce began to write on the drawing paper, several other students began to take notes on their own papers about contributions they wanted to make.

Analysis of Scenario

The students in Ms. Ling's class had worked in discussion groups many times and were ready to participate when they came to the table. Tonya acted the part of a good leader by getting the discussion started and by collecting materials for the webbing and delegating the task of actually constructing the web to another student. Ms. Ling had taught a valuable skill, webbing, in earlier lessons, and these students remembered it and put it to use.

Teachers can incorporate the use of a variety of materials, in addition to content area textbooks, into thematic units. Whatever materials are chosen, the teacher must make several instructional decisions and plan the unit carefully.

Materials for Thematic Content Units. Thematic content units involve linking reading of fiction and nonfiction about a content topic, along with other media, in order to help the students obtain a more complete picture of the topic. As Doiron (1994) points out, facts can be embedded in fiction, and narrative structures can be used to convey facts presented in nonfiction. Thus, both types of books are useful, and students need to be able to read both types. Text sets (for example, sets of books on one topic, by the same author, of the same genre, or about the same culture) are useful in unit instruction. Reading of related texts allows synthesis of ideas and more complete understanding of the topic. Nonfiction trade books need to be available on a number of difficulty levels, and teachers need to show students how to locate them and use them to find information. Assignments involving these books should require synthesis and critical thinking (Palmer and Stewart, 1997).

Teachers should not overlook the possible value of picture books in content units for the middle-school grades. These books are often relegated to the primary grades, but many are appropriate for older students, and they add motivation and variety to lessons (Danielson, 1992). Eve Bunting has written a number of books that would be appropriate for these students, although they can be used with younger students as well. They include *How Many Days to America?* (1988), *Terrible Things* (1989), and *The Wall* (1990). Thematically focused alphabet books by Jerry Pallotta, George Ella Lyon, Gisela Jernigan, Abbie Zabar, Malka Drucker, and John Agard are also good. They cover a variety of topics, with many focusing on science and social studies concepts. For example, books by Zabar, Drucker, Red Hawk, and Agard introduce other cultures. Many of Pallotta's books have science and social studies themes (Chaney, 1993; Thompson, 1992).

Magazines are also useful. Middle-school students can benefit from *National Geographic, Reader's Digest, Discover,* and some news magazines. Children's magazines, such as *National Geographic World, Cobblestone, Calliope, Odyssey,* and *Ranger Rick,* are useful, especially for struggling readers (Short, 2002). Nonfiction offers information in many forms, including text, pictures, and maps. It frequently has useful headings and subheadings, as well as other typographic aids (Harvey, 2002).

TECHNOLOGY

Use of computer programs in thematic units should not be ignored. Morden (1994) reports an interdisciplinary simulation project in which she and a colleague involved students with literature selections about traveling, followed by the use of simulation software, such as *Oregon Trail* (MECC) and *Country Canada* (Didatech). Simulation programs replicate as closely as possible selected aspects of real-life events. The students take on the part of a particular character in the simulated event and respond as they think that person would. Simulations are frequently interdisciplinary, combining reading, writing, health, science, history, geography, and math experiences, for example, as *The Oregon Trail II* (MECC) program does (Bigelow, 1997). Students who use them make critical reading/thinking decisions and see the consequences of these decisions.

Morden's students chose travel destinations and gathered information about them, using letter writing with word processors and communication with people all over the world through *WorldClassroom,* a curriculum-based educational telecommunications network. Databases were used as organizational tools, and CDs and laserdiscs were viewed. Students had a budget, and they had to use a spreadsheet to plan an itinerary, staying within the budget. They "earned" money by doing jobs for the class or winning test review games. They planned a bon voyage party and even made invitations with *Print Shop* (Broderbund). As they "traveled" to their destinations, they collected information from people in those locations through telecommunications, CDs, laserdiscs, and traditional print. They kept logs of their travels, one year on paper and the next year on audiotape, and developed a multimedia scrapbook.

DIVERSITY

As with all other materials, teachers must be aware of possible hazards of using simulation programs without properly preparing the students. For example, while acknowledging that *The Oregon Trail II* program and the associated trail guide provide information about many facets of the journey, including geography of the area covered, ailments the pioneers suffered, treatments that the travelers used, and equipment and supplies, Bigelow (1997) believes *The Oregon Trail* and many other simulations are "sexist, racist, culturally insensitive, and contemptuous of the earth" (p. 85). He explains that these simulations cast players as white males, who would have different motivations and responsibilities than females or blacks would have. He also says that *The Oregon Trail* does not have students behave toward the Native Americans whom they meet along the trail in a culturally sensitive way, and it does not point out the impact of movement on the trail on the native people and their land. Of course, a single simulation program will not encompass every aspect of any situation, and historical simulations are not likely to take on modern attitudes toward ecological and cultural issues.

Simulations are simplified versions of reality. Teachers do need to take into account the particular perspective of each program and make students aware of this perspective. Students can learn from the simulation without believing that everyone had the outlook and reactions that the protagonist of the program takes. Other resources, such as CDs, Internet sites, books, and videos, can help students see how the trail affected pioneers other than white males and how it affected the Native Americans in the area.

Planning Thematic Content Units. Some thematic units are related to a single discipline; some are interdisciplinary, linking content and skills from different disciplines through authentic tasks; and some are integrative, in which the theme is the focus and boundaries between the disciplines are not evident. (Students may collaborate with the teacher in theme selection, or the content may be mandated by the school district.) Teachers should choose broad themes that lend themselves to good instructional activities (Lapp and Flood, 1994). Good themes can focus on such wide-ranging areas as the horrors of the Holocaust and life long ago contrasted with life today.

A web of resources for the content topic can be elaborated with fiction and nonfiction selections, textbooks, magazines, newspapers, videos, and software for use with each subtopic. However, such a web is not a complete plan. Teachers still must decide on goals and objectives for their units, because not all concepts presented in all of the sources can possibly be used. Then they must choose instructional procedures and related activities to meet these goals, gather related materials, schedule unit activities, and decide how to assess the outcomes. Shanahan (1997) points out that the teacher needs to have a clear idea of the desired learning outcomes, since thematic unit instruction does not automatically result in learning. He adds the caution that instruction in the separate fields, accompanied by drill and practice, is still needed when integration is implemented, because "a common problem in integrated instruction can be that the focus is so much on relevance that students never practice anything enough to get good at it" (p. 18).

Thematic units connect information from language arts, science, social studies, math, art, music, and drama. Shanahan (1997) indicates that the different disciplines involved all need sufficient attention; some disciplines may not fit into a particular thematic study. At times a discipline such as math may need to be taught separately from the thematic unit to give it appropriate attention. During thematic studies, the ways text is used in the different disciplines should receive attention, because scientists, mathematicians, historians, and practitioners in other fields think and write differently.

To set reading purposes, students can brainstorm questions about a topic. The students learn to read selectively to answer their questions. They can sort their questions into categories, discovering that by doing so they can find answers to more than one question at a time by locating the proper sections of books and becoming aware of the organization of nonfiction. When they share information with the class, they may refer to the text to prove points (Hess, 1991).

Schmidt (1999) suggests a modification of the K-W-L procedure—KWLQ—to aid students in forming questions for inquiry during thematic units. The first three steps are the same as K-W-L (which is described in Chapter 5). The *Q* step asks for more questions, to show that learning is continuous. Students are not likely to be successful with inquiry procedures if they are not explicitly taught the steps in such procedures and have not seen how the procedures work. They may first need much exposure to nonfiction writing and the differences in the ways fiction and nonfiction are organized and used (Tower, 2000).

Literature-Based Units Across the Curriculum

Literature can be the basis of a unit that will include activities from many curricular areas. Related science, social studies, math, art, and drama content may be taught with the literature as the focal point. Language learning can take place along with reading, discussion, and writing done in relation to the literature selections. Example 8.5 on page 314 shows one such unit.

Specific Content Areas

Special reading challenges are associated with each of the content areas. It is best to teach skills for handling these challenges when students need the skills in order to read their assignments.

Language Arts

The ***language arts*** block of the middle-school curriculum involves instruction in listening, speaking, reading, writing, viewing, and visually representing. It includes the subjects of reading, literature, and English. Since basal readers that may be used during

EXAMPLE 8.5 Literature-Based Unit Across the Curriculum

Theme: Slavery in America produced many significant reactions.
Goal: To understand the impact that slavery had on people and events in America.
Web:

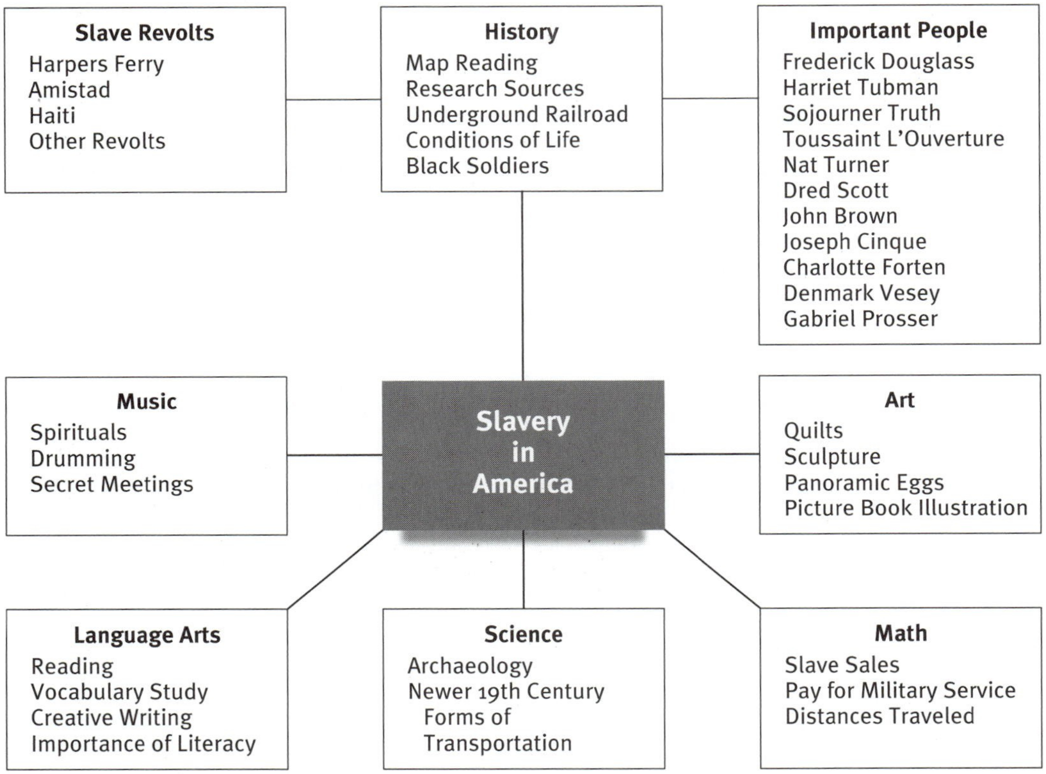

Slavery in America

Slave Revolts
Harpers Ferry
Amistad
Haiti
Other Revolts

History
Map Reading
Research Sources
Underground Railroad
Conditions of Life
Black Soldiers

Important People
Frederick Douglass
Harriet Tubman
Sojourner Truth
Toussaint L'Ouverture
Nat Turner
Dred Scott
John Brown
Joseph Cinque
Charlotte Forten
Denmark Vesey
Gabriel Prosser

Music
Spirituals
Drumming
Secret Meetings

Art
Quilts
Sculpture
Panoramic Eggs
Picture Book Illustration

Language Arts
Reading
Vocabulary Study
Creative Writing
Importance of Literacy

Science
Archaeology
Newer 19th Century Forms of Transportation

Math
Slave Sales
Pay for Military Service
Distances Traveled

Core Texts

Freedom Roads: Searching for the Underground Railroad by Joyce Hansen and Gary McGowan. (Chicago: Cricket Books, 2003).

Now Is Your Time! The African-American Struggle for Freedom by Walter Dean Myers. (New York: HarperCollins, 1991).

Core Websites

Aboard the Underground Railroad: **http://www.cr.nps.gov/nr/travel/underground/ugrrhome.htm**
HistoricCamdenCounty.com: **http://www.historiccamdencounty.com/ccnews16.shtml**

Core Video

Underground Railroad. Produced by Triage, Inc. for the History Channel, A&E Television Networks, 100 minutes, 1999.

Core Music CD

Steal Away: Songs of the Underground Railroad by Kim and Reggie Harris. (Appleseed Recordings, 1997).

Continued

EXAMPLE 8.5 Literature-Based Unit Across the Curriculum (*cont.*)

Supplementary Texts

**Narrative of the Life of Frederick Douglass, An American Slave* by Frederick Douglass. (New York: Anchor Books, 1989).
Frederick Douglass Fights for Freedom by Margaret Davidson. (New York: Scholastic, 1968). For struggling readers.
Frederick Douglass: Freedom Fighter by Garnet Nelson Jackson. (New York: Modern Curriculum Press, 1993). For struggling readers. (PB)
**Harriet Tubman: Conductor on the Underground Railroad* by Ann Petry (New York: Archway, 1955).
Minty: A Story of Young Harriet Tubman by Alan Schroeder. (New York: Puffin Books, 1996). For struggling readers. (PB)
A Picture Book of Harriet Tubman by David A. Adler. (New York: Scholastic, 1992). For struggling readers. (PB)
**Sojourner Truth: Ain't I a Woman?* by Patricia C. McKissack and Fredrick McKissack. (New York: Scholastic, 1992).
A Picture Book of Sojourner Truth by David Adler. (New York: Holiday House, 1994). For struggling readers. (PB)
John Brown: One Man Against Slavery by Gwen Everett. (New York: Rizzoli, 1993). (PB)
Toussaint L'Ouverture: The Fight for Haiti's Freedom by Walter Dean Myers. (New York: Simon & Schuster Books for Young Readers, 1996). (PB)
**Rebels Against Slavery: American Slave Revolts* by Patricia C. McKissak and Fredrick L. McKissack. (New York: Scholastic, 1996).
**The Amistad Slave Revolt and American Abolition* by Karen Zeinert. (North Haven, Conn.: Linnet Books, 1997).
Amistad by Joyce Annette Barnes, based on the screenplay by David Franzoni. (New York: Puffin, 1997). (Movie tie-in)
**War Comes to Willy Freeman* by James Lincoln Collier and Christopher Collier. (New York: Dell, 1983). (Fiction)
**Jump Ship to Freedom* by James Lincoln Collier and Christopher Collier. (New York: Dell, 1981). (Fiction)
**Who Is Carrie?* by James Lincoln Collier and Christopher Collier. (New York: Dell, 1984). (Fiction)
**True North: A Novel of the Underground Railroad* by Kathryn Lasky. (New York: Blue Sky Press, 1996). (Fiction)
From Slave Ship to Freedom Road by Julius Lester. (New York: Puffin, 1998). (PB for older students)
Secret Signs Along the Underground Railroad by Anita Riggio. Honesdale, Pa.: Boyds Mills Press, 1997). For struggling readers. (PB)
Sweet Clara and the Freedom Quilt by Deborah Hopkinson. (New York: Knopf, 1993). For struggling readers. (PB)
Follow the Drinking Gourd by Jeanette Winter. (New York: Knopf, 1988). For struggling readers. (PB)
**Nightjohn* by Gary Paulsen. (New York: Delacorte, 1993).
**Steal Away Home* by Lois Ruby. (New York: Macmillan, 1994).

Possible Unit Activities

- Read aloud selected excerpts from the two core nonfiction texts: *Now Is Your Time! The African-American Struggle for Freedom; Freedom Roads: Searching for the Underground Railroad.*
- View and discuss the video *Underground Railroad.*
- Play and discuss the CD *Steal Away: Songs of the Underground Railroad.*
- Form literature circles to read some of the supplementary books (or others that are appropriate). Let groups present information about their books after the reading is complete.
- Let students choose books from the supplementary books (or others that are appropriate) to read independently and report on to the class through a formal book report, a mural or diorama, a skit (with others who have read the same book), or a mock interview with a book character (with someone else who has read the same book).
- Have students keep literature logs on their readings.

Continued

EXAMPLE 8.5 Literature-Based Unit Across the Curriculum (*cont.*)

- Let students write historical fiction, diaries from the viewpoints of book characters, poetry, or songs based on their readings.
- Have students discuss the advantages of literacy for all people and the ways that illiteracy worked to the disadvantage of many African Americans during the days of slavery.
- Have students study and share visual aids in the books that they read.
- Have students make maps of common escape routes used by slaves.
- Let students form special interest research groups to study in detail some aspect of slavery or the Underground Railroad. They may want to study about a particular person or a particular revolt, or they may want to study living conditions for the slaves and the owners of the time. Prepare them for this activity by discussing and sometimes modeling research techniques, primary and secondary sources, proper citations, and other related topics. Visit the two websites listed above as core websites (and/or other appropriate ones) and describe finding information on the Web and the need for critical analysis for information found on the Web. Encourage students to present their findings in a multimedia presentation.

*Appropriate for read-alouds; PB = picture books.

reading class were discussed in other chapters in this textbook, they will not be considered here. Although literature is treated briefly in this chapter, more thorough coverage is found in Chapter 6.

LITERATURE 

Literature

Ideally, a literature program should encourage students to learn about their literary heritages and the heritages of others, expand their imaginations, develop reading preferences, evaluate literature, increase their awareness of language, and grow socially, emotionally, and intellectually. These goals can be reached through a well-planned program in which the teacher reads aloud to students daily and provides them with opportunities to read and respond to literature. Teachers may teach literary skills directly through a unit on poetry or a novel, or they may integrate these skills with basal reader and language arts lessons.

Teaching Literature Skills. When developing literature programs, teachers can organize instruction by genres (forms or categories), literary elements, or topics in order to vary students' experiences, and they should introduce students to the specialized vocabulary and skills they need to develop an appreciation of literature.

In literature classes, students are asked to read and understand many literary forms, including short stories, novels, plays, poetry, biographies, and autobiographies. One characteristic of all these forms is the frequent occurrence of ***figurative,*** or nonliteral, ***language,*** which is sometimes a barrier to understanding. Students tend to interpret such language literally. Chapter 2 covers teaching students to deal with figurative expressions.

Literary Elements. To understand literary passages, students need to be able to recognize and analyze plots, themes, characterization, settings, and authors' styles. The *plot* is the overall plan for the story; the *theme* is the main idea the writer wishes to convey; and *characterization* is the way in which the writer makes the reader aware of the characteristics and motives of each person in the story. The *setting* consists of time and place, and the *style* is the writer's mode of expressing thoughts. Teacher-directed questioning can make students aware of these literary elements and help students understand the interrelationships among them. Following are some points related to major story elements:

1. *Setting.* Teachers should point out how time and place affect the plot, characterization, and mood of a story. Stories must be true to their settings: characters behave differently today from the way they behaved a hundred years ago, and city life involves situations different from those that occur in country life. All of these facts make understanding the setting of a story important. *Bud, Not Buddy* by Christopher Paul Curtis is a good book to use in helping students see the importance of setting.

2. *Characterization.* Students who examine literature with strong characterization find that writers develop their characters through dialogue, actions, interactions with others, and insights into their thoughts and feelings, as well as through description. Looking for these clues will make the students more attuned to the characters and should increase their overall understanding of the piece of literature. Students can also take note of how characters grow and change as the story progresses. The characterizations in Cynthia Voigt's *Dicey's Song* and those in Lois Lowry's *Number the Stars* make good discussion material.

3. *Plot.* Students may analyze short, simple stories to see how writers introduce their stories, develop them through a series of incidents, create interest and suspense, and reach satisfying conclusions. Awareness of the ways plots are developed can increase understanding of narratives. *Red Midnight* by Ben Mikaelsen and *A Wrinkle in Time* by Madeline L'Engle are good books for examining plot with students. A more complex book, such as *The View from Saturday* by E. L. Konigsburg, has intertwined plots that make up the overall plot. Teachers should start with relatively easy books and work up to the more difficult ones.

4. *Style.* Students should examine written material to analyze the authors' choices of words, sentence patterns, and manners of expression. Teachers and students can discuss and compare the styles of writing in Patricia MacLachlan's *Sarah, Plain and Tall,* Avi's *Nothing But the Truth,* and Karen Hesse's *Witness.*

5. *Theme.* The concept of *theme* is abstract. Smit (1990) suggests selecting two stories that have the same theme but different settings, plots, and other elements to allow students to see how the same theme can be developed in different ways. She suggests *Why the Chimes Rang* by Raymond MacDonald Alden and *The Grateful Statues,* a Japanese folktale, for helping the students discover the theme of *giving.*

One way that teachers may work on these elements is through journal writing. (See Chapters 5 and 6 for more on journal writing.) The students may be asked to respond to a story by selecting a character from the story and writing a journal entry as though that character were writing it. The entries can be dated according to the time in which the book takes place. The journal writers can leave clues in their entries to the identities of the characters doing the writing. These entries can be shared orally, with the other students trying to decide which character wrote each entry. Such an activity encourages attention to characterization, point of view, and mood (Jossart, 1988).

Webbing literary elements related to a story can help students clarify their concepts of these elements. The teacher can read the story and have the students listen for the elements that need to be added to the web.

Literary Forms. Literature for children and adolescents consists of a variety of genres, or literary forms, including historical and realistic fiction, biographies, poetry, plays, informational books, and fantasy and folklore. Historical fiction, biographies, and informational books are all useful for integrating with content areas, whereas good realistic fiction serves as a model for helping young people to understand others and solve problems in their own lives. Nonfiction selections allow students a way to investigate and understand the world, offering a wide range of subjects and ideas to explore (Harvey, 2002). Poetry encourages readers to explore their emotions, and plays offer the pleasure of acting out favorite stories. Both modern fantasy and folklore allow readers to escape into worlds of imaginary characters and events. Teachers should use all of these forms in their literature programs, and they can enhance students' understanding of them by reading literature of all forms aloud and pointing out the characteristics of each genre. More information on literary genres appears in Chapter 6.

English

English textbooks cover the areas of listening, speaking, and writing and generally consist of a series of sections of instructional material followed by practice exercises. The technical vocabulary includes such terms as *noun, pronoun, cursive,* and *parliamentary procedure.* The concepts presented in the informational sections are densely packed; each sentence is usually important for understanding, and examples are abundant. Students need to be encouraged to study the examples because they help to clarify the information presented in the narrative portion of the textbook.

Teachers are wise to plan oral activities in class to accompany the listening and speaking portions of the English textbook, since such practice allows students to apply the concepts immediately and helps them retain the material. Similarly, it is wise to ask students to apply the concepts encountered in the writing section as soon as possible in relevant situations to aid retention.

Writing instruction can form the basis for reading activities. Students read to obtain information to include in their compositions, and they read to learn different styles of writing. For example, they read poems to absorb the style of writing before attempting to write poetry, and they read informational books for ideas about the structure needed to write their own books. Students can also read their own material in order to revise it to enhance accuracy, improve clarity, or ensure correct use of language conventions. They may read it aloud to peers for constructive criticism, or their peers may read it themselves.

LITERATURE

Multigenre writing, or writing that organizes a series of writing genres into a multidimensional product with a common theme, is a relatively unused form in the middle school, but it has been highly effective on high-school and college levels. Grierson, Anson, and Baird (2002) have described its use with sixth graders in a unit study of Yolan's *The Devil's Arithmetic.* They chose this type of writing partly because Utah's state core curriculum stipulates that students must understand "functional, informational, and literary texts from different periods, cultures, and genres" (Utah State Office of Education, 1999). The writing assignment was for the students to research and write about one of their own ancestors whom they believed should be remembered, just as Hannah in *The Devil's Arithmetic* is urged to remember her ancestors who died in the Holocaust. Some genres that were used were documents such as birth certificates, letters, passports, obituaries, lists, train tickets, wanted posters, and telegrams. Books that can be used as examples of multigenre writing include Molly Bang's *Nobody Particular,* Diane Hoyt-Goldsmith's *Celebrating Ramadan,* Sharon Draper's *Tears of a Tiger,* and Avi's *Nothing But the Truth.*

Much of a student's formal vocabulary instruction takes place in English classes. Trade books can be the basis for vocabulary lessons. Fred Gwynne's *The King Who Rained* and *A Chocolate Moose for Dinner* offer good examples of figurative expressions, homonyms, and words with multiple meanings that can be used to interest students in word study. In the Amelia Bedelia books by Peggy Parish, Amelia takes everything literally, with disastrous results: her sponge cake is made of sponges! Emily Hanlon's *How a Horse Grew Hoarse on the Site Where He Sighted a Bare Bear* offers examples of homonyms in nonsense verses.

Social Studies

Social studies texts in particular have been criticized for being difficult to read, often requiring more reading ability than prospective readers have, and varying four or more years in difficulty from passage to passage. Social studies texts have often been found to assume unrealistic levels of background knowledge on the part of the students and to lack coherence (Beck and McKeown, 1991a; Stetson and Williams, 1992), interest, and meaning for them (Guzzetti, Kowalinski, and McGowan, 1992).

Social studies materials are generally written in a very precise and highly compact expository style in which many ideas are expressed in a few lines of print. Authors may discuss a hundred-year span in a single page or even a single paragraph or may cover complex issues in a few paragraphs, even though whole books could be devoted to these issues. Study guides are recommended for helping students read social studies materials with understanding and purpose.

Social studies materials are organized in a variety of ways, including cause-and-effect relationships, chronological order, comparisons and/or contrasts, and topical order (for example, by regions, such as Asia and North America, or by concepts, such as transportation and communication). The content selection in Example 8.1 is an example of the cause/effect pattern, but it also offers comparisons and contrasts of the effects of the war on different groups. Knowing the organizational pattern of the selection allows students to approach the reading with an appropriate mental set, which aids greatly in comprehension of the material. To help students deal with cause-and-effect and chronological-order arrangements, teachers can use the ideas found in Chapter 4 for helping students determine such relationships and sequences. Drawing time lines is one good way to work with chronological order, and pattern guides such as the one in Example 8.2 on page 302 are ways to work on cause/effect or comparison/contrast relationships.

In social studies reading, students encounter such technical terms as *democracy, tropics, hemisphere, decade,* and *century,* as well as many words with meanings that differ from their meanings in general conversation. When students first hear that a candidate is going to *run* for office, they may picture a foot race, an illusion that is furthered if they read that a candidate has decided to enter the *race* for governor. If the term *race* is applied to people in their texts, the students may become even more confused. Students who know that you *strike* a match or make a *strike* when bowling may not understand a labor union *strike.* Discussions about the *mouth* of a river could bring unusual pictures to the minds of students. The teacher is responsible for seeing that the students understand the concepts these terms represent.

Harmon and Hedrick (2000) have developed a technique called "Zooming In and Zooming Out" to enhance vocabulary and conceptual learning in social studies. The Zooming Out refers to situating the term or concept within a larger context, and the Zooming In refers to looking closely at the concept itself. The procedure begins with the students brainstorming about their current knowledge about the concept, with the teacher listing the ideas. Then the students read to find out more about the concept and confirm the brainstormed ideas, making notes as they read. Discussion about their findings then ensues, with the students identifying the most and least important facts about the concept, after the teacher models this process. The discussion also involves concepts or people and places that are similar to, related to, or unrelated to the target concept. At the end of the discussion, the students summarize information about the concept in a single statement. Harmon and Hedrick suggest putting this information into a web that provides a visual display of the information collected.

Social studies materials also present readers with maps, charts, and graphs to read. Ways of teaching the use of such reading aids are suggested in Chapter 7. Social studies materials must be read critically. Students should be taught to check copyright dates to determine timeliness and to be alert for such problems as outdated geography materials that show boundaries or place names that have changed.

Some social studies materials contain embedded texts such as diary entries, personal letters, and newspaper articles that may be helpful to some students in making the text more interesting and understandable, while making the reading more challenging for other students. Diary entries, for example, may offer more personal connections to events for some students and cause problems for others because of the unfamiliar vocabulary terms and sentence structure. Some students may not be able to understand that the writer of a diary entry in the past would have a different cultural perspective than would a writer of the present.

Students can learn much social studies content by writing about the topics. Multicultural education generally falls in the realm of social studies, but it is often not covered in an active way that links the learning to the students' lives. Means and Olson (1994) have described how one fifth-grade teacher in California met the challenge of finding easy-to-read materials about community leaders from different cultural backgrounds by having his students produce them. The Classroom Scenario on using technology on page 321 to produce classroom materials summarizes his class activity.

CLASSROOM SCENARIO Using Technology to Produce Classroom Materials

Students in a fifth-grade class in California needed funds to go to a science camp, and they also needed appropriate materials, on easy reading levels, about Hispanic leaders. They decided on a project that used technology to develop their own materials, not only about local Hispanic heroes, but also about African American and Vietnamese American community leaders as well. They planned to sell the materials to others to raise funds for science camp.

The fifth graders identified people whom they wished to interview; planned, conducted, and videotaped the interviews; and wrote up the main points from each one.

The students carried out their plans by first studying existing interviews of famous people to help them construct their questions; then they formed groups and practiced interviewing skills on each other. The actual interviews were conducted by collaborative groups, with one student videotaping, one asking questions, and one taking notes. The interviews were critiqued and transcribed, and the key points were summarized. This task involved much proofreading and editing. The teacher, Mr. Gilkey, moved from group to group, monitoring progress and offering assistance.

Analysis of Scenario

The students were working on an authentic task to meet two real-life needs. The technology was used as a tool to help meet these needs. The process involved a number of important literacy skills as the students read interviews, composed questions, took notes, summarized material, and proofread and edited material. Mr. Gilkey was a coach and a facilitator of learning.

LITERATURE

Using Literature in Social Studies

Social studies materials are frequently written in a very impersonal style and may be concerned with unfamiliar people or events that are often remote in time or place. Students may also lack interest in the subject. For these reasons, teachers should use many interesting trade books to personalize the content and to expand on topics that are covered very briefly in the textbook.

DIVERSITY 

The five fundamental themes in geography are location (where a story takes place and why); place (what the place is like); relationships within places (including human/environmental relationships); movement of people, materials, and ideas (descriptions and consequences); and regions (including how they change) (*GEONews Handbook*, 1990; Norton, 1993a). Norton (1993a) shows how the books *People of the Breaking Day* by Marcia Sewell, *Christopher Columbus: Voyager to the Unknown* by Nancy Smiler Levinson, *Encounter* by Jane Yolen, and *The Other Fourteen Ninety-Two: Jewish Settlement in the New World* by Norman H. Funkelstein can help students learn about these five themes in the context of literature rather than textbook discussions. This treatment, supplemented with other books about the period, offers diverse perspectives on the geographic concepts being studied.

STANDARDS AND ASSESSMENT

Trade books provide causal relationships between concepts and give students a chance to answer their own questions about the content from their reading. Trade books offer opportunities to meet curricular objectives for both reading and social studies simultaneously. Maps in trade books can be used to teach map-reading skills, to locate the places being studied, and to identify the features of the land in these places, for example. When using such books, brainstorming about prior knowledge and form-

DIVERSITY ing semantic maps can be helpful. Then teachers can have students use think sheets on which they list their questions about a central question posed by the teacher, their ideas about how the questions would be answered, and how the text answered the questions. They may eventually produce their own question-and-answer books about the topic (Guzzetti, Kowalinski, and McGowan, 1992).

Teachers can choose from a wide variety of literature when picking trade books for social studies, including picture books, biographies and fictionalized biographies, and historical fiction. All have something to offer.

Picture Books. Picture books can be valuable for presenting many social studies concepts to middle-school students. These books elaborate on topics that would otherwise get limited attention. Sensitive issues that are ignored in textbooks can often be treated effectively in fictional accounts. Readers become emotionally involved with other people and historical situations through these books (Farris and Fuhler, 1994).

Biographies and Fictionalized Biographies. Biographies of famous people who lived during different historical periods add spice to textbook accounts, and use of literature DIVERSITY about different peoples is one way to approach multicultural issues (Pugh and Garcia, 1990; Rasinski and Padak, 1990). Walker-Dalhouse (1992) believes the use of multicultural literature can decrease negative stereotyping of people from other cultures.

Use of biographies can help students think about social issues and individuals' involvement with them, assessing the importance of events and understanding the objective and subjective dimensions of the events. This can lead to lessons on determining fact and opinion (Miller, Clegg, and Vanderhoff, 1992).

Fictionalized biographies and diaries used for social studies instruction are excellent for teaching middle-school students to evaluate the accuracy and authenticity of material, since authors have invented dialogue and thoughts for the characters to make the material seem more realistic. Teachers should lead students to see that these stories try to add life to facts but are not completely factual, perhaps by having them check reference books for accuracy of dates, places, and names. Sometimes reading an author's foreword or postscript will offer clues to the fictional aspects of a story; for example, at times only the historical events mentioned are true. Students should be aware that authors use first-person narrative accounts to make the action seem more personal but that in reality, the supposed speaker is not the person who did the writing. Any first-person account necessarily offers a limited perspective, because the person speaking cannot know everything that all the characters in the story do or everything that is happening at one time. Teachers should alert students to look for the author's bias and ask them to check to see how much the author depended on actual documents if a bibliography of sources is given (Storey, 1982; Zarnowski, 1988).

Another approach to reading biographical material is to have students choose a famous person; read that person's biography; do additional research on the person using multiple sources; make time lines of events in the person's life; and take on the role of that person in role-playing sessions. Since reading research strategies should be taught in context, this procedure provides a fertile ground for such teaching. Such studies can also naturally link social studies with science and language.

Historical Fiction. Students can also be drawn into historical periods and issues through historical fiction. Historical fiction transforms a series of events into an interpretation of these events, providing humanizing details. It can help students understand the times in which historical events occurred. Readers are able to become emotionally involved with people from the past. As they identify with the actual historical characters in the books they read, they face conflicting viewpoints that require them to do critical thinking. They read to interpret the moral and ethical issues posed during these events. They see multiple perspectives and can make informed judgments (Johnson and Ebert, 1992; Levstick, 1990).

DIVERSITY

For example, a book such as Ben Mikaelsen's *Red Midnight* provides a gripping story of a twelve-year-old boy managing to make his way with his little sister from the scene of the military massacre of his family and friends in Guatemala to the United States. The descriptions in the book are specific and evocative. The problems with travel over land and ocean are believable, as described. The reception that they receive in the United States, although generally positive, does not omit the negative reactions of some people, providing material for discussion to which many students can relate more directly than they would be able to react to the ocean voyage. As students study such materials, teachers can read related materials to them to build background. Newspaper articles about boat people can help students see that, although this particular story is fiction, the situation is potentially real. Other books about actions of oppressive governments or about ocean travel without adequate supplies may also provide comparative information. If the books are too advanced for middle-school students to read, the teacher can read them, or excerpts from them, aloud.

Irene Hernandez's novel *Heartbeat, Drumbeat* depicts the main character exploring her Hispanic and Navajo heritages. This can lead to discussing and writing about such topics as Navajo burial ceremonies and gender issues (Bean, 2000).

Students can do activities such as making time lines based on their readings, marking maps to show where events in the reading occurred, classifying characters as to beliefs or allegiances, producing mock newspapers from the times, illustrating events and places described, writing diaries for characters in the reading, or writing letters to characters with comments and advice (Johnson and Ebert, 1992).

DIVERSITY

Award-winning trade books can be found for nearly every period of history. Elizabeth Speare's *The Bronze Bow* is a novel about a boy who encounters Jesus in Rome; Marguerite De Angeli's *The Door in the Wall* treats the situation of a boy with a physical disability in fourteenth-century England; *The Courage of Sarah Noble,* by Alice Dalgliesh, describes a young girl who must face the difficulties of living in Connecticut in early pioneer days; *The Sign of the Beaver,* by Elizabeth Speare, is the story of a boy's struggle to survive in the Maine wilderness in the 1700s; Carol Brink's *Caddie Woodlawn* brings the reader into the excitement of living on the Wisconsin frontier during the last half of the nineteenth century; Paula Fox's *The Slave Dancer* tells about a boy who becomes involved in the slave trade with Africa during pre–Civil War days; Patricia MacLachlan's *Sarah, Plain and Tall* unites a woman from the East with a motherless family on a prairie farm during pioneer days; and David Klass's *California Blue* tells of the discovery of an endangered butterfly in a logging area in northern California in more recent times.

Using the Newspaper to Teach Social Studies

Teachers may use special student newspapers or regular newspapers in class. The newspaper is a living textbook for social studies through which students learn about tomorrow's history as it is happening today. Different parts of the newspaper require different reading skills, as noted here:

1. *News stories*—identifying main ideas and supporting details (*who, what, where, when, why, how*), determining sequence, recognizing cause-and-effect relationships, making inferences, drawing conclusions
2. *Editorials*—discriminating between fact and opinion, discovering the author's point of view, detecting author bias and propaganda techniques, making inferences, drawing conclusions
3. *Comics*—interpreting figurative language and idiomatic expressions, recognizing sequence of events, making inferences, detecting cause-and-effect relationships, drawing conclusions, making predictions
4. *Advertisements*—detecting propaganda, making inferences, drawing conclusions, distinguishing between fact and opinion
5. *Entertainment section*—reading charts, such as the TV schedule, and evaluating material presented
6. *Weather*—reading maps

Each of these skills is discussed fully in both Chapter 4 and Chapter 7.

Following are several activities for practice in reading newspapers more effectively:

1. Have students locate the *who, what, where, when, why,* and *how* in news stories.
2. Using news stories with the headlines cut off, have students write their own headlines and compare them with the actual headlines.
3. Give students copies of news stories about the same event from two different newspapers. Then ask them to point out and discuss likenesses and differences.
4. Using copies of conflicting editorials, have students underline facts in one color and opinions in another color and discuss the results. Also, have them locate emotional language and propaganda techniques in each editorial.
5. Discuss the symbolism and the message conveyed by each of several editorial cartoons. Then ask students to draw their own editorial cartoons.
6. Have students compare an editorial and a news story on the same topic. Discuss differences in approach.
7. Tell students to locate comics that are funny. Then ask them to explain why they are funny.
8. Have students study the entertainment section and decide which movies or plays would be most interesting to them or locate time slots for certain television programs.

9. Encourage students to try to solve crossword puzzles.
10. Have students compare human interest features with straight news stories to discover which type of writing is more objective, which has more descriptive terms, and so on. Have them dramatize appropriate ones.
11. Ask students to search grocery advertisements from several stores for the best buy on a specified item or to study the classified advertisements to decide what job they would most like to have and why. Then ask them to write their own classified ads.
12. Have the students study the display advertisements for examples of propaganda techniques.
13. Ask students to use the index of the paper to tell what page to look on for the television schedule, weather report, and other items.
14. Ask the students to search through the newspaper for typographical errors. Then discuss the effects of these errors on the material in which they appear.
15. Have students search the sports page for synonyms for the terms *won* and *lost*. Ask them why these synonyms are used.

Mathematics

Mathematics material is concise and abstract in nature and involves complex relationships. A high density of ideas per page appears in this kind of material, and understanding each word is very important, for one word may be the key to understanding an entire section. Yet teachers too often approach a math lesson in terms of developing only computational skill, apparently not realizing that reading skills can be advanced during mathematics lessons or that mathematics statement problems would be more comprehensible if attention were given to reading skills. Draper (2002, p. 528) says, "As long as mathematicians pose problems, solve problems, and analyze problems (Copes, 1996), and as long as those problems, solutions, and analyses appear as text, teachers have an obligation to help their students negotiate and make meaning of the text in order to keep mathematics within the reach of all students." She suggests that teachers adapt literacy activities such as the DR-TA (see Chapter 5 and this chapter) and K-W-L (see Chapter 3) for use in mathematics instruction.

Reading in mathematics poses a number of special difficulties. First is the technical and specialized vocabulary. Middle-school students encounter such terms as *polygon, arc, perimeter,* and *diameter.* Words with multiple meanings also appear frequently. Discussions about *volume, planes, figures,* finding the *difference,* or raising a number to the third *power* can confuse students who know more common meanings for these words. Nevertheless, many mathematics terms have root words, prefixes, or suffixes that students can use in determining their meanings. For example, *triangle* means "three angles," and a *quadrilateral* has "four sides." Students need to be able to recognize and use formal definitions for mathematics terms. They can develop understanding of mathematical definitions by examining examples and nonexamples of mathematical concepts (Adams, 2003).

Students use many diverse reading and study skills in their mathematics class as they follow directions, interpret diagrams, learn symbols, and work story problems.
(© Elizabeth Crews)

Mountain (1993) suggests constructing stories that require the use of math synonyms in context to help students build concepts. Here is an example:

> Mother needed *one yard* of material to make the cover.
> "Mr. Huffer sells the material by the foot," Jamie complained.
> "Then buy *three feet* of material," said Mother. "You're lucky he doesn't sell it by the inch. Then you'd have to remember to get *thirty-six inches.*"

Some of the synonyms in the story can be provided and others left out, to be filled in by the students from the context. Whitin and Whitin (1997) encourage teachers to postpone the use of technical mathematics vocabulary until students have had a chance to explain significant concepts in their own words.

Difficulties with words are not the only problems students have with math textbooks. They are also required to understand a different symbol system and to read numerals as well as words, which involves understanding place value. They must be able to interpret such symbols as plus and minus signs, multiplication and division signs, symbols for union and intersection, equal signs and signs indicating inequalities, and many others, as well as abbreviations such as *ft.*, *lb.*, *in.*, *qt.*, *mm*, and *cm*.

Symbols are often particularly troublesome to middle-school students, perhaps partly because some symbols mean other things in other contexts; for example, − means *minus* in math but is a hyphen in regular print. Matching exercises such as the one described in the Model Activity below encourage students to learn the meanings of symbols.

To read numbers, students must understand place value. They must note, for example, that the number 312.8 has three places to the left of the decimal point (which they must discriminate from a period), which means that the left-most numeral indicates a particular number of hundreds, the next numeral tells how many tens, and the next numeral tells how many ones (in this case, three hundreds, one ten, and two ones, or three hundred twelve). To determine the value to the right of the decimal, they must realize that the first place is tenths, the second place is hundredths, and so forth. In this example, there are eight tenths; therefore, the entire number is three hundred twelve and eight-tenths. This is obviously a complex procedure, involving not merely reading from left to right but also reading back and forth.

Mathematical sentences also present reading problems. Students must recognize numbers and symbols and translate them into verbal sentences, reading $9 \div 3 = 3$, for example, as "nine divided by three equals three."

Students will need help in reading and analyzing word problems as well. Teachers should arrange such problems according to difficulty and avoid assigning too many at one time. Story problems can present special comprehension difficulties. They require all of the basic comprehension skills (determining main ideas and details, seeing relationships among details, making inferences, drawing conclusions, analyzing critically, and following directions). Chapter 7 contains a description of the SQRQCQ study method for mathematics, which takes these requirements into account.

MODEL ACTIVITIES

Matching Activity for Symbols

Place the symbols $=$, $\neq$, $>$, $<$, $-$, $+$, and $\div$ on separate index cards. Write *equals, is not equal to, is greater than, is less than, minus, plus,* and *divided by* on other individual cards. Shuffle the cards and give them out randomly to students. Then let one student with a symbol card go to the front of the room and hold up his or her card. The student with the matching card should go up to join the first student. If nobody moves, the students with the definition cards all hold them up so that the first student can see them, and he or she calls the student with the matching card to the front. If the student at the front cannot choose correctly, a student without a card may volunteer to make the match. After the match is made, the pair, or the trio if outside help was used, watches as other matches are made. Then each pair or trio thus formed makes up a math problem using its own symbol for the rest of the class to solve. These problems are written on the board. All students go to their seats and work the problems on their own papers. Students who were not involved in constructing the problems volunteer to work them on the board, with the original pairs or trios acting as verifiers.

Sometimes students find it useful to draw a picture of the situation a problem describes or to manipulate actual objects, and teachers should encourage such approaches to problem solving when they are appropriate. Teachers should watch their students solve word problems and decide where they need the most help: with computation, with problem interpretation (understanding of problems that they are not required to read for themselves), with reading, or with integration of the three skills in order to reach a solution. Small groups of students who need help in different areas of problem solving can be formed (Cunningham and Ballew, 1983).

Since story problems are not written in a narrative style, students often lack the familiarity with the text structure needed for ease of comprehension. The pattern of writing for story problems is procedural, with important details at the beginning and the topic sentence near the end. This pattern fails to offer students an early purpose for their reading (Reutzel, 1983).

Braselton and Decker (1994) suggest that teachers have students think of the word problems as short stories that they could comprehend by using their prior knowledge. They suggest the use of a graphic organizer to help students visualize the steps in problem solution. The use of the organizer can be taught through modeling by the teacher, followed by guided practice and independent practice by the students.

A good way to teach mathematics includes presenting mathematics content in ways that are like real-life uses. Therefore, the mathematics program would have problems related to students' everyday experiences, with the problems being written by teachers and students. Language and mathematics strategy lessons would be interwoven as students performed such tasks as shopping for groceries within a budget, figuring tax on purchases, conducting surveys, and constructing graphs.

STANDARDS AND ASSESSMENT

Hadaway and Young (1994) agree that students will benefit from creating story problems related to their own experiences after a group language experience approach with classroom-related math problems. A research study showed that students who made up their own math story problems to solve performed better on tests of application skills than did those who practiced textbook word problems. They are likely to interpret a story problem more successfully if they have constructed a similar problem (Ferguson and Fairburn, 1985). Fortescue (1994, p. 576) says, "To write about a mathematical problem, one must separate the problem into a series of steps that lead to a solution. So, in writing about math problems or activities, students become familiar with analytical writing while gaining and displaying a deeper understanding of the math concept."

Donna Strohauer uses a technique called "mathematician's circle" in which students (one at a time) share problems they have generated with a group and invite other students to solve the problems. Answers and explanations of answers follow, and peers of the students presenting the problems are asked to make suggestions about the problems (Winograd and Higgins, 1994/1995).

Study guides can be useful for working with mathematics materials. Students may be given a reaction guide composed of statements about the mathematics material that are either true or false and, working in cooperative groupings, they can complete the guide by agreeing or disagreeing with each statement and providing the reason (Wood, 1992).

Graphs, maps, charts, and tables, which often occur in mathematics materials, were discussed in Chapter 7. Students need help with these graphic aids in order to perform well on many mathematical assignments. Students can learn about making graphs by graphing predictions that they make about stories that they read in class. Numbers of students who make specific predictions can be graphed on bar graphs and fractions or percentages of the class who make specific predictions can be graphed on circle or pie graphs (McDonald, 1999).

LITERATURE

Using Literature in Mathematics

Teachers can use literature to help them teach mathematical material. Many mathematical concepts that middle-school students need to learn are presented well in picture books. These books work especially well for struggling readers. Through the humorous situations in Rod Clement's *Counting on Frank,* readers can begin to think like mathematicians—experimenting, calculating, and estimating. Two excellent books for developing concepts of large numbers are *How Much Is a Million?* and *On Beyond a Million* by David M. Schwartz. A book for getting students to work with division is *The Doorbell Rang* by Pat Hutchins. Carr and others (2001) suggest the use of Demi's *One Grain of Rice* when studying how numbers that are doubled grow rapidly. Other books that may be used with middle-school students profitably are *Sir Cumference and the First Round Table* and *Sir Cumference and the Dragon of Pi* by Cindy Neuschwander and *Math Curse* by Jon Scieszka and Lane Smith. Picture books are not the only useful sources for mathematics. *The Phantom Tollbooth* by Norton Juster contains a good discussion of infinity, for example.

The Focus on Strategies on page 330 shows a mathematics lesson for struggling fifth-grade math students that is based on literature. The use of a picture book takes away some of the intimidation that many of these students feel when studying math.

Science and Health

Scientific literacy involves asking and finding answers to questions about experiences and being able to describe and explain natural phenomena. "Observing, questioning, predicting, describing, explaining, and investigating" are scientific practices that are related to literacy (Ebbers, 2002). Ebbers (p. 41) points out, "A current emphasis on inquiry encourages the participation of students in genuine scientific activity, gradually developing their abilities to test theories and construct explanatory models." El-Hindi (2003) emphasizes the importance of getting students to reason out loud about scientific concepts during inquiry learning activities, promoting instructional conversations that develop both understanding of the science concepts and their linguistic competence. Writing about scientific concepts, such as keeping logs of observations, can also be helpful.

Having students brainstorm questions about material read in the science text, categorize the questions, and work as cooperative groups to investigate them can result in students' interacting with the text as a group and sharing information (Sampson, Sampson, and Linek, 1994/1995). Such active involvement tends to facilitate learning.

Extremely heavy use of technical vocabulary is typical in science and health textbooks, in which students will encounter terms like *lever, extinct, rodent, pollen, stamen, bacteria, inoculation,* and *electron.* Some of the words that have technical meanings also have more common meanings, for example, *shot, matter, solution,* and *pitch.* In

FOCUS ON STRATEGIES

Mathematics Lesson Based on Literature

Ms. Barnes opened the class by displaying the book *The Doorbell Rang* by Pat Hutchins. "From the picture on the cover of this book and the title *The Doorbell Rang*, what do you think it will be about?" she asked the students.

"There are lots of people in the picture," Sammy said. "I think a lot of people have come to visit. The doorbell rings every time somebody comes."

"What else does the picture make you think?" Ms. Barnes asked.

"They've tracked up the kitchen," said Monica. "The mom is going to have to clean it up. She'll send them all out."

"Does anybody else have something to add?" Ms. Barnes asked.

"The children don't look happy. Maybe she is running them out," Tasha suggested.

"They are looking out the slot in the door. Maybe the person that just rang the bell is someone they don't like," Jimmy said.

"Or maybe the kids don't want anyone else to come," Don added.

"Listen carefully as I read the story to see if your predictions were right," Ms. Barnes said. "Also listen to see what this book has to do with math."

Ms. Barnes read the story. When she finished, she asked, "Were your predictions right?"

"I was right that lots of people came, and the bell rang every time," Sammy said.

"Mom didn't send them out of the kitchen, so Tasha and I were wrong," Monica said.

"I was wrong," Jimmy said. "They acted like they liked the people who came."

"But I'll bet they really didn't want all of those people to come and share the cookies. I think I was right, even though they were nice to the people," Don said.

"How does all of this fit into a math problem?" asked Ms. Barnes.

"They have to decide how many cookies to give each person," Don replied.

"That's right. Now we are going to see how they figured it all out," Ms. Barnes said. "Now," she said, "listen carefully and answer my questions as I go back through the story."

She read the first two pages. "How many children were there?" she asked.

"Two," the students chorused.

"How many cookies did each one get?" she asked.

"Six," answered the students.

"We need to know how many cookies there were in all," she said. "What do we do to get this answer?"

"We multiply," answered Joey.

"Joey, write the multiplication problem on the board and solve it." she said.

Joey went to the board and wrote "$6 \times 2 = 12$".

"Thank you, Joey," she said. Then she read further in the book.

"How many children were there after Tom and Hannah came?" she asked.

The students chorused, "Four." "How did Sam and Victoria know that each one would get three cookies?" Ms. Barnes asked. Laticia replied, "They divided four into twelve and got three."

She repeated the procedure for the entrance of Peter and his brother and again for the entrance of Joy and Simon and their four cousins. At the end of the lesson, the students counted the cookies on the tray that Grandma brought, added the number to twelve, and divided by twelve to see how many each one would have before they let in that last person at the door.

these classes, as in all other content area classes, the teacher is responsible for seeing that students understand the concepts represented by the technical and specialized terms in their subjects. For example, a science teacher might bring in a flower to explain what the stamens are and where they are located. Although diagrams are also useful, a diagram is still a step removed from the actual object, and the more concrete an experience students have with a concept, the more likely it is that they will develop a complete understanding of it.

Comprehension strategies, such as recognizing main ideas and details, making inferences, drawing conclusions, recognizing cause-and-effect relationships, classifying items, recognizing sequence, and following directions, are important in reading science and health materials, as are critical reading strategies. The scientist's inquiring attitude is exactly the same as that of the critical reader. Students must determine the author's purpose for writing and check the completeness, timeliness, and accuracy of the material. Because material can rapidly become outdated, it is very important that students be aware of the copyright dates of these materials.

Armbruster (1992/1993) points out that students need to learn how to read scientific material in order to obtain valid scientific information. She says, "The same skills that make good scientists also make good readers" (p. 347). Casteel and Isom (1994) have clearly illustrated the relationship of literacy processes to understanding of scientific material. The literacy processes form the root system that supports the branches that represent the parts of the scientific method, which in turn support the scientific facts, concepts, laws, and theories of science. (See Example 8.6 on page 332.)

Science and health materials must be read slowly and deliberately, and rereading may be necessary to fully grasp the information presented. These materials, like social studies materials, are written in a highly compact, expository style that often involves classification, explanations, and cause-and-effect relationships. The suggestions in Chapter 7 for teaching outlining skills can be especially useful in working with classification, which involves arranging information under main headings and subheadings. The suggestions given in Chapter 4 for recognizing cause-and-effect relationships will help students handle this type of arrangement when it occurs in science textbooks.

The ability to use such reading aids as maps, tables, charts, and graphs is also necessary. Explanations in science and health materials often describe processes, such as pasteurization of milk, that may be illustrated by pictures, charts, or diagrams designed to clarify the textual material. Teachers might apply the material in Chapter 7 on reading diagrams and illustrations or the material in Chapter 4 on detecting sequence, since a process is generally explained in sequence.

Science textbooks often contain instructions for performing experiments. Readers must be able to comprehend the purpose of an experiment, read the list of materials to determine what must be assembled in order to perform the experiment, and determine the order of steps to be followed. The suggestions in Chapter 4 on locating main ideas, details, and sequential order and learning to follow directions should be useful when reading material of this nature. Before they perform an experiment, students should attempt to predict the outcome, based on their prior knowledge. Afterward they should compare their predicted results with the actual results, investigating the reasons for differences. Did they perform each step correctly? Can they check special references to find out what actually should have happened?

EXAMPLE 8.6 Relationship of Literacy Processes and Scientific Content

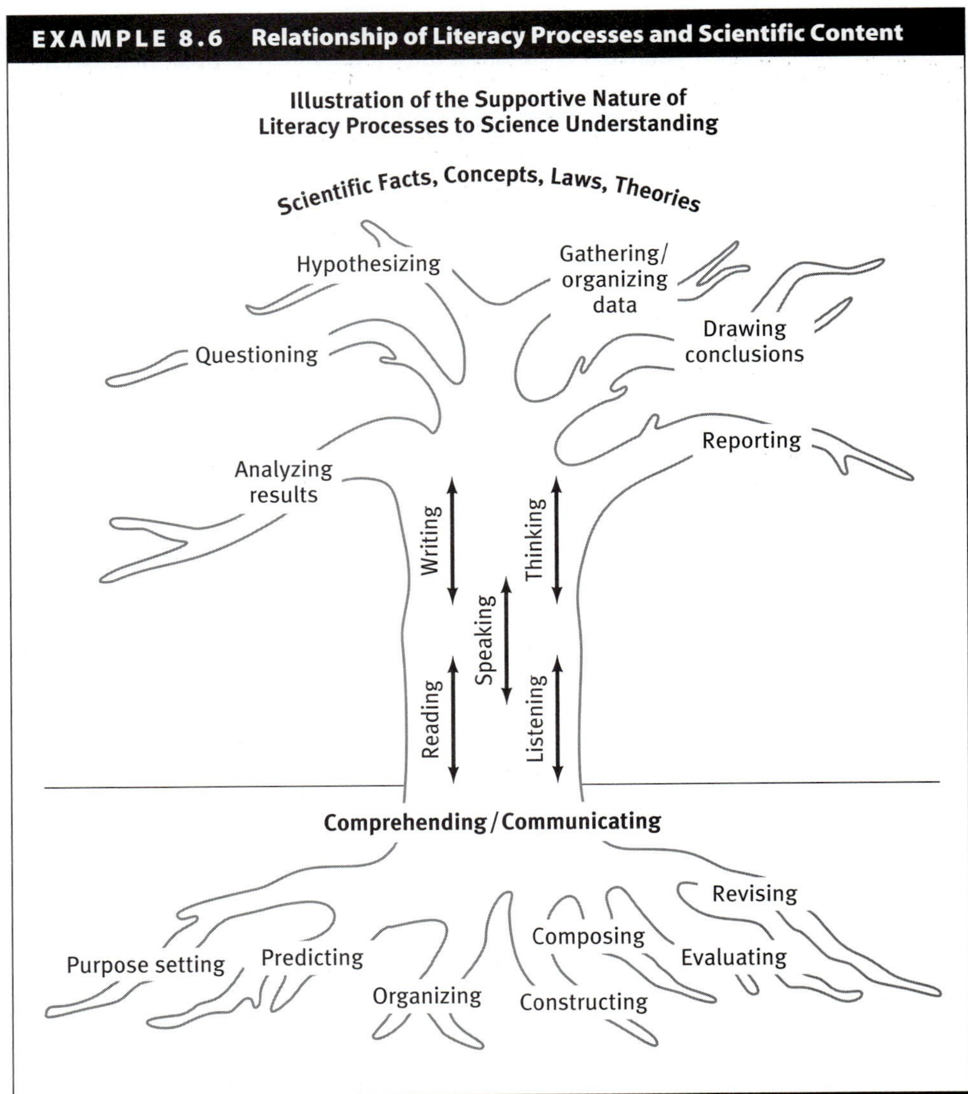

Source: Carolyn P. Casteel and Bess A. Isom, "Reciprocal Processes in Science and Literacy Learning," *The Reading Teacher*, 47 (April 1994), 540. Reprinted with permission of Carolyn P. Casteel and the International Reading Association.

Because science textbooks are often written at higher difficulty levels than the basal readers for the same grade level, some students will need alternate materials for science instruction. Trade books are available on all levels of difficulty to meet this need. One advantage of using the trade books is that they are written to minimize the need for prior knowledge of science concepts in order to understand them (Collard, 2003).

Keeping a science log or journal is a traditional practice for scientists and makes a natural connection to language instruction. Students can enter a short science-related passage in a journal each day. They can also write reports on science projects, detailing the procedures and the findings. These reports may be taken through the writing process from initial drafts and revisions to the finished products.

Science activities that involve direct experiences, such as using manipulative materials, doing experiments, or making observations of phenomena, can be the basis for language experience stories or charts that will provide reading material in science. The experience is accompanied and/or followed by class discussion, after which the students produce a chart or a story about the experience. Reading of related concept books, such as the ones mentioned later in this chapter, may provide students with material to use in expanding their stories.

Franks (2001) had middle-school students link science, art, drama, and writing in his language arts class. The students made daily weather observations, especially of clouds, and responded to one of five writing prompts asking them to write about weather memories, tell how the weather was affecting their mood, observe their surroundings, forecast their future, or list questions. Following a day of observation, the students created sketches of the three main cloud types after the teacher modeled the sketching activity. Students also swapped journals and highlighted sentences in their classmates' journals that grabbed their attention. Then groups of students used costumes from the teacher's costume boxes to act out those lines. In this way they learned the cloud types.

Another middle-school teacher, Tevebaugh (2001), tied the scientific study of insects and arachnids into other curricular areas. The students did much work in language arts as they researched and compiled information, took their writing through the writing process, organized information, and participated in mini-writing lessons on problem areas. They also read and wrote poems about insects and wrote and presented speeches. They ended by reading, writing about, and discussing books that related to the unit, such as George Selden's *The Cricket in Times Square.*

LITERATURE

Using Literature in Science and Health

Teachers can use trade books that deal with scientific concepts to help students distinguish between real and make-believe situations. Both fiction and nonfiction selections can help teachers clarify scientific information (Cerullo, 1997; El-Hindi, 2003). Ebbers (2002) identifies seven nonfiction genres that can help students learn about science: reference books, explanation books, field guides, how-to books, narrative expository books (books that give information through a story format), biographies, and journals. The Magic School Bus series by Joanna Cole uses multiple genres. Discussion of the books offers students a chance to ask questions, share their opinions and background knowledge, make predictions, and engage in inferential and critical thinking. Literature circles and book club discussions that focus on books about scientific topics can be very effective (El-Hindi, 2003). Science books can help students understand scientific processes and progress as well as specific topics. As Ebbers (2002, p. 45) says, "The stories of Copernicus, Galileo, and other astronomers, for example, can be used not just to describe planetary motion but to illustrate how scientific explanations involve debate, political context, cultural perspectives, and ultimately acceptance by a majority of peers."

Teachers should make a wealth of science trade books available for Sustained Silent Reading or Drop Everything and Read (DEAR) periods, so that students can discover the books for themselves. Some books that can be useful for particular scientific concepts and topics, include the following:

Aliki. *Fossils Tell of Long Ago*. New York: HarperCollins, 1990. (fossils)

Arnosky, Jim. *Crinkleroot's Guide to Knowing Animal Habitats*. New York: Aladdin, 1998. (animal habitats)

Fletcher, Ralph. *Spider Boy*. New York: Bantam Doubleday Dell, 1997. (arachnids)

Jackson, D. M. *The Wildlife Detectives: How Forensic Scientists Fight Crimes Against Nature*. Boston: Houghton Mifflin, 2000. (forensic science)

Kramer, Stephen. *Hidden Worlds: Looking through a Scientist's Microscope,* Boston: Houghton Mifflin, 2001. (microscience)

Montgomery, S. *The Snake Scientist*. Boston: Houghton Mifflin, 1999. (snakes)

Pringle, Laurence. *An Extraordinary Life: The Story of a Monarch Butterfly.* New York: Orchard, 1997. (monarch butterfly)

Weatherford, C. B. *The Sound That Jazz Makes.* New York: Walker, 2000. (sound)

Presenting scientific ideas and pointing out common misconceptions in narrative, or story, format, rather than in a straight expository format, can help students learn scientific information (Maric and Johnson, 1990; Schumm, 1991). Kaser (2001) told legends and folktales about constellations and the sky to enhance learning in an astronomy unit. For example, he told "The Never-Ending Bear Story," a legend explaining why the constellation Canis Major seems to change position in the sky as the seasons change. The scientific explanation, with a visual demonstration, followed the telling of the legend. The legend helped the students remember the scientific material. Nonfiction books were also used in this study as read-alouds. Seymour Simon's *Venus* was read while students watched slides of Venus on a screen in a dimly lit room with soft background music. Students read more of Simon's books about astronomy. They also listened to or read and discussed science fiction such as Monica Hughes's *Invitation to the Game,* John Christopher's *The White Mountains* trilogy, and books by Madeleine L'Engle. They considered science issues that the science fiction raised.

The color photographs and realistic illustrations found in many science books enhance a reader's enjoyment and understanding (Norton, 1995). Science informational books, such as Laurence Pringle's *Into the Woods: Exploring the Forest Ecosystem,* help students understand the laws of nature. Lynne Cherry's beautifully illustrated *A River Ran Wild: An Environmental History* documents the story of the Nashua River—its pollution and revitalization—and her *The Great Kapok Tree* relates how the animals of a Brazilian rain forest convince a man not to cut down their home. In Chris Van Allsburg's *Just a Dream,* Walter's dream helps him realize the importance of caring for the environment (Galda, 1991; Galda and MacGregor, 1992; Pierce and Short, 1993/1994). *Tree of Life: The World of the African Baobab* by Barbara Bash and *The Hidden Life of the Desert* by Thomas Wiewandt emphasize the interrelatedness of plant and animal life. Another type of ecosystem is explored in *Life in a Tidal Pool* by Alvin and Virginia Silverstein (Martinez and Nash, 1990b). Animal life in general is depicted in Doris Gove's *A Water Snake's Year,* Miriam Schliess's *Squirrel Watching,* and Jan Sterling's *Bears* (Galda and MacGregor, 1992).

Endangered species are discussed in *Saving Endangered Mammals: A Field Guide to Some of the Earth's Rarest Animals* by Thane Maynard; *The Endangered Florida Panther* by Margaret Goff Clark; and *On the Brink of Extinction: The California Condor* by Caroline Arnold. *Four Against the Odds: The Struggle to Save Our Environment* by Stephen Krensky and *The Fire Bug Connection* by Jean Craighead George are biographies of environmental activists. *Earthways: Simple Environmental Activities for Children* by Carol Petrash and *What to Do About Pollution* by Anne Shelby contain environmental activities for students (Pierce and Short, 1993/1994). Rule and Atkinson (1994) have analyzed books about ecology to help teachers choose wisely books that show realistic ecology problems, address possible solutions, have positive tones, avoid stereotypes, and are appropriate for the intended audience.

Ebbers (2002) has used text sets to teach a unit on sound and hearing. As students carried out class inquiries about sound that were sparked by a read-aloud, they also generated questions about such topics as the production of sound and the mechanics of sound. They posted questions that they had and carried out hands-on activities, such as constructing musical instruments and experimenting with them and studying diagrams of the ear and writing explanations of how sound moves from its source to a person's brain. The children read all genres of nonfiction books in order to collect information about their unit inquiries.

TIME for REFLECTION

Some teachers believe that literacy instruction should take place only during reading or language arts classes. Others believe it should also take place whenever students need literacy skills in content areas. **What do *you* think, and why?**

SUMMARY

Teachers must be aware that basal reading instruction alone is not likely to prepare students thoroughly to read in the content areas. Students need to learn reading skills that are appropriate to specific subject areas, as well as general techniques that are helpful in reading expository text. Content texts present more reading difficulties than do basal reader materials. They have a greater density of ideas presented, and they lack the narrative style that is most familiar to the students. They may also contain many graphic aids that have to be interpreted. Teachers need to be aware of the readability levels of the materials they give students to read, and they must adjust their expectations and reading assignments based on the students' reading levels in relation to the readability of available instructional materials.

Many techniques can be used to help students read content area materials more effectively. Among them are the Directed Reading-Thinking Activity, the guided reading procedure, Press Conference, the language experience approach, feature analysis plus writing, keeping learning logs, webbing, creative mapping, structured overviews, every-pupil-response activities, readers' theater, use of study guides, computer approaches, integrated approaches, thematic content units, and literature-based units across the curriculum.

Each content area presents special reading challenges, such as specialized vocabulary. Reading in literature involves comprehending many literary forms, including short stories, novels, plays, poetry, biographies, and autobiographies. English textbooks cover the areas of listening, speaking, and writing. The techniques presented in these areas need to be practiced through authentic oral and written experiences. Social studies materials abound with graphic aids to be interpreted and require much application of critical reading skills. The newspaper is a good teaching aid for the social studies area. Mathematics has a special symbol system to be learned, but perhaps the greatest difficulty in this content area is the reading of story problems. Students need to learn a procedure for approaching the reading of such problems. Science and health materials contain many graphic aids. They also often include instructions for performing experiments, which must be read carefully to ensure accurate results.

Use of literature selections to work with content area concepts is effective in every content area. In addition, including real-life activities and connections to the students' backgrounds of experiences enhances learning.

TEST YOURSELF

True or False

______ 1. Content area textbooks are carefully graded in terms of difficulty and are generally appropriate to the grade levels for which they are designed.

______ 2. One difficulty encountered in all content areas is specialized vocabulary, especially common words that have additional specialized meanings.

______ 3. All students in the sixth grade benefit from the use of a single science textbook designated for the sixth grade.

______ 4. Students often must acquire early concepts and vocabulary in content textbooks before they can understand later content passages.

______ 5. Offering students instruction in basal readers is sufficient to teach reading skills needed in content area textbooks.

______ 6. Story problems in mathematics are generally extremely easy to read.

______ 7. Mathematics materials require a learner to learn a new symbol system.

______ 8. Concrete examples are helpful in building an understanding of new concepts.

______ 9. Science materials need not be read critically, since they are written by experts in the field.

______ 10. An expository style of writing is very precise and highly compact.

______ 11. The cause-and-effect pattern of organization is found in social studies and science and health materials.

______ 12. Social studies materials frequently have a chronological organization.

______ 13. All parts of the newspaper require identical reading skills.

_______ 14. Study guides may set purposes for reading.

_______ 15. The Directed Reading-Thinking Activity is a general plan for teaching either basal reader stories or content area selections.

_______ 16. Expository text structure can be taught through the language experience approach.

_______ 17. Anticipation guides are used before reading a selection and can be the basis for discussion after reading has taken place.

_______ 18. Literature for young people can be used to teach social studies and science concepts.

_______ 19. Real-life mathematics problems produced by students are effective teaching tools.

_______ 20. Expository paragraph frames can scaffold students' attempts to write about content area topics.

_______ 21. Passages using math synonyms can help students build concepts.

_______ 22. Use of picture books should be avoided above the third grade.

For your journal . . .

1. Write about the usefulness of newspaper reading in your particular content area.
2. Describe how you can make use of trade books in a particular content area.

. . . and your portfolio

1. Develop a directed reading-thinking activity (DR-TA) for a content area lesson. Then try it out in a middle-school classroom, and write an evaluation of its effectiveness.
2. Develop a lesson for teaching students the multiple meanings of words encountered in science and health, social studies, mathematics, or literature. Try out the lesson in a middle-school classroom, and write an evaluation of its effectiveness.
3. Select a passage from a social studies or science textbook. Prepare a study guide for students to use in reading/studying the passage.
4. Develop a bibliography of trade books for students who are unable to read a particular content area textbook.
5. Prepare a comparison/contrast chart for some topic in your content area.

9

Assessment of Student Progress and Text Difficulty

STANDARDS AND ASSESSMENT

KEY VOCABULARY

Pay close attention to these terms when they appear in the chapter.

- adequate yearly progress
- alternative assessment
- anecdotal record
- assessment
- authentic assessment
- cloze procedure
- criterion-referenced test
- disaggregated data
- frustration level
- independent reading level
- informal reading inventory (IRI)
- instructional reading level
- listening comprehension level
- maze procedure
- miscue
- norm-referenced, standardized test
- readability
- reading miscue inventory
- rubric
- running record
- text leveling

SETTING OBJECTIVES

When you finish reading this chapter, you should be able to

- Discuss current trends in assessment.
- Describe some appropriate multiple measures of assessment for middle-school readers and writers.
- Identify some features and appropriate uses of norm-referenced and criterion-referenced assessment measures.
- Construct and interpret informal tests.
- Describe some ways in which authentic assessment differs from traditional assessment.
- Explain the importance of observation, and identify some ways to record observations.
- Implement portfolio assessment in a middle-school classroom.
- Recognize and analyze the significance of reading miscues.
- Identify some ways for middle-school students to assess their own progress.
- Use a cloze test to determine the difficulty of written materials.
- Identify some readability formulas that can be used to assess the difficulty of written materials.
- Discuss text leveling.

Assessment is the collection and evaluation of data for the purpose of understanding the strengths and weaknesses of student learning (Harris and Hodges, 1995). Evaluating student progress is important because it enables the teacher to discover each student's strengths and weaknesses, plan instruction accordingly, communicate student progress, and evaluate the effectiveness of teaching strategies. Assessing student learning is essential for effective teaching and should be an integral part of instructional procedures.

Chapter 9 Organization

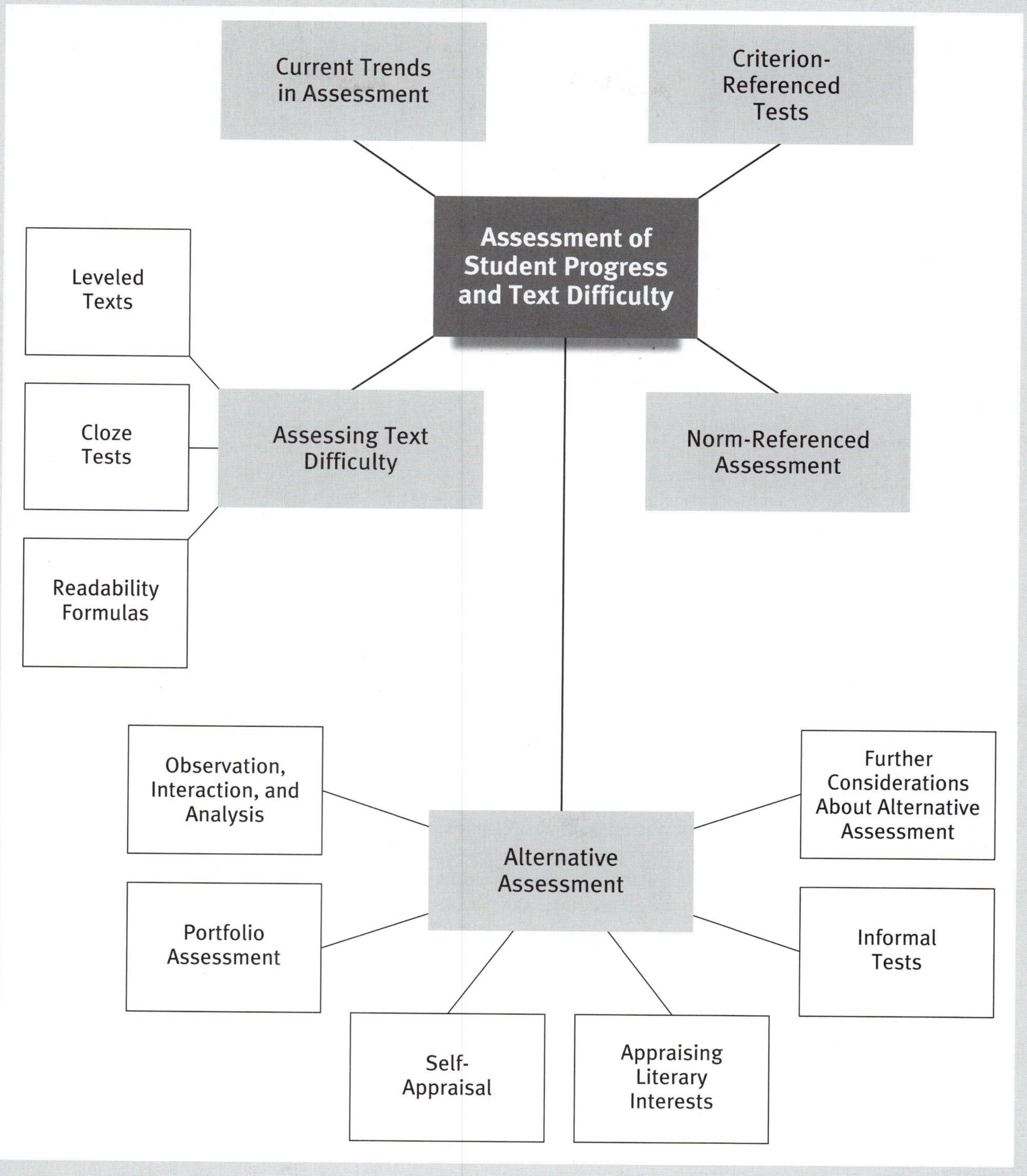

Assessment should not be simply equated with testing. It should involve the collection of data from multiple measures, such as day-to-day observation, student conferences and interviews, and analysis of samples of students' work, as well as formal means. Profiles of student learning based on multiple sources of data provide a more valid evaluation of students' capabilities and facilitate differentiated instruction for all students (Brimijoin, Marquissee, and Tomlinson, 2003). By reflecting on quantitative and qualitative data from multiple sources, teachers can gain an understanding of each student's performance in order to plan long- and short-term instruction, determine lesson content, drive instructional decisions, and decide which students need to be engaged in certain types of learning experiences (Parker et al., 1995).

The field of assessment is undergoing a great many changes as researchers and educators strive to make procedures correspond more closely with current views about the development of literacy. This chapter first examines current trends in assessment as the result of the impact of federal legislation and changes in middle-level education. Assessment is further discussed as it relates to the use of data collection from multiple sources and the implementation of recent education reform movements. Types of assessment are defined, and sources that provide multiple measures of assessment data are outlined. The chapter presents several types of authentic assessment procedures, many of which reflect the current emphasis on using real-life reading and writing tasks to evaluate student progress (Tombari and Borich, 1999). Finally, the assessment of text difficulty is reviewed. Text leveling and the use of readability formulas to determine the difficulty of written materials are discussed.

Current Trends in Assessment

Assessment serves many purposes (Leslie and Jett-Simpson, 1997; Serafini, 1997; Walberg, Haertel, and Gerlach-Downie, 1994). Three primary reasons to evaluate students are to (1) provide accountability, (2) classify students, and, most important, (3) guide instruction. Some assessment procedures are used as accountability instruments, while others provide indicators of overall strengths and weaknesses of students in a class. Norm-referenced tests, for example, yield scores that school districts use for comparing student achievement with that from previous years and for comparing district scores with national norms. Other assessment procedures described in this chapter, including observation, samples of students' work, and other informal techniques, can provide guidance for teachers in individualizing instruction.

The 2001 Elementary and Secondary Education Act (ESEA) mandates that each state establish a rigorous assessment plan that provides both quantitative and qualitative data from multiple sources. Often referred to as the No Child Left Behind (NCLB) Act, this legislation seeks to improve K–12 education. States must plan annual testing programs that determine whether or not students in the state are making ***adequate yearly progress (AYP)*** toward learning objectives in key subject areas. In addition, the annual tests must provide the states with ***disaggregated data***—scores that show the progress of subgroups of students, including racial/ethnic groups, economically disadvantaged students, students with disabilities, and students with limited English proficiency (Tennessee State Department of Education, 2003). To achieve AYP, states must set academic achievement standards and outline measurable objectives in reading/language

DIVERSITY

arts and mathematics for all students. Anderson, MacDonald, and Sinnemann (2004, p. 737) state that "implementation of a systemwide student performance assessment is critical to school improvement." They suggest that without such data, it is difficult to identify curricular goals and establish performance targets.

With recent education reforms and legislation, it is expected that states, schools, and school districts include students with special needs in assessment plans, especially when the assessment is completed for accountability purposes. States must also offer other appropriate assessments for those individuals who are unable to participate in the mandated assessments, even with approved accommodations (Salvia and Ysseldyke, 2004).

Current trends in assessment involve the development or revision of standards for what a student should know and be able to do in many subject areas. Numerous education agencies and professional associations are critically viewing curriculum and assessment through a standards lens. The International Reading Association (IRA) and the National Council of Teachers of English (NCTE) have jointly developed and published a set of reading and language arts standards (IRA/NCTE Joint Task Force on Assessment, 1996). Issues of accountability and effectiveness abound. The type of assessment method a teacher selects should match the state or district standards and accurately report how students perform. According to Snow, Burns, and Griffin (1998, p. 300), "Standards can serve as the common reference point for developing curricula, instructional materials, tests, accountability systems, and professional development."

Teachers must be able to rely on assessment to make informed instructional and curricular decisions (Serafini, 1997). It is extremely important that educators be familiar with a variety of assessment measures. As reflective practitioners in the current high-stakes testing atmosphere, teachers must use appropriate data to guide their instruction and develop curricula. As faculty members work collaboratively in learning communities to implement school improvement plans and develop curricula, the understanding of assessment data and implications for classroom use is of paramount importance in helping students learn (Guskey, 2003).

Effective assessment at middle-school levels provides consistent feedback to the student, offers clear recommendations for improvement, and should be connected to the learning process. During the planning process, middle-school students and their teachers should all be involved in identifying learning objectives. Cooperatively developed learning goals are likely to be understood by the students and teachers from the beginning of a teaching and learning task. This planning process helps eliminate ambiguity of expectations and supports the development of students' metacognitive processes (Wormeli, 2001).

Furthermore, Wormeli (2001) suggests that effective assessment should incorporate multiple disciplines and use a variety of formats to reflect what a student knows and is able to do. The interdisciplinary approach to assessment reflects the type of instructional format often implemented at middle-school levels. This type of instruction frequently requires an alternative assessment approach to sample students' knowledge and skills appropriately. It often includes the collection of performance-based data that reflect learning that has taken place over a period of time and throughout various subject areas or disciplines.

Assessment is part of good instruction when it occurs during typical learning activities, periods of social interaction, and times for reflection (Kapinus, 1994). Assessment should be a continuous process in which teachers observe and interact with students in these types of activities throughout the day. To provide a match between the strategies students use when they read and the strategies and skills that are being assessed, many educators have turned to the use of checklists, rubrics, and the analysis of portfolios, response journals, and retellings. They are evaluating debates, collaborative activities, presentations, projects, journals, performances, exhibitions, process writing, and experiments (Sugarman, Allen, and Keller-Cogan, 1993; Wiggins, 1990).

Norm-Referenced Assessment

Norm-referenced assessments are standardized; that is, they are administered, scored, and interpreted according to specified criteria (Lipson and Wixson, 1997; Rubin, 1997). Norm-referenced assessments are designed to compare the progress of students to that of other students.

Many educators have concerns about the emphasis on ***norm-referenced, standardized tests.*** Assessment that corresponds with instruction should relate to students' prior knowledge, use complete text passages, accept different interpretations, and allow the reader to vary reading strategies. Many norm-referenced tests do not exhibit these features (Kapinus, 1994; Shepard, 1989). Large-scale norm-referenced tests are objective, formal, time- and cost-efficient, widely applicable, centrally processed, and presented in a form useful to policymakers. They usually consist of multiple-choice items that primarily measure literal comprehension and isolated skills. Many of these tests fail to measure thinking and problem-solving skills, in-depth knowledge of subjects, and students' abilities to direct their own learning (Harp, 1994; Sugarman, Allen, and Keller-Cogan, 1993). Later in this section, we review efforts that have been made to create norm-referenced assessment tools that more closely resemble authentic or real-life tasks, but few changes in the norm-referenced, standardized-test format have actually been implemented. Nevertheless, use of norm-referenced, standardized tests remains widespread.

Norm-referenced tests are standardized on groups. They measure a student's relative standing in relation to comparable groups of students across the nation or locally. Authors of these tests sample large populations of students to determine the appropriateness of test items. They seek to verify the *validity* and *reliability* of test results so that schools can be confident that the tests measure what they are intended to measure and that results will not vary significantly if students take the same test more than once.

Results of norm-referenced tests are most commonly expressed quantitatively, or numerically, as standard scores, such as grade equivalents (or grade scores), percentile ranks, or stanines. A *grade equivalent* indicates the grade level, in years and months, for which a given score was the average score in the standardization sample. *Percentile rank* (PR) expresses a score in terms of its position within a set of 100 scores. The PR indicates the percentage of scores in a reference group that is equal to or lower than the given score; therefore, a score ranked at the fortieth percentile is equal to or better than the scores of 40 percent of the people in the reference group. On a *stanine scale,* the scores are divided into nine equal parts, with a stanine of 5 as the mean.

Schools administer norm-referenced, standardized *achievement tests* in the spring or fall every year to assess the gains in achievement of groups of students. Most of these tests are commercially-prepared batteries, or collections of tests on different subjects, and should be administered under carefully controlled conditions and often over the course of several days. Generally the completed tests are sent to the publisher for scoring.

Many standardized achievement tests contain subtests in reading and language that provide useful information for identifying students' general strengths and weaknesses in reading. However, these tests have limitations. In order to understand their limitations, teachers should consider the following questions.

Do tests really measure what we know about the reading process today? Some norm-referenced, standardized tests do not reflect current thinking about reading comprehension as a strategic process for the following reasons:

- The test may check knowledge of vocabulary by asking students to find one of several words that most closely matches an isolated key word, instead of asking students to identify vocabulary in context, in the manner in which readers nearly always encounter words.

Norm-referenced tests can provide teachers with quantitative data about general reading achievement, scholastic aptitude, and areas of strengths and weaknesses. *(© Charles Gupton/CORBIS)*

- The test may assess reading comprehension on the basis of answers to series of short, unrelated paragraphs, instead of asking students to read longer passages, as they would in real reading situations.
- The test may present material without regard for students' prior knowledge, instead of considering the way students' existing schemata interact with the text as students construct meaning.

DIVERSITY

Is the test fair to diverse learners? Test publishers have been giving increasing attention to the question of the fairness of their tests. They do not want to state questions in a way that will give certain individuals an unfair advantage or discourage some students so that they will not do their best. Many writers and editors from different backgrounds are involved in test construction, and members of several ethnic groups review questions to correct unintentional, built-in biases.

DIVERSITY

How are test scores being used? Too much emphasis is being placed on standardized test scores if they are the only source used to classify students as gifted or learning disabled, group students according to achievement levels, match materials designed for a particular reading level with students who scored at that level, or place students in remedial classes. Although norm-referenced, standardized tests may be one consideration, placement in special groups should be the result of evaluating multiple assessments (Eby, 1998; Flippo, 1997).

DIVERSITY

With the inclusion of students with special needs in the assessment plan, educators are especially concerned with the accuracy of the assessment data. It is critical that decisions are made regarding appropriate accommodations for those students who may need them. Accommodations include changes from the standardized materials or procedures. Some examples include conducting the assessment in the student's native language, offering extended testing time, arranging for alternative test settings, and repeating directions. Assessment accommodations should be discussed and noted on the Individualized Education Plan for those students with an IEP. Accommodations should not destroy the purpose of the test but allow students to have their proficiencies or achievement assessed, not their disabilities (Salvia and Ysseldyke, 2004).

Some education agencies, such as those in the state of Tennessee and the Chicago public schools, include longitudinal achievement data as a value-added feature of their assessment programs. Whereas norm-referenced tests attempt to determine evidence of achievement in comparison with a normed sample of the population, value-added scores attempt to profile the academic growth of an individual student. By collecting value-added testing information over a period of time, teachers are better able to profile academic growth, identify learning trends, and note the impact on a student's performance of possible intervening variables such as the school system, the school, and the individual teacher (Holloway, 2000).

TIME for REFLECTION

Many teachers believe that students should not have to take norm-referenced, standardized tests, yet most administrators and legislators require them. **What do *you* think, and why?**

Researchers have been seeking to establish more authentic ways to assess reading ability, by taking into consideration students' thought processes and reading strategies. Educators believe that because test scores often are used to direct instruction and predict performance, tests should measure the high-level thinking strategies students actually employ when reading. Therefore, developers of standardized tests have been seeking ways to measure a student's ability to apply reading strategies in a variety of authentic reading tasks.

Rather than focusing on single correct answers, researchers have been considering the entire process of reading and the strategies used. Three ways that test developers have adapted new ideas about comprehension to their tests are (1) setting purposes for reading, (2) analyzing incorrect responses to multiple-choice questions to aid in diagnosing sources of difficulties, and (3) assessing vocabulary by asking readers to identify words embedded in text instead of words in isolation (Farr and Carey, 1986). Some tests attempt to evaluate students' use of the reading process, application of prior knowledge, and depth of understanding (Harp, 1994).

Despite efforts to include more authentic tasks on standardized tests, however, "there is little evidence of their wide-scale feasibility, practicality, and utility" (Walberg, Haertel, and Gerlach-Downie, 1994, p. 37). During the last decade, concerns related to the current high-stakes testing envionment have risen. The pressure to achieve good results has led to several testing scandals. Test publishers admit to rushing test construction and scoring, therefore resulting in errors, sometimes extremely serious errors (Goldberg, 2004). Difficulties arise from lack of information about technical characteristics of the new assessments, from the inability to establish consistent ratings among judges, and from the variability in a student's scores, depending on which performance task is given.

Criterion-Referenced Tests

A ***criterion-referenced test*** (or objective-referenced test) is designed to yield scores that are interpretable in terms of specific performance standards, for example, to indicate that a student can identify the main idea of a paragraph 90 percent of the time. Criterion-referenced tests are designed to match the standards or expectations of what students should know at successive points, or benchmarks, throughout their school careers. Such tests, which may be commercially prepared or teacher constructed, are intended to be used as guides for developing instructional prescriptions. For example, if a student cannot perform the task of identifying cause-and-effect relationships, the teacher should provide instruction in that area. When assessment data are collected in an effort to assist the teacher in planning, instruction, and evaluating progress for learners, criterion-referenced data are preferred (Salvia and Ysseldyke, 2004). Such specific applications make these tests useful in day-to-day decisions about instruction. The National Assessment of Educational Progress (NAEP) uses criterion-referenced assessment data to report on what American students in public and private schools know and can do in a number of subject areas (Snow, Burns, and Griffin, 1998).

Criterion-referenced testing has both advantages and disadvantages. It is an effective way to determine what a student is able to do, or to diagnose a student's knowledge of reading skills. Analyzing the results of a criterion-referenced assessment helps in prescribing appropriate instruction. Furthermore, students do not compete with other students; rather, they try to achieve mastery of each criterion or objective. One disadvantage of criterion-referenced testing is the impact it may have on instructional approaches. Reading can appear to the teacher to be nothing more than a series of skills to be taught and tested, and skills may be taught in isolation rather than in combination. Knowledge gained in this way may be difficult for students to apply to actual reading situations.

Another consideration in criterion-referenced assessment is establishing appropriate standards. Establishing standards that are too high results in larger numbers of students who may fail to meet expectations. If standards are set too low, many students who are experiencing difficulty in reading will remain unidentified and may not receive appropriate instructional programs with interventions needed for success.

Alternative Assessment

Alternative assessment refers to the gathering of data through performance measures. Concern about the inadequacies of norm-referenced, standardized tests and the need to look carefully at students' work in order to evaluate student performance have caused educators to take more interest in alternative assessment. Alternative assessment often involves the collection of qualitative data, involves use of multiple progress indicators, includes authentic tasks, and reveals progress as growth over time rather than as a one-time evaluation (Cole, 1998). With it students create and evaluate their own work, thus developing a sense of responsibility and ownership.

Alternative assessment should be based on the following principles (IRA/NCTE Joint Task Force on Assessment, 1994; Lipson and Wixson, 1997; Neill, 1997; Tombari and Borich, 1999):

1. The major purpose of assessment is improvement of student learning.
2. Assessment is fair and equitable for all students.

3. Assessment involves all members of the educational community: parents, students, administrators, and the public.
4. Communication about assessment is clear and regular.
5. Assessment includes a variety of perspectives and data.
6. Professional collaboration supports assessment.
7. Activities assessed are authentic, meaningful, and contextualized (within daily instruction rather than on tests).
8. Assessment is continuous.

Knowledge of recent brain research and its implications is important as middle-school teachers create authentic assessment tasks. According to Irvin (2002), some findings from brain research provide guidance for the type of enriched teaching and learning environment that can strengthen connections and lead to improved memory and retention. Teachers working to create such an enriched environment for middle-school students would:

- Provide experiences that engage all the senses and emotions.
- Encourage students to complete learning tasks through problem-based or inquiry approaches.

- Use simulations to involve their students and prompt discussions.
- Pose thought-provoking or challenging problems or puzzles on a routine basis.
- Implement cooperative learning or collaborative learning approaches.
- Develop an interdisciplinary curriculum.
- Have students write reflectively each day.

Observation, Interaction, and Analysis

Three aspects of informal evaluation that effective teachers use are observation, interaction, and analysis (Goodman, Goodman, and Hood, 1989). During *observation,* the teacher carefully watches the activities of a single student, a group of students, or the whole class in order to evaluate students' language use and social behaviors. Longer observations will reveal more information regarding students' progress.

The observer may want to join or participate in a cooperative group activity in an effort to assess and analyze the depth of interaction informally. *Interaction* takes place when the teacher raises questions, responds to journal writing, and confers with students in order to stimulate further language and cognitive growth. During *analysis,* the teacher gets information by listening to a student read or discuss ideas and by examining a student's work. The teacher then applies knowledge of learning principles to analyze the student's ability to use language or demonstrate specific knowledge and skills.

Observation Strategies

Since much student assessment occurs informally, teachers need to interpret their observations with insight and accuracy. Johnston (1987) suggests several characteristics of teachers who successfully evaluate students' literacy development:

- Expert evaluators recognize patterns of behavior and understand how reading and writing processes develop. They notice, for example, that one student is unable to make reasonable predictions or that another uses context clues effectively.
- Observant teachers listen attentively at scheduled conferences and during the course of each day.
- Effective observers evaluate as they teach, and they accept the responsibility for assessing students' needs and responding to them instead of relying only on test data.

On the basis of informal observations and even intuition, teachers can modify instructional strategies, clarify explanations, give individual help, use a variety of motivational techniques, adjust classroom management techniques, and provide reinforcement as needed.

Recordkeeping is an essential part of observation, and it may be done in different ways. Some teachers keep a notebook with a separate page to record observations for

TIME for REFLECTION

How might observation data be more useful than test scores in guiding instruction in the middle grades?

each student; others jot dated notes on sticky notes or on file cards that they later place in the students' files or portfolios. Use of anecdotal records, checklists, and rating forms can help to focus observations on important areas of literacy learning.

Anecdotal Records. ***Anecdotal records*** are written accounts of specific incidents in the classroom. The teacher records information about a significant language event: the time and place, the students involved, what caused the incident, what happened, and possibly the implications. Such records may be kept of individual students, groups, or the whole class. Anecdotal records are useful in evaluating progress, planning and individualizing instruction, informing others (including the students) of progress, noting changes in language development, and understanding attitudes and behaviors (Parker et al., 1995; Rhodes and Nathenson-Mejia, 1992). Anecdotal records

are especially helpful when discussing progress of students with special needs, including English language learners. Individualized Education Plan (IEP) team members often use anecdotal records to assist in the development of an initial IEP or in the revision of an existing one. Teachers who keep anecdotal records regularly become more sensitive to their students' special interests and needs than they were before they kept such records (Baskwill and Whitman, 1988). (See Example 9.1 for a sample anecdotal record.)

Checklists and Rating Scales. Some teachers keep checklists, which are useful for recording information about student accomplishments and seeing at a glance what a particular student has achieved and what skills and strategies need further work. Rating scales provide additional information. Teachers can assign numbers to each item, perhaps from 1 (lowest) to 5 (highest), according to each student's level of performance or achievement. Teachers can make several copies of the checklist or rating scale for each student and keep them in a folder. By filling out the forms periodically and dating each one, teachers have a written record of each student's progress over time.

EXAMPLE 9.1 Anecdotal Record

It was Lee's first day in our fifth-grade classroom. He appeared hesitant about joining the other students during our advisory group meeting. I had previously asked another student, Steve, to partner with Lee and help him through the first day. Steve agreed, so I assigned Lee to the desk next to Steve. Steve and Lee ate lunch together, and Steve did help include Lee in a game of basketball during physical education class. Before language arts class, another student showed Lee where the classroom library was located, and Steve suggested one of his own favorite books, *The Great Kapok Tree*. Although Lee spoke and read little English, Steve partner-read with him, pointing to pictures and words and discussing the story. By the end of the day, Lee was smiling and interacting with small groups of students in the classroom. Before leaving at the end of the day, Steve told me that he thought Lee had had a good day.

CLASSROOM SCENARIO

Evaluation of Literature Circles

Ms. Knox reminds the students of their responsibilities for reading, discussing, writing in their literature logs, and planning for their next session while they are in their groups. She tries to meet with each group as both a participant and an evaluator. As she joins a group that is reading Lois Lowry's *Number the Stars*, she enters the discussion and also keeps a checklist of each student's status. One day's checklist is shown in Example 9.2 on page 350.

Analysis of Scenario

As she visits different groups, Ms. Knox is gaining a great deal of information over a period of time about each student's interests and enthusiasm, insights into characters and plot development, and skill in group interaction. From her observations, she can make judgments about progress in student responses to literature and social interactions. The informal records of her observations can serve as a basis for parent conferences and entries on report cards.

An example of using a checklist for evaluation during literature circles comes from Natalie Knox's sixth-grade class. (See the Classroom Scenario above.) This was Ms. Knox's and the students' first time to use multiple sets of books from quality literature instead of basal readers.

Rubrics

A ***rubric*** provides specific criteria for describing student performance at different levels of proficiency in different content areas (O'Neil, 1994). With this performance-based assessment, students receive a number of points that represent minimal to high-quality work, depending on the type of response. For example, during group reading, the criterion for a high-quality response that would earn the highest number of points might be "Carries on a meaningful conversation about reading," and the criterion for a minimal response with low or no points might be "Unable to express thoughts or feelings about reading material" (Winograd, 1994, p. 421). Example 9.3 on page 351 is a sample rubric.

A well-constructed rubric lets students know in advance what is expected of them and helps teachers grade students' work fairly. When students receive their grades, they are more likely to understand them because they can refer to the criteria instead of just getting a letter grade without explanation.

The effective use of rubrics at the middle-school level should involve students during the design stage. When constructing rubrics, teachers may invite students to suggest criteria to include (Batzle, 1992). Students should begin their involvement when teacher-generated rubrics used for assessment and instruction are introduced. They should then be encouraged to view rubrics critically and to generate components of their own. As the process continues, the students should assume more control in the rubric design and development. The process of developing and implementing student-generated rubrics helps develop critical thinking and metacognitive skills.

When used correctly, rubrics are effective instructional and assessment tools (Andrade, 2000). Although rubrics vary in format, all share two features: *standards,* which refer to the levels at which students should be able to perform tasks, and *criteria,* or what is being evaluated. In some cases, educators establish criteria for district- or

EXAMPLE 9.2 Checklist for Literature Response Groups

Number the Stars Meeting # 1	Attended	Read to page	Shared # of items	Asked questions for clarification	Made predictions &/or connections within the book (or other books)	Made connections to real situations	Responded to others in group	Read from response journal
Kristine Zerr	✓	60	✓	-Ellen's family?		-Far away relatives	✓	hesitant
Marie Orly	✓	60	✓✓	-Why star? -Buttons?	-Sister's death?		✓	excellent
Katie Smith	✓	125	✓✓✓✓✓	-Symbols? -Religion?			✓ Missy Marie	thorough
Missy Guy	✓	65	✓✓✓	-Peter's involvement?		-Family friends religious difference		detailed
Magan Clifton	✓	60	✓✓✓✓✓✓	-Symbols?	-Fishing? -Mom's ?s	-Aunt's death	✓ Marie	-skipped around -sequence?
Next meeting: 11/19 Read to: p. 94								

EXAMPLE 9.3 Rubric for Oral or Written Retelling of a Narrative

3	2	1
Characterization		
Accurately recalls both primary characters and secondary characters	Accurately recalls only primary or secondary characters, not both	Incorrectly identifies the characters
Uses vivid, appropriate descriptive words when discussing the characters	Provides limited, correct descriptions of the character	Provides no descriptions or inaccurate descriptions of the characters
Setting		
Recalls the setting: both place and time	Recalls only the time or place, not both	Provides minimal information or inaccurately describes the setting
Plot		
Recalls the action or plot in correct sequence as it happens in the story	Describes some of the events as they occur in the story sequence	Inaccurately describes events as they happen in the story sequence or describes events out of sequence
Conflict/Resolution		
Accurately discusses both the conflict and the resolution	Discusses only the conflict or the resolution, not both	Discusses fragmented sections of story with little mention of a conflict or problem with a resulting resolution

Name of student: ______________________________

Story: ______________________________

Circle type of response: Written Oral

statewide standards and train scorers to be consistent in their grading (Garcia and Verville, 1994). Some guidelines for writing rubrics include the following:

- Base standards on samples of student work that represent each level of proficiency.
- Use precise wording that describes observable behaviors in terms that students can understand.
- Avoid negative statements, such as "Cannot make predictions."
- Construct rubrics with 3-, 4-, or 5-point scales, with the highest number representing the most desirable level.
- Limit criteria to a reasonable number.

Conferences and Interviews

Another type of informal assessment occurs when teachers have conferences with students (or interview them) about their attitudes, interests, and progress in reading.

Conferences provide opportunities for teachers to assess students' attitudes, interests, and progress in reading. *(© Stefanie Felix)*

Conferences may be scheduled or may occur spontaneously when opportunities arise. Sample questions for teachers to ask include the following:

"Do you enjoy reading? Why or why not?"

"Do you think reading is important? Why or why not?"

"What books have you read recently? What did you like or dislike about them?"

"What do you do when you have a problem understanding what you are reading?"

"What do you do when you come to a word that you don't know?"

Through interviews, teachers learn how students make interpretations and construct meaning. They also gain insights into the reasoning behind students' task performances as the students explain their answers.

Student-led conferences are often successfully implemented at middle-school levels. During such conferences, students assume the responsibility for sharing authentic work samples with parents or family members and/or discussing assessment results during a specific event. Student-led conferences encourage students to approach their learning metacognitively and take ownership of it.

FAMILY

Retellings

LITERATURE 

Retelling occurs when a student tells a story or informational selection she or he has heard or read. Retellings can be done with material from different genres, such as biographies, fables, and mysteries, so that the reader can explore different types of texts. At first, the teacher encourages the student to retell without offering assistance, but when the student appears to have finished, the teacher may prompt by asking open-ended questions, or together they may complete a graphic organizer that might stimulate further retelling. By listening carefully and analyzing documentation, the teacher can learn much about a student's understanding and appreciation of the story. Retellings are effective assessment tools and may be used with both oral and written responses. As an instructional technique, retellings benefit students by improving their comprehension, sense of structure, and use of oral language (Fisette, 1993). A rubric, such as the one in Example 9.3 on page 351, may be used to specify the criteria and standards for the retelling and serve as documentation for the task.

Portfolio Assessment

Many teachers are adopting a portfolio approach to assessment. A *portfolio* is defined as a purposeful recording of learning that focuses on the work of the student and involves his or her reflection on that work (National Education Association, 1993). Student portfolios may be kept in expandable file folders, three-ring binders, or storage boxes or saved digitally on computers. Some teachers take advantage of Internet technologies to maintain a classroom presence and display student portfolio artifacts. Some websites, such as Homestead (**http://www.homestead.com**) and TeacherWeb (**http:// teacherweb.com**), allow students and teachers to create personal or school sites using design templates. Web addresses are assigned and can be accessed easily with an Internet connection. Maintaining portfolio artifacts in this manner makes viewing and sharing convenient. It also facilitates communication between the school and home.

TECHNOLOGY

FAMILY

Portfolios enable students and teachers to analyze and reflect on student work in order to evaluate progress. Danielson and Abrutyn (1997) believe that it is not the portfolio itself but the process of portfolio implementation that helps establish a classroom climate in which both teachers and students recognize that learning is valued.

Implementing portfolio assessment is not easy (Stowell and Tierney, 1995). Moving from traditional testing practices to assessing student progress with portfolios can be a difficult transition that may take several years. There is no single way to implement portfolios unless a district mandates procedures and inclusions, so teachers and students must decide what works best for them. Teachers face many difficult decisions, such as what to include in order to provide evidence representing the range of activities students are pursuing and the extent of students' capabilities. They need to consider how to analyze the material, how to evaluate the contents for grading purposes, and how to guide students' selections of their best work. Teachers therefore must ask themselves: Who will see the portfolios? What should a portfolio look like? Who decides what to include? How should information be shared? Among the types of portfolios are the following (Batzle, 1992; Leslie and Jett-Simpson, 1997; Salinger, 1996):

- A *working portfolio*—a sampling of representative student work, usually chosen by the student in collaboration with the teacher

- A *showcase portfolio*—student-selected samples of best work only, likely to be shared with family members during conferences
- A *recordkeeping portfolio*—records of evaluation and test scores kept by the teacher, often for purposes of accountability

Both students and teachers should decide on the *artifacts* to be included in the portfolio—for example: writing samples (from first draft to published work, to show growth); literacy goals; accounts of classroom experiences; a variety of products that demonstrate purposeful use of language; communications with others; audiotapes or videotapes; multimedia presentations; reasons for selecting certain pieces; and reflections and self-evaluations (Fiderer, 1995; Wiener and Cohen, 1997). Artifacts should be dated and will vary according to the purposes for using them and the criteria for selection.

Portfolios provide opportunities for innovative ways to reveal information that is not always evident from traditional assessments. Some examples are evidence of service-learning, culminating performances from an interdisciplinary unit, and creative student products that demonstrate subject or skill area proficiency (Danielson and Abrutyn, 1997).

Although it is important for teachers and students to review portfolios together periodically, such reviews can consume considerable time. Teachers should develop rotating schedules in order to have a conference with each student at least once a month. The Focus on Strategies on using portfolio assessment on page 355 illustrates one teacher's procedure for conferences.

Self-Appraisal

Assessment should help students develop the ability to judge their own accomplishments—to set their own goals, decide how to achieve those goals, and evaluate their progress in meeting the goals—in order to experience a sense of ownership in the assessment process (Au, 1990). Teachers can guide students toward self-assessment in a number of ways (Hansen, 1992; Winograd, Paris, and Bridge, 1991). By sharing audiotapes or videotapes of oral reading and checklists, teachers can help students become aware of their strengths and ways they might improve. Through interviews, they can help students focus on their own progress by asking such questions as "How has your reading improved in the last month?" and "What goals would you like to set for yourself in reading and writing?" By including student self-evaluations as part of report card grades, teachers show students that they value their judgments.

Students who display metacognition are aware of how they learn and of their personal strengths and weaknesses in relation to specific learning tasks. They ask themselves questions in order to assess the difficulty of an assignment, the learning strategies they might use, any potential problems, and their likelihood of success. While reading or studying, their self-questioning might proceed as follows:

1. Do I understand exactly what I am supposed to do for this assignment?
2. What am I trying to learn?

FOCUS ON STRATEGIES

Using Portfolio Assessment

Although this was Mr. Fernandez's first year using portfolios, he was quickly becoming aware of their usefulness. They were very helpful during parent conferences, because he could show the parents exactly what their students had done during a six-week period—the progress they had made or, in a few cases, the lack of progress. The parents seemed to understand better what their students were doing by looking at their work than just by looking at grades.

Mr. Fernandez had also found the samples of students' work useful when it was time to give report card grades. He had always believed that grades should be more than averages of test scores, and now he could use students' work samples to supplement the test score averages. Quite often, an examination of their work told him that his students had done better work than their tests indicated. If anyone questioned his judgment about his grades, he would be able to show these samples, along with the test scores, to support his evaluation.

Perhaps best of all, many students enjoyed working on their portfolios. They really enjoyed looking back through their papers, recalling different pieces they had worked on, and realizing they were getting better. They also liked being able to choose which pieces to include, although sometimes Mr. Fernandez suggested additions.

Mr. Fernandez moved throughout the room, visiting with the students at their desks while they were engaged in an independent reading assignment. The students had been asked to have their portfolios ready and be prepared for the individual conferences. When Mr. Fernandez completed his interviews, he realized how much he had learned about the students' work as they explained their portfolios to him. He learned that he would need to help students make judgments about their work so that they could decide which selections merited inclusion in their portfolios. He would need to spend more time with some students. Some needed help with organizing and completing work. He saw opportunities for peer coaching, integration of special interests, and use of technology and other resources. Mr. Fernandez realized that periodic portfolio reviews were an effective way to get to know his students better, understand their work, and encourage them to think and reflect.

Mr. Fernandez planned to do a few things differently next year. He had heard of placing an audiotape in each portfolio and recording the students' oral reading periodically. That would be another way to measure their progress. He also needed a better system of weeding out some of the students' work; otherwise, their portfolios would be quite bulky by the end of the year. He would try to get some ideas from teachers who were already using portfolios so that he could make the procedure run more smoothly next time. "We're off to a good start this year, though," Mr. Fernandez thought, "and next year will be even better."

TIME for REFLECTION

Traditionally, teachers have felt that assessment was their job and that students should have little or nothing to say about their own work. How might you encourage middle-school students to appraise their own work?

3. What do I already know about this subject that will help me understand what I read?
4. What is the most efficient way for me to learn this material?
5. What parts of this chapter may give me problems?
6. What can I do so that I will understand the hard parts?
7. Now that I am finished reading, do I understand what I read?

The self-appraisal form in Example 9.4 on page 356 is designed primarily for middle-school students. It enables them to

EXAMPLE 9.4 Self-Check Exercise

Directions: Read the following sentences and put a number beside each one.

Put 1 beside the sentence if it is nearly always true.
Put 2 beside the sentence if it is sometimes true.
Put 3 beside the sentence if it is hardly ever true.

______ I understand what I read.
______ I can find the main idea of a paragraph.
______ I think about what I read and what it really means to me.
______ I can "read between the lines" and understand what the author is trying to say.
______ I think about what I already know about the subject as I read.
______ I can figure out new words by reading the rest of the sentence.
______ I can figure out new words by sounding them out.
______ I can use a dictionary to figure out how to pronounce new words.
______ I can use a dictionary to find word meanings.
______ I know how to find information in the library.
______ I can find books I like to read in the library.
______ I can read aloud easily and with expression.
______ I know what is important to learn in my textbooks.
______ I know how to use the indexes in my books.
______ I know how to study for a test.
______ I ask myself questions as I read to make sure I understand.

assess their competency in various reading skills and recognize areas of strength or weakness. Teachers can use the results to understand students' perceptions of their own needs and plan appropriate instruction. Another application for self-appraisal is found in Natalie Knox's literature circles (see the Classroom Scenario on page 357).

LITERATURE

Appraising Literary Interests

An observant teacher who takes time to be a sensitive yet critical evaluator of students' progress is probably the best judge of the quality of their reactions to literature. The following questions will help the teacher in the evaluation process:

- Are the students gaining an appreciation of good literature? How do I know?
- Are the students making good use of time in the library and during free reading of books and periodicals?
- Are the students enjoying storytelling, reading aloud, choral reading, and creative drama?

Teachers can obtain answers to these questions through students' spontaneous remarks ("Do you know any other good books about space travel?"), through directed conversation with the class ("What books would you like to add to our classroom li-

CLASSROOM SCENARIO

Literature Circle Self-Evaluation

The students have completed the book for their literature circle, and it is time to fill out the self-evaluations Ms. Knox has given them. They rate themselves from 0 (not at all) to 3 (above average) on criteria related to their reading, their group responses, and their writing logs. After carefully rating themselves, they give themselves grades and justify their grades with reasons. Some of the students wrote as follows:

The grade I think I deserve for this literature group is ___A___ because

most of the answers above are number threes. And I love discussing questions and other things about my book.

The grade I think I deserve for this literature group is ___B___ because

I think I deserve a B because I sometimes took my vocabulary folder home and left it and then didn't have it.

The grade I think I deserve for this literature group is ___C___ because

I think I can do better in keeping up with my journal. Mostly, I keep my voice level down and rarely get called down.

Analysis of Scenario

Such self-evaluation encourages students to reflect on their work and to become aware of their strengths and weaknesses. In so doing, they become independent learners.

brary?"), and during individual conferences, when students have opportunities to describe books they like and dislike.

An excellent device for showing changes in literary taste over a period of time is a *reading record,* in which students record each book they read, giving the author, title, kind of book, date of report, and a brief statement of how well they liked the book. Reading records are often maintained separately by (or for) each student. They may classify reading selections by genre or topic, such as poetry, fantasy, adventure, mystery, myths and folklore, animals, biography, other lands, and sports. By focusing on different areas of interests or genres of literature the students read, teachers may encourage them to read about new topics and to expand their reading interests.

Informal Tests

In addition to such informal assessments as observations, checklists, rubrics, and portfolios, teachers may administer informal tests for specific purposes. Teachers may construct these tests or may find them in commercially available manuals or books.

Informal Tests of Specific Content or Skills

Sometimes the classroom teacher needs to administer an informal test to check students' knowledge and understanding of a specific skill or content area. For instance, the teacher might construct a vocabulary test from words students have studied during a thematic unit. Basal reader programs usually include tests to be used for determining how well students have learned the content of a specific unit of instruction. Whenever such tests are given, they should be used for diagnosing students' strengths and weaknesses, deciding if reteaching is needed, and providing direction for future learning experiences.

Cloze Procedure

The ***cloze procedure,*** introduced in Chapter 2 as an instructional strategy, can also be used as a tool to assess student comprehension. It provides information regarding a student's use of semantics, syntax, and context clues. By filling in words that have been deleted from a textbook selection, the student reveals his or her familiarity with the subject and ability to read the text with understanding. Test results give information about the student's independent, instructional, or frustration levels for both narrative and expository material. (Independent, instructional, and frustration levels are discussed further in the Informal Reading Inventory section that follows, and the use of cloze tests to determine text difficulty is discussed on pages 363–366.)

Maze Procedure

Originated by Guthrie (1974), the ***maze procedure,*** a modification of the cloze procedure, requires the reader to choose from alternatives rather than to fill in a blank. To construct a maze test, the teacher must first select the textbook passage. The first and last sentences should be left intact. Beginning with the second sentence, every fifth or tenth word is deleted, with three alternatives offered from which the reader must choose. One choice is the correct word; another is a word that is syntactically acceptable but semantically unacceptable; the final choice is both syntactically and semantically unacceptable. The order in which the three words are presented should vary from deletion to deletion.

TECHNOLOGY

Multimedia and Computer Approaches

Teachers can use computers for assessment in several ways. Online testing allows students to work at computers with software that analyzes their responses. Software is also available to help teachers modify test items and entire tests, perform test and item analysis, collect and analyze test scores and student grades, record grades for various assignments, and compute final grades. Many teachers use spreadsheets and grade book programs to record and compute a student's average grade.

Multimedia and computers also provide motivational alternatives to traditional testing. Photographs of completed projects, audio recordings of students retelling stories or reading orally, and video recordings of student performances and students at work are useful for documenting students' learning experiences throughout the year. Multimedia computer presentations, prepared by students, show evidence of facility with a number of literacy skills. Web-based technologies also allow teachers and students to create webpages that can be used to display and share portfolio artifacts.

Informal Reading Inventory

Teachers administer ***informal reading inventories (IRIs)*** to get a general idea of a student's reading levels and strengths and weaknesses in word recognition and comprehension. IRIs help teachers identify specific types of word recognition and comprehension difficulties so that they can use this information to plan appropriate instruction. An IRI can indicate a student's reading levels:

- ***Independent reading level***—level the student can read on his or her own
- ***Instructional reading level***—level of the material the student can read with teacher guidance
- ***Frustration level***—level that thwarts or baffles
- ***Listening comprehension level***—potential reading level

An IRI typically consists of an analysis of oral and silent reading, as well as listening comprehension. The oral reading sequence in an informal reading inventory should begin at the highest level at which the student achieves 100 percent on a sight word recognition test. After the oral reading, the teacher asks questions about the selection; then the student reads the silent reading part and is asked questions about that selection.

Material is written at a student's *independent* reading level when he or she correctly pronounces 99 words in 100 (99 percent correct) and correctly responds to at least 90 percent of the questions. The material for which the student correctly pronounces 95 percent of the words and correctly answers at least 75 percent of the questions is roughly at the student's *instructional* level—the level at which teaching of reading may most effectively take place. If a student needs help on more than 1 word out of 10 or responds correctly to less than 50 percent of the questions, the material is too advanced and is at the student's *frustration* level. After the frustration level has been reached, the teacher should read aloud higher levels of material until the student reaches the highest reading level for which he or she can correctly answer 75 percent of the comprehension questions. The highest level achieved indicates the student's probable *listening comprehension* (potential reading) level.

Teachers may make their own informal reading inventories or use commercially prepared inventories. Example 9.5 on page 360 shows a sample reading selection with comprehension questions and a scoring aid from the *Burns/Roe Informal Reading Inventory*.

It is important to remember that the result of an IRI is an *estimate* of a student's reading levels. The percentages the student achieves are a significant indication of levels of performance, but the teacher's observations of the student taking the test are equally important.

Miscue Analysis

Similar in form and procedures to the informal reading inventory, the ***reading miscue inventory (RMI)*** considers both the quantity and quality of ***miscues,*** or unexpected responses. Instead of simply considering the number of errors with equal weight for each, the teacher analyzes the student responses for the significance of each miscue.

EXAMPLE 9.5 Reading Selection and Questions from an Informal Reading Inventory

☆ TEACHER 5 FORM A 5 PASSAGE ☆

INTRODUCTORY STATEMENT: Read this story to find out about a harbor seal pup that has a special problem.

In the sea, a harbor seal pup learns to catch and eat fish by watching its mother. By the time it is weaned, at the age of four or five weeks, it is able to feed on its own.

Without a mother, and living temporarily in captivity, Pearson had to be taught what a fish was and how to swallow it. Eventually, he would have to learn to catch one himself.

Holly started his training with a small herring—an oily fish which is a favorite with seals. Gently, she opened his mouth and slipped the fish in headfirst. Harbor seals have sharp teeth for catching fish but no teeth for grinding and chewing. They swallow their food whole.

But Pearson didn't seem to understand what he was supposed to do. He bit down on the fish and then spit it out. Holly tried again. This time, Pearson got the idea. He swallowed the herring in one gulp and looked eagerly for more.

Within a week, he was being hand-fed a pound of fish a day in addition to his formula. This new diet made him friskier than ever. He chased the other pups in the outside pen. He plunged into the small wading pool and rolled in the shallow water, splashing both seals and people.

Source: Pearson, A Harbor Seal Pup, by Susan Meyers, New York: E.P. Dutton, 1980, pp. 15–16.

[Note: Do not count as a miscue mispronunciation of the name Pearson. You may pronounce this name for the student if needed.]

COMPREHENSION QUESTIONS

_______	main idea	1. What is this story about? (teaching a harbor seal pup to catch and eat fish; teaching Pearson to catch and eat fish)
_______	detail	2. How does a harbor seal pup learn to catch and eat fish in the sea? (by watching its mother)
_______	vocabulary	3. What does the word "temporarily" mean? (for a short time; not permanently)
_______	vocabulary	4. What does the word "captivity" mean? (the condition of being held as a prisoner or captive; confinement; a condition in which a person or animal is not free)
_______	cause and effect/inference	5. What caused Pearson to need to be taught what a fish was and how to swallow it? (He didn't have a mother to show him.)
_______	inference	6. What is an oily fish that seals like? (herring)
_______	cause and effect/inference	7. What causes harbor seals to swallow their food whole? (They have no teeth for grinding and chewing.)
_______	sequence	8. Name in order the two things that Pearson did the first time Holly put a fish in his mouth. (bit down on the fish and then spit it out)
_______	inference	9. How fast did Pearson learn how to eat a fish? (He learned on the second try.)
_______	detail	10. What made Pearson get friskier? (his new diet of fish and formula; his new diet)

SCORING AID

Word Recognition
%—Miscues

99–3
95–11
90–22
85–33

Comprehension
%—Errors

100–0
90–1
80–2
70–3
60–4
50–5
40–6
30–7
20–8
10–9
0–10

214 Words
(for word recognition)

217 Words
(for rate)

WPM
13020

Source: Betty D. Roe, *Burns/Roe Informal Reading Inventory,* Sixth Edition.

Knowing the type of miscue and what might have caused it provides more information about reading difficulties than knowing only the number of miscues. (Some commercial IRIs, such as the one in Example 9.5, also include a qualitative analysis.)

Miscue analysis helps teachers gain insight into the reading process and helps them analyze students' oral reading (Y. Goodman, 1995). Analysis of the types of miscues each student makes helps the teacher interpret why students are having difficulties. To some extent, miscues are the result of the thought and language the student brings to the reading situation. Therefore, analyzing miscues in terms of the student's background or schemata enables the teacher to understand why some miscues were given and to provide appropriate instructional strategies that build on strengths.

Teachers should consider whether miscalled words indicate lack of knowledge about phonics or structural analysis, show inability to use context, reveal limited sight word knowledge, result from dialect differences, or suggest some other type of difficulty. Therefore, while listening to a student read, a teacher must evaluate the significance of different miscues. Some miscues do not interfere with meaning, but many miscues do reflect problems.

In studying the miscues, the teacher should check for specific items such as the following:

1. Is the miscue a result of the reader's dialect? If the reader says *foe* for *four,* he or she may simply be using a familiar pronunciation that does not affect meaning.
2. Does the miscue change the meaning? If the reader says *dismal* for *dismiss,* the meaning is changed, and the substitution would not make sense.
3. Does the reader self-correct? If a student says a word that does not make sense but self-corrects, he or she is trying to make sense of reading.
4. Is the reader using syntactic cues? If a student says *run* for *chase,* the student still shows some use of syntactic cues, but if the student says *boy* for *beautiful,* he or she is probably losing the syntactic pattern.
5. Is the student using graphic cues? Comparing the sounds and spellings of miscues and expected words in substitutions will reveal how a reader is using graphic cues. Examples of graphic miscues include *house* for *horse, running* for *run, is* for *it,* and *dogs* for *dog.*

Running Records

The ***running record*** is a detailed account of a student's oral reading behavior that helps a teacher determine how well the student is recognizing print (Clay, 1979; Harris and Hodges, 1995). The procedure for completing the running record is similar to that used with the IRI or RMI. While a student is reading, the teacher places a check above every word read correctly. When a student makes a miscue, the teacher uses a coding system to mark the type of miscue. After completing the running record, the teacher considers why the student made each miscue.

TIME for REFLECTION

Some educators believe that counting the total number of miscues a reader makes is sufficient for purposes of evaluation, but others consider it important to analyze miscues to find the reasons for unexpected responses. **What do *you* think, and why?**

Running records are particularly useful for classroom teachers because they can be made quickly and easily in any oral reading situation in which the teacher can see the text that a student is reading (Lipson and Wixson, 1997). Students' miscues offer insights into how well they use various reading strategies, construct meaning from text, and/or monitor their own reading (e.g., self-correct if something doesn't make sense). As a result, teachers become aware of students' strengths and weaknesses and gain information to guide their instruction (Salinger, 1996). Information regarding a student's miscues on a running record may assist in the process of leveling texts according to difficulty (discussed later in this chapter).

Further Considerations About Alternative Assessment

Although alternative assessment gives a great deal of information about how well a student uses reading strategies, it has some limitations that teachers should consider. First, alternative assessment is subjective; that is, the teacher's personal biases may influence judgments about student performance. Therefore, it is possible for two teachers to assess the same work differently. Also, some teachers may not be knowledgeable about the use of informal strategies or may not have realistic expectations for students at a certain level, so their assessments may not be fair appraisals of student performance. Alternative assessment can also place a heavy burden on teacher time if teachers write frequent narrative reports on student progress instead of simply assigning numerical or letter grades based on objective test results. In addition, teachers must know how to interpret and apply information from informal records to help students improve their reading strategies.

Assessing Text Difficulty

In planning instruction based on assessment, the teacher must not only be aware of the student's levels of performance but also be prepared to select materials that provide the appropriate scaffolding. In selecting materials to teach in the content areas, teachers must be aware of the level of difficulty of the textbook or literature assignments they make. Methods of identifying text difficulty include the use of readability formulas, cloze tests, and, more recently, the leveling of texts.

Readability Formulas

Readability formulas often rank text by numerical values based on syntactic and semantic construction. When teachers have determined the students' reading levels with tests, they can obtain an approximate idea of whether a textbook or literature selection is appropriate by testing it with a standard measure of readability. Among widely used readability formulas, the *Dale-Chall Readability Formula* is designed for materials from the fourth-grade through college levels (Dale and Chall, 1948, 1995), and the *Fry Readability Graph* (Fry, 1977) can be used on material at all levels.

Because readability formulas are strictly text based, they do not give information related to the interactive nature of reading. For example, they cannot gauge a reader's background knowledge about the topic, motivation to read the material, or interest in the topic, although these are important factors in determining the difficulty of a text for a particular student. Furthermore, they cannot separate reasonable prose from a series of unconnected words (Rush, 1985). They cannot measure the effects of an author's writing style or the complexity of concepts presented, and they do not consider the format of the material (typeface and type size, spacing, amount of white space on the page, numbers of illustrations and pictures, and so on). For these reasons, no formula offers more than an approximation of level of difficulty for material. Formulas do, however, generally give reliable information about the relative difficulty levels of textbook passages and other printed materials, and this information can be extremely helpful to teachers. Example 9.6 on page 264 shows a quick way to estimate readability. Computer programs designed to test readability can also ease the burden of making calculations by hand. Grammar and style checking programs may run several formulas.

TECHNOLOGY

Many content area textbooks are written at much higher readability levels than basal readers for the corresponding grades, and subject matter textbooks also often vary in difficulty from chapter to chapter. Unfamiliar content vocabulary is a major factor in the higher difficulty levels of many content area materials. A good way to decrease the readability levels of content passages for students, therefore, is to teach the content vocabulary thoroughly before the material containing the vocabulary is assigned to be read.

Cloze Tests

One way for the teacher to estimate the suitability of a textbook or literature selection for students is to construct and administer a ***cloze test.*** The procedure for doing this follows:

1. Select a passage of approximately 250 consecutive words. The passage should be one the students have not read, or tried to read, before.
2. Type the passage, leaving the first sentence intact and deleting every fifth word thereafter. In place of deleted words, substitute blanks of uniform length.
3. Give students the passage, and tell them to fill in the blanks. Allow them all the time they need.
4. Score the test by counting as correct only the exact words that were in the original text. Determine each student's percentage of correct answers.

If a student had less than 44 percent of the answers correct, the material is probably at his or her frustration level and is therefore too difficult. Thus, the teacher should offer alternative ways of learning the material. If the student had from 44 to 57 percent of the answers correct, the material is probably at that student's instructional level, and he or she will be able to learn from the text if the teacher provides careful guidance in the reading by developing readiness, helping with new concepts and unfamiliar vocabulary, and providing reading purposes to aid comprehension. If the student had more than 57 percent of the answers correct, the material is probably at that student's independent level, and he or she should be able to benefit from the material when reading it independently (Bormuth, 1968).

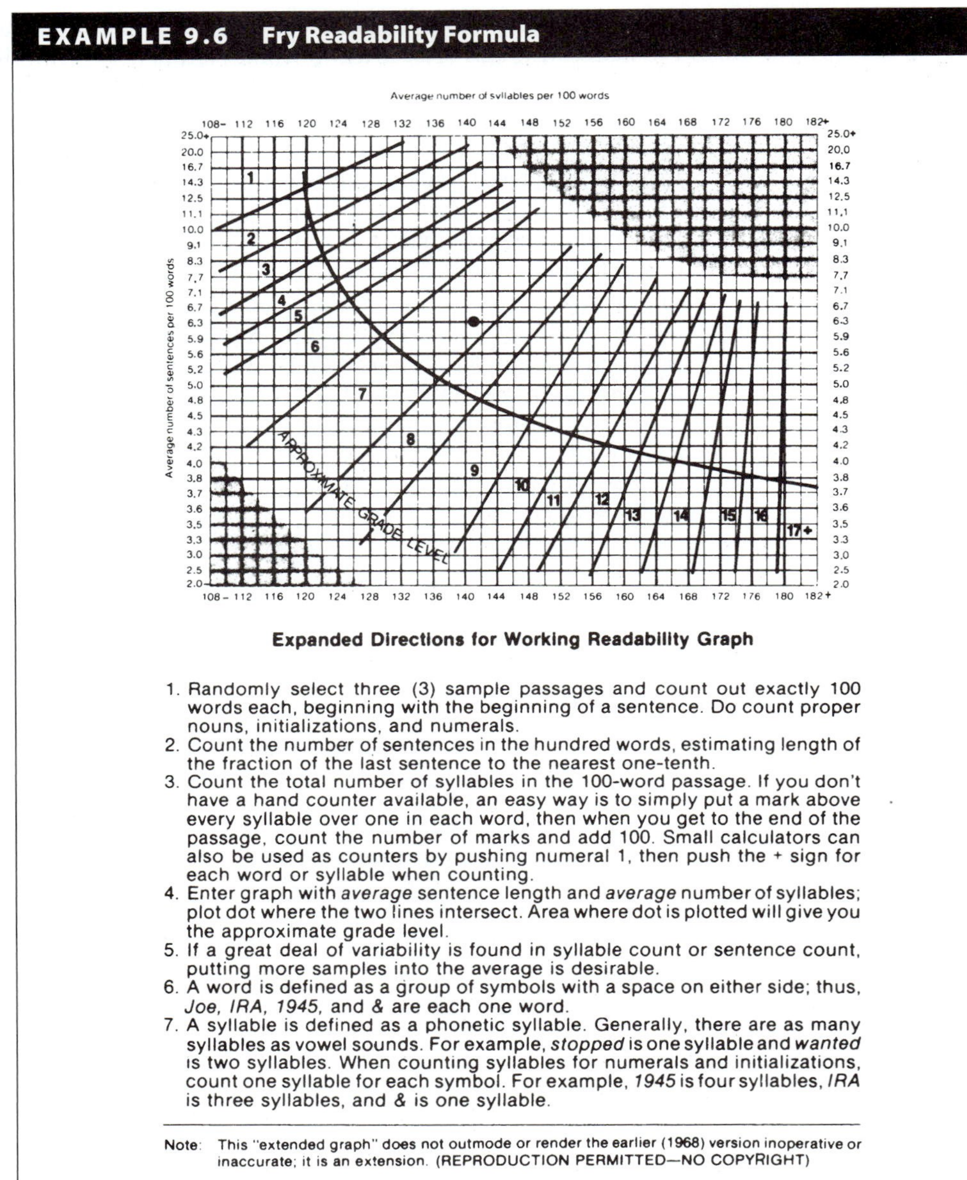

EXAMPLE 9.6 Fry Readability Formula

Expanded Directions for Working Readability Graph

1. Randomly select three (3) sample passages and count out exactly 100 words each, beginning with the beginning of a sentence. Do count proper nouns, initializations, and numerals.
2. Count the number of sentences in the hundred words, estimating length of the fraction of the last sentence to the nearest one-tenth.
3. Count the total number of syllables in the 100-word passage. If you don't have a hand counter available, an easy way is to simply put a mark above every syllable over one in each word, then when you get to the end of the passage, count the number of marks and add 100. Small calculators can also be used as counters by pushing numeral 1, then push the + sign for each word or syllable when counting.
4. Enter graph with *average* sentence length and *average* number of syllables; plot dot where the two lines intersect. Area where dot is plotted will give you the approximate grade level.
5. If a great deal of variability is found in syllable count or sentence count, putting more samples into the average is desirable.
6. A word is defined as a group of symbols with a space on either side; thus, *Joe, IRA, 1945,* and *&* are each one word.
7. A syllable is defined as a phonetic syllable. Generally, there are as many syllables as vowel sounds. For example, *stopped* is one syllable and *wanted* is two syllables. When counting syllables for numerals and initializations, count one syllable for each symbol. For example, *1945* is four syllables, *IRA* is three syllables, and *&* is one syllable.

Note: This "extended graph" does not outmode or render the earlier (1968) version inoperative or inaccurate; it is an extension. (REPRODUCTION PERMITTED—NO COPYRIGHT)

Source: "Fry's Readability Graph: Clarifications, Validity, and Extension to Level 17," *Journal of Reading,* 21 (December 1977), 249.

A teacher using the percentages given here must count *only* exact words as correct, since the percentages were derived using only exact words. Synonyms must be counted as incorrect, along with obviously wrong answers and unfilled blanks.

Because all the material in a given book is unlikely to be written on the same level, teachers should choose several samples for a cloze test from several places in the book in order to determine the book's suitability for a particular child.

Example 9.7 below shows a cloze passage for a social studies textbook. This passage contains 283 words. No words have been deleted from the first sentence in order to give the student an opportunity to develop an appropriate mental set for the material that follows, and the entire paragraph in which the fiftieth blank occurs has been included in order to complete the thought that was in progress. A score of fewer than 22 correct responses indicates that the material is too difficult; a score of 22 to 28 indicates that the student can manage the material if the teacher gives assistance; and a score of more than 28 indicates that the student can read the material independently.

EXAMPLE 9.7 Cloze Test

Directions: Read the following passage and fill in each blank with a word that makes sense in the sentence.

The first battle in July 1861 began like a holiday outing. Union supporters packed picnic ______ (1) and followed soldiers from ______ (2), D.C., into Virginia. Newspaper ______ (3) also came to get ______ (4) story.
Armies from the ______ (5) and the South met ______ (6) a stream called Bull ______ (7), about 25 miles from ______ (8), D.C.
At first Confederates ______ (9) the Union soldiers back. ______ (10) the Confederates attacked. Fierce ______ (11) broke out, and the ______ (12) army won the battle.

______ (13) Battle of Bull Run ______ (14) the North that it ______ (15) not win the war ______ (16). Congress passed laws calling ______ (17) troops to serve three ______ (18). President Lincoln's generals had ______ (19) plan to save the ______ (20).
The Union's "anaconda plan" ______ (21) named for the snake ______ (22) squeezes its prey to ______ (23). The Union planned to ______ (24) the strength out of ______ (25) South by a blockade, ______ (26) closing of southern ocean ______ (27).
Union ships would stop ______ (28) and keep Southerners from ______ (29) money by selling cotton ______ (30) other countries.

Under the ______ (31) plan, Union ships would ______ (32) control of the Mississippi ______ (33). Confederate states would then ______ (34) unable to send boats ______ (35) supplies and soldiers to ______ (36) Confederate states. Finally, Union ______ (37) would try to capture ______ (38), the Confederate capital.

The ______ (39) also had plans. One ______ (40) to destroy Union ships. ______ (41) 1862, the South sent ______ (42) iron-sided steamship, *Merrimack*, up ______ (43) James River. (The South ______ (44) the ship the *Virginia*.) ______ (45) *Merrimack* was far stronger ______ (46) the Union's wooden ships. ______ (47) Union ships fired at ______ (48), the cannonballs could not ______ (49) the ship's sides.

The ______ (50) day, the Union sent its own iron ship, the Monitor, to attack the Merrimack. The two ships battled, with no clear winner.

Answers: (1) lunches, (2) Washington, (3) reporters, (4) the, (5) North, (6) near, (7) Run, (8) Washington, (9) held, (10) Then, (11) fighting, (12) Confederate, (13) The, (14) showed, (15) would, (16) easily, (17) for, (18) years, (19) a, (20) Union, (21) was, (22) that, (23) death, (24) squeeze, (25) the, (26) or, (27) ports, (28) supplies, (29) earning, (30) to, (31) anaconda, (32) take, (33) River, (34) be, (35) with, (36) other, (37) forces, (38) Richmond, (39) South, (40) was, (41) In, (42) its, (43) the, (44) renamed, (45) The, (46) than, (47) When, (48) it, (49) pierce, (50) next.

Some authorities prefer cloze tests to informal reading inventories for matching textbooks to students because these tests put the student in direct contact with the author's language without having the teacher as a mediator (through the written questions). Frequently a student can understand the text but not the teacher's questions related to it, which can cause the teacher to underestimate the student's comprehension of the material. On the other hand, some students react with frustration to cloze materials; these students would fare better if tested with an IRI. Students should have experience with cloze-type exercises before teachers use this procedure to help match students with the appropriate levels of textbooks.

Leveled Texts

Text leveling involves organizing texts according to a defined continuum of characteristics so that teachers can match students with the appropriate materials (Fountas and Pinnell, 1996; Fry, 2002; Walker, 2004). The leveling of texts does not rely only on a quantitative formula; it involves consideration of more text factors (Fountas and Pinnell, 1996; Fry, 2002). Whereas readability is determined in an objective manner, leveling of texts occurs more subjectively. In some cases, individual teachers or teams of teachers work collaboratively to level texts and compile a collection of appropriate reading materials. Fountas and Pinnell (1996) offer lists of texts that have been leveled and are suggested for use in the implementation of guided reading. Characteristics of texts are first identified; then decisions regarding the level of difficulty are made. Some characteristics or text factors that are often included in the process of leveling include:

- format or size and layout of print
- content, including concepts and vocabulary
- length
- illustration support
- genre
- predictability
- language structure

The readability may also be one of the characteristics of the text to be considered in the leveling process. The leveling of texts involves observation of students' reading behavior as they interact with the text over a period of time. Running records are maintained and provide information to identify benchmark texts for the various levels. Benchmark texts are those that remain reliable for the level for approximately 90 percent of the students.

SUMMARY

Assessment procedures are constantly changing as educators seek ways to measure student progress in reading that reflect current views of the reading process. More than ever before, assessment is merging with instruction as teachers continuously observe students, interact with them, and analyze their strengths and weaknesses.

Although teachers may use information from norm-referenced and criterion-referenced assessments, much information is gathered informally on a daily basis in authentic circumstances. As students engage in learning experiences, the teacher collects and analyzes data to determine appropriate instructional strategies to scaffold and support the development of literacy skills.

Norm-referenced tests are administered, scored, and interpreted according to designated procedures. They compare students with other students across the nation on the basis of standard scores. Most schools require that achievement tests be administered annually to measure the progress students have made in overall academic achievement. Most traditional standardized tests measure mastery by requiring students to answer multiple-choice questions. Test developers are seeking ways to include more authentic tasks on standardized tests, but progress has been slow.

The teacher can use criterion-referenced tests to determine how well a student has mastered a specific skill. Skill mastery, however, does not always indicate whether or not the student can apply the skill to actual reading situations.

Alternative assessment can take many forms. Teachers can learn much about their students by using observation strategies. Daily observation is a key to effective assessment, and teachers can record their observations in a variety of ways, including anecdotal records and checklists and rating scales. Rubrics make students aware of expectations by giving specific criteria for scoring their work, and teachers gain insight into students' reading abilities through conferences, interviews, and retelling. Portfolios are useful for keeping samples of student work, and self-appraisal helps students evaluate their own accomplishments.

Informal tests over specific areas, including teacher-made tests on content or skills, provide information about student mastery of material. Cloze procedures and maze procedures enable teachers to assess a student's comprehension of material, while multimedia and computers are also used in various ways to assess students' knowledge. The informal reading inventory, reading miscue inventory, and running records are similar forms for informal measures that help the teacher identify students' strengths and weaknesses.

The teacher's most useful assessment tool is day-to-day observation. Informal tests may be used to reinforce or supplement such observation, whereas norm-referenced assessments are usually given only as mandated by the school system. The following lists summarize the purposes and characteristics of alternative and formal assessment:

Alternative Assessment	*Norm-Referenced Assessment*
Gives teacher useful day-to-day information about student progress	Compares students with other students across the nation
Informs teacher about planning instruction to meet students' needs	Provides accountability for school systems
Identifies individual strengths and weaknesses	Gives scores that can be interpreted quantitatively or statistically
Occurs continuously	Occurs once or twice a year
Uses classroom-based materials and procedures	Uses standardized materials and procedures

Teachers use various readability formulas and cloze tests to determine whether written material is too easy or too difficult for students so that the appropriate materials are selected for instruction. Leveling is also a method of determining text difficulty according to designated characteristics or text factors that may include readability based on a formula as one criterion used for the rankings.

TEST YOURSELF

True or False

_____ 1. Large-scale assessment practices haven't changed much in the last decade.

_____ 2. Norm-referenced tests are more helpful than multiple assessment measures for guiding instruction.

_____ 3. Instruction and assessment should be separate procedures.

_____ 4. Teachers must devise their own informal reading inventories, since none are commercially available.

_____ 5. Most norm-referenced tests consist primarily of multiple-choice items.

_____ 6. Material written on a student's independent reading level is less difficult than material written on his or her instructional level.

_____ 7. Miscue analysis can help a teacher understand the nature of a student's unexpected responses in reading.

_____ 8. Self-questioning is an effective tool for reading and studying.

_____ 9. Teachers are not allowed to provide accommodations for students with special needs when participating in norm-referenced, standardized testing procedures.

_____ 10. A criterion-referenced assessment relates an individual's test performances to absolute standards rather than to the performances of others.

_____ 11. At present there are no computer programs for assessing reading skills.

_____ 12. Test publishers have given less attention to the issue of test fairness during recent years.

_____ 13. Authentic assessment focuses on small, separate skills.

_____ 14. Three significant aspects of informal evaluation are observation, interaction, and analysis.

_____ 15. Recordkeeping is an essential part of observation.

_____ 16. Anecdotal records are written accounts of specific classroom incidents.

_____ 17. Story retelling enables teachers to learn about a student's comprehension of a story.

_____ 18. A rubric is used for scoring cloze tests.

_____ 19. It is considered desirable for students to assess their own progress.

_____ 20. In evaluating the results of a reading miscue inventory, the teacher focuses on the types of miscues rather than on the total number of miscalled words.

_____ 21. A running record is a narrative report of a student's overall progress.

_____ 22. Rubrics consist of standards (levels of proficiency) and criteria (skills or behaviors being evaluated).

_____ 23. The cloze procedure is an example of a norm-referenced test.

_____ 24. When portfolios are used, samples of a student's work should be collected and reviewed by both the student and the teacher.

_____ 25. The best questions for a teacher to ask during a student conference or interview are those that can be answered with *yes* or *no*.

_____ 26. Norm-referenced, standardized tests are the most appropriate form of assessment for identifying how well middle-school students have mastered curriculum standards in math.

_____ 27. Web-based technologies allow teachers and students to maintain portfolios that can be accessed via the Internet.

_____ 28. Readability formulas and text leveling are similar in that both attempt to provide a ranking of written materials based on characteristics that contribute to text difficulty.

For your journal . . .

1. Reflect on the various types of alternative assessment discussed in this chapter. Which of them do you consider most useful? Why?
2. How can the misuse of norm-referenced, standardized tests hurt both students and teachers? What can be done to avoid misusing them?
3. What do you think it means to merge instruction and assessment? How can one support the other?

. . . and your portfolio

1. Collect samples of student work that you could use as examples for each proficiency level, or standard, of a rubric. Be sure to focus on what you intend to measure.
2. Interview an ESL teacher. Identify different approaches to the assessment of English language learners in the middle schools. Outline the advantages and the disadvantages of the different assessment approaches.
3. Plan ways to use portfolio assessment in your classroom. Consider your purposes, a desirable format, ways to involve students in the selection and maintenance of portfolios, and ways to organize and store them.

APPENDIX A

Answers to "Test Yourself"

Chapter 1 *True or False*

1. F	11. T	21. T
2. T	12. F	22. F
3. T	13. F	23. T
4. T	14. T	24. T
5. T	15. T	25. T
6. F	16. F	26. F
7. F	17. F	27. T
8. T	18. T	28. F
9. F	19. T	29. T
10. T	20. T	

Chapter 2 *True or False*

1. F	17. T	33. T
2. F	18. T	34. T
3. T	19. T	35. T
4. T	20. F	36. T
5. T	21. T	37. T
6. T	22. F	38. T
7. T	23. T	39. T
8. F	24. F	40. F
9. T	25. F	41. T
10. F	26. T	42. F
11. F	27. T	43. T
12. T	28. T	44. T
13. F	29. T	45. T
14. T	30. T	46. F
15. F	31. T	47. T
16. T	32. F	48. F

Chapter 3 *True or False*

1. T	7. F	13. T
2. T	8. T	14. F
3. F	9. T	15. T
4. T	10. T	16. F
5. F	11. F	17. F
6. T	12. T	18. F

Chapter 4 *True or False*

1. T	8. F	15. F
2. T	9. T	16. F
3. T	10. T	17. F
4. F	11. T	18. T
5. T	12. T	19. T
6. F	13. F	20. T
7. T	14. T	

Chapter 5 *True or False*

1. F	9. T	17. F
2. T	10. F	18. T
3. F	11. T	19. T
4. F	12. T	20. T
5. F	13. T	21. T
6. T	14. F	22. T
7. F	15. T	23. T
8. T	16. T	24. T

Chapter 6 *True or False*

1. T	9. F	17. F
2. T	10. T	18. F
3. F	11. T	19. F
4. F	12. F	20. F
5. F	13. T	21. T
6. F	14. F	22. T
7. T	15. F	
8. F	16. T	

Chapter 7 *True or False*

1. F	10. T	19. T
2. T	11. T	20. T
3. T	12. F	21. F
4. T	13. T	22. F
5. F	14. F	23. T
6. T	15. T	24. T
7. F	16. T	25. T
8. F	17. F	26. T
9. T	18. T	27. F

Chapter 8 *True or False*

1. F
2. T
3. F
4. T
5. F
6. F
7. T
8. T
9. F
10. T
11. T
12. T
13. F
14. T
15. T
16. T
17. T
18. T
19. T
20. T
21. T
22. F

Chapter 9 *True or False*

1. F
2. F
3. F
4. F
5. T
6. T
7. T
8. T
9. F
10. T
11. F
12. F
13. F
14. T
15. T
16. T
17. T
18. F
19. T
20. T
21. F
22. T
23. F
24. T
25. F
26. F
27. T
28. T

GLOSSARY

achievement test A measure of the extent to which a person has assimilated a body of information.

adequate yearly progress (AYP) The progress of students in meeting established assessment growth or progress in key subject areas.

affective Relating to attitudes, interests, values, appreciations, and opinions.

allusion An indirect reference to a person, place, thing, or event considered to be known to the reader.

alternative assessment All types of assessment other than norm-referenced tests.

analogies Comparisons of two similar relationships, stated in the form of the following example: *Author* is to *book* as *artist* is to *painting*.

anaphora Use of a word as a substitute for another word or group of words.

anecdotal record A written account of specific incidents or behaviors in the classroom.

anticipation guides Sets of declarative statements related to materials about to be read that are designed to stimulate thinking and discussion.

antonyms A pair of words that have opposite meanings.

appositive A word or a phrase placed beside another word or phrase as a restatement.

artifacts The contents in portfolios that provide evidence of growth over a period of time.

assessment The collection of data, such as test scores and informal records, to measure student achievement.

auditory acuity Sharpness of hearing.

auditory discrimination The ability to differentiate among sounds.

authentic assessment Measurement of a student's performance on activities that reflect real-world learning experiences.

automaticity The ability to carry out a task without having to give it much attention.

bar graphs Graphs that use vertical or horizontal bars to compare quantities.

bottom-up models of reading Models that depict reading as being initiated by examination of the printed symbols, with little input being required from the reader.

Caldecott Medal An annual award, presented by the American Library Association, for excellence in illustration.

categorization Classification into related groups.

CD-ROM Compact disc–read only memory. A digital data storage device from which information can be accessed in nonlinear fashion.

checklist A convenient form on which the teacher can record observations about specific student behaviors or attitudes.

circle or pie graphs Graphs that show relationships of individual parts to a whole circle.

cloze procedure Method of estimating reading difficulty by omitting every *n*th (usually fifth) word in a reading passage and observing the number of correct words a reader can supply; an instructional technique in which words or other structures are deleted from a passage by the teacher, with blanks left in their places for students to fill in by using the surrounding context.

compound words Two (or sometimes three) words that have been joined together to form a new word.

computer-assisted instruction Instruction that makes use of a computer to administer a programmed instructional sequence or other educational experience.

content area textbooks Textbooks in areas of information, such as literature, social studies, science, and mathematics.

content literacy The reader's ability to read information and write information on a variety of topics through strategically selected organizational structures and appropriate styles.

context clues Clues to word meanings or pronunciations found in the surrounding words or sentences.

contractions Words made by combining two words that use an apostrophe to indicate that one or more letters from the separate words have been left out of the combined word.

Coretta Scott King Awards Annual awards to authors and illustrators of African descent whose books promote peace and world brotherhood.

creative reading Reading beyond the lines.

criterion-referenced test Test designed to yield measurements interpretable in terms of specific performance standards.

critical literacy The ability to evaluate a variety of textual and visual materials critically.

critical reading Reading for evaluation.

cumulative tales Traditional tales displaying rhythm and a pattern with a repetitive sequence of events or refrain.

database An organized body of information that can be sorted and searched electronically.

desktop publishing Application of computers combining text and graphics for classroom publishing.
dialect Regional or social modifications of a language; distinguishing features may include pronunciation, vocabulary, and syntax.
directed reading activity A strategy in which detailed lesson plans are followed to teach the reading of stories.
directed reading-thinking activity A general plan for directing the reading of content area reading selections or basal reader stories and for encouraging students to think as they read, to predict, and to check their predictions.
direct instruction Instruction with clearly stated goals that students understand, carefully sequenced and structured materials, detailed explanations and extensive modeling of reading processes, and monitoring of student work with immediate feedback.
disaggregated data Scores that show the progress of subgroups of students, including racial/ethnic groups, economically disadvantaged students, students with disabilities, and students with limited English proficiency.

eclectic approaches Approaches to teaching reading that combine desirable aspects of a number of major approaches.
ellipsis The omission of a word or group of words that are to be "understood" by the reader.
E-mail (electronic mail) Messages sent electronically from one computer user to another.
etymology The origin and history of words.
euphemism The substitution of a less offensive word or phrase for an unpleasant term or expression.
expository text Material written in a precise, factual writing style.

fable A brief moral tale in which animals or inanimate objects speak.
fantasy A genre of literature including highly imaginative fictional stories, with fanciful or supernatural elements.
fiction Stories that are not true, written in a narrative style, for the purpose of entertainment.
figurative language Nonliteral language.
frustration level A level of reading difficulty with which a reader is unable to cope. When reading material is on this level, the reader usually recognizes 90 percent or fewer of the words he or she reads or comprehends 50 percent or less of what he or she reads.

genre A type or classification of literature, such as historical fiction, biography, or folktales.
grapheme A written symbol that represents a phoneme.
graphic organizers Visual depictions of text material, such as webs.
guide words Words used in dictionaries, encyclopedias, and other reference books to aid users in finding entries. The first guide word names the first entry on the page; the second guide word names the final entry on the page.
guided reading procedure A method designed to help readers improve organizational skills, comprehension, and recall.

hearing impairment A condition that exists when the sense of hearing is defective but functional for ordinary purposes.
homographs Words that have identical spellings but sound different and have different meanings.
homonyms Pairs or groups of words that are spelled differently but are pronounced alike; homophones.
homophones Pairs or groups of words that are spelled differently but are pronounced alike; homonyms.
hyperbole An extreme exaggeration.
hypermedia Text, sound, or pictures (still or animated) linked in a nonsequential manner, allowing access to the material in an order the user chooses.
hypertext Information that is linked in a nonsequential manner, allowing students to choose the paths they will take through the information.

idiom A group of words that, taken as a whole, has a meaning different from that of the sum of the meanings of the individual words.
independent reading level A level of reading difficulty low enough that the reader can progress without noticeable hindrance. The reader can ordinarily recognize at least 99 percent of the words and comprehend at least 90 percent of what he or she reads.
individualized reading approach An approach to reading instruction that is characterized by students' self-selection of reading materials and self-pacing and by student-teacher conferences.
informal reading inventory An informal instrument designed to help the teacher determine a reader's independent, instructional, frustration, and capacity levels.
inflectional endings Endings that, when added to nouns, change the number, case, or gender; when added to verbs, change the tense or person; and when added to adjectives, change the degree.
instructional reading level A level of difficulty at which the reader can read with understanding with teacher assistance. The reader can ordinarily recognize at least 95 percent of

the words in a selection and comprehend at least 75 percent of what he or she reads.

interactive theories of reading Theories that depict reading as a combination of reader-based and text-based processing.

Internet International "network of networks" that links a multitude of computers.

interpretive reading Reading between the lines.

Investigative Questioning (InQuest) A comprehension strategy that combines student questioning with creative drama.

journals Written records of reflections, events, and ideas.

kinesthetic Pertaining to body movement and muscle feelings.

knowledge-based processing Bringing one's prior world knowledge and background of experiences to the interpretation of the text.

K-W-L Teaching Model A teaching model for expository text; stands for What I *Know*, What I *Want* to Learn, What I *Learned*.

language arts Listening, speaking, reading, writing, viewing, and visually representing skills.

language experience approach An approach in which reading and the other language arts are interrelated in the instructional program and the experiences of students are used as the basis for reading materials.

legend (of a map) The map's key to symbols used.

legends Unverified historical stories that originated orally.

line graphs Graphs that show changes in amounts by connecting with line segments points representing the amounts.

listening comprehension level Potential reading level.

literature-based approaches Approaches to teaching reading that use quality literature as a basis for reading instruction.

literature circles Groups established to allow students to exchange ideas about books they are reading.

literal comprehension Understanding ideas that are directly stated.

maze procedure A procedure, similar to the cloze procedure, requiring the reader to complete missing sections of text by choosing from three provided alternatives.

meaning vocabulary Words for which meanings are understood.

media literacy Critical evaluation of materials in various media that incorporates consideration of how media messages are created, marketed, and distributed and how they can affect attitudes and behavior.

metaphor A direct comparison not using the word *like* or *as*.

metacognition A person's knowledge of the functioning of his or her own mind and his or her conscious efforts to monitor or control this functioning.

metacognitive strategies Techniques for thinking about and monitoring one's own thought processes.

miscue An unexpected oral reading response (that is, an error).

modality A sensory system for receiving and processing information (visual, auditory, kinesthetic, tactile).

morphemes The smallest units of meaning in a language.

motivation Incentive to act.

multimedia The use of a number of different media (e.g., graphics, text, moving images, sound effects) in the same application.

multiple intelligences Several distinct areas of potential that people possess to different degrees.

myths Traditional literature selections that feature characters such as gods, heroes, or supernatural beings.

narrative text Written material with a storylike presentation.

Newbery Award An annual award presented by the American Library Association for the most distinguished contribution to American literature for children.

nonfiction True material designed to inform or instruct.

norm-referenced, standardized test Test designed to yield results interpretable in terms of a norm, the average or mean results of a sample population.

perception The interpretation of sensory impressions.

personification Giving the attributes of a person to an inanimate object or abstract idea.

phoneme The smallest unit of sound in a language.

picture graphs Graphs that express quantities with pictures.

portfolio A collection of a student's work over a period of time.

***pourquoi* tales** Traditional literature selections that often explain "why."

programmed instruction A method of presenting instructional material in which small, sequential steps; active involvement of the learner; immediate reinforcement; and self-pacing are emphasized.

propaganda techniques Techniques of writing used to influence people's thinking and actions, including bandwagon technique, card stacking, glittering generalities, name calling, plain folks talk, testimonials, and transfer techniques.

rating scale A device for recording estimates of the levels of student functioning.

readability The difficulty of written material.

readability level The level of difficulty of written material.

readers' theater Reading aloud from scripts in a dramatic style.

reading and writing workshops Instructional procedures consisting of a minilesson, a status-of-the-class report, reading or writing, and sharing.

reading miscue inventory An informal instrument that considers both the quality and quantity of miscues made by the reader.

reading rate Speed of reading, often reported in words per minute.

reading/study techniques Techniques designed to enhance comprehension and retention of written material.

reciprocal teaching A technique to develop comprehension and metacognition in which the teacher and students take turns being "teacher." They predict, generate questions, summarize, and clarify ideas.

reinforcement A reward or a positive consequence that makes a behavior more likely to be repeated or a negative consequence that makes a behavior less likely to be repeated.

reliability The extent to which an assessment tool measures a consistent score with multiple applications of the same assessment tool.

retelling A student's recounting of a story or other material that he or she has read or heard.

relative clauses Clauses that refer to an antecedent (may be restrictive or nonrestrictive).

rubric A set of criteria used to describe and evaluate a student's level of proficiency in a particular subject area.

running record A record of word recognition miscues during a student's oral reading.

scaffolding Offering support through modeling or feedback, and then withdrawing support gradually as the learner gains competence.

scale (of a map) The part of a map showing the relationship of a given distance on a map to the same distance on the area represented.

schema A preexisting knowledge structure developed about a thing, place, or idea. Plural: schemata.

self-concept An individual's perception of himself or herself as a person, his or her abilities, appearance, performance, and so on.

semantic clues (or cues) Meaning clues.

semantic feature analysis A technique in which the presence or absence of particular features in the meaning of a word is indicated through symbols on a chart, allowing comparisons of word meanings.

semantic maps Graphic representations of relationships among words and phrases in written material.

semantic webbing Making a graphic representation of relationships in written material through the use of a core question, strands (answers), strand supports (facts and inferences from the story), and strand ties (relationships of the strands to each other).

sight words Words that are recognized immediately, without having to resort to analysis.

simile A comparison using *like* or *as*.

SQRQCQ A study method consisting of six steps: Survey, Question, Read, Question, Compute, Question.

SQ3R A study method consisting of five steps: Survey, Question, Read, Recite, Review

story grammar A set of rules that define story structures.

story mapping Making graphic representations of stories that make clear the specific relationships of story elements.

structural analysis Analysis of words by identifying prefixes, suffixes, root words, inflectional endings, contractions, word combinations forming compound words, and syllabication.

study guides Duplicated sheets prepared by the teacher and distributed to the students to help guide reading in content fields and alleviate some difficulties that interfere with understanding.

subskill theories of reading Theories that depict reading as a set of subskills that children must master and integrate.

Sustained Silent Reading (SSR) A program for setting aside a certain period of time daily for silent reading without interruption.

syllable A letter or group of letters that forms a pronunciation unit.

synonyms Groups of words that have the same, or very similar, meanings.

syntactic clues (or cues) Clues derived from the word order in sentences.

tactile Pertaining to the sense of touch.

tall tales Humorous folktales displaying a great deal of exaggeration.

text-based processing Trying to extract the information that resides in the text.

text leveling The categorization of books on a continuum based on a set of criteria that may include readability, genre, interest, format, links across the curriculum, or other characteristics.

thematic unit An integrated learning experience with a topic or concept that is the core of the curriculum for an extended period of time.

think-alouds Verbalizing aloud the thought processes present as one reads a selection orally.

top-down models of reading Models that depict reading as beginning with the generation of hypotheses or predictions about the material by the reader.

topic sentence A sentence that sets forth the central thought of the paragraph in which it occurs.

trade book A book marketed to the general public.

traditional literature (folklore) A literary genre of stories, without identified authors, which are passed from generation to generation through oral narration.

transactive theories of reading Theories based on Rosenblatt's idea that every reading act is a transaction that involves a reader and a text and occurs at a particular time in a specific context, with meaning coming into being during the transaction between the reader and the text.

validity The extent to which an assessment tool measures what it was designed to measure.

vicarious experiences Indirect experiences.

videoconferencing The holding of conferences over the Internet with others who can be seen on their computer monitors and heard through the speakers.

visual acuity Sharpness of vision.

visual discrimination Ability to differentiate between different shapes.

visual impairment A condition described as partially sighted but able to read print.

visualization Picturing events, places, and people described by the author.

webbing A technique that graphically connects a central topic or theme to related ideas.

WebQuests Inquiry-based Internet activities that assign students to collect, analyze and apply information from the Internet related to the topic of the quest.

word bank A collection of sight words that have been mastered by an individual student, usually recorded on index cards.

word-processing software Computer software designed to allow entry, manipulation, and storage of text (and sometimes images).

word webs Graphic representations of the relationships among words that are constructed by connecting the related terms with lines.

word sorts Categorization activities involving classifying words into categories.

World Wide Web (WWW) A part of the Internet that allows users to choose special words or symbols with a mouse click or keyboard stroke and be automatically connected to related Web locations.

writing process A procedure for writing consisting of prewriting, drafting, revising, editing, and publishing.

REFERENCES

Aaron, Ira E., Jeanne S. Chall, Dolores Durkin, Kenneth Goodman, and Dorothy Strickland. "The Past, Present, and Future of Literacy Education: Comments from a Panel of Distinguished Educators, Part II." *The Reading Teacher,* 43 (February 1990), 370–380.

Adams, Marilyn Jager. *Beginning to Read: Thinking and Learning about Print.* Cambridge, Mass.: MIT Press, 1990.

Adams, Marilyn Jager. "Modeling the Connections Between Word Recognition and Reading." In *Theoretical Models and Processes of Reading,* 4th ed., edited by Robert B. Ruddell, Martha Rapp Ruddell, and Harry Singer. Newark, Del.: International Reading Association, 1994, 838–863.

Adams, Marilyn Jager, et al. "Beginning to Read: A Critique by Literacy Professionals and a Response by Marilyn Jager Adams." *The Reading Teacher,* 44 (February 1991), 370–395.

Adams, Thomasenia Lott. "Reading Mathematics: More Than Words Can Say." *The Reading Teacher*, 56 (May 2003), 786–794.

Agnew, William J., ed. *Standards Based Language Arts Curriculum.* Boston: Allyn and Bacon, 2000.

Airasian, Peter W., and Mary E. Walsh. "Constructivist Cautions." *Phi Delta Kappan,* 78 (February 1997), 444–449.

Allen, Linda. "An Integrated Strategies Approach: Making Word Identification Instruction Work for Beginning Readers." *The Reading Teacher,* 52 (November 1998), 254–268.

Allington, Richard L. "What I've Learned About Effective Reading Instruction From a Decade of Studying Exemplary Elementary Classroom Teachers." *Phi Delta Kappan,* 83 (June 2002), 740–747.

Anderson, Barry D., Scott McDonald, and Christina Sinnemann. "Can Measurement of Results Help Improve the Performance of Schools?" *Phi Delta Kappan*, 85 (June 2004), 735–739.

Anderson, C., J. Mason, and L. Shirey. *The Reading Group: An Experimental Investigation of a Labyrinth.* Technical Report No. 271. Urbana-Champaign, Ill.: Center for the Study of Reading, University of Illinois, 1983.

Anderson, Nancy A. "Teaching Reading as a Life Skill." *The Reading Teacher,* 42 (October 1988), 92.

Anderson, Richard C., Elfrieda H. Hiebert, Judith A. Scott, and Ian A. G. Wilkinson. *Becoming a Nation of Readers: The Report of the Commission on Reading.* Washington, D.C.: National Institute of Education, 1985.

Anderson, Richard C., and William E. Nagy. "Word Meanings." In *Handbook of Reading Research,* Vol. II, edited by Rebecca Barr, Michael L. Kamil, Peter Mosenthal, and P. David Pearson. New York: Longman, 1991, 690–724.

Anderson-Inman, Lynne. "Electronic Text: Literacy Medium of the Future." *Journal of Adolescent &Adult Literacy,* 41 (May 1998), 678–682.

Andrade, Heidi G. "Using Rubrics to Promote Thinking and Learning." *Educational Leadership,* 57, no. 5 (February 2000), 13–18.

Ankney, Paul, and Pat McClurg. "Testing Manzo's Guided Reading Procedure." *The Reading Teacher,* 34 (March 1981), 681–685.

Armbruster, Bonnie B. "On Answering Questions." *The Reading Teacher,* 45 (May 1992), 724–725.

Armbruster, Bonnie B. "Science and Reading." *The Reading Teacher,* 46 (December 1992/January 1993), 346–347.

Armbruster, Bonnie B., and William E. Nagy. "Vocabulary in Content Area Lessons." *The Reading Teacher*, 45 (March 1992), 550–551.

Armitage, Rita. "The Press to Test." *The Reading Teacher*, 53 (April 2000), 596–597.

Armstrong, Thomas. *Multiple Intelligences in the Classroom.* Alexandria, Va.: Association for Supervision and Curriculum Development, 1994.

Ashby-Davis, Claire. "Improving Students' Comprehension of Character Development in Plays." *Reading Horizons,* 26, no. 4 (1986), 256–261.

Ashton-Warner, Sylvia. *Teacher.* New York: Simon & Schuster, 1963.

Atwell, Nancie. *In the Middle: Writing, Reading, and Learning with Adolescents.* Upper Montclair, N.J.: Boynton/Cook, 1987.

Atwell, Nancie. "Writing and Reading from the Inside Out." In *Breaking Ground: Teachers Relate Reading and Writing in the Elementary School,* edited by Jane Hansen, Thomas Newkirk, and Donald Graves. Portsmouth, N.H.: Heinemann, 1985.

Au, Kathryn. *Literacy Instruction in Multicultural Settings.* Fort Worth: Harcourt Brace, 1993.

Au, Kathryn H. "Constructing the Theme of a Story." *Language Arts,* 69 (February 1992), 106–111.

Au, Kathryn H. "An Overview of New Concepts of Assessment: Impact on Decision Making and Instruction." Paper presented at the International Reading Association Convention, Atlanta, May 6, 1990.

Avery, Charles W., and Beth Faris Avery. "Merging Reading and Cooperative Strategies Through Graphic Organizers." *Journal of Reading,* 37 (May 1994), 689–690.

Babbs, Patricia J., and Alden J. Moe. "Metacognition: A Key for Independent Learning from Text." *The Reading Teacher,* 36 (January 1983), 422–426.

Bagford, Jack. "What Ever Happened to Individualized Reading?" *The Reading Teacher,* 39 (November 1985), 190–193.

Baker, Marianne. "Reading Resistance in Middle School: What Can Be Done?" *Journal of Adolescent & Adult Literacy,* 45 (February 2002), 364–366.

Barnitz, John G. "Developing Sentence Comprehension in Reading." *Language Arts,* 56 (November/December 1979), 902–908, 958.

Barone, Tom, Maryann Eeds, and Kathleen Mason. "Literature, the Disciplines, and the Lives of Elementary School Children." *Language Arts,* 72 (January 1995), 30–38.

Baroni, Dick. "Have Primary Children Draw to Expand Vocabulary." *The Reading Teacher,* 40 (April 1987), 819–820.

Barrentine, Shelby. "Engaging with Reading Through Interactive Read-Alouds." *The Reading Teacher,* 50 (September 1996), 36–43.

Barta, Jim, and Martha Crouthers Grindler. "Exploring Bias Using Multicultural Literature for Children." *The Reading Teacher,* 50 (November 1996), 269–270.

Barton, James. "Interpreting Character Emotions for Literature Comprehension." *Journal of Adolescent and Adult Literacy,* 40 (September 1996), 22–28.

Barton, James, and Donna M. Sawyer. "Our Students *Are* Ready for This: Comprehension Instruction in the Elementary School." *The Reading Teacher,* 57 (December 2003/January 2004), 334–347.

Barton, Keith C., and Lynne A. Smith. "Themes or Motifs? Aiming for Coherence Through Interdisciplinary Outlines." *The Reading Teacher*, 54 (September 2000), 54–63.

Basden, Jonathan C. "Authentic Tasks as the Basis for Multimedia Design Curriculum." *T.H.E Journal,* 29 (November 2001), 16–21.

Baskwill, Jane, and Paulette Whitman. *Evaluation: Whole Language, Whole Child.* Toronto: Scholastic, 1988.

Batzle, Janine. *Portfolio Assessment and Evaluation.* Cypress, Calif.: Creative Teaching Press, 1992.

Baumann, James F., Helene Hooten, and Patricia White. "Teaching Comprehension Through Literature: A Teacher-Research Project to Develop Fifth Graders' Reading Strategies and Motivation." *The Reading Teacher,* 53 (September 1999), 38–51.

Baumann, James F., Leah A. Jones, and Nancy Seifert-Kessell. "Using Think-Alouds to Enhance Children's Comprehension Monitoring Abilities." *The Reading Teacher,* 47 (November 1993), 184–193.

Baumann, James F., and Maribeth C. Schmitt. "The What, Why, How, and When of Comprehension Instruction." *The Reading Teacher,* 39 (March 1986), 640–646.

Beach, R., and S. Hynds. "Research on Response to Literature." In *Handbook of Reading Research, Vol. II,* edited by R. Barr, M.L. Kamil, P. Mosenthal, and P.D. Pearson. New York: Longman, 1991, 453–489.

Bean, Thomas W. "Reading in the Content Areas: Social Constructivist Dimensions." In *Handbook of Reading Research: Volume 3,* edited by Michael L. Kamil, Peter B. Mosenthal, P. David Pearson, and Rebecca Barr. Mahwah, N.J.: Lawrence Erlbaum, 2000, 629–644.

Beck, Isabel L. "Reading and Reasoning." *The Reading Teacher,* 42 (May 1989), 676–682.

Beck, Isabel L., and Margaret G. McKeown. "Research Directions: Social Studies Texts Are Hard to Understand: Mediating Some of the Difficulties." *Language Arts,* 68 (October 1991a), 482–490.

Beck, Isabel L., and Margaret McKeown. "Conditions of Vocabulary Acquisition." In *Handbook of Reading Research,* Vol. II, edited by Rebecca Barr, Michael L. Kamil, Peter Mosenthal, and P. David Pearson. New York: Longman, 1991b, 789–814.

Beck, Isabel L., and Margaret G. McKeown. "Learning Words Well—A Program to Enhance Vocabulary and Comprehension." *The Reading Teacher,* 36 (March 1983), 622–625.

Beck, I. L., C. A. Perfetti, and M. G. McKeown. "Effects of Long-Term Vocabulary Instruction on Lexical Access and Reading Comprehension." *Journal of Educational Psychology,* 74 (1982), 506–521.

Bell, Barbara. "Literature Response Groups." Paper presented at the Richard C. Owen Workshop "Whole Language in the Classroom." Oak Ridge, Tenn., June 12, 1990.

Bellows, Barbara Plotkin. "Running Shoes Are to Jogging as Analogies Are to Creative/Critical Thinking." *Journal of Reading,* 23 (March 1980), 507–511.

Berger, Linda R. "Reader Response Journals: You Make the Meaning . . . and How." *Journal of Adolescent & Adult Literacy,* 39 (February 1996), 380–385.

Bergeron, Bette S. "Seeking Authenticity: What Is 'Real' About Thematic Literacy Instruction." *The Reading Teacher,* 49 (April 1996), 544–551.

Bernhardt, Bill. "Reading and Writing Between the Lines: An Interactive Approach Using Computers." *Journal of Reading,* 37 (March 1994), 458–463.

Bidwell, Sandra M. "Ideas for Using Drama to Enhance Reading Instruction." *The Reading Teacher,* 45 (April 1992), 653–654.

Bigelow, Bill. "On the Road to Cultural Bias: A Critique of *The Oregon Trail* CD-ROM." *Language Arts,* 74 (1997), 84–93.

Blachowicz, Camille L. Z. "Making Connections: Alternatives to the Vocabulary Notebook." *Journal of Reading,* 29 (April 1986), 643–649.

Blachowicz, Camille L. Z. "Showing Teachers How to Develop Students' Predictive Reading." *The Reading Teacher,* 36 (March 1983), 680–683.

Blachowicz, Camille L. Z. "Vocabulary Development and Reading: From Research to Instruction." *The Reading Teacher,* 38 (May 1985), 876–881.

Blachowicz, Camille L. Z., and Barbara Zabroske. "Context Instruction: A Metacognitive Approach for At-Risk Readers." *Journal of Reading,* 33 (April 1990), 504–508.

Blachowicz, Camille L. Z., and John J. Lee. "Vocabulary Development in the Whole Literacy Classroom." *The Reading Teacher,* 45 (November 1991), 188–195.

Blanton, William E., Gary B. Moorman, and Karen D. Wood. "A Model of Direct Instruction Applied to the Basal Skills Lesson." *The Reading Teacher,* 40 (December 1986), 299–304.

Blanton, William E., Karen D. Wood, and Gary B. Moorman. "The Role of Purpose in Reading Instruction." *The Reading Teacher,* 43 (March 1990), 486–493.

Bluestein, N. Alexandra. "Comprehension through Characterization: Enabling Readers to Make Personal Connections with Literature," *The Reading Teacher* 55 (February 2002), 431–434.

Boodt, Gloria M. "Critical Listeners Become Critical Readers in Remedial Reading Class." *The Reading Teacher,* 37 (January 1984), 390–394.

Borkowski, J.G., and B.E. Kurtz. "Metacognition and Executive Control." *Cognition in Special Children: Comparative Approaches to Retardation, Learning Disabilities, and Giftedness,* edited by J. G. Borkowski and J. D. Day. Norwood, N. J.: Ablex, 1987, 123–152.

Bormuth, J. R. "The Cloze Readability Procedure." In *Readability in 1968,* edited by J. R. Bormuth. Champaign, Ill.: National Council of Teachers of English, 1968.

Brabham, Edna Greene, and Susan Kidd Villaume. "Continuing Conversations About Literature Circles." *The Reading Teacher,* 54 (November 2000), 278–280.

Brabham, Edna Greene, and Susan Kidd Villaume. "Vocabulary Instruction: Concerns and Visions." *The Reading Teacher,* 56 (November 2002), 264–268.

Bransford, John D., and Barry S. Stein. *The IDEAL Problem Solver.* New York: W. H. Freeman, 1984.

Braselton, Stephania, and Barbara C. Decker. "Using Graphic Organizers to Improve the Reading of Mathematics." *The Reading Teacher,* 48 (November 1994), 276–281.

Breen, Leonard. "Connotations." *Journal of Reading,* 32 (February 1989), 461.

Brimijoin, Kay, Ede Marquissee, and Carol Ann Tomlinson. "Using Data to Differentiate Instruction." *Educational Leadership,* 60 (February 2003), 70–73.

Bristow, Page Simpson. "Are Poor Readers Passive Readers? Some Evidence, Possible Explanations, and Potential Solutions." *The Reading Teacher,* 39 (December 1985), 318–325.

Bromley, Karen D. "Buddy Journals Make the Reading-Writing Connection." *The Reading Teacher,* 43 (November 1989), 122–129.

Bromley, Karen D'Angelo. "Teaching Idioms." *The Reading Teacher,* 38 (December 1984), 272–276.

Brown, A. L., and J. D. Day. "Macrorules for Summarizing Texts: The Development of Expertise." *Journal of Verbal Learning and Verbal Behavior,* 22, no. 1 (1983), 1–14.

Brown, A. L., J. D. Day, and R. Jones. "The Development of Plans for Summarizing Texts." *Child Development,* 54 (1983), 968–979.

Burns, Paul C., Betty D. Roe, and Elinor P. Ross. *Word Recognition and Meaning Vocabulary: A Literacy Skills Primer.* Boston: Houghton Mifflin, 1999.

Busching, Beverly A., and Betty Ann Slesinger. "Authentic Questions: What Do They Look Like? Where Do They Lead?" *Language Arts,* 72 (September 1995), 341–351.

Buss, Kathleen, and Lee Karnowski. *Reading and Writing Literary Genres.* Newark, Del.: International Reading Association, 2000.

Butler, Andrea, and Jan Turbill. *Towards a Reading-Writing Classroom.* Portsmouth, N.H.: Heinemann, 1987.

Cadiero-Kaplan, Karen. "Literacy Ideologies: Critically Engaging the Language Arts Curriculum," *Language Arts,* 79 (May 2002), 372–381.

Cairney, T. *Teaching Reading Comprehension.* Milton Keynes, U.K.: Open University Press, 1990.

Cambourne, Brian. "Why Do Some Students Fail to Learn to Read? Ockham's Razor and the Conditions of Learning." *The Reading Teacher,* 54 (May 2001), 784–786.

Camp, Deanne. "It Takes Two: Teaching with Twin Texts of Fact and Fiction." *The Reading Teacher,* 53 (February 2000), 400–408.

Carney, J. J., D. Anderson, C. Blackburn, and D. Blessing. "Preteaching Vocabulary and the Comprehension of Social Studies Materials by Elementary School Children." *Social Education,* 48 (1984), 71–75.

Carr, Eileen, and Karen K. Wixson. "Guidelines for Evaluating Vocabulary Instruction." *Journal of Reading,* 29 (April 1986), 588–595.

Carr, Kathryn S., Dawna L. Buchanan, Joanna B. Wentz, Mary L. Weiss, and Kitty J. Brant. "Not Just for the Primary Grades: A Bibliography of Picture Books for Secondary Content Teachers." *Journal of Adolescent & Adult Literacy,* 45 (October 2001), 146–153.

Carroll, John B., Peter Davies, and Barry Richman. *The American Heritage Word Frequency Book.* Boston: Houghton Mifflin, 1971.

Casteel, Carolyn P., and Bess A. Isom. "Reciprocal Processes in Science and Literacy Learning." *The Reading Teacher,* 47 (April 1994), 538–545.

Ceprano, Maria A. "A Review of Selected Research on Methods of Teaching Sight Words." *The Reading Teacher,* 35 (December 1981), 314–322.

Cerullo, Mary. *Reading the Environment: Children's Literature in the Science Curriculum.* Portsmouth, N.H.: Heinemann, 1997.

Chamberlain, Julia, and Dorothy Leal. "Caldecott Medal Books and Readability Levels: Not Just 'Picture' Books." *The Reading Teacher,* 52 (May 1999), 898–902.

Chaney, Jeanne H. "Alphabet Books: Resources for Learning." *The Reading Teacher,* 47 (October 1993), 96–104.

Cheng, Pui-wan. "Metacognition and Giftedness: The State of the Relationship." *Gifted Child Quarterly,* 37 (Summer 1993), 105–112.

Clay, Marie. *The Early Detection of Reading Difficulties.* Auckland, New Zealand: Heinemann, 1979.

Clemmons, Joan, and Lois Laase. *Language Arts Mini-Lessons.* New York: Scholastic, 1995.

Coelho, Elizabeth. *Learning Together in the Multicultural Classroom.* Markham, Ontario: Pippin, 1994.

Cohen, Ruth. "Self-Generated Questions as an Aid to Reading Comprehension." *The Reading Teacher,* 36 (April 1983), 770–775.

Coiro, Julie. "Reading Comprehension on the Internet: Expanding Our Understanding of Reading Comprehension to Encompass New Literacies." *The Reading Teacher,* 56 (February 2003), 458–464.

Cole, Ardith Davis. "Beginner-Oriented Texts in Literature-Based Classrooms: The Segue for a Few Struggling Readers." *The Reading Teacher,* 51 (March 1998), 488–501.

Collard, Sneed B., III. "Using Science Books to Teach Literacy—and Save the Planet." *The Reading Teacher*, 57 (November 2003), 280–283.

Combs, Martha, and John D. Beach. "Stories and Storytelling: Personalizing the Social Studies." *The Reading Teacher,* 47 (March 1994), 464–471.

Commeyras, M. "Were Janell and Neesie in the Same Classroom? Children's Questions as the First Order of Reality in Storybook Discussion." *Language Arts,* 71 (1994), 517–523.

Commeyras, Michelle. "Using Literature to Teach Critical Thinking." *Journal of Reading,* 32 (May 1989), 703–707.

Conrad, Lori L. "Charting Effect and Cause in Informational Books." *The Reading Teacher,* 42 (February 1989), 451–452.

Cooney, S. Leading the Way: State Actions to Improve Student Achievement in the Middle Grades. Atlanta: Southern Regional Education Board, 1999.

Cooper, Charles R., and Anthony R. Petrosky. "A Psycholinguistic View of the Fluent Reading Process." *Journal of Reading,* 20 (December 1976), 184–207.

Copes, L. "Teaching What Mathematicians Do." In *The Teacher Educator's Handbook: Building a Knowledge Base for the Preparation of Teachers,* edited by R. B. Murray. New York: Cambridge University Press, 1996, 261–276.

Cornett, Claudia E. "Beyond Retelling the Plot: Student-led Discussions." *The Reading Teacher,* 50 (March 1997), 527–528.

Cotton, Eileen Giuffre. *The Online Classroom: Teaching with the Internet.* Bloomington, Ind.: ERIC Clearinghouse on Reading, English, and Communication, 1996.

Cowan, Hilary. "Software At-a-Glance: New and Hot!: *Classroom Publisher.*" *Electronic Learning,* 15 (May–June 1996), 61–62.

Cox, Carole. "Literature-Based Teaching: A Student Response–Centered Curriculum." In *Reader Response in Elementary Classrooms,* edited by Nicholas Karolides. Mahwah, N.J.: Erlbaum, 1997.

Cox, Carole, and Joyce Many. "Toward an Understanding of the Aesthetic Response to Literature." *Language Arts,* 69 (January 1992), 28–33.

Cox, Carole, and Paul Boyd-Batstone. *Crossroads.* Upper Saddle River, N.J.: Merrill, 1997.

Cox, Susan, and Lee Galda. "Multicultural Literature: Mirrors and Windows on a Global Community." *The Reading Teacher,* 43 (April 1990), 582–589.

Cudd, Evelyn T., and Leslie L. Roberts. "A Scaffolding Technique to Develop Sentence Sense and Vocabulary." *The Reading Teacher*, 47 (December 1993/January 1994), 346–349.

Cudd, Evelyn T., and Leslie Roberts. "Using Writing to Enhance Content Area Learning in the Primary Grades." *The Reading Teacher,* 42 (February 1989), 392–404.

Cullinan, Bernice E. "Whole Language and Children's Literature." *Language Arts,* 69 (October 1992), 426–430.

Cullinan, Bernice E., and Lee Galda. *Literature and the Child,* 3d ed. Fort Worth, Tex.: Harcourt Brace, 1994.

Cunningham, James W., and Hunter Ballew. "Solving Word Problem Solving." *The Reading Teacher,* 36 (April 1983), 836–839.

Cunningham, James W., and Lisa K. Wall. "Teaching Good Readers to Comprehend Better." *Journal of Reading,* 37 (March 1994), 480–486.

Cunningham, Patricia M., and James W. Cunningham. "Content Area Reading-Writing Lessons." *The Reading Teacher,* 40 (February 1987), 506–512.

Daisey, Peggy. "Three Ways to Promote the Values and Uses of Literacy at Any Age." *Journal of Reading,* 36 (March 1993), 436–440.

Dale, Edgar, and Jeanne S. Chall. "A Formula for Predicting Readability." *Educational Research Bulletin,* 27 (January 21, 1948), 11–20, 28; (February 18, 1948), 37–54.

Dale, Edgar, and Jeanne S. Chall. *Manual for Use of the New Dale-Chall Readability Formula.* Newton Upper Falls, Mass.: Brookline Books, 1995.

Daneman, Meredyth. "Individual Differences in Reading Skills." In *Handbook of Reading Research*, Vol. II, edited by R. Barr, M. L. Kamil, P. Mosenthal, and P. D. Pearson. New York: Longman, 1991, pp. 512–538.

Danielson, Charlotte, and Leslye Abrutyn. *An Introduction to Using Portfolios in the Classroom.* Alexandria, Va.: Association for Supervision and Curriculum Development, 1997.

Danielson, Kathy Everts. "Picture Books to Use with Older Students." *Journal of Reading,* 35 (May 1992), 652–654.

Davis, Anita P., and Thomas R. McDaniel. "An Essential Vocabulary: An Update." *The Reading Teacher,* 52 (November 1998), 308–309.

Davis, Susan J. "Synonym Rally: A Vocabulary Concept Game." *Journal of Reading,* 33 (February 1990), 380.

Davis, Zephaniah T., and Michael D. McPherson. "Story Map Instruction: A Road Map for Reading Comprehension." *The Reading Teacher,* 43 (December 1989), 232–240.

Deaton, Cheryl D. "Idioms As a Means of Communication: Writing in the Middle Grades." *The Reading Teacher,* 45 (February 1992), 473.

DeSerres, Barbara. "Putting Vocabulary in Context." *The Reading Teacher,* 43 (April 1990), 612–613.

Dever, Christine T. "Press Conference: A Strategy for Integrating Reading with Writing." *The Reading Teacher,* 46 (September 1992), 72–73.

Diamond, Barbara, and Margaret Moore. *Multicultural Literacy.* White Plains, N.Y.: Longman, 1995.

Dixon-Krauss, Lisbeth. "Using Literature as a Context for Teaching Vocabulary." *Journal of Adolescent & Adult Literacy*, 45 (December 2001/January 2002), 310–318.

Doda, Nancy M. and Sue C. Thompson. *Transforming Ourselves, Transforming Schools: Middle School Change.* Westerville, Ohio: National Middle School Association, 2002.

Dodge, Bernie. "Some Thoughts About WebQuests." (May 5, 1997). Available at http://edweb.sdsu.edu/courses/edtec596/ about_webquests.html.

Dodge, Bernie. "WebQuests: A Strategy for Scaffolding Higher Level Learning." (1998). Available at http://edweb.sdsu.edu/webquest/necc98.htm.

Doiron, Ray. "Using Nonfiction in a Read-Aloud Program: Letting the Facts Speak for Themselves." *The Reading Teacher,* 47 (May 1994), 616–624.

Dowd, Cornelia A., and Richard Sinatra. "Computer Programs and the Learning of Text Structure." *Journal of Reading,* 34 (October 1990), 104–112.

Dowhower, Sarah L. "Supporting a Strategic Stance in the Classroom: A Comprehension Framework for Helping Teachers Help Students to Be Strategic." *The Reading Teacher,* 52 (April 1999), 672–688.

Downing, John. "Reading—Skill or Skills?" *The Reading Teacher*, 35 (February 1982), 534–537.

Draper, Roni Jo. "School Mathematics Reform, Constructivism, and Literacy: A Case for Literacy Instruction in the Reform-Oriented Math Classroom." *Journal of Adolescent & Adult Literacy*, 45 (March 2002), 520–529.

Dreher, Mariam Jean. "Motivating Children to Read More Nonfiction." *The Reading Teacher,* 52 (December 1998/January 1999), 414–416.

Dreher, Mariam Jean, and Harry Singer. "Story Grammar Instruction Unnecessary for Intermediate Grade Students." *The Reading Teacher*, 34 (December 1980), 261–268.

Drucker, Mary J. "What Reading Teachers Should Know About ESL Learners." *The Reading Teacher,* 57 (September 2003), 22–29.

Duchein, M. A., and D. L. Mealey. "Remembrance of Books Past . . . Long Past: Glimpses into Aliteracy." *Reading Research and Instruction,* 33, no. 1 (1993), 12–28.

Duffelmeyer, Frederick A. "Effective Anticipation Guide Statements for Learning from Expository Prose." *Journal of Reading,* 37 (March 1994), 452–457.

Duffelmeyer, Frederick A. "The Influence of Experience-Based Vocabulary Instruction on Learning Word Meanings." *Journal of Reading,* 24 (October 1980), 35–40.

Duffelmeyer, Frederick A. "Introducing Words in Context." *The Reading Teacher,* 35 (March 1982), 724–725.

Duffelmeyer, Frederick A. "Teaching Word Meaning from an Experience Base." *The Reading Teacher,* 39 (October 1985), 6–9.

Duffelmeyer, Frederick A., and Barbara Blakely Duffelmeyer. "Developing Vocabulary Through Dramatization." *Journal of Reading,* 23 (November 1979), 141–143.

Duffelmeyer, Frederick A., and Dale D. Baum. "The Extended Anticipation Guide Revisited." *Journal of Reading,* 35 (May 1992), 654–656.

Duffy, Gerald G., and James V. Hoffman. "In Pursuit of an Illusion: The Flawed Search for a Perfect Method." *The Reading Teacher,* 53 (September 1999), 10–16.

Duffy, Gerald G., Laura R. Roehler, and Beth Ann Herrmann. "Modeling Mental Processes Helps Poor Readers Become Strategic Readers." *The Reading Teacher,* 41 (April 1988), 762–767.

Dugan, Jo Ann. "Transactional Literature Discussions: Engaging Students in the Appreciation and Understanding of Literature." *The Reading Teacher,* 51 (October 1997), 86–96.

Duke, Nell K., and P. David Pearson. "Effective Practices for Developing Reading Comprehension." In Alan E. Farstrup and S. Jay Samuels, eds. *What Research Has to Say About Reading Instruction.* Newark, Delaware: International Reading Assosiation, 2002, 205–242.

Duncan, Patricia H. "I Liked the Book Better: Comparing Film and Text to Build Critical Comprehension." *The Reading Teacher,* 46 (May 1993), 720–725.

Durkin, Dolores. "What Classroom Observations Reveal about Reading Comprehension Instruction." *Reading Research Quarterly,* 14 (1978/1979), 481–533.

Durkin, Dolores. "What Is the Value of the New Interest in Reading Comprehension?" *Language Arts,* 58 (January 1981), 23–43.

Dwyer, Edward J. "Solving Verbal Analogies." *Journal of Reading,* 32 (October 1988), 73–75.

Dymock, Susan. "Reading But Not Understanding." *Journal of Reading,* 37 (October 1993), 86–91.

Eads, Maryann. "What to Do When They Don't Understand What They Read—Research-Based Strategies for Teaching Reading Comprehension." *The Reading Teacher,* 34 (February 1981), 565–571.

Ebbers, Margaretha. "Science Text Sets: Using Various Genres to Promote Literacy and Inquiry." *Language Arts,* 80 (September 2002), 40–50.

Eby, Judy. *Reflective Planning, Teaching, and Evaluation K–12,* 2d ed. Upper Saddle River, N.J.: Merrill, 1998.

Edwards, Anthony T., and R. Allan Dermott. "A New Way with Vocabulary." *Journal of Reading,* 32 (March 1989), 559–561.

Eken, Ali Nihat. "The Third Eye." *Journal of Adolescent & Adult Literacy,* 46 (November 2002), 220–230.

El-Hindi, Amelia E. "Beyond Classroom Boundaries: Constructionist Teaching with the Internet." *The Reading Teacher,* 51 (May 1998), 694–700.

El-Hindi, Amelia E. "Integrating Literacy and Science in the Classroom: From Ecomysteries to Readers Theatre." *The Reading Teacher,* 56 (March 2003), 536–538.

Emery, Donna W. "Helping Readers Comprehend Stories from the Characters' Perspectives." *The Reading Teacher,* 49 (April 1996), 534–541.

Englot-Mash, Christine. "Tying Together Reading Strategies." *Journal of Reading,* 35 (October 1991), 150–151.

Farr, Roger, and Robert F. Carey. *Reading: What Can Be Measured?* 2d ed. Newark, Del.: International Reading Association, 1986.

Farrar, Mary Thomas. "Asking Better Questions." *The Reading Teacher,* 38 (October 1984a), 10–15.

Farrar, Mary Thomas. "Why Do We Ask Comprehension Questions? A New Conception of Comprehension Instruction." *The Reading Teacher,* 37 (February 1984b), 452–456.

Farris, Pamela J., and Carol J. Fuhler. "Developing Social Studies Concepts Through Picture Books." *The Reading Teacher,* 47 (February 1994), 380–387.

Fawson, Parker C., and D. Ray Reutzel. "But I Only Have a Basal: Implementing Guided Reading in the Early Grades." *The Reading Teacher,* 54 (September 2000), 84–97.

Fay, Leo. "Reading Study Skills: Math and Science." In *Reading and Inquiry,* edited by J. Allen Figurel. Newark, Del.: International Reading Association, 1965.

Felber, Sheila. "Story Mapping for Primary Students." *The Reading Teacher,* 43 (October 1989), 90–91.

Fennessey, Sharon. "Living History Through Drama and Literature." *The Reading Teacher,* 49 (September 1995), 16–19.

Ferguson, Anne M., and Jo Fairburn. "Language Experience for Problem Solving in Mathematics." *The Reading Teacher,* 38 (February 1985), 504–507.

Fiderer, Adele. *Practical Assessments.* New York: Scholastic, 1995.

Fielding, L. G., R. C. Anderson, and P. D. Pearson. *How Discussion Questions Influence Story Understanding* (Tech. Rep. No. 490). Urbana-Champaign, Ill.: University of Illinois, Center for the Study of Reading, January 1990.

Fischer, Cynthia. "Revisiting the Reader's Rudder: A Comprehension Strategy." *Journal of Adolescent & Adult Literacy,* 47 (November 2003), 248–256.

Fisette, Dolores. "Practical Authentic Assessment: Good Kid Watchers Know What to Teach Next." *The California Reader,* 26 (Summer 1993), 4–7.

Fisk, Candace, and Beth Hurst. "Paraphrasing for Comprehension." *The Reading Teacher,* 57 (October 2003), 182–183.

Fitzgerald, Jill. "Enhancing Two Related Thought Processes: Revision in Writing and Critical Reading." *The Reading Teacher,* 43 (October 1989a), 42–48.

Fitzgerald, Jill. "Helping Readers Gain Self-Control over Reading Comprehension." *The Reading Teacher,* 37 (December 1983), 249–253.

Fitzgerald, Jill. "Research on Stories: Implications for Teachers." In *Children's Comprehension of Text: Research into Practice,* edited by K. Denise Muth. Newark, Del.: International Reading Association, 1989b.

Flippo, Rona. *Reading Assessment and Instruction: A Qualitative Approach to Diagnosis.* Fort Worth, Tex.: Harcourt Brace, 1997.

Flitterman-King, Sharon. "The Role of the Response Journal in Active Reading." *Quarterly of the National Writing Project and the Center for the Study of Writing,* 10, no. 3 (1988), 4–11.

Flood, James, and Diane Lapp. "Conceptual Mapping Strategies for Understanding Information Texts." *The Reading Teacher,* 41 (April 1988), 780–783.

Flood, James, and Diane Lapp. "Reading and Writing Relations: Assumptions and Directions." In *The Dynamics of Language Learning,* edited by James R. Squire. Urbana, Ill.: ERIC Clearinghouse on Reading and Communication Skills, 1987.

Flynn, Linda L. "Developing Critical Reading Skills Through Cooperative Problem Solving." *The Reading Teacher,* 42 (May 1989), 664–668.

Flynn, Rosalind M., and Gail A. Carr. "Exploring Classroom Literature Through Drama: A Specialist and a Teacher Collaborate." *Language Arts,* 71 (January 1994), 38–43.

Ford, Michael, and Marilyn Ohlhausen. "Tips from Reading Clinicians for Coping with Disabled Readers in Regular Classrooms." *The Reading Teacher,* 42 (October 1988), 18–23.

Forell, Elizabeth. "The Case for Conservative Reader Placement." *The Reading Teacher,* 38 (May 1985), 857–862.

Fortescue, Chelsea M. "Using Oral and Written Language to Increase Understanding of Math Concepts." *Language Arts,* 71 (December 1994), 576–580.

Foss, Abigail. "Peeling the Onion: Teaching Critical Literacy with Students of Privilege," *Language Arts,* 79 (May 2002), 393–403.

Fountas, Irene C., and Gay Su Pinnell. *Guided Reading: Good First Teaching for All Children.* Portsmouth, N.H.: Heinemann, 1996.

Fountas, Irene, and Gay Su Pinnell. *Guiding Readers and Writers: Grades 3–6.* Portsmouth, N.H.: Heinemann, 2001.

Fournier, David N. E., and Michael F. Graves. "Scaffolding Adolescents' Comprehension of Short Stories." *Journal of Adolescent & Adult Literacy,* 46 (September 2002), 30–39.

Fowler, Gerald. "Developing Comprehension Skills in Primary Students Through the Use of Story Frames." *The Reading Teacher,* 36 (November 1982), 176–179.

Frager, Alan M. "Affective Dimensions of Content Area Reading." *Journal of Reading,* 36 (May 1993), 616–622.

Franks, Leslie. "Charcoal Clouds and Weather Writing: Inviting Science to a Middle School Language Arts Classroom." *Language Arts,* 78 (March 2001), 319–324.

Fredericks, Anthony D. "Mental Imagery Activities to Improve Comprehension." *The Reading Teacher,* 40 (October 1986), 78–81.

Freedman, Glenn, and Elizabeth G. Reynolds. "Enriching Basal Reader Lessons with Semantic Webbing." *The Reading Teacher,* 33 (March 1980), 667–684.

French, Joyce, Nancy Ellsworth, and Marie Amoruso. *Reading and Learning Disabilities: Research and Practice.* New York: Garland, 1995.

Fry, Edward. "Fry's Readability Graph: Clarifications, Validity, and Extension to Level 17." *Journal of Reading,* 21 (December 1977), 249.

Fry, Edward. "Readability versus Leveling," *The Reading Teacher,* 56 (November 2002), 286–291.

Fuhler, Carol J. "Let's Move Toward Literature-Based Reading Instruction." *The Reading Teacher,* 43 (January 1990), 312–315.

Fuhler, Carol J. "Response Journals: Just One More Time with Feeling." *Journal of Reading,* 37 (February 1994), 400–405.

Furleigh, Mary A. "Teaching Comprehension with Editorials." *The Reading Teacher,* 44 (March 1991), 523.

Galda, Lee. "Saving Our Planet, Saving Ourselves." *The Reading Teacher,* 45 (December 1991), 310–317.

Galda, Lee, and Kathy G. Short. "Visual Literacy: Exploring Art and Illustration in Children's Books." *The Reading Teacher,* 46 (March 1993), 506–516.

Galda, Lee, and Pat MacGregor. "Nature's Wonders: Books for a Science Curriculum." *The Reading Teacher,* 46 (November 1992), 236–245.

Gallagher, Janice Mori. "Pairing Adolescent Fiction with Books from the Canon." *Journal of Adolescent & Adult Literacy,* 39 (September 1995), 8–14.

Gambrell, Linda. "Creating Classroom Cultures that Foster Reading Motivation." *The Reading Teacher,* 50 (September 1996), 14–25.

Garcia, Mary, and Kathy Verville. "Redesigning Teaching and Learning: The Arizona Student Assessment Program." In *Authentic Reading Assessment: Practices and Possibilities,* edited by Sheila Valencia, Elfrieda Hiebert, and Peter Afflerbach. Newark, Del.: International Reading Association, 1994.

Gardner, Howard. "Reflections on Multiple Intelligences: Myths and Messages." *Phi Delta Kappan,* 77 (November 1995), 200–209.

Gardner, Michael K., and Martha M. Smith. "Does Perspective Taking Ability Contribute to Reading Comprehension?" *Journal of Reading,* 30 (January 1987), 333–336.

Garrison, James W., and Kenneth Hoskisson. "Confirmation Bias in Predictive Reading." *The Reading Teacher,* 42 (March 1989), 482–486.

Gaskins, Irene West, et al. "Classroom Talk About Text: Learning in Science Class." *Journal of Reading,* 37 (April 1994), 558–565.

Gaskins, Robert W. "The Missing Ingredients: Time on Task, Direct Instruction, and Writing." *The Reading Teacher,* 41 (April 1988), 750–755.

Geisert, Paul G., and Mynga K. Futrell. *Teachers, Computers, and Curriculum: Microcomputers in the Curriculum.* 2d ed. Boston: Allyn and Bacon, 1995.

GEONews Handbook, November 11–17, 1990, 7.

Gill, Sharon Ruth. "Reading with Amy: Teaching and Learning Through Reading Conferences." *The Reading Teacher,* 53 (March 2000), 500–509.

Gillet, Jean Wallace, and J. Richard Gentry. "Bridges Between Nonstandard and Standard English with Extensions of Dictated Stories." *The Reading Teacher,* 36 (January 1983), 360–365.

Gipe, Joan P. "Use of a Relevant Context Helps Kids Learn New Word Meanings." *The Reading Teacher,* 33 (January 1980), 398–402.

Glass, Gerald G. "The Strange World of Syllabication." *The Elementary School Journal,* 67 (May 1967), 403–405.

Glynn, Shawn. "Teaching with Analogies: Building on the Science Textbook." *The Reading Teacher,* 49 (March 1996), 490–492.

Goldberg, Mark F. "The Test Mess." *Phi Delta Kappan,* 85 (January 2004), 361–366.

Golden, Joanne M. "Children's Concept of Story in Reading and Writing." *The Reading Teacher,* 37 (March 1984), 578–584.

Golden, Joanne M., Annyce Meiners, and Stanley Lewis. "The Growth of Story Meaning." *Language Arts,* 69 (January 1992), 22–27.

Goldenberg, Claude. "Instructional Conversations: Promoting Comprehension through Discussion." *The Reading Teacher,* 46 (December 1992/January 1993), 316–326.

Goldman, S. R. "Learning from Text: Reflections on the Past and Suggestions for the Future." *Discourse Processes,* 23 (1997), 357–398.

Goodman, Kenneth S. "Reading: A Psycholinguistic Guessing Game." In *Perspectives on Elementary Reading,* edited by Robert Karlin. New York: Harcourt Brace Jovanovich, 1973.

Goodman, Kenneth S. "Reading, Writing, and Written Texts: A Transactional Sociopsycholinguistic View." In *Theoretical Models and Processes of Reading,* 4th ed., edited by Robert B. Ruddell, Martha Rapp Ruddell, and Harry Singer. Newark, Del.: International Reading Association, 1994, 1093–1130.

Goodman, Kenneth S. "Unity in Reading." In *Theoretical Models and Processes of Reading,* 3d ed., edited by Harry Singer and Robert B. Ruddell. Newark, Del.: International Reading Association, 1985.

Goodman, Kenneth S., and Catherine Buck. "Dialect Barriers to Reading Comprehension Revisited." *The Reading Teacher,* 50 (March 1997), 454–459.

Goodman, Kenneth S., Yetta M. Goodman, and Wendy J. Hood, eds. *The Whole Language Evaluation Book.* Portsmouth, N.H.: Heinemann, 1989.

Goodman, Yetta. "Miscue Analysis for Classroom Teachers: Some History and Some Procedures." *Primary Voices K–6,* 3 (November 1995), 2–9.

"Good News, Bad News: Latest NAEP Scores Indicate Gains at 4th and 8th Grade Levels, Decreases at 12th Grade Level." *Reading Today,* 21 (August/September, 2003), 1–4.

Gordon, Christine, and P. David Pearson. *Effects of Instruction in Metacomprehension and Inferencing on Students' Comprehension Abilities* (Technical Report No. 269). Urbana-Champaign, Ill.: University of Illinois, Center for the Study of Reading, 1983.

Gough, Philip B. "Word Recognition." In *Handbook of Reading Research,* edited by P. David Pearson et al. New York: Longman, 1984.

Gove, Mary. "Clarifying Teachers' Beliefs about Reading." *The Reading Teacher,* 37 (December 1983), 261–268.

Grabe, Mark, and Cindy Grabe. "The Microcomputer and the Language Experience Approach." *The Reading Teacher,* 38 (February 1985), 508–511.

Graves, Michael F., and Maureen C. Prenn. "Costs and Benefits of Various Methods of Teaching Vocabulary." *Journal of Reading,* 29 (April 1986), 596–602.

Graves, Michael F., and Susan M. Watts-Taffe. "The Place of Word Consciousness in a Research-Based Vocabulary Program." In Alan E. Farstrup and S. Jay Samuels, eds. *What Research Has to Say About Reading Instruction.* Newark, Del.: International Reading Association, 2002.

Greenewald, M. Jane, and Rosalind L. Rossing. "Short-Term and Long-Term Effects of Story Grammar and Self-Monitoring Training on Children's Story Comprehension." In *Solving Problems in Literacy: Learners, Teachers, and Researchers,* edited by Jerome A. Niles and Rosary V. Lalik. Rochester, N.Y.: National Reading Conference, 1986.

Greenlaw, James. *English Language Arts and Reading on the Internet: A Resource for K–12 Teachers.* Upper Saddle River, N.J.: Prentice Hall, 2002.

Grierson, Sirpa T., Amy Anson, and Jacoy Baird. "Exploring the Past Through Multigenre Writing." *Language Arts,* 80 (September 2002), 51–59.

Guillaume, Andrea M. "Learning with Text in the Primary Grades." *The Reading Teacher,* 51 (March 1998), 476–486.

Gunderson, Lee. "Voices of the Teenage Diasporas." *Journal of Adolescent & Adult Literacy,* 43 (May 2000), 692–706.

Guskey, Thomas R. "How Classroom Assessments Improve Learning." *Educational Leadership,* 60 (February 2003), 7–11.

Guthrie, John. "The Maze Technique to Assess, Monitor Reading Comprehension." *The Reading Teacher,* 28 (1974), 161–168.

Guthrie, John T. "Children's Reasons for Success and Failure." *The Reading Teacher,* 36 (January 1983), 478–480.

Guthrie, John T. "Models of Reading and Reading Disability." *Journal of Educational Psychology,* 65 (1973), 9–18.

Guzzetti, Barbara J., Barbara J. Kowalinski, and Tom McGowan. "Using a Literature-Based Approach to Teaching Social Studies." *Journal of Reading,* 36 (October 1992), 114–122.

Hadaway, Nancy, and Viola Florez. "Teaching Multiethnic Literature, Promoting Cultural Pluralism." *The Dragon Lode,* 8 (Winter 1990), 7–13.

Hadaway, Nancy L., and Terrell A. Young. "Content Literacy and Language Learning: Instructional Decisions." *The Reading Teacher,* 47 (April 1994), 522–527.

Haggard, Martha Rapp. "Developing Critical Thinking with the Directed Reading-Thinking Activity." *The Reading Teacher,* 41 (February 1988), 526–533.

Haggard, Martha Rapp. "The Vocabulary Self-Collection Strategy: Using Student Interest and World Knowledge to Enhance Vocabulary Growth." *Journal of Reading,* 29 (April 1986), 634–642.

Hamann, Lori S., Loree Schultz, Michael W. Smith, and Brian White. "Making Connections: The Power of Autobiographical Writing Before Reading." *Journal of Reading,* 35 (September 1991), 24–28.

Hancock, Marjorie R. "Character Journals: Initiating Involvement and Identification through Literature." *Journal of Reading,* 37 (September 1993), 42–50.

Hancock, Marjorie R. "Literature Response Journals: Insights Beyond the Printed Page." *Language Arts,* 69 (January 1992), 36–42.

Handloff, Elaine, and Joanne Golden. "Writing as a Way of 'Getting to' What You Think and Feel About a Story." In *Book Talk and Beyond,* edited by Nancy Roser and Miriam Martinez. Newark, Del.: International Reading Association, 1995.

Hansell, Stevenson F. "Stepping Up to Outlining." *Journal of Reading,* 22 (December 1978), 248–252.

Hansen, Jane. "Students' Evaluations Bring Reading and Writing Together." *The Reading Teacher,* 46 (October 1992), 100–105.

Hansen, Jane. "Synergism of Classroom and School Libraries." *The New Advocate,* 6 (Summer 1993), 201–211.

Hansen, Jane, and P. David Pearson. "An Instructional Study: Improving the Inferential Comprehension of Fourth Grade Good and Poor Readers." *Journal of Educational Psychology,* 75, no. 6 (1983), 821–829.

Hansen, Jane, and Ruth Hubbard. "Poor Readers Can Draw Inferences." *The Reading Teacher,* 37 (March 1984), 586–589.

Harmon, Janis M. "Vocabulary Teaching and Learning in a Seventh-Grade Literature-Based Classroom." *Journal of Adolescent & Adult Literacy,* 41 (April 1998), 518–529.

Harmon, Janis M., and Wenda B. Hedrick. "Zooming In and Zooming Out: Enhancing Vocabulary and Conceptual Learning in Social Studies." *The Reading Teacher,* 54 (October 2000), 155–159.

Harp, Bill. "Principles of Assessment and Evaluation in Whole Language Classrooms." In *Assessment and Evaluation for Student Centered Learning,* 2d ed., edited by Bill Harp. Norwood, Mass.: Christopher-Gordon, 1994, 47–66.

Harp, Bill. "When the Principal Asks, 'How Are We Using What We Know About Literacy Processes in the Content Areas?' " *The Reading Teacher,* 42 (May 1989a), 726–727.

Harp, Bill. "When the Principal Asks, 'Why Are You Doing Guided Imagery During Reading Time?' " *The Reading Teacher,* 41 (February 1988), 588–590.

Harris, Albert J., and Edward R. Sipay. *How to Increase Reading Ability,* 8th ed. New York: Longman, 1985.

Harris, Sandra. "Bringing About Change in Reading Instruction." *The Reading Teacher,* 49 (May 1996), 612–618.

Harris, Theodore L., and Richard E. Hodges, eds. *The Literacy Dictionary: The Vocabulary of Reading and Writing.* Newark, Del.: International Reading Association, 1995.

Harvey, Stephanie. "Nonfiction Inquiry: Using Real Reading and Writing to Explore the World." *Language Arts,* 80 (September 2002), 12–22.

Hashey, Jane M., and Dianne J. Connors. "Learn from Our Journey: Reciprocal Teaching Action Research." *The Reading Teacher,* 57 (November 2003), 224–232.

Heald-Taylor, B. Gail. "Three Paradigms for Literature Instruction in Grades 3 to 6." *The Reading Teacher,* 49 (March 1996), 456–466.

Heald-Taylor, Gail. *Whole Language Strategies for ESL Students.* San Diego, Calif.: Dormac, 1989.

Heilman, Arthur W. *Phonics in Proper Perspective.* Upper Saddle River, New Jersey: Merrill/Prentice Hall, 2002.

Heimlich, Joan E., and Susan D. Pittelman. *Semantic Mapping: Classroom Applications.* Newark, Del.: International Reading Association, 1986.

Heine, Patricia. "The Power of Related Books." *The Reading Teacher,* 45 (September 1991), 75–77.

Heller, Mary F. "Comprehending and Composing Through Language Experience." *The Reading Teacher,* 42 (November 1988), 130–135.

Henke, Linda. "Beyond Basal Reading: A District's Commitment to Change." *The New Advocate,* 1, no. 1 (1988), 4251.

Herman, Patricia A., Richard C. Anderson, P. David Pearson, and William E. Nagy. "Incidental Acquisition of Word Meaning from Expositions with Varied Text Features." *Reading Research Quarterly,* 22, no. 3 (1987), 263–284.

Herrell, Adrienne L. *Fifty Strategies for Teaching English Language Learners.* Upper Saddle River, NJ: Prentice Hall, Inc., 2000.

Herrmann, Beth Ann. "Two Approaches for Helping Poor Readers Become More Strategic." *The Reading Teacher,* 42 (October 1988), 24–28.

Hess, Mary Lou. "Understanding Nonfiction: Purpose, Classification, Response." *Language Arts,* 68 (March 1991), 228–232.

Hibbing, Anne Nielsen, and Joan L. Rankin-Erickson. "A Picture is Worth a Thousand Words: Using Visual Images to Improve Comprehension for Middle School Struggling Readers." *The Reading Teacher,* 56 (May 2003), 758–770.

Hickman, Janet. "Not by Chance: Creating Classrooms That Invite Responses to Literature." In *Book Talk and Beyond,* edited by Nancy Roser and Miriam Martinez. Newark, Del.: International Reading Association, 1995.

Hiebert, Elfrieda H., and Jacalyn Colt. "Patterns of Literature-Based Reading Instruction." *The Reading Teacher,* 43 (October 1989), 1420.

Hoffman, James V. "Critical Reading/Thinking Across the Curriculum: Using I-Charts to Support Learning." *Language Arts,* 69 (February 1992), 121–127.

Holloway, John H. "A Value-Added View of Pupil Performance." *Educational Leadership,* 57 (February 2000), 84–85.

Hornsby, David, Deborah Sukarna, and Jo-Ann Parry. *Read On: A Conference Approach to Reading.* Portsmouth, N.H.: Heinemann, 1986.

Hoyt, Linda. "Many Ways of Knowing: Using Drama, Oral Interactions, and the Visual Arts to Enhance Reading Comprehension." *The Reading Teacher,* 45 (April 1992), 580–584.

Huck, Charlotte S., Susan Hepler, and Janet Hickman. *Children's Literature in the Elementary School,* 6th ed. Fort Worth, Tex.: Harcourt Brace, 1997.

Hughes, Sandra M. "Impact of Whole Language on Four Elementary School Libraries." *Language Arts,* 70 (September 1993), 393–399.

International Reading Association. "International Reading Association Calls upon Government Leaders to Make Reading and Literacy the Cornerstone of Education Reform and Consider the Best Long-Term Investment You Can Make." *Tennessee Reading Teacher*, 32 (Fall 2003) 17–18.

International Reading Association and National Middle School Association. *Supporting Young Adolescents' Literacy Learning A Joint Position Statement of the International Reading Association and the National Middle School Association.* Available at www.nmsa.org and www.reading.org.

IRA/NCTE Joint Task Force on Assessment. *Standards for the Assessment of Reading and Writing.* Newark, Del.: International Reading Association, 1996.

Irvin, Judith L. "Implications of Brain Research for Teaching Young Adolescents." *Middle School Journal,* 34 (September 2002), 57–61.

Irwin, Judith Westphal. *Teaching Reading Comprehension Processes,* 2d ed. Englewood Cliffs, N.J.: Prentice-Hall, 1991.

Iwicki, Ann L. "Vocabulary Connections." *The Reading Teacher,* 45 (May 1992), 736.

Jackson, Anthony W. and Gayle A. Davis. *Turning Points 2000: Educating Adolescents in the Twenty-First Century,* New York: Teachers College Press, 2000.

Jasmine, Julia. *Middle School Assessment.* Huntington Beach, Calif.: Teacher Created Press, 1994.

Jenks, Carolyn, and Janice Roberts. "Reading, Writing, and Reviewing: Teacher, Librarian, and Young Readers Collaborate." *Language Arts,* 67 (November 1990), 742–745.

Jett-Simpson, Mary. "Writing Stories Using Model Structures: The Circle Story." *Language Arts,* 58 (March 1981), 293–300.

Johnson, Dale D., and Bonnie von Hoff Johnson. "Highlighting Vocabulary in Inferential Comprehension Instruction." *Journal of Reading,* 29 (April 1986), 622–625.

Johnson, Dale D., and P. David Pearson. *Teaching Reading Vocabulary,* 2d ed. New York: Holt, Rinehart and Winston, 1984.

Johnson, Dale D., Susan D. Pittelman, and Joan E. Heimlich. "Semantic Mapping." *The Reading Teacher,* 39 (April 1986), 778–783.

Johnson, Lori Beckmann. "Windows Computing: Finding the Right Words: Dictionaries, Thesauruses, and Quotations." *PC Novice,* 5 (September 1994), 21–23.

Johnson, Nancy M., and M. Jane Ebert. "Time Travel Is Possible: Historical Fiction and Biography—Passport to the Past." *The Reading Teacher,* 45 (March 1992), 488–495.

Johnson, Terry D., and Daphne R. Louis. *Literacy Through Literature.* Portsmouth, N.H.: Heinemann, 1987.

Johnston, Francine R. "Improving Student Response in DR-TAs and DL-TAs." *The Reading Teacher,* 46 (February 1993), 448–449.

Johnston, Peter H. *Constructive Evaluation of Literate Activity.* New York: Longman, 1992.

Johnston, Peter H. "Teachers as Evaluation Experts." *The Reading Teacher,* 40 (April 1987), 744–748.

Jones, Linda L. "An Interactive View of Reading: Implications for the Classroom." *The Reading Teacher,* 35 (April 1982), 772–777.

Jones, Margaret B., and Denise D. Nessel. "Enhancing the Curriculum with Experience Stories." *The Reading Teacher,* 39 (October 1985), 18–22.

Joranko, Joyce. "Reading and Writing Informational Texts." *The Reading Teacher,* 44 (November 1990), 276–277.

Jossart, Sarah A. "Character Journals Aid Comprehension." *The Reading Teacher,* 42 (November 1988), 180.

Kachuck, Beatrice. "Relative Clauses May Cause Confusion for Young Readers." *The Reading Teacher,* 34 (January 1981), 372–377.

Kane, Sharon. "The View from the Discourse Level: Teaching Relationships and Text Structure." *The Reading Teacher,* 52 (October 1998), 182–184.

Kapinus, Barbara. "Looking at the Ideal and the Real in Large-Scale Reading Assessment: The View from Two Sides of the River." *The Reading Teacher,* 47 (April 1994), 578–580.

Karlin, R. *Teaching Elementary Reading: Principles and Strategies,* 3d ed. New York: Harcourt Brace Jovanovich, 1980.

Kaser, Sandy. "Searching the Heavens with Children's Literature: A Design for Teaching Science." *Language Arts,* 78 (March 2001), 348–356.

Kimmel, Susan, and Walter H. MacGinitie. "Helping Students Revise Hypotheses While Reading." *The Reading Teacher,* 38 (April 1985), 768–771.

Kitagawa, Mary M. "Improving Discussions or How to Get the Students to Ask the Questions." *The Reading Teacher,* 36 (October 1982), 42–45.

Klein, Perry D., and David R. Olson. "Text, Technology, and Thinking: Lessons from the Great Divide." *Language Arts,* 78 (January 2001), 227–236.

Knickerbocker, Joan, and James Rycik. "Growing into Literature: Adolescents' Literary Interpretation and Appreciation." *Journal of Adolescent & Adult Literacy,* 46 (November 2002), 196–206.

Koskinen, Patricia S., Linda B. Gambrell, Barbara A. Kapinus, and Betty S. Heathington. "Retelling: A Strategy for Enhancing Students' Reading Comprehension." *The Reading Teacher,* 41 (May 1988), 892–896.

Koskinen, Patricia S., Robert M. Wilson, Linda B. Gambrell, and Susan B. Neuman. "Captioned Video and Vocabulary Learning: An Innovative Practice in Literacy Instruction." *The Reading Teacher,* 47 (September 1993), 36–43.

Kotrla, Melissa. "What's Literacy?" *The Reading Teacher,* 50 (May 1997), 702–703.

Krieger, Evelyn. "Developing Comprehension Through Author Awareness." *Journal of Reading,* 33 (May 1990), 618–619.

Kupiter, Karen, and Patricia Wilson. "Updating Poetry Preferences: A Look at the Poetry Children Really Like." *The Reading Teacher,* 47 (September 1993), 28–35.

Kuta, Katherine Wiesolek. "Teaching Text Patterns to Remedial Readers." *Journal of Reading,* 35 (May 1992), 657–658.

Laase, Lois. "Study Skills: Note-Taking Strategies That Work." *Instructor,* 106 (May/June 1997), 58.

LaBerge, David, and S. Jay Samuels. "Toward a Theory of Automatic Information Processing in Reading." In *Theoretical Models and Processes of Reading,* 3d ed., edited by Harry Singer and Robert B. Ruddell. Newark, Del.: International Reading Association, 1985.

Lamme, Linda Leonard, and Linda Ledbetter. "Libraries: The Heart of Whole Language." *Language Arts,* 67 (November 1990), 735–741.

Lancia, Peter. "Literary Borrowing: The Effects of Literature on Children's Writing." *The Reading Teacher,* 50 (March 1997), 470–475.

Lange, Bob. "Making Sense with Schemata." *Journal of Reading,* 24 (February 1981), 442–445.

Lapp, Diane, and James Flood. "Integrating the Curriculum: First Steps." *The Reading Teacher,* 47 (February 1994), 416–419.

Lauritzen, Carol, Michael Jaeger, and M. Ruth Davenport. "Integrating Curriculum: Contexts for Integrating Curriculum." *The Reading Teacher,* 49 (February 1996), 404–406.

Layton, Kent, and Martha E. Irwin. "Enriching Your Reading Program with Databases." *The Reading Teacher,* 42 (May 1989), 724.

Lazear, David. *Teaching for Multiple Intelligences.* Bloomington, Ind.: Phi Delta Kappa, 1992.

Leal, Dorothy J., and Julia Chamberlain-Solecki. "A Newbery Medal–Winning Combination: High Student Interest Plus Appropriate Readability Levels." *The Reading Teacher,* 51 (May 1998), 712–714.

Leal, Dorothy L. "The Power of Literary Peer-Group Discussions: How Children Collaboratively Negotiate Meaning." *The Reading Teacher,* 47 (October 1993), 114–120.

Lee, Gretchen. "Technology in the Language Arts Classroom: Is It Worth the Trouble?" *Voices from the Middle,* 7 (March 2000), 24–32.

Leslie, Lauren, and Mary Jett-Simpson. *Authentic Literacy Assessment.* New York: Longman, 1997.

Leu, Donald J., Jr. "Exploring Literacy Within Multimedia Environments." *The Reading Teacher,* 50 (October 1996), 162–165.

Leu, Donald J., Jr. "Our Children's Future: Changing the Focus of Literacy and Literacy Instruction." *The Reading Teacher,* 53 (February 2000), 424–427.

Leu, Donald J., Jr., Jill Castek, Laurie A. Henry, Julie Coiro, and Melissa McMullan. "The Lessons That Children Teach Us: Integrating Children's Literature and the New Literacies of the Internet." *The Reading Teacher,* 57 (February 2004), 496–503.

Leu, Donald J., Jr., Rachel A. Karchmer, and Deborah Diadiun Leu. "The Miss Rumphius Effect: Envisionments for Literacy and Learning That Transform the Internet." *The Reading Teacher,* 52 (March 1999), 636–642.

Levstick, Linda S. "Research Directions: Mediating Content Through Literary Texts." *Language Arts,* 67 (December 1990), 848–853.

Lewis, Maureen, David Wray, and Patricia Rospigliosi. ". . . And I Want It in Your Own Words." *The Reading Teacher,* 47 (April 1994), 528–536.

Lipman, Doug. *Improving Your Storytelling: Beyond the Basics for All Who Tell Stories in Work or Play.* Little Rock, Ark.: August House, 1999.

Lipson, Marjorie, and Karen Wixson. *Assessment & Instruction of Reading and Writing Disability,* 2d ed. New York: Longman, 1997.

Lipson, Marjorie Y., Sheila W. Valencia, Karen K. Wixon, and Charles W. Peters. "Integration and Thematic Teaching: Integration to Improve Teaching and Learning." *Language Arts,* 70 (April 1993), 252–263.

Long, Emily S. "Using Acrostic Poems for Research Reporting." *The Reading Teacher,* 46 (February 1993), 447–448.

Lunsford, Susan H. " 'And They Wrote Happily Ever After': Literature-Based Mini-Lessons in Writing." *Language Arts,* 74 (January 1997), 42–48.

Mandler, Jean M., and Nancy S. Johnson. "Remembrance of Things Parsed: Story Structure and Recall." *Cognitive Psychology,* 9 (January 1977), 111–151.

Mandler, J. M. *Stories, Scripts, and Scenes: Aspects of Schema Theory.* Hillsdale, N.J.: Erlbaum, 1984.

Manz, Suzanne Liff. "A Strategy for Previewing Textbooks: Teaching Readers to Become THIEVES." *The Reading Teacher,* 55 (February 2002), 434–435.

Maria, Katherine. "Developing Disadvantaged Children's Background Knowledge Interactively." *The Reading Teacher,* 42 (January 1989), 296–300.

Maric, K., and J. M. Johnson. "Correcting Misconceptions: Effect of Type on Text." In *Literacy Theory and Research: Analyses from Multiple Paradigms,* edited by S. McCormick and J. Zutell. Chicago: National Reading Conference, 1990.

Maring, Gerald H. "Video Conferencing." Paper presented at the International Reading Association Convention, San Francisco, May 1, 2002.

Marshall, Nancy. "Using Story Grammar to Assess Reading Comprehension." *The Reading Teacher,* 36 (March 1983), 616–620.

Martinez, Miriam, and Marcia F. Nash. "Bookalogues: Talking About Children's Literature." *Language Arts,* 67 (December 1990b), 854–861.

Martinez-Roldan, Carmen M., and Julia M. Lopez-Robertson. "Initiating Literature Circles in a First-Grade Bilingual Classroom." *The Reading Teacher,* 53 (December 1999/January 2000), 270–281.

Marzano, Lorraine. "Connecting Literature with Cooperative Writing." *The Reading Teacher,* 43 (February 1990), 429–430.

Marzano, Robert J. "A Cluster Approach to Vocabulary Instruction: A New Direction from the Research Literature." *The Reading Teacher,* 38 (November 1984), 168–173.

Mason, George. "The Word Processor and Teaching Reading." *The Reading Teacher,* 37 (February 1984), 552–553.

Mathison, Carla. "Activating Student Interest in Content Area Reading." *Journal of Reading,* 33 (December 1989), 170–176.

Maudeville, Thomas F. "KWLA: Linking the Affective and Cognitive Domains." *The Reading Teacher,* 47 (May 1994), 679–680.

Maxwell, Rhonda, and Mary Jordan Metser. *Teaching English in Middle and Secondary Schools.* Upper Saddle River, NJ: Merrill, 2001.

McCarthy, Robert. "Assessing the Whole Student." *Instructor Special Supplement* (May–June 1994), 18.

McClure, Amy A., and Connie S. Zitlow. "Not Just the Facts: Aesthetic Response in Elementary Content Area Studies." *Language Arts,* 68 (January 1991), 27–33.

McDonald, Jacqueline. "Graphs and Prediction: Helping Children Connect Mathematics and Literature." *The Reading Teacher,* 53 (September 1999), 25–29.

McGee, Lea M. "Exploring the Literature-Based Reading Revolution." *Language Arts,* 69 (November 1992), 529–537.

McGee, Lea M., and Donald J. Richgels. "Teaching Expository Text Structure to Elementary Students." *The Reading Teacher,* 38 (April 1985), 739–748.

McGee, Lea M., and Gail E. Tompkins. "Literature-Based Reading Instruction: Who's Guiding the Instruction?" *Language Arts,* 72 (October 1995), 405–414.

McGee, Lea M., and Gail E. Tompkins. "The Videotape Answer to Independent Reading Comprehension Activities." *The Reading Teacher,* 34 (January 1981), 427–433.

McKenna, Michael C., David Reinking, Linda D. Labbo, and R.D. Kieffer. "The Electronic Transformation of Literacy and Its Implications for the Struggling Reader." *Reading & Writing Quarterly,* 15 (1999), 111–126.

McKeown, M. G., I. L. Beck, R. C. Omanson, and C. A. Perfetti. "The Effects of Long-Term Vocabulary Instruction on Reading Comprehension: A Replication." *Journal of Reading Behavior,* 15 (1983), 3–18.

McKeown, Margaret G., Isabel L. Beck, and M. Jo Worthy. "Grappling with Text Ideas: Questioning the Author." *The Reading Teacher,* 46 (April 1993), 560–566.

McKeown, Margaret G., Isabel L. Beck, Richard C. Omanson, and Martha T. Pople. "Some Effects of the Nature and Frequency of Vocabulary Instruction on the Knowledge and Use of Words." *Reading Research Quarterly,* 20, no. 5 (1985), 522–535.

McWhirter, Anna M. "Whole Language in the Middle School." *The Reading Teacher,* 43 (April 1990), 562–565.

Means, Barbara, and Kerry Olson. "The Link Between Technology and Authentic Learning." *Educational Leadership,* 51 (April 1994), 15–18.

Meir, Margaret. "Comprehension Monitoring in the Elementary Classroom." *The Reading Teacher,* 37 (April 1984), 770–774.

Memory, David M., and Carol Y. Yoder. "Improving Concentration in Content Classrooms." *Journal of Reading,* 31 (February 1988), 426–435.

Menke, Deborah J., and Michael Pressley. "Elaborative Interrogation: Using 'Why' Questions to Enhance the Learning from Text." *Journal of Reading,* 37 (May 1994), 642–645.

Merkley, Donna J. "Modified Anticipation Guide." *The Reading Teacher,* 50 (December 1996/January 1997), 365–368.

Merkley, Donna M., and Debra Jefferies. "Guidelines for Implementing a Graphic Organizer." *The Reading Teacher,* 54 (December 2000–January 2001), 350–357.

Mesmer, Heidi Anne E., and Elizabeth J. Hutchins. "Using QARs with Charts and Graphs," *The Reading Teacher,* 56 (September 2002), 21-27.

Michener, Darlene M. "Test Your Reading Aloud IQ." *The Reading Teacher,* 42 (November 1988), 118–122.

Miller, Etta, Luther B. Clegg, and Bill Vanderhoff. "Creating Postcards from the Famous for Social Studies Class." *Journal of Reading,* 36 (October 1992), 134–135.

Miller, G. Michael, and George E. Mason. "Dramatic Improvisation: Risk-Free Role Playing for Improving Reading Performance." *The Reading Teacher,* 37 (November 1983), 128–131.

Moldofsky, Penny Baum. "Teaching Students to Determine the Central Story Problem: A Practical Application of Schema Theory." *The Reading Teacher,* 36 (April 1983), 740–745.

Moore, Margaret. "Electronic Dialoguing: An Avenue to Literacy." *The Reading Teacher,* 45 (December 1991), 280–286.

Morden, Dawn L. "Crossroads to the World." *Educational Leadership,* 51 (April 1994), 36–38.

Morrell, Ernest. "Toward a Critical Pedagogy of Popular Culture: Literacy Development Among Urban Youth." *Journal of Adolescent & Adult Literacy,* 46 (September 2002), 72–77.

Morrow, Lesley Mandel. "Using Story Retelling to Develop Comprehension." In *Children's Comprehension of Text: Research into Practice,* K. Denise Muth. Newark, Del.: International Reading Association, 1989.

Mosenthal, P., and T. J. Na. "Quality of Children's Recall under Two Classroom Testing Tasks: Toward a Socio-Psycholinguistic Model of Reading Comprehension." *Reading Research Quarterly,* 15 (1980a), 501–528.

Mosenthal P., and T. J. Na. "Quality of Text Recall as a Function of Children's Classroom Competence." *Journal of Experimental Child Psychology,* 30 (1980b), 1–21.

Mosenthal, Peter B. "The Whole Language Approach: Teachers Between a Rock and a Hard Place." *The Reading Teacher,* 42 (April 1989), 628–629.

Moss, Barbara, and Judith Hendershot. "Exploring Sixth Graders' Selection of Nonfiction Trade Books." *The Reading Teacher,* 56 (September 2002), 6–17.

Moss, Joy F., and Sherri Oden. "Children's Story Comprehension and Story Learning." *The Reading Teacher,* 36 (April 1983), 784–789.

Mountain, Lee. "Flip-a-Chip to Build Vocabulary." *Journal of Adolescent & Adult Literacy,* 48 (September 2002), 62–68.

Mountain, Lee. "Math Synonyms." *The Reading Teacher,* 46 (February 1993), 451–452.

Moustafa, Margaret. "Comprehensible Input PLUS the Language Experience Approach: A Longterm Perspective." *The Reading Teacher,* 41 (December 1987), 276–286.

Moustafa, Margaret, and Joyce Penrose. "Comprehensible Input PLUS the Language Experience Approach: Reading Instruction for Limited English Speaking Students." *The Reading Teacher,* 38 (March 1985), 640–647.

Muller, Dorothy H., and Liz Savage. "Mapping the Library." *The Reading Teacher,* 35 (April 1982), 840–841.

Nagy, William E. *Teaching Vocabulary to Improve Reading Comprehension.* Urbana, Ill.: National Council of Teachers of English, 1988.

Nagy, William E., Patricia A. Herman, and Richard C. Anderson. "Learning Words from Context." *Reading Research Quarterly,* 20, no. 2 (1985), 233–253.

National Education Association. *Student Portfolios.* Washington, D.C.: National Education Association, 1993.

Naughton, Victoria M. "Creative Mapping for Content Reading." *Journal of Reading,* 37 (December 1993/January 1994), 324–326.

Neill, Monty. "Principles for 'Assessment.' " *Talking Points,* 8 (February/March 1997), 26–27.

Nelson-Herber, Joan. "Expanding and Defining Vocabulary in Content Areas." *Journal of Reading,* 29 (April 1986), 626–633.

Neuman, Susan B., and Patricia S. Koskinen. "Captioned Television as Comprehensible Input: Effects of Incidental Word Learning in Context for Language Minority Students." *Reading Research Quarterly,* 27 (1992), 95–106.

Neville, Rita. "Critical Thinkers Become Critical Readers." *The Reading Teacher,* 35 (May 1982), 947–948.

Newman, Gayle. "Comprehension Strategy Gloves." *The Reading Teacher,* 55 (December 2001/January 2002), 329–332.

Nicholson, Tom. "The Flashcard Strikes Back." *The Reading Teacher,* 52 (October 1998), 188–192.

Nolan, Thomas E. "Self-Questioning and Prediction: Combining Metacognitive Strategies." *Journal of Reading,* 35 (October 1991), 132–138.

Nolte, Ruth Yopp, and Harry Singer. "Active Comprehension: Teaching a Process of Reading Comprehension and Its Effects on Reading Achievement." *The Reading Teacher,* 39 (October 1985), 24–31.

Norton, Donna E. "Circa 1942 and the Integration of Literature, Reading, and Geography." *The Reading Teacher,* 46 (April 1993a), 610–614.

Norton, Donna E. "Modeling Inferencing of Characterization." *The Reading Teacher,* 46 (September 1992a), 64–67.

Norton, Donna E. *Through the Eyes of a Child,* 4th ed. Columbus, Ohio: Merrill, 1995.

Norton, Donna E. *Through the Eyes of a Child: An Introduction to Children's Literature.* Upper Saddle River, N.J.: Merrill, 1999.

Norton, Donna E. *Through the Eyes of a Child: An Introduction to Children's Literature.* Upper Saddle River, N.J.: Merrill, 2003.

Norton, Donna E. "Understanding Plot Structures." *The Reading Teacher,* 46 (November 1992b), 254–258.

Norton, Donna E. "Webbing and Historical Fiction." *The Reading Teacher,* 46 (February 1993), 432–436.

Ogle, Donna M. "K-W-L: A Teaching Model that Develops Active Reading of Expository Text." *The Reading Teacher,* 39 (February 1986), 564–570.

Ogle, Donna M. "The Know, Want to Know, Learn Strategy." In *Children's Comprehension of Text: Research into Practice,* edited by K. Denise Muth. Newark, Del.: International Reading Association, 1989.

Oja, Leslie Anne. "Using Story Frames to Develop Reading Comprehension." *Journal of Adolescent & Adult Literacy,* 40 (October 1996), 129–130.

Oldfather, Penny. "Commentary: What's Needed to Maintain and Extend Motivation for Literacy in the Middle Grades." *Journal of Reading,* 36 (March 1995), 420–422.

Ollmann, Hilda E. "Creating Higher Level Thinking with Reading Response." *Journal of Adolescent & Adult Literacy,* 39 (April 1996), 576–581.

Ollmann, Hilda E. "Integrating Content Area Skills with Fiction Favorites." *Journal of Reading,* 34 (February 1991), 398–399.

O'Neil, John. "Making Assessment Meaningful." *ASCD Update,* 36 (August 1994), 1, 4–5.

Oster, Lester. "Using the Think-Aloud for Reading Instruction." *The Reading Teacher,* 55 (September 2001), 64–69.

Ovando, Carlos J., and Virginia P. Collier. *Bilingual and ESL Classrooms.* New York: McGraw-Hill, 1985.

Owens, Roxanne Farwick, Jennifer L. Hester, and William H. Teale. "Where Do You Want To Go Today? Inquiry-Based Learning and Technology Integration," *The Reading Teacher,* 55 (April 2002), 616-625.

Owston, R. D., S. Murphy, and H. H. Wideman. "The Effects of Word Processing on Students' Writing Quality and Revision Strategies." *Research in the Teaching of English,* 26 (1992), 249–276.

Palincsar, Annemarie Sullivan, and Ann. L. Brown. "Interactive Teaching to Promote Independent Learning from Text." *The Reading Teacher,* 39 (April 1986), 771–777.

Palmer, Rosemary G., and Roger A. Stewart. "Nonfiction Trade Books in Content Area Instruction: Realities and Potential." *Journal of Adolescent & Adult Literacy,* 40 (May 1997), 630–641.

Papalia, Diane, Sally W. Olds, and Ruth Duskin Feldman. *A Child's World: Infancy Through Adolescence.* Columbus: McGraw-Hill, 2002.

Paris, Scott G., Barbara A. Wasik, and Julianne C. Turner. "The Development of Strategic Readers." In *Handbook of Reading Research, Vol.II,* edited by Rebecca Barr, Michael L. Kamil, Peter B. Mosenthal, and P. David Pearson. White Plains, N.Y.: Longman, 1991, 609–640.

Parker, Emelie, Regla Armengol, Leigh Brooke, Kelly Carper, Sharon Cronin, Anne Denman, Patricia Irwin, Jennifer McGunnigle, Tess Pardini, and Nancy Kurtz. "Teachers' Choices in Classroom Assessment." *The Reading Teacher,* 48 (April 1995), 622–624.

Pavonetti, Linda M. "Joan Lowery Nixon: The Grande Dame of Young Adult Mystery." *Journal of Adolescent & Adult Literacy,* 39 (March 1996), 454–461.

Pearson, P. David. "Changing the Face of Comprehension Instruction." *The Reading Teacher,* 38 (April 1985), 724–738.

Pearson, P. David, and Dale D. Johnson. *Teaching Reading Comprehension.* New York: Holt, Rinehart and Winston, 1978.

Pearson, P. David, and Kaybeth Camperell. "Comprehension of Text Structures." In *Comprehension and Teaching: Research Reviews,* edited by John T. Guthrie. Newark, Del.: International Reading Association, 1981, 815–860.

Pearson, P. David, and Linda Fielding. "Comprehension Instruction." In *Handbook of Reading Research,* Vol. 2, edited by Rebecca Barr, Michael L. Kamil, Peter Mosenthal, and P. David Pearson. New York: Longman, 1991, 815–860.

Pearson, P. David, et al. *The Effect of Background Knowledge on Young Children's Comprehension of Explicit and Implicit Information.* Urbana-Champaign, Ill.: University of Illinois, Center for the Study of Reading, 1979.

Peck, Jackie. "Using Storytelling to Promote Language and Literacy Development." *The Reading Teacher,* 43 (November 1989), 138–141.

Pehrsson, Robert, and Peter Denner. *Semantic Organizers: A Study Strategy for Special Needs Learners.* Rockville, Md.: Aspen, 1989.

Perkins-Gough, Deborah. "Special Report: RAND Report on Reading Comprehension." *Educational Leadership,* 60 (November 2002), 92.

Petrick, Pamela Bondi. "Creative Vocabulary Instruction in the Content Area." *Journal of Reading,* 35 (March 1992), 481–482.

Pettersen, Nancy-Laurel. "Grate/Great Homonym Hunt." *Journal of Reading,* 31 (January 1988), 374–375.

Pierce, Kathryn Mitchell, and Kathy G. Short, eds. "Children's Books: Environmental Issues and Actions." *The Reading Teacher,* 47 (December 1993/January 1994), 328–335.

Poole, Bernard J. *Education for an Information Age.* Boston: WCB/McGraw-Hill, 1997.

Popp, Marcia. *Learning Journals in the K–8 Classroom.* Mahwah, N.J.: Erlbaum, 1997.

Powell, Janet L. "How Well Do Tests Measure Real Reading?" *ERIC Clearinghouse on Reading and Communication Skills* (June 1989), 1.

Powell, William R. "Teaching Vocabulary Through Opposition." *Journal of Reading,* 29 (April 1986), 617–621.

Pressley, Michael. *Advanced Educational Psychology.* New York: HarperCollins, 1995.

Pressley, Michael. "Comprehension Instruction: What Makes Sense Now, What Might Make Sense Soon," *Reading Online,* 5 (September 2001), 14 pages. Available at http://www.readingonline.org.

Pressley, Michael. "Metacognition and Self-Regulated Comprehension." In Alan E. Farstrup and S. Jay Samuels, eds. *What Research Has to Say About Reading Instruction.* Newark, Delaware: International Reading Association, 2002, 291–309.

Probst, Robert E. "Transactional Theory in the Teaching of Literature." *Journal of Reading,* 31 (January 1988), 378–381.

Pugh, Sharon L., and Jesus Garcia. "Portraits in Black: Establishing African American Identity Through Nonfiction Books." *Journal of Reading,* 34 (September 1990), 20–25.

Quiocho, Alice. "The Quest to Comprehend Expository Text: Applied Classroom Research." *Journal of Adolescent & Adult Literacy,* 40 (March 1997), 450–455.

Rand, Muriel K. "Story Schema: Theory, Research and Practice." *The Reading Teacher,* 37 (January 1984), 377–382.

RAND Reading Study Group. *Reading for Understanding: Towards an R&D Program in Reading Comprehension,* 2002. Available at http://www.rand.org/multi/achievementforall/reading/readreport.html.

Raphael, Taffy E. "Question-Answering Strategies for Children." *The Reading Teacher,* 36 (November 1982), 186–190.

Raphael, Taffy E. "Teaching Learners about Sources of Information for Answering Comprehension Questions." *Journal of Reading,* 27 (January 1984), 303–311.

Raphael, Taffy E. "Teaching Question-Answer Relationships, Revisited." *The Reading Teacher,* 39 (February 1986), 516–522.

Raphael, Taffy E., and P. David Pearson. *The Effect of Metacognitive Awareness Training on Children's Question Answering Behavior* (Technical Report No. 238). Urbana–Champaign, Ill.: University of Illinois, Center for the Study of Reading, 1982.

Raphael, Taffy, et al. "Research Directions: Literature and Discussion in the Reading Program." *Language Arts,* 69 (January 1992), 54–61.

Rasinski, Timothy V. "Mental Imagery Improves Comprehension." *The Reading Teacher,* 41 (April 1988), 867–868.

Rasinski, Timothy V., and Nancy D. Padak. "Multicultural Learning Through Children's Literature." *Language Arts,* 67 (October 1990), 576–580.

Readence, John E., R. Scott Baldwin, and Martha H. Head. "Direct Instruction in Processing Metaphors." *Journal of Reading Behavior,* 18, no. 4 (1986), 325–339.

Readence, John E., R. Scott Baldwin, and Martha H. Head. "Teaching Young Readers to Interpret Metaphors." *The Reading Teacher,* 40 (January 1987), 439–443.

Reardon, S. Jeanne. "The Development of Critical Readers: A Look Into the Classroom." *The New Advocate,* 1, no. 1 (1988), 52–61.

Recht, Donna. "Teaching Summarizing Skills." *The Reading Teacher,* 37 (March 1984), 675–677.

Reinking, David. "Me and My Hypertext :) A Multiple Digression Analysis of Technology and Literacy (Sic)." *The Reading Teacher,* 50 (May 1997), 626–643.

Resnick, Lauren B. *Education and Learning to Think* (report). Washington, D.C.: National Academy Press, 1987.

Reutzel, D. Ray. "C6: A Reading Model for Teaching Arithmetic Story Problem Solving." *The Reading Teacher,* 37 (October 1983), 28–34.

Reutzel, D. Ray, and Robert Cooter. "Organizing for Effective Instruction: The Reading Workshop." *The Reading Teacher,* 44 (April 1991), 548–554.

Rhoder, Carol. "Mindful Reading: Strategy Training that Facilitates Transfer," *Journal of Adolescent & Adult Literacy,* 45 (March 2002), 498–512.

Rhoder, Carol, and Patricia Huerster. "Use Dictionaries for Word Learning with Caution." *Journal of Adolescent & Adult Literacy,* 45 (May 2002), 730–735.

Rhodes, Lynn K., and Curt Dudley-Marling. *Readers and Writers with a Difference.* Portsmouth, N.H.: Heinemann, 1988.

Rhodes, Lynn, and Sally Nathenson-Mejia. "Anecdotal Records: A Powerful Tool for Ongoing Literacy Assessment." *The Reading Teacher,* 45 (March 1992), 502–509.

Richards, Janet Clarke, and Joan P. Gipe. "Activating Background Knowledge: Strategies for Beginning and Poor Readers." *The Reading Teacher,* 45 (February 1992), 474–478.

Richek, Margaret Ann. "Relating Vocabulary Learning to World Knowledge." *Journal of Reading,* 32 (December 1988), 262–267.

Richler, Howard. "Word Play: You're Likely to be Clipped." *Notes Plus* (March 1996), 11–12.

Robertson, Julie Fisher, and Donna Rane-Szostak. "Using Dialogues to Develop Critical Thinking Skills." *Journal of Adolescent & Adult Literacy,* 39 (April 1996), 552–556.

Robinson, Francis P. *Effective Study,* rev. ed. New York: Harper & Row, 1961.

Robinson, H. Alan, Vincent Faraone, Daniel R. Hittleman, and Elizabeth Unruh. *Reading Comprehension Instruction: 1783–1987.* Newark: Del.: International Reading Association, 1990.

Roe, Betty D. *Report on Non-Instructional Assignment.* Cookeville, Tenn.: Tennessee Technological University, 1990.

Roe, Betty D. *Use of Storytelling/Storyreading in Conjunction with Follow-up Language Activities to Improve Oral Communication of Rural First Grade Students: Phase I.* Cookeville, Tenn.: Rural Education Consortium, 1985.

Roe, Betty D. *Use of Storytelling/Storyreading in Conjunction with Follow-up Language Activities to Improve Oral Communication of Rural Primary Grade Students: Phase II.* Cookeville, Tenn.: Rural Education Consortium, 1986.

Roe, Betty D. "Using Technology for Content Area Literacy." In *Linking Literacy and Technology: A Guide for K–8 Classrooms,* edited by Shelley B. Wepner, William J. Valmont, and Richard Thurlow. Newark, Del.: International Reading Association, 2000, 133–158.

Roe, Betty D., and Sandy H. Smith. "University/Public Schools Keypals Project: A Collaborative Effort for Electronic Literature Conversations." In *Rethinking Teaching and Learning through Technology.* Proceedings of the Mid-South Instructional Technology Conference. Murfreesboro, Tenn.: Mid-South Technology Conference, 1997.

Roe, Betty D., Suellen Alfred, and Sandy H. Smith. *Teaching Through Stories: Yours, Mine, and Theirs.* Norwood, Mass.: Christopher Gordon, 1998.

Roe, Mary F. "Reading Strategy Instruction: Complexities and Possibilities in Middle School." *Journal of Reading,* 36 (November 1992), 190–196.

Rosenbaum, Catherine. "A Word Map for Middle School: A Tool for Effective Vocabulary Instruction." *Journal of Adolescent and Adult Literacy,* 45 (September 2001), 44–49.

Rosenblatt, Louise M. *Literature as Exploration.* New York: Noble & Noble, 1938/1983.

Rosenblatt, Louise M. "Literature—S.O.S.!" *Language Arts,* 68 (1991), 444–448.

Rosenblatt, Louise M. *The Reader, the Text, and the Poem: The Transactional Theory of the Literary Work.* Carbondale, Ill.: Southern Illinois University Press, 1978.

Rosenblatt, Louise M. "The Transactional Theory of Reading and Writing." In *Theoretical Models and Processes of Reading,* 4th ed., edited by Robert B. Ruddell, Martha Rapp Ruddell, and Harry Singer. Newark, Del.: International Reading Association, 1994, 1057–1092.

Rosenshine, Barak, and Carla Meister. "Reciprocal Teaching: A Review of the Research." *Review of Educational Research,* 64 (Winter 1994), 479–530.

Roser, N., and C. Juel. "Effects of Vocabulary Instruction on Reading Comprehension." In *New Inquiries in Reading Research and Instruction, Thirty-First Yearbook of the National Reading Conference,* edited by J.A. Niles and L.A. Harris, Rochester, N.Y.: National Reading Conference, 1982.

Roser, Nancy L., James Hoffman, Linda D. Labbo, and Cindy Forest. "Language Charts: A Record of Story Time Talk." *Language Arts,* 69 (January 1992), 44–52.

Ross, Elinor. *The Workshop Approach: A Framework for Literacy.* Norwood, Mass.: Christopher-Gordon, 1996.

Ross, Elinor Parry. "Checking the Source: An Essential Component of Critical Reading." *Journal of Reading,* 24 (January 1981), 311–315.

Rubin, Dorothy. *Diagnosis and Correction in Reading Instruction,* 3d ed. Needham Heights, Mass.: Allyn & Bacon, 1997.

Ruddell, Martha Rapp, and Brenda A. Shearer. "'Extraordinary,' 'Tremendous,' 'Exhilarating,' 'Magnificent': Middle School At-Risk Students Become Avid Word Learners with the Vocabulary Self-Collection Strategy (VSS)." *Journal of Adolescent & Adult Literacy,* 45 (February 2002), 352–363.

Ruddell, Robert B. "A Whole Language and Literature Perspective: Creating a Meaning-Making Instructional Environment." *Language Arts,* 69 (December 1992), 612–620.

Ruddell, Robert B., and Norman J. Unrau. "Reading as a Meaning-Construction Process: The Reader, the Text, and the Teacher." In *Theoretical Models and Processes of Reading,* 4th ed., edited by Robert B. Ruddell, Martha Rapp Ruddell, and Harry Singer. Newark, Del.: International Reading Association, 1994, 996–1056.

Rule, Audrey, and Joan Atkinson. "Choosing Picture Books About Ecology." *The Reading Teacher,* 47 (April 1994), 586–591.

Rumelhart, David E. "Schemata: The Building Blocks of Cognition." In *Comprehension and Teaching: Research Reviews,* edited by John T. Guthrie. Newark, Del.: International Reading Association, 1981.

Rupley, William H., John W. Logan, and William D. Nichols. "Vocabulary Instruction in a Balanced Reading Program." *The Reading Teacher,* 52 (December 1998/January 1999), 336–356.

Rush, R. Timothy. "Assessing Readability: Formulas and Alternatives." *The Reading Teacher,* 39 (December 1985), 274–283.

Russell, David L. *Literature for Children,* 2d ed. New York: Longman, 1994.

Saccardi, Marianne. "Predictable Books: Gateways to a Lifetime of Reading." *The Reading Teacher,* 49 (April 1996a), 588–590.

Sadow, Marilyn W. "The Use of Story Grammar in the Design of Questions." *The Reading Teacher,* 35 (February 1982), 518–522.

Salinger, Terry S. *Literacy for Young Children,* 2d ed. Englewood Cliffs, N.J.: Merrill, 1996.

Salvia, John, and James E. Ysseldyke. *Assessment in Special and Inclusive Education.* Boston, Mass: Houghton Mifflin Company, 2004.

Sampson, Mary Beth, Michael R. Sampson, and Wayne Linek. "Circle of Questions." *The Reading Teacher,* 48 (December 1994/January 1995), 364–365.

Samuels, S. Jay. "Decoding and Automaticity: Helping Poor Readers Become Automatic at Word Recognition." *The Reading Teacher,* 41 (April 1988), 756–760.

Samuels, S. Jay. "Toward a Theory of Automatic Information Processing in Reading, Revisited." In *Theoretical Models and Processes of Reading,* 4th ed., edited by Robert

B. Ruddell, Martha Rapp Ruddell, and Harry Singer. Newark, Del.: International Reading Association, 1994, 816–837.

Samuels, S. Jay, and Sumner W. Schachter. "Controversial Issues in Beginning Reading Instruction: Meaning Versus Subskill Emphasis." In *Readings on Reading Instruction,* edited by Albert J. Harris and Edward R. Sipay. New York: Longman, 1984.

Sandholtz, Judith Haymore, Cathy Ringstaff, and David C. Dwyer. *Teaching with Technology.* New York: Teachers College Press, 1997.

Savage, John F. *Teaching Reading Using Literature.* Madison, Wis.: WCB Brown & Benchmark, 1994.

Sawyer, John Michael. "Using Media Knowledge to Enhance the Literary Schema of Literarily Impoverished Students." *Journal of Reading,* 37 (May 1994), 683–684.

Scharer, Patricia L., and Deana B. Detwiler. "Changing as Teachers: Perils and Possibilities of Literature-Based Language Arts Instruction." *Language Arts,* 69 (March 1992), 186–192.

Scharrer, Erica. "Making a Case for Media Literacy in the Curriculum: Outcomes and Assessment." *Journal of Adolescent & Adult Literacy,* 46 (December 2002/January 2003), 354–358.

Schmidt, Patricia Ruggiano. "KWLQ: Inquiry and Literacy Learning in Science." *The Reading Teacher,* 52 (April 1999), 789–792.

Schmitt, M. C., and D. O'Brien. "Story Grammars: Some Cautions about the Translation of Research into Practice." *Reading Research Quarterly,* 26, no. 1 (1986), 1–8.

Schmitt, Maribeth Cassidy, and James F. Baumann. "How to Incorporate Comprehension Monitoring Strategies into Basal Reader Instruction." *The Reading Teacher,* 40 (October 1986), 28–31.

Schmoker, Mike, and Robert J. Marzano. "Realizing the Promise of Standards-Based Education." *Educational Leadership,* 56 (March 1999), 17–21.

Schumm, Jeanne Shay. "Overcoming Students' Misconceptions About Science." *Journal of Reading,* 35 (October 1991), 161

Schumm, Jeanne Shay, and Linda Saumell. "Aliteracy: We Know It Is a Problem, But Where Does It Start?" *Journal of Reading,* 37 (May 1994), 701.

Schumm, Jeanne Shay, and Linda Saumell. "Word Processors: Their Impact on Process and Product." *Journal of Reading,* 37 (November 1993), 190.

Schwartz, Robert M. "Learning to Learn Vocabulary in Content Area Textbooks." *Journal of Reading,* 32 (November 1988), 108–118.

Schwartz, Robert M. "Self-Monitoring in Beginning Reading." *The Reading Teacher,* 51 (September 1997), 40–48.

Schwartz, Robert M., and Taffy E. Raphael. "Concept of Definition: A Key to Improving Students' Vocabulary." *The Reading Teacher,* 39 (November 1985), 198–205.

Sears, Sue, Cathy Carpenter, and Nancy Burstein. "Meaningful Reading Instruction for Learners with Special Needs." *The Reading Teacher,* 47 (May 1994), 632–638.

Sebesta, Sam Leaton, James William Calder, and Lynne Nelson Cleland. "A Story Grammar for the Classroom." *The Reading Teacher,* 36 (November 1982), 180–184.

Seda, Ileana, and P. David Pearson. "Interviews to Assess Learners' Outcomes." *Reading Research and Instruction,* 31 (Fall 1991), 22–32.

Sefton-Green, Julian. "Computers, Creativity, and the Curriculum: The Challenge for Schools, Literacy, and Learning," *Journal of Adolescent & Adult Literacy,* 44 (May 2001), 726–728.

Seitz, Ernest R., Jr. "Using Media Presentations to Teach Notetaking, Main Idea, and Summarization Skills." *Journal of Adolescent and Adult Literacy,* 40 (April 1997), 562–563.

Seminoff, Nancy Wiseman. "Children's Periodicals Throughout the World: An Overlooked Educational Resource." *The Reading Teacher,* 39 (May 1986), 889–895.

Serafini, Frank. "Stances to Assessment." *Talking Points,* 8 (February/March 1997), 2–4

Shanahan, Timothy. "Reading-Writing Relationships, Thematic Units, Inquiry Learning . . . In Pursuit of Effective Integrated Literacy Instruction." *The Reading Teacher,* 51 (September 1997), 12–19.

Shanahan, T., and S. Neuman. "Conversations: Literacy Research That Makes a Difference." *Reading Research Quarterly,* 32 (1997), 202–211.

Shanklin, Nancy L., and Lynn K. Rhodes. "Comprehension Instruction as Sharing and Extending." *The Reading Teacher,* 42 (March 1989), 496–500.

Shaw, Evelyn. "A Novel Journal." *The Reading Teacher,* 41 (January 1988), 489.

Shepard, Lorrie. "Why We Need Better Assessments." *Educational Leadership,* 46 (April 1989), 4–9.

Shiflett, Anne Chalfield. "Marketing Literature: Variations on the Book Talk Theme." *Journal of Adolescent & Adult Literacy,* 41 (April 1998), 568–570.

Shoop, Mary. "InQuest: A Listening and Reading Comprehension Strategy." *The Reading Teacher,* 39 (March 1986), 670–674.

Short, Kathy G. "Informational Magazines for Children." *Language Arts,* 80 (September 2002), 21.

Simpson, Anne. "Critical Questions: Whose Questions?" *The Reading Teacher,* 50 (October 1996), 118–127.

Singer, Harry, John D. McNeil, and Lory L. Furse. "Relationship Between Curriculum Scope and Reading Achievement in Elementary Schools." *The Reading Teacher,* 37 (March 1984), 608–612.

Sippola, Arne E. "K-W-L-S." *The Reading Teacher,* 48 (March 1995), 542–543.

Smagorinsky, Peter. "Standards Revisited: The Importance of Being There." *English Journal,* 88 (March 1999), 82–88.

Smit, Edna K. "Teaching Theme to Elementary Students." *The Reading Teacher,* 43 (May 1990), 699–701.

Smith, Carl B. "Prompting Critical Thinking." *The Reading Teacher,* 42 (February 1989), 424.

Smith, Frank. *Essays into Literacy.* Exeter, N.H.: Heinemann, 1983.

Smith, Henry P., and Emerald V. Dechant. *Psychology in Teaching Reading.* Englewood Cliffs, N.J.: Prentice-Hall, 1961, 22.

Smith, J. Lea, and Holly Johnson. "Models for Implementing Literature in Content Studies." *The Reading Teacher,* 48 (November 1994), 198–209.

Smith, Marilyn, and Thomas W. Bean. "Four Strategies That Develop Children's Story Comprehension and Writing." *The Reading Teacher,* 37 (December 1983), 295–301.

Smith, Richard J., et al. *The School Reading Program.* Boston: Houghton Mifflin, 1978.

Smolen, Lynn Atkinson, and Victoria Ortiz-Castro. "Dissolving Borders and Broadening Perspectives Through Latino Traditional Literature." *The Reading Teacher,* 53 (April 2000), 566–578.

Snow, Catherine, M. Susan Burns, and Peg Griffin, eds. *Preventing Reading Difficulties in Young Children.* Washington, D.C.: National Academy Press, 1998.

Southern Prairie Area Education Agency 15. "Reading Matters." Available at http://www.aea15.k12.ia.us/reading.htm.

Spiegel, Dixie Lee. "Blending Whole Language and Systematic Direct Instruction." *The Reading Teacher,* 46 (September 1992), 38–44.

Spiegel, Dixie Lee. "The Role of Trust in Reader-Response Groups." *Language Arts,* 73 (September 1996), 332–339.

Spiegel, Dixie Lee. "Silver Bullets, Babies, and Bath Water: Literature Response Groups in a Balanced Literacy Program." *The Reading Teacher,* 52 (October 1998), 114–124.

Spiegel, Dixie Lee, and Jill Fitzgerald. "Improving Reading Comprehension Through Instruction about Story Parts." *The Reading Teacher,* 39 (March 1986), 676–682.

Spiro, Rand J. *Etiology of Comprehension Style.* Urbana-Champaign, Ill.: University of Illinois, Center for the Study of Reading, 1979.

Staal, Laura A. "The Story Face: An Adaptation of Story Mapping that Incorporates Visualization and Discovery Learning to Enhance Reading and Writing," *The Reading Teacher,* 54 (September 2000), 26–31.

Stahl, S. "Instructional Models in Reading: An Introduction." In *Instructional Models in Reading,* edited by S. Stahl and D. Hayes. Mahwah, N.J.: Erlbaum, 1997.

Stahl, Steven A. "Three Principles of Effective Vocabulary Instruction." *Journal of Reading,* 29 (April 1986), 662–668.

Stahl, Steven A., and Barbara A. Kapinus. "Possible Sentences: Predicting Word Meanings to Teach Content Area Vocabulary." *The Reading Teacher,* 45 (September 1991), 36–43.

Stahl, Steven A., and Sandra J. Vancil. "Discussion Is What Makes Semantic Maps Work in Vocabulary Instruction." *The Reading Teacher,* 40 (October 1986), 62–67.

Standards for the English Language Arts. Prepared jointly by the IRA/NCATE Joint Task Force on Assessment. Newark, Del.: International Reading Association, 1996.

Stauffer, Russell G. "Reading as a Cognitive Process." *Elementary English,* 44 (April 1968), 348.

Stauffer, Russell G. *Teaching Reading as a Thinking Process.* New York: Harper & Row, 1969.

Stetson, Elton G., and Richard P. Williams. "Learning from Social Studies Textbooks: Why Some Students Succeed and Others Fail." *Journal of Reading,* 36 (September 1992), 22–30.

Stevens, Kathleen C. "Can We Improve Reading by Teaching Background Information?" *Journal of Reading,* 25 (January 1982), 326–329.

Stewart, Roger A., Edward E. Paradis, Bonita D. Ross, and Mary Jane Lewis. "Student Voices: What Works in Literature-Based Developmental Reading." *Journal of Adolescent & Adult Literacy,* 39 (March 1996), 468–478.

Stivers, Jan. "The Writing Partners Project." *Phi Delta Kappan,* 77 (June 1996), 694–695.

Stoll, Donald R. *Magazines for Kids and Teens.* Newark, Del.: International Reading Association, 1997.

Storey, Dee C. "Reading in the Content Areas: Fictionalized Biographies and Diaries for Social Studies." *The Reading Teacher,* 35 (April 1982), 796–798.

Stotsky, Sandra. "Research on Reading/Writing Relationships: A Synthesis and Suggested Directions." *Language Arts,* 60 (May 1983), 627–642.

Stowell, Laura, and Robert Tierney. "Portfolios in the Classroom: What Happens When Teachers and Students Negotiate Assessment?" In *No Quick Fix,* edited by Richard Allington and Sean Walmsley. Newark, Del.: International Reading Association, 1995, 78–94.

Strange, Michael. "Instructional Implications of a Conceptual Theory of Reading Comprehension." *The Reading Teacher,* 33 (January 1980), 391–397.

Strube, Penny. *Getting the Most from Literature Groups.* New York: Scholastic, 1996.

Struggling Readers, Day 1: Closing the Decoding Crack. Bothell, Wash.: The Wright Group, 2000.

Sudol, Peg, and Caryn King. "A Checklist for Choosing Nonfiction Trade Books." *The Reading Teacher,* 49 (February 1996), 422–424.

Sugarman, Jay, James Allen, and Meg Keller-Cogan. "Make Authentic Assessment Work for You." *Instructor,* 103 (July/August 1993), 66–68.

Sullivan, Joanne. "The Global Method: Language Experience in the Content Areas." *The Reading Teacher,* 39 (March 1986), 664–668.

Swindall, Vickie, and R. Jeffrey Cantrell. "Character Interviews Help Bring Literature to Life." *The Reading Teacher,* 53 (September 1999), 23–25.

"A Talk with Marilyn Adams." *Language Arts,* 68 (March 1991), 206–212.

Teclehaimanot, Berhane, and Annette Lamb. "Reading, Technology, and Inquiry-based Learning Through Literature-Rich WebQuests." *Reading Online,* 7 (March/April 2004). Available at http://www.readingonline.org/articles/art_index.asp?HREF eclehaimanot/index.html.

Tennessee State Department of Education. *No Child Left Behind Executive Summary,* Nashville, Tenn.: Author, 2003.

Tevebaugh, Tara. "Welcome to Our Web: Integrating Subjects Through Entomology." *Language Arts,* 78 (March 2001), 343–347.

Thelen, Judith N. "Vocabulary Instruction and Meaningful Learning." *Journal of Reading,* 29 (April 1986), 603–609.

Thompson, Deborah L. "The Alphabet Book as a Content Area Resource." *The Reading Teacher,* 46 (November 1992), 266–267.

Tierney, Robert J., and James W. Cunningham. "Research on Teaching Reading Comprehension." In *Handbook of Reading Research,* edited by P. David Pearson et al. New York: Longman, 1984.

Tinker, Miles A., and Constance M. McCullough. *Teaching Elementary Reading,* 4th ed. Englewood Cliffs, N.J.: Prentice-Hall, 1975, 9.

Tombari, Martin, and Gary Borich. *Authentic Assessment in the Classroom: Applications and Practice.* Upper Saddle River, N.J.: Prentice Hall, 1999.

Tower, Cathy. "Questions that Matter: Preparing Elementary Students for the Inquiry Process." *The Reading Teacher,* 53 (April 2000), 550–557.

Trelease, Jim. *The New Read-Aloud Handbook,* 4th ed. New York: Viking Penguin, 1995.

Trelease, Jim. *Read All About It! Great Read-Aloud Stories, Poems, and Newspaper Pieces for Preteens and Teens.* New York, NY: Penguin Books, 1993.

Turner, Julianne, and Scott Paris. "How Literacy Tasks Influence Children's Motivation for Literacy." *The Reading Teacher,* 48 (May 1995), 662–673.

Tyson, Eleanore S., and Lee Mountain. "A Riddle or Pun Makes Learning Words Fun." *The Reading Teacher,* 36 (November 1982), 170–173.

Utah State Office of Education. "Core Curriculum." 1999. Available at http://www.usoe.k12.ut.us.

Valenza, Joyce Kasman. "Library as Multimedia Studio." *Electronic Learning,* 16 (November–December 1996), 56–57.

Valmont, William J. *Creating Videos for School Use.* Boston: Allyn & Bacon, 1995.

Van Hoose, John, David Strahan, and Mark L'Esperance. *Promoting Harmony: Young Adolescent Development and School Practices.* Westerville, OH: National Middle School Association, 2001.

Van Horn, Leigh. "The Character Within Us: Readers Connect with Characters to Create Meaning and Understanding." *Journal of Adolescent & Adult Literacy,* 40 (February 1997), 342–347.

VanLeirsburg, Peggy. "Standardized Reading Tests: Then and Now." In *Literacy: Celebration and Challenge,* edited by Jerry Johns. Bloomington, Ill.: Illinois Reading Council, 1993, 31–54.

Villaume, Susan Kidd, and Edna Greene Brabham. "Comprehension Instruction: Beyond Strategies." *The Reading Teacher,* 55 (April 2002), 672–675.

Wade, Suzanne E., and Elizabeth B. Moje. "The Role of Text in Classroom Learning." In *Handbook of Reading Research: Volume 3,* edited by Michael L. Kamil, Peter B. Mosenthal, P. David Pearson, and Rebecca Barr. Mahwah, N.J.: Lawrence Erlbaum, 2000, 609–627.

Walberg, Herbert, Geneva Haertel, and Suzanne Gerlach-Downie. *Assessment Reform: Challenges and Opportunities.* Bloomington, Ind.: Phi Delta Kappa, 1994.

Walberg, Herbert J., Victoria Chou Hare, and Cynthia A. Pulliam. "Social-Psychological Perceptions and

Reading Comprehension." In *Comprehension and Teaching: Research Reviews,* edited by John T. Guthrie. Newark, Del.: International Reading Association, 1981, 140–159.

Walker, Barbara. *Diagnostic Teaching of Reading: Techniques for Instruction and Assessment.* Upper Saddle River, N.J.: Prentice-Hall, 2000.

Walker, Barbara. *Diagnostic Teaching of Reading: Techniques for Instruction and Assessment.* Upper Saddle River, N.J.: Pearson, 2004.

Walker-Dalhouse, Doris. "Using African-American Literature to Increase Ethnic Understanding." *The Reading Teacher,* 45 (February 1992), 416–422.

Walker-Dalhouse, Doris, A. Derick Dalhouse, and Dennis Mitchell. "Development of a Literature-Based Middle School Reading Program: Insights Gained." *Journal of Adolescent & Adult Literacy,* 40 (February 1997), 362–370.

Walpole, Sharon. "Changing Texts, Changing Thinking: Comprehension Demands of New Science Textbooks." *The Reading Teacher,* 52 (December 1998/January 1999), 358–369.

Watson, Jerry. "An Integral Setting Tells More Than When and Where." *The Reading Teacher, 44* (May 1991), 638–646.

Watson, Kenneth Lee. "WebQuests in the Middle School." *Meridian: A Middle School Computer Technologies Journal,* 2 (July 1999). Available at http://www.ncsu.edu/meridian/jul99/webquest/webquest2.html.

Waugh, Joyce Clark. "Using LEA in Diagnosis." *Journal of Reading,* 37 (September 1993), 56–57.

Weaver, Phyllis, and Fredi Shonhoff. "Subskill and Holistic Approaches to Reading Instruction." In *Readings on Reading Instruction,* edited by Albert J. Harris and Edward R. Sipay. New York: Longman, 1984.

Weissman, Kathleen E. "Using Paragraph Frames to Complete a K-W-L." *The Reading Teacher,* 50 (November 1996), 271–272.

Wepner, Shelley B. "Technology and Thematic Units: A Primary Example." *The Reading Teacher,* 46 (November 1992b), 260–263.

Wepner, Shelley B. "Using Technology with Content Area Units." *The Reading Teacher,* 45 (April 1992c), 644–646.

Wepner, Shelley B., and Lucinda C. Ray. "Using Technology for Reading Development." In *Linking Literacy and Technology: A Guide for K–8 Classrooms*, edited by Shelley B. Wepner, William J. Valmont, and Richard Thurlow. Newark, Del.: International Reading Association, 2000.

Wertheim, Judy. "Teaching Guides for Novels." *The Reading Teacher,* 42 (December 1988), 262.

Whaley, Jill Fitzgerald. "Story Grammars and Reading Instruction." *The Reading Teacher,* 34 (April 1981), 762–771.

White, Thomas G., Joanne Sowell, and Alice Yanagihara. "Teaching Elementary Students to Use Word-Part Clues." *The Reading Teacher,* 42 (January 1989), 302–308.

Whitin, Phyllis. "Leading into Literature Circles Through the Sketch-to-Stretch Strategy." *The Reading Teacher,* 55 (February 2002), 444–450.

Whitin, Phyllis E., and David J. Whitin. "The Numbers and Beyond: Language Lessons for the Mathematics Classroom." *Language Arts,* 74 (February 1997), 108–115.

Wicklund, LaDonna. "Shared Poetry: A Whole Language Experience Adapted for Remedial Readers." *The Reading Teacher,* 42 (March 1989), 478–481.

Wiener, Roberta, and Judith Cohen. *Literacy Portfolios.* Upper Saddle River, N.J.: Merrill, 1997.

Wiesendanger, Katherine D. "Comprehension: Using Anticipation Guides." *The Reading Teacher,* 39 (November 1985), 241–242.

Wiggins, Grant. *The Case for Authentic Assessment.* Washington, D.C.: ERIC Clearinghouse, 1990 [ED328611].

Wiggins, Grant, and Jay McTighe. *Understanding by Design.* Alexandria, Va.: Association for Supervision and Curriculum Development, 1998.

Wiggins, Robert A. "Large Group Lesson/Small Group Follow-Up: Flexible Grouping in a Basal Reading Program." *The Reading Teacher,* 47 (March 1994), 450–460.

Wilhelm, Jeff. "Literacy by Design: Why Is All This Technology So Important?" *Voices from the Middle,* 7 (March 2000), 4–14.

Wilkinson, Phyllis A., and Del Patty. "The Effects of Sentence Combining on the Reading Comprehension of Fourth Grade Students." *Research in the Teaching of English,* 27 (February 1993), 104–125.

Williams, Bronwyn T. "What They See Is What We Get: Television and Middle School Writers," *Journal of Adolescent & Adult Literacy,* 46 (April 2003), 546–554.

Williams, Joanna P. "Reading Comprehension Strategies and Teacher Preparation." In Alan E. Farstrup and S. Jay Samuels, eds. *What Research Has to Say About Reading Instruction.* Newark, Delaware: International Reading Association, 2002, pp. 243-260.

Wilson, Cathy Roller. "Teaching Reading Comprehension by Connecting the Known to the New." *The Reading Teacher,* 36 (January 1983), 382–390.

Winograd, Peter. "Developing Alternative Assessments: Six Problems Worth Solving." *The Reading Teacher,* 47 (February 1994), 420–423.

Winograd, Peter, and Karen W. Higgins. "Writing, Reading, and Talking Mathematics: One Interdisciplinary Possibility." *The Reading Teacher,* 48 (December 1994/January 1995), 310–318.

Winograd, Peter, Scott Paris, and Connie Bridge. "Improving the Assessment of Literacy." *The Reading Teacher,* 45 (October 1991). 108–116.

Wixson, Karen K. "Questions about a Text: What You Ask about Is What Children Learn." *The Reading Teacher,* 37 (December 1983), 287–293.

Wolfe, Ronald, and Alice Lopez. "Structured Overviews for Teaching Science and Terms." *Journal of Reading,* 36 (December 1992/January 1993), 315–317.

Wollman-Bonilla, Julie E. "Reading Journals: Invitations to Participate in Literature." *The Reading Teacher,* 43 (November 1989), 112–120.

Wong-Kam, Jo Ann, and Kathryn Au. "Improving a 4th Grader's Reading and Writing: Three Principles." *The Reading Teacher,* 41 (April 1988), 768–772.

Wood, Judy. *Mainstreaming,* 2d ed. Columbus, Ohio: Merrill, 1993.

Wood, Karen D. "Fostering Collaborative Reading and Writing Experiences in Mathematics." *Journal of Reading,* 36 (October 1992), 96–103.

Wormeli, Rick. *Meet Me in the Middle: Becoming an Accomplished Middle-Level Teacher.* Portland, Me.: Stenhouse Publishers, 2001.

Worthing, Bernadette, and Barbara Laster. "Strategy Access Rods: A Hands-On Approach," *The Reading Teacher,* 56 (October 2002), 122–123.

Worthy, Jo. "A Matter of Interest: Literature That Hooks Reluctant Readers and Keeps Them Reading." *The Reading Teacher,* 50 (November 1996), 204–212.

Yopp, Ruth Helen, and Hallie Kay Yopp. "Sharing Informational Text with Young Children." *The Reading Teacher,* 53 (February 2000), 410–423.

Young, Terrell A., and Sylvia Vardell. "Weaving Readers Theatre and Nonfiction into the Curriculum." *The Reading Teacher,* 46 (February 1993), 396–406.

Zarillo, James. "Teachers' Interpretations of Literature-Based Reading." *The Reading Teacher,* 43 (October 1989), 22–28.

Zarillo, James, and Carole Cox. "Efferent and Aesthetic Teaching." In *Stance and Literary Understanding: Exploring the Theories, Research, and Practice,* edited by Joyce Many and Carole Cox. Norwood, N.J.: Ablex, 1992.

Zarnowski, Myra. "Learning About Fictionalized Biographies: A Reading and Writing Approach." *The Reading Teacher,* 42 (November 1988), 136–142.

Zimet, Sara Goodman. "Teaching Children to Detect Social Bias in Books." *The Reading Teacher,* 36 (January 1983), 418–421.

Zogby, Grace. "Literature Groups: Empowering the Reader." Paper presented at the Whole Language Umbrella Conference, St. Louis, Mo., August 4, 1990.

Zorfass, Judith, Patricia Corley, and Arlene Remz. "Helping Students with Disabilities Become Writers." *Educational Leadership,* 51 (April 1994), 62–66.

Zucker, Carol. "Using Whole Language with Students Who Have Language and Learning Disabilities." *The Reading Teacher,* 46 (May 1993), 660–670.

NAME INDEX

SUBJECT INDEX

About the Authors

Betty Roe is Professor Emerita at Tennessee Technological University. She is the former Director of Doctoral Studies for the College of Education and Professor of Reading and Language Arts. She earned her Ed. D. at the University of Tennessee (1969) in Curriculum and Instruction with Reading emphasis. She is the senior author of Roe/Smith/Burns, *Teaching Reading in Today's Elementary Schools*, 9/e (HMCo., 2005), Roe/Stoodt/Burns, *Secondary School Literacy Instruction*, 8/e (HMCo., 2004) and Burns/Roe, *Informal Reading Inventory*, 6/e (HMCo., 2002). Dr. Roe is an active speaker at inservice workshops and at the annual International Reading Association convention and other professional conferences and conventions. Her most recent area of interest is the use of technology in the teaching of reading. She has received numerous awards for her scholarship and service to the profession, including the Tennessee Reading Association's Distinguished Professor Award and the TTU Chapter Phi Delta Kappa Educator of the Year Award. She is a past president of the Tennessee Reading Association, the founder and past president of the Tennessee Tech Council of IRA, and the past chair of two special interest groups of the International Reading Association. She has also served on a number of IRA Committees.

Sandra Hope Smith is an Assistant Professor in the Department of Curriculum and Instruction and serves as the Director of the Teacher Education Program at Tennessee Technological University. She received her MA in Special Education in 1981 and a Specialist in Education Degree in Reading/Curriculum from Tennessee Technological University in 1989. She is currently completing her doctoral studies at Tennessee State University. In 1997, she was awarded the Tennessee Reading Association's Distinguished Professor Award, and has received numerous other accolades over the last 20 years-including TTU Chapter Phi Delta Kappa Educator of the Year Award, Overton County Teacher of the Year Award, and the Tennessee CEC Special Education Teacher of the Year Award. She has presented papers at numerous state and national conferences, including the annual International Reading Association convention.